1996
KEY INDICATORS OF
DEVELOPING ASIAN AND
PACIFIC COUNTRIES

Published for the Asian Development Bank
by Oxford University Press

Asian Development Bank
P.O. Box 789
0980 Manila, Philippines

© 1996 by Asian Development Bank
Published for the Asian Development Bank
By Oxford University Press
July 1996

Inquiries and orders may be addressed to: Publications Unit,
Information Office, Asian Development Bank, P.O. Box 789,
0980 Manila, Philippines. Tel. Nos.: 632-4444 or for international calls
(632) 711-3851; Facsimile Nos.: (632) 636-2648; 636-2640; E-mail
address: adbpub@mail.asiandevbank.org; Telex: 63587 ADB PN (ETPI);
42205 ADB PM (ITT); 29066 ADB PH (RCA). Orders can also be placed
directly to Oxford University Press offices, associated companies and
agents worldwide.

ISBN 0-19-587836-1
ISSN 0116-3000

British Library Cataloguing in Publication Data
Library of Congress Cataloguing in Publication Data

In this publication, the term "country" does not
imply any judgment by the Asian Development Bank
as to the legal or other status of any territorial entity.

FOREWORD

Key Indicators of Developing Asian and Pacific Countries is an annual statistical publication of the Asian Development Bank, presenting the most current economic, financial and social data on the Bank's developing member countries (DMCs).

Key Indicators comprises two parts. Part 1 presents standard socioeconomic data comparable among DMCs. Part 2 presents detailed data for each country. Data on **Uzbekistan** and **Nauru** are included in Part 1 for the first time. Also, new **Kazakstan** and **Kyrgyz Republic** country tables are presented in Part 2.

The 1996 *Key Indicators* was prepared by the Statistics and Data Systems Division of the Bank's Economics and Development Resource Center under the overall direction of Isidoro P. David, Assistant Chief Economist. Contributions were made by Bishnu Dev Pant, Senior Statistician, Peter Blok, Economist, Jani Damiri, Abuzar Asra and Dalisay Maligalig, Statisticians. Data compilation was undertaken by Belen Villaflor, Fernanda Fernandez, Adelina Nenette Mendoza, Gina Marie Umali, Barbara Carreon, Modesta de Castro, Marichu Duka and Ma. Olivia Nuestro, all of the Statistics and Data Systems Division. A special word of thanks is due to the Bank's Printing Section for its production assistance.

The cooperation of DMC governments and international agencies in providing data is gratefully acknowledged.

We hope that *Key Indicators* remains a valuable resource for its users. Suggestions for improving the publication are welcome.

Vishvanath V. Desai
Director and Chief Economist
Economics and Development Resource Center

CONTENTS

PART 2 - COUNTRY TABLES

ACKNOWLEDGEMENTS

We thank our statistical contacts in the following agencies of the DMCs for their continued cooperation in updating and revising the country tables.

Afghanistan	–	Central Statistics Office; Ministry of Planning
Bangladesh	–	Bangladesh Bureau of Statistics; Bangladesh Bank
Bhutan	–	Central Statistical Organization; Royal Monetary Authority of Bhutan
Cambodia	–	National Institute of Statistics, Ministry of Planning; National Bank of Cambodia
China, People's Republic of	–	State Statistical Bureau; People's Bank of China
Cook Islands	–	Statistics Office
Fiji	–	Bureau of Statistics
Hong Kong	–	Census and Statistics Department
India	–	Central Statistical Organization, Department of Statistics, Ministry of Planning and Program Implementation; Ministry of Finance; Reserve Bank of India
Indonesia	–	Central Bureau of Statistics; Bank Indonesia
Kazakstan	–	State Committee on Statistics and Analysis
Kiribati	–	Statistics Office, Ministry of Finance and Economic Planning
Korea, Republic of	–	National Statistical Office; Bank of Korea
Kyrgyz Republic	–	National Statistical Committee
Lao People's Democratic Republic	–	National Statistical Centre; Bank of the Lao PDR
Malaysia	–	Department of Statistics; Ministry of Finance; Bank Negara Malaysia

Maldives	–	Department of External Resources, Ministry of Finance and Treasury; Ministry of Planning, Human Resources and Environment; Maldives Monetary Authority
Marshall Islands	–	Office of Planning and Statistics
Micronesia, Federated States of	–	Office of Planning and Statistics
Mongolia	–	State Statistical Office
Myanmar	–	Central Statistical Organization; Foreign Economic Relations Department, Ministry of National Planning and Economic Development
Nauru	–	Bureau of Statistics
Nepal	–	Central Bureau of Statistics; Ministry of Finance; Nepal Rastra Bank
Pakistan	–	Federal Bureau of Statistics; Ministry of Finance and Economic Affairs
Papua New Guinea	–	National Statistical Office; Ministry of Finance and Planning; Bank of Papua New Guinea
Philippines	–	National Statistical Coordination Board; Bangko Sentral ng Pilipinas
Singapore	–	Department of Statistics, Ministry of Trade and Industry; Trade Development Board; Economic Development Board; Ministry of Labor
Solomon Islands	–	Statistics Office, Ministry of Finance and Economic Planning; Central Bank of Solomon Islands
Sri Lanka	–	Department of Census and Statistics; Central Bank of Sri Lanka
Taipei,China	–	Directorate-General of Budget, Accounting and Statistics; Central Bank of China; Department of Statistics
Thailand	–	National Statistical Office; National Economic and Social Development Board; Bank of Thailand
Tonga	–	Statistics Department; Ministry of Finance; National Reserve Bank of Tonga

Tuvalu	–	Central Statistics Division, Ministry of Finance, Economic Planning, Commerce and Industry
Uzbekistan	–	State Committee on Forecasting and Statistics; Department for Coordination of External Economic Activity
Vanuatu	–	Statistics Office
Viet Nam	–	General Statistical Office; State Bank of Viet Nam
Western Samoa	–	Department of Statistics; Central Bank of Samoa

For this issue, the assistance of colleagues in the following intergovernmental agencies is also gratefully acknowledged: Food and Agriculture Organization (FAO), International Monetary Fund (IMF), Organization for Economic Co-operation and Development (OECD), South Pacific Commission (SPC), UN Department for Economic and Social Information and Policy Analysis (DESIPA), UN Development Programme (UNDP), UN Economic and Social Commission for Asia and the Pacific (ESCAP), UN Statistical Division (UNSD), and the World Bank (WB).

INTRODUCTORY NOTES

Concepts, Definitions and Estimation Methodology

The data series are compiled from two major sources, namely, the developing member countries (DMCs) of ADB and international statistics agencies. The data obtained from the DMCs are comparable to the extent that the individual countries follow the standard statistical concepts, definitions and estimation methods recommended by the United Nations and other applicable international agencies. However, countries invariably develop and apply their own concepts, definitions and estimation methodology to suit their individual conditions and these may not necessarily conform with the recommended international standards. Hence, although attempts are made to present the data in comparable and uniform format, they are subject to variations in the statistical methods used by individual countries. These variations are shown in the footnotes of the country tables.

General Guidelines

The cut-off date for data to be included in this issue was 13 May 1996.

Sixteen countries have varying fiscal years not corresponding to the calendar year. Whenever the statistical series, e.g., national accounts or government finance, are compiled by fiscal year, these are presented under single year captions corresponding to the period in which most of the fiscal year falls, as follows:

Country	Fiscal Year	Year Caption
Afghanistan	21 March 1995 to 20 March 1996	1995
Cook Islands Hong Kong India Indonesia Myanmar Singapore	1 April 1995 to 31 March 1996	1995
Bangladesh Bhutan Pakistan Taipei,China Tonga Western Samoa	1 July 1994 to 30 June 1995	1995
Nepal	16 July 1994 to 15 July 1995	1995

Exceptions are Marshall Islands and Federated States of Micronesia, whose statistical series can be, and are, recompiled and presented here on calendar year basis, although the fiscal year of these countries ends on 30 September of the following year.

Key Symbols

...	Data not available at cut-off date
–	Magnitude zero
0 or 0.0	Magnitude less than half of unit employed
*	Provisional / Preliminary
I	Marked break in series

Measurement Units

bbl	barrel
bn	billion
c	cent
cu m	cubic meter
ha	hectare
kg	kilogram
kgoe	kilogram of oil equivalent
kl	kiloliter
km	kilometer
kWh	kilowatt-hour
lb	pound
m	meter
mn	million
m t	metric ton
pc	piece
sq m	square meter
'000	thousand
tr	trillion
toe	ton of oil equivalent

Abbreviations and Acronyms

ADB	Asian Development Bank
cif	cost, insurance and freight
DAC	Development Assistance Committee
DMC	Developing Member Country of the ADB
ERBOP	Economic Review and Bank Operations
ESCAP	Economic and Social Commission for Asia and the Pacific
FAO	Food and Agriculture Organization
fc	factor cost
fob	free on board
GDI	Gross Domestic Investment
GDP	Gross Domestic Product
GDS	Gross Domestic Saving
GNP	Gross National Product
IEA	International Energy Agency
ILO	International Labour Office
IMF	International Monetary Fund
LDC	Least Developed Country
LT	long term
mp	market prices
NCDS	National Centre for Development Studies
NMP	Net Material Product
ODA	Official Development Assistance
OECD	Organization for Economic Co-operation and Development
OPEC	Organization of the Petroleum Exporting Countries
SDRs	Special Drawing Rights

SITC	Standard International Trade Classification
UN	United Nations
UNCTAD	UN Conference on Trade and Development
UNDP	UN Development Programme
UNEP	UN Environment Programme
UNESCO	UN Educational, Scientific and Cultural Organization
WB	World Bank

Publications

ADB,	GIDAPC	Gender Indicators of Developing Asian and Pacific Countries
ESCAP,	APF	Asia-Pacific in Figures
	SIAP	Statistical Indicators for Asia and the Pacific
	SYAP	Statistical Yearbook for Asia and the Pacific
FAO,	PY	Production Yearbook
ILO,	YLS	Yearbook of Labor Statistics
IMF,	BOP	Balance of Payments Yearbook
	DOTS	Direction of Trade Statistics
	IFS	International Financial Statistics
OECD,	FEDDC	Financing and External Debt of Developing Countries
	GDFFDC	Geographical Distribution of Financial Flows to Developing Countries
UN,	CSISW	Compendium of Statistics and Indicators on the Situation of Women
	ESY	Energy Statistics Yearbook
	MBS	Monthly Bulletin of Statistics
	SY	Statistical Yearbook
	WES	Yearbook of World Energy Statistics
	WISTAT	Women's Indicators and Statistics Database
	WPP	World Population Prospect
UNCTAD,	HITDS	Handbook of International Trade and Development Statistics
UNDP,	HDR	Human Development Report
UNESCO,	SY	Statistical Yearbook
	WER	World Education Report
WB,	PPMC	Price Prospects for Major Commodities
	SID	Social Indicators of Development
	WDR	World Development Report
	WDT	World Debt Tables
	WT	World Tables

Notes

1.   Data on GDP estimates converted through purchasing power parities (PPP) under the International Comparison Program (ICP) coordinated by the United Nations are not shown in this publication, mainly because of the lack of consistent data.

2.   Data on Direction of Trade contained in country tables are based on data shown in the Direction of Trade Statistics (DOTS) yearbooks and tapes of the IMF, which in turn are reported by the respective countries. However, such data may not be fully consistent with those reported by their trading partners.

3.   Data on Germany in the Direction of Trade refer to those of the former Federal Republic of Germany through June 1990. As from July 1990, the data cover the area of united Germany.

REGIONAL TABLES

PART 1

KEY INDICATORS OF DEVELOPING ASIAN AND PACIFIC COUNTRIES

Table 1: POPULATION

DMC	Mid-year Population (Million) [a]									Growth Rates (%)		
	1975	1980	1985	1990	1991	1992	1993	1994	1995	Annual Growth Rate between Census Years	Annual Growth Rate 1990-95	Rate of Natural Increase 1990-95
Afghanistan	11.8	13.4	14.7	16.1	16.4	16.8	17.1	17.4 *	17.8 *	... (1979-)	2.0 [d]	2.8
Bangladesh	78.2	88.5	97.4	106.8	108.6	110.6	112.7	114.8	116.9 *	1.9 (1981-91)	1.8	2.4
Bhutan	1.1	1.3	1.4	1.5	1.6	1.6	1.7	1.7	1.7	1.1 (1969-80)	2.4	2.4
Cambodia	7.1	6.5	7.5	8.6	8.8	9.3	9.7 *	9.9 *	10.2 *	... (1962-)	3.4 [d]	2.9
China, People's Rep. of	930.5	981.2	1051.0	1135.2	1150.8	1165.0	1178.4	1191.8	1204.9 *	1.5 (1982-90)	1.2	1.1
Cook Islands	18.1	17.9	17.2	18.4	18.5	18.6	19.2	19.6	20.2	1.1 (1986-91)	1.9	...
Fiji	576.0	634.0	697.0	732.0 *	742.0 *	753.0 *	765.0 *	779.0 *	793.3 *	2.0 (1976-86)	1.6	1.9
Hong Kong	4.4	5.1	5.5	5.7	5.8	5.8	5.9	6.1	6.2	0.5 (1986-91)	1.6	0.6
India	602.8	673.4	750.9	834.7	851.7	867.8	883.9	900.0	916.5 *	2.1 (1981-91)	1.9	1.9
Indonesia	132.0	148.0	164.6	179.2 [c]	182.9	186.0	189.1	192.2	195.3	2.0 (1980-90)	1.7	1.6
Kazakstan	14.1	14.8	15.8	16.7	16.9	17.0	17.0	16.8	16.6	1.2 (1979-89)	-0.2	1.2
Kiribati	53.6	56.7	64.0 [c]	72.3 [c]	73.9 *	75.6 *	77.3 *	79.1 *	80.8 *	2.3 (1985-90)	2.3	...
Korea, Rep. of	35.3	38.1	40.8	42.9	43.3	43.7	44.1	44.5	44.9	1.4 (1985-90)	0.9	1.0
Kyrgyz Republic	3.3	3.6	4.0	4.3	4.4	4.5	4.5	4.5	4.5 *	2.0 (1979-89)	0.7	2.2
Lao PDR	3.4	3.2	3.6	4.1	4.2	4.4	4.5	4.6	4.7	2.5 (1985-95)	2.6	3.0
Malaysia	12.3	13.8	15.7	17.8	18.2	18.6	19.1	19.5	20.1	2.6 (1980-91)	2.5	2.4
Maldives	135.0	157.6	180.1	213.2	223.3	230.0	238.4	245.0	253.3	3.5 (1985-90)	3.5	3.3
Marshall Islands	26.0	31.7	38.7	46.2	48.0	50.0	52.0	53.8	55.6	4.3 (1980-88)	3.8	...
Micronesia, Fed. States of	...	73.2 [c]	91.0	100.5	101.5	102.5	103.5	104.7	106.0 *	3.3 (1980-90)	1.1	2.7
Mongolia	1.4	1.7	1.9	2.1	2.2	2.2	2.2	2.3	2.3	2.5 (1979-89)	1.6	2.0
Myanmar	29.9	33.1	37.1	40.8	41.6	42.3	43.1	43.9	44.7	... (1983-)	1.9	2.1
Nauru	...	7.9	8.5	9.4	9.6	9.8	10.0	...	...	2.8 (1983-92)	1.9 [e]	...
Nepal	12.6	14.6	16.3	18.1	18.5	19.0	19.5	20.1 *	20.6 *	2.1 (1981-91)	2.6	2.6
Pakistan	71.0	82.6	96.2	112.1	115.5	119.1	122.8	126.6	129.8	3.1 (1972-81)	3.0	3.2
Papua New Guinea	2.7	3.0	3.3	3.7	3.8	3.8	3.9	4.0	4.1	1.9 (1980-90)	2.0	2.3
Philippines	42.1 [c]	48.3	54.7	62.0	63.7	65.3	67.0	68.6	70.3	2.3 (1980-90)	2.5	2.4
Singapore	2.3	2.3 [c]	2.5	2.7 [c]	2.8	2.8	2.9	2.9	3.0	1.1 (1980-90)	2.0	1.0
Solomon Islands	192.0	225.0	267.3	318.7	330.2	342.4	355.0	368.1	381.7	3.5 (1976-86)	3.7	3.3
Sri Lanka	13.5	14.8	15.8	17.0	17.2	17.4	17.6	17.8 *	18.0 *	1.7 (1971-81)	1.2	1.5
Taipei,China	16.0	17.6	19.1	20.2	20.5	20.7	20.8	21.0	21.2	1.2 (1980-90)	1.0	0.0
Thailand	41.4	46.7	51.7	55.8	56.6	57.3	58.0	58.7	59.4	2.0 (1980-90)	1.2	1.3
Tonga	88.8	91.8	94.1	96.4	96.9	97.4	97.7	97.1	97.7	0.5 (1976-86)	0.3	...
Tuvalu	...	...	8.2	9.0	9.0	9.2	9.4	9.5	9.7 *	1.9 (1979-91)	1.4	...
Uzbekistan	...	15.9	18.2	20.5	21.0	21.5	21.9	22.4	...	... (- 89)	2.2 [e]	2.5
Vanuatu	95.4	115.1	129.1	147.3	151.5	155.6	159.8	164.2	168.4	2.5 (1979-89)	2.7	2.8
Viet Nam	47.7	53.7	59.9	66.2	67.8	69.4	71.0	72.5 *	74.0 *	2.1 (1979-89)	2.2	2.3
Western Samoa	149.0	156.0	159.5	164.0	164.7	165.4	166.2	166.9	167.6 *	0.3 (1981-91)	0.4	3.1
TOTAL DMCs [b]	2118.1	2326.7	2551.3	2797.0	2846.5	2893.9	2940.5	2986.6 *	3009.6 *		1.5	
WORLD	4079.0	4453.2	4851.4	5292.2	5385.3	5480.0	5544.0	5629.6 *	5716.4 *		1.6	

a   Except for Cook Islands, Fiji, Kiribati, Maldives, Marshall Islands, Micronesia, Nauru, Solomon Islands, Tonga, Tuvalu, Vanuatu and Western Samoa, where units are in thousands.
b   For all reporting countries only.
c   Census figure.
d   Figures may be influenced by refugees to an unknown extent.
e   Annual population growth rates refer to the growth of the population for the last five years available.

Sources: Country sources.
ESCAP, *APF 1995*.
UN, *World Population 1994*.
UN, *WPP 1994* and past issues.
UN, *Population and Vital Statistics Report*, January 1995 and past issues.
UN, *Demographic Yearbook 1993*.

Table 2: DEMOGRAPHIC INDICATORS

DMC	Population Density (Persons/sq km)			Crude Birth Rate (Per 1000 Persons)			Crude Death Rate (Per 1000 Persons)		
	1975	1985	1993	1975	1985	1993	1975	1985	1993
Afghanistan	18	22	26	51	49 [a]	51	31	23 [a]	22
Bangladesh	543	676	782	46	40	35	18	15	11
Bhutan	24	29	35	43	43	39	20	21	16
Cambodia	39	41	53	47	46	40	18	20	15
China, People's Rep. of	97	109	123	26	18	19	9	7	8
Cook Islands	79	75	81	27	25	26	6	8	5
Fiji	32	38	42	29	28	25	7	5	5
Hong Kong	4231	5246	5637	18	14	11	5	5	6
India	183	228	269	36	33	29	15	12	10
Indonesia	69	86	99	40	32	24	17	12	8
Kazakstan	5	6	6	...	25	20	...	8	7
Kiribati	75	90	108	...	26	31 [b]	...	9	11 [b]
Korea, Rep. of	357	412	444	24	21	16	8	6	6
Kyrgyz Republic	17	20	23	...	32	28	...	8	7
Lao PDR	14	15	19	42	42	44	22	19	15
Malaysia	37	48	58	31	32	28	6	5	5
Maldives	450	600	800	40	50	33	11	9	6
Marshall Islands	143	214	287	...	39	32 [c]	...	5	3 [c]
Micronesia, Fed. States of	...	130	148	...	31	35 [b]	...	4	8 [b]
Mongolia	1	1	1	38	35	27	9	8	7
Myanmar	44	55	64	34	30	32	11	11	11
Nauru	...	425	500	...	...	24 [d]	...	...	5 [d]
Nepal	89	116	139	46	43	39	20	18	13
Pakistan	89	121	154	47	44	40	16	15	9
Papua New Guinea	6	7	8	41	37	33	17	13	11
Philippines	140	182	223	36	33	30	10	8	6
Singapore	3645	4000	4588	18	17	16	5	5	6
Solomon Islands	7	9	12	45 [e]	47	37	12 [e]	6 [a]	4
Sri Lanka	206	241	269	27	25	20	9	6	6
Taipei,China	445	532	579	23	18	16	5	5	5
Thailand	81	101	113	34	26	19	10	8	6
Tonga	118	125	131	30	30	23	4	4	4
Tuvalu	...	317	360	...	...	25 [f]	...	...	11 [f]
Uzbekistan	...	...	49	...	...	31	...	...	6
Vanuatu	8	11	13	...	...	35 [b]	...	...	7 [b]
Viet Nam	144	181	214	41	34	30	16	8	8
Western Samoa	52	56	59	22	35	32 [d]	4	...	7 [d]

a Refers to the period 1980-85.
b Refers to 1994.
c Refers to 1989.
d Refers to 1992.
e Refers to 1976.
f Refers to 1990.

Table 2: DEMOGRAPHIC INDICATORS (Continued)

Total Fertility Rate (Births Per Woman)			Net Reproduction Rate			DMC
1975	1985	1993	1975 [g]	1985 [a]	1995 [h]	
7.1[g]	6.9[a]	6.9[i]	2.0	2.0	2.1	Afghanistan
6.6	5.7	4.3	2.3	2.1	1.7	Bangladesh
6.2	6.2	5.9[d]	1.8	1.9	2.1	Bhutan
5.5[g]	5.1[a]	5.1[i]	1.7	1.8	2.0	Cambodia
3.8	2.3	2.0	2.0	1.1	0.9	China, People's Rep. of
...	...	...	...	...	...	Cook Islands
3.7[g]	3.5[a]	2.8[i]	1.9	1.8	1.4	Fiji
3.0	1.8	1.2	1.4	0.9	0.6	Hong Kong
5.7	4.5	3.7	1.9	1.7	1.5	India
5.5	4.1	2.8	1.8	1.6	1.3	Indonesia
3.3[g]	3.1[a]	2.3[i]	1.6	1.4	1.2	Kazakstan
5.7[g]	4.9[a]	3.8[i]	...	...	...	Kiribati
4.0	2.4	1.7	1.7	1.1	0.8	Korea, Rep. of
4.9[g]	4.2[a]	3.3[i]	2.1	1.9	1.7	Kyrgyz Republic
6.2	6.4	6.6	1.9	2.3	2.4	Lao PDR
5.7	3.7	3.5	2.2	1.9	1.7	Malaysia
7.0[g]	6.8[a]	6.7[i]	2.5	2.6	2.8	Maldives
8.4[j]	7.9[k]	7.2[i]	...	...	...	Marshall Islands
7.1[g]	6.5[a]	5.1[i]	...	...	...	Micronesia, Fed. States of
5.6	4.9	3.5	2.2	2.2	1.5	Mongolia
5.5	3.9	4.1	2.1	1.8	1.7	Myanmar
...	...	...	...	...	...	Nauru
6.2	6.3	5.3	1.9	2.2	2.0	Nepal
7.2	6.1	6.1	2.4	2.7	2.5	Pakistan
6.0	5.4	5.0	2.2	2.2	2.0	Papua New Guinea
6.4	4.3	3.9	2.2	2.0	1.8	Philippines
2.8	1.7	1.7	1.2	0.8	0.8	Singapore
...	6.4[a]	5.2[i]	3.1	2.9	2.5	Solomon Islands
4.2	3.2	2.4	1.7	1.5	1.2	Sri Lanka
2.8	1.9	1.8	1.4	0.9	0.8 [b]	Taipei,China
6.3	3.2	2.1	2.1	1.3	1.0	Thailand
...	4.7[a]	3.4[i]	...	...	...	Tonga
...	...	...	...	...	...	Tuvalu
5.7[g]	4.7[a]	3.8[i]	2.7	2.1	1.8	Uzbekistan
6.6[g]	...	5.1[i]	2.5	2.2	2.1	Vanuatu
6.2	4.6	3.8	2.2	2.0	1.7	Viet Nam
5.9[g]	5.5[a]	4.3[i]	2.8	2.4	1.9	Western Samoa

g   Refers to the period 1970-75.
h   Refers to the period 1990-95.
i   Refers to the period 1989-94.
j   Refers to 1973.
k   Refers to 1980.
l   Refers to 1994/95.

Table 2: DEMOGRAPHIC INDICATORS (Continued)

DMC	Contraceptive Prevalence Rate (% of Women 15-49 years)		Maternal Mortality Rate (Per 100, 000 Live Births)		Human Development Index
	1985 [a]	1993 [b]	1985 [c]	1994 [d]	1992
Afghanistan	...	...	600	1835	0.228
Bangladesh	25	40	3000	887	0.364
Bhutan	...	...	773	370	0.305
Cambodia	...	...	500	900	0.337
China, People's Rep. of	74	83	...	115	0.594
Cook Islands	...	...	...	...	...
Fiji	...	...	...		0.860
Hong Kong	72	81	6	...	0.905
India	35	43	460	437	0.439
Indonesia	40	50	450	...	0.637
Kazakstan	...	...	56	53	0.798
Kiribati	...	...	...	...	...
Korea, Rep. of	70	77	42	30	0.882
Kyrgyz Republic	...	...	...	43	0.717
Lao PDR	...	...	200	660	0.420
Malaysia	51	56	40	34	0.822
Maldives	...	...	...	480	0.554
Marshall Islands	...	...	...	...	...
Micronesia, Fed. States of	...	...	...	...	...
Mongolia	...	...	...	240	0.604
Myanmar	5	...	460	518	0.457
Nauru	...	...	...	...	...
Nepal	15	15	...	...	0.343
Pakistan	11	14	600	...	0.483
Papua New Guinea	4	...	900	700	0.508
Philippines	44	40	...	208	0.677
Singapore	74	...	11	...	0.878
Solomon Islands	...	...	...	...	0.511
Sri Lanka	62	62	90	30	0.704
Taipei,China	...	...	...	...	...
Thailand	65	66	270	155	0.827
Tonga	...	...	...	...	...
Tuvalu	...	...	...	...	...
Uzbekistan	...	...	46	43	0.706
Vanuatu	...	...	...	...	0.541
Viet Nam	20	53	110	105	0.539
Western Samoa	...	...	...	...	0.651

a   If estimates for the captioned year are not available, data refer to the most recent year prior to the captioned year.
b   Refers to the period 1988-93.
c   Refers to the period 1980-85.
d   Refers to the period 1989-94.
e   Refers to the period 1970-75.
f   Refers to 1975.

Infant Mortality Rate (Per 1,000 Live Births)			Life Expectancy at Birth (Years)						DMC
			1975 [e]		1985 [c]		1993		
1975 [e]	1985 [c]	1993	F	M	F	M	F	M	
194	183	...	38	38	41	40	45 [d]	43 [d]	Afghanistan
140	128	106	44	46	50	50	56	56	Bangladesh
...	...	...	...	...	...	...	...	...	Bhutan
181	160	110 [d]	41	39	47	45	54 [d]	50 [d]	Cambodia
48	37	30	65	63	69	67	71	68	China, People's Rep. of
...	...	...	...	...	...	...	...	...	Cook Islands
45	31	22 [d]	67	63	71	67	74 [d]	70 [d]	Fiji
15	9	7	74	68	79	73	82	76	Hong Kong
132	108	80	49	51	55	55	61	61	India
114	80	56	50	48	58	54	65	61	Indonesia
...	30	29	...	...	74	64	74	65	Kazakstan
120	82	65 [d]	50	48	54	52	58 [d]	56 [d]	Kiribati
47	30	11	64	59	71	65	75	68	Korea, Rep. of
...	42	34	...	...	69	61	73	65	Kyrgyz Republic
145	122	95	41	39	48	45	53	50	Lao PDR
32 [f]	17 [g]	11	65	61	70	66	73	69	Malaysia
121	94	55 [d]	50	52	56	58	61 [d]	63 [d]	Maldives
...	...	55 [h]	60 [f]	57 [f]	62 [g]	59 [g]	64 [i]	61 [i]	Marshall Islands
...	...	37 [d]	59	57	64	62	...	...	Micronesia, Fed. States of
98	78	58	55	53	60	58	65	63	Mongolia
122	106	82	52	48	55	51	60	57	Myanmar
...	...	...	...	...	...	...	...	...	Nauru
153	139	96	42	44	47	49	54	55	Nepal
140	120	88	48	50	54	54	63	61	Pakistan
100	65	67	48	48	53	51	57	56	Papua New Guinea
53 [f]	38 [g]	22 [j]	60 [f]	57 [f]	65 [g]	61 [g]	68 [k]	64 [k]	Philippines
14	9	6	72	67	75	69	78	73	Singapore
...	64	42 [d]	...	...	62	60	63 [d]	61 [d]	Solomon Islands
48	30	17	66	64	71	67	74	70	Sri Lanka
14 [f]	7 [g]	5	73 [f]	68 [f]	76 [g]	71 [g]	78 [l]	72 [l]	Taipei,China
65	44	36	62	58	67	63	72	66	Thailand
...	43	19 [d]	...	...	64	61	71 [d]	67 [d]	Tonga
...	...	38 [m]	...	...	...	...	...	...	Tuvalu
...	45	40	...	...	71	65	72	66	Uzbekistan
89	63	47 [d]	51	51	57	55	61 [d]	59 [d]	Vanuatu
90	53	41	60	56	66	62	68	63	Viet Nam
...	...	23 [d]	...	...	64	62	71 [d]	67 [d]	Western Samoa

g Refers to 1985.
h Refers to 1989.
i Refers to 1994/95.
j Refers to 1992.
k Refers to 1995.
l Refers to 1993.
m Refers to 1990.

Sources: Country sources.
ESCAP, *AFP 1995*.
FAO, *PY 1994* and past issues.
UN, *WPP 1994*.
UNDP, *HDR 1995*.
WB, *WDR 1995* and past issues.
WB, *SID 1996*.

Table 3: POPULATION BY AGE GROUP

| DMC | Age Distribution (As % of Total Population) | | | | | | | | |
| | 1975 | | | 1985 | | | 1995 [a] | | |
	0-14	15-64	65 +	0-14	15-64	65 +	0-14	15-64	65 +
Afghanistan	43.8	53.8	2.4	41.8	55.5	2.7	40.8	56.4	2.8
Bangladesh	45.9	50.5	3.6	44.8	52.0	3.2	39.5	57.4	3.1
Bhutan	39.9	56.9	3.2	40.4	56.3	3.3	41.1	55.4	3.5
Cambodia	41.6	55.6	2.8	40.9	56.4	2.7	44.9	52.5	2.6
China, People's Rep. of	39.5	56.1	4.4	30.3	64.5	5.2	26.4	67.5	6.1
Cook Islands [b]	47.0	48.4	4.6	36.9	58.4	4.7	34.1	60.9	5.0
Fiji	39.9	57.4	2.7	38.3	58.8	2.9	34.7	61.5	3.8
Hong Kong	30.4	64.2	5.4	23.4	69.2	7.4	19.2	70.6	10.2
India	39.8	56.4	3.8	37.5	58.3	4.2	35.2	60.2	4.6
Indonesia	42.0	54.8	3.2	38.7	57.7	3.6	33.0	62.7	4.3
Kazakstan	34.6	59.7	5.7	32.0	62.3	5.7	29.8	63.2	7.0
Kiribati [b]	41.1	55.3	3.6	38.9	57.5	3.6	40.3	56.3	3.4
Korea, Rep. of	37.8	58.6	3.6	30.0	65.7	4.3	23.6	70.8	5.6
Kyrgyz Republic	39.8	54.3	5.9	37.0	57.8	5.2	37.1	57.1	5.8
Lao PDR	42.1	55.2	2.7	42.7	54.4	2.9	44.8	52.2	3.0
Malaysia	42.1	54.2	3.7	38.7	57.6	3.7	38.0	58.1	3.9
Maldives	41.8	53.8	4.4	45.6	51.3	3.1	46.6	50.0	3.4
Marshall Islands [b]	...	...	...	51.0	46.1	2.9	50.6	46.5	2.9
Micronesia, Fed. States of [b]	...	...	...	46.4	50.1	3.5	...	...	...
Mongolia	43.7	53.4	2.9	42.3	54.7	3.0	38.0	58.5	3.5
Myanmar	40.7	55.5	3.8	39.2	57.0	3.8	37.4	58.5	4.1
Nauru [b]	...	...	...	46.5	52.3	1.2	...	...	...
Nepal	42.3	54.5	3.2	44.2	53.1	2.7	42.4	54.2	3.4
Pakistan	45.4	51.6	3.0	43.7	53.4	2.9	44.3	52.7	3.0
Papua New Guinea	41.9	55.0	3.1	41.8	56.3	1.9	39.5	57.6	2.9
Philippines	43.6	53.7	2.7	41.0	56.1	2.9	38.3	58.3	3.4
Singapore	32.8	63.1	4.1	24.4	70.4	5.2	22.7	70.6	6.7
Solomon Islands	47.7	49.0	3.3	47.3	50.4	2.3	44.2	53.0	2.8
Sri Lanka	39.3	56.6	4.1	34.3	61.0	4.7	30.6	63.6	5.8
Taipei,China	35.7	60.9	3.4	29.9	65.2	5.0	24.1	68.4	7.5
Thailand	44.9	52.1	3.0	35.5	60.6	3.9	28.3	66.7	5.0
Tonga [b]	44.4	52.3	3.3	40.6	55.2	4.2	...	...	...
Tuvalu [b]	31.8	63.1	5.1	...	...	...	...	...	...
Vanuatu	46.0	51.7	2.3	44.7	52.1	3.2	43.4	53.2	3.4
Uzbekistan	43.4	51.1	5.5	40.5	55.1	4.4	39.9	55.7	4.4
Viet Nam	43.7	52.3	4.0	40.5	55.0	4.5	37.4	57.7	4.9
Western Samoa	50.1	47.3	2.6	48.2	48.7	3.1	46.3	50.6	3.1

a   Estimated data using medium variant projections except for Cook Islands, Kiribati and Marshall Islands.
b   Based on actual census results.

Sources: UN, *World Population Prospects*, The 1994 Revision, 1995.
DGBAS, *Statistical Yearbook 1995* for Taipei,China.
ESCAP, *SYAP 1994* and past issues for Cook Islands, Kiribati, Marshall Islands, Fed. States of Micronesia, Nauru, Tonga and Tuvalu.

Table 4: URBAN POPULATION[a] INDICATORS

DMC	As % of Total Population			Annual Growth Rate of Urban Population (%)		
	1975	1985	1995	1970-75	1980-85	1990-95
Afghanistan	13.3	16.9	20.0	6.1	-0.5	7.7
Bangladesh	9.3	13.4	18.3	6.7	5.6	5.3
Bhutan	3.5	4.5	6.4	4.0	5.1	4.8
Cambodia	10.3	14.8	20.7	-2.1	6.6	6.2
China, People's Rep. of	17.3	22.5	30.3	2.0	4.2	4.0
Cook Islands	54.0	55.6	60.4	-1.4	-1.0	1.8
Fiji	36.7	38.5	40.7	3.1	2.4	2.2
Hong Kong	89.7	92.9	95.0	2.6	1.9	0.8
India	21.3	24.3	26.8	3.8	3.2	2.9
Indonesia	19.4	26.1	35.4	4.9	5.3	4.5
Kazakstan	52.2	55.8	59.7	2.3	1.8	1.2
Kiribati	30.1	33.5	35.7	5.3	2.9	2.4
Korea, Rep. of	48.0	64.9	81.3	5.3	4.0	2.9
Kyrgyz Republic	37.9	38.2	38.9	2.4	1.9	2.1
Lao PDR	11.4	15.9	21.7	5.5	5.6	6.1
Malaysia	37.7	45.9	53.7	4.8	4.4	3.9
Maldives	18.0	25.7	26.8	8.2	5.8	4.0
Marshall Islands	60.7	62.0	69.1	2.5	4.2	4.0
Micronesia, Fed. States of	24.6	25.3	28.0	3.4	3.1	4.0
Mongolia	48.7	55.0	60.9	4.4	3.9	3.0
Myanmar	23.9	24.0	26.2	3.3	2.1	3.3
Nepal	5.0	8.5	13.7	7.3	8.0	7.1
Nauru	100.0	100.0	100.0	2.9	2.6	2.6
Pakistan	26.4	29.8	34.7	3.8	4.9	4.4
Papua New Guinea	11.9	14.0	16.0	6.3	3.6	3.6
Philippines	35.6	43.0	54.2	4.2	5.2	4.2
Singapore	100.0	100.0	100.0	1.7	1.2	1.0
Solomon Islands	9.1	12.4	17.1	3.8	6.8	6.5
Sri Lanka	22.0	21.1	22.4	1.8	1.2	2.2
Taipei,China	43.9	50.7	57.4	5.0	3.5	2.0
Thailand	15.1	17.9	20.0	5.5	2.8	2.5
Tonga	20.3	29.1	41.1	1.5	3.9	3.5
Tuvalu	25.2	35.0	46.2	5.1	3.7	4.1
Uzbekistan	39.1	40.7	41.3	4.4	2.5	2.6
Vanuatu	15.7	18.2	19.3	6.7	2.8	3.4
Viet Nam	18.8	19.6	20.8	2.9	2.5	3.1
Western Samoa	21.0	21.1	21.0	1.8	0.1	1.1

a   Based on national definitions incorporated in the latest available census.

Sources: UN, *World Urbanization Prospects*, 1994 Revision.
Country source for Taipei,China.

Table 5: ECONOMICALLY ACTIVE POPULATION (EAP) BY GENDER AND INDUSTRY

DMC	EAP (% of working age population) [a]						EAP in Agriculture / EAP (%)					
	1975 [b]		1985 [c]		1994 [d]		1975 [b]		1985 [c]		1994 [d]	
	Female	Male	Female	Male	Female	Male	Female	Male	Female	Male	Female	Male
Afghanistan	20.1	91.0	6.5	86.4	...	...	...	...	3.2	65.3	...	...
Bangladesh	19.4	90.2	...	...	62.6	88.3	73.0	78.1	...	...	84.9	54.4
Bhutan	58.6	93.0	...	...	...	...	...	...	...	...	...	...
Cambodia	...	...	...	...	55.4	58.1	...	...	...	...	79.0	70.8
China, People's Rep. of	53.0	83.7	70.1	86.2	72.9	84.9	...	...	78.0	69.4	76.1	69.2
Cook Islands	34.1	83.6	46.8	83.0	43.6	71.4	1.7	32.8	9.7	23.4	6.3	15.8
Fiji	17.1	84.0	23.3	85.5	...	...	27.1	50.7	28.5	52.7	...	...
Hong Kong	43.4	83.2	49.5	82.5	47.1	77.6	2.5	2.6	1.6	1.7	0.4	0.8
India	18.6	85.5	21.2	81.7	...	...	83.1	70.3	81.2	65.6	78.1	60.9
Indonesia	33.6	84.5	43.5	81.7	49.1	82.6	68.6	66.1	53.6	55.3	53.6	52.5
Kazakstan	...	...	62.8	78.5	...	...	...	...	17.0	27.2	...	...
Kiribati	8.7	37.3	...	...	14.2	38.2	1.2	9.2	...	...	0.9	10.1
Korea, Rep. of	37.8	78.8	41.7	67.4	47.9	76.4	51.9	42.4	27.8	23.1	17.2	13.0
Kyrgyz Republic	...	...	...	...	...	...	...	...	...	...	...	...
Lao PDR	15.3	87.8	...	...	...	...	...	...	...	...	...	...
Malaysia	37.2	79.3	40.2	82.2	35.1	74.8	67.9	49.7	49.3	37.5	19.0	22.2
Maldives	62.5	90.8	23.8	77.6	20.2	77.3	44.0	63.3	14.8	34.8	14.2	29.2
Marshall Islands	...	...	30.1	77.2	...	...	...	...	2.6	28.4	...	...
Micronesia, Fed. States of	...	...	15.6	36.5	...	...	...	...	1.0	3.4	...	...
Mongolia	42.9	86.1	71.3	81.5	...	...	...	...	...	...	...	...
Myanmar	33.8	76.4	38.9	73.8	...	...	58.3	66.7	63.0	67.8	...	...
Nauru	...	...	...	...	...	...	...	...	...	...	...	...
Nepal	58.1	91.8	45.2	87.7	...	...	92.9	88.1	96.8	89.7	...	...
Pakistan	8.8	86.8	11.3	85.1	14.0	83.5	66.3	58.8	75.1	47.9	66.0	44.8
Papua New Guinea	69.0	91.2	...	...	...	...	...	...	83.3	50.4	...	...
Philippines	50.0	79.0	48.0	80.3	47.3	81.6	26.1	64.5	35.0	58.3	30.5	52.8
Singapore	30.2	80.4	44.9	79.9	50.9	79.6	2.0	2.1	0.5	0.8	0.1	0.4
Solomon Islands	7.8	35.0	13.5	37.2	...	...	...	...	51.3	44.2	...	...
Sri Lanka	21.3	69.8	31.9	80.2	38.1	76.7	65.7	51.6	55.0	49.8	41.0	31.7
Taipei,China	30.9	81.8	32.7	79.0	45.4	72.4	48.4	35.1	15.7	22.1	...	...
Thailand	71.5	85.3	76.3	87.8	65.2	83.8	75.7	70.7	64.1	63.0	39.7	43.1
Tonga	13.5	71.8	17.5	67.7	36.1	75.6	3.5	62.8	5.3	59.6	9.1	51.6
Tuvalu [e]	10.2	39.0	14.7	37.5	15.2	26.1	...	...	...	...	...	...
Uzbekistan	...	...	...	...	...	...	...	...	...	...	...	...
Vanuatu	78.1	89.4	79.3	88.6	...	...	84.7	71.6	78.4	70.8	...	...
Viet Nam	72.8	79.7	62.3	81.5	...	...	73.3	67.6	72.6	69.1	...	...
Western Samoa	16.5	77.1	14.6	78.5	...	...	25.1	68.7	15.8	68.5	...	...

a   Data on working age population refer to ages 15 years and over for most countries.
b   Around 1975.
c   Around 1985.
d   Around 1994.
e   Data refer to age group 15-54 years in the formal cash economy.

EAP in Industry / EAP (%)						EAP in Services / EAP (%)						DMC
1975 [b]		1985 [c]		1994 [d]		1975 [b]		1985 [c]		1994 [d]		
Female	Male	Female	Male	Female	Male	Female	Male	Female	Male	Female	Male	
...	...	83.4	8.2	...	...	...	...	13.4	26.5	...	...	Afghanistan
5.2	5.3	...	...	8.8	15.7	21.8	16.6	...	...	6.3	29.9	Bangladesh
...	...	...	...	...	...	...	...	...	...	...	...	Bhutan
...	...	...	...	3.2	5.9	...	...	...	...	17.8	23.3	Cambodia
...	...	13.7	17.2	13.5	16.8	...	...	8.3	13.4	10.4	14.0	China, People's Rep. of
25.7	15.9	12.5	20.2	6.9	18.0	72.6	51.4	77.8	56.4	86.9	66.2	Cook Islands
8.0	18.4	11.3	16.0	...	...	64.9	30.8	60.3	31.3	...	...	Fiji
61.4	46.9	47.0	42.8	19.7	32.9	36.1	50.5	51.4	55.5	79.9	66.3	Hong Kong
8.1	12.3	9.5	15.1	...	...	8.8	17.4	9.3	19.2	...	...	India
8.5	9.4	12.2	14.6	13.1	14.7	23.0	24.6	34.1	30.6	33.3	32.7	Indonesia
...	...	22.9	36.1	...	...	...	...	60.1	36.7	...	...	Kazakstan
7.7	29.9	...	...	6.2	15.6	91.1	60.9	...	...	92.9	74.3	Kiribati
18.1	27.0	24.4	34.9	25.3	39.0	30.0	30.6	47.9	42.0	57.5	48.0	Korea, Rep. of
...	...	...	...	...	...	...	...	...	...	...	...	Kyrgyz Republic
...	...	...	...	...	...	...	...	...	...	...	...	Lao PDR
9.5	15.7	17.7	19.9	31.9	32.1	22.6	34.6	33.0	42.7	49.1	45.7	Malaysia
48.1	13.4	59.8	22.2	40.6	19.1	7.8	23.3	25.4	42.9	45.2	51.7	Maldives
...	...	33.0	16.5	...	...	...	...	64.4	55.2	...	...	Marshall Islands
...	...	...	...	...	...	...	...	...	...	...	...	Micronesia, Fed. States of
...	...	...	...	...	...	...	...	...	...	...	...	Mongolia
...	...	13.5	10.6	...	...	...	...	23.5	21.6	...	...	Myanmar
...	...	...	...	...	...	...	...	...	...	...	...	Nauru
0.4	1.0	0.3	0.9	...	...	6.7	10.9	3.0	9.5	...	...	Nepal
...	...	11.8	21.0	14.7	20.6	...	...	13.1	30.4	19.3	34.6	Pakistan
...	...	...	...	...	...	...	...	...	...	...	...	Papua New Guinea
18.3	13.9	12.8	14.5	13.5	17.1	55.6	21.6	52.2	27.3	56.0	30.1	Philippines
36.6	30.5	33.5	36.3	29.5	35.3	61.3	67.0	66.1	62.5	70.4	64.3	Singapore
...	...	9.1	16.3	...	...	...	...	39.6	39.5	...	...	Solomon Islands
13.3	14.1	20.2	19.3	21.4	20.1	21.0	34.2	24.7	31.0	37.6	48.2	Sri Lanka
19.8	21.0	42.5	35.2	...	...	31.8	43.9	41.7	42.7	...	...	Taipei,China
7.4	10.3	10.7	14.8	20.2	26.5	16.9	19.0	25.2	22.2	40.1	30.4	Thailand
7.8	10.1	9.7	12.9	41.4	11.0	88.7	27.1	84.9	27.5	49.5	37.5	Tonga
...	...	...	...	...	...	...	...	...	...	...	...	Tuvalu
...	...	...	...	...	...	...	...	...	...	...	...	Uzbekistan
2.1	6.2	1.0	6.1	...	...	13.2	22.3	20.6	23.1	...	...	Vanuatu
12.9	16.9	10.9	17.2	...	...	13.8	15.5	16.4	13.7	...	...	Viet Nam
3.7	8.7	6.1	8.9	...	...	71.2	22.6	78.1	22.6	...	...	Western Samoa

Sources: ADB, *GIDAPC*, 1993.
ILO, *YLS 1995* and past issues.
NCDS, *South Pacific Economic and Social Database*, March 1996.
Country sources.

Table 6: POVERTY AND INEQUALITY INDICATORS

DMC	Population in Poverty (%) [a]				Income Ratio of Highest 20% to Lowest 20%	Gini Coefficient
	Total	Urban	Rural		1989-94	1975-90
Afghanistan	...	...	...		...	...
Bangladesh	51.6	56.0	51.0	(1985/86)	4.2	0.3
Bhutan	...	...	...		...	...
Cambodia	30.0	19.0	32.0	(1994)	22.5	0.4
China, People's Rep. of	8.6	0.4	11.5	(1990)	7.3	0.3
Cook Islands	...	...	...		...	...
Fiji	...	...	...		...	...
Hong Kong	...	...	...		...	0.5
India	29.9	20.1	33.4	(1987-88)	5.4	0.4
Indonesia	13.7	13.4	13.8	(1993)	4.8	0.3
Kazakstan	55.0	...	...	(1995)	5.7	0.3
Kiribati	...	...	...		...	...
Korea, Rep. of	4.5	4.6	4.4	(1984)	...	0.4
Kyrgyz Republic	25.0	...	...	(1995)	6.0	...
Lao PDR	46.1	...	...	(1992-93)	4.0	...
Malaysia	10.5	4.4	14.9	(1993)	10.8	0.5
Maldives	...	...	...		...	...
Marshall Islands	...	...	...		...	...
Micronesia, Fed. States of	...	...	...		...	...
Mongolia	25.0	...	...	(1995)	...	...
Myanmar	...	...	...		...	...
Nepal	42.6	19.2	43.1	(1984/85)	...	0.5
Nauru	...	...	...		...	...
Pakistan	...	20.0	31.0	(1984/85)	5.0	0.4
Papua New Guinea	65.0	10.0	75.0	(1979)	...	...
Philippines	41.3	28.8	53.7	(1994)	10.6	0.5
Singapore	...	...	...		9.6	0.4
Solomon Islands	...	...	...		...	...
Sri Lanka	39.4	27.6	45.7	(1985/86)	4.3	0.5
Taipei,China	...	...	...		5.4	...
Thailand	43.2	27.8	49.3	(1988)	8.8	0.5
Tonga	...	...	...		...	...
Tuvalu	...	...	...		...	...
Uzbekistan	...	...	...		...	...
Vanuatu	...	...	...		...	...
Viet Nam	51.0	27.0	57.0	(1992-93)	5.5	...
Western Samoa	...	...	...		...	...

a   Based on the concept of an "absolute" poverty line, expressed in monetary terms, that is, the income or expenditure level below which a minimum nutritionally adequate diet plus essential non-food requirements are not affordable.

Sources: UNDP, *HDR 1995* and past issues.
WB, *SID 1996*.
ILO, *The Incidence of Poverty in Developing Countries: An ILO Compendium of Data*, 1993.
Country sources.
ADB data file.

Table 7: EDUCATION INDICATORS

DMC	Adult Literacy Rate (%) [a]						Gross Primary School Enrolment Ratio (%)					
	1975 [b]		1985 [c]		1995		1975		1985		1994 [d]	
	Female	Male	Female	Male	Female	Male	Female	Male	Female	Male	Female	Male
Afghanistan	5	30	...	...	15	47	8	41	13	27	16	46
Bangladesh	13	37	18	40	26	49	51	95	54	72	73	84
Bhutan	...	...	...	...	28	56	5	13	19	34	60	81
Cambodia	...	...	...	...	22	48	35	48	...	...	46	48
China, People's Rep. of	...	...	51	79	73	90	114	130	114	132	116	120
Cook Islands	...	...	...	...	...	...	...	...	...	...	...	...
Fiji	74	84	84	90	89	94	137	138	122	122	127	128
Hong Kong	64	90	...	...	88	96	117	122	105	106	...	...
India	19	48	26	55	38	66	64	96	80	110	91	113
Indonesia	45	70	58	78	78	90	78	94	114	120	112	116
Kazakstan	...	...	96	99	...	...	...	...	...	...	86	86
Kiribati	...	...	...	...	...	...	...	...	...	...	...	...
Korea, Rep. of	81	94	...	...	97	99	107	107	98	96	99	97
Kyrgyz Republic	...	...	96	99	...	...	...	...	...	...	...	...
Lao PDR	...	...	76 [f]	92 [f]	44	69	77	106	100	121	92	123
Malaysia	47	69	60	80	78	89	92	97	100	101	93	93
Maldives	82	83	92	91	93	93	...	...	...	...	133	136
Marshall Islands	...	...	...	...	...	...	...	...	...	...	...	...
Micronesia, Fed. States of	...	...	...	...	...	...	...	...	...	...	...	...
Mongolia	...	...	77	89	...	...	104	111	107	107	100	95
Myanmar	58	84	72	86	78	89	82	88	96	101	104	107
Nauru	...	...	...	...	...	...	...	...	...	...	...	...
Nepal	5	33	9	32	14	41	16	86	47	101	87	130
Pakistan	12	35	15	35	24	50	25	56	30	56	30	57
Papua New Guinea	24	39	...	...	63	81	44	69	63	74	67	80
Philippines	81	84	83	84	94	95	...	...	107	108	111	113
Singapore	54	83	74	92	86	96	107	113	113	117	107	109
Solomon Islands	...	...	...	...	...	...	...	...	65	85	87	102
Sri Lanka	69	86	82	91	87	93	74	81	101	104	105	106
Taipei,China	63 [g]	88 [g]	78 [g]	94 [g]	86 [g]	96 [g]	...	...	...	...	...	...
Thailand	70	87	85	93	92	96	80	87	97	100	97	98
Tonga	100	100	...	...	...	...	...	...	...	...	...	...
Tuvalu	...	...	...	...	...	...	...	...	...	...	...	...
Uzbekistan	...	...	96	99	...	...	...	...	...	...	79	80
Vanuatu	48	57	...	...	...	...	...	...	106	112	107	105
Viet Nam	78	91	...	...	91	97	108	106	100	106	99	105
Western Samoa	98	98	...	...	...	...	...	...	90	87	107	106

a Adult literacy rate refer to population of 15 years old and over.
b Data relate to years 1970 through 1979.
c Data relate to years 1980 through 1989.
d Data relate to years 1990 through 1994.
e Refers to the percentage of children starting primary school who eventually attain Grade 4.
f Refers to population of 15-45 years old.
g Refers to population of 25 years old and over.

Table 7: EDUCATION INDICATORS (Continued)

DMC	Percentage of Cohort reaching Grade 4 [e]				Gross Secondary School Enrolment Ratio (%)					
	1970		1988		1975		1985		1994 [d]	
	Female	Male	Female	Male	Female	Male	Female	Male	Female	Male
Afghanistan	...	...	...	...	2	13	6	12	8	22
Bangladesh	...	...	46	44	8	29	11	26	13	25
Bhutan	...	...	...	...	...	...	...	...	...	...
Cambodia	...	...	...	...	...	...	...	...	...	...
China, People's Republic of	...	...	78	98	38	54	33	45	51	60
Cook Islands	...	...	...	...	...	...	...	...	...	...
Fiji	...	...	...	...	4443	51	51	65	64	
Hong Kong	96	95	...	...	47	51	73	69	...	...
India	44	49	...	...	18	37	26	48	38	59
Indonesia	67	89	83	99	15	25	41	50	39	48
Kazakstan	...	...	...	...	...	...	...	...	91	89
Kiribati	...	...	...	...	...	...	...	...	...	...
Korea, Rep. of	95	94	100	100	48	64	91	93	96	97
Kyrgyz Republic	...	...	...	...	...	...	...	...	...	...
Lao PDR	...	...	...	...	...	...	19	27	19	31
Malaysia	...	...	99	98	39	53	53	53	61	56
Maldives	...	...	...	...	...	...	...	...	49	49
Marshall Islands	...	...	...	...	...	...	...	...	...	...
Micronesia, Fed. States of	...	...	...	...	...	...	...	...	...	...
Mongolia	...	...	...	...	84	77	97	85	...	...
Myanmar	...	...	...	...	20	24	22	24	23	23
Nauru	...	...	...	...	...	...	...	...	...	...
Nepal	...	...	...	...	4	23	12	37	23	46
Pakistan	50	62	45	55	7	22	10	24	13	28
Papua New Guinea	82	90	70	72	7	16	9	16	10	15
Philippines	...	...	85	84	...	...	65	64	75	71
Singapore	98	99	100	100	52	51	64	61	71	69
Solomon Islands	...	...	...	...	...	...	9	22	13	21
Sri Lanka	...	...	99	99	49	47	66	60	78	71
Taipei,China	...	...	...	...	69	78	91	89	98	94
Thailand	75	75	...	...	22	28	28	30	37	38
Tonga	...	...	...	...	...	...	...	...	...	...
Tuvalu	...	...	...	...	...	...	...	...	...	...
Uzbekistan	...	...	...	...	...	...	...	...	92	96
Vanuatu	...	...	...	...	...	...	14	18	18	23
Viet Nam	...	...	...	...	41	38	41	44	40	43
Western Samoa	...	...	...	...	...	...	67	61	...	...

Sources: UNESCO, *SY 1995* and past issues.
UNDP, *HDR 1995* and past issue.
WB, *WDR 1995*.
WB, *SID 1996*.
Country sources.

Table 8: HEALTH INDICATORS

DMC	Persons per Hospital Bed			Persons per Physician			Daily Per Capita Protein Supply (grams)			Daily Per Capita Calorie Supply (calories)		
	1975	1985	1993	1975	1985	1993	1975	1985	1992	1975	1985	1992
Afghanistan	5025[a]	3699[b]	4003[c]	15417[a]	13237[b]	7001[c]	...	55	43	2010	1970	1523
Bangladesh	5110	3638	3265	12689	6703	5143	39	43	43	1760	1953	2019
Bhutan	...	1500	1500[d]	...	11300	10922[e]	...	...	...	...	...	...
Cambodia	925[a]	...	491[c]	16248[a]	16489[b]	9727[c]	42	50	50	1710	2062	2021
China, People's Rep. of	584	480	424	3184	752	645	52	62	67	2210	2596	2727
Cook Islands	114[f]	...	121[g]	968[f]	...	931[g]	...	...	...	...	...	...
Fiji	358	400	431[h]	2391	1708	2074[h]	57	60	74	2540	2710	3089
Hong Kong	237	223	223	1528	1126	845	79	84	94	2580	2724	3129
India	1264	1143	1037	3039	2437	2106	45	54	58	1790	2179	2395
Indonesia	1222[a]	1796[b]	1503[c]	26988[a]	9412[b]	7028[c]	42	54	61	2040	2578	2752
Kazakstan	79[a]	74	75	361[a]	267	252	...	...	...	...	...	...
Kiribati	81[a]	205[b]	...	1633[a]	1900[b]	5143[c]	58	64	66	2160	2637	2651
Korea, Rep. of	1661	549	349	2100	1379	855	74	75	86	2700	2822	3285
Kyrgyz Republic	88[a]	83[b]	92[c]	402[a]	296[b]	303[c]	...	...	...	...	...	...
Lao PDR	1078[a]	...	405[c]	15156[a]	1362[b]	4446[c]	49	67	63	1840	2434	2259
Malaysia	343[i]	408	489	3981[i]	3175	2302	54	55	60	2540	2688	2888
Maldives	3500[j]	1500	1192	...	7889	5297	62	88	...	1750	2335	2580
Marshall Islands	...	...	...	...	...	...	...	...	...	...	...	...
Micronesia, Fed. States of	...	290	330[d]	...	2614	3294[d]	...	...	...	...	...	...
Mongolia	133	89	101	497	409	401	...	88	69	...	2435	1899
Myanmar	1180	1448	1548[h]	5370	3714	3565[h]	57	64	64	2220	2460	2598
Nauru	...	...	...	...	...	...	...	...	...	...	...	...
Nepal	5823	4634	3894[h]	36453	23584	12612[h]	49	50	50	2030	1950	1957
Pakistan	2061	1695	1548	3971	3153	1918	59	58	56	2210	2128	2315
Papua New Guinea	202[a]	208[b]	297[c]	14495	12416	10083[d]	43	49	49	2220	2418	2613
Philippines	606	645	935	2661[j,k]	6413[k]	9689[k]	49	49	52	2050	2182	2257
Singapore	249	248	275	1395	985	722	78	80	...	2850	2929	...
Solomon Islands	139[a]	178[b]	...	5135	8438	...	38	58	53	1980	2293	2173
Sri Lanka	341	358	360	6389	8276[k]	4745	40	50	47	2020	2423	2273
Taipei,China	526	258	208	1492[l]	1130[l]	802[l]	75	83	90	2722	2874	3111
Thailand	786	614	606[g]	8270	5975	4425[g]	48	49	54	2330	2286	2432
Tonga	301	270	266[d]	3259	2703	2235[d]	59	69	68	3050	2890	2946
Tuvalu	...	...	...	2367[j]	...	...	...	...	...	...	...	...
Uzbekistan	96[a]	81[b]	106[c]	393[a]	293[b]	282[c]	...	...	...	...	...	...
Vanuatu	...	273	405[e]	...	4789	7365[e]	65	68	63	2400	2717	2739
Viet Nam	336	284	365[d]	5668	3135	2491	52	48	52	2100	2152	2250
Western Samoa	229	232	253[d]	2745	3383	4075[d]	54	49	76	2260	2415	2828

a   Refers to the period 1970-1975.
b   Refers to the period 1980-1985.
c   Refers to the period 1989-1994.
d   Refers to 1989.
e   Refers to 1990.
f   Refers to 1976.
g   Refers to 1991.
h   Refers to 1992.
i   Refers to Peninsular Malaysia only.
j   Refers to 1977.
k   Physicians include doctors in government service only.
l   Physicians include doctors practicing herbal medicine.

Table 8: HEALTH INDICATORS (Continued)

	Child Malnutrition (Percent of under age 5)			Population with Access to Safe Water (%)		Population with Access to Sanitation (%)	
				Urban	Rural	Urban	Rural
	1975 [a]	1985 [b]	1994 [c]	1988-93		1988-93	
Afghanistan	...	...	...	40	19	13	...
Bangladesh	84.4	70.1	67.0	82	85	63	26
Bhutan	...	...	...	60	30	50	7
Cambodia	...	20.0	...	65	33	81	8
China, People's Rep. of	...	...	17.5	99	60	58	3
Cook Islands	...	...	...	...	...	...	...
Fiji	...	...	...	...	...	...	...
Hong Kong	...	...	...	100	96	90	50
India	...	...	63.0	85	78	62	12
Indonesia	...	...	38.7	68	43	64	36
Kazakstan	...	...	...	...	...	...	...
Kiribati	...	...	...	...	...	...	...
Korea, Rep. of	...	...	...	100	76	100	100
Kyrgyz Republic	...	...	...	...	...	...	...
Lao PDR	...	36.5	40.0	54	33	97	8
Malaysia	...	26.6	23.3	96	66	...	...
Maldives	...	56.1	...	...	...	...	...
Marshall Islands	...	...	...	...	...	...	...
Micronesia, Fed. States of	...	...	...	...	...	...	...
Mongolia	...	...	10.2	100	58	100	47
Myanmar	...	42.1	31.2	37	...	39	35
Nauru	...	...	...	...	...	...	...
Nepal	69.6	...	69.6	67	39	52	3
Pakistan	...	...	40.4	85	50	60	17
Papua New Guinea	...	34.7	...	94	20	57	10
Philippines	...	33.2	29.6	85	79	79	62
Singapore	14.4	...	14.4	100	...	99	...
Solomon Islands	20.3	...	...	...	...	...	...
Sri Lanka	...	47.5	37.6	...	...	...	...
Taipei,China	...	...	...	...	...	...	...
Thailand	...	36.0	13.0	87	72	80	72
Tonga	...	...	...	...	...	...	...
Tuvalu	...	...	...	...	...	...	...
Uzbekistan	...	...	...	...	...	...	...
Vanuatu	...	19.7	...	...	...	...	...
Viet Nam	...	52.0	44.9	39	21	34	14
Western Samoa	...	...	...	...	...	...	...

Sources: Country sources.
ESCAP, *APF 1995* and past issues.
FAO, Statistics Division, 14 February 1995 and past communication.
FAO, *PY 1994*.
UNDP, *HDR 1995*.
WB, *SID 1996*.

Table 9: ENVIRONMENT INDICATORS

DMC	Average Annual Rate of Deforestation (As % of Forest Area) 1981-90	National Protected Areas [a] (As % of total land area) 1985	National Protected Areas [a] (As % of total land area) 1993	Per Capita Carbon Dioxide Emissions [b] (metric tons) 1991	Greenhouse Index (Carbon Heating Equiv. in MT Per Capita) 1988-89
Afghanistan	...	0.0	0.3	0.3	0.2
Bangladesh	3.3	0.2	0.7	0.2	0.3
Bhutan	0.6	20.2	19.3	0.1	0.2
Cambodia	1.0	0.1	0.0	0.0	...
China, People's Rep. of	...	0.2	3.2	2.2	0.6
Cook Islands	...	...	0.7	...	...
Fiji	...	0.3	0.3	1.0	0.4
Hong Kong	...	...	...	4.6	...
India	0.6	3.7	4.0	0.8	0.5
Indonesia	1.0	7.6	10.2	0.9	1.3
Kazakstan	...	...	0.3	...	...
Kiribati	...	...	38.9 [c]	...	...
Korea, Rep. of	...	4.8	7.6	6.1	1.2
Kyrgyz Republic	...	...	1.0	...	...
Lao PDR	0.9	0.0	0.0	0.1	...
Malaysia	1.8	4.7	4.5	3.3	3.2
Maldives	...	...	...	...	...
Marshall Islands	...	...	...	...	...
Micronesia, Fed. States of	...	...	...	...	...
Mongolia	...	3.0	3.9	4.4	1.5
Myanmar	1.2	0.0	0.3	0.1	4.3
Nauru	...	...	...	14.7	...
Nepal	1.0	7.1	7.9	0.0	0.7
Pakistan	2.9	8.4	4.6	0.6	0.2
Papua New Guinea	0.3	0.0	0.1	0.6	0.6
Philippines	2.9	1.3	1.9	0.7	0.9
Singapore	0.0	4.3	2.6	15.1	4.2
Solomon Islands	...	0.0	0.0	0.5	0.1
Sri Lanka	1.3	9.9	11.9	0.3	0.5
Taipei,China	...	...	8.0	...	...
Thailand	2.9	5.3	12.6	1.8	1.8
Tonga	...	...	...	0.8	...
Tuvalu	...	...	...	...	...
Uzbekistan	...	...	0.5	...	...
Vanuatu	...	...	...	0.4	...
Viet Nam	1.4	0.5	2.7	0.3	0.8
Western Samoa	...	...	...	...	...

a Refers to all protected areas at least 1000 ha. listed in categories I - V of the International Union for Conservation of Nature and Natural Resources (IUCN).
b Refers to carbon dioxide emissions from industrial processes.
c National protected areas include marine areas.

Sources: UNDP, *HDR 1995* and past issues.
           ESCAP, *State of the Environment in Asia and the Pacific 1995.*
           UNEP, *Environmental Data Report 1993-94.*
           World Resources Institute, *World Resources 1994/1995* and past issues.

Table 10: LAND USE

DMC	Total Area (1000 sq.km.) 1993	Share in Total Land Area (%)								Cropped Land Per Capita (Ha.)	
		Agriculture (Cropped Land)		Permanent Pastures		Forest & Woodland		Others			
		1975	1993	1975	1993	1975	1993	1975	1993	1975	1993
Afghanistan	652.1	12.3	12.4	46.0	46.0	2.9	2.9	38.7	38.7	0.52	0.46
Bangladesh	144.0	70.1	74.5	4.6	4.6	16.9	14.6	8.4	6.3	0.12	0.08
Bhutan	47.0	2.4	2.9	5.6	5.8	55.0	66.0	37.1	25.4	0.10	0.08
Cambodia	181.0	11.9	13.6	3.3	11.3	74.7	65.7	10.1	9.4	0.30	0.25
China, People's Rep. of	9597.0	10.8	10.3	32.3	42.9	15.1	14.0	41.8	32.8	0.11	0.08
Cook Islands	0.2	26.1	21.7	–	–	–	–	73.9	78.3	0.32	0.26
Fiji	18.3	8.5	14.2	4.9	9.6	64.9	64.9	21.7	11.3	0.27	0.34
Hong Kong	1.0	9.9	7.1	0.0	1.0	20.8	22.2	69.3	69.7	0.00	0.00
India	3287.6	56.5	57.1	4.3	3.8	22.1	23.0	17.1	16.1	0.27	0.19
Indonesia	1904.6	14.4	17.1	6.8	6.5	67.5	61.7	11.4	14.7	0.19	0.16
Kazakstan	2717.3	13.4	12.8	69.2	68.7	3.9	3.5	13.5	15.0	2.57	2.05
Kiribati	0.7	49.3	50.7	–	–	2.7	2.7	47.9	46.6	0.65	0.49
Korea, Rep. of	99.0	22.7	20.8	0.3	0.9	67.1	65.4	9.9	12.8	0.06	0.05
Kyrgyz Republic	198.5	7.6	7.2	45.8	43.8	4.3	3.5	42.3	45.5	0.45	0.31
Lao PDR	236.8	2.9	3.5	3.5	3.5	61.5	54.2	32.1	38.9	0.22	0.17
Malaysia	329.8	14.2	14.9	0.1	0.1	68.4	67.9	17.3	17.2	0.38	0.25
Maldives	0.3	10.0	10.0	3.3	3.3	3.3	3.3	83.3	83.3	0.02	0.01
Marshall Islands	0.2	...	...	...	...	...	...	...	...	...	...
Micronesia, Fed. States of	0.7	...	...	...	...	...	...	...	...	...	...
Mongolia	1566.5	0.5	0.9	89.3	79.8	9.7	8.8	0.5	10.5	0.57	0.60
Myanmar	676.6	15.2	15.3	0.6	0.5	48.9	49.3	35.4	34.8	0.33	0.23
Nauru	0.0	...	...	...	...	...	...	...	...	...	...
Nepal	140.8	17.0	17.2	13.2	14.6	42.9	42.0	26.9	26.1	0.18	0.11
Pakistan	796.1	25.7	27.6	6.5	6.5	3.7	4.5	64.1	61.4	0.27	0.16
Papua New Guinea	462.8	0.8	0.9	0.2	0.2	92.7	92.7	6.2	6.2	0.13	0.10
Philippines	300.0	25.7	30.8	2.8	4.3	45.2	45.6	26.3	19.3	0.18	0.14
Singapore	0.6	13.1	1.6	–	–	4.9	4.9	82.0	93.4	0.00	0.00
Solomon Islands	28.9	1.8	2.0	1.4	1.4	91.5	87.5	5.4	9.0	0.26	0.16
Sri Lanka	65.6	29.6	29.4	6.8	6.8	27.9	32.5	35.8	31.3	0.14	0.11
Taipei,China [a]	36.0	25.5	24.3	...	...	61.8	51.8	12.7	23.9	0.06	0.04
Thailand	513.1	32.6	40.7	1.1	1.6	36.2	26.4	30.1	31.3	0.40	0.36
Tonga	0.8	63.9	66.7	5.6	5.6	11.1	11.1	19.4	16.7	0.52	0.49
Tuvalu	0.0	–	–	–	–	–	–	100.0	100.0	–	–
Uzbekistan	447.4	8.0	10.1	53.0	46.5	5.9	2.9	33.1	40.5	0.26	0.21
Vanuatu	12.2	8.3	11.8	2.1	2.1	75.0	75.0	14.7	11.2	0.99	0.89
Viet Nam	331.7	19.2	20.6	0.8	1.0	41.6	29.6	38.4	48.8	0.13	0.09
Western Samoa	2.8	41.7	43.1	0.4	0.4	48.8	47.3	9.2	9.2	0.77	0.73

a   Agriculture refers to cultivated land area consisting of all types of registered and unregistered land, including reclaimed river bed, reclaimed tidal land, slope-land, and virgin land, which have been used for farming purposes.

Sources: FAO, *FAOSTAT* v3.0, *PY 1994* and *Agrostat* PC v3.0.
DGBAS, *Statistical Yearbook 1995* for Taipei,China.

DMC	Total GNP (Million US$)			Per Capita GNP (US$)		
	1992 [b]	1993 [c]	1994 [d]	1992 [b]	1993 [c]	1994 [d]
Afghanistan	...	...	...	...	...	...
Bangladesh	25130	25630	26640	220	220	230
Bhutan	280	260	270	440	400	400
Cambodia	1990	2240	2360	210	230	240
China, People's Rep. of	558000	580380	630200	480	490	530
Cook Islands	70	70	80	3870	3880	4150
Fiji	1570	1660	1780	2090	2180	2320
Hong Kong [e]	95170	110280	126290	16670	19010	21650
India	278240	263010	278740	320	290	310
Indonesia	137200	151350	167630	750	810	880
Kazakstan	29350 *	24640 *	18900 *	1740 *	1410 *	1110 *
Kiribati	50	50	60	720	710	730
Korea, Rep. of	315400	337940	366480	7220	7660	8220
Kyrgyz Republic	4600 *	3890 *	2820 *	1020 *	850 *	610 *
Lao PDR	1130	1300	1500	250	280	320
Malaysia	52660	59670	68670	2830	3140	3520
Maldives	170	200	220	740	820	900
Marshall Islands	...	80	90	...	1610	1680
Micronesia, Fed. States of	...	190	200	...	1840	1890
Mongolia	1050	750	800	460	320	340
Myanmar	...	...	...	...	...	...
Nauru	...	...	...	...	...	...
Nepal	4100	4050	4170	200	190	200
Pakistan	51340	54030	55560	430	440	440
Papua New Guinea	4010	4860	4860	1000	1180	1160
Philippines	51110	55160	63310	810	850	960
Singapore	48160	56160	65840	17440	20130	23360
Solomon Islands	240	260	290	710	740	800
Sri Lanka	9600	10620	11630	550	600	640
Taipei,China	209340	229310	251080	10130	11000	11930
Thailand	109330	123420	129860	1910	2110	2210
Tonga	140	150	160	1460	1540	1640
Tuvalu	...	...	...	...	...	...
Uzbekistan	21470 *	21520 *	21140 *	1010 *	980 *	950 *
Vanuatu	170	185	190	1110	1150	1150
Viet Nam	...	12050	13780	...	170	190
Western Samoa	150	160	160	960	960	970

a   Total and per capita GNP are estimated according to World Bank Atlas method of converting data in national currency to current U.S. dollars.
    All figures are rounded to the nearest ten.
b   In 1990-92 base.
c   In 1991-93 base.
d   In 1992-94 base.
e   Data refer to GDP.

Sources: WB, *The World Bank Atlas 1996* and past issues.
           WB, 8 February 1996.

Table 12: GROWTH RATES OF REAL GDP AND MAJOR SECTORS [a]
(Percent)

DMC	Real GDP						Agriculture					
	1990	1991	1992	1993	1994	1995	1990	1991	1992	1993	1994	1995
Afghanistan	-0.1	-8.4	-12.5	-10.8	...	...	-9.1	0.5	4.7	-8.6	...	...
Bangladesh	6.6	3.4	4.2	4.5	4.2	4.1	10.0	1.6	2.2	1.8	0.3	-1.6
Bhutan [b]	6.6	3.5	4.1	6.3	6.5	5.5	3.1	3.2	-1.8	3.9	2.0	3.2
Cambodia	1.2	7.6	7.0	4.1	4.0	7.0	1.2	6.7	1.9	-1.0	0.0	5.5
China, People's Rep. of	3.9	9.3	14.2	13.5	11.8	10.2	7.4	2.4	4.7	4.7	4.0	4.5
Cook Islands	1.7	2.1	2.0	1.7	1.5	1.3	-0.6	4.6	2.0	1.7	1.5	1.3
Fiji [b]	3.5	0.5	3.2	1.8	4.5	2.2	-4.1	-1.3	3.1	3.4	8.5	-1.9
Hong Kong	3.4	5.1	6.3	6.1	5.4	4.6	...	...	...	...	...	...
India [b]	5.4	0.8	5.1	5.0	6.3	3.3	3.8	-2.3	6.0	3.2	4.9	0.1
Indonesia	9.0	8.9	7.2	7.3	7.5*	8.1*	3.1	2.9	6.3	1.7	0.5*	4.0*
Kazakstan	...	-14.8	-14.9	-12.9	-25.5	-8.9*	...	-23.6	0.0	-12.7	-22.9	...
Kiribati [b]	0.7	0.5	4.0	...	...	...	-8.2	12.2	1.6	...	...	...
Korea, Rep. of	9.5	9.1	5.1	5.8	8.6	9.0	-4.6	0.4	6.0	-2.9	1.6	2.8
Kyrgyz Republic [c]	...	-7.8	-13.8	-15.5	-20.1	-6.0	...	-8.2	-3.2	-9.1	-8.7	-2.0
Lao PDR [b]	7.3	3.4	7.0	5.2	8.0	7.0*	8.7	-1.7	8.3	2.7	8.3	4.9*
Malaysia	9.7	8.6	7.8	8.3	9.2	9.6*	0.4	0.0	4.7	4.3	-1.0	4.2*
Maldives	16.2	7.6	6.3	6.2	6.6	7.2	6.0	3.8	3.8	3.9	3.8	3.3
Marshall Islands	7.0	1.1	0.0	4.1	-3.8	10.9	...	...	...	...	...	...
Micronesia, Fed. States of	-3.9	4.5	-1.3	5.7	1.3	1.0	...	...	...	...	...	...
Mongolia	-2.5	-9.2	-9.5	-3.0	2.3	6.3	-1.3	-4.4	-2.1	-2.7	2.7	4.2
Myanmar	2.8	-0.6	9.7	5.9	6.8	7.7	1.8	-2.4	10.5	4.2	6.1	7.3
Nauru	...	...	...	...	...	...	...	...	...	...	...	...
Nepal [b]	4.5	6.4	4.6	3.1	7.1	2.1*	5.8	2.2	-1.1	-0.6	7.2	-0.7*
Pakistan [b]	4.6	5.6	7.7	2.3	4.5	4.4	3.0	5.0	9.5	-5.4	5.4	5.8
Papua New Guinea	-3.0	9.5	11.8	16.5	0.8	...	2.2	-2.6	6.0	9.4	7.2	...
Philippines	3.0	-0.6	0.3	2.1	4.4	4.8	0.5	1.4	0.4	2.1	2.6	0.9
Singapore	9.0	7.0	6.2	10.4	10.2	8.9	-7.6	-9.4	1.1	-2.4	5.6	7.7
Solomon Islands [b]	1.5	3.9	3.8	...	...	...	2.0	2.7	9.5	...	...	...
Sri Lanka	6.2	4.8	4.4	6.9	5.6	5.6	8.5	1.8	-1.8	6.8	3.3	2.3
Taipei,China	5.4	7.6	6.8	6.3	6.5	6.1	2.1	1.8	-2.9	5.4	-4.4	2.4
Thailand	11.2	8.5	8.1	8.3	8.7*	8.7*	-4.6	6.5	6.0	-1.9	5.5*	2.1*
Tonga [b]	-2.7	5.4	3.5	2.8	5.7	1.8	-5.0	9.8	7.3	2.7	7.1	5.4
Tuvalu [b]	19.8	13.0	1.6	-7.4	16.8	7.0	...	...	...	...	...	...
Uzbekistan	...	...	...	...	...	...	...	...	...	...	...	...
Vanuatu	4.8	4.4	1.0	4.0	2.0	2.0	15.1	-2.0	1.9	8.2	...	...
Viet Nam	2.3	6.0	8.6	8.1	8.8	9.5*	-1.2	2.2	7.2	3.8	3.9	4.5*
Western Samoa	-7.5	-27.9	-4.3	9.5	-7.8	6.7	...	...	...	...	...	...

a Unless otherwise indicated, growth rates are based on GDP at constant market prices in national currency.
b Based on GDP at constant factor cost.
c Based on NMP at constant prices.

Sources: Country sources.
          ADB data file.

Table 12: GROWTH RATES OF REAL GDP AND MAJOR SECTORS [a] (Continued)
(Percent)

Industry						Services						DMC
1990	1991	1992	1993	1994	1995	1990	1991	1992	1993	1994	1995	
11.4	-24.1	-44.5	-11.4	...	...	6.1	4.0	-5.6	-18.2	...	...	Afghanistan
6.4	4.3	7.1	8.0	7.8	8.5	4.0	4.6	4.8	5.3	5.8	5.9	Bangladesh
1.7	2.4	12.9	9.8	16.1	8.5	16.1	4.8	5.9	6.9	4.8	5.6	Bhutan
-2.1	8.9	15.5	13.1	7.5	9.5	2.7	8.4	11.2	7.2	7.5	7.5	Cambodia
3.2	13.3	21.7	20.7	17.4	13.6	2.0	10.0	11.6	9.5	8.2	8.0	China, People's Rep.
-13.3	44.7	2.0	1.7	1.5	1.3	3.9	-2.2	2.0	1.7	1.5	1.4	Cook Islands
0.7	6.2	5.8	-4.5	8.0	2.6	7.3	-0.4	2.4	3.1	2.1	3.6	Fiji
...	...	...	...	...	...	...	...	...	...	...	...	Hong Kong
7.2	-1.1	3.9	4.2	8.3	4.6	5.2	4.9	5.1	6.8	6.0	4.7	India
11.5	11.7	8.2	9.8	11.2*	10.3*	9.8	9.3	6.8	7.4	6.9*	7.5*	Indonesia
...	-13.3	-23.3	-19.3	-26.6	...	...	-12.7	-9.9	-5.6	-25.5	...	Kazakstan
7.3	-20.1	-10.8	...	...	...	3.8	-0.5	7.6	...	...	...	Kiribati
13.7	10.4	3.4	6.2	9.0	10.3	8.8	9.5	6.4	6.8	9.3	8.6	Korea, Rep. of
...	-7.4	-26.0	-22.7	-37.3	-9.9	...	-7.9	-11.6	-16.3	-19.7	-9.2	Kyrgyz Republic
16.2	19.9	7.5	10.3	10.7	11.4*	-0.4	6.5	3.9	7.7	5.6	8.5*	Lao PDR
13.2	11.2	8.9	10.1	12.4	13.5*	11.0	9.9	8.0	8.1	9.9	7.2*	Malaysia
17.8	9.8	9.0	8.4	6.1	8.3	17.2	7.6	6.0	5.9	7.0	7.3	Maldives
...	...	...	...	...	...	...	...	...	...	...	...	Marshall Islands
...	...	...	...	...	...	...	...	...	...	...	...	Micronesia, Fed. States of
-2.7	-12.8	-12.9	-6.9	2.1	14.6	-3.4	-9.8	-13.2	1.0	2.0	0.2	Mongolia
5.5	1.5	12.7	12.0	8.9	11.4	3.1	0.7	7.6	5.8	6.8	6.8	Myanmar
...	...	...	...	...	...	...	...	...	...	...	...	Nauru
2.8	12.5	16.8	4.8	8.4	2.9*	3.4	9.9	6.4	7.1	6.2	5.0*	Nepal
6.5	6.9	7.7	5.2	4.9	3.6	4.4	5.2	6.8	4.9	3.9	4.1	Pakistan
-2.5	30.0	28.5	35.8	-4.9	...	-7.4	6.5	2.9	3.0	2.9	...	Papua New Guinea
2.6	-2.7	-0.5	1.6	5.8	7.3	4.9	0.2	1.0	2.5	4.3	4.9	Philippines
9.1	7.8	5.7	9.4	13.4	9.8	9.0	6.6	6.6	11.0	8.4	8.4	Singapore
0.4	-0.1	-42.9	...	...	...	1.0	6.2	6.6	...	...	...	Solomon Islands
7.8	4.4	7.5	9.7	8.6	8.0	4.2	6.4	5.4	5.4	5.0	5.4	Sri Lanka
1.1	6.8	4.3	4.1	5.7	5.8	9.2	8.5	9.3	7.9	7.8	6.4	Taipei,China
16.1	12.1	9.9	10.6	9.9*	12.4*	12.8	6.1	7.2	9.2	8.5*	7.1*	Thailand
1.0	-10.1	0.3	5.8	6.7	-2.4	-2.2	7.0	1.6	2.1	4.5	0.2	Tonga
...	...	...	...	...	...	...	...	...	...	...	...	Tuvalu
...	...	...	...	...	...	...	...	...	...	...	...	Uzbekistan
8.1	8.3	-8.4	2.7	...	...	0.9	5.6	3.0	3.0	...	...	Vanuatu
2.6	9.0	14.0	13.1	14.0	12.0*	6.3	8.1	6.9	9.1	10.0	12.2*	Viet Nam
...	...	...	...	...	...	...	...	...	...	...	...	Western Samoa

Table 13: SHARES OF MAJOR SECTOS IN GDP [a]
(Percent)

DMC	Agriculture			Industry						Services		
				All			Manufacturing only					
	1975	1985	1995	1975	1985	1995	1975	1985	1995	1975	1985	1995
Afghanistan	...	...	...	...	...	...	...	...	...	...	...	...
Bangladesh	59.1	41.8	...	11.1	16.0	...	6.7	9.9	...	29.8	42.3	...
Bhutan [b]	...	52.6	...	...	19.0	...	...	5.5	...	...	28.4	...
Cambodia	...	...	...	...	...	...	...	...	...	...	...	...
China, People's Rep. of	...	28.4	19.7	...	43.1	49.0	...	38.5 [c]	42.8 [c]	...	28.5	31.3
Cook Islands	22.0	14.9	18.1	10.0	7.2	9.3	...	4.4	4.1	68.0	77.9	72.6
Fiji [b]	...	18.3	...	...	19.5	...	...	9.5	...	...	62.2	...
Hong Kong [b]	1.3	0.5	...	32.5	29.9	...	25.1	22.1	...	66.2	69.6	...
India [b]	40.5	33.0	...	23.7	28.2	...	16.7	17.9	...	35.8	38.8	...
Indonesia	31.7	23.2	17.2 *	33.8	35.8	41.5 *	8.9	16.0	24.3 *	34.6	40.9	41.3 *
Kazakstan [d]	...	29.4	16.6	...	49.0	47.1	...	32.9 [c]	35.6 [c]	...	21.5	36.3
Kiribati [b]	...	27.1	...	...	10.0	...	...	2.3	...	...	62.9	...
Korea, Rep. of	24.5	12.5	6.6	33.6	41.0	43.6	26.2	29.3	26.9	42.0	46.5	49.8
Kyrgyz Republic [d]	...	...	43.6	...	...	23.9	...	...	16.8 [e]	...	...	32.5
Lao PDR [b]	...	53.9	55.9 *	...	17.7	18.7 *	...	10.0	13.4 *	...	28.4	25.4 *
Malaysia	...	...	...	...	...	...	...	...	...	...	...	...
Maldives	...	...	...	...	...	...	...	...	...	...	...	...
Marshall Islands	...	...	...	...	...	...	...	...	...	...	...	...
Micronesia, Fed. States of	...	...	...	...	...	...	...	...	...	...	...	...
Mongolia [f]	22.4	14.5	...	30.1	35.1	...	...	30.8 [c]	...	47.5	50.4	...
Myanmar	47.1	48.2	62.1	10.8	13.1	9.9	9.0	9.9	7.2	42.2	38.7	28.0
Nauru	...	...	...	...	...	...	...	...	...	...	...	...
Nepal [b]	71.8	51.7	42.4 *	8.2	15.1	21.7 *	4.2	5.7	9.2 *	20.1	33.2	35.9 *
Pakistan [b]	32.4	28.5	26.0	22.2	22.5	24.4	15.3	15.9	17.2	45.5	49.0	49.6
Papua New Guinea	29.6	33.3	...	27.2	26.6	...	8.6	10.9	...	43.2	40.1	...
Philippines	30.3	24.6	21.7	35.0	35.1	32.1	25.7	25.2	22.9	34.7	40.4	46.3
Singapore	1.9	0.8	0.2	34.1	36.6	35.5	23.9	23.6	26.7	64.0	62.6	64.3
Solomon Islands [b]	...	51.7	...	...	8.4	...	...	3.8	...	...	39.9	...
Sri Lanka	28.0	24.4	...	30.6	26.8	...	24.2	16.6	...	41.4	48.8	...
Taipei,China	12.7	5.8	3.5	39.9	46.3	36.3	30.9	37.6	28.2	47.4	47.9	60.2
Thailand	26.9	15.8	10.9 *	25.8	31.8	39.8 *	18.7	21.9	29.2 *	47.3	52.3	49.2 *
Tonga [b]	50.1	37.8	35.2	10.4	14.9	13.0	5.3	5.7	5.2	39.5	47.3	51.8
Tuvalu [b]	...	10.8	...	...	13.5	...	...	2.1 [e]	...	...	75.6	...
Uzbekistan	...	...	...	...	...	...	...	...	...	...	...	...
Vanuatu	...	29.5	...	...	8.1	...	...	3.8	...	...	62.4	...
Viet Nam [g]	...	47.2	27.5 *	...	34.5	29.1 *	...	30.0 [c]	21.9 * [c]	...	18.3	43.4 *
Western Samoa	...	...	...	...	...	...	...	...	...	...	...	...

a   Unless otherwise indicated, data are based on GDP at current market prices.
b   Based on GDP at current factor cost.
c   Includes mining and electricity, gas and water.
d   Based on NMP at current prices.
e   Includes mining.
f   Data for 1975 refer to NMP, and data for 1985 refer to GDP at factor cost.
g   Data for 1985 refer to NMP, and data for 1995 refer to GDP at market prices.

Sources: Country sources.

Table 14: EXPENDITURE SHARES IN GDP [a]
(Percent)

DMC	Private Consumption			Government Consumption			Gross Capital Formation			Net Exports [b]		
	1975	1985	1995	1975	1985	1995	1975	1985	1995	1975	1985	1995
Afghanistan	...	...	...	...	...	...	...	...	...	...	...	...
Bangladesh	96.0	85.5	78.5	3.1	12.2	13.7	5.9	12.8	16.6	-5.0	-10.5	-8.9
Bhutan	...	63.0	41.5	...	23.5	22.5	...	45.4	54.5	...	-31.8	-18.5
Cambodia	...	...	...	...	...	...	...	...	...	...	...	...
China, People's Rep. of	...	51.2	45.6	...	13.2	12.1	...	37.8	39.5	...	-2.2	2.8
Cook Islands	...	...	...	...	...	...	...	...	...	...	...	...
Fiji	68.0	63.7	...	12.0	19.2	...	20.6	19.1	...	-0.6	-1.9	...
Hong Kong	67.4	61.7	58.8	7.5	7.3	8.6	24.1	21.6	34.9	1.0	9.4	-2.3
India	73.1	67.4	61.8 *	9.4	11.1	13.0 *	20.8	23.9	20.9 *	-3.3	-2.4	4.3 *
Indonesia	69.2	59.0	56.0 *	9.9	11.2	8.2 *	20.3	28.0	37.8 *	0.6	1.8	-2.0 *
Kazakstan [c]	...	79.9	...	...	13.4	...	...	42.8	...	...	-36.1	...
Kiribati	37.4	67.8	...	18.0	51.1	...	4.8	53.9	...	39.8	-72.7	...
Korea, Rep. of	70.9	58.5	52.9	11.0	10.1	10.4	27.1	29.6	37.1	-8.9	1.8	-0.4
Kyrgyz Republic	...	...	67.3	...	...	22.6	...	...	15.7	...	...	-5.6
Lao PDR	...	...	...	...	...	...	...	...	...	...	...	...
Malaysia	58.6	52.0	50.7 *	17.6	15.3	12.2 *	23.4	27.6	40.6 *	0.5	5.1	-3.4 *
Maldives	...	...	...	...	...	...	...	...	...	...	...	...
Marshall Islands	...	...	...	...	...	...	...	...	...	...	...	...
Micronesia, Fed. States of	...	...	...	...	...	...	...	...	...	...	...	...
Mongolia [d]	...	80.8	84.1	...	–	–	...	56.4	24.7	...	-37.2	-8.8
Myanmar [d]	91.1	88.5	87.8	–	–	–	10.0	15.5	13.0	-1.1	-4.0	-0.8
Nauru	...	...	...	...	...	...	...	...	...	...	...	...
Nepal	...	77.2	...	...	9.4	...	...	21.9	...	...	-8.5	...
Pakistan	81.9	81.6	73.1	10.7	12.1	11.1	16.4	18.3	18.7	-9.0	-12.0	-3.0
Papua New Guinea	55.3	66.6	...	34.4	23.8	...	18.1	20.0	...	-7.8	-10.4	...
Philippines	62.5	73.6	74.1	10.7	7.6	11.2	30.9	14.3	22.3	-4.1	4.5	-7.7
Singapore	60.4	45.1	39.5	10.6	14.3	8.5	39.9	42.5	33.2	-10.9	-1.9	18.8
Solomon Islands	...	64.2	...	...	28.1	...	...	26.2	...	...	-18.5	...
Sri Lanka	80.2	74.9	...	10.0	12.2	...	17.2	25.7	...	-7.3	-12.7	...
Taipei,China	57.1	51.0	59.5	15.8	16.1	14.4	30.4	19.1	23.8	-3.3	13.8	2.3
Thailand	69.7	62.2	54.7 *	10.3	13.5	9.7 *	26.7	28.2	43.1 *	-6.7	-4.0	-7.5 *
Tonga	88.9	99.8	...	13.0	16.0	...	27.6	26.4	...	-29.5	-42.1	...
Tuvalu	...	...	...	...	...	...	...	...	...	...	...	...
Uzbekistan	...	...	...	...	...	...	...	...	...	...	...	...
Vanuatu	...	56.6	...	...	35.9	...	...	28.3	...	...	-20.8	...
Viet Nam [d]	...	...	81.0 *	...	...	– *	...	...	27.1 *	...	...	-8.2 *
Western Samoa	...	90.2	...	...	18.0	...	...	28.4	...	...	-36.7	...

a   Unless otherwise indicated, GDP data are at current market prices.
b   Includes statistical discrepancy.
c   Figures are based on NMP at current prices.
d   Private consumption includes government consumption.

Sources: Country sources.

Table 15: DOMESTIC SAVING, CAPITAL FORMATION AND RESOURCE GAP
(Percent of GDP)

DMC	Gross Domestic Saving			Capital Formation			Resource Gap		
	1975	1985	1995	1975	1985	1995	1975	1985	1995
Afghanistan	...	...	...	...	...	...	...	...	...
Bangladesh	-0.9	2.3	7.7	5.9	12.8	16.6	5.0	10.5	8.9
Bhutan	...	13.5	36.0	...	45.4	54.5	...	31.8	18.5
Cambodia	...	...	8.3	...	...	21.5	...	...	13.2
China, People's Rep. of	...	35.6	42.3	...	37.8	39.5	...	2.2	-2.8
Cook Islands	...	...	...	...	...	...	...	...	...
Fiji	20.0	17.2	...	20.6	19.1	...	0.6	1.9	...
Hong Kong	25.1	31.1	32.6	24.1	21.6	34.9	-1.0	-9.4	2.3
India	19.0	21.4	25.2 *	20.8	23.9	20.9 *	1.9	2.4	-4.3 *
Indonesia	21.0	29.8	35.8 *	20.3	28.0	37.8 *	-0.7	-1.8	2.0 *
Kazakstan	...	...	...	...	...	...	...	...	...
Kiribati	44.6	-18.9	...	4.8	53.9	...	-39.8	72.7	...
Korea, Rep. of	18.1	31.4	36.7	27.1	29.6	37.1	8.9	-1.8	0.4
Kyrgyz Republic	...	...	10.1	...	...	15.7	...	...	5.6
Lao PDR	...	...	...	...	...	...	...	...	...
Malaysia	23.8	32.7	37.2 *	23.4	27.6	40.6 *	-0.5	-5.1	3.4 *
Maldives	...	...	...	...	...	...	...	...	...
Marshall Islands	...	...	...	...	...	...	...	...	...
Micronesia, Fed. States of	...	...	...	...	...	...	...	...	...
Mongolia	...	19.2	15.9	...	56.4	24.7	...	37.2	8.8
Myanmar	8.9	11.5	12.2	10.0	15.5	13.0	1.1	4.0	0.8
Nauru	...	...	...	...	...	...	...	...	...
Nepal	10.0	13.4	10.3	14.5	21.9	20.2	4.5	8.5	9.9
Pakistan	7.4	6.3	15.7	16.4	18.3	18.7	9.0	12.0	3.0
Papua New Guinea	14.8	9.6	...	18.1	20.0	...	3.3	10.4	...
Philippines	26.8	18.8	14.7	30.9	14.3	22.3	4.1	-4.5	7.7
Singapore	29.0	40.6	52.0	39.9	42.5	33.2	10.9	1.9	-18.8
Solomon Islands	...	7.7	...	...	26.2	...	...	18.5	...
Sri Lanka	9.9	13.0	15.9	17.2	25.7	25.7	7.3	12.7	9.8
Taipei,China	27.1	32.9	26.1	30.4	19.1	23.8	3.2	-13.8	-2.3
Thailand	20.6	24.8	36.5 *	26.7	28.2	43.1 *	6.2	3.4	6.6 *
Tonga	-1.9	-15.7	...	27.6	26.4	...	29.5	42.1	...
Tuvalu	...	...	...	...	...	...	...	...	...
Uzbekistan	...	...	...	...	...	...	...	...	...
Vanuatu	...	7.5	...	...	28.3	...	...	20.8	...
Viet Nam	...	...	19.0 *	...	...	27.1 *	...	...	8.2 *
Western Samoa	...	-8.3	...	...	28.4	...	...	36.7	...

Sources: Country sources.
ADB data file.

Table 16: CEREAL PRODUCTION [a]
('000 Metric Tons)

DMC	1985	1986	1987	1988	1989	1990	1991	1992	1993	1994	1995
Afghanistan	3242	3084	3394	2997	2834	2705	2724	2420	2540	2612	2562
Bangladesh	24135	24266	24304	24453	27882	27749	28465	28654	28310	26452	26041
Bhutan	167	164	140	95	95	106	106	106	106	106	106
Cambodia	1863	2144	1853	2541	2726	2588	2460	2281	2429	2288	1867
China, People's Rep. of	336761	349164	356366	348997	364820	401629	392306	397678	403150	390734	415750
Cook Islands	...	...	...	...	...	...	...	...	...	...	...
Fiji	29	27	24	34	33	28	31	23	21	20	18
Hong Kong	0	0	0	0	0	0	0	0	0	0	0
India	165682	164955	156117	183895	199403	193897	193054	201669	206692	212316	214893
Indonesia	43364	45647	45236	48332	50923	51914	50946	56235	54640	53510	58083
Kazakstan	...	...	25540	20785	18632	28305	11928	29654	21544	16401	...
Kiribati	...	...	...	...	...	...	...	...	...	...	...
Korea, Rep. of	8807	8636	8467	9164	8950	8434	7852	7845	7046	7269	6923
Kyrgyz Republic	...	...	1818	1667	1597	1503	1375	1516	1506	996	...
Lao PDR	1431	1491	1243	1054	1448	1558	1292	1561	1298	1730	1491
Malaysia	1873	1773	1730	1815	1873	1995	2175	2106	2069	2080	2120
Maldives	0	0	0	0	0	0	0	0	0	0	0
Marshall Islands	...	...	...	...	...	...	...	...	...	...	...
Micronesia, Fed. States of	...	...	...	...	...	...	...	...	...	...	...
Mongolia	884	869	689	814	841	720	597	496	492	431	450
Myanmar	15100	14861	14240	13640	14253	14422	13647	15342	17260	18859	20690
Nauru	...	...	...	...	...	...	...	...	...	...	...
Nepal	4374	4000	4759	5307	5672	5847	5520	4919	5723	5372	5440
Pakistan	17700	20866	18458	19245	21018	20962	21143	22119	23843	22264	23686
Papua New Guinea	2	2	2	3	3	3	3	3	3	3	3
Philippines	12728	13338	12818	13399	13981	14739	14329	14003	14947	15058	15163
Singapore	...	...	...	...	...	...	...	...	...	...	...
Solomon Islands	6	2	...	...	...	...	...	...	...	...	...
Sri Lanka	2703	2639	2177	2524	2101	2579	2430	2374	2606	2722	2722
Taipei,China	3033	2842	2793	2750	2740	2703	2709	2486	2738	2554	2422
Thailand	25613	23400	21416	26164	25239	21166	24463	23887	22016	25339	25358
Tonga	...	...	...	...	...	...	...	...	...	...	...
Tuvalu	...	...	...	...	...	...	...	...	...	...	...
Uzbekistan	...	...	1725	2068	1541	1885	1902	2252	2135	2432	...
Vanuatu	1	1	1	1	1	1	1	1	1	1	1
Viet Nam	16466	16578	15666	17820	19843	19906	20297	22343	23728	24535	25206
Western Samoa	...	...	...	...	...	...	...	...	...	...	...
TOTAL DMCs (Reporting)	685964	700749	720975	749564	788448	827344	801752	841973	846841	836083	850994
WORLD	1826989	1837306	1769295	1726594	1870299	1947396	1879404	1960582	1889254	1953400	1899430

a   Cereal production refers to all cereals including rice as paddy, mixed grains and buckwheat.

Sources: FAO, Statistics Division, 22 May 1996 and past communication.

Table 17: PADDY PRODUCTION [a]
('000 Metric Tons)

DMC	1985	1986	1987	1988	1989	1990	1991	1992	1993	1994	1995
Afghanistan	317	336	324	343	320	333	335	300	300	350	300
Bangladesh	22556	23110	23120	23320	26780	26780	27380	27510	27060	25248	24659
Bhutan	62	63	65	43	43	43	43	43	43	43	43
Cambodia	1812	2093	1815	2500	2672	2500	2400	2221	2383	2223	1817
China, People's Rep. of	168569	172224	174260	169110	180130	189331	183813	186220	177700	175933	190000
Cook Islands	...	...	...	...	...	...	...	...	...	...	...
Fiji	28	25	23	32	32	26	29	22	20	18	17
Hong Kong	0	0	0	0	0	0	0	0	0	0	0
India	95818	90779	85340	106400	110300	111500	112000	109000	118400	121997	122372
Indonesia	39033	39727	40080	41680	44730	45180	44690	48240	48180	46642	49860
Kazakstan	...	...	606	626	555	579	515	467	403	283	...
Kiribati	...	...	...	...	...	...	...	...	...	...	...
Korea, Rep. of	7855	7871	7596	8260	8100	7722	7293	7303	6507	6932	6519
Kyrgyz Republic	...	...	1	1	2	2	3	3	2	2	...
Lao PDR	1395	1449	1207	1003	1404	1491	1224	1502	1251	1653	1409
Malaysia	1849	1747	1700	1783	1839	1960	2140	2070	2031	2040	2080
Maldives	...	...	...	...	...	...	...	...	...	...	...
Marshall Islands	...	...	...	...	...	...	...	...	...	...	...
Micronesia, Fed. States of	...	...	...	...	...	...	...	...	...	...	...
Mongolia	...	...	...	...	...	...	...	...	...	...	...
Myanmar	14317	14126	13640	13160	13800	13970	13200	14840	16760	18351	20109
Nauru	...	...	...	...	...	...	...	...	...	...	...
Nepal	2804	2372	2982	3283	3390	3502	3223	2585	3500	2928	2906
Pakistan	4378	5230	4861	4800	4830	4891	4865	4674	5962	5096	4815
Papua New Guinea	1	1	1	1	1	1	1	1	1	1	1
Philippines	8806	9247	8540	8971	9459	9885	9673	9513	9922	10538	11002
Singapore	...	...	...	...	...	...	...	...	...	...	...
Solomon Islands	6	2	0	0	0	0	0	0	0	0	0
Sri Lanka	2661	2588	2128	2477	2063	2538	2389	2340	2570	2684	2684
Taipei,China	2717	2467	2376	2306	2331	2258	2273	2035	2275	2099	1966
Thailand	20264	18868	18430	21260	20600	17190	20400	19940	18450	21111	21130
Tonga	...	...	...	...	...	...	...	...	...	...	...
Tuvalu	...	...	...	...	...	...	...	...	...	...	...
Uzbekistan	...	...	506	581	484	503	515	539	545	490	...
Vanuatu	...	...	...	...	...	...	...	...	...	...	...
Viet Nam	15875	16003	15100	17000	19000	19230	19620	21590	22840	23528	24000
Western Samoa	...	...	...	...	...	...	...	...	...	...	...
TOTAL DMCs (Reporting)	411123	410328	404701	428941	452864	461416	458022	462958	467105	470189	487687
WORLD	470984	471262	463425	489660	516696	520478	518128	526642	524741	537318	554003

a   Data refer to the calendar year in which the whole harvest or bulk of harvest took place.

Sources: FAO, Statistics Division, 22 May 1996 and past communication.

Table 18: MAIZE PRODUCTION [a]
('000 Metric Tons)

DMC	1985	1986	1987	1988	1989	1990	1991	1992	1993	1994	1995
Afghanistan	577	567	514	494	458	480	420	300	350	360	360
Bangladesh	3	3	3	3	3	3	3	3	3	3	3
Bhutan	76	74	50	31	31	40	40	40	40	40	40
Cambodia	51	51	38	41	54	88	60	60	45	65	50
China, People's Rep. of	63826	70856	79240	77351	78930	96819	98773	95383	102700	99275	104000
Cook Islands	...	...	...	...	...	...	...	...	...	...	...
Fiji	2	2	1	1	1	2	2	1	1	2	2
Hong Kong	...	...	...	...	...	...	...	...	...	...	...
India	6644	7593	5721	8229	9651	8962	8064	10040	9406	9490	9800
Indonesia	4330	5920	5156	6652	6193	6734	6256	7995	6460	6869	8223
Kazakstan	...	...	477	561	479	442	330	370	355	233	...
Kiribati	...	...	...	...	...	...	...	...	...	...	...
Korea, Rep. of	132	113	127	106	121	120	75	92	82	89	90
Kyrgyz Republic	...	...	460	497	452	406	365	281	184	129	...
Lao PDR	36	42	36	51	44	67	69	59	48	77	82
Malaysia	24	26	30	32	34	35	35	36	38	40	40
Maldives	0	0	0	0	0	0	0	0	0	0	0
Marshall Islands	...	...	...	...	...	...	...	...	...	...	...
Micronesia, Fed. States of	...	...	...	...	...	...	...	...	...	...	...
Mongolia	...	...	...	...	...	...	...	...	...	...	...
Myanmar	299	285	224	193	194	187	191	209	205	285	272
Nauru	...	...	...	...	...	...	...	...	...	...	...
Nepal	874	868	902	1072	1201	1231	1205	1291	1200	1273	1302
Pakistan	1009	1111	1127	1204	1179	1185	1203	1184	1213	1318	1275
Papua New Guinea	1	1	1	1	1	1	2	2	2	2	2
Philippines	3922	4091	4278	4428	4522	4854	4655	4490	5025	4519	4161
Singapore	...	...	...	...	...	...	...	...	...	...	...
Solomon Islands	...	...	...	...	...	...	...	...	...	...	...
Sri Lanka	30	41	42	39	31	33	34	29	29	32	32
Taipei,China	226	272	307	321	329	339	321	339	346	345	345
Thailand	4934	4309	2781	4675	4393	3722	3793	3672	3328	3965	3965
Tonga	...	...	...	...	...	...	...	...	...	...	...
Tuvalu	...	...	...	...	...	...	...	...	...	...	...
Uzbekistan	...	...	421	520	460	431	431	367	404	276	...
Vanuatu	1	1	1	1	1	1	1	1	1	1	1
Viet Nam	587	570	561	815	838	671	672	748	882	1001	1200
Western Samoa	...	...	...	...	...	...	...	...	...	...	...
TOTAL DMCs (Reporting)	87584	96796	102497	107317	109599	126852	126998	126990	132345	129688	135244
WORLD	487040	476716	449058	398577	472933	476829	490430	528451	469271	570611	504980

a   Data refer to the calendar year in which the whole harvest or bulk of harvest took place.

Sources: FAO, Statistics Division, 22 May 1996 and past communication.

Table 19: COCONUT PRODUCTION [a]
('000 Metric Tons)

DMC	1985	1986	1987	1988	1989	1990	1991	1992	1993	1994	1995
Afghanistan	...	...	...	...	...	...	...	...	...	...	...
Bangladesh	83	83	83	86	84	82	76	82	93	94	94
Bhutan	...	...	...	...	...	...	...	...	...	...	...
Cambodia	38	41	42	44	46	46	48	50	51	53	53
China, People's Rep. of	70	75	80	62	67	65	67	68	68	75	77
Cook Islands	11	8	5	8	5	4	4	4	5	4	4
Fiji	215	259	190	173	193	251	203	244	200	200	200
Hong Kong	...	...	...	...	...	...	...	...	...	...	...
India	5030	4738	5402	6346	6954	7230	7489	8452	7700	7800	8000
Indonesia	12471	12363	12520	12920	12100	14180	14400	14200	14310	13868	13868
Kazakstan	...	...	...	...	...	...	...	...	...	...	...
Kiribati	67	50	52	104	75	47	67	73	65	65	65
Korea, Rep. of	...	...	...	...	...	...	...	...	...	...	...
Kyrgyz Republic	...	...	...	...	...	...	...	...	...	...	...
Lao PDR	...	...	...	...	...	...	...	...	...	...	...
Malaysia	1262	1188	1022	1134	1131	1190	979	1023	1103	1043	1043
Maldives	11	11	10	10	13	13	12	14	13	13	13
Marshall Islands	...	...	...	...	...	...	...	...	...	...	...
Micronesia, Fed. States of	...	...	...	...	...	...	...	...	...	...	...
Mongolia	...	...	...	...	...	...	...	...	...	...	...
Myanmar	224	250	321	222	181	183	187	217	196	320	310
Nauru	...	...	2	2	2	2	2	2	2	2	2
Nepal	...	...	...	...	...	...	...	...	...	...	...
Pakistan	...	...	0	1	1	1	1	1	1	1	1
Papua New Guinea	1098	1011	1014	918	904	796	618	794	790	700	700
Philippines	8600	11283	10520	7942	7866	11020	8638	9384	9063	9800	10300
Singapore	7	5	5	3	2	1	1	1	0	0	0
Solomon Islands	209	209	208	209	201	180	210	208	210	220	220
Sri Lanka	2096	2310	1742	1469	1888	1924	1660	1745	1597	1997	1997
Taipei,China	...	...	...	...	...	...	...	...	...	...	...
Thailand	1226	1280	1310	1378	1437	1426	1379	1411	1462	1476	1465
Tonga	52	70	45	32	30	25	25	25	25	25	25
Tuvalu	...	...	2	2	2	2	3	3	2	2	2
Uzbekistan	...	...	...	...	...	...	...	...	...	...	...
Vanuatu	322	343	338	304	242	357	262	260	259	259	259
Viet Nam	612	711	791	857	922	894	1053	1140	1207	1190	1000
Western Samoa	178	191	170	160	159	138	95	100	130	130	130
TOTAL DMCs (Reporting)	33882	36479	35873	34384	34503	40056	37477	39498	38551	39335	39826
WORLD	38571	41267	40628	39353	39366	45048	42421	42518	41997	44482	45001

a   Coconut production is expressed in terms of weight of the whole nut, excluding only the fibrous outer husk.

Sources: FAO, Statistics Division, 22 May 1996 and past communication.

Table 20: YIELD OF PADDY AND MAIZE [a]
(Kg/Ha)

DMC	Paddy			Maize		
	1975	1985	1995	1975	1985	1995
Afghanistan	2071	2248	1765	1612	1688	1565
Bangladesh	1853	2169	2348	902	867	903
Bhutan	1098	1938	1654	1111	1357	889
Cambodia	1429	1239	1367	1182	1109	1667
China, People's Rep.	3518	5256	6271	2542	3607	4837
Cook Islands	...	...	...	...	...	...
Fiji	2255	2366	2369	2000	3400	2416
Hong Kong	1792	2500	–	...	...	...
India	1858	2329	2879	1203	1146	1633
Indonesia	2630	3942	4343	1187	1774	2255
Kazakstan	...	...	...	...	...	...
Kiribati	...	...	...	...	...	...
Korea, Rep. of	5324	6351	6179	1715	4362	3913
Kyrgyz Republic	...	...	...	...	...	...
Lao PDR	1338	2087	2701	1556	1184	2150
Malaysia	2661	2780	3152	1281	1600	1905
Maldives	...	...	...	1000	1000	1000
Marshall Islands	...	...	...	...	...	...
Micronesia, Fed. States of	...	...	...	...	...	...
Mongolia	...	...	...	...	...	...
Myanmar	1816	1749	3106	457	1749	1663
Nauru	...	...	...	...	...	...
Nepal	2074	2016	2124	1651	1422	1688
Pakistan	2296	2350	2179	1294	1256	1428
Papua New Guinea	1740	3000	3023	1151	2200	1500
Philippines	1721	2588	2654	839	1117	1540
Singapore	...	...	...	...	...	...
Solomon Islands	2065	2744	–	...	...	...
Sri Lanka	1933	3071	2993	1091	915	1003
Taipei,China	4135	4820	5386	2773	3667	4604
Thailand	1825	2061	2343	2426	2572	2807
Tonga	...	...	...	...	...	...
Tuvalu	...	...	...	...	...	...
Uzbekistan	...	...	...	...	...	...
Vanuatu	...	...	...	500	520	515
Viet Nam	2133	2783	3636	1625	1479	2181
Western Samoa	...	...	...	...	...	
TOTAL DMCs (Reporting)	2461	3270	3762	1965	1564	3546
WORLD	2525	3273	3710	2887	3745	3752

a   FAO estimates derived from official (i.e. country) estimates of total production and total area.

Sources: For 1975, FAO, *PY 1982*.
           For 1985 and 1995, FAO, Statistics Division, 22 May 1996 and past communication.

Table 21: ENERGY INDICATORS

DMCs	Per Capita Energy Consumption (kgoe)			Energy Intensity in GDP [a] (toe/'000 1993 US$)			Net Oil Import Dependency (%) [b]		
	1975	1985	1993	1975	1985	1993	1975	1985	1993
Afghanistan	59	84	29 [d]	...	...	...	...	...	...
Bangladesh	28	43	63	0.17	0.24	0.30	59.6	36.0	27.0
Bhutan	2	17	35	...	...	...	...	...	...
Cambodia	2	19	19	...	...	...	...	...	...
China, People's Rep. of [c]	342	513	676	...	...	...	-3.8	-0.9	-1.0
Cook Islands	...	407	412	...	...	...	...	...	...
Fiji	...	390	466 [d]	...	0.21	...	...	69.1	76.6
Hong Kong	...	1251	2184	...	0.10	0.11	100.0	42.4	100.0
India	119	174	285	0.62	0.74	0.96	21.6	12.6	17.0
Indonesia [c]	103	226	330	0.29	0.43	0.39	-400.6	-154.7	-50.4
Kazakstan	...	133	117	...	...	0.19	...	...	...
Kiribati	205	110	95 [d]	...	...	...	...	...	...
Korea, Rep. of	665	1273	2801	0.43	0.31	0.37	64.3	49.1	64.5
Kyrgyz Republic	...	...	1240 [d]	...	...	...	...	...	...
Lao PDR	29	23	26	...	...	...	...	...	...
Malaysia [c]	556	805	1691	0.37	0.35	0.51	15.3	-103.1	44.0
Maldives	15	114	145 [d]	...	...	...	...	...	...
Marshall Islands	...	...	...	...	...	...	...	...	...
Micronesia, Fed. States of	...	...	...	...	...	...	...	...	...
Mongolia	...	1577	1176 [d]	...	...	...	...	...	20.4
Myanmar	...	57	40	...	0.04	0.03	...	0.1	...
Nauru	...	...	...	...	...	...	...	...	...
Nepal	10	18	38	0.08	0.12	0.21	62.6	53.3	60.8
Pakistan	137	210	261	0.58	0.65	0.67	38.3	31.0	30.9
Papua New Guinea	189	219	193	...	...	...	...	...	...
Philippines	243	195	285	0.30	0.25	0.35	93.2	62.9	43.3
Singapore	...	6551	6627	...	0.53	0.33	...	99.4	100.0
Solomon Islands	99	184	155 [d]	...	...	...	...	...	...
Sri Lanka	102	109	149	0.31	0.23	0.25	79.7	70.3	72.3
Taipei,China	1385	1875	2730	0.48	0.30	0.26	76.3	50.2	61.8
Thailand	215	314	705	0.28	0.27	0.33	90.0	53.8	59.2
Tonga	124	159	309 [d]	...	...	...	...	...	...
Tuvalu	...	...	...	...	...	...	...	...	...
Uzbekistan	...	...	...	...	...	...	...	...	...
Vanuatu	189	155	146 [d]	...	...	...	...	...	...
Viet Nam [c]	...	78	97	...	...	0.54	...	36.0	-13.7
Western Samoa	134	250	285 [d]	...	...	...	...	...	...

a Defined as total primary commercial energy consumed divided by GDP at constant prices.
b Defined as the ratio of net oil imports (including bunkers) to total primary energy requirements.
c Net oil exporting countries.
d Refers to previous year.

Sources: ADB, *Energy Indicators of Developing Member Countries of ADB*, December 1994 .
ADB data file.
OECD/IEA, *Energy Statistics and Balances of Non-OECD Countries 1992-93*.
UN, *ESY 1992* and past isssues.

Table 22: ELECTRICITY INDICATORS

DMCs	Per Capita Electricity Generation (kWh)			Per Capita Electricity Consumption (kWh)			Electricity Intensity in GDP [a] (kWh/1993 US$)			Population with Access to Electricity (%) [b]
	1975	1985	1993	1975	1985	1993	1975	1985	1993	1994
Afghanistan	50	72	42 [c]	50	47	44 [c]	...	...	...	6 [c]
Bangladesh	17	47	82	11	29	51	0.06	0.16	0.24	12 [c]
Bhutan	10	9	1021	10	9	105	...	...	0.74	11 [c]
Cambodia	21	20	14	21	9	8	...	...	0.04	10
China, People's Rep. of	210	391	711	183	363	601	...	...	...	80
Cook Islands	442	694	839	442	520	724	...	...	0.19	35
Fiji	297	466	537	297	409	489	...	0.23	0.23	50
Hong Kong	1674	3525	6233	1460	2919	4684	...	0.24	0.29	100
India	143	244	367	109	179	270	0.56	0.76	0.91	88 [d]
Indonesia	29	103	247	21	77	206	0.06	0.15	0.25	39
Kazakstan	...	...	4782 [c]	...	...	4768	...	...	...	...
Kiribati	75	94	109	75	78	91	...	...	...	29 [c]
Korea, Rep. of	562	1422	2973	562	1422	2616	0.37	0.34	0.38	100 [c]
Kyrgyz Republic	...	...	2672 [c]	...	...	2170	...	...	...	...
Lao PDR	102	251	206	61	35	59	...	...	0.20	12 [c]
Malaysia	417	955	1713	367	799	1466	0.24	0.35	0.44	85 [c]
Maldives	7	60	145	7	49	121	...	...	0.13	30
Marshall Islands	...	...	1479	...	...	1244	...	...	0.74	50 [c]
Micronesia, Fed. States of	...	...	760	...	...	650	...	...	0.35	30 [c]
Mongolia	587	1512	1514 [c]	579	1237	883	...	...	...	...
Myanmar	25	57	79	19	39	47	0.02	0.03	0.04	10 [c]
Nauru	...	...	...	...	...	...	...	...	...	...
Nepal	6	21	44	6	18	34	0.05	0.12	0.19	14
Pakistan	140	239	397	95	183	297	0.40	0.57	0.78	37
Papua New Guinea	...	139	159	...	134	136	...	...	0.10	22
Philippines	244	416	400	202	331	327	0.25	0.43	0.74	57
Singapore	1820	3999	6449	1625	3577	5973	0.24 ·	0.29	0.30	100
Solomon Islands	83	81	129	83	66	118	...	...	...	15
Sri Lanka	80	156	226	71	130	186	0.22	0.28	0.36	44 [c]
Taipei,China	1495	2864	5080	1291	2499	4756	0.44	0.41	0.41	100
Thailand	204	446	1062	181	388	970	0.24	0.33	0.86	74
Tonga	68	149	278	68	128	231	...	...	0.16	80 [c]
Tuvalu	...	...	183	...	...	163	...	...	0.15	...
Uzbekistan	...	...	...	...	...	...	...	...	...	...
Vanuatu	157	155	173	157	147	161	...	...	...	...
Viet Nam	...	85	81	39	65	58	...	...	0.05	35
Western Samoa	174	225	330	174	188	277	...	...	0.41	90

a   Defined as total electricity consumed divided by GDP at constant prices.
b   Households with access to electricity as percentage of total households.
c   Refers to previous year.
d   Villages with access to electricity as percentage of total villages.

Sources :   ADB, *Energy Indicators of Developing Member Countries of ADB*, December 1994;
            ADB data file.
            OECD/IEA, *Energy Statistics and Balances of Non-OECD Countries 1992-93.*
            UN, *ESY 1992* and past isssues.

Table 23: PRICES OF SELECTED PRIMARY COMMODITIES

COMMODITY	1982	1983	1984	1985	1986	1987	1988	1989	1990	1991	1992	1993	1994	1995
FOOD														
Wheat (US), $/mt	132.6	137.3	140.2	128.7	118.4	112.1	140.7	161.3	136.0	129.0	151.0	140.0	150.0	177.0
Rice, $/mt	292.9	276.9	252.1	215.9	210.5	230.3	301.4	320.2	271.0	293.0	268.0	235.0	268.0	321.0
Maize, $/mt	109.3	136.0	135.9	112.2	87.6	75.7	106.9	111.5	109.0	107.0	104.0	102.0	108.0	123.0
Sugar (US), ¢/kg	18.6	18.7	11.5	8.9	13.3	14.9	22.5	28.2	27.7	19.8	20.0	22.1	26.7	29.3
Tea (US), ¢/kg	193.2	232.8	345.8	198.3	192.8	170.8	178.9	201.9	203.0	184.0	200.0	186.0	183.0	164.0
Copra, $/mt	314.2	496.0	710.3	386.0	197.5	309.2	397.7	347.9	231.0	286.4	380.0	295.0	417.0	439.0
Palm Oil, $/mt	445.1	501.4	728.8	500.6	257.0	342.6	437.2	350.4	290.0	339.0	394.0	378.0	528.0	628.0
NON-FOOD														
Cotton (A Index), ¢/kg	159.7	185.4	179.0	131.8	105.6	164.8	139.9	167.4	182.0	168.0	128.0	128.0	176.0	213.0
Jute, $/mt	285.8	302.2	530.8	582.9	270.1	321.9	370.0	373.3	408.0	378.0	320.0	273.0	298.0	368.0
Rubber (US), ¢/kg	100.2	123.8	109.6	92.4	94.5	111.7	128.8	111.7	86.0	83.0	86.0	83.0	113.0	158.0
Logs (Malaysia), $/m³ a	156.0	145.0	167.0	132.0	151.3	221.4	233.4	224.6	210.4	191.0	209.5 I	390.0	308.0	256.0
Logs (Cameroon), $/m³	175.9	160.8	175.6	173.9	221.6	258.9	271.3	273.8	343.5	316.0	331.3	310.0	330.0	340.0
METALS AND MINERALS														
Copper, ¢/kg	148.0	159.2	137.7	141.7	137.4	178.2	260.2	284.8	266.2	233.9	228.1	191.3	230.7	293.6
Tin (UK I Malaysia), ¢/kg b	1295.0	1303.0	1246.0	1154.0 I	616.1	669.0	705.2	853.4	609.0	560.0	610.0	561.0	546.0	621.0
Lead, ¢/kg	54.6	42.5	44.3	39.1	40.6	59.7	65.6	67.3	81.1	55.8	54.1	40.6	54.8	63.1
Petroleum, $/bbl	31.0	28.1	27.5	27.2	13.6	17.2	13.6	16.3	22.9	19.4	19.0	16.8	15.9	17.2
Price Index (1990=100)														
FOOD														
Wheat (US)	97.5	101.0	103.1	94.6	87.1	82.4	103.5	118.6	100.0	94.9	111.0	102.9	110.3	130.1
Rice	108.1	102.2	93.0	79.7	77.7	85.0	111.2	118.2	100.0	108.1	98.9	86.7	98.9	118.5
Maize	100.3	124.8	124.7	102.9	80.4	69.4	98.1	102.3	100.0	98.2	95.4	93.6	99.1	112.8
Sugar (US)	67.1	67.5	41.5	32.1	48.0	53.8	81.2	101.8	100.0	71.5	72.2	79.8	96.4	105.8
Tea (US)	95.2	114.7	170.3	97.7	95.0	84.1	88.1	99.5	100.0	90.6	98.5	91.6	90.1	80.8
Copra	136.0	214.7	307.5	167.1	85.5	133.9	172.2	150.6	100.0	124.0	164.5	127.7	180.5	190.0
Palm Oil	153.5	172.9	251.3	172.6	88.6	118.1	150.8	120.8	100.0	116.9	135.9	130.3	182.1	216.6
NON-FOOD														
Cotton (A Index)	87.7	101.9	98.4	72.4	58.0	90.5	76.9	92.0	100.0	92.3	70.3	70.3	96.7	117.0
Jute	70.0	74.1	130.1	142.9	66.2	78.9	90.7	91.5	100.0	92.6	78.4	66.9	73.0	90.2
Rubber (US)	116.5	144.0	127.4	107.4	109.9	129.9	149.8	129.9	100.0	96.5	100.0	96.5	131.4	183.7
Logs (Malaysia) a	74.1	68.9	79.4	62.7	71.9	105.2	110.9	106.7	100.0	90.8	99.6 I	185.4	146.4	121.7
Logs (Cameroon)	51.2	46.8	51.1	50.6	64.5	75.4	79.0	79.7	100.0	92.0	96.4	90.2	96.1	99.0
METALS AND MINERALS														
Copper	55.6	59.8	51.7	53.2	51.6	67.0	97.8	107.0	100.0	87.9	85.7	71.9	86.7	110.3
Tin (UK I Malaysia) b	212.6	214.0	204.6	189.5 I	101.2	109.9	115.8	140.1	100.0	92.0	100.2	92.1	89.7	102.0
Lead	67.3	52.4	54.6	48.2	50.1	73.6	80.9	83.0	100.0	68.8	66.7	50.1	67.6	77.8
Petroleum	135.5	122.8	120.2	118.9	59.4	75.2	59.4	71.2	100.0	84.8	83.0	73.6	69.4	75.1

a From 1982 onward, data refer to Malaysian Sabah and Sarawak logs; beginning February 1993, data refer to Malaysian Sarawak logs only as a result of the recent export restrictions in Malaysia.

b From 1986 onward, data refer to Malaysian tin.

Source: WB, *Commodity Markets and the Developing Countries*, May 1996 and past issues.

Table 24: CONSUMER PRICE INDEX [a]
(1990=100)

DMC	1982	1983	1984	1985	1986	1987	1988	1989	1990	1991	1992	1993	1994	1995	Annual Change (%) 1993	1994	1995
Afghanistan [b]	12.6	18.6	22.3	23.7	25.5	30.1	40.4	74.8	100.0	165.8	181.1	...	...	...	...	...	...
Bangladesh [b]	46.9	51.5	56.5	62.7	68.9	76.1	84.7	91.5	100.0	108.9	114.5	116.0	118.1	124.3	1.3	1.8	5.2
Bhutan	50.4	59.5	63.7	64.9	71.4	75.9	83.6	90.9	100.0	112.3	130.2	144.8	155.0	...	11.2	7.0	...
Cambodia [c]	...	...	...	...	...	...	...	41.4	100.0	265.1	733.7	961.0	1212.0	...	31.0	26.1	...
China, People's Rep. of	...	...	...	60.5	64.5	69.2	82.2	97.0	100.0	103.4	110.0	126.2	156.5	...	14.7	24.1	...
Cook Islands [d]	...	...	...	...	...	...	...	95.0	100.0	105.8	109.5	117.5	120.6	121.7	7.3	2.7	0.9
Fiji	61.7	65.9	69.4	72.4	73.7	77.9	87.1	92.5	100.0	106.5	111.7	117.5	118.5	121.0	5.2	0.8	2.2
Hong Kong [e]	57.9	63.5	68.8	71.0	73.0	77.0	82.7	91.1	100.0	111.6	122.0	132.5	143.2	155.7	8.5	8.1	8.7
India	53.7	60.1	65.1	68.7	74.7	81.3	87.6	91.8	100.0	113.9	127.3	135.4	149.2	164.5	6.4	10.2	10.2
Indonesia [f]	54.9	61.4	67.8	71.0	75.2	82.1	88.7	94.4	100.0	109.2	117.3	128.7	139.7	152.9	9.7	8.5	9.5
Kazakstan [c]	...	...	...	...	...	...	...	...	...	...	100.0	2265.0	28500.0	45695.0	2165.0	1158.3	60.3
Kiribati [d]	68.1	72.4	76.3	79.7	85.0	90.5	91.5	96.4	100.0	105.7	110.0	116.7	123.0	127.4	6.1	5.3	3.6
Korea, Rep. of [d]	70.8	73.3	74.9	76.8	78.8	81.4	87.0	91.9	100.0	109.7	115.9	121.7	129.0	134.0	5.0	6.0	3.9
Kyrgyz Republic	...	...	...	...	...	...	...	...	100.0	185.8	1766.7	23112.5	87382.5	124833.0	1208.2	278.1	42.9
Lao PDR	...	...	...	...	...	...	46.1	73.6	100.0	113.2	124.4	133.5	142.5	179.0	7.3	6.7	25.7
Malaysia	84.2	87.3	90.4	90.7	91.4	92.0	94.4	96.9	100.0	104.3	109.3	113.1	117.4	121.4	3.5	3.7	3.4
Maldives	...	...	...	69.9	77.1	84.6	90.1	96.5	100.0	114.7	134.0	161.1	...	...	20.2	...	...
Marshall Islands [d]	...	87.1	91.7	91.5	95.4	94.8	97.2	99.3	100.0	104.0	114.7	120.4	127.2	136.4	5.0	5.7	7.3
Micronesia, Fed. States of	...	...	...	...	...	...	...	...	...	...	...	...	...	...	...	...	...
Mongolia [c]	...	...	...	...	...	...	...	...	...	...	100.0	368.4	691.0	1083.2	268.4	87.6	56.8
Myanmar [d]	35.7	37.7	39.6	42.3	46.2	57.2	66.9	85.0	100.0	132.3	161.3	212.4	263.9	330.3	31.7	24.2	25.2
Nauru	...	...	...	...	...	...	74.6	81.6	100.0	114.7	118.1	113.2	112.4	...	-4.1	-0.7	...
Nepal [b]	45.8	52.3	55.6	57.9	67.0	75.9	84.3	89.7	100.0	109.8	132.9	144.7	157.7	169.8	8.9	8.9	7.6
Pakistan [b]	62.7	65.6	70.4	74.3	77.6	80.4	85.4	94.3	100.0	112.7	123.5	135.0	149.9	188.6	9.3	11.1	25.8
Papua New Guinea [d]	63.3	72.9	74.5	76.6	81.9	85.1	90.3	93.1	100.0	107.4	112.2	116.7	121.2	...	4.0	3.9	...
Philippines	36.5	38.5	56.6	69.9	69.6	71.7	78.1	87.6	100.0	118.7	129.3	139.1	151.7	163.9	7.6	9.0	8.1
Singapore	90.0	91.1	93.4	93.9	92.6	93.0	94.5	96.7	100.0	103.4	105.8	108.2	111.5	113.5	2.2	3.1	1.7
Solomon Islands [d, h]	...	...	...	54.3	61.7	68.5	80.4	91.9	100.0	115.0	127.4	139.1	157.5	...	9.2	13.3	...
Sri Lanka	41.3	47.0	54.8	55.6	60.1	64.7	73.8	82.3	100.0	112.2	125.0	139.6	151.4	163.1	11.7	8.4	7.7
Taipei,China	88.7	89.9	89.9	89.7	90.3	90.8	92.0	96.1	100.0	103.6	108.3	111.4	115.9	120.2	2.9	4.0	3.7
Thailand	77.1	80.0	80.7	82.6	84.2	86.3	89.6	94.4	100.0	105.7	110.0	113.7	119.5	126.4	3.4	5.1	5.8
Tonga	48.2	52.9	53.0	61.9	75.3	78.8	86.6	90.2	100.0	109.3	118.1	119.2	120.3	120.8	0.9	0.9	0.4
Tuvalu [d]	68.8	75.0	77.9	80.7	86.9	89.8	95.6	98.0	100.0	107.9	110.3	112.8	114.4	120.1	2.3	1.4	5.0
Uzbekistan	...	...	...	...	...	...	...	...	...	...	...	...	...	...	...	...	...
Vanuatu [d, g]	61.5	62.5	65.9	66.6	69.8	81.4	88.7	95.6	100.0	106.1	111.1	115.9	119.0	121.0	4.3	2.6	1.7
Viet Nam [h]	...	...	...	0.4	2.2	9.1	37.4	73.3	100.0	183.1	252.3	273.3	298.9	...	8.3	9.4	...
Western Samoa	47.8	55.8	62.3	67.9	71.8	75.1	81.7	86.8	100.0	98.6	107.0	108.8	128.8	130.1	1.7	18.4	1.0

a   Unless otherwise indicated, data refer to annual average consumer prices for the country.
b   Data refer to period averages for the fiscal year.
c   Base year is other than 1990.
d   Data refer to capital city only.
e   Data refer to urban areas/selected cities only.

f   Data for 1982-89 refer to 17 cities only; starting 1990, data refer to 27 cities.
g   Data for 1982-86 refer to low-income group only.
h   Data refer to retail price index.

Sources: Country sources.

31

Table 25: CHANGES IN MONEY SUPPLY
(Percent)

DMC	Narrow Money (M1)						Broad Money (M2)					
	1990	1991	1992	1993	1994	1995	1990	1991	1992	1993	1994	1995
Afghanistan	39.8	...	...	...	...	...	40.6	...	...	...	...	...
Bangladesh	16.6	13.1	14.6	9.8	23.2	18.0	14.4	10.8	12.3	9.5	13.4	13.8
Bhutan	-1.2	39.0	12.2	-0.9	25.3	34.9	29.6	13.5	23.1	22.6	21.2	15.6
Cambodia	240.6	27.4	121.3	18.7	-2.1	40.8	70.7	22.2	68.2	25.6	25.9	31.2
China, People's Rep. of	20.1	28.2	30.3	21.6	51.2	18.7	28.9	26.7	30.8	23.6	56.0	29.4
Cook Islands	...	...	...	...	...	...	...	...	...	...	...	...
Fiji	-0.7	6.9	15.1	14.4	-4.7	12.4	19.7	13.4	12.3	6.0	2.9	4.6
Hong Kong	13.3	19.5	21.1	20.6	-1.2	2.3	22.4	13.3	10.8	15.9	12.9	13.9
India	14.6	23.6	-0.4	8.4	21.5	...	15.1	19.4	-0.1	15.7	18.4	...
Indonesia	18.4	10.6	9.3	27.9	23.3	16.1	30.6	14.6	16.8	18.0	16.8	21.6
Kazakstan	...	...	...	...	...	41.6	...	...	...	...	...	...
Kiribati	...	...	...	...	...	...	...	...	...	...	...	...
Korea, Rep. of	11.0	36.8	13.0	18.1	11.9	-4.9	17.2	21.9	14.9	16.6	18.7	15.6
Kyrgyz Republic	...	...	563.0	570.5	131.9	75.4	...	...	428.2	179.9	117.8	77.5
Lao PDR	-0.1	12.5	24.5	48.6	17.4	9.5	7.8	15.7	49.0	64.6	31.9	16.4
Malaysia	14.1	11.0	13.0	37.5	11.2	11.7	12.8	14.5	19.1	22.1	14.7	24.0
Maldives	18.9	28.5	15.4	49.7	22.5	5.7	18.7	24.9	13.0	36.3	24.2	15.6
Marshall Islands	...	...	...	...	...	...	...	...	...	...	...	...
Micronesia, Fed.States of	...	...	...	...	...	...	...	...	...	...	...	...
Mongolia [a]	35.5	54.0	4.5	142.8	77.2	29.7	10.8	76.0	31.6	227.6	79.5	32.9
Myanmar	50.1	35.3	37.6	24.6	31.1	34.0	29.3	23.7	26.3	21.1	25.3	29.3
Nepal	20.8	14.5	19.5	22.5	19.6	12.4	18.6	19.5	21.1	27.7	19.6	14.4
Nauru	...	...	...	...	...	...	...	...	...	...	...	...
Pakistan	20.0	9.0	24.7	9.2	12.5	12.8	14.4	19.9	35.2	11.2	15.5	13.8
Papua New Guinea	0.4	29.6	11.2	3.6	8.3	10.9	4.3	17.7	12.6	13.6	2.4	10.9
Philippines	13.3	13.9	10.6	19.4	13.5	21.7	15.5	13.6	9.9	19.7	21.1	20.2
Singapore	11.0	7.7	12.7	23.6	2.3	8.3	20.0	12.4	8.9	8.5	14.4	8.5
Solomon Islands	...	...	...	...	...	...	...	...	...	...	...	...
Sri Lanka	12.8	18.0	6.4	18.6	18.7	-0.2	19.1	23.2	15.8	23.4	19.7	10.1
Taipei,China	-6.6	12.1	12.4	15.3	12.2	0.9	9.9	19.3	19.3	15.1	14.0	8.6
Thailand	11.9	13.8	12.3	18.6	17.0	12.1	26.7	19.8	15.6	18.4	12.9	17.0
Tonga	-12.8	10.9	8.8	10.6	-3.5	1.0	2.4	7.1	9.1	22.6	-5.3	8.8
Tuvalu	...	...	...	...	...	...	...	...	...	...	...	...
Uzbekistan	...	...	...	...	...	...	...	...	...	...	...	...
Vanuatu	-12.9	27.4	11.6	4.2	0.0	2.6	11.3	23.1	-2.7	9.8	4.5	6.9
Viet Nam	44.2	55.6	58.5	31.4	16.1	25.1	53.1	78.7	33.7	19.0	19.0	22.9
Western Samoa	42.6	-9.2	-11.3	17.4	5.6	29.0	19.2	-1.9	0.7	2.3	12.9	21.8

a   In May 1993, the government of Mongolia adopted a free market exchange rate.

Sources: Country sources.

Table 26: GOVERNMENT FINANCE INDICATORS
(Percent of GDP)

DMC	Taxes			Total Expenditures			Fiscal Deficit		
	1975	1985	1994	1975	1985	1994	1975	1985	1994
Afghanistan	...	...	...	...	...	...	...	...	...
Bangladesh	3.9	8.2	9.5	8.2	14.9	17.6	3.1	6.1	-0.9
Bhutan	...	5.7	6.0	...	50.9	43.8	...	40.1	24.8
Cambodia	...	...	6.0	...	...	16.5	...	...	6.7
China, People's Rep. of	...	22.7	10.5	...	27.0	...	...	7.3	1.2
Cook Islands	...	21.1	...	...	61.9	69.3	...	0.3	3.5
Fiji	15.8	5.1	4.6	24.0	30.6	27.9	-2.4	...	-1.1
Hong Kong	8.6	10.4	3.0	12.8	15.3	14.4	1.9	0.4	-1.1
India	7.6	...	...	12.0	18.4	16.2	2.4	5.2	1.8
Indonesia	16.9	18.3	14.6	21.6	23.5	16.0	3.9	3.7	-0.2
Kazakstan	...	30.3	13.6	...	34.5	22.8	...	...	...
Kiribati	60.0	15.3	...	77.8	51.6	...	8.4	-1.8	...
Korea, Rep. of	13.8	14.8	16.5	15.7	16.3	17.7	2.1	1.2	0.5
Kyrgyz Republic	...	...	...	...	...	25.9	...	...	8.2
Lao PDR	...	1.7	9.4	...	23.3	24.4	...	7.7	...
Malaysia	20.5	21.6	20.2	31.4	32.9	25.0	8.5	5.7	0.3
Maldives	...	15.1	19.7	...	33.6	48.8	...	5.9	12.7
Marshall Islands	...	...	19.2	...	...	83.9	...	...	54.8
Micronesia, Fed. States of	...	...	9.7	...	...	82.1	...	...	55.1
Mongolia	...	47.1	23.9	...	60.8	30.1	8.5	8.4	6.5
Myanmar	7.9	8.3	3.8	11.2	12.8	9.3	1.6	-0.9	2.9
Nauru	...	...	...	...	...	...	...	...	...
Nepal	5.1	6.8	7.7	9.0	17.6	15.9	3.0	9.2	6.1
Pakistan	10.0	13.2	15.4	25.1	27.5	27.2	10.7	8.7	6.4
Papua New Guinea	13.1	17.9	19.4	37.4	31.8	31.1	20.8	11.4	8.0
Philippines	13.2	10.7	16.0	16.0	14.1	13.7	1.4	1.9	-0.9
Singapore	17.1	17.3	...	26.3	39.1	...	-0.8	4.4	...
Solomon Islands	13.4	20.0	...	35.2	31.0	...	15.8	9.6	...
Sri Lanka	15.5	19.3	17.2	26.6	34.3	27.2	7.8	12.0	10.0
Taipei,China	16.5	8.5	10.3	21.4	14.0	15.9	-1.3	0.2	1.8
Thailand	11.5	13.7	17.2	14.9	18.9	16.1	1.7	4.3	-2.7
Tonga	16.8	18.3	18.9	22.5	31.4	...	-6.3	...	...
Tuvalu	...	16.6	...	...	95.4	...	...	41.7	...
Uzbekistan	...	...	...	...	...	...	...	...	...
Vanuatu	...	18.3	...	...	45.9	...	...	23.5	...
Viet Nam	...	4.0	19.7	...	46.3	26.2	...	21.2	1.5
Western Samoa	...	31.1	43.1	...	53.5	71.9	...	16.4	19.2

Sources: Country sources.

Table 26: GOVERNMENT FINANCE INDICATORS (Continued)
(Percent of GDP)

DMC	Health			Education			Housing & Community Amenities		
	1975	1985	1994	1975	1985	1994	1975	1985	1994
Afghanistan	...	...	...	...	...	...	...	...	...
Bangladesh	0.4	0.9	1.4	0.9	1.4	2.3	0.3	0.6	0.2
Bhutan	...	...	...	...	...	4.5	...	...	0.2
Cambodia	...	...	...	...	...	1.0	...	...	...
China, People's Rep. of	...	–	...	...	–	...	...	...	...
Cook Islands	...	...	...	...	...	...	...	...	...
Fiji	1.5	2.3	2.1	3.1	5.3	5.2	...	0.1	0.1
Hong Kong	1.2	1.4	1.9	2.7	2.8	2.9	2.2	3.3	3.3
India	...	...	...	...	...	...	...	...	...
Indonesia	0.3	0.4	0.4	0.9	1.5	0.8	1.6	1.4	1.6
Kazakstan	...	...	...	...	...	...	...	...	...
Kiribati	...	...	...	...	...	...	...	...	...
Korea, Rep. of	0.2	0.2	...	2.2	3.0	...	0.2	0.9	...
Kyrgyz Republic	...	...	3.5	...	...	6.6	...	...	1.1
Lao PDR	...	0.7	0.1	...	0.3	0.3	...	...	0.3
Malaysia	1.9	1.4	1.3	6.1	5.6	5.2	0.2	1.3	0.2
Maldives	...	1.8	4.6	...	3.7	7.6	...	6.1	2.0
Marshall Islands	...	...	...	...	...	...	...	...	...
Micronesia, Fed. States of	...	...	...	...	...	...	...	...	...
Mongolia	...	–	4.1	...	–	5.8	...	–	1.9
Myanmar	...	...	...	...	...	...	...	...	...
Nauru	...	...	...	...	...	...	...	...	...
Nepal	0.5	0.8	0.5	0.9	1.7	2.3	0.4	1.3	1.0
Pakistan	...	...	...	...	...	...	...	...	...
Papua New Guinea	...	3.0	2.7	...	5.4	5.3	...	0.6	1.1
Philippines	0.7	0.5	0.5	1.9	2.0	3.1	0.4	0.1	0.3
Singapore	1.2	1.3	...	3.1	4.6	...	6.4	...	1.3
Solomon Islands	...	2.8	...	...	5.9	...	...	0.4	...
Sri Lanka	1.5	1.3	...	2.6	2.8	...	0.3	0.4	...
Taipei,China	...	0.2	0.3	0.7	0.8	1.8	...	0.1	0.1
Thailand	...	...	...	...	...	...	...	...	...
Tonga	2.6	3.0	3.0	2.7	3.3	4.4	...	...	...
Tuvalu	...	2.8	...	...	22.4	...	...	0.7	...
Uzbekistan	...	...	...	...	...	...	...	...	...
Vanuatu	...	3.5	...	...	6.3	...	...	...	...
Viet Nam	...	...	...	...	...	...	...	...	...
Western Samoa	...	3.0	...	...	4.1	...	...	...	...

Table 27: MERCHANDISE EXPORTS, F.O.B.
(US$ Million)

DMC	1982	1983	1984	1985	1986	1987	1988	1989	1990	1991	1992	1993	1994	1995
Afghanistan	708	729	633	567	552	512	395	236	235	188	...	...	...	...
Bangladesh	769	724	931	999	887	1067	1291	1305	1671	1689	2098	2272	2661	3473 *
Bhutan	17	16	18	22	34	55	75	70	75	72	63	60	...	...
Cambodia	...	...	...	...	...	36	45	79	86	253	265	283	490	856
China, People's Rep. of	21896	22195	24982	27555	31447	39542	47540	51858	61269	71910	84940	90970	121047	148797
Cook Islands	4	3	4	3	5	7	4	3	5	5	3	4	4	5
Fiji	377	306	332	307	336	380	431	494	615	462	407	405	509	...
Hong Kong	21006	21959	28323	30187	35439	48476	63163	73140	82160	98577	119512	135248	151395	176711 *
India	9358	9148	9916	9140	9399	11298	13325	15846	17975	17664	19563	21553	25075	30539
Indonesia	22293	21152	21902	18590	16075	17135	19465	22160	25674	29142	33967	36823	40054	44700 *
Kazakstan [a]	...	...	...	...	...	...	...	...	1402	928	1451	1486	2691	4110
Kiribati	2	4	11	4	2	2	5	5	3	3	5	3	5	6 *
Korea, Rep. of	21853	24446	29245	30282	34715	47182	60696	62377	65016	71870	76632	82236	96013	125058
Kyrgyz Republic	...	...	...	...	...	...	...	...	...	...	258	340	340	409
Lao PDR	40	41	44	54	55	64	58	63	79	97	133	241	300	347
Malaysia	12031	14130	16590	15442	13753	17939	21110	25053	29416	34349	40713	47122	58756	74045
Maldives	10	13	18	23	25	31	40	45	52	54	40	35	46	...
Marshall Islands	2	3	6	3	1	2	2	2	2	3	9	8	22	23
Micronesia, Fed. States of	2	2	2	3	1	1	3	2	3	11	...	...	...	...
Mongolia	562	610	674	689	716	718	739	722	661	348	388	383	368	512
Myanmar	391	378	301	303	288	219	147	215	325	419	537	583	771	846
Nauru [b]	133	94	68	63	55	59	73	80	66	26	35	41	...	...
Nepal	88	94	128	160	142	151	190	158	210	264	374	390	364	348
Pakistan	2397	3077	2558	2740	3384	4172	4522	4709	5589	6528	7317	6688	7365	7992
Papua New Guinea	771	813	892	912	1033	1161	1399	1404	1144	1338	1810	2491	2640	2627 *
Philippines	4968	4890	5274	4607	4770	5649	7032	7755	8068	8767	9752	11089	13304	17316 *
Singapore	20787	21833	24070	22812	22495	28687	39306	44665	52752	59025	63484	74012	96826	118265
Solomon Islands	58	62	93	70	66	64	82	75	70	83	102	94	...	...
Sri Lanka	1030	1066	1451	1293	1215	1368	1479	1545	1983	2039	2455	2859	3208	3798
Taipei,China	22090	25094	30424	30704	39644	53483	60493	66085	67142	76115	81395	84678	92847	111585
Thailand	6945	6368	7413	7121	8872	11654	15953	20078	23070	28428	32472	37168	45261	55375 *
Tonga	4	5	9	5	6	6	7	9	11	13	12	16	14	17 *
Tuvalu	1	1	1	0	0	0	0	0	0	0	0	0	0	...
Uzbekistan	...	...	...	...	...	...	...	...	...	...	1497	2838	3235	3771 *
Vanuatu	23	30	44	31	17	18	20	22	19	18	24	23	25	28
Viet Nam	527	617	650	699	789	854	1038	1946	2404	2087	2581	2971	3600	5220 *
Western Samoa	13	18	20	16	11	12	15	13	9	6	6	6	4	9
(A) TOTAL DMCs (Reporting)	171157	179920	207027	205406	226229	292004	360144	402220	449260	512781	584300	645418	769240	936787
(B) TOTAL WORLD [c]	1739100	1696400	1799300	1832800	2009500	2366200	2698500	2921700	3334400	3566200	3807600	3824600	4364300	...
(A) / (B) %	9.8	10.6	11.5	11.2	11.3	12.3	13.3	13.8	13.5	14.4	15.3	16.9	17.6	...

a   Excludes trade with other states of the former USSR for 1990-93.
b   Covers trade with Australia and New Zealand only; refers to fiscal year ending 30 June.
c   Includes only those countries reporting to IMF.

Sources: IMF, *IFS*, May 1996.
IMF, *IFS Yearbook 1995*.
ADB, *Annual Report 1995*.
Country sources.

Table 28: MERCHANDISE IMPORTS, C.I.F.
(US$ Million)

DMC	1982	1983	1984	1985	1986	1987	1988	1989	1990	1991	1992	1993	1994	1995
Afghanistan	962	1064	1390	1194	1404	996	900	822	936	616	...	...	...	...
Bangladesh	2307	2165	2825	2772	2486	2680	3046	3648	3598	3401	3888	4001	4701	6633 *
Bhutan [a]	68	72	73	84	102	92	135	99	108	102	74	114	...	...
Cambodia [a]	...	...	...	...	...	152	169	176	164	285	443	471	726	1188
China, People's Rep. of	18906	21345	26482	42896	43411	43392	55278	58437	52523	63791	80585	103088	115681	129113
Cook Islands	20	23	21	25	26	34	42	44	52	55	59	67	85	106
Fiji	509	484	450	442	435	379	462	581	743	642	614	634	724	...
Hong Kong	23575	24017	28568	29703	35367	48465	63896	72155	82474	100255	123430	138658	161777	210367 *
India	14786	14061	15322	15928	15421	16675	19149	20535	23642	20418	23580	22761	26846	34399
Indonesia	16859	16352	13882	10262	10718	12891	13249	16360	21837	25869	27280	28328	31985	44576
Kazakstan [b]	...	...	...	...	...	...	...	...	1490	584	566	472	4213	5320
Kiribati [a]	23	18	18	15	14	18	22	23	27	26	37	28	26	37 *
Korea, Rep. of	24251	26192	30631	31136	31585	41020	51811	61465	69844	81525	81775	83800	102348	135119
Kyrgyz Republic	...	...	...	...	...	...	...	...	...	...	332	503	398	537
Lao PDR	132	150	162	193	186	216	149	194	185	210	244	432	654	587
Malaysia	12395	13198	14069	12301	10823	12701	16551	22496	29258	36648	39926	45657	59581	79853 *
Maldives	43	57	53	53	45	81	90	113	138	161	189	185	222	...
Marshall Islands [a]	19	18	23	29	31	34	34	44	56	56	62	61	70	75
Micronesia, Fed. States of [a]	43	49	38	41	44	42	68	73	84	89	...	...	...	...
Mongolia	791	928	975	1096	1840	1105	1114	963	924	361	418	379	258	389
Myanmar	409	268	239	283	304	268	244	201	270	646	651	814	886	1272
Nauru [c]	13	13	13	9	11	11	14	14	16	21	...	...	...	...
Nepal	395	464	416	453	459	570	681	580	686	758	792	880	1159	1374
Pakistan	5465	5329	5853	5890	5374	5822	6590	7143	7376	8439	9379	9500	8889	11461
Papua New Guinea	1170	1120	1110	1008	1080	1165	1393	1530	1193	1614	1485	1299	1521	1741 *
Philippines	8263	7976	6432	5459	5394	7144	8721	11171	13041	12786	15449	18754	22546	28192 *
Singapore	28167	28158	28667	26285	25511	32559	43864	49667	60899	66293	72179	85234	102670	124507
Solomon Islands	71	74	79	83	72	81	98	114	94	110	98	101	...	...
Sri Lanka	1831	1820	1867	1843	1857	2058	2262	2188	2685	3054	3445	3991	4776	5185
Taipei,China	18827	20308	22002	20124	24230	34802	49763	52507	54830	63078	72181	77099	85507	103698
Thailand	8549	10287	10398	9242	9173	13023	20285	25771	33379	37591	40686	46208	54459	68554 *
Tonga	42	38	41	41	41	48	55	54	62	59	63	61	69	74 *
Tuvalu [a]	3	3	3	3	3	3	5	4	4	5	5	7	7	...
Uzbekistan	...	...	...	...	...	...	...	...	...	...	1756	3180	3203	3619 *
Vanuatu	60	64	69	70	58	70	70	71	96	83	82	79	89	95 *
Viet Nam	1472	1527	1745	1857	2155	2455	2757	2566	2752	2338	2541	3415	4500	7125 *
Western Samoa	50	48	50	51	47	62	76	75	80	94	110	105	82	95
(A) TOTAL DMCs (Reporting)	190477	197689	213966	220871	229707	281112	363043	411884	465545	532063	604403	680365	800659	1005291
(B) TOTAL WORLD [d]	1840500	1781600	1898200	1907700	2089300	2443900	2788100	3023300	3455400	3580700	3823300	3766700	4285700	...
(A) / (B) %	10.3	11.1	11.3	11.6	11.0	11.5	13.0	13.6	13.5	14.9	15.8	18.1	18.7	...

a   Refers to imports in fob for entire series for Cambodia, Kiribati and Fed. States of Micronesia;
    Refers to imports in fob for 1993 for Bhutan, for 1980-88 for Marshall Islands and for 1993-94 for Tuvalu.
b   Excludes trade with other states of the former USSR for 1990-93.
c   Covers trade with Australia and New Zealand only; refers to fiscal year ending 30 June.
d   Includes only those countries reporting to IMF.

Sources: IMF, *IFS*, May 1996.
          IMF, *IFS Yearbook 1995.*
          ADB, *Annual Report 1995.*
          Country sources.

Table 29: DIRECTION OF TRADE – MERCHANDISE EXPORTS
(Percent)

From \ To	Asia 1985	Asia 1994	Western Europe 1985	Western Europe 1994	North and Central America 1985	North and Central America 1994	Middle East 1985	Middle East 1994	South America 1985	South America 1994	Africa 1985	Africa 1994	Oceania 1985	Oceania 1994	Rest of the World 1985	Rest of the World 1994
Afghanistan	18.3	32.8	53.1	45.0	3.2	7.8	2.2	2.5	0.0	0.1	0.4	0.6	0.1	0.3	22.7	11.0
Bangladesh	21.8	12.4	22.1	42.8	19.9	36.5	15.4	3.5	0.1	0.7	11.4	2.1	1.9	0.8	7.5	1.3
Bhutan	...	...	...	...	...	...	...	...	...	...	...	...	...	...	...	...
Cambodia	44.3	87.8	31.8	2.2	5.6	0.5	1.0	0.0	0.0	0.0	0.0	0.0	0.0	9.5	17.3	0.0
China, People's Rep. of	61.5	57.5	10.1	13.6	9.6	20.1	6.4	2.4	1.7	1.1	1.6	1.2	0.8	1.5	8.4	2.7
Cook Islands	...	...	...	...	...	...	...	...	...	...	...	...	...	...	...	...
Fiji	16.2	16.3	36.4	21.4	8.2	21.4	0.0	0.0	0.0	0.6	0.0	0.0	39.2	40.3	0.0	0.0
Hong Kong	42.4	50.0	15.3	16.6	35.0	27.0	2.7	1.7	0.4	1.4	1.2	1.2	2.5	1.7	0.5	0.5
India	20.2	28.1	21.7	30.0	20.4	21.5	10.7	10.5	0.1	0.8	2.2	3.4	1.5	1.6	23.3	4.1
Indonesia	64.8	55.6	6.7	18.4	24.2	19.4	1.3	2.2	0.0	0.3	0.7	1.0	1.2	2.4	1.0	0.7
Kazakstan	...	8.1	...	14.8	...	3.1	...	0.3	...	...	...	...	...	0.0	...	73.7
Kiribati	4.3	60.5	88.0	15.8	0.0	17.2	...	...	...	0.0	...	...	7.7	0.6	0.0	6.0
Korea, Rep. of	29.3	47.4	14.9	13.1	44.4	28.7	5.8	3.5	0.7	2.1	3.5	2.2	1.5	1.6	0.0	1.6
Kyrgyz Republic	...	51.7	...	39.3	...	3.9	...	2.9	...	0.0	...	...	...	0.0	...	2.2
Lao PDR	78.5	32.0	4.4	65.0	3.9	2.8	0.1	0.0	0.0	0.0	3.1	0.1	5.6	0.0	4.6	0.2
Malaysia	64.3	54.8	15.8	15.4	13.9	23.8	1.9	2.4	0.3	0.6	0.3	0.7	2.0	2.2	1.5	0.3
Maldives	61.0	44.4	6.6	36.9	32.2	18.7	0.2	0.0	...	...	0.0	0.0	0.0	0.0	...	...
Marshall Islands	...	...	...	...	...	...	...	...	...	...	...	...	...	...	...	...
Micronesia, Fed. States of	...	...	...	...	...	...	...	...	...	...	...	...	...	...	...	...
Mongolia [a]	2.3	52.4	6.1	12.0	0.0	3.4	0.0	0.0	0.0	0.0	0.0	0.0	0.0	0.0	91.6	32.4
Myanmar	70.6	76.5	14.8	9.3	1.0	10.3	4.7	0.7	0.0	0.0	2.4	1.5	0.0	0.9	6.5	0.8
Nauru	...	...	...	...	...	...	...	...	...	...	...	...	...	...	...	...
Nepal	42.1	5.7	21.7	58.3	35.8	34.9	0.0	0.1	0.0	0.7	0.0	0.1	0.1	0.3	0.2	0.0
Pakistan	28.7	27.6	27.8	35.8	11.4	19.4	18.8	11.5	1.0	0.8	4.7	2.5	1.2	2.0	6.4	0.5
Papua New Guinea	31.5	42.3	47.5	14.5	8.0	4.6	0.1	0.1	0.0	0.0	0.0	0.1	12.9	38.4	0.1	0.1
Philippines	39.2	35.4	17.3	18.4	38.5	42.2	1.6	1.8	0.1	0.3	0.2	0.3	2.3	1.4	0.8	0.2
Singapore	48.7	55.7	12.2	15.1	23.9	21.2	5.9	2.0	0.6	0.7	1.8	1.0	5.6	3.3	1.4	1.1
Solomon Islands	63.9	81.5	30.1	14.2	2.5	0.9	...	0.2	...	0.3	...	0.0	3.6	2.9	...	0.0
Sri Lanka	17.4	12.1	22.3	36.8	26.7	36.4	23.6	6.6	0.6	0.7	2.9	1.2	1.9	1.4	4.7	4.8
Taipei,China	27.2	49.4	9.8	13.9	52.8	29.2	3.7	2.1	0.5	1.3	1.8	1.5	2.9	2.1	1.3	0.5
Thailand	41.6	49.6	21.6	17.2	21.6	23.7	7.4	3.6	0.5	0.5	4.0	1.6	2.0	1.9	1.5	2.0
Tonga	0.2	58.5	2.5	3.8	3.2	28.6	0.0	0.0	0.0	0.0	0.0	...	94.2	9.2	...	...
Tuvalu	...	0.0	30.4	23.9	0.0	0.0	...	...	...	10.1	...	65.2	69.6	0.7	0.0	0.0
Uzbekistan	...	7.4	...	39.2	...	0.8	...	0.1	...	0.7	...	0.0	...	0.0	...	51.9
Vanuatu	18.0	27.7	76.2	40.6	0.0	14.1	0.0	0.0	...	3.1	...	0.0	5.7	14.5	...	0.0
Viet Nam	24.7	58.1	10.3	25.1	0.0	1.9	0.5	0.4	0.0	1.2	0.0	1.2	0.4	5.4	64.2	6.7
Western Samoa	0.9	3.6	5.8	1.4	59.4	3.6	...	...	...	...	0.0	0.0	33.9	91.4	...	...

a   Figures are based on data published by the State Statistical Office of Mongolia as a result of Mongolia's exclusion in the IMF, DOTS tape for 1996.

Sources: IMF, *DOTS* tape, May 1996 .
Country sources for Cambodia, Mongolia and Taipei,China.

Table 30: DIRECTION OF TRADE – MERCHANDISE IMPORTS
(Percent)

From / To	Asia		Western Europe		North and Central America		Middle East		South America		Africa		Oceania		Rest of the World	
	1985	1994	1985	1994	1985	1994	1985	1994	1985	1994	1985	1994	1985	1994	1985	1994
Afghanistan	71.5	71.8	21.0	20.2	1.0	1.8	0.5	0.5	0.0	0.1	0.0	0.1	0.0	0.1	6.0	5.4
Bangladesh	44.0	66.2	19.5	15.3	16.3	8.0	12.5	4.0	0.6	1.6	0.3	0.3	1.9	2.3	5.0	2.1
Bhutan	...	...	...	...	...	...	...	...	...	...	...	...	...	...	...	...
Cambodia	72.0	93.0	18.2	4.7	0.0	0.0	0.0	0.2	0.0	0.8	0.0	0.6	2.0	0.8	7.7	0.0
China, People's Rep. of	51.4	51.6	18.3	20.3	15.5	16.0	0.4	1.2	4.2	2.0	0.8	0.8	3.2	2.9	6.3	5.2
Cook Islands	...	...	...	...	...	...	...	...	...	...	...	...	...	...	...	...
Fiji	29.2	22.1	12.1	3.9	4.8	18.0	0.0	0.1	0.1	0.2	0.1	0.2	53.2	55.4	0.5	0.2
Hong Kong	68.2	75.0	15.4	12.8	11.3	8.5	0.9	1.3	0.8	0.5	1.2	0.4	2.0	1.2	0.4	0.3
India	16.8	20.8	29.4	29.8	13.9	10.9	20.4	24.3	2.3	2.8	2.7	5.1	2.8	3.6	11.7	2.9
Indonesia	41.9	52.1	20.6	22.6	19.8	12.7	9.2	3.3	1.4	1.8	1.4	0.7	5.3	6.1	0.3	0.7
Kazakstan	...	5.3	...	28.0	...	3.5	...	0.4	...	0.1	...	...	...	0.1	...	62.6
Kiribati	24.1	9.7	18.4	34.4	0.0	26.3	...	...	...	0.1	0.0	...	57.5	28.2	0.0	1.3
Korea, Rep. of	38.4	41.5	13.7	15.7	27.4	25.4	9.8	8.5	4.2	1.9	1.9	0.8	4.6	4.6	0.0	1.5
Kyrgyz Republic	...	17.7	...	33.3	...	35.2	...	1.3	...	...	...	...	...	0.0	...	12.6
Lao PDR	86.2	72.4	11.0	21.4	0.4	1.0	0.0	0.1	0.0	0.1	0.2	0.0	0.1	4.9	2.1	0.2
Malaysia	54.3	57.5	17.9	17.9	17.0	18.2	4.0	0.7	0.9	1.0	0.5	0.5	5.1	3.8	0.4	0.4
Maldives	91.1	80.6	8.5	10.3	0.0	0.6	...	6.4	...	0.1	0.0	0.8	0.3	0.8	...	0.4
Marshall Islands	...	...	...	...	...	...	...	...	...	...	...	...	...	...	...	...
Micronesia, Fed. States of	...	...	...	...	...	...	...	...	...	...	...	...	...	...	...	...
Mongolia [a]	1.1	27.0	3.1	7.0	0.0	4.4	0.0	0.0	0.0	0.0	0.0	0.0	0.0	0.0	95.7	61.6
Myanmar	53.2	87.7	27.8	8.9	6.3	0.8	0.4	0.1	0.0	0.0	1.3	0.5	1.7	1.2	9.4	0.8
Nauru	...	...	...	...	...	...	...	...	...	...	...	...	...	...	...	...
Nepal	78.2	79.7	16.6	12.7	3.2	1.7	0.0	0.5	0.0	0.1	0.0	0.0	0.9	5.2	1.2	0.1
Pakistan	26.5	31.5	24.0	29.3	15.5	10.8	25.3	21.1	1.0	0.9	2.0	1.8	4.2	2.3	1.5	2.3
Papua New Guinea	34.1	35.7	8.1	4.1	9.0	4.8	0.1	0.0	0.3	0.4	0.1	0.4	48.2	54.6	0.0	0.0
Philippines	43.7	51.4	10.6	12.6	26.8	20.5	12.7	7.8	1.2	1.8	0.2	0.6	4.4	3.9	0.5	1.5
Singapore	50.8	58.2	14.0	15.3	16.2	16.7	14.4	6.6	0.4	0.6	0.6	0.3	3.3	1.8	0.3	0.4
Solomon Islands	40.6	40.9	6.4	5.0	2.1	1.0	...	0.0	...	0.0	0.7	0.3	50.2	52.9	...	0.0
Sri Lanka	40.3	54.7	19.2	27.2	9.7	5.9	22.5	4.8	1.0	0.8	2.0	1.4	4.2	4.0	1.1	1.2
Taipei,China	27.2	48.0	9.8	18.7	52.8	22.8	3.7	3.7	0.5	2.0	1.8	1.6	2.9	3.1	1.3	0.1
Thailand	53.7	57.4	18.8	18.1	13.5	14.1	8.4	3.8	1.2	1.1	1.3	0.9	2.2	2.4	1.0	2.3
Tonga	13.0	16.1	10.4	2.2	5.8	9.2	0.3	0.0	0.0	0.2	0.0	0.0	70.5	72.2	0.0	0.0
Tuvalu	0.0	1.9	14.2	8.3	0.0	0.7	...	...	0.0	0.2	...	...	85.8	89.1	0.0	0.0
Uzbekistan	...	7.6	...	35.2	...	6.3	...	0.3	...	0.0	...	...	...	0.0	...	50.7
Vanuatu	23.6	51.6	13.5	14.6	0.8	0.8	0.1	0.0	0.0	0.1	0.0	...	62.0	32.9	...	0.0
Viet Nam	46.1	77.7	27.5	12.4	0.2	3.0	0.0	0.1	0.0	0.1	0.0	0.0	1.5	2.1	24.7	4.7
Western Samoa	31.1	13.7	6.7	2.1	10.8	11.9	...	...	...	0.0	...	...	51.4	72.3	...	...

a   Figures are based on data published by the State Statistical Office of Mongolia as a result of Mongolia's exclusion in the IMF, DOTS tape for 1996.

Sources: IMF, *DOTS* tape, May 1996.
Country sources for Cambodia, Mongolia, and Taipei,China.

Table 31: TERMS OF TRADE
(1990 = 100)

DMC	1982	1983	1984	1985	1986	1987	1988	1989	1990	1991	1992	1993	1994	1995
Afghanistan	...	...	...	...	...	...	...	...	...	...	...	...	...	...
Bangladesh [a]	98.4	90.1	107.7	138.2	104.6	90.0	93.6	121.1	100.0	90.0	89.0	83.1	...	...
Bhutan	...	...	...	...	...	...	...	...	...	...	...	...	...	...
Cambodia	...	...	...	...	...	...	...	...	...	...	...	...	...	...
China, People's Rep. of	99.5	89.3	82.0	55.6	62.0	78.4	73.8	76.3	100.0	96.8	...	...	...	...
Cook Islands	...	...	...	...	...	...	...	...	...	...	...	...	...	...
Fiji	...	...	...	...	...	...	...	...	...	...	...	...	...	...
Hong Kong	99.0	98.0	99.0	103.0	100.0	99.0	98.0	100.0	100.0	101.0	101.0	102.0	100.0	99.0
India [b]	88.8	111.4	96.0	98.4	117.9	111.5	114.2	110.8	100.0	109.4	115.7	132.7	181.9	...
Indonesia	...	122.9	126.2	134.7	108.1	106.7	89.4	86.7	100.0	91.9	83.9	89.1	82.1	...
Kazakstan	...	...	...	...	...	...	...	...	...	...	...	...	...	...
Kiribati	...	...	...	...	...	...	...	...	...	...	...	...	...	...
Korea, Rep. of	86.9	87.7	89.7	90.1	98.1	100.5	103.6	101.8	100.0	100.0	100.0	104.5	105.4	105.4
Kyrgyz Republic	...	...	...	...	...	...	...	...	...	...	...	...	...	...
Lao, PDR	...	...	...	...	...	...	...	...	...	...	...	...	...	...
Malaysia	86.4	95.6	99.6	93.1	89.2	95.8	100.3	100.8	100.0	99.5	99.7	...	...	...
Maldives	...	...	...	...	...	...	...	...	...	...	...	...	...	...
Marshall Islands	...	...	...	...	...	...	...	...	...	...	...	...	...	...
Micronesia, Fed. States of	...	...	...	...	...	...	...	...	...	...	...	...	...	...
Mongolia	110.6	102.4	97.6	101.2	89.4	90.6	91.8	97.6	100.0	...	...	...	...	...
Myanmar [b]	150.0	150.6	156.0	134.2	110.0	88.2	99.7	108.7	100.0	88.1	70.7	63.4	75.1	...
Nepal	101.4	101.5	96.7	104.4	113.7	106.7	105.2	102.2	100.0	103.2	103.3	...	...	...
Nauru	...	...	...	...	...	...	...	...	...	...	...	...	...	...
Pakistan [a]	99.0	99.1	105.7	104.2	100.1	107.5	107.3	99.9	100.0	86.9	92.2	89.8	91.5	98.7
Papua New Guinea	134.8	140.8	152.4	138.5	134.9	124.7	141.1	113.1	100.0	100.4	113.1	131.7	...	...
Philippines	84.4	81.9	78.2	91.5	98.8	108.1	120.1	111.0	100.0	106.5	93.9	90.7	92.7	94.0
Singapore	113.8	111.2	107.6	108.5	105.6	100.9	98.9	98.6	100.0	97.7	94.5	94.3	91.4	...
Solomon Islands	140.2	141.1	199.0	193.8	150.2	195.0	165.3	183.6	100.0	96.6	90.5	...	...	...
Sri Lanka	73.8	89.9	110.0	90.5	84.2	92.1	89.8	94.7	100.0	90.1	97.5	98.4	93.5	...
Taipei,China	77.0	79.4	80.3	82.6	88.0	94.3	93.3	99.7	100.0	100.8	102.7	101.7	97.0	98.7
Thailand	99.7	107.1	104.6	98.7	110.3	109.1	107.1	103.0	100.0	98.9	99.6	100.3	101.3	98.1
Tonga	103.6	101.0	100.8	97.5	94.1	92.8	117.0	97.6	100.0	99.3	97.3	102.9	109.5	...
Tuvalu	...	...	...	...	...	...	...	...	...	...	...	...	...	...
Uzbekistan	...	...	...	...	...	...	...	...	...	...	...	...	...	...
Vanuatu	...	...	...	...	...	...	...	...	...	...	...	...	...	...
Viet Nam	...	...	...	...	...	...	...	...	...	...	...	...	...	...
Western Samoa	126.8	139.8	202.9	150.9	103.3	108.8	127.3	109.1	100.0	124.1	130.5	142.2	116.3	103.9

a   Averages for the fiscal year ending 30 June.
b   Averages for the fiscal year beginning 1 April.

Sources: Country sources.
WB, *World Tables 1995* and past issues for Nepal and Papua New Guinea.
ADB data file for PRC and Mongolia.

Table 32: FOREIGN TRADE INDICATORS
(Percent of GNP)

DMC	Total Trade			Trade Balance			Current Account Balance		
	1975	1985	1995	1975	1985	1995	1975	1985	1995
Afghanistan	...	...	...	...	...	...	...	...	...
Bangladesh	10.5	22.7	30.5	-5.8	-10.1	-7.8	-1.8	-1.5	-0.5
Bhutan	...	67.7	67.4 [c]	...	-39.6	-12.6 [c]	...	-10.4	-18.5 [c]
Cambodia [a]	...	...	69.8	...	...	-11.3	...	...	-5.4
China, People's Rep. of [b]	11.0	22.7	40.7	-0.2	-4.9	2.4	...	-3.7	1.2 [c]
Cook Islands [a]	92.2	101.4	106.7	-58.1	-78.9	-97.8	...	...	...
Fiji	65.4	60.9	75.3 [c]	-14.3	-18.5	-15.3 [c]	-2.2	-1.2	-3.2 [c]
Hong Kong [a]	146.7	175.2	239.9 [c]	-8.4	1.4	-8.0 [c]	...	...	...
India	11.8	11.7	18.5 [c]	-1.6	-3.3	-0.8 [c]	-0.2	-2.0	-1.5 [d]
Indonesia	40.8	34.4	45.4	8.0	9.9	2.5	-3.8	-2.3	-1.7 [c]
Kazakstan	...	...	57.9	...	...	-7.4	...	...	-6.2
Kiribati [a]	88.0	84.9	123.3 [d]	43.9	-47.7	-95.2 [d]	42.1	-10.8	-36.6 [d]
Korea, Rep. of	59.4	67.4	57.6	-10.5	-0.9	-2.2	-9.1	-1.0	-2.0
Kyrgyz Republic [a]	...	...	65.5	...	...	-8.9	...	...	-9.2
Lao PDR [a]	...	13.2	53.9	...	-7.4	-13.8	...	-5.0	-5.8
Malaysia	82.2	95.1	175.5 [c]	3.2	10.5	-1.3 [c]	-5.5	-2.1	-8.8
Maldives [a]	...	98.7	118.4	...	-38.4	-55.7	...	-6.5	-6.1
Marshall Islands [a]	...	83.0	93.2	...	-69.0	-49.4	...	...	36.1 [g]
Micronesia, Fed. States of [a]	...	...	59.3 [e]	...	...	-46.2 [e]	...	...	30.1 [g]
Mongolia	...	81.2	107.6	...	-18.5	14.7	...	-37.1	11.7 [c]
Myanmar	12.5	13.5	3.2 [c]	-1.3	-3.9	-0.7 [c]	-2.1	-3.1	-0.9 [e]
Nauru	...	...	...	...	...	...	...	...	...
Nepal	16.1	22.2	34.9 [c]	-5.5	-10.6	-15.9 [c]	...	-4.7	-8.6 [c]
Pakistan	27.9	25.1	30.5	-9.3	-10.0	-3.7	-9.4	-4.0	-4.0
Papua New Guinea [a]	73.1	74.4	76.1 [c]	6.3	1.6	25.5 [c]	-2.7	-6.4	10.7 [f]
Philippines	40.9	33.7	59.8	-10.0	-2.7	-14.2	-6.0	-0.3	-2.5
Singapore	236.1	267.8	287.8	-48.0	-18.9	-7.4	-10.2	-0.0	13.3
Solomon Islands [a]	84.0	87.2	109.5 [f]	-24.9	0.5	-4.1 [f]	-24.1	-12.9	-0.9 [d]
Sri Lanka	34.2	54.5	66.6 [c]	-4.9	-9.1	-11.0 [c]	-2.9	-7.4	-6.6 [c]
Taipei,China	73.0	80.5	81.5	-4.3	16.7	3.0	-3.8	14.6	2.0
Thailand	36.9	42.8	78.0	-7.2	-5.6	-9.0	-4.2	-4.0	-8.0
Tonga [a]	70.6	77.6	54.4	-33.8	-59.5	-37.5	6.2	-1.7	-5.2
Tuvalu [a]	...	92.4	...	...	-71.5	...	...	16.2	9.0 [c]
Uzbekistan	...	...	...	...	...	...	...	...	...
Vanuatu	...	82.2	59.7 [c]	...	-31.9	-32.1 [c]	...	1.1	-7.6 [f]
Viet Nam	...	...	...	...	...	...	...	...	...
Western Samoa [a]	...	79.1	67.7	...	-41.3	-55.9	...	2.1	6.8

a   GDP at current market prices was used in the computation.
b   For 1975, Net Material Product (NMP) at current market prices was used in the computation.
c   Refers to 1994.
d   Refers to 1992.
e   Refers to 1991.
f   Refers to 1993.
g   Refers to 1990.

Sources: Country sources.

DMC	1982	1983	1984	1985	1986	1987	1988	1989	1990	1991	1992	1993	1994
Afghanistan	...	...	...	...	...	...	...	...	...	...	...	...	...
Bangladesh	...	0.4	0.6	...	2.4	3.2	1.8	0.2	3.2	1.4	3.7	14.0	11.0
Bhutan	...	...	...	...	...	...	...	...	...	...	...	...	...
Cambodia	...	...	...	...	...	...	109.6	10.9	94.2	25.2	33.0	54.1	69.0
China, People's Rep. of	386.0	543.0	1124.0	1030.0	1425.0	1669.0	2344.0	2613.0	2657.0	3453.0	7156.0	23115.0	31787.0
Cook Islands	...	...	...	...	...	...	...	...	...	...	...	...	...
Fiji	28.7	32.0	23.1	8.2	9.3	-14.5	30.1	-18.5	75.5	19.4	48.7	42.9	...
Hong Kong	...	...	...	...	...	...	...	...	...	...	...	...	...
India	–	–	–	–	–	–	–	–	–	–	–	–	...
Indonesia	225.0	292.0	222.0	310.0	258.0	385.0	576.0	682.0	1093.0	1482.0	1777.0	2004.0	2109.0
Kazakstan	...	...	...	...	...	...	...	...	...	...	...	1272.2	635.0
Kiribati	...	...	...	...	...	...	...	...	...	...	...	...	...
Korea, Rep. of	-76.0	-57.0	73.0	200.0	325.0	418.0	720.0	505.0	-268.0	-320.0	-481.0	-773.0	-1715.0
Kyrgyz Republic	...	...	...	...	...	...	...	...	...	...	...	10.0	...
Lao PDR	...	...	...	...	...	...	2.0	4.0	6.0	8.0	9.0	59.8	60.1
Malaysia	1397.0	1261.0	797.0	695.0	489.0	423.0	719.0	1668.0	2332.0	3998.0	5183.0	5006.0	4348.0
Maldives	...	...	...	...	4.2	5.1	1.2	4.4	5.6	6.5	6.6	6.9	...
Marshall Islands	...	...	...	...	-6.5	11.7	6.5	13.5	-9.5	...	...	...	...
Micronesia, Fed.States of	...	...	...	...	...	...	...	...	...	...	...	...	...
Mongolia	...	...	...	...	...	...	...	...	...	...	...	2.0	7.7	7.0
Myanmar	–	–	–	–	–	–	–	8.0	161.0	238.0	...	...	...
Nauru	...	...	...	...	...	...	...	...	...	...	...	...	...
Nepal	–	–	–	–	–	–	–	–	–	–	–	...	...
Pakistan	64.0	29.0	60.0	139.0	106.0	110.0	173.0	167.0	242.0	261.0	347.0	348.0	...
Papua New Guinea	84.1	137.8	113.4	113.4	82.4	99.5	115.4	221.3	155.4	202.5	293.6	-1.7	-4.9
Philippines	16.0	105.0	9.0	12.0	127.0	307.0	936.0	563.0	530.0	544.0	228.0	763.0	1861.0
Singapore	1298.0	1085.0	1210.0	809.0	1529.0	2630.0	3537.0	2005.0	3541.0	3855.0	1034.0	3232.0	3411.0
Solomon Islands	1.0	0.4	2.0	0.7	3.1	10.5	1.7	11.6	10.4	14.5	14.2	...	...
Sri Lanka	63.6	37.8	32.6	24.8	29.2	58.2	43.6	17.7	35.4	43.9	121.0	187.6	158.1
Taipei,China	71.0	130.0	131.0	261.0	260.0	11.0	-3161.0	-5347.0	-3913.0	-583.0	-990.0	-1534.0	-1085.0
Thailand	189.0	349.0	400.0	162.0	262.0	182.0	1081.0	1725.0	2304.0	1847.0	1969.0	1505.0	147.0
Tonga	...	...	...	0.0	0.1	0.2	0.1	0.2	0.2	0.3	1.2	2.2	...
Tuvalu	...	...	...	...	...	...	...	...	...	...	...	...	...
Uzbekistan	...	...	...	...	...	...	...	...	...	...	...	...	...
Vanuatu	6.9	5.9	7.4	4.6	2.0	12.9	10.8	9.2	13.1	25.5	26.5	26.7	29.8
Viet Nam	...	...	...	...	...	...	...	100.0	120.0	213.0	260.0	300.0	1048
Western Samoa	–	–	–	–	–	–	–	–	–	–	–	–	...
Total DMCs (Reporting)	3754.4	3951.3	4205.1	3769.7	4907.2	6321.8	7247.8	4963.2	9188.7	15335.3	17042.4	35648.3	42876.1

a   Data are taken from the balance of payments statistics.

Sources: For 1982-1988, IMF, *IFS Yearbook 1995*.
For 1989-1994, IMF, *IFS*, April 1996.
Country sources for Kazakstan, Kyrgyz Republic, Marshall Islands ,Taipei,China and Viet Nam.

Table 34: INTERNATIONAL RESERVES AND RATIO TO IMPORTS

DMC	1982	1983	1984	1985	1986	1987	1988	1989	1990	1991	1992	1993	1994	1995
							International Reserves [a] (End of year; US$ Million)							
Afghanistan	698.7	582.3	526.2	610.8	635.7	746.8	657.0	630.7	637.9	576.1	...	...	...	...
Bangladesh	208.6	545.8	408.1	356.1	434.9	876.0	1076.5	532.0	659.5	1307.9	1853.6	2446.7	3174.7	2376.1
Bhutan	35.5 [b]	40.2	44.8	50.3	61.0	74.9	94.1	98.5	86.0	98.9	77.9	90.2	115.2	115.9
Cambodia	...	...	...	...	...	...	...	...	...	...	...	24.2	118.5	191.9
China, People's Rep. of [c]	17151.6	19832.1	21281.4	16880.9	16417.4	22453.1	23751.2	23052.7	34475.5	48164.7	24852.3	27348.3	57781.3	80288.7
Cook Islands	...	...	...	...	...	...	...	...	...	...	...	...	...	...
Fiji	131.9	120.0	120.8	134.4	175.3	132.7	233.8	212.0	261.2	271.8	317.2	269.9	273.5	349.4
Hong Kong	...	...	...	...	...	...	...	...	...	...	...	...	...	...
India	8241.6	8215.6	8535.6	9492.8	10480.5	11512.4	9185.7	8049.0	5637.4	7616.3	9538.7	14674.7	24220.4	22864.7
Indonesia	4562.2	4902.2	5730.0	5989.0	5264.4	7094.6	6321.4	6699.9	8656.7	10358.0	11482.4	12474.4	13321.5	14907.3
Kazakstan [d]	...	...	...	...	...	...	...	...	...	...	...	581.0	907.0	982.0
Kiribati [e]	80.0	87.0	74.0	94.0	...	...	...	...	...	...	...	...	...	...
Korea, Rep. of [f]	7092.6	6993.7	7713.9	7819.7	8135.5	9316.6	20991.0	23209.9	24448.2	24519.6	30133.2	36565.8	46701.9	60610.2
Kyrgyz Republic [g]	...	...	...	...	...	...	...	...	...	...	...	63.4 *	97.9 *	78.0 *
Lao PDR [h]	8.3	19.4	11.2	25.9	32.4	21.2	16.7	2.0	2.4	29.3	40.9	63.6	61.5	92.7
Malaysia	4832.6	4672.9	4441.3	5677.2	6941.7	8572.6	7491.1	8733.4	10658.8	11717.0	18024.5	28182.7	26339.0	24698.3
Maldives	8.4	4.5	5.1	4.6	6.9	8.2	21.6	24.8	24.4	23.5	28.2	26.2	31.2	48.0
Marshall Islands	...	...	...	...	...	...	...	...	...	...	...	...	...	...
Micronesia, Fed. States of	...	...	...	...	...	...	...	...	...	...	...	...	...	...
Mongolia [i]	24.5	20.8	35.0	58.7	71.5	146.9	150.0	279.1	145.5	125.6	40.5	65.1	92.4	151.5
Myanmar	219.0	185.2	139.5	116.0	131.2	148.7	180.4	364.1	409.4	347.2	363.7	401.0	518.2	650.4
Nauru	...	...	...	...	...	...	...	...	...	...	...	...	...	...
Nepal	268.2	190.9	128.6	105.4	145.7	251.3	282.7	273.0	354.2	451.1	518.4	700.0	752.2	645.6
Pakistan	1813.4	2683.4	1610.0	1429.0	1465.0	1441.2	1192.9	1302.5	1046.4	1220.4	1523.5	1995.5	3715.4	2527.8
Papua New Guinea	481.2	464.1	454.7	463.2	450.1	467.3	419.3	409.6	427.3	345.3	259.6	166.1	120.2	266.8
Philippines	1740.6	857.3	844.3	1098.3	2611.0	2311.9	2168.5	2398.2	2035.9	4436.2	5335.4	5934.3	7125.4	7756.6
Singapore [j]	8480.0	9264.0	10416.0	12847.0	12939.0	15227.0	17073.0	20345.0	27748.0	34133.0	39885.0	48361.0	58177.0	68695.0
Solomon Islands	37.2	47.3	44.7	35.6	29.6	36.8	39.6	26.2	17.6	8.5	23.5	20.1	13.7	15.0
Sri Lanka	379.8	321.0	530.4	471.6	377.6	309.5	247.8	269.3	447.3	724.2	980.3	1685.6	2046.0 [k]	2088.0 [k]
Taipei,China	10243.1	13047.0	17040.3	24194.9	48488.9	80459.6	79430.0	78652.3	77652.7	87191.7	86819.5	88869.4	97652.8	95559.0
Thailand	2674.3	2555.8	2687.7	3003.2	3776.2	5205.6	7112.8	10507.9	14258.3	18392.5	21183.5	25439.5	30280.2	36938.8
Tonga [l]	15.6	21.0	26.0	27.5	22.5	28.9	30.5	24.9	31.3	32.3	31.8	37.1	35.5	28.7
Tuvalu	...	...	...	...	...	...	...	...	...	...	...	...	...	...
Uzbekistan	...	...	...	...	...	...	...	...	...	...	...	...	...	...
Vanuatu	5.7	6.6	8.1	10.6	21.4	40.2	40.7	35.1	37.7	39.8	42.5	45.6	43.6	50.1
Viet Nam [m]	...	...	16.0	16.0	14.6	14.6	14.6	...	...	...	...	...	...	...
Western Samoa	3.5	7.2	10.6	14.0	23.8	37.2	49.2	55.1	69.1	67.8	61.2	50.7	50.8	55.3
TOTAL (Reporting)	69438.1	75687.2	82884.2	91026.7	119153.9	166935.7	178272.1	186187.0	210228.6	252198.9	253417.3	296581.6	373766.9	423031.6

a   Data refer to total international reserves with gold valued at London market prices, unless otherwise specified. For Bhutan, Cambodia, Maldives, Solomon Islands, Vanuatu and Western Samoa, data refer to total international reserves excluding gold; for Taipei,China, data refer to foreign exchange and gold only.
b   Refers to foreign exchange and reserve position in the Fund only.
c   The component, foreign exchange, comprises the holdings of the People's Bank of China and the Bank of China. Beginning December 1984, it includes foreign government securities. Starting July 1992, foreign exchange includes holdings of People's Bank of China only.
d   Refers to net reserves of the National Bank of Kazakstan.
e   Refers to foreign exchange only.
f   Series includes other bank assets. Beginning 1988, data for the component, other bank assets, include claims of foreign banks' branches on non-residents.
g   Refers to gross official reserves.

Table 34: INTERNATIONAL RESERVES AND RATIO TO IMPORTS (Continued)

Ratio of International Reserves to Imports [n] (Months)

1982	1983	1984	1985	1986	1987	1988	1989	1990	1991	1992	1993	1994	1995	DMC
10.1	7.8	5.2	8.0	6.7	9.9	10.8	12.1	...	...	...	...	...	...	Afghanistan
1.1	3.1	2.3	1.8	2.5	4.5	4.8	2.1	2.3	5.0	7.1	8.2	10.1	...	Bangladesh
6.4	6.9	7.6	7.5	7.5	9.8	...	10.2	11.2	17.7	11.3	9.5	14.2	12.6	Bhutan
...	...	...	...	...	...	...	...	...	...	...	0.6	2.0	1.9	Cambodia
12.2	12.7	10.7	5.3	5.6	7.4	6.1	5.7	9.8	11.5	4.6	3.8	7.3	7.3 [o]	China, People's Rep. of
...	...	...	...	...	...	...	...	...	...	...	...	...	...	Cook Islands
3.6	3.4	3.4	4.1	5.7	4.9	7.0	5.2	4.9	5.9	7.1	5.0	4.5	5.8	Fiji
...	...	...	...	...	...	...	...	...	...	...	...	...	...	Hong Kong
7.0	7.1	7.2	7.6	8.0	7.8	5.5	4.3	2.9	4.3	5.2	7.4 [o]	9.3 [o]	6.9 [o]	India
3.1	3.3	4.6	5.7	5.3	6.8	5.5	4.9	4.8	5.0	5.1	5.3	4.9	4.4 [o]	Indonesia
...	...	...	...	...	...	...	...	...	...	...	1.5	2.6	2.0	Kazakstan
41.4	59.0	48.4	52.3	...	...	...	...	...	...	...	...	...	...	Kiribati
3.6	3.4	3.4	3.5	3.3	2.9	5.2	4.9	4.5	3.8	4.7	5.5	5.8	5.7	Korea, Rep. of
...	...	...	...	...	...	...	...	...	...	...	1.5 *	2.9 *	1.7 *	Kyrgyz Republic
0.8	1.6	0.8	1.6	2.1	1.2	1.3	0.1	0.2	1.7	2.0	1.8	1.3	1.9	Lao PDR
4.6	4.2	4.0	5.9	8.1	8.6	5.9	5.0	4.9	4.3	6.0	7.9	5.8	4.1	Malaysia
2.2	0.9	1.0	0.9	1.3	1.5	3.0	2.7	2.4	2.0	2.0	1.8	1.9	2.4	Maldives
...	...	...	...	...	...	...	...	...	...	...	...	...	...	Marshall Islands
...	...	...	...	...	...	...	...	...	...	...	...	...	...	Micronesia, Fed. States of
0.3	0.2	0.4	0.7	0.6	1.3	1.3	1.8	1.7	3.0	1.2	2.1	3.2	4.7 [o]	Mongolia
2.9	3.1	3.0	2.7	2.5	3.9	5.8	14.4	9.4	13.8	6.7 [b]	3.7 [o]	3.7 [o]	4.1 [o]	Myanmar
...	...	...	...	...	...	...	...	...	...	...	...	...	...	Nauru
7.9	4.9	3.8	2.8	4.0	5.9	5.1	5.8	6.4	7.2	8.3	9.8	7.8	6.1	Nepal
3.8	5.7	3.2	2.9	2.9	2.8	2.0	2.1	1.6	1.7	2.0	2.4	5.1	3.0	Pakistan
5.7	5.7	5.7	6.4	5.8	5.0	3.6	3.7	4.6	3.0	2.4	1.8	1.1	1.8 * [o]	Papua New Guinea
2.7	1.4	1.7	2.6	6.2	4.1	3.2	2.8	2.0	4.4	4.4	4.0	4.0	3.5	Philippines
3.9	4.2	4.7	6.3	6.6	6.1	5.1	5.3	6.0	6.7	7.1	7.2	7.3	9.7	Singapore
7.6	9.2	7.9	5.9	5.3	6.3	4.5	3.3	2.7	1.1	3.2	1.7 [o]	1.2 [o]	...	Solomon Islands
2.3	2.0	3.3	2.8	2.3	1.8	1.3	1.5	2.0	2.9	3.4	5.0	5.1	7.3 [o]	Sri Lanka
6.8	8.3	9.8	15.0	25.7	29.2	20.5	19.0	18.0	17.5	15.3	14.7	14.6	11.8	Taipei,China
4.2	3.3	3.5	4.3	5.4	5.2	4.8	5.5	5.8	6.5	7.0	7.5	7.6	6.9	Thailand
5.3	7.0	10.4	10.3	8.2	9.1	7.7	6.4	7.0	6.7	8.2	9.2	7.5	5.5	Tonga
...	...	...	...	...	...	...	...	...	...	...	...	...	...	Tuvalu
...	...	...	...	...	...	...	...	...	...	...	...	...	...	Uzbekistan
1.6	1.7	1.9	2.4	5.5	8.4	8.4	7.3	5.7	6.5	7.6	8.5	6.3	6.4 [o]	Vanuatu
...	...	0.1	0.1	0.1	0.1	0.1	...	...	...	...	...	...	...	Viet Nam
0.9	2.0	2.8	3.6	6.7	8.0	8.9	9.9	11.8	10.5	8.2	7.0	8.8	8.3	Western Samoa

h   Data refer to gold (in national valuation), foreign exchange and SDRs.
i   Prior to1991, data refer to gold (in national valuation) and foreign exchange. From 1991 onwards, data refer to total international reserves including gold (in national valuation).
j   Refers to total international reserves including gold (in national valuation).
k   Refers to total international reserves excluding gold.
l   Prior to 1985, data refer to foreign exchange only. From 1985 onwards, data refer to SDRs, reserve position in the Fund and foreign exchange.
m   Refers to gold (in national valuation) and foreign exchange.
n   Merchandise imports, fob from balance of payments was used in the computation, unless otherwise specified. For entire series for Kyrgyz Rep. and Lao PDR, merchandise imports, cif
    from balance of payments section was used in the computation.
o   Merchandise imports, cif from trade statistics was used in the computation.

Sources: Country sources.
           IMF, *IFS*, May 1996.
           IMF, *IFS Yearbook 1995*.

Table 35: TOTAL EXTERNAL DEBT AND DEBT SERVICE PAYMENTS
(US$ Million)

DMC	1982	1983	1984	1985	1986	1987	1988	1989	1990	1991	1992	1993	1994
						Total External Debt [a]							
Afghanistan	2020.0	2639.0	2060.0	2274.0	2753.0	4041.0	5155.0	5055.4	5085.7	5305.4	5404.4	5420.3	...
Bangladesh	5412.0	5950.3	6229.3	7278.1	8723.1	10584.1	11108.7	11504.5	13070.0	13812.2	14166.9	14938.5	16568.8
Bhutan	1.1	1.8	2.7	8.8	21.0	40.2	67.0	73.9	83.6	86.4	83.6	84.9	87.4
Cambodia	...	...	...	...	...	...	...	1716.6	1887.3	1894.6	1872.6	1862.1	1943.4
China, People's Rep. of	8358.1	9609.4	12081.9	16695.9	23719.4	35339.5	42438.9	44932.5	52750.5	59779.2	69508.4	84177.6	100535.5
Cook Islands	...	...	...	...	...	...	...	...	...	...	...	...	...
Fiji	401.9	437.4	413.3	443.8	441.2	468.3	472.1	414.2	412.6	360.5	338.6	330.0	298.7
Hong Kong	5685.0	6580.0	6925.0	8555.0	11784.0	12069.0	11864.0	12136.0	12566.0	13455.0	14092.0	16463.0	20444.0
India	27438.2	32004.1	33826.0	40970.8	48277.9	55727.2	58443.4	73388.9	81982.9	83946.9	89822.4	92104.1	98989.9
Indonesia	25133.6	30229.6	32020.3	36709.0	42921.6	52500.4	54095.3	59394.2	69955.2	79778.0	88296.4	89477.2	96499.6
Kazakstan	...	...	...	...	...	...	...	...	...	...	35.0	1654.6	2704.2
Kiribati	9.0	10.0	9.0	10.0	10.0	17.0	13.0	14.8	14.7	14.9	16.0	16.3	...
Korea, Rep. of	37329.5	40419.1	42099.0	47133.3	46724.5	39807.7	35716.1	32798.6	34986.7	39733.8	44156.7	47202.7	54542.3
Kyrgyz Republic	...	...	...	...	...	...	...	...	...	...	0.6	309.0	441.3
Lao PDR	428.5	450.5	518.1	618.7	868.2	1161.4	1330.2	1472.5	1768.1	1874.7	1917.0	1985.3	2080.1
Malaysia	13353.7	17550.2	18733.4	20269.1	21879.7	22839.1	18567.0	16277.7	16079.5	17811.3	19959.2	23300.6	24766.6
Maldives	65.2	77.2	82.9	83.0	68.7	72.9	71.3	66.8	78.0	81.2	97.1	114.7	126.7
Marshall Islands	...	...	...	...	...	...	...	...	...	...	...	...	...
Micronesia, Fed. States of	...	...	...	...	...	...	...	...	...	...	...	...	...
Mongolia	...	...	...	...	...	...	...	...	...	...	350.3	374.6	443.0
Myanmar	2043.2	2323.2	2332.9	3090.8	3792.2	4387.4	4414.2	4171.2	4673.1	4852.6	5326.6	5730.3	6502.0
Nauru	...	...	...	...	...	...	...	...	...	...	...	...	...
Nepal	352.8	452.5	470.2	589.9	754.6	1000.3	1178.0	1368.5	1640.0	1771.4	1801.9	2003.8	2319.8
Pakistan	11640.4	11939.9	12141.0	13371.1	14868.0	16707.2	16983.5	18346.0	20660.5	23046.2	24193.7	26173.4	29578.7
Papua New Guinea	1627.6	1867.6	2029.4	2112.1	1984.0	2276.0	2249.9	2305.7	2571.4	2733.5	3740.0	3223.8	2878.5
Philippines	24412.5	24211.0	24356.6	26639.9	28206.2	29786.2	29011.1	28721.6	30614.5	32456.4	32997.0	35926.4	39301.6
Singapore	3607.0	3911.0	4128.0	4407.0	3787.0	4196.0	4192.0	4575.0	4204.0	4825.0	4705.0	5511.0	7868.0
Solomon Islands	28.0	34.4	44.0	65.9	77.6	98.5	104.8	100.8	121.6	130.4	95.2	151.1	165.1
Sri Lanka	2625.5	2884.2	2993.1	3540.0	4079.8	4748.3	5200.4	5169.3	5840.1	6544.8	6419.4	6793.1	7811.0
Taipei,China	9631.0	10866.0	9645.0	9146.0	12757.0	20102.0	18595.0	17890.0	18459.0	19900.0	19858.0	23243.0	26161.0
Thailand	12237.9	13902.4	15012.8	17551.7	18505.0	20305.3	21673.6	23452.0	28204.1	35894.1	39612.1	45835.6	60990.4
Tonga	...	...	...	...	28.9	36.1	37.6	39.2	53.6	45.0	43.4	44.3	64.4
Tuvalu	...	...	...	...	...	...	...	...	...	...	...	...	...
Uzbekistan	...	...	...	...	...	...	...	...	...	...	8.1	981.4	1156.4
Vanuatu	4.0	10.5	12.9	15.9	18.1	23.7	26.8	30.3	40.3	39.3	40.4	42.4	46.5
Viet Nam	...	...	...	...	...	...	...	19516.2	22268.2	22449.7	23840.0	24359.6	25115.4
Western Samoa	69.8	74.6	75.5	76.0	75.7	80.6	75.9	73.7	91.9	140.6	117.9	194.3	154.9

a   Refers to long-term public and publicly guaranteed debt, long-term private non-guaranteed debt, short-term debt, and use of IMF credit.
b   Refer to long-term principal repayments, long-term interest payments, short-term interest payments, and IMF repurchases and charges.

Table 35: TOTAL EXTERNAL DEBT AND DEBT SERVICE PAYMENTS (Continued)
(US$ Million)

1982	1983	1984	1985	1986	1987	1988	1989	1990	1991	1992	1993	1994	DMC
						Total Debt Service Payments [b]							
50.0	38.0	43.0	47.0	46.0	50.0	40.0	102.0	130.0	119.0	120.0	95.0	...	Afghanistan
255.4	220.2	289.0	359.8	486.2	555.2	511.3	523.0	809.3	634.0	583.2	575.8	652.9	Bangladesh
0.0	0.0	0.0	0.0	0.2	0.5	1.3	6.6	5.1	7.3	5.9	6.7	6.8	Bhutan
...	...	...	...	...	...	...	11.7	30.0	16.1	13.0	34.3	2.0	Cambodia
2124.9	2691.5	2284.6	2478.1	2973.3	3851.7	4564.7	5650.3	6955.1	8258.2	8618.0	10168.2	11135.4	China, People's Rep. of
...	...	...	...	...	...	...	...	...	...	...	...	...	Cook Islands
37.2	40.7	53.8	63.4	66.7	67.3	67.4	91.1	105.8	102.8	84.2	78.2	80.7	Fiji
814.0	956.0	1232.0	1132.0	1441.0	1314.0	1440.0	2481.0	1718.0	1467.0	...	...	...	Hong Kong
2041.5	2608.1	2959.5	3533.4	5273.9	5693.6	5952.5	7032.8	7888.0	7502.4	7323.1	8453.3	10515.7	India
3856.3	3741.4	4846.6	5823.9	5984.9	7003.2	8640.9	9708.8	9921.8	11461.3	12577.9	14267.4	14791.9	Indonesia
...	...	...	...	...	...	...	...	...	...	0.0	9.6	59.5	Kazakstan
0.0	0.0	0.0	1.0	2.0	1.0	1.0	1.0	1.0	1.0	1.0	1.0	...	Kiribati
6348.1	6429.1	7160.6	9047.6	11222.3	18196.0	10460.7	8765.0	8279.2	6051.0	6973.3	9172.9	7922.5	Korea, Rep. of
...	...	...	...	...	...	...	...	...	...	0.0	1.4	16.4	Kyrgyz Republic
4.6	3.8	6.7	7.0	8.5	10.3	10.7	17.7	8.9	8.7	9.6	28.5	20.0	Lao PDR
1524.7	1874.6	2683.9	5398.6	3526.7	4453.1	6057.0	4337.7	3570.6	3042.0	3099.2	4204.7	5042.3	Malaysia
4.0	7.4	19.2	10.2	12.0	7.4	9.8	9.9	8.8	7.6	7.0	8.5	9.4	Maldives
...	...	...	...	...	...	...	...	...	...	...	...	...	Marshall Islands
...	...	...	...	...	...	...	...	...	...	...	...	...	Micronesia, Fed. States of
...	...	...	...	...	...	...	...	...	...	67.5	19.9	39.9	Mongolia
142.9	174.1	178.3	226.1	290.1	225.8	129.5	196.9	61.1	80.1	54.2	105.1	173.0	Myanmar
...	...	...	...	...	...	...	...	...	...	...	...	...	Nauru
17.9	19.4	18.8	23.3	28.0	36.5	48.6	63.3	71.2	66.9	67.9	71.0	82.3	Nepal
848.8	1309.7	1185.4	1416.9	1650.8	1816.4	1812.4	1782.4	1916.8	2010.2	2370.9	2512.8	3423.2	Pakistan
232.9	286.7	412.6	340.2	321.9	355.4	498.1	516.0	557.2	508.1	660.1	847.0	870.0	Papua New Guinea
3513.2	3028.0	2703.3	2534.2	2961.2	3364.5	3396.7	3245.1	3591.9	3398.2	4302.1	4908.2	4534.1	Philippines
718.0	711.0	657.0	1317.0	914.0	949.0	556.0	858.0	586.0	543.0	...	...	...	Singapore
0.5	0.6	2.5	3.6	4.8	5.3	7.3	9.9	11.6	13.3	7.6	10.0	17.4	Solomon Islands
244.7	265.4	273.8	320.1	398.7	496.8	487.2	422.3	389.2	429.7	485.4	418.4	405.1	Sri Lanka
2034.0	2031.0	2427.0	2312.0	1757.0	2833.0	1806.0	1899.0	1862.0	1928.0	...	...	...	Taipei,China
1939.8	2213.4	2677.1	3263.3	3654.8	3463.2	4386.0	4394.1	5293.6	4918.0	5907.2	9120.6	9237.2	Thailand
...	...	...	...	1.0	1.1	1.3	1.3	1.9	1.6	1.5	1.8	2.8	Tonga
...	...	...	...	...	...	...	...	...	...	...	...	...	Tuvalu
...	...	...	...	...	...	...	...	...	...	0.0	27.9	112.0	Uzbekistan
0.5	1.3	1.3	1.3	1.6	3.5	2.4	1.9	2.4	1.7	1.6	1.5	1.9	Vanuatu
...	...	...	...	...	...	...	279.7	208.7	230.8	498.4	496.4	300.1	Viet Nam
4.4	5.9	6.2	7.6	8.1	8.0	8.6	6.6	5.4	5.4	4.8	5.4	5.0	Western Samoa

Sources: WB, *WDT* 1996 (STARS version).
For Hong Kong, Singapore and Taipei,China:
OECD, *Financing and External Debt of Developing Countries, 1992 Survey* and past issues for 1982-91,
OECD, *External Debt Statistics Annual Report 1994* for 1992, and
OECD, *External Debt Statistics, 1995 Edition* for 1993-94.

Table 36: DEBT INDICATORS
(Percent)

DMC	Total External Debt/GNP [a]					Total External Debt/Exports [b]				
	1975	1985	1992	1993	1994	1975	1985	1992	1993	1994
Afghanistan	34.0	...	...	...	...	...	326.1	...	...	...
Bangladesh	12.9	46.8	59.8	62.5	63.4	411.0	459.6	416.0	378.8	384.4
Bhutan	...	5.6	33.9	36.3	32.1	...	23.2	98.0	...	...
Cambodia	...	...	93.6	84.5	83.5	...	...	594.5	653.4	375.9
China, People's Rep. of	...	5.5	16.6	19.6	19.3	...	56.0	82.1	92.3	80.4
Cook Islands	...	...	...	...	...	...	...	...	...	...
Fiji	8.8	40.5	21.4	20.5	17.7	20.1	81.5	37.7	34.7	26.2
Hong Kong [d]	4.2 [c]	26.7	15.5	14.8	16.2	5.2 [c]	23.6	...	...	...
India	15.1	19.3	33.6	36.3	34.2	218.5	263.7	334.9	284.9	247.5
Indonesia	36.7	44.3	66.4	58.9	57.4	163.8	181.7	221.8	211.9	195.8
Kazakstan	...	...	0.1	6.5	14.9	...	...	0.8	48.0	86.8
Kiribati	...	31.7	31.1	31.9	...	...	60.6	30.4	31.5	...
Korea, Rep. of	40.3	51.7	14.4	14.4	15.3	143.0	142.4	48.4	47.6	46.9
Kyrgyz Republic	...	...	...	8.1	16.2	...	...	0.2	91.8	129.8
Lao PDR	...	...	161.8	148.9	135.6	...	826.0	960.4	613.5	803.1
Malaysia	22.3	69.9	36.4	38.7	36.9	47.9	114.0	42.7	43.5	37.7
Maldives	...	116.1	55.5	55.3	50.9	...	90.8	43.7	52.2	45.7
Marshall Islands	...	...	...	...	...	...	...	...	...	...
Micronesia, Fed. States of	...	...	...	...	...	...	...	...	...	...
Mongolia	...	...	33.6	62.7	61.3	...	...	89.6	95.4	105.2
Myanmar	9.1	45.5	...	...	...	170.9	727.1	615.6	607.9	578.0
Nauru	...	...	...	...	...	...	...	...	...	...
Nepal	2.1	22.2	50.1	52.5	57.3	22.6	184.0	314.6	322.2	236.1
Pakistan	51.2	39.7	49.0	50.1	56.6	386.7	228.2	246.6	262.5	300.4
Papua New Guinea	39.4	90.4	95.8	68.0	57.5	90.3	157.4	166.1	110.4	95.9
Philippines	28.1	89.1	60.8	64.1	59.3	131.6	331.8	187.1	187.0	160.6
Singapore	11.4 [c]	23.4	10.4	9.5	11.9	8.7 [c]	14.8	5.4	5.4	6.0
Solomon Islands	17.8	42.9	40.8	55.2	53.0	49.2	78.5	68.6	...	...
Sri Lanka	21.7	59.5	66.3	66.4	67.6	125.9	182.8	181.4	163.2	190.5
Taipei,China	12.4 [c]	14.5	9.2	10.3	10.7	30.5 [c]	25.8	20.1	22.2	23.1
Thailand	12.5	45.9	36.2	37.1	43.1	62.4	171.7	91.8	93.0	103.1
Tonga	...	...	30.2	30.5	40.5	...	...	81.9	83.6	...
Tuvalu	...	...	...	...	...	...	...	...	...	...
Uzbekistan	...	...	...	4.5	5.4	...	...	...	34.4	32.5
Vanuatu	...	13.0	23.1	24.8	24.7	...	17.6	36.2	41.5	41.1
Viet Nam	...	...	241.6	189.8	161.3	...	...	735.6	666.8	510.7
Western Samoa	...	88.7	77.8	125.7	87.5	73.6	149.3	134.4	249.7	305.5

a   Total external debt is the sum of public and publicly guaranteed long-term debt, private non-guaranteed long-term debt, short-term debt, and the use of IMF credit. It also includes interest arrears on long-term debt whenever available.
b   Exports refer to exports of goods and services.
c   Total external debt refers to long-term debt only.
d   GDP is used in lieu of GNP.
e   Total debt service includes principal and interest payments on total long-term debt, interest payments on short-term debt, and IMF repurchases and charges.
f   Refers to the ratio of long-term concessional debt to total long-term debt.
g   Total debt service refers to long-term debt only.

Table 36: DEBT INDICATORS (Continued)
(Percent)

Total Debt Service/Exports [e]					Concessional Debt/Long-term Debt [f]					DMC
1975	1985	1992	1993	1994	1975	1985	1992	1993	1994	
...	6.7	...	...	...	100.0	99.8	99.9	99.3	...	Afghanistan
23.3	22.7	17.1	14.6	15.1	92.2	97.2	97.8	98.0	98.3	Bangladesh
...	...	6.9	...	...	...	100.0	83.6	86.4	89.6	Bhutan
...	...	4.1	12.0	0.4	...	...	100.0	100.0	100.0	Cambodia
...	8.3	10.2	11.2	8.9	...	24.7	19.5	19.1	18.8	China, People's Rep. of
...	...	...	...	...	...	...	...	...	...	Cook Islands
4.0	11.6	9.4	8.2	7.1	18.4	7.4	16.4	18.3	20.5	Fiji
2.7 [g]	3.1	...	...	...	0.9	0.1	...	...	...	Hong Kong
13.1	22.7	27.3	26.1	26.3	92.0	62.7	53.7	52.2	53.2	India
15.1	28.8	31.6	33.8	30.0	47.4	30.4	31.9	35.0	36.4	Indonesia
...	...	...	0.3	1.9	...	...	0.0	0.0	0.1	Kazakstan
...	6.1	1.9	1.9	...	...	10.0	45.5	42.6	...	Kiribati
12.9	27.3	7.6	9.2	6.8	27.7	8.8	14.1	13.5	12.1	Korea, Rep. of
...	...	...	0.4	4.8	...	...	100.0	12.4	30.1	Kyrgyz Republic
...	9.3	4.8	8.8	7.7	83.0	99.4	99.8	99.8	99.8	Lao PDR
5.1	30.4	6.6	7.8	7.7	20.1	7.0	16.0	17.3	17.9	Malaysia
...	11.2	3.1	3.9	3.4	...	77.3	90.5	78.0	80.8	Maldives
...	...	...	...	...	...	...	...	...	...	Marshall Islands
...	...	...	...	...	...	...	...	...	...	Micronesia, Fed. States of
...	...	17.3	5.1	9.5	...	...	55.3	59.9	67.3	Mongolia
20.7	53.2	6.3	11.1	15.4	80.6	85.8	92.9	92.8	92.8	Myanmar
...	...	...	...	...	...	...	...	...	...	Nauru
1.1	7.3	11.9	11.4	8.4	90.2	95.7	94.9	96.2	97.1	Nepal
20.6	24.2	24.2	25.2	34.8	81.8	82.1	68.4	65.4	67.0	Pakistan
18.2	25.4	29.3	29.0	29.0	5.9	17.8	21.6	26.9	30.6	Papua New Guinea
14.4	31.6	24.4	25.5	18.5	17.8	15.5	33.5	35.1	34.6	Philippines
1.5 [g]	4.4	...	...	...	16.3	3.0	...	...	...	Singapore
...	4.3	5.5	...	...	100.0	75.1	79.6	52.8	55.2	Solomon Islands
26.1	16.5	13.7	10.0	9.9	74.2	71.4	86.3	88.5	90.2	Sri Lanka
5.2 [g]	6.5	...	...	...	8.8	3.5	...	...	...	Taipei,China
12.0	31.9	13.7	18.5	15.6	23.1	15.3	20.3	22.8	21.6	Thailand
...	...	2.8	3.4	...	...	...	98.8	99.1	83.6	Tonga
...	...	...	...	...	...	...	...	...	...	Tuvalu
...	...	...	1.0	3.1	...	...	...	16.1	16.5	Uzbekistan
...	1.4	1.4	1.5	1.7	68.6	71.0	95.2	95.7	96.6	Vanuatu
...	...	15.4	13.6	6.1	...	...	90.4	92.2	92.3	Viet Nam
4.7	14.9	5.5	6.9	9.9	44.9	85.7	98.8	99.5	100.0	Western Samoa

Sources: WB, *WDT 1996* (STARS version).
For Hong Kong, Singapore, and Taipei,China:
OECD, *External Debt of Developing Countries, 1986 Survey* for 1975,
OECD, *Financing and External Debt of Developing Countries, 1992 Survey* for 1985,
OECD, *External Debt Statistics Annual Report 1994* for 1992,
OECD, *External Debt Statistics, 1995 Edition* for 1993-94.
WB, *WT* 1995.
Country sources.

Table 37: TOTAL NET FLOWS[a] OF FINANCIAL RESOURCES FROM ALL SOURCES TO DMCs
(US$ Million)

DMC	1982	1983	1984	1985	1986	1987	1988	1989	1990	1991	1992	1993	1994
Afghanistan	12.3	13.2	5.6	-5.9	2.5	45.7	74.9	164.7	135.4	519.5	204.1	299.0	170.5
Bangladesh	1351.0	1088.5	1239.7	1099.2	1400.0	1763.5	1615.8	1817.7	2151.4	2028.5	1935.0	1491.0	1618.7
Bhutan	11.3	13.0	17.9	24.1	40.1	42.1	59.5	40.6	50.9	63.4	43.6	73.7	74.3
Cambodia	43.7	36.7	14.8	12.9	13.5	14.2	18.5	17.3	41.6	94.4	214.3	319.8	351.3
China, People's Rep. of	678.1	748.1	938.1	2297.2	3441.5	4285.4	5202.9	5620.2	4842.4	5133.1	6092.6	9001.0	12574.7
Cook Islands	12.1	11.3	7.6	10.6	27.3	11.0	14.2	20.3	15.9	22.7	73.2	-116.8	-240.3
Fiji	75.6	65.3	31.9	22.5	46.7	22.2	56.6	56.2	70.2	59.4	127.9	33.5	22.9
Hong Kong	1183.1	1100.8	1254.4	-1206.4	-1385.3	4164.5	2606.3	1267.0	3509.4	2523.1	1747.0	3437.9	6785.5
India	2269.0	2327.2	2193.6	2506.8	3694.4	3363.1	3875.6	5055.5	4186.8	4378.1	3108.0	2096.9	3857.5
Indonesia	2891.7	3137.3	3308.9	1683.0	1585.7	3159.8	3210.5	4786.8	3377.9	5766.4	5832.1	3877.7	5415.3
Kazakstan	–	–	–	–	–	–	–	–	–	111.5	110.2	361.7	626.40
Kiribati	15.2	16.7	11.4	12.0	13.8	18.3	16.3	17.5	20.5	20.1	27.5	15.5	-11.8
Korea, Rep. of	1516.0	1306.9	1916.2	1592.2	385.3	-2437.7	-1908.4	-807.4	1081.6	2825.4	2412.6	2235.5	4332.2
Kyrgyz Republic	–	–	–	–	–	–	–	–	–	3.5	93.6	154.8
Lao PDR	38.1	30.1	35.2	64.1	45.4	55.1	73.9	145.5	151.2	143.8	165.3	206.6	218.5
Malaysia	833.8	1750.0	1418.5	232.4	54.3	389.7	627.8	516.6	1612.3	1469.9	1205.2	4777.8	3292.8
Maldives	9.0	9.0	5.5	9.9	16.2	23.7	25.1	59.1	37.7	43.8	40.5	38.9	40.9
Marshall Islands	–	–	–	–	–	–	–	–	–	–	7.7	34.0	53.0
Micronesia, Fed. States of	–	–	–	–	–	–	–	–	–	–	13.9	64.7	105.5
Mongolia	–	–	0.1	3.3	4.7	2.8	3.1	8.4	11.9	83.1	135.1	146.1	167.5
Myanmar	418.0	297.5	278.1	310.8	358.8	336.6	459.1	79.1	108.5	166.9	128.2	111.2	171.0
Nauru	–	–	–	–	–	–	26.8	-8.9	1.2	16.4	-43.1	19.4	13.7
Nepal	199.4	197.4	200.1	244.0	327.6	379.7	440.3	503.9	431.7	449.3	496.3	349.8	449.2
Pakistan	1197.3	762.7	708.6	897.0	950.9	915.3	1822.9	2660.6	1724.5	2206.8	1751.9	1773.8	2757.7
Papua New Guinea	600.6	574.8	519.3	330.2	193.7	300.5	441.0	738.6	604.2	682.5	631.9	367.2	241.7
Philippines	944.8	1542.6	930.7	583.2	1052.3	912.8	1252.2	1204.5	1976.8	1665.2	1440.9	3295.3	2815.3
Singapore	914.3	191.9	1314.1	-267.3	-109.1	912.7	1657.9	2963.2	3369.0	1565.5	3263.8	3694.8	4778.2
Solomon Islands	28.5	30.9	25.5	22.0	29.9	70.4	65.1	49.9	57.7	38.5	46.9	58.9	45.6
Sri Lanka	471.9	530.4	632.7	567.7	491.8	519.3	617.1	818.2	737.8	868.4	666.2	816.4	665.7
Taipei,China	427.6	-48.1	-73.7	-518.0	-476.0	-305.0	-79.2	732.1	450.3	-1410.4	-1408.6	-1148.7	765.6
Thailand	1238.2	1277.0	1460.0	856.8	544.7	884.7	315.1	2277.7	2794.6	3689.8	3682.5	2437.1	7022.4
Tonga	17.4	17.9	15.7	13.6	15.1	36.6	5.9	31.7	29.5	19.7	24.0	31.4	35.3
Tuvalu	5.9	4.2	5.5	3.3	4.4	25.7	14.0	6.9	5.0	6.2	13.3	4.2	7.7
Uzbekistan	–	–	–	–	–	–	–	–	–	–	1.4	5.8	99.0
Vanuatu	33.1	35.6	45.3	38.5	-28.4	35.2	38.6	79.2	148.8	77.2	10.1	69.0	12.9
Viet Nam	137.8	76.7	103.7	93.3	122.8	83.7	161.0	138.5	187.1	269.0	590.8	348.7	1134.1
Western Samoa	22.6	31.0	13.4	20.1	22.5	34.2	30.4	30.3	54.2	60.0	53.0	52.0	48.7
TOTAL DMCs	17597.4	17176.6	18578.4	11553.1	12887.1	20065.8	22840.8	31091.5	33978.0	35657.2	34848.8	40774.4	60674.0
TOTAL DEVELOPING COUNTRIES	86913.4	72233.9	81338.0	46207.7	69695.8	65637.7	78937.2	89331.9	82997.5	99494.1	115948.0	137842.4	164615.4

a Total net flows represent the actual international transfer of financial resources less repayments of principal in respect of earlier loans. Such flows may be recorded at one of several stages: provision of goods and services, placing of funds at the disposal of the recipient in an earmarked fund or account, withdrawal of funds by the recipient from an earmarked fund or account, payment by the donor of invoices on behalf of the recipient, etc.

Sources: OECD, *Geographical Distribution of Financial Flows to Aid Recipients, 1990-1994.*
OECD, *Geographical Distribution of Financial Flows to Developing Countries, 1989/1992* and past issues.

Table 38: OFFICIAL DEVELOPMENT ASSISTANCE FLOWS[a] FROM ALL SOURCES TO DMCs
(US$ Million)

DMC	1982	1983	1984	1985	1986	1987	1988	1989	1990	1991	1992	1993	1994
Afghanistan	9.3	13.5	6.7	16.8	2.3	45.0	72.4	167.0	137.2	511.9	204.3	227.2	228.5
Bangladesh	1341.2	1049.0	1189.8	1130.8	1427.2	1790.3	1615.9	1806.9	2100.5	1889.1	1820.7	1383.4	1757.1
Bhutan	11.3	13.0	17.9	24.1	40.0	42.1	41.5	41.7	47.9	64.2	56.2	65.8	76.5
Cambodia	43.9	36.7	16.9	12.9	13.2	14.2	18.5	30.3	41.6	91.0	206.8	316.8	336.8
China, People's Rep. of	524.0	669.6	798.2	940.0	1097.5	1381.6	1924.4	2076.7	2092.5	1998.7	3049.6	3271.2	3232.0
Cook Islands	10.4	9.3	8.1	9.7	26.4	11.0	12.0	12.6	12.3	13.5	17.2	12.8	14.3
Fiji	35.4	32.7	31.3	31.9	42.5	35.9	54.3	43.1	50.4	44.7	63.4	61.5	40.4
Hong Kong	7.9	8.8	13.8	20.5	18.5	19.4	22.1	40.6	38.2	36.1	-39.0	30.3	26.9
India	1643.9	1840.0	1672.3	1592.0	1996.2	1702.9	1956.0	1778.1	1407.0	2744.9	2423.0	1459.0	2324.9
Indonesia	906.3	744.5	672.7	603.2	710.9	1245.9	1631.8	1839.3	1747.0	1874.4	2078.9	2017.6	1642.1
Kazakstan	–	–	–	–	–	–	–	–	–	111.5	9.5	14.1	48.4
Kiribati	15.1	16.8	11.9	12.0	13.4	18.4	16.3	17.5	20.5	20.1	26.8	16.0	15.4
Korea, Rep. of	34.0	8.0	-36.6	-8.6	-17.3	11.2	9.7	51.6	52.5	54.8	-3.0	-40.8	-113.6
Kyrgyz Republic	–	–	–	–	–	–	–	–	–	–	3.5	93.6	154.5
Lao PDR	38.3	29.7	34.1	37.0	45.3	55.0	73.6	145.0	151.2	143.3	164.9	206.4	217.7
Malaysia	135.3	176.6	326.6	229.2	192.0	363.4	103.7	140.2	468.8	289.5	205.5	94.1	68.2
Maldives	5.4	11.0	5.6	9.3	16.3	18.6	27.5	28.2	21.7	35.3	38.1	29.1	30.2
Marshall Islands	–	–	–	–	–	–	–	–	–	–	7.7	32.4	49.3
Micronesia, Fed. States of	–	–	–	–	–	–	–	–	–	–	13.9	64.3	104.2
Mongolia	–	–	0.1	3.3	4.6	3.0	3.1	6.4	13.1	69.5	122.9	126.0	184.1
Myanmar	318.9	302.0	269.0	345.7	402.0	352.6	437.4	176.3	164.0	179.4	115.1	101.5	161.6
Nauru	–	–	–	–	–	–	0.2	0.1	0.2	0.4	0.2	0.3	2.4
Nepal	200.6	200.8	196.9	234.0	297.7	353.0	411.0	501.5	429.0	453.4	433.2	364.4	448.2
Pakistan	915.6	735.0	729.4	769.6	916.5	820.2	1355.4	1446.0	1129.7	1370.9	1009.3	1004.8	1605.6
Papua New Guinea	310.7	332.8	320.1	257.2	258.9	317.7	374.4	336.5	413.4	396.8	442.1	309.3	325.7
Philippines	333.4	429.0	381.8	460.4	920.4	732.2	820.4	825.3	1277.4	1053.0	1718.0	1486.9	1057.5
Singapore	20.5	14.6	41.0	23.9	29.4	23.3	21.9	94.8	-2.9	7.8	19.9	23.6	16.9
Solomon Islands	28.4	27.5	19.4	20.8	30.1	57.1	58.3	49.2	45.3	35.2	44.7	55.4	47.0
Sri Lanka	415.5	472.6	456.9	468.3	547.9	477.0	634.8	620.1	729.9	890.5	638.0	659.4	594.7
Taipei,China	-6.4	8.2	5.4	-9.7	-10.1	-8.5	-6.9	2.1	36.3	3.4	5.9	7.4	6.2
Thailand	388.9	431.7	462.0	458.6	465.4	469.9	533.2	722.2	796.9	721.5	772.5	811.1	578.2
Tonga	17.4	17.9	15.7	13.6	15.1	21.3	18.8	24.5	29.7	19.3	23.6	31.3	35.2
Tuvalu	6.2	4.2	5.5	3.3	4.4	25.7	14.0	6.9	5.0	5.4	8.4	4.2	7.4
Uzbekistan	–	–	–	–	–	–	–	–	–	–	1.4	5.7	23.3
Vanuatu	26.0	26.9	24.5	21.8	24.4	51.0	39.3	39.8	49.9	52.6	40.6	35.3	41.8
Viet Nam	135.5	105.9	108.8	114.0	146.5	111.0	147.8	120.0	189.8	237.5	575.1	258.1	897.1
Western Samoa	22.8	26.7	20.0	19.1	22.8	34.6	30.2	31.1	48.0	56.8	53.4	52.5	48.7
TOTAL DMCs	7895.7	7795.0	7825.8	7864.7	9700.4	10596.0	12473.0	13221.6	13744.0	15476.4	16372.3	14692.0	16335.4
TOTAL DEVELOPING COUNTRIES	30622.1	30067.0	30984.9	32260.2	37813.9	41674.2	44959.2	46766.9	58035.9	61865.2	61437.1	56809.1	60968.9

a Official Development Assistance (ODA) is defined as those concessional flows to developing countries and multilateral institutions provided by official agencies, including state and local governments, or by their executive agencies administered with the promotion of economic development and welfare of the developing countries and contains a grant element of at least 25 percent.

Sources: OECD, *Geographical Distribution of Financial Flows to Aid Recipients, 1990-1994.*
OECD, *Geographical Distribution of Financial Flows to Developing Countries, 1989/1992* and past issues.

Table 39: NET PRIVATE FLOWS[a] FROM DAC COUNTRIES TO DMCs
(US$ Million)

DMC	1982	1983	1984	1985	1986	1987	1988	1989	1990	1991	1992	1993	1994
Afghanistan	3.1	-0.1	0.2	0.1	0.3	0.6	2.5	-2.2	-1.8	7.6	-0.2	-3.9	-58.0
Bangladesh	40.4	6.3	37.9	-16.8	-1.5	1.2	12.7	-5.1	49.7	123.0	89.5	38.2	-155.5
Bhutan	–	–	–	–	–	–	18.0	-1.1	3.0	-0.8	-13.2	8.0	-2.3
Cambodia	-0.1	–	-2.1	–	0.4	–	–	-13.0	0.0	3.4	0.3	-0.6	-3.2
China, People's Rep. of	131.2	-60.0	-138.8	908.9	1816.1	3579.1	2312.2	2175.7	1490.8	2216.0	2135.0	3944.4	72131.1
Cook Islands	0.6	–	-0.4	-0.2	-0.1	–	2.2	7.5	4.4	2.1	31.2	-105.0	-218.0
Fiji	8.1	1.5	-5.6	-1.3	-0.6	-7.7	-7.8	23.9	34.4	24.5	70.3	-11.1	1.0
Hong Kong	1155.4	1097.4	1259.2	-1205.7	-1384.5	4154.0	2591.5	1233.6	3477.9	2486.7	1810.9	3440.8	6782.6
India	217.1	153.9	266.2	635.1	1127.7	1059.3	405.4	1764.4	1276.0	3.8	-236.5	-294.7	533.8
Indonesia	1291.3	1596.7	1469.9	470.0	94.2	-275.7	-422.2	1063.3	103.9	1734.8	1372.3	125.5	3557.2
Kazakstan	–	–	–	–	–	–	–	–	–	–	100.7	345.0	300.8
Kiribati	0.1	-0.1	-0.5	-0.1	0.3	-0.1	–	0.0	–	0.0	0.8	-0.5	-27.2
Korea, Rep. of	385.1	376.3	1338.8	1446.1	578.8	-1033.4	-850.0	-123.9	1572.3	3111.8	2742.4	3258.3	4917.3
Kyrgyz Republic	–	–	–	–	–	–	–	–	–	–	–	–	0.3
Lao PDR	-0.2	0.3	1.1	27.1	0.2	0.1	0.3	0.5	–	0.5	0.5	0.1	0.8
Malaysia	568.7	1391.4	964.7	-147.2	-155.4	-4.5	557.9	548.3	1073.9	1019.4	662.0	4778.5	3193.0
Maldives	-3.4	–	–	–	–	–	-1.7	-0.5	12.6	9.8	3.7	8.7	12.0
Marshall Islands	–	–	–	–	–	–	–	–	–	–	–	1.6	3.6
Micronesia, Fed. States of	–	–	–	–	–	–	–	–	–	–	–	0.4	0.3
Mongolia	–	–	–	–	–	–	–	2.0	-1.3	13.6	-18.4	11.6	-7.7
Myanmar	101.0	-2.8	3.6	-35.2	-40.8	-14.1	16.4	-30.3	-78.7	-36.9	-15.0	-12.4	-3.4
Nauru	–	–	–	–	–	–	26.7	-8.9	1.0	16.1	-43.4	19.2	11.3
Nepal	-0.9	-3.4	0.8	6.5	30.2	26.6	28.7	0.7	-6.6	-3.3	63.1	-17.5	0.0
Pakistan	224.4	-34.8	-112.5	-48.8	58.0	-95.9	150.6	665.0	80.7	257.2	228.6	213.4	740.9
Papua New Guinea	150.5	108.2	128.2	74.0	-26.2	-38.5	27.2	349.9	128.3	164.8	138.6	85.5	-56.3
Philippines	323.3	260.0	161.5	-247.9	-40.1	-225.6	-2.6	-165.6	-206.9	65.2	-1076.5	977.2	1574.3
Singapore	891.2	222.3	1227.2	-211.4	79.5	950.4	1681.8	2899.2	3216.7	1443.2	3320.2	3549.0	4896.6
Solomon Islands	0.0	–	1.0	1.4	-0.8	2.5	4.7	2.0	11.9	-1.0	1.0	-0.7	0.2
Sri Lanka	43.8	28.2	138.3	81.2	-57.3	11.2	-7.1	194.4	17.9	-6.0	40.8	149.1	86.8
Taipei,China	318.3	-44.4	71.7	-236.2	-159.6	715.9	-60.9	701.9	425.7	-1411.7	-1354.3	-1208.2	780.5
Thailand	416.1	246.0	602.0	72.8	-7.7	495.2	350.7	1504.9	1689.5	2619.0	2962.3	1432.8	6050.0
Tonga	–	–	0.0	–	–	15.3	-12.9	7.3	0.0	0.0	-0.1	0.1	0.1
Tuvalu	–	–	–	–	–	–	–	–	–	0.8	4.9	–	0.4
Uzabekistan	–	–	–	–	–	–	–	–	–	–	0.0	0.1	9.1
Vanuatu	6.2	7.7	19.7	15.8	-16.9	-17.1	-1.8	38.7	94.3	22.5	-30.8	33.7	-27.9
Viet Nam	2.3	-29.6	-5.5	-21.8	-24.2	-28.8	12.7	7.3	-2.7	29.1	-12.2	29.0	104.0
Western Samoa	0.1	4.6	-6.4	0.4	0.1	0.2	0.7	-0.2	6.3	3.8	–	0.0	0.2
TOTAL DMCs	6273.7	5325.6	7420.2	1566.8	1870.1	9270.2	6835.9	12839.7	14473.2	13919.0	12978.5	20795.6	105128.7
TOTAL DEVELOPING COUNTRIES	43142.5	31041.5	36485.6	2401.2	21802.4	13999.2	21729.0	30470.5	6887.2	24183.3	43000.1	66901.3	91926.7

a   Net private flows refer to the combined direct investment, portfolio investment, and net export credits of Development Assistance Committe countries (DAC) to the country.

Sources: OECD, *Geographical Distribution of Financial Flows to Aid Recipients, 1990-1994.*
OECD, *Geographical Distribution of Financial Flows to Developing Countries, 1989/1992* and past issues.

Table 40: BORROWING OF DMCs IN INTERNATIONAL CAPITAL MARKETS
(US$ Million)

DMC	Bonds [a]			Long-Term Bank Loans [b]			Total		
	1975	1985	1995	1975	1985	1995	1975	1985	1995
Afghanistan	...	...	...	...	...	...	...	...	...
Bangladesh	...	...	...	...	...	...	...	...	...
Bhutan	...	...	...	...	...	...	...	...	...
Cambodia	...	...	...	...	...	...	...	...	...
China, People's Rep. of	–	972.8	1790.0	142.7	2191.5	4226.1	142.7	3164.3	6016.1
Cook Islands	...	...	...	...	...	...	...	...	...
Fiji	...	...	...	...	...	...	...	...	...
Hong Kong	24.5	118.1	5822.1	533.4	107.5	1000.4	557.9	225.6	6822.5
India	–	417.8	800.0	–	173.8	1312.6	–	591.6	2112.6
Indonesia	17.5	–	1008.9	1607.5	81.0	6386.4	1625.0	81.0	7395.3
Kazakstan	...	...	...	...	...	...	...	...	...
Kiribati	...	...	...	...	...	...	...	...	...
Korea, Rep. of	–	1730.9	8640.0	325.7	3104.2	5285.0	325.7	4835.1	13925.0
Kyrgyz Republic	...	...	...	...	...	...	...	...	...
Lao PDR	...	...	...	...	...	...	...	...	...
Malaysia	–	2001.8	2132.3	425.0	58.6	895.9	425.0	2060.4	3028.2
Maldives	...	...	...	...	...	...	...	...	...
Marshall Islands	...	...	...	...	...	...	...	...	...
Micronesia, Fed. States	...	...	...	...	...	...	...	...	...
Mongolia	...	...	...	...	...	...	...	...	...
Myanmar	...	...	...	...	...	...	...	...	...
Nauru	...	...	...	...	...	...	...	...	...
Nepal	...	...	...	...	...	...	...	...	...
Pakistan	...	...	...	7.5	281.9	691.8	7.5	281.9	691.8
Papua New Guinea	25.0	20.3	...	–	45.0	...	25.0	65.3	...
Philippines	–	–	1172.1	253.1	925.0	100.0	253.1	925.0	1272.1
Singapore	12.0	155.0	–	–	173.3	1037.5	12.0	328.3	1037.5
Solomon Islands	...	...	...	...	...	...	...	...	...
Sri Lanka	...	...	...	...	...	...	...	...	...
Taipei,China	–	–	401.5	–	–	1300.1	–	–	1701.6
Thailand	–	861.7	1386.9	5.0	482.2	5196.8	5.0	1343.9	6583.7
Tonga	...	...	...	...	...	...	...	...	...
Tuvalu	...	...	...	...	...	...	...	...	...
Uzbekistan	...	...	...	...	...	...	...	...	...
Vanuatu	...	...	...	...	...	...	...	...	...
Viet Nam	...	...	-	...	...	94.0	...	...	94.0
Western Samoa	...	...	...	...	...	...	...	...	...
TOTAL (Reporting)	79.0	6278.4	23153.8	3299.9	7624.0	27526.6	3378.9	13902.4	50680.4
TOTAL WORLD [c]	11912.7	157031.5	460658.0	12429.1	53996.1	367841.2	24341.8	211027.6	828499.2

a   Refer to international issues and traditional foreign issues of bonds.
b   Refer to international medium and long-term bank loans.
c   Excludes borrowings of international development institutions.

Sources: OECD, *Financial Statistics Monthly*, January 1996 and past issues.

COUNTRY TABLES

PART 2

	Item	1978	1979	1980	1981	1982	1983	1984	1985
001	**POPULATION** [a]	12.72	13.05	13.39	13.75	14.12	14.09	14.37	*Million;* 14.65
002	**LABOR FORCE** [b]	3600	3633	3730	3829	3978	5299	5403	*Thousand;* 5560
003	Productive Sector	2700	2751	2827	2902	3015	4356	4441	4566
004	Agriculture	2100	2080	2138	2195	2280	3546	3615	3721
005	Manufacturing								
006	Mining	600	671	689	707	735	810	826	845
007	Others								
008	Non-productive Sector	700	684	699	717	745	739	784	829
009	Unemployed & unclassified	200	198	204	210	218	204	177	165
010	Unemployment rate, %	6	5	5	5	5	4	3	3
	NATIONAL ACCOUNTS								
	At Constant 1978/79 Prices								*Billion Afghanis;*
011	GDP by Industrial Origin	142.9	139.9	134.7	137.6	140.4	147.3	150.0	150.3
012	Agriculture	82.0	84.3	83.6	86.2	86.6	88.5	88.1	87.6
013	Mining								
014	Manufacturing	32.6	30.7	28.8	28.2	29.5	32.5	33.2	36.1
015	Electricity, gas and water								
016	Construction	8.6	7.6	5.9	6.3	6.1	7.4	8.0	8.0
017	Trade	11.5	10.3	9.8	10.1	11.1	11.2	12.4	12.1
018	Transport and communications	6.1	5.2	4.8	4.8	5.0	5.5	5.9	4.3
019	Finance								
020	Public administration	2.1	1.8	1.8	2.0	2.1	2.2	2.4	2.2
021	Others								
022	Net factor income from abroad	...	...	...	...	...	...	...	...
023	GNP	...	...	...	...	...	...	...	...
024	*Per Capita GDP, Afghanis* Constant *1978/79* prices	11234	10720	10060	10007	9943	10454	10438	10259
	PRODUCTION Agriculture, *crop year*								*Thousand metric tons;*
025	1. Wheat	2813	2663	2550	2470	2391	2306	2194	2081
026	2. Maize	780	760	752	701	663	639	608	577
027	3. Grapes	...	...	...	...	444	434	418	408
028	4. Rice, paddy	428	439	415	390	364	350	334	317
029	5. Potatoes	250	265	266	273	273	268	260	248
030	6. Barley	325	318	321	330	276	266	254	240
031	7. Sugarcane	64	64	70	70	63	62	60	58
	Mining								
032	1. Natural gas *(petajoules)*	90	85	102	98	95	99	106	111
033	2. Coal	218	132	119	125	145	145	148	151
034	3. Salt	81	68	37	31	45	52	53	51
	Manufacturing								
035	1. Wheat flour	97.0	122.6	113.1	122.9	123.9	136.4	153.5	173.9
036	2. Woolen textile, *'000 meters*	550.9	401.0	405.0	244.8	276.9	284.6	320.0	245.3
037	3. Fertilizer	105.7	106.2	106.3	107.8	112.8	125.3	120.5	125.5
038	4. Cement	126.5	99.3	87.2	75.1	87.0	130.5	111.6	127.6
039	5. Dry fruits incl. raisins	38.3	46.6	47.2	57.2	45.1	65.1	52.1	48.3
040	6. Casing, *'000 coils*	2246.0	1700.0	1880.0	1390.0	1413.0	1803.0	1551.9	...
	Production Indexes								*Period*
041	Agriculture, *1979-81 = 100*	103.5	101.4	100.1	98.5	96.6	94.4	90.4	84.3
042	Mining	...	...	...	...	...	...	...	...
043	Manufacturing	...	...	...	...	...	...	...	...

	1986	1987	1988	1989	1990	1991	1992	1993	1994	1995	
As of 1 July											
	14.93	15.22	15.51	15.81	16.12	16.43	16.75	17.08	17.42 *	17.76 *	001
Fiscal year beginning 21 March											
	5668	5778	5890	6004	6120	...	...	...	...	...	002
	4644	4734	4826	4925	5020	...	...	...	...	...	003
	3792	3870	3950	4037	4115	...	...	...	...	...	004
						...	...	...	...	...	005
	852	864	876	888	905	...	...	...	...	...	006
						...	...	...	...	...	007
	833	849	866	877	894	...	...	...	...	...	008
	192	195	199	202	206	...	...	...	...	...	009
	3	3	3	3	3	...	...	...	...	...	010
Fiscal year beginning 21 March											
	154.9	139.0	127.5	124.7	124.6	114.1	99.8	89.0	...	...	011
	89.0	72.1	67.3	65.6	59.6	59.9	62.7	57.3	...	...	012
									...	...	013
	37.9	37.3	32.8	35.6	40.4	29.2	14.3	12.3	...	...	014
									...	...	015
	9.1	10.6	10.2	7.2	7.3	7.0	5.8	5.5	...	...	016
	12.6	12.0	10.6	9.9	10.5	11.1	10.5	10.1	...	...	017
	4.0	4.9	4.6	4.4	4.7	4.8	4.5	2.0	...	...	018
									...	...	019
	2.3	2.1	2.0	2.0	2.1	2.1	2.0	1.8	...	...	020
									...	...	021
	...	...	...	...	...	...	...	...	...	...	022
	...	...	...	...	...	...	...	...	...	...	023
	10375	9133	8221	7887	7730	6945	5958	5211	...	...	024
Fiscal year beginning 21 March											
	1925	2300	1900	1800	1650	1726	1650	1700	1700	1700	025
	567	514	494	458	480	420	300	350	360	360	026
	365	360	365	365	365	365	330	330	...	...	027
	336	324	343	320	333	335	300	300	350	300	028
	238	217	218	203	224	223	224	228	...	...	029
	231	231	235	231	216	217	150	170	180	...	030
	60	60	62	60	55	38	38	38	...	...	031
	111	113	114	115	114	92	...	...	...	...	032
	160	167	138	145	143	135	...	...	...	...	033
	37	15	37	35	35	...	...	...	...	...	034
	187.0	203.0	165.9	164.9	186.0	...	...	...	...	...	035
	268.2	225.2	162.9	171.3	167.2	...	...	...	...	...	036
	126.1	123.4	117.0	105.2	105.5	...	...	...	...	...	037
	103.4	104.0	70.0	100.0	100.0	109.0	...	...	...	...	038
	69.3	51.0	46.7	45.4	32.8	...	...	...	...	...	039
	...	...	...	...	...	...	...	...	...	...	040
averages											
	77.8	79.8	78.0	76.2	76.9	78.8	75.2	76.0	77.7	76.6	041
	...	...	...	...	...	...	...	...	...	...	042
	...	...	...	...	...	...	...	...	...	...	043

Item	1978	1979	1980	1981	1982	1983	1984	1985
ENERGY								*Annual*
Coal, *'000 m.t.*								
044 Production	218	132	145	125	145	145	148	151
045 Consumption	217	132	145	125	145	145	148	151
Natural gas, *terajoules*								
046 Production	90223	85354	102302	98058	94743	99482	105940	111240
047 Exports	84134	77500	98489	91855	86705	87000	87000	87000
048 Consumption	6089	7854	2813	3703	5038	11482	17940	23240
Electricity, *Mn kWh*								
049 Production	857	908	970	1018	976	1025	1045	1060
050 Consumption	857	908	970	1018	976	1025	1045	1060
PRICE INDEXES								*Fiscal year*
Consumer, *21 March 1978/*								
051 *20 March 1979 = 100*	100	112	120	143	136	201	241	256
052 Food	100	111	116	139	172	210	251	254
053 Non-food	100	115	128	150	153	182	221	258
MONEY AND BANKING								*Million Afghanis;*
054 Money supply (M1)	28625	34187	39779	45665	52973	...	68638	76359
055 Currency in circulation	21667 I	26641	32316	38750 I	46674	53782	58716	64390
056 Demand deposits	6958 I	7546	7463	6915 I	6299	...	9922	11969
057 Quasi-money	4826	5474	6566	8768	11439	...	13476	14282
058 Money supply (M2)	33451	39661	46345	54433	64412	...	82114	90641
059 Foreign assets (net)	20107	21915	39353	44960	40328	...	26264	22723
060 Domestic credit	22958	29176	20670	28083	32964	...	66732	83082
061 Claims on govt. sector (net) [c]	16188	19386	11067	18030	27879	...	60728	75126
062 Claims on private sector	6770	9790	9603	10053	4185	...	4788	6728
063 Claims on other financial insts.	...	...	...	...	900	...	1216	1227
064 Other items	-9614	-11430	-13678	-18610 I	-8880	...	-10882	-15164
Deposit Money Banks								
065 Demand deposits	1407	1788	1786	2128 I	1850	...	2946	3705
066 Savings deposits [d]	2326	2533	3161	4059 I	5217	...	7339	7156
GOVERNMENT FINANCE								*Million Afghanis;*
Central Government								
067 Current revenue	16455	15788	26295	29978	33629	34744	37615	...
068 Taxes	9448	7253	9926	9041	10808	13952	17081	...
069 Non-taxes	7007	8535	16369	20937	22821	20792	20534	...
070 Current expenditure	12385	16782	19575	26831	30064	37760	43177	...
071 Current surplus/deficit	4070	-994	6720	3147	3565	-3016	-5562	...
072 Capital receipts	...	...	...	...	...	...	...	...
073 Capital expenditure	6844	5374	4978	5579	5262	5433	8000	...
074 Capital account surplus/deficit	...	...	...	...	...	...	...	...
075 Net lending	...	...	...	...	...	...	...	...
076 Overall surplus/deficit	...	...	...	...	...	...	...	...
EXTERNAL TRADE								*Million Afghanis;*
077 Exports, fob	15122	21279	32514	35644	38990	44006	75819	74878
078 Imports, cif	26613	29837	25323	31680	35247	51098	131504	120102
079 Trade balance	-11491	-8558	7191	3964	3743	-7092	-55685	-45224
Exports, by SITC section								
080 Food and live animals	5980	8972	9749	11467	11524	15604	17512	15938
081 Beverage and tobacco	...	...	...	...	...	...	...	...
082 Crude materials excl. fuels	4648	4619	3305	2577	3398	4085	10863	11412
083 Mineral fuels, etc.	2492	4474	10794	13793	15627	18439	37656	40870
084 Animal, vegetable oil & fats	...	...	...	...	...	...	...	...
085 Chemicals	6	6	...	...	...	...	...	...

	1986	1987	1988	1989	1990	1991	1992	1993	1994	1995	
values											
	160	167	138	127	105	94	8	...	...	...	044
	160	167	138	127	105	94	8	...	...	...	045
	111444	112890	113977	115425	114485	91950	...	...	...	...	046
	87000	88000	34465 *	40000 *	40000 *	35000 *	...	...	...	...	047
	23644	23890	78512	74425	73685	55450	...	...	...	...	048
	1171	1257	1109	1119	1128	1015	703	...	...	...	049
	1171	1257	1109	1119	1128	1015	834	...	...	...	050
beginning 21 March											
	276	326	437	809	1082	1794	1960	...	...	...	051
	285	351	560	934	...	...	...	...	...	...	052
	266	296	350	550	...	...	...	...	...	...	053
As of end of period											
	85113	131419	179414	251062	351025	...	...	...	...	...	054
	71402	112488	152330	222720	311929	454750	...	...	...	...	055
	13711	18931	27084	28342	39096	...	...	...	...	...	056
	16678	21866	26732	31604	46305	...	...	...	...	...	057
	101791	153285	206146	282666	397330	...	...	...	...	...	058
	17918	25260	26126	20574	4163	...	...	...	...	...	059
	103956	155278	210073	301072	447411	...	...	...	...	...	060
	93879	140743	190856	279691	419334	...	...	...	...	...	061
	8773	12699	17580	19973	26547	...	...	...	...	...	062
	1305	1836	1637	1409	1529	...	...	...	...	...	063
	-20083	-27253	-30053	-38980	-54244	...	...	...	...	...	064
	4127	5642	9531	11699	18217	...	...	...	...	...	065
	9218	12223	15604	17132	25269	...	...	...	...	...	066
Fiscal year beginning 21 March											
	...	...	...	...	...	...	...	...	...	...	067
	...	...	...	...	...	...	...	...	...	...	068
	...	...	...	...	...	...	...	...	...	...	069
	...	...	...	...	...	...	...	...	...	...	070
	...	...	...	...	...	...	...	...	...	...	071
	...	...	...	...	...	...	...	...	...	...	072
	...	...	...	...	...	...	...	...	...	...	073
	...	...	...	...	...	...	...	...	...	...	074
	...	...	...	...	...	...	...	...	...	...	075
	...	...	...	...	...	...	...	...	...	...	076
Fiscal year beginning 21 March											
	81794	93414	87988	97774	140698	...	...	...	...	...	077
	129169	132495	151379	282425	433591	...	...	...	...	...	078
	-47375	-39081	-63391	-184651	-292893	...	...	...	...	...	079
	23559	28449	28806	47146	60423	...	...	...	...	...	080
	...	...	...	...	...	...	...	...	...	...	081
	...	...	...	...	...	...	...	...	...	...	082
	8603	13328	22629	25150	28206	...	...	...	...	...	083
	38469	37328	20785	...	...	...	...	...	...	...	084
	...	...	...	...	...	...	...	...	...	...	085

	Item	1978	1979	1980	1981	1982	1983	1984	1985
086	Basic manufactures	1938	3098	4867	3578	4450	3048	5059	3540
087	Machines, transport equipment	...	...	...	...	...	...	...	...
088	Misc. manufactured goods	58	110	10	12	16	15	21	29
089	Unclassified goods	0	0	3789	4217	3975	2815	4708	3089
	Exports, by principal commodity								
090	1. Dried fruits & nuts	4715	7599	7777	8852	7791	15604	17512	15938
091	2. Carpets & rugs	1719	2484	4754	3678	4086	3048	5059	3540
092	3. Wool	287	468	565	1322	1131	1533	3123	2966
093	4. Raw cotton	1680	1592	1820	1142	453	615	2687	2580
094	5. Karakul skins	872	1053	1629	1020	1184	579	1102	754
	Imports, by SITC section								
095	Food and live animals	3861	3167	3438	5360	4715	5484	8925	5862
096	Beverage and tobacco	207	343	234	366	503	773	1821	1564
097	Crude materials excl. fuels	235	48	106	...	...	248	779	95
098	Mineral fuels, etc.	2399	2919	5692	5706	5024	9785	18533	17204
099	Animal, vegetable oil & fats	946	1183	794	1332	1060	1842	4409	4148
100	Chemicals	1598	679	803	1217	948	701	2504	2353
101	Basic manufactures	6267	2818	4310	4184	6251	9471	3417	22875
102	Machines, transport equipment	3480	3970	4535	7844	10307	15601	51095	46471
103	Misc. manufactured goods	1116	1287	1584	1762	1901	2089	2284	2103
104	Unclassified goods [e]	6504	13423	3827	3909	4538	5104	37737	17427
	Direction of Trade							*Million US dollars;*	
105	Exports, Total	269.2	435.0	670.5	638.1	200.9	195.4	176.0	203.1
106	1. China, People's Republic of	–	–	0.2	–	3.0	0.3	–	0.3
107	2. Pakistan	41.1	52.9	52.1	61.2	47.4	21.2	21.8	20.4
108	3. Germany	22.5	32.5	51.5	41.8	36.0	36.5	30.2	22.2
109	4. Russia	0.0	0.0	0.0	0.0	0.0	0.0	0.0	0.0
110	5. Belgium-Luxembourg	–	–	–	–	3.5	3.7	2.3	1.0
111	6. United States	11.3	4.1	4.9	9.7	10.3	8.0	12.6	6.1
112	7. United Kingdom	30.2	32.6	51.8	36.3	39.5	27.5	24.4	59.9
113	8. Greece	0.0	0.0	0.0	0.0	0.0	0.1	0.0	0.0
114	9. Italy	–	–	–	–	2.8	4.5	6.1	4.5
115	10. India	37.5	42.1	54.7	43.2	18.9	12.7	13.0	14.2
116	Imports, Total	450.5	551.2	494.8	541.5	322.0	372.6	392.1	395.9
117	1. Japan	102.8	80.8	98.2	78.7	106.0	132.8	123.1	108.5
118	2. Singapore	–	–	–	–	36.3	34.3	32.1	56.5
119	3. China, People's Rep. of	–	–	8.2	1.1	2.4	8.1	8.6	19.1
120	4. Pakistan	16.9	13.7	14.9	11.7	18.9	17.3	21.3	16.7
121	5. Germany	22.2	22.6	17.0	16.8	26.1	23.4	25.1	23.5
122	6. Thailand	–	–	–	–	3.8	2.9	2.9	7.4
123	7. Hong Kong	–	–	18.6	27.4	21.7	21.0	23.2	21.7
124	8. India	37.1	22.3	20.6	17.0	16.8	15.6	15.5	14.8
125	9. Russia	0.0	0.0	0.0	0.0	0.0	0.0	0.0	0.0
126	10. France	–	–	–	–	20.9	12.4	10.3	13.1
	BALANCE OF PAYMENTS							*Million US dollars;*	
127	Merchandise exports, fob	...	494	705	691	708	729	788	628
128	Merchandise imports, fob	...	-629	-774	-897	-829	-891	-1205	-922
129	Trade balance	...	-136	-69	-207	-121	-162	-417	-293
130	Other goods, services and income	...	-46	-63	-108	-70	-95	-161	-94
131	Credit	...	122	88	76	90	77	54	69
132	Debit	...	-168	-151	-183	-161	-172	-215	-163
133	Unrequited transfer	...	82	185	108	124	118	127	144
134	Private	...	...	14	-5	16	8	...	...
135	Official	...	82	171	113	108	110	127	144

1986	1987	1988	1989	1990	1991	1992	1993	1994	1995	
5859	8930	8918	15747	26803	...	...	...	...	...	086
...	...	...	...	...	...	...	...	...	...	087
28	30	26	50	...	...	...	...	...	...	088
5276	5349	6824	9681	25266	...	...	...	...	...	089
23559	28449	28806	47146	58953	...	...	...	...	...	090
5859	8930	8918	15747	26803	...	...	...	...	...	091
2161	684	9186	2818	8088	...	...	...	...	...	092
1452	1624	1777	352	3977	...	...	...	...	...	093
1554	1506	1382	1561	2273	...	...	...	...	...	094
11228	10987	10726	27737	44622	...	...	...	...	...	095
1769	3157	3074	2861	5748	...	...	...	...	...	096
270	110	153	373	...	...	...	...	...	...	097
12003	3614	4077	1617	1765	...	...	...	...	...	098
6641	3833	6387	24296	14705	...	...	...	...	...	099
2893	3084	3397	4975	9157	...	...	...	...	...	100
23774	32193	37692	62439	20160	...	...	...	...	...	101
44850	59021	69978	12207	208997	...	...	...	...	...	102
2291	2376	2580	2741	6082	...	...	...	...	...	103
23450	14120	13315	143179	122355	...	...	...	...	...	104

Calendar year

1986	1987	1988	1989	1990	1991	1992	1993	1994	1995	
166.3	336.2	175.1	174.7	131.1	189.0	181.0	677.4	75.9	85.0	105
–	–	–	0.3	0.5	1.4	1.9	2.3	10.7	15.3	106
45.2	66.2	11.3	7.1	5.8	4.7	6.0	9.1	10.1	14.0	107
30.8	62.1	28.7	32.2	24.0	23.3	14.0	14.6	9.2	8.8	108
0.0	0.0	0.0	0.0	0.0	0.0	0.0	617.6	6.9	8.9	109
–	9.8	18.5	25.3	18.6	18.7	10.3	6.4	7.1	8.0	110
7.2	11.8	4.5	5.4	4.5	4.2	2.0	2.5	5.7	6.6	111
26.8	49.4	18.3	12.3	15.0	8.5	7.4	5.8	5.6	1.8	112
0.0	0.0	0.0	0.0	0.1	0.1	0.1	0.0	2.2	2.6	113
0.0	4.5	5.3	6.9	4.9	4.9	2.6	2.5	3.8	1.0	114
31.9	52.8	16.9	10.5	12.8	9.9	5.2	2.4	1.8	2.1	115
597.0	681.2	524.5	425.8	479.3	443.1	398.4	417.8	344.1	347.7	116
129.9	156.4	123.7	122.1	133.1	127.7	96.1	100.9	88.8	92.0	117
57.7	78.9	83.3	90.4	79.9	61.6	57.1	37.4	43.7	23.7	118
76.1	76.2	27.4	11.4	25.8	28.1	26.0	35.6	30.1	34.8	119
29.1	27.8	35.4	4.4	2.2	8.2	17.6	16.9	28.4	19.5	120
24.9	32.3	19.9	24.3	22.8	18.8	11.8	12.0	20.3	21.4	121
6.0	10.1	7.3	3.3	4.1	5.9	7.0	8.4	18.8	19.0	122
33.4	26.7	26.0	21.8	18.4	19.2	24.8	29.8	25.8	11.9	123
16.2	23.9	29.6	43.6	64.7	19.8	37.0	31.5	16.0	18.5	124
0.0	0.0	0.0	0.0	0.0	0.0	0.0	54.9	17.1	16.2	125
14.2	15.1	13.0	9.9	17.1	26.3	26.8	17.9	17.0	14.5	126

Calendar year

1986	1987	1988	1989	1990	1991	1992	1993	1994	1995	
497	539	454	252	...	...	...	...	...	...	127
-1139	-905	-732	-624	...	...	...	...	...	...	128
-642	-366	-278	-371	...	...	...	...	...	...	129
-163	-113	-39	-83	...	...	...	...	...	...	130
53	55	93	28	...	...	...	...	...	...	131
-216	-168	-132	-111	...	...	...	...	...	...	132
267	312	343	311	...	...	...	...	...	...	133
...	...	...	-1	...	...	...	...	...	...	134
267	312	343	312	...	...	...	...	...	...	135

Item	1978	1979	1980	1981	1982	1983	1984	1985
136 Current balance	...	-100	54	-206	-67	-139	-451	-243
137 Direct investment	...	...	...	...	...	...	...	...
138 Portfolio investment	...	...	...	...	...	...	...	...
139 Other long-term capital	...	...	...	...	...	...	...	...
140 Other short-term capital	...	115	-105	67	137	184	313	101
141 Net errors and omissions	...	-22	-20	101	-77	-100	203	168
142 Overall balance	...	-6	-72	-38	-8	-55	65	26
143 Allocation of SDRs	...	...	...	...	...	...	...	...
144 Monetary movements	...	6	72	38	8	55	-65	-26
INTERNATIONAL RESERVES								*Million US dollars;*
145 Total	430.6	484.2	641.5	519.3	502.8	459.2	473.8	540.3
146 Gold, national valuation	40.0	43.0	270.3	245.0	245.0	245.1	245.1	245.1
147 Foreign exchange	371.9	411.1	336.5	237.8	223.9	198.7	210.8	276.3
148 Reserve position in the Fund	11.7	12.4	19.2	17.6	16.7	5.0	4.7	5.3
149 SDRs	7.0	17.7	15.5	19.0	17.2	10.4	13.2	13.6
EXCHANGE RATES								*Afghanis*
150 End of period	45.0	42.3	45.9	50.6	50.6	50.6	50.6	50.6
151 Average of period	45.0	43.7	44.1	49.5	50.6	50.6	50.6	50.6
EXTERNAL INDEBTEDNESS								*Million US dollars;*
152 Total outstanding and disbursed	1227	1291	1201	1248	2020	2640	2060	2275
153 Long-term	1221	1285	1195	1242	2010	2631	2054	2270
154 Public and publicly guaranteed	1221	1285	1195	1242	2010	2631	2054	2269
155 Private non-guaranteed	...	...	...	...	...	...	...	...
156 Short-term	6	6	6	6	10	8	6	5
157 Use of IMF credit	...	...	...	...	...	...	...	...
								Transactions
158 Debt service	–	26	28	29	50	38	43	47
159 Principal repayments on LT debt	–	–	–	–	19	7	8	26
160 Interest on long-term debt	–	25	27	28	30	30	34	20
161 Interest on short-term debt	–	1	1	1	1	1	1	0
Average terms of new commitments								
162 Interest (%)	...	...	...	...	...	...	...	...
163 Maturity (years)	...	...	...	...	...	...	...	...
164 Grace Period (years)	...	...	...	...	...	...	...	...
165 Grant element (%)	...	...	...	...	...	...	...	...

Footnotes:

a   Beginning 1983, population excludes nomads.
b   The labor force data were derived from the settled population and include the population between ages 10-59 years. Productive sector refers to agriculture, industries including small-scale and handicrafts, construction and geology, transport and communications. Non-productive sector refers to education and health, government departments and public services.
c   Includes claims on government and non-financial public enterprises.
d   Includes time and foreign currency deposits.
e   Includes loan and grant imports reported in total imports.

1986	1987	1988	1989	1990	1991	1992	1993	1994	1995	
-537	-167	26	-143	...	...	...	...	...	...	136
...	...	...	...	...	...	...	...	...	...	137
...	...	...	...	...	...	...	...	...	...	138
...	...	...	...	...	...	...	...	...	...	139
302	-34	-4	-60	...	...	...	...	...	...	140
216	212	-48	183	...	...	...	...	...	...	141
-19	11	-26	-20	...	...	...	...	...	...	142
...	...	...	...	...	...	...	...	...	...	143
19	-11	26	20	...	...	...	...	...	...	144
As of end of period										
503.6	524.7	506.2	488.8	511.5	480.0	...	...	...	...	145
245.1	245.1	245.1	245.1	245.1	245.1	...	...	...	...	146
238.6	257.9	241.8	226.7	250.4	221.2	...	...	...	...	147
5.9	6.9	6.5	6.4	7.0	7.0	6.8	6.8	7.2	7.3	148
14.0	14.9	12.8	10.6	9.0	6.7	4.4	2.8	1.4	...	149
per US dollar										
50.6	50.6	50.6	50.6	50.6	50.6	50.6	50.6	50.6	50.6	150
50.6	50.6	50.6	50.6	50.6	50.6	50.6	50.6	50.6	50.6	151
As of end of year										
2753	4041	5154	5054	5086	5305	5405	5579	5586	...	152
2735	4026	5134	5019	5046	5269	5381	5569	5577	...	153
2735	4026	5134	5019	5046	5269	5381	5569	5577	...	154
...	...	...	...	...	...	...	...	...	...	155
18	15	21	35	40	35	24	10	9	...	156
...	...	...	...	...	...	...	...	...	...	157
during the year										
46	50	39	43	115	70	...	...	...	...	158
12	9	10	11	12	11	...	...	...	...	159
33	40	28	30	101	57	...	...	...	...	160
1	1	1	3	3	2	...	...	...	...	161
...	...	...	...	...	...	...	...	...	...	162
...	...	...	...	...	...	...	...	...	...	163
...	...	...	...	...	...	...	...	...	...	164
...	...	...	...	...	...	...	...	...	...	165

Item	1978	1979	1980	1981	1982	1983	1984	1985
								Million;
001 **POPULATION** [a]	84.48	86.46	88.47	90.49	92.17	93.88	95.62	97.40
								Million;
002 **LABOR FORCE** [b]	29.40	30.05	30.75	26.90	27.40	28.00	28.50	29.41
003 Employed	18.20	18.60	18.92	19.53	20.45	20.50	25.23	28.91
004 Agriculture	12.80	12.90	13.00	13.30	14.00	13.70	14.00	16.71
005 Manufacturing	1.40	1.50	1.50	1.60	1.67	1.70	2.40	2.69
006 Mining	...	...	...	...	...	...	...	...
007 Others	4.00	4.20	4.42	4.63	4.78	5.10	8.83	9.51
008 Unemployed [c]	11.20	11.45	11.83	7.37	6.95	7.50	3.27	0.50
009 Unemployment rate, % [c]	38.1	38.1	38.5	27.4	25.4	26.8	11.5	1.7
NATIONAL ACCOUNTS								*Billion Taka;*
At Current Market Prices								
010 GDP by Industrial Origin	145.19	174.05	196.05	231.43	259.03	294.19	355.19	406.93
011 Agriculture	68.93	77.95	80.82	94.80	104.56	117.58	148.26	169.97
012 Mining	0.00	0.01	0.00	0.00	0.01	0.00	0.00	0.00
013 Manufacturing	14.65	17.18	22.02	25.19	27.92	32.76	37.74	40.12
014 Electricity, gas and water	0.42	0.48	0.61	0.74	0.96	1.61	1.94	2.35
015 Construction	6.06	9.66	9.31	13.01	15.86	15.03	18.10	22.52
016 Trade	13.84	15.82	19.17	20.15	22.76	26.26	32.82	38.82
017 Transport and communications	14.70	19.87	22.65	28.68	32.04	39.87	41.80	45.66
018 Finance	1.57	2.28	3.10	3.85	4.19	4.63	5.96	6.89
019 Public administration	4.24	5.01	5.50	6.61	6.67	8.73	8.93	13.24
020 Others	20.78	25.80	32.87	38.40	44.06	47.72	59.64	67.36
021 Net factor income from abroad	1.23	1.84	3.47	5.82	5.78	11.63	12.15	8.62
022 GNP	146.42	175.89	199.52	237.25	264.81	305.82	367.34	415.55
023 Expenditure on GDP	145.19	174.05	196.05	231.43	259.03	294.19	355.19	406.93
024 Private consumption	123.51	147.68	165.27	192.81	223.83	255.72	306.49	347.75
025 Government consumption	19.16	23.52	26.38	30.83	33.92	36.64	44.03	49.69
026 Gross fixed capital formation	15.20	17.72	22.30	30.58	40.14	38.61	43.38	46.06
027 Increase in stocks	1.85	1.79	6.70	6.65	-0.30	0.60	-0.30	6.04
028 Exports of goods and services	8.21	10.64	14.02	16.98	18.84	24.08	26.07	31.19
029 Less: Imports of goods and services	22.86	27.51	39.59	46.71	57.66	61.78	64.95	74.36
030 Statistical discrepancy	0.12	0.21	0.97	0.29	0.25	0.32	0.47	0.56
At Constant 1984/85 Prices								
031 GDP by Industrial Origin	323.03	338.52	341.30	352.89	357.21	374.71	395.03	406.93
032 Agriculture	150.57	149.57	149.81	156.07	156.31	162.94	168.81	169.97
033 Mining	0.00	0.00	0.00	0.00	0.00	0.00	0.00	0.00
034 Manufacturing	33.96	37.76	38.30	37.12	37.22	37.92	40.77	40.12
035 Electricity, gas and water	0.85	0.86	1.00	1.11	1.32	2.02	2.17	2.35
036 Construction	11.55	17.53	13.94	16.71	17.30	16.71	20.07	22.52
037 Trade	29.38	30.97	33.48	32.55	32.68	35.11	38.30	38.82
038 Transport and communications	35.04	36.50	36.71	37.52	38.93	41.74	43.51	45.66
039 Finance	3.17	4.12	5.08	5.77	5.78	5.81	6.65	6.89
040 Public administration	8.97	9.60	9.13	9.80	8.76	10.73	9.98	13.24
041 Others	49.54	51.61	53.85	56.24	58.91	61.73	64.77	67.36
042 Net factor income from abroad	2.73	3.58	6.04	8.87	7.97	14.82	13.52	8.62
043 GNP	325.76	342.10	347.34	361.76	365.18	389.53	408.55	415.55
Investment Financing, at current prices								
044 Gross domestic capital formation	17.05	19.51	29.00	37.23	39.84	39.21	43.08	52.10
045 Gross national saving	3.75	4.69	7.87	13.61	7.06	13.46	16.82	18.11
046 Gross domestic saving	2.52	2.85	4.40	7.79	1.28	1.83	4.67	9.49
047 Net factor income from abroad	1.23	1.84	3.47	5.82	5.78	11.63	12.15	8.62
048 Foreign saving	13.30	14.82	21.13	23.62	32.78	25.75	26.26	33.99
049 Net transfer from abroad	6.04	9.67	10.32	10.71	13.35	18.28	17.94	19.04
050 Net borrowing from abroad	7.26	5.15	10.81	12.91	19.43	7.47	8.32	14.95

	1986	1987	1988	1989	1990	1991	1992	1993	1994	1995	
As of 1 July											
	99.21	101.05	102.93	104.84	106.79	108.61	110.62	112.68	114.77	116.90 *	001
Fiscal year ending 30 June											
	30.96	...	...	50.75	...	51.16	...	...	...	...	002
	30.56	...	...	50.15	...	50.16	...	...	...	...	003
	17.46	...	...	32.57	...	33.30	...	...	...	...	004
	3.02	...	...	6.98	...	5.93	...	...	...	...	005
	...	...	...	0.09	...	0.02	...	...	...	...	006
	10.08	...	...	10.51	...	10.91	...	...	...	...	007
	0.40	...	...	0.60	...	1.00	...	...	...	...	008
	1.3	...	...	1.2	...	2.0	...	...	...	...	009
Fiscal year ending 30 June											
	466.23	539.19	597.15	659.60	737.56	834.40	906.50	947.91	1030.36	1170.25	010
	188.38	219.76	231.62	245.39	271.79	300.60	312.44	288.84	305.89	...	011
	0.01	0.00	0.00	0.00	0.09	0.11	0.13	0.16	0.19	...	012
	43.56	47.63	50.44	55.61	64.51	72.80	82.57	92.01	101.46	...	013
	2.71	3.55	4.60	6.72	8.82	11.20	14.01	17.00	20.53	...	014
	26.06	28.84	34.60	39.26	43.11	47.26	53.59	56.72	60.40	...	015
	41.51	45.88	50.40	55.02	61.58	68.28	73.77	78.31	86.16	...	016
	54.61	61.90	65.95	71.77	75.06	97.70	108.67	122.47	129.22	...	017
	8.94	10.12	11.44	13.13	15.11	16.30	17.79	19.61	21.50	...	018
	17.37	20.87	24.74	29.20	32.76	38.19	43.41	49.21	55.04	...	019
	83.08	100.64	123.36	143.50	164.73	181.96	200.12	223.58	249.97	...	020
	11.93	15.55	20.46	22.53	22.27	26.51	33.85	38.80	48.64	55.67	021
	478.16	554.74	617.61	682.13	759.83	860.91	940.35	986.71	1079.00	1225.92	022
	466.23	539.19	597.15	659.60	737.56	834.40	906.50	947.91	1030.36	1170.25	023
	392.80	458.90	509.43	551.73	614.26	685.20	728.63	747.70	806.32	918.76	024
	58.44	61.25	69.97	90.46	103.22	114.73	124.94	134.30	147.28	160.80	025
	46.20	67.50	59.44	65.99	107.28	87.22	112.74	120.79	154.63 ⎫	194.65	026
	11.07	0.08	12.42	14.72	-12.85	8.74	-2.89	10.06	-9.86 ⎭		027
	33.86	37.59	45.02	51.19	61.42	73.63	90.70	104.17	121.89	165.71	028
	77.31	88.11	101.58	118.96	135.75	135.13	147.61	173.49	187.74	263.13	029
	1.17	2.00	2.44	4.48	0.00	0.00	-0.01	4.38	-2.16	-6.54	030
	424.60	442.35	455.13	466.61	497.53	514.44	536.18	560.22	583.83	...	031
	175.55	176.25	174.90	173.04	190.35	193.42	197.66	201.23	201.92	...	032
	0.00	0.00	0.00	0.00	0.07	0.08	0.09	0.11	0.12	...	033
	41.16	44.41	44.68	45.93	49.26	50.42	54.12	59.03	63.67	...	034
	2.64	3.22	3.74	4.82	5.56	6.70	7.88	8.93	10.18	...	035
	22.91	24.47	27.48	28.82	29.75	31.09	32.47	34.03	36.07	...	036
	39.39	40.39	41.68	43.66	44.97	46.71	48.56	50.63	53.28	...	037
	47.12	52.34	54.29	56.61	59.02	60.84	63.35	66.42	70.09	...	038
	8.70	9.18	9.31	9.42	9.52	9.76	10.00	10.30	10.66	...	039
	15.94	17.19	18.55	19.84	20.36	22.33	24.18	26.24	28.48	...	040
	71.19	74.90	80.50	84.47	88.67	93.09	97.87	103.30	109.36	...	041
	10.86	12.76	15.59	15.94	15.02	16.37	20.03	22.93	27.56	...	042
	435.46	455.11	470.72	482.55	512.55	530.81	556.21	583.15	611.39	...	043
	57.27	67.58	71.86	80.71	94.43	95.96	109.85	130.85	144.77	194.65	044
	26.92	34.59	38.21	39.94	42.35	60.98	86.78	104.71	125.40	146.36	045
	14.99	19.04	17.75	17.41	20.08	34.47	52.93	65.91	76.76	90.69	046
	11.93	15.55	20.46	22.53	22.27	26.51	33.85	38.80	48.64	55.67	047
	30.35	32.99	33.65	40.77	52.08	34.98	23.07	26.14	19.37	48.29	048
	17.03	21.56	23.33	21.85	25.27	29.67	31.18	32.03	28.40	35.78	049
	13.32	11.43	10.32	18.92	26.81	5.31	-8.11	-5.89	-9.03	12.51	050

Item	1978	1979	1980	1981	1982	1983	1984	1985
Per Capita GNP, Taka								
051 Current prices	1733	2034	2255	2622	2873	3258	3842	4266
052 Constant *1984/85* prices	3856	3957	3926	3998	3962	4149	4273	4267
PRODUCTION								*Thousand metric tons;*
Agriculture								
053 1. Rice	12968	12849	12740	13881	13631	14216	14501	14622
054 2. Sugarcane	6670	6828	6676	6599	7138	7358	7169	6878
055 3. Jute	957	1150	1082	842	885	946	928	928
056 4. Pulses	238	231	220	216	219	216	176	204
057 5. Oilseeds	264	264	250	251	256	255	469	269
058 6. Condiments and spices, *m.t.*	303	182	303	242	288	295	289	298
059 7. Tobacco	49	43	40	48	50	49	47	50
060 8. Tea	37	38	40	39	41	42	38	38
Mining								
061 1. Limestone	60	58	45	39	45	32	34	40
062 2. China clay	6	7	10	10	6	2	3	4
Manufacturing								
063 1. Fertilizer	260	358	438	422	416	454	820	809
064 2. Cement	339	322	336	345	326	307	278	240
065 3. Sugar	178	133	95	155	220	197	165	88
066 4. Jute pressing	101	110	118	90	230	236	229	209
067 5. Molasses	83	62	47	67	93	80	71	42
068 6. Steel ingot	117	126	138	139	109	47	73	101
069 7. Cotton yarn	41	44	43	46	43	44	46	48
070 8. Paper	32	32	32	33	32	26	28	39
Production Indexes								*Period*
071 Agriculture, *1979-81 = 100*	99	98	101	100	104	107	107	113
072 Mining, *1973/74\ 1981/82 = 100* [d]	111	123	135	144	177	109	127	145
073 Manufacturing, *1973/74\ 1981/82 = 100* [d]	125	132	132	143	143	97	107	122
ENERGY								*Annual*
Crude petroleum, *'000 m.t.*								
074 Production	...	...	6	6	9	20	20	22
075 Imports	1064	1040	1278	1305	1178	1030	1004	992
076 Consumption	1050	1073	1238	1319	1221	1024	1061	1028
Coal, *'000 m.t.*								
077 Imports	319	201	235	246	299	163	62	98
078 Consumption	319	201	235	246	299	163	62	98
Natural gas, *terajoules*								
079 Production	37483	42916	45241	49582	64322	71593	90816	103396
080 Consumption	37483	42916	45241	49582	64322	71593	90816	103396
Electricity, *Mn kWh*								
081 Production	2219	2402	2653	2962	3336	3758	4292	4592
082 Consumption	2219	2402	2653	2962	3336	3758	4292	4592
PRICE INDEXES [d]								*Period*
083 Consumer (Dhaka, Mid. Class), *1973/74 = 100*	176.7	191.2	226.6	255.0	296.5	325.9	357.5	396.6
084 Food	173.7	185.5	225.2	244.7	288.2	312.8	355.5	387.0
085 Non-food	181.8	201.0	228.9	272.3	310.6	348.1	369.3	442.0
086 Wholesale, *1969/70 = 100* [e]	407.8	446.4	501.5	541.2	608.6	642.7	746.9	874.7
087 Implicit GDP deflator, *1984/85 = 100*	44.9	51.4	57.4	65.6	72.5	78.5	89.9	100.0
MONEY AND BANKING								*Million Taka;*
088 Money supply (M1)	12241	15248	17318	19863	20121	26343	35499	42318
089 Currency in circulation	5043	6133	6934	9148	8775	11386	15563	17229
090 Demand deposits	7198	9115	10384	10715	11346	14957	19936	25089

1986	1987	1988	1989	1990	1991	1992	1993	1994	1995	
4820	5490	6000	6506	7115	7927	8501	8757	9401	10487	051
4389	4504	4573	4603	4800	4887	5028	5175	5327	...	052

Fiscal year ending 30 June

1986	1987	1988	1989	1990	1991	1992	1993	1994	1995	
15038	15407	15413	15544	17856	17852	18252	18340	18042	16833	053
6640	6896	7207	6707	7423	7682	7446	7507	7111	7446	054
1572	1226	853	805	842	962	957	893	808	964	055
194	403	545	501	512	523	519	517	530	534	056
267	438	448	428	438	443	462	476	470	480	057
294	289	305	304	325	319	322	321	325	318	058
47	40	42	39	38	34	34	36	38	38	059
44	38	41	44	41	45	46	49	51	47	060
22	46	33	29	38	42	43	23	24	26	061
3	12	10	7	7	7	2	2	3	5	062
946	878	1409	1599	1621	1533	1736	2051	2366	2145	063
287	310	310	344	337	275	272	207	324	316	064
82	182	178	110	184	246	195	187	221	270	065
295	324	277	275	235	273	232	201	139	213	066
38	85	82	50	76	113	...	...	...	...	067
96	82	70	86	75	58	37	7	6	25	068
43	45	47	49	51	56	61	61	58	49	069
42	43	92	86	93	90	88	90	90	83	070

averages

1986	1987	1988	1989	1990	1991	1992	1993	1994	1995	
114	113	113	124	125	129	130	130	123	133	071
162	192	225	240	256	264	292	321	314	368	072
127	145	146	148	167	171	189	214	235	262	073

values

1986	1987	1988	1989	1990	1991	1992	1993	1994	1995	
23	25	8	15	19	16	12	8	6	...	074
983	1000	1212	1147	948	1182	1018	1169	...	...	075
1018	1042	1420	1658	1632	1545	1675	...	...	...	076
148	233	202	54	563	180	169	...	...	...	077
148	233	202	54	563	180	...	...	...	...	078
116644	137255	158754	170334	183496	188861	205999	230547	244636	270419	079
110661	129574	153891	159912	173885	179482	195307	212753	230200	255559	080
4573	5302	6143	6720	7135	7817	8378	8563	9221	10166	081
3307	3485	3792	4695	5294	4809	6326	6785	7457	8376	082

averages

1986	1987	1988	1989	1990	1991	1992	1993	1994	1995	
436.0	481.2	536.0	578.9	632.7	689.3	724.4	734.0	747.5	786.3	083
429.5	483.4	535.4	565.9	606.2	647.9	683.8	676.5	679.2	731.6	084
447.1	477.0	537.0	600.8	641.1	759.0	792.8	830.9	862.3	878.2	085
914.4	988.5	1047.8	1129.4	1225.4	1276.5	1322.9	1345.8	1412.9	1478.5	086
109.8	121.9	131.2	141.4	148.2	162.2	169.1	169.2	176.5	...	087

Fiscal year ending 30 June

1986	1987	1988	1989	1990	1991	1992	1993	1994	1995	
49279	43516	50477	54607	63687	72037	82572	90626	111671	131794	088
19531	20756	24150	26156	31883	36118	40726	44801	54160	65651	089
29748	22760	26327	28451	31804	35919	41846	45825	57511	66143	090

	Item	1978	1979	1980	1981	1982	1983	1984	1985
091	Quasi-money	9169	12352	15131	21497	25366	32639	48359	63024
092	Money supply (M2)	21410	27600	32449	41360	45487	58982	83858	105342
093	Foreign assets (net)	556	678	-2660	7902	-8804	1278	1876	-2398
094	Domestic credit	30563	37603	48808	65821	67223	84068	89154	121084
095	Claims on govt. sector (net)	10106	10712	14471	20017	16627	20903	22301	19883
096	Claims on private sector	9408	12955	16761	22423	26566	37799	59386	68906
097	Claims on other financial insts.	11049	13936	17576	23381	24030	25366	7467	32295
098	Other items	-9709	-10681	-13699	-32363	-12932	-26364	-7172	-13344
	Deposit Money Banks								
099	Demand deposits	7195	9114	10382	10713	11345	14950	19934	25087
100	Time deposits	9169	12352	15131	21497	25365	32639	48359	63024
101	Domestic credits outstanding [f]	18344	23381	30167	37483	48441	57427	79616	103029
	Interest Rates								**Per cent;**
	On deposits								
102	Savings [g]	7.00	7.00	7.04	10.00	10.00	10.00	10.00	10.00
103	Time: 6 months	7.50	7.50	10.25	13.00	13.00	13.00	13.00	13.00
104	12 months	8.25	8.25	11.12	14.00	14.00	14.00	14.00	14.00
	On loans and discounts								
105	Export credit	10.50	10.50	10.44	12.00	12.00	12.00	12.00	12.00
	GOVERNMENT FINANCE								**Million Taka;**
	Central Government								
106	Current revenue	10981	15813	15333	17551	25725	28666	24288	35825
107	Taxes	9034	12682	13251	13935	20405	23487	22025	33438
108	Non-taxes	1947	3131	2082	3616	5320	5179	2263	2387
109	Current expenditure	8477	10876	11408	13254	16531	18358	20457	25729
110	Current surplus/deficit	2504	4937	3925	4297	9194	10308	3831	10096
111	Capital receipts	...	...	...	...	...	...	...	...
112	Capital expenditure	12029	15546	21726	24683	25529	24272	29739	34837
113	Capital account surplus/deficit	-12029	-15546	-21726	-24683	-25529	-24272	-29739	-34837
114	Net lending	...	...	...	...	...	...	...	...
115	Overall surplus/deficit	-9525	-10609	-17801	-20386	-16335	-13964	-25908	-24741
	Financing								
116	Domestic borrowing	...	...	2920	5075	...	...	...	...
117	Foreign borrowing	...	11882	13144	10552	...	...	...	...
118	Foreign grants	...	...	...	...	...	...	...	...
119	Use of cash balances [h]	...	-1273	1737	4759	16335	13964	25908	24741
	Expenditure by Function, Central Govt.								
120	Total	20822	26551	33536	38642	42828	50742	50196	60566
121	General public services	3956	5656	5953	6321	8524	10493	8406	10781
122	Defence	1624	1485	1782	2118	2742	4241	4643	5068
123	Education	1767	2026	2219	2731	3177	4073	3054	5661
124	Health	1168	1293	1430	1508	2083	2374	2855	3746
125	Social security & welfare	129	169	289	373	372	447	501	572
126	Housing & community amenities	1447	1661	2021	2608	1561	1342	3343	2251
127	Economic services	10071	14026	19591	22758	24122	27373	26888	32374
128	Agriculture	1880	4011	5065	4823	6474	8098	8130	9338
129	Industry	2417	2431	2649	3102	2266	3436	2879	2211
130	Electricity, gas & water	2945	3902	6038	8186	8834	9293	10754	14419
131	Transport and communications	2403	2933	4969	5727	5631	5451	4670	5727
132	Other economic services	426	749	870	920	917	1095	455	679
133	Others	660	235	251	225	247	399	506	113
	EXTERNAL TRADE								**Million Taka;**
134	Exports, fob	7178	9632	10997	11484	12387	18016	20136	26225
135	Imports, cif	18216	21727	30525	37288	38729	45265	50874	68263
136	Trade balance	-11038	-12095	-19528	-25804	-26342	-27249	-30738	-42038

	1986	1987	1988	1989	1990	1991	1992	1993	1994	1995	
	74102	95132	113603	136175	159290	178007	202687	224730	252359	290329	091
	123381	138648	164080	190781	222976	250044	285259	315356	364030	422123	092
	1410	3885	5998	7773	4275	17517	40249	60811	91528	104637	093
	141822	157724	169735	192638	230308	253684	272083	292738	304003	362264	094
	18532	26470	17175	12704	20147	21878	36256	39221	38084	45091	095
	83562	89636	108963	133597	160045	178229	179392	193174	209725	259210	096
	39728	41618	43597	46337	50116	53577	56435	60343	56194	57963	097
	-19851	-22961	-11653	-9630	-11607	-21157	-27073	-38193	-31501	-44778	098
	29748	22760	26327	28451	31804	35919	41846	45825	57511	66143	099
	74102	95132	113603	136174	159290	178007	202687	224730	252359	290329	100
	123283	135702	154660	183118	212992	238718	266485	288389	300612	366164	101

Period averages

	1986	1987	1988	1989	1990	1991	1992	1993	1994	1995	
	10.00	10.00	10.00	10.00	9.50	8.10	6.94	5.42	5.30	...	102
	13.00	12.50	12.50	12.50	12.13	11.88	9.99	7.90	6.36	...	103
	14.00	13.25	13.25	13.25	12.13	11.88	10.29	8.29	8.60	...	104
	10.38	9.00	9.00	9.00	10.50	10.50	10.00	9.50	9.50	...	105

Fiscal year ending 30 June

	1986	1987	1988	1989	1990	1991	1992	1993	1994	1995	
	38354	46185	51519	61015	65194	81769	97236	113189	122800	136370	106
	32110	37253	42062	49560	55725	67978	78234	90989	97601	104751	107
	6244	8932	9457	11455	9469	13791	19002	22200	25199	31619	108
	36870	39605	46998	61304	66358	72651	78386	86428	91556	96001	109
	1484	6580	4521	-289	-1164	9118	18850	26761	31244	40369	110
	...	...	50856	47412	55060	64779	65390	66400	67610	80570	111
	33803	38499	40471	46454	54306	52898	60240	65404	89830	96102	112
	-33803	-38499	10385	958	754	11881	5150	996	-22220	-15532	113
	...	...	...	...	...	...	...	...	...	...	114
	-32319	-31919	14906	669	-410	20999	24000	27757	9024	24837	115
	...	...	...	...	...	...	...	...	...	...	116
	...	...	...	...	...	...	...	...	...	...	117
	...	...	...	...	...	...	...	...	...	...	118
	32319	31919	-14906	-669	410	-20999	-24000	-27757	-9024	-24837	119
	70673	78421	87638	108339	120665	125549	138627	151832	181386	192103	120
	19174	17639	21065	31424	32666	37269	38301	37961	38926	37649	121
	5815	7259	8162	10045	11080	11205	12937	15855	16355	18260	122
	7291	9282	10923	11290	13506	12528	14972	17044	23955	27894	123
	3685	3895	4697	5512	6239	7147	8301	11356	14170	15617	124
	644	635	734	885	839	906	965	1006	1781	2522	125
	2426	2927	4203	3550	5414	4656	5988	4130	5620	5778	126
	31558	36784	37854	45633	50921	51838	57163	64480	80011	80403	127
	2944	3587	3919	5150	6494	7024	7195	10312	7330	7371	128
	5563	8289	5656	6552	7248	11691	8225	8719	7130	9122	129
	17112	17972	20083	21965	24659	20542	24193	35666	37248	36187	130
	4953	6758	8118	11911	12484	12451	17456	9609	28125	27425	131
	986	178	78	55	36	130	94	174	178	298	132
	80	–	–	–	–	–	–	–	568	3980	133

Fiscal year ending 30 June

	1986	1987	1988	1989	1990	1991	1992	1993	1994	1995	
	27396	30643	37045	41161	48929	59559	72627	92575	100976	139285	134
	62930	80261	93286	108477	123743	123782	132114	159335	167660	234547	135
	-35533	-49618	-56241	-67316	-74814	-64223	-59487	-66760	-66684	-95262	136

	Item	1978	1979	1980	1981	1982	1983	1984	1985
	Exports, by SITC section [i]								
137	Food & live animals	1010	1222	1328	1435	2210	3161	4134	4265
138	Beverage & tobacco	0	0	0	0	37	49	42	68
139	Crude materials excl.fuels	1601	2239	2190	1952	2089	2802	2836	4026
140	Mineral fuels, etc.	36	79	0	0	110	826	346	537
141	Animal, vegetable oil & fats	2	11	1	1	2	2	2	4
142	Chemicals	8	34	93	150	20	274	140	47
143	Basic manufactures	4475	5788	7156	7591	7538	9696	11272	13111
144	Machines, transport equipment	10	68	69	176	124	718	231	292
145	Misc. manufactured goods	15	14	52	82	207	388	1036	3758
146	Unclassified goods	21	177	108	97	52	101	98	117
	Exports, by principal commodity								
147	1. Jute manufactures	3609	4386	5771	6565	6331	8009	8712	10952
148	2. Fish	202	451	657	602	1004	1673	2031	2333
149	3. Leather	692	1266	1057	871	1073	1581	2198	1921
150	4. Raw jute and mesta	1539	2186	2137	1875	2000	2580	2730	3900
151	5. Tea	651	612	564	672	812	1100	1700	1570
	Imports, by SITC section [i]								
152	Food & live animals	4728	2537	6408	3421	6575	7653	8400	15017
153	Beverage & tobacco	53	38	51	40	75	69	117	93
154	Crude materials excl.fuels	1900	2947	2011	3076	2461	2934	4672	4094
155	Mineral fuels, etc.	2665	2282	4906	8262	7136	10254	9966	10589
156	Animal, vegetable oil & fats	949	1127	1560	1994	1971	2995	3535	4957
157	Chemicals	1241	3013	3530	3749	4564	4253	5574	7158
158	Basic manufactures	3413	4220	5067	7019	8016	7716	8968	13099
159	Machines, transport equipment	2911	4997	6373	9063	7147	8609	8511	11835
160	Misc. manufactured goods	313	492	572	599	682	691	1018	1327
161	Unclassified goods	43	74	48	64	103	92	113	93
	Direction of Trade								*Million US dollars;*
162	Exports, Total	513.2	656.0	790.1	791.3	768.0	724.4	931.3	998.8
163	1. United States	79.0	86.9	73.2	80.1	78.3	104.2	129.4	180.5
164	2. Germany	7.8	15.3	14.7	10.4	14.5	11.7	16.1	19.3
165	3. United Kingdom	27.7	54.2	39.8	34.1	38.0	42.5	67.6	50.6
166	4. France	5.0	6.2	8.2	4.7	7.3	7.0	11.3	4.7
167	5. Italy	23.7	47.2	29.7	23.8	24.2	32.3	63.9	35.1
168	6. Belgium-Luxembourg	12.6	18.6	25.3	13.9	20.4	33.0	54.3	44.5
169	7. Netherlands	8.3	11.4	12.2	15.2	12.8	14.3	13.7	14.1
170	8. Hong Kong	1.6	2.4	16.6	12.8	4.2	4.4	5.6	10.0
171	9. Japan	24.0	40.0	30.8	27.1	45.6	53.5	61.9	71.8
172	10. Canada	6.9	7.1	7.5	5.7	3.9	7.6	10.9	12.2
173	Imports, Total	1502.1	1927.7	2610.6	2651.4	2418.5	2291.1	2692.8	2526.2
174	1. India	43.0	40.0	55.6	64.0	43.3	37.9	60.1	64.9
175	2. Japan	196.6	262.3	295.1	288.5	305.7	167.4	260.7	310.3
176	3. Hong Kong	4.1	5.2	9.8	16.6	7.5	16.9	42.0	51.0
177	4. Singapore	41.8	63.2	91.4	62.7	50.5	162.2	259.9	210.2
178	5. China, People's Rep. of	44.5	67.8	99.7	113.4	108.2	58.4	108.9	82.8
179	6. Korea, Rep. of	17.3	21.1	30.2	33.5	15.1	28.4	40.9	63.2
180	7. United States	192.5	211.9	359.5	155.9	209.0	271.5	256.2	256.8
181	8. Germany	59.8	82.6	103.3	118.2	86.2	98.7	81.8	88.9
182	9. Pakistan	21.5	22.0	34.9	46.5	25.5	17.2	18.6	17.7
183	10. United Kingdom	86.1	159.7	147.2	114.1	80.2	105.4	113.1	87.4
	Trade Indexes [d]								*1976/77 = 100;*
	Unit value index								
184	Exports	112.1	128.4	166.6	158.1	150.7	173.3	208.2	300.6
185	Imports	111.5	114.5	123.7	137.7	153.7	193.1	194.0	218.5
186	Terms of Trade	100.5	112.1	134.7	114.8	98.0	89.7	107.3	137.6

1986	1987	1988	1989	1990	1991	1992	1993	1994	1995	
5503	5700	6695 I	7021	7071	7981	8881	11218	...	...	137
27	23	22 I	61	73	60	237	114	...	...	138
3661	2644	2344 I	4925	6194	5380	4127	3435	...	...	139
475	202	412 I	518	553	465	311	796	...	...	140
2	2	2 I	1	2	0	0	0	...	...	141
35	25	608 I	1759	581	1648	581	2176	...	...	142
11861	11644	12745 I	12562	13892	15415	17632	19974	...	...	143
258	908	562 I	42	65	31	199	96	...	...	144
5459	9412	13525 I	14270	20498	28477	40540	54561	...	...	145
114	84	130 I	3	0	102	119	206	...	...	146
9068	8906	9320	9261	9484	8946	10155	10477	...	...	147
3580	4453	5075	5241	5571	5708	6331	8274	...	...	148
2362	3653	4579	4514	3582	4422	4982	5392	...	...	149
3438	2754	2486	2813	2425	3231	3474	2795	...	...	150
996	903	1293	1208	1393	1544	1296	1555	...	...	151
7718	13329	17827 I	17726	18918	9960	9744	13310	...	...	152
60	186	314 I	370	481	303	628	1035	...	...	153
3616	4482	5515 I	4589	6843	22946	39113	48878	...	...	154
12161	11872	13469 I	13993	15796	19773	18388	15261	...	...	155
5139	5007	6580 I	6785	6894	8308	6989	8619	...	...	156
9963	7187	8053 I	9858	12342	10751	12820	10605	...	...	157
13261	19115	22792 I	33756	37366	24579	20865	28507	...	...	158
11449	16605	15273 I	17700	21433	21349	17892	21676	...	...	159
16399	2169	3162 I	2845	2919	5115	5302	10191	...	...	160
175	308	302 I	854	751	698	374	1254	...	...	161
Calendar year										
888.9	1076.8	1291.1	1304.9	1671.8	1687.4	2037.5	2277.3	2703.8	3259.2	162
210.6	322.5	335.6	370.5	510.1	449.5	734.0	764.7	919.5	1058.6	163
24.9	40.8	64.9	56.2	108.0	175.4	166.3	226.1	236.6	289.5	164
48.6	56.4	75.8	76.5	119.3	142.5	151.2	195.8	250.7	328.6	165
5.2	12.8	24.0	28.9	62.1	90.5	106.7	128.4	162.3	195.3	166
45.2	82.1	126.5	88.8	106.6	112.4	137.3	119.5	159.4	201.4	167
37.0	31.2	40.7	34.0	52.6	72.1	68.7	86.8	101.0	121.9	168
16.7	18.6	25.3	22.3	38.0	57.9	67.0	74.8	102.5	120.9	169
9.0	16.3	12.3	14.5	16.5	24.2	41.5	60.7	83.8	107.1	170
71.4	62.1	74.1	55.6	64.7	53.4	51.6	58.3	69.0	106.5	171
13.6	17.7	17.4	14.0	27.3	23.2	29.2	39.2	49.7	62.3	172
2550.4	2730.3	3034.1	3617.6	3656.1	3421.0	3730.8	4014.5	5026.8	6758.6	173
57.2	74.4	90.0	120.7	170.3	189.5	283.9	380.2	573.1	664.8	174
318.8	381.3	477.2	457.2	482.2	306.6	293.6	502.5	368.3	382.3	175
47.1	87.3	120.9	132.6	167.7	199.9	289.7	320.0	476.9	550.4	176
184.0	163.1	158.4	215.8	407.2	292.3	222.2	183.1	473.6	549.4	177
74.0	82.1	97.1	134.4	124.1	146.9	215.0	204.1	407.5	696.2	178
58.6	75.5	94.4	105.2	156.1	171.3	213.8	279.4	...	569.8	179
211.0	189.5	181.7	285.2	186.0	176.4	257.9	173.6	256.7	344.0	180
111.5	83.3	32.8	104.8	125.4	125.9	117.6	117.4	175.1	222.7	181
26.3	37.3	62.5	26.0	70.1	57.4	88.0	90.2	130.6	175.1	182
90.8	86.7	120.7	92.4	118.2	100.3	132.0	124.1	92.0	151.9	183
Period averages										
256.7	232.0	259.0	287.0	269.0	302.0	296.0	285.0	...	...	184
246.3	259.0	278.0	238.0	270.0	337.0	334.0	344.0	...	...	185
104.2	89.6	93.2	120.6	99.6	89.6	88.6	82.8	...	...	186

Item	1978	1979	1980	1981	1982	1983	1984	1985
BALANCE OF PAYMENTS								*Million US dollars;*
187 Merchandise exports, fob	506	575	751	817	665	759	934	971
188 Merchandise imports, fob	-1289	-1488	-2126	-2403	-2211	-2111	-2146	-2358
189 Trade balance	-783	-913	-1375	-1586	-1546	-1352	-1212	-1387
190 Other goods, services and income	-178	-197	-280	-256	-319	-319	-275	57
191 Credit	...	152	256	274	227	223	276	175
192 Debit	...	-349	-536	-530	-546	-542	-551	-118
193 Unrequited transfers	...	777	949	1070	975	1340	1277	1102
194 Private	...	140	212	397	353	581	546	398
195 Official	...	637	737	673	622	759	731	704
196 Current balance	-961	-333	-706	-772	-890	-331	-210	-228
197 Direct investment	...	...	...	...	...	...	...	...
198 Portfolio investment	...	...	...	...	...	...	...	2
199 Other long-term capital	...	462	541	561	490	588	481	488
200 Other short-term capital	...	-22	-16	10	190	-136	68	-23
201 Net errors and omissions	22	33	16	47	75	65	-36	-4
202 Overall balance	-939	140	-165	-154	-135	186	303	235
203 Allocation of SDRs	...	...	...	...	...	...	...	...
204 Monetary movements [j]	939	-140	165	154	135	-186	-303	-235
INTERNATIONAL RESERVES								*Million US dollars;*
205 Total	316.4	402.0	321.2	155.3	207.1	541.6	405.8	349.4
206 Gold, national valuation	1.2	15.7	21.5	16.9	24.5	17.5	15.8	12.9
207 Foreign exchange	315.1	374.2	299.2	138.3	173.5	487.1	367.7	298.8
208 Reserve position in the Fund	0.0	0.0	0.0	0.0	8.3	23.5	22.0	24.6
209 SDRs	0.1	12.1	0.5	0.1	0.8	13.5	0.3	13.1
EXCHANGE RATES								*Taka per*
210 End of period	14.934	15.643	16.251	19.847	24.074	25.000	26.000	31.000
211 Average of period	15.016	15.552	15.454	17.987	22.118	24.615	25.354	27.995
EXTERNAL INDEBTEDNESS								*Million US dollars;*
212 Total outstanding and disbursed	3108.2	3308.1	4327.0	4815.2	5412.0	5950.3	6229.3	7278.1
213 Long-term	2736.6	2852.4	3690.8	4122.9	4655.6	5215.0	5634.0	6623.1
214 Public and publicly guaranteed	2736.6	2852.4	3690.8	4122.9	4655.6	5215.0	5634.0	6623.1
215 Private non-guaranteed	–	–	–	–	–	–	–	–
216 Short-term	72.4	111.1	212.0	228.0	209.0	170.0	133.0	135.1
217 Use of IMF credit	299.2	344.6	424.2	464.3	547.4	565.3	462.3	519.9
Debt Service								*Transactions*
218 Principal repayments on LT debt	64.3	86.4	64.1	82.1	98.0	69.4	91.0	117.4
219 Interest on long-term debt	38.6	42.4	49.8	59.4	65.8	73.1	80.0	101.1
220 Interest on short-term debt	4.2	11.0	16.1	21.0	21.8	18.9	15.1	13.4
Average terms of new commitments								
221 Interest (%)	2.0	1.4	1.7	2.1	1.8	1.6	1.5	1.4
222 Maturity (years)	37.1	40.0	36.0	30.6	40.0	37.1	39.7	37.7
223 Grace period (years)	10.0	9.4	8.9	7.8	10.2	8.8	9.6	9.3
224 Grant element (%)	67.6	73.6	68.5	61.8	70.7	69.4	72.6	70.8

Footnotes:

a ADB staff estimates based on the 1974, 1981 and 1991 census figures adjusted for undercount and mid-year reporting.
b Labor force data for 1989 are on a calendar year basis.
c Include underemployed for 1978-84.
d Period averages of fiscal year.
e Refers to agricultural and industrial products.
f Total advances and investment of Deposit Money Banks.

	1986	1987	1988	1989	1990	1991	1992	1993	1994	1995	
Fiscal year ending 30 June											
	909	1000	1186	1281	1486	1667	1904	2138	2525	3465	187
	-2126	-2346	-2687	-3033	-3379	-3122	-3118	-3573	-3765	-5247	188
	-1217	-1346	-1501	-1752	-1893	-1455	-1214	-1435	-1240	-1782	189
	49	23	-144	-150	-110	-28	28	-410	-436	-683	190
	180	188	308	389	444	457	563	617	670	819	191
	-131	-165	-452	-539	-554	-485	-535	-1027	-1106	-1502	192
	1073	1293	1613	1516	1567	1676	1793	1883	1956	2315	193
	525	629	788	836	799	844	976	1065	1246	1425	194
	548	664	825	680	768	832	817	818	710	890	195
	-95	-30	-32	-386	-436	193	607	38	280	-150	196
	2	2	3	...	2	1	4	7	16	6	197
	-7	...	...	1	1	1	6	10	53	61	198
	512	635	606	867	820	671	512	564	533	513	199
	56	-71	-136	-94	-173	-132	-90	-38	-52	-212	200
	6	-45	-12	-41	-76	-96	-80	-27	-149	106	201
	474	491	429	347	138	638	959	554	681	324	202
	-13	-60	51	6	1	-48	-74	-31	19	-50	203
	-461	-431	-480	-353	-139	-590	-885	-523	-700	-274	204
As of end of period											
	425.9	866.0	1070.0	522.8	649.5	1299.7	1847.3	2436.7	3165.9	2366.6	205
	16.8	22.8	24.0	21.4	20.8	21.5	22.7	25.9	27.2	26.9	206
	371.4	758.1	961.9	469.0	602.9	1206.9	1783.2	2387.9	3102.6	2180.1	207
	27.4	31.8	30.1	29.4	0.0	0.0	0.0	0.1	0.1	0.1	208
	10.3	53.3	54.0	3.0	25.8	71.3	41.4	22.8	36.0	159.5	209
US dollar											
	30.800	31.200	32.270	32.270	35.790	38.580	39.000	39.850	40.250	40.750	210
	30.407	30.950	31.733	32.270	34.569	36.596	38.951	39.567	40.212	40.278	211
As of end of year											
	8723.1	10584.1	11108.7	11504.5	13070.0	13812.2	14166.9	14938.5	16568.8	...	212
	8059.2	9669.3	10219.4	10718.3	12288.6	12867.1	13203.2	14106.4	15713.4	...	213
	8059.2	9669.3	10219.4	10718.3	12288.6	12867.1	13203.2	14106.4	15713.4	...	214
	–	–	–	–	–	–	–	–	–	...	215
	125.1	74.0	49.8	67.6	155.9	218.1	231.3	149.8	186.3	...	216
	538.8	840.8	839.5	718.6	625.5	727.0	732.4	682.3	669.1	...	217
during the year											
	162.7	180.2	212.6	194.5	375.5	289.6	309.8	296.7	374.8	...	218
	121.0	151.4	154.7	153.4	172.0	168.4	159.4	172.7	207.1	...	219
	13.1	11.9	5.1	8.6	9.3	13.1	15.4	10.4	11.4	...	220
	1.3	1.3	1.6	1.2	2.3	1.0	1.2	1.1	1.3	...	221
	40.6	41.2	33.3	37.1	32.6	38.4	35.8	35.3	33.4	...	222
	10.0	10.5	9.7	10.0	9.1	9.7	9.7	9.7	9.0	...	223
	75.1	75.7	70.3	75.6	64.8	77.2	74.7	75.1	70.8	...	224

g   Refers to savings accounts without chequeing facilities.
h   Refers to financing of the overall balance.
i   Bangladesh Bureau of Statistics has stopped compilation of trade data by SITC and replaced it with the harmonized system. Data presented for 1989-93 are estimates based on ESCAP trade data by SITC in US dollars.
j   Refers to total change in reserves and related items.

	Item	1978	1979	1980	1981	1982	1983	1984	1985
001	**POPULATION** [a]	1.20	1.22	1.25	1.27	1.29	1.32	1.35	*Million;* 1.38
	LABOR FORCE								*Thousand;*
002	Employed	600	620	...	650	...	...	721	...
003	Agriculture	560	580	...	610	...	...	629	...
004	Manufacturing	...	...	...	10	...	...	...	...
005	Mining	...	...	...	...	...	...	...	...
006	Others	40	40	...	30	...	...	92	...
007	Unemployed	...	...	...	...	...	...	...	...
008	Unemployment Rate, %	...	...	...	...	...	...	...	...
	NATIONAL ACCOUNTS *At Current Factor Cost*								*Million Ngultrum;*
009	GDP by Industrial Origin	...	...	1095.0	1280.1	1498.1	1753.5	2059.9	2349.6
010	Agriculture	...	...	621.4	676.7	804.3	934.2	1117.6	1236.2
011	Mining	...	...	6.8	8.9	12.5	10.2	23.3	20.2
012	Manufacturing	...	...	35.8	63.5	70.1	96.5	109.5	128.3
013	Electricity, gas and water	...	...	2.5	2.7	3.7	6.7	5.9	6.8
014	Construction	...	...	88.5	142.8	188.2	238.6	276.5	290.5
015	Trade	...	...	121.5	155.6	162.1	170.0	182.4	203.0
016	Transport and communications	...	...	47.9	58.1	66.2	76.8	80.6	104.1
017	Finance	...	...	70.2	80.3	84.2	100.5	129.6	149.3
018	Public administration	...	...	120.4	121.5	139.8	155.0	178.5	262.2
019	Others	...	...	...	...	...	...	...	...
020	Less: Imputed bank service charges	...	...	20.0	30.0	33.0	35.0	44.0	51.0
021	Indirect taxes less subsidies	...	...	17.9	21.2	23.5	35.3	45.6	41.8
022	GDP at current market prices	...	...	1112.9	1301.3	1521.6	1788.8	2105.5	2391.4
023	Net factor income from abroad	...	...	-200.0	-269.7	-321.6	-456.1	-387.8	-449.7
024	GNP at current market prices	...	...	912.9	1031.6	1200.0	1332.7	1717.7	1941.7
	At Current Market Prices								
025	Expenditure on GDP [b]	...	...	1112.9	1301.3	1521.6	1788.8	2105.5	2391.4
026	Private consumption	...	...	748.6	922.2	1053.8	1195.1	1435.8	1506.7
027	Government consumption	...	...	275.9	287.3	326.7	442.9	513.2	560.9
028	Gross fixed capital formation	...	...	330.4	425.8	555.7	690.7	754.9	1002.9
029	Increase in stocks	...	...	14.7	74.7	59.8	21.3	10.4	81.6
030	Exports of goods and services	...	...	145.4	207.4	213.2	227.8	290.2	367.5
031	Less: Imports of goods and services	...	...	402.1	616.2	687.6	789.0	898.9	1127.8
032	Statistical discrepancy	...	...	0.0	0.1	0.0	-0.0	-0.1	-0.4
	At Constant 1980 Factor Cost								
033	GDP by Industrial Origin	...	...	1095.0	1204.8	1269.2	1370.2	1465.7	1519.8
034	Agriculture	...	...	621.4	636.1	692.2	742.2	806.5	833.9
035	Mining	...	...	6.8	8.9	12.1	8.9	15.8	12.6
036	Manufacturing	...	...	35.8	59.1	59.6	62.9	67.2	75.4
037	Electricity, gas and water	...	...	2.5	2.7	3.1	6.0	5.2	6.0
038	Construction	...	...	88.5	131.0	157.7	185.2	173.5	169.0
039	Trade	...	...	121.5	140.3	132.0	122.0	123.4	132.4
040	Transport and communications	...	...	47.9	54.9	57.4	64.8	66.4	79.4
041	Finance	...	...	70.2	80.3	77.0	91.1	109.4	110.1
042	Public administration	...	...	120.4	121.5	102.1	113.1	130.3	126.0
043	Others	...	...	...	...	...	...	...	...
044	Less: Imputed bank service charges	...	...	20.0	30.0	24.0	26.0	32.0	25.0
045	Indirect taxes less subsidies	...	...	...	...	...	...	...	...
046	GDP at *1980* market prices	...	...	...	...	...	...	...	...
047	Net factor income from abroad	...	...	...	...	...	...	...	...
048	GNP at *1980* market prices	...	...	...	...	...	...	...	...

	1986	1987	1988	1989	1990	1991	1992	1993	1994	1995	
As of 1 July											
	1.41	1.44	1.47	1.51	1.54	1.58	1.61	1.65	1.69	1.73	001
Calendar year											
	...	...	...	...	527	...	...	...	...	...	002
	...	...	...	...	...	...	...	...	...	...	003
	...	...	...	...	...	...	...	...	...	...	004
	...	...	...	...	...	...	...	...	...	...	005
	...	...	...	...	...	...	...	...	...	...	006
	...	...	...	...	...	...	...	...	...	...	007
	...	...	...	...	...	...	...	...	...	...	008
Calendar Year											
	2758.6	3530.8	3850.9	4307.9	4848.2	5342.1	6177.7	7007.4	8012.5	9039.5	009
	1399.2	1623.5	1746.3	1924.3	2094.9	2305.1	2460.5	2801.8	3154.4	...	010
	37.4	37.0	33.4	41.8	44.8	90.0	98.8	102.3	118.7	...	011
	137.1	204.7	226.5	302.5	396.7	499.5	647.4	752.3	831.6	...	012
	96.6	377.0	388.0	391.0	384.7	384.4	445.3	560.9	553.5	...	013
	267.5	349.9	309.0	365.4	398.7	359.7	595.1	616.8	989.0	...	014
	234.1	248.2	258.5	282.3	321.6	382.9	479.7	551.2	647.2	...	015
	114.2	126.0	180.6	235.6	346.7	398.5	471.2	587.4	614.3	...	016
	170.7	210.5	263.9	306.9	378.0	409.4	438.8	457.7	477.4	...	017
	350.8	416.0	507.8	525.1	540.5	564.4	608.9	645.0	715.3	...	018
	...	...	...	...	...	...	...	...	...	...	019
	49.0	62.0	63.1	67.0	58.4	51.8	68.1	68.0	89.0	...	020
	43.0	76.7	82.8	73.7	133.8	159.4	176.2	184.8	304.9	373.2	021
	2801.6	3607.5	3933.7	4381.6	4982.0	5501.5	6353.9	7192.2	8317.4	9412.7	022
	-467.0	-349.5	-344.3	-172.0	-296.0	-440.0	-645.0	-579.0	-654.0	...	023
	2334.6	3258.0	3589.4	4209.6	4686.0	5061.5	5708.9	6613.2	7663.4	...	024
	2801.6	3607.5	3933.7	4381.6	4982.0	5501.5	6353.9	7192.2	8317.4	9412.7	025
	1837.9	2321.0	2558.2	2581.8	2926.3	3292.7	3453.6	3044.3	3201.0	3904.7	026
	576.3	633.6	641.1	879.0	948.7	1015.1	1215.2	1901.2	2065.1	2116.5	027
	1103.1	1249.7	1508.0	1573.5	1685.6	1781.6	2562.7	3245.4	4312.3 ⎫	5131.7	028
	32.0	-161.5	10.4	-121.1	-33.9	-71.3	351.0	-93.7	− ⎬		029
	550.5	838.0	1101.0	1239.0	1405.0	1829.0	2000.0	2367.0	2522.0	2685.9	030
	1297.8	1286.0	2006.0	1788.0	2025.0	2281.0	3555.0	3272.0	3783.0	4426.1	031
	-0.4	12.7	121.0	17.4	75.3	-64.6	326.4	-0.0	-0.0	0.0	032
	1674.5	1973.1	1993.6	2087.1	2224.6	2303.4	2397.2	2549.4	2716.3	2865.3	033
	881.0	925.8	939.7	962.9	992.8	1024.6	1006.4	1045.3	1066.2	1100.5	034
	22.2	21.6	19.0	21.7	19.3	27.4	23.5	26.2	29.8	32.7	035
	71.0	105.0	110.3	129.2	158.1	186.7	208.8	217.3	223.6	254.9	036
	60.4	229.0	225.1	222.3	204.1	200.4	210.0	232.0	229.8	236.7	037
	141.8	152.3	129.0	136.2	136.8	116.2	156.6	181.8	279.8	303.9	038
	143.4	142.4	129.2	133.6	134.7	145.1	160.7	163.8	170.2	175.3	039
	83.9	91.3	122.1	142.4	172.1	182.0	192.3	223.4	231.0	237.9	040
	126.2	135.7	141.0	162.9	212.2	208.8	215.4	238.1	245.4	268.5	041
	168.6	200.0	210.0	217.0	223.3	233.2	251.6	266.5	295.6	315.1	042
	...	...	...	...	...	...	...	...	...	...	043
	24.0	30.0	31.8	41.1	28.8	21.0	28.1	45.0	55.0	60.2	044
											045
	...	...	...	...	...	...	...	...	...	...	046
	...	...	...	...	...	...	...	...	...	...	047
	...	...	...	...	...	...	...	...	...	...	048

	Item	1978	1979	1980	1981	1982	1983	1984	1985
	Investment Financing, at current prices								
049	Gross domestic capital formation	...	...	345.1	500.5	615.5	712.0	765.3	1084.5
050	Gross national saving	...	...	-111.6	-177.9	-180.5	-305.3	-231.3	-125.9
051	Gross domestic saving	...	...	88.4	91.8	141.1	150.8	156.5	323.8
052	Net factor income from abroad	...	...	-200.0	-269.7	-321.6	-456.1	-387.8	-449.7
053	Foreign saving	...	...	486.9	652.9	789.2	1085.0	989.0	1230.6
054	Net transfer from abroad	...	...	486.9	650.2	780.8	887.5	672.1	906.0
055	Net borrowing from abroad	...	...	...	2.7	8.4	197.5	316.9	324.6
	Per Capita GDP, Ngultrum								
056	Current market prices	...	...	890	1026	1176	1353	1560	1734
057	Constant *1980* factor cost	...	...	876	950	981	1036	1086	1102
	PRODUCTION								*Thousand metric tons;*
	Agriculture								
058	1. Rice, paddy	54	55	57	59	60	66	62	63
059	2. Maize	75	76	78	81	81	83	80	76
060	3. Potatoes	23	24	24	25	25	26	33	27
061	4. Millet	5	6	6	7	7	7	9	7
062	5. Apple	3	3	3	3	3	3	4	4
063	6. Wheat	8	8	9	9	10	11	12	11
	Production Indexes								*Period*
064	Agriculture, *1979-81 = 100*	95.4	97.4	100.3	102.3	104.0	107.3	116.6	109.1
065	Mining	...	...	...	...	...	...	...	...
066	Manufacturing	...	...	...	...	...	...	...	...
	ENERGY								*Annual*
	Electricity, *Mn kWh*								
067	Production	19	20	20	22	24	22	20	21
068	Exports	–	–	–	–	–	–	–	–
069	Imports	–	–	–	–	–	4	9	9
070	Consumption	19	20	20	22	24	26	29	30
	PRICE INDEXES								*Period*
071	Consumer, *December 1979 = 100*	...	100.0	104.4	115.1	126.5	149.3	159.8	162.8
072	Implicit GDP deflator, *1980 = 100*[c]	...	...	100.0	106.3	118.0	128.0	140.5	154.6
	MONEY AND BANKING								*Million Ngultrum;*
073	Money supply (M1)[d]	...	...	125.3	144.3	165.7	177.2	209.8	261.7
074	Currency in circulation[e]	...	...	63.1	76.1	92.2	22.1	46.2	70.4
075	Demand deposits	...	...	62.2	68.2	73.5	155.1	163.6	191.3
076	Quasi-money	...	...	29.7	57.8	73.8	147.4	157.2	202.3
077	Money supply (M2)	...	...	155.0	202.1	239.5	324.6	367.0	464.0
078	Foreign assets (net)	...	...	205.3	311.9	372.3	345.7	490.2	595.5
079	Domestic credit	...	...	13.1	-13.9	-65.3	110.4	45.1	101.7
080	Claims on govt. sector (net)	...	...	-79.5	-101.4	-160.5	10.0	-54.0	19.7
081	Claims on private sector	...	...	41.0	52.0	49.5	43.1	57.8	55.4
082	Claims on other financial insts.[f]	...	...	51.6	35.5	45.7	57.3	41.3	26.6
083	Other items	...	...	-63.4	-95.9	-67.5	-131.5	-168.3	-233.1
	Deposit Money Banks								
084	Demand deposits ⎫	...	...	...	...	...	155.1	163.6	191.3
085	Savings deposits ⎬	...	...	...	...	...			
086	Time deposits ⎭	...	...	...	...	...	146.9	156.7	201.0
087	Domestic credits outstanding	...	...	...	...	...	...	...	...

1986	1987	1988	1989	1990	1991	1992	1993	1994	1995	
1135.1	1088.2	1518.4	1452.4	1651.7	1710.3	2913.7	3151.7	4312.3	5131.6	049
-79.6	303.4	390.1	748.8	811.0	753.7	1040.1	1667.7	2397.3	...	050
387.4	652.9	734.4	920.8	1107.0	1193.7	1685.1	2246.7	3051.3	3391.5	051
-467.0	-349.5	-344.3	-172.0	-296.0	-440.0	-645.0	-579.0	-654.0	...	052
1262.4	871.6	1108.0	293.4	434.0	1110.0	2218.0	1846.0	2257.0	...	053
982.3	630.0	602.0	277.0	398.0	796.0	1838.0	1820.0	1969.0	...	054
280.1	241.6	506.0	16.4	36.0	314.0	380.0	26.0	288.0	...	055
1988	2505	2672	2911	3237	3493	3942	4359	4924	5444	056
1188	1370	1354	1387	1445	1462	1487	1545	1608	1657	057
Calendar year										
63	65	43	43	43	43	43	43	43	43	058
74	50	31	31	40	40	40	40	40	40	059
39	40	40	31	31	33	34	34	34	...	060
7	7	7	7	7	7	7	7	7	...	061
4	4	4	5	5	5	5	5	6	...	062
11	8	4	4	5	5	5	5	5	6	063
averages										
110.1	122.6	98.5	99.6	104.9	88.1	89.1	108.5	109.5	109.7	064
...	...	...	...	...	...	...	...	...	...	065
...	...	...	...	...	...	...	...	...	...	066
values										
21	1182	1544	1544	1564	1580	1627	1650	1686 *	...	067
–	1109	1396	1396	1395	1400	1445	...	...	...	068
10	17	4	4	3	3	3	1	5 *	...	069
31	90	152	152	172	183	185	...	...	...	070
averages										
179.0	190.4	209.6	228.0	250.8	281.6	326.6	363.2	388.8	...	071
164.7	178.9	193.2	206.4	217.9	231.9	257.7	274.9	295.0	...	072
As of end of period										
277.0	316.8	412.1	545.9	539.5	749.7	840.9	833.1	1044.0 *	...	073
90.7	103.5	149.1	187.7	194.1	246.0	345.0	346.0	347.5 *	...	074
186.3	213.3	263.0	358.2	345.4	503.7	495.9	487.1	696.5 *	...	075
221.8	235.7	311.6	430.2	539.3	648.2	746.1	1120.2	1351.0 *	...	076
498.8	552.5	723.7	976.2	1078.8	1397.9	1586.9	1953.3	2395.0 *	...	077
700.1	1077.0	1384.4	1446.2	1487.6	2480.0	1882.5	2811.2	3194.9 *	...	078
53.9	-208.9	-250.5	3.3	143.2	83.8	1149.0	1028.0	1175.0 *	...	079
-33.1	-304.7	-398.8	-216.5	-125.9	-287.1	-46.9	-256.4	-164.7 *	...	080
67.3	82.3	115.9	192.2	215.9	306.1	425.8	488.8	540.0 *	...	081
19.7	13.5	32.4	27.6	53.2	64.8	770.1	795.6	799.7 *	...	082
-255.2	-315.6	-410.2	-473.4	-551.8	-1165.8	-1444.6	-1886.0	-1974.9 *	...	083
186.3	213.3	263.0	358.2	345.4	503.7	495.9	487.1	696.5	...	084
									...	085
212.6	223.4	289.1	415.1	515.2	622.8	691.1	1054.9	1266.8	...	086
...	...	...	...	...	...	...	...	...	...	087

Item	1978	1979	1980	1981	1982	1983	1984	1985
Interest Rates [g]								**Per cent;**
On deposits								
088 Savings	...	...	...	...	5.0	5.0	5.0	5.0
089 Time: 6 months	...	...	...	...	5.5	5.5	5.5	6.1
090 12 months	...	...	...	...	7.0	7.0	7.0	8.0
GOVERNMENT FINANCE [h]								**Million Ngultrum;**
Central government								
091 Current revenue	93	94	102	89	128	177	250	233
092 Taxes	49	52	53	65	76	114	134	136
093 Non-taxes	44	43	49	24	52	63	116	97
094 Current expenditure	133	155	170	170	213	223	304	442
095 Current surplus/deficit	-40	-61	-68	-81	-85	-46	-54	-208
096 Capital receipts	...	...	...	31	10	19	26	24
097 Capital expenditure [i]	120	170	160	267	275	476	454	776
098 Capital account surplus/deficit	-120	-170	-160	-236	-265	-457	-428	-752
099 Overall surplus/deficit	-160	-231	-228	-317	-350	-503	-482	-960
Financing								
100 Domestic borrowing	...	...	...	...	...	12	0	–
101 Foreign borrowing	...	...	...	...	...	11	21	132
102 Foreign grants	165	206	206	300	360	478	512	702
103 Use of cash balances	-5	25	22	17	-10	2	-51	127
								...
Expenditure by Function, Central Govt.								
104 Total	...	...	...	...	488	698	753	1098
105 General public services	...	...	...	...	77	81	155	...
106 Education	...	...	...	...	62	100	86	...
107 Health	...	...	...	...	24	40	42	...
108 Social security & welfare	...	...	...	...	8	15	11	...
109 Housing and community amenities [j]	...	...	...	...	16	19	42	...
110 Economic services	...	...	...	...	277	407	393	...
111 Agriculture	...	...	...	...	119	161	164	...
112 Industry	...	...	...	...	9	19	20	...
113 Electricity, gas and water	...	...	...	...	13	13	19	...
114 Transport and communications	...	...	...	...	116	181	132	...
115 Other economic services [k]	...	...	...	...	21	33	57	...
116 Others	...	...	...	...	23	36	24	...
EXTERNAL TRADE [h]								**Million Ngultrum;**
117 Exports, fob	...	...	131.5	171.7	159.4	160.7	206.4	272.0
118 Imports, cif	...	...	394.6	585.9	646.5	730.0	825.2	1041.6
119 Trade balance	...	...	-263.1	-414.2	-487.1	-569.3	-618.8	-769.6
Exports, by principal commodity [l, m]								
120 1. Timber	...	...	...	16.0	10.1	8.2	14.0	46.8
121 2. Cement	...	...	...	35.7	34.3	35.2	41.8	55.0
122 3. Electricity	...	...	...	–	–	–	–	–
123 4. Wood products (Block boards)	...	...	...	–	–	0.1	6.3	14.8
BALANCE OF PAYMENTS [h, n]								**Million US dollars;**
124 Merchandise exports, fob [m]	13	15	16	20	17	16	19	22
125 Merchandise imports, fob [m]	-19	-34	-43	-66	-66	-70	-71	-80
126 Trade balance	-6	-19	-27	-46	-49	-54	-52	-58
127 Other goods, services and income	...	-14	-17	-31	-34	-48	-33	-39
128 Unrequited transfer	21	39	47	76	85	95	63	81
129 Private	...	...	...	2	2	2	3	3
130 Official	21	39	...	74	84	93	61	79
131 Current balance	15	6	3	-1	3	-7	-22	-16
132 Direct investment	–	–	–	–	–	–	–	–
133 Portfolio investment	–	–	–	–	–	–	–	–

1986	1987	1988	1989	1990	1991	1992	1993	1994	1995	

As of end of period

5.0	5.0	5.0	5.0	5.0	5.0	5.0	5.0	5.0	5.0	088
6.5	6.5	6.5	6.5	6.5	6.5	8.0	8.0	8.0	8.0	089
8.0	8.0	8.0	8.0	8.0	8.0	9.0	9.0	9.0	9.0	090

Fiscal year beginning 1 July

313 I	728	... I	790	946	996	1155	1595	1574 *	1805 *	091
174 I	236	... I	232	232	281	328	457	503 *	651 *	092
139 I	492	... I	558	714	715	827	1138	1071 *	1154 *	093
523 I	775	... I	908	1069	1082	1152	1241	1606 *	1826 *	094
-210 I	-47	... I	-118	-123	-86	3	354	-32 *	-21 *	095
27 I	114	... I	38	...	...	...	...	...	...	096
698 I	966	... I	1182	790	512	1180	1436	2034 *	3086 *	097
-671 I	-852	... I	-1144	-790	-512	-1180	-1436	-2034 *	-3086 *	098
-881 I	-899	... I	-1262	-913	-598	-1177	-1082	-2066 *	-3107 *	099
6 I	-242	... I	-8	333	-208	301	-171	-145 *	28 *	100
170 I	210	... I	491	57	53	91	23	90 *	135 *	101
782 I	930	... I	791	523	753	786	1230	2121 *	2944 *	102
-77 I	1	... I	-12	0	0	-1	0	0	0	103
1064 I	1621	... I	1573	1780	1753	2075	2397	3559 *	4903 *	104
241 I	352	... I	330	445	558	652	704	1106 *	1079 *	105
102 I	169	... I	201	230	201	266	240	371 *	534 *	106
55 I	93	... I	89	103	106	139	168	304 *	407 *	107
20 I	22	... I	44	...	...	...	...	...	...	108
49 I	52	... I	45	9	9	11	11	20 *	33 *	109
554 I	843	... I	797	993	879	1007	1274	1758 *	2850 *	110
180 I	272	... I	241	290	359	396	433	582 *	672 *	111
100 I	113	... I	69	112	62	56	61	75 *	137 *	112
137 I	202	... I	147	140	130	60	90	286 *	866 *	113
134 I	241	... I	329	113	90	108	394	434 *	322 *	114
4 I	16	... I	12	338	238	387	297	380 *	854 *	115
43 I	91	... I	67	–	–	–	–	–	–	116

Fiscal year beginning 1 July

377.0 I	705.2	... I	1040.7	1132.3	1308.5	1632.0	1837.3	2097.9 *	2225.0 *	117
1285.4 I	1194.6	... I	1874.5	1613.9	1525.5	2148.5	3470.9	3064.1 *	3562.4 *	118
-908.4 I	-489.4	... I	-833.8	-481.6	-217.0	-516.6	-1633.6	-966.2 *	-1337.4 *	119
53.3	121.2	197.1	96.9	107.2	120.4	139.6	134.7	158.0	...	120
79.6	103.2	110.5	135.5	137.0	164.3	164.1	190.0	268.0	...	121
42.0	275.9	337.3	280.2	374.4	397.3	355.1	537.3	519.0	...	122
21.2	29.3	31.0	56.6	72.6	172.5	164.5	175.3	81.0	...	123

Fiscal year beginning 1 July

34 I	54	... I	64	65	58	63	60 *	67 *	69 *	124
-97 I	-92	... I	-116	-92	-67	-83	-114 *	-98 *	-110 *	125
-63 I	-38	... I	-51	-28	-10	-20	-54 *	-31 *	-41 *	126
-35 I	-19	... I	-15	0	-4	-5	-10 *	-14 *	-14 *	127
85 I		... I								128
3 I		... I								129
82 I		... I								130
-14 I	-57	... I	-66	-27	-14	-25	-64 *	-45 *	-55 *	131
– I	–	... I	–	–	0	1	–	–	–	132
– I	...	... I	...	...	...	...	...	...	...	133

	Item	1978	1979	1980	1981	1982	1983	1984	1985
134	Other long-term capital	–	–	–	–	–	–	–	–
135	Other short-term capital	0	0	0	0	1	20	27	27
136	Net errors and omissions	0	0	0	8	3	-6	7	-5
137	Overall balance	16	7	4	7	6	7	11	5
138	Allocation of SDRs	...	...	...	...	...	...	...	...
139	Monetary movements	-16	-7	-4	-7	-6	-7	-11	-5
	INTERNATIONAL RESERVES								*Million US dollars;*
140	Total	–	–	–	31.1	35.5	40.2	44.8	50.3
141	Gold, national valuation	–	–	–	...	...	...	...	...
142	Foreign exchange	–	–	–	31.1	35.1	39.8	44.2	49.6
143	Reserve position in the fund	–	–	–	–	0.4	0.4	0.6	0.6
144	SDRs	–	–	–	–	–	0.0	0.1	0.1
	EXCHANGE RATES [o]								*Ngultrum*
145	End of period	8.188	7.907	7.930	9.099	9.634	10.493	12.451	12.166
146	Average of period	8.193	8.126	7.863	8.659	9.455	10.099	11.363	12.369
	EXTERNAL INDEBTEDNESS								*Million US dollars;*
147	Total outstanding and disbursed	–	–	–	0.3	1.1	1.8	2.7	8.8
148	Long-term	–	–	–	0.3	1.1	1.8	2.7	8.8
149	Public and publicly guaranteed	–	–	–	0.3	1.1	1.8	2.7	8.8
150	Private non-guaranteed	–	–	–	–	–	–	–	–
151	Short-term	–	–	–	–	–	–	–	–
152	Use of IMF credit	–	–	–	–	–	–	–	–
	Debt service								*Transactions*
153	Principal repayments on LT debt	–	–	–	–	–	–	–	–
154	Interest on long-term debt	–	–	–	–	–	–	–	–
155	Interest on short-term debt	–	–	–	–	–	–	–	–
	Average terms of new commitments								
156	Interest (%)	–	–	1.0	–	–	1.6	1.3	1.3
157	Maturity (years)	–	–	50.0	–	–	27.6	36.1	38.1
158	Grace Period (years)	–	–	10.5	–	–	6.6	7.8	8.6
159	Grant element (%)	–	–	81.0	–	–	62.2	69.3	72.1

Footnotes:

a   Data for 1978 and 1979 are adjusted to reflect an annual growth rate of 2% based on the 1980 census given by the Ministry of Home Affairs. Starting 1990, the Government has come up with new population estimates based on new definition as follows: 1990: 600,000; 1991: 610,000; 1992: 630,000; 1993: 650,000 and 1994: 675,000.

b   A sharp rise in consumption of fixed capital in 1987 is due to coming into operation of Chukha Hydel Project.

c   Computations are based on factor cost data.

d   Money supply excludes rupees in circulation, but includes Nu 6.2 million currency issue ending March for 1978-1980.

e   Refers to currency outside banks. From 1983 onward, data exclude rupees in circulation.

f   Refers to Government corporations.

g   Rates for 6-month period are rates offered by the Bank of Bhutan for 3-to 6-month deposits, while rates for 12 month period are for 9-month to 1-year deposits.

h   Up to 1986, data refer to the twelve-month fiscal year 1 April to 31 March. For 1987, data refer to the fifteen-month fiscal year 1 April to 30 June. Starting 1989, fiscal year refers to 1 July to 30 June.

i   Up to 1982, data refer to development expenditure. From 1983 onward, includes net lending.

j   From 1990, data refers to urban development and municipal corporations.

k   From 1990, data include public works services and business, commerce and trade affairs.

l   Refers to trade with India only.

m   Data are for corresponding calendar years.

n   Data from 1987 were reported in Ngultrum and were converted using the average exchange rate to the US dollar.

o   Since its introduction in 1974, the Ngultrum has been pegged to the Indian Rupee at a rate of Nu = RS1.

	1986	1987	1988	1989	1990	1991	1992	1993	1994	1995	
	– I										134
	22 I	86	... I	92	41	43	46	67 *	63 *	66 *	135
	7 I	-2	... I	-4	-17	-14	3	9 *	2 *	1 *	136
	15 I	28	... I	22	-3	16	26	12 *	20 *	12 *	137
	... I	...	... I	...	...	...	...	...	...		138
	-15 I	-28	... I	-22	3	-16	-26	-12 *	-20 *	-12 *	139
As of end of period											
	61.0	74.9	94.1	98.5	86.0	98.9	77.9	...	115.2	...	140
	...	...	...	...	...	...	...	...	...	...	141
	60.2	73.9	93.1	97.5	84.8	97.7	76.6	–	113.8	–	142
	0.7	0.8	0.8	0.8	0.8	0.8	0.8	0.8	0.8	0.9	143
	0.1	0.2	0.2	0.3	0.4	0.4	0.5	0.5	0.6	0.7	144
per US Dollar											
	13.122	12.877	14.949	17.035	18.073	25.834	26.200	31.380	31.380	35.180	145
	12.611	12.962	13.917	16.200	17.500	22.700	25.918	30.500	31.374	32.400	146
As of end of period											
	21.0	40.2	67.0	73.9	83.6	86.4	83.6	84.9	...	...	147
	21.0	40.2	67.0	71.9	80.3	84.9	82.7	83.2	...	...	148
	21.0	40.2	67.0	71.9	80.3	84.9	82.7	83.2	86.7	...	149
	–	–	–	–	–	–	–	–	...	...	150
	–	–	–	2.0	3.3	1.5	0.9	1.7	0.7	...	151
	–	–	–	–	–	–	–	–	...	...	152
during the year											
	–	–	0.6	4.1	2.9	5.3	4.1	4.7	5.1	...	153
	0.2	0.5	0.7	2.3	2.0	1.9	1.8	1.9	1.7	...	154
	–	–	–	0.2	0.2	0.1	–	0.1	–	...	155
	1.4	1.0	5.5	1.0	0.0	1.0	1.9	0.7	...	...	156
	37.0	39.5	19.0	39.5	0.0	39.2	29.7	39.9	...	...	157
	8.0	10.0	3.3	10.0	0.0	9.7	7.0	10.4	...	...	158
	68.6	77.8	29.0	77.0	0.0	78.1	59.4	80.8	77.5	...	159

Item	1978	1979	1980	1981	1982	1983	1984	1985
								Million;
001 **POPULATION**	6.59	6.44	6.50	6.59	6.76	6.99	7.23	7.46
NATIONAL ACCOUNTS								
At Current Market Prices								**Million Riels;**
002 GDP by Industrial Origin	...	...	...	...	...	...	...	...
003 Agriculture	...	...	...	...	...	...	...	...
004 Mining	...	...	...	...	...	...	...	...
005 Manufacturing	...	...	...	...	...	...	...	...
006 Electricity, gas and water	...	...	...	...	...	...	...	...
007 Construction	...	...	...	...	...	...	...	...
008 Trade	...	...	...	...	...	...	...	...
009 Transport and communications	...	...	...	...	...	...	...	...
010 Finance	...	...	...	...	...	...	...	...
011 Public administration	...	...	...	...	...	...	...	...
012 Others [a]	...	...	...	...	...	...	...	...
013 Net factor income from abroad	...	...	...	...	...	...	...	...
014 GNP	...	...	...	...	...	...	...	...
015 Expenditure on GDP	...	...	...	...	...	...	...	...
016 Private consumption	...	...	...	...	...	...	...	...
017 Government consumption	...	...	...	...	...	...	...	...
018 Gross fixed capital formation	...	...	...	...	...	...	...	...
019 Increase in stocks	...	...	...	...	...	...	...	...
020 Exports of goods and services	...	...	...	...	...	...	...	...
021 Less: Imports of goods and services	...	...	...	...	...	...	...	...
022 Statistical discrepancy	...	...	...	...	...	...	...	...
At Constant 1989 Prices								
023 GDP by Industrial Origin	...	...	...	...	...	...	...	...
024 Agriculture	...	...	...	...	...	...	...	...
025 Mining	...	...	...	...	...	...	...	...
026 Manufacturing	...	...	...	...	...	...	...	...
027 Electricity, gas and water	...	...	...	...	...	...	...	...
028 Construction	...	...	...	...	...	...	...	...
029 Trade	...	...	...	...	...	...	...	...
030 Transport and communications	...	...	...	...	...	...	...	...
031 Finance	...	...	...	...	...	...	...	...
032 Public administration	...	...	...	...	...	...	...	...
033 Others [a]	...	...	...	...	...	...	...	...
034 Net factor income from abroad	...	...	...	...	...	...	...	...
035 GNP	...	...	...	...	...	...	...	...
036 Expenditure on GDP	...	...	...	...	...	...	...	...
037 Private consumption	...	...	...	...	...	...	...	...
038 Government consumption	...	...	...	...	...	...	...	...
039 Gross fixed capital formation	...	...	...	...	...	...	...	...
040 Increase in stocks	...	...	...	...	...	...	...	...
041 Exports of goods and services	...	...	...	...	...	...	...	...
042 Less: Imports of goods and services	...	...	...	...	...	...	...	...
043 Statistical discrepancy	...	...	...	...	...	...	...	...
Investment Financing, at current prices								
044 Gross domestic capital formation	...	...	...	...	...	...	...	...
045 Gross national saving	...	...	...	...	...	...	...	...
046 Gross domestic saving	...	...	...	...	...	...	...	...
047 Net factor income from abroad	...	...	...	...	...	...	...	...
048 Foreign saving	...	...	...	...	...	...	...	...
049 Net transfer from abroad	...	...	...	...	...	...	...	...
050 Net borrowing from abroad	...	...	...	...	...	...	...	...

1986	1987	1988	1989	1990	1991	1992	1993	1994	1995	
As of 1 July										
7.69	7.92	8.15	8.38	8.61	8.83	9.30	9.65 *	9.87 *	10.20 *	001
Calendar year										
...	101636	195587	240909	598636	1335968	2508000	5414000	6048000	7178000	002
...	45422	122048	125862	333107	666463	1198300	2894100	...	...	003
...	1562	1953	2500	3124	4689	8500	16150	...	...	004
...	10609	13904	18022	31355	71005	126900	248025	...	...	005
...	522	588	600	2155	6966	16300	29695	...	...	006
...	7930	10436	16000	30115	79001	178200	328000	...	...	007
...	13724	18951	29351	58407	173640	327100	607330	...	...	008
...	3226	4222	6500	22547	43155	86100	173062	...	...	009
...	...	...	...	...	...	...	...	...	...	010
...	3562	5729	9300	28301	62487	108400	215960	...	...	011
...	15079	17756	32774	89525	228562	458200	901678	...	...	012
...	...	...	...	...	...	...	...	...	...	013
...	...	...	...	...	...	...	...	...	...	014
...	...	195587	240909	598636	1335968	2508000	5414000	6048000	...	015
...	...	182845	213470	541324	992007	2066400	4595600	4994400	...	016
...	...	10500	18476	43293	238000	255000	373200	605400	...	017
...	...	17533	26463	49719	125861	245400	789800	1162700	...	018
...	...	...	...	...	...	...	...	...	...	019
...	...	3500	7200	14600	60000	126600	719000	969900	...	020
...	...	18791	24700	50300	79900	185400	1063600	1684400	...	021
...	...	–	–	–	–	–	–	–	...	022
...	211979	232773	240909	243704	262193	280600	292100	303700	324900	023
...	110311	117495	125862	127358	135937	138500	137100	137100	144700	024
...	2066	2273	2500	2750	3025	3200	3400	3700	4000	025
...	13836	15818	18022	17247	18419	19000	20500	22100	24100	026
...	566	612	600	541	467	600	700	700	800	027
...	15459	17778	16000	15792	17642	22900	27100	29100	32000	028
...	27107	32761	29351	26894	30954	39900	42300	44800	48300	029
...	6252	6505	6500	6411	7000	8100	8900	9700	10700	030
...	...	...	...	...	...	...	...	...		031
...	6943	9760	9300	10995	10980	11000	11500	12500	} 60300	032
...	29439	29771	32774	35716	37769	37400	40600	44000		033
...	...	...	...	...	...	...	...	...	...	034
...	...	...	...	...	...	...	...	...	...	035
...	...	232773	240909	243704	262193	280600	292100	...	...	036
...	...	217340	213470	218839	222598	232700	245000	...	...	037
...	...	12496	18476	17625	19417	26700	25500	...	...	038
...	...	20866	26463	20240	24701	27500	28600	...	...	039
...	...	...	...	...	...	...	...	...	...	040
...	...	4435	7200	5505	9921	16500	19400	...	...	041
...	...	22364	24700	18505	14443	22800	26400	...	...	042
...	...	–	–	–	–	–	–	...	...	043
...	...	17533	26463	49719	125861	245400	789800	1162700	...	044
...	...	...	...	...	...	...	...	...	...	045
...	...	2242	8963	14019	105961	186600	445200	448200	...	046
...	...	...	...	...	...	...	...	...	...	047
...	...	...	...	...	...	...	...	...	...	048
...	...	...	...	...	...	...	...	...	...	049
...	...	...	...	...	...	...	...	...	...	050

Item	1978	1979	1980	1981	1982	1983	1984	1985
Per Capita GDP, Riels								
051 Current prices	...	...	...	...	...	...	...	...
052 Constant *1989* prices	...	...	...	...	...	...	...	...
PRODUCTION								
Agriculture								*Thousand metric tons;*
053 1. Rice (paddy)	1500	1000	1717	1490	1949	2039	1260	1812
054 2. Maize	80	50	101	85	51	43	48	42
055 3. Rubber	...	...	1	4	7	9	13	18
056 4. Logs, *'000 cu. m.*	...	...	0	11	68	90	73	97
057 5. Fish	...	...	20	52	69	68	64	71
Production Indexes								
058 Agriculture, *1979-81 = 100*	115	76	114	110	129	146	123	151
059 Mining	...	...	...	...	...	...	...	...
060 Manufacturing	...	...	...	...	...	...	...	...
ENERGY								*Annual*
Electricity, *Mn kWh*								
061 Production	...	...	...	...	...	...	...	...
062 Exports	...	...	...	...	...	...	...	...
063 Imports	...	...	...	...	...	...	...	...
064 Consumption	...	...	...	...	...	...	...	...
PRICE INDEXES								*Period*
065 Consumer, *March 1988 = 100*	...	...	...	...	...	...	...	...
066 Implicit GDP deflator, *1989 = 100*	...	...	...	...	...	...	...	...
MONEY AND BANKING								*Million Riels;*
067 Money supply (M1)	...	...	...	...	...	...	...	...
068 Currency in circulation	...	...	...	...	...	...	...	...
069 Demand deposits	...	...	...	...	...	...	...	...
070 Quasi-money	...	...	...	...	...	...	...	...
071 Money supply (M2)	...	...	...	...	...	...	...	...
072 Foreign assets (net)	...	...	...	...	...	...	...	...
073 Domestic credit	...	...	...	...	...	...	...	...
074 Claims on govt. sector (net)	...	...	...	...	...	...	...	...
075 Claims on private sector	...	...	...	...	...	...	...	...
076 Claims on other financial insts.	...	...	...	...	...	...	...	...
077 Other items	...	...	...	...	...	...	...	...
Deposit Money Banks								
078 Demand deposits	...	...	...	...	...	...	...	...
079 Savings deposits	...	...	...	...	...	...	...	...
080 Time deposits	...	...	...	...	...	...	...	...
081 Domestic credits outstanding	...	...	...	...	...	...	...	...
GOVERNMENT FINANCE								*Million Riels;*
Central government								
082 Current revenue	...	...	...	...	...	...	...	...
083 Taxes	...	...	...	...	...	...	...	...
084 Non-taxes	...	...	...	...	...	...	...	...
085 Current expenditure	...	...	...	...	...	...	...	...
086 Current surplus/deficit	...	...	...	...	...	...	...	...
087 Capital receipts	...	...	...	...	...	...	...	...
088 Capital expenditure	...	...	...	...	...	...	...	...
089 Capital account surplus/deficit	...	...	...	...	...	...	...	...
090 Net lending	...	...	...	...	...	...	...	...
091 Overall surplus/deficit	...	...	...	...	...	...	...	...

1986	1987	1988	1989	1990	1991	1992	1993	1994	1995	
...	12830	23993	28741	69528	151299	269561	560862	613636	703725	051
...	26758	28554	28741	28305	29693	30159	30260	30814	31853	052

Calendar year

1986	1987	1988	1989	1990	1991	1992	1993	1994	1995	
2093	1815	2500	2672	2500	2400	2221	2384	2223	3373	053
51	38	41	54	88	60	60	54	45	55	054
25	25	31	34	35	35	28	22	27	...	055
214	306	283	245	257	322	370	765	282	...	056
74	82	87	82	111	118	111	109	94	113	057
164	159	193	199	194	194	202	209	207	193	058
...	...	...	...	...	...	...	...	...	...	059
...	...	...	...	...	...	...	...	...	...	060

values

1986	1987	1988	1989	1990	1991	1992	1993	1994	1995	
...	173	192	216	199	128	176	...	...	...	061
...	...	...	...	...	...	...	...	...	...	062
...	...	...	...	...	...	...	...	...	...	063
...	173	192	216	199	128	176	...	...	...	064

averages

1986	1987	1988	1989	1990	1991	1992	1993	1994	1995	
...	*	...	177.2	428.4	1135.5	3143.0	4117.0	5192.0	5198.0	065
...	47.9	84.0	100.0	245.6	509.5	893.8	1853.5	1991.4	2209.3	066

As of end of period

1986	1987	1988	1989	1990	1991	1992	1993	1994	1995	
...	6300	10553	17888	60932	77620	171773	203820	199561	281000 *	067
...	6300	8845	15290	45715	64811	158731	189718	...	...	068
...	...	1708	2598	15217	12809	13042	14102	...	...	069
...	840	65	142	533	1404	76364	129649	250366	373000 *	070
...	7140	10618	18030	61465	79023	248137	333469	449927	654000 *	071
...	-532	-1797	-2614	3097	-1706	24187	119152	391000	538000 *	072
...	12158	13717	23643	59192	87667	267421	343139	386000	445000 *	073
...	10669	3739	8112	41197	55282	156913	175317	...	...	074
...	295	1033	3851	5087	9927	98790	161609	...	...	075
...	1194	8945	11680	12908	22458	11718	6213	...	...	076
...	-4486	-1302	-2998	-823	-6939	-43471	-128822	-327073	-329000 *	077
...	...	1708	2598	15217	12809	13042	14102	25381	...	078
...	...	...	...	...	...	...	...	...	...	079
...	...	47	69	129	682	11016	8514	17798	...	080
...	...	...	...	...	...	...	...	...	...	081

Fiscal year ending 31 December

1986	1987	1988	1989	1990	1991	1992	1993	1994	1995	
3900	6200	8800	15400	23300	58700	156100	290700	590400	642200	082
...	...	3400	6200	13300	38800	110200	234700	364600	445500	083
...	...	5400	9200	10000	19900	45900	56000	225800	196700	084
6900	3100	10500	18500	43300	98900	239000	373000	662400	689600	085
-3000	3100	-1700	-3100	-20000	-40200	-82900	-82300	-72000	-47400	086
...	...	–	–	–	–	–	–	–	–	087
...	...	2800	3500	6900	5300	7000	235000	335300	459400	088
...	...	-2800	-3500	-6900	-5300	-7000	-235000	-335300	-459400	089
...	...	–	–	–	–	–	–	–	–	090
-3000	3100	-4500	-6600	-26900	-45500	-89900	-317300	-407300	-506800	091

Item	1978	1979	1980	1981	1982	1983	1984	1985
Financing								
092 Domestic borrowing	...	...	...	...	...	...	...	...
093 Foreign borrowing	...	...	...	...	...	...	...	...
094 Foreign grants	...	...	...	...	...	...	...	...
095 Use of cash balances	...	...	...	...	...	...	...	...
Expenditure by Function, Central Govt.								
096 Total	...	...	...	...	...	...	...	...
097 General public services	...	...	...	...	...	...	...	...
098 Defence	...	...	...	...	...	...	...	...
099 Education	...	...	...	...	...	...	...	...
100 Health	...	...	...	...	...	...	...	...
101 Social security & welfare	...	...	...	...	...	...	...	...
102 Economic services	...	...	...	...	...	...	...	...
103 Agriculture	...	...	...	...	...	...	...	...
104 Industry	...	...	...	...	...	...	...	...
105 Power	...	...	...	...	...	...	...	...
106 Transport and communications	...	...	...	...	...	...	...	...
107 Other services	...	...	...	...	...	...	...	...
108 Others [b]	...	...	...	...	...	...	...	...
EXTERNAL TRADE								*Million US dollars;*
109 Exports, fob	...	...	...		...	...	...	...
110 Imports, fob	...	...	...		...	...	...	...
111 Trade balance	...	...	...		...	...	...	...
Exports, by principal commodity								
112 1. Rubber	...	...	...	...	...	...	...	...
113 2. Timber	...	...	...	...	...	...	...	...
114 3. Soya beans	...	...	...	...	...	...	...	...
115 4. Maize	...	...	...	...	...	...	...	...
116 5. Sesame	...	...	...	...	...	...	...	...
Direction of Trade								*Million US dollars;*
117 Exports, Total	...	...	...	2.4	4.9	2.1	4.0	3.8
118 1. Thailand	0.0	0.0	0.0	0.0	0.0	0.0	0.0	0.0
119 2. Japan	0.4	0.3	0.5	0.5	0.5	0.3	0.2	0.2
120 3. Germany	0.1	0.0	0.0	0.0	0.0	0.0	0.0	0.0
121 4. Malaysia	0.0	0.0	0.0	0.0	0.0	0.0	0.0	0.3
122 5. Canada	0.0	0.0	0.0	0.0	0.0	0.0	0.0	0.0
123 6. Italy	0.0	0.0	0.2	0.0	0.1	0.1	0.0	0.0
124 7. Netherlands	0.0	0.0	0.0	0.0	0.0	0.0	0.0	0.0
125 8. France	0.0	0.0	0.0	0.0	0.0	0.0	0.0	0.0
126 9. Indonesia	0.0	0.0	0.0	0.0	0.1	0.0	0.0	0.0
127 10. Egypt	0.0	0.0	0.0	0.1	0.4	0.2	0.0	0.1
128 Imports, Total	...	...	...	78.4	50.8	52.1	49.1	27.4
129 1. Japan	0.0	0.8	28.2	11.4	5.8	3.6	5.9	1.9
130 2. Thailand	0.0	9.2	35.4	5.4	1.7	0.2	0.0	0.4
131 3. Australia	0.0	0.0	0.0	0.4	0.0	0.0	0.0	0.5
132 4. Indonesia	0.0	0.0	0.0	0.0	0.0	0.2	0.0	0.0
133 5. Hong Kong	8.5	0.5	6.0	3.4	0.6	2.4	0.3	0.0
134 6. United States	0.3	0.1	28.6	12.8	1.8	2.6	1.2	0.0
135 7. France	1.5	0.7	2.1	0.6	1.5	1.5	0.7	1.5
136 8. China, People's Rep. of	0.0	0.0	0.0	0.3	0.6	0.7	0.0	0.6
137 9. Malaysia	0.0	0.0	0.2	0.0	0.1	0.0	0.8	1.2
138 10. Germany	0.0	0.8	4.4	0.9	0.2	0.1	0.1	0.1

1986	1987	1988	1989	1990	1991	1992	1993	1994	1995	
1700	600	1400	4600	19700	39200	88100	36200	3200	2000	092
1300	1400	3200	2000	7200	6100	1500	59900	404100	483400	093
...	...	...	...	...	...	...	...	...	–	094
...	-5100	-100	–	–	200	300	221200	–	21400	095
5700	6636	13400	22000	50200	102900	245500	612900	950600	...	096
...	...	4800	...	...	...	...	...	190100	...	097
2500	2418	3700	7200	18700	46800	118600	180500	333400	...	098
1700	2418	...	3400	4900	...	26600	47700	60300	...	099
...	...	...	3200	9100	...	5600	7800	29800	...	100
...	...	...	...	...	...	10800	26300	2500	...	101
1500	1800	4900	8200	12300	25700	51100	268000	76000	...	102
...	...	...	...	...	...	...	...	13200	...	103
...	...	...	...	...	...	...	...	...	...	104
...	...	...	...	...	...	...	...	7200	...	105
...	...	...	...	...	...	...	...	36500	...	106
...	...	...	...	...	...	...	...	19100	...	107
...	...	...	...	5200	30400	32800	82600	258500	...	108
Calendar year										
...	36.2	44.8	79.2	85.8	252.6	264.5	283.0	489.8	855.8	109
...	151.9	169.3	176.0	163.5	285.1	443.4	471.0	725.9	1188.0	110
...	-115.7	-124.5	-96.8	-77.7	-32.5	-178.9	-188.0	-236.1	-332.2	111
4.4	2.8	7.2	6.8	4.7	18.6	12.6	13.9	25.6	...	112
0.5	0.5	1.4	4.8	4.8	20.9	25.0	84.9	197.6	...	113
...	0.4	0.7	2.1	2.0	9.9	2.0	...	...	...	114
0.5	0.1	0.3	0.8	0.3	2.3	0.6	...	...	...	115
0.2	...	0.1	0.7	...	1.2	0.2	...	...	...	116
Calendar year										
2.5	9.6	8.4	20.8	41.8	57.4	165.4	261.5	...	...	117
0.0	0.0	0.0	2.2	8.6	10.5	84.7	94.7	...	...	118
0.2	0.6	1.2	2.0	3.2	5.0	8.5	78.5	...	...	119
0.0	0.0	0.0	0.4	0.8	15.2	24.3	26.6	...	...	120
0.0	0.1	3.1	6.8	14.9	9.4	13.2	12.1	...	...	121
0.0	0.0	0.0	0.0	0.0	1.1	5.7	0.8	...	...	122
0.2	0.1	0.0	0.1	0.0	0.0	1.2	3.8	...	...	123
0.0	0.0	0.0	0.0	0.0	0.1	1.2	2.9	...	...	124
0.0	0.1	0.1	0.1	0.9	2.6	3.1	0.7	...	...	125
0.1	0.5	0.0	0.0	0.7	0.9	0.2	1.1	...	...	126
0.0	4.4	0.0	0.0	0.0	0.8	0.1	0.1	...	...	127
9.9	13.3	23.9	51.9	56.0	62.0	806.3	874.0	...	...	128
1.9	1.2	5.3	3.9	5.0	7.4	251.7	54.8	...	...	129
0.0	0.0	0.7	0.1	0.9	5.1	72.3	197.3	...	...	130
0.0	0.4	0.1	0.4	1.2	3.4	65.9	7.1	...	...	131
0.0	0.0	1.1	14.9	11.5	6.0	26.0	43.6	...	...	132
1.5	0.0	0.1	1.6	1.8	5.9	24.8	33.9	...	...	133
0.1	0.1	0.0	0.0	0.0	0.0	17.7	20.0	...	...	134
1.1	1.1	0.7	2.1	2.9	4.7	14.8	22.2	...	...	135
0.1	0.2	0.4	1.4	3.3	2.4	14.1	22.4	...	...	136
1.2	0.3	2.2	0.6	0.1	2.0	9.4	13.6	...	...	137
0.0	0.3	0.4	1.0	8.7	3.1	5.3	2.6	...	...	138

Item	1978	1979	1980	1981	1982	1983	1984	1985
BALANCE OF PAYMENTS								*Million US dollars;*
139 Merchandise exports, fob	...	...	...	...	...	...	...	...
140 Merchandise imports, fob	...	...	...	...	...	...	...	...
141 Trade balance	...	...	...	...	...	...	...	...
142 Other goods, services and income	...	...	...	...	...	...	...	...
143 Credit	...	...	...	...	...	...	...	...
144 Debit	...	...	...	...	...	...	...	...
145 Unrequited transfer	...	...	...	...	...	...	...	...
146 Private	...	...	...	...	...	...	...	...
147 Official	...	...	...	...	...	...	...	...
148 Current balance	...	...	...	...	...	...	...	...
149 Direct investment	...	...	...	...	...	...	...	...
150 Portfolio investment	...	...	...	...	...	...	...	...
151 Other long-term capital [c]	...	...	...	...	...	...	...	...
152 Other short-term capital	...	...	...	...	...	...	...	...
153 Net errors and omissions	...	...	...	...	...	...	...	...
154 Overall balance	...	...	...	...	...	...	...	...
155 Allocation of SDRs	...	...	...	...	...	...	...	...
156 Monetary movements	...	...	...	...	...	...	...	...
INTERNATIONAL RESERVES								*Million US dollars;*
157 Total	...	...	...	...	...	...	...	...
158 Gold, national valuation	...	...	...	...	...	...	...	...
159 Foreign exchange	...	...	...	...	...	...	...	...
160 Reserve position in the Fund	0.01	0.01	0.01	0.01	0.01	0.01	0.01	0.01
161 SDRs	...	2.50	4.82	5.28	3.44	1.65	...	...
EXCHANGE RATES								*Riels per*
162 End of period	...	...	...	...	...	...	...	...
163 Average of period	...	...	...	4.0	4.0	4.2	7.0	7.0
EXTERNAL INDEBTEDNESS								*Million US dollars;*
164 Total outstanding and disbursed	...	...	...	...	...	...	...	...
165 Long-term	...	...	...	...	...	...	...	...
166 Public and publicly guaranteed	...	...	...	...	...	...	...	...
167 Private non-guaranteed	...	...	...	...	...	...	...	...
168 Short-term	...	...	...	...	...	...	...	...
169 Use of IMF credit	...	...	...	...	...	...	...	...
Debt service								*Transactions*
170 Principal repayments on LT debt	...	...	...	...	...	...	...	...
171 Interest on long-term debt	...	...	...	...	...	...	...	...
172 Interest on short-term debt	...	...	...	...	...	...	...	...
Average terms of new commitments								
173 Interest (%)	...	...	...	...	...	...	...	...
174 Maturity (years)	...	...	...	...	...	...	...	...
175 Grace period (years)	...	...	...	...	...	...	...	...
176 Grant element (%)	...	...	...	...	...	...	...	...

Footnotes:

a   Includes home ownership and import duties.
b   For 1990-1993, figure includes information, government (other agencies) and contingencies.
c   Includes other short-term capital.

	1986	1987	1988	1989	1990	1991	1992	1993	1994	1995	
Calendar year											
	34.6	36.2	44.8	79.2	85.8	212.5	264.5	283.0	489.8	855.6	139
	-120.7	-151.9	-169.3	-176.0	-163.5	-245.0	-443.4	-471.0	-725.9	-1188.0	140
	-86.1	-115.7	-124.5	-96.8	-77.7	-32.5	-178.9	-188.0	-236.1	-332.4	141
	1.6	8.7	-11.6	-12.2	-16.5	1.3	-60.5	-72.7	-126.0	-113.9	142
	...	...	...	...	...	...	...	64.3	56.6	110.6	143
	...	...	...	...	...	...	...	-137.0	-182.6	-224.5	144
	2.0	3.0	20.5	19.8	44.6	6.0	271.3	279.6	254.8	289.1	145
	1.0	1.5	2.0	2.5	3.0	3.5	...	9.0	20.0	20.0	146
	1.0	1.5	18.5	17.3	41.6	2.5	...	270.6	234.8	269.1	147
	-82.5	-104.0	-115.6	-89.2	-49.6	-25.2	31.9	18.9	-107.3	-157.2	148
	...	109.3	109.6	109.0	94.2	25.2	33.0	54.1	69.0	101.7	149
	...	...	...	...	...	...	...	...	...	...	150
	...	...	...	...	...	...	-26.9	-54.0	14.3	10.9	151
	...	...	...	...	...	...	...	...	...	...	152
	...	-6.1	-1.8	-21.7	-34.8	-10.0	-41.2	-3.5	60.0	58.7	153
	...	-0.8	-7.8	-1.9	9.8	-10.0	-3.2	15.5	36.0	14.1	154
	...	...	...	...	...	...	...	...	...	...	155
	...	0.8	7.8	1.9	-9.8	10.0	3.2	-15.5	-36.0	-14.1	156
As of end of period											
	...	...	...	...	...	...	...	24.18	118.50	191.88	157
	...	...	...	...	...	...	...	...	...	...	158
	...	...	...	...	...	...	...	8.50	102.60	176.70	159
	0.01	0.01	0.01	0.01	0.01	0.01	1.28	–	–	–	160
	...	...	...	...	...	...	...	15.68	15.90	15.18	161
US dollar											
	...	...	142.0	218.0	600.0	520.0	2000.0	2305.0	2575.0	2526.0	162
	19.6	51.3	108.8	167.2	418.3	703.0	1266.6	2689.0	2545.2	2450.8	163
As of end of period											
	...	...	...	1717	1887	1895	1873	1862	1943	...	164
	...	...	...	1578	1721	1721	1713	1718	1774	...	165
	...	...	...	1578	1721	1721	1713	1718	1774	...	166
	...	...	...	–	–	–	–	–	–	...	167
	...	...	...	114	140	146	145	135	140	...	168
	23	27	25	25	27	27	15	9	30	...	169
during the year											
	...	...	...	–	–	–	–	–	–	...	170
	...	...	...	11	29	15	1	–	0	...	171
	...	...	...	1	1	1	1	1	1	...	172
	...	...	...	–	–	–	–	0.9	0.7	...	173
	...	...	...	–	–	–	–	39.9	40.0	...	174
	...	...	...	–	–	–	–	10.4	10.4	...	175
	...	...	...	–	–	–	–	79.6	80.7	...	176

	Item	1978	1979	1980	1981	1982	1983	1984	1985
001	**POPULATION**	956.2	969.0	981.2	993.9	1008.6	1023.3	1036.8	*Million;* 1051.0
002	**LABOR FORCE** [a]	406.82	415.92	429.03	441.65	456.74	467.07	484.33	*Million;* 501.12
003	Employed [b]	401.52	410.24	423.61	437.25	452.95	464.36	481.97	498.73
004	Agriculture	283.18	286.34	291.22	297.77	308.59	311.51	308.68	311.30
005	Industry [c]	60.91	62.98	67.14	69.75	72.04	73.97	79.30	83.49
006	Services	57.43	60.92	65.25	69.73	72.32	78.88	93.99	103.94
007	Unemployed [d]	5.30	5.68	5.42	4.40	3.79	2.71	2.36	2.39
008	Unemployment rate, % [d]	5.3	5.4	4.9	3.8	3.2	2.3	1.9	1.8
	NATIONAL ACCOUNTS *At Current Market Prices*								*Billion Yuan;*
009	GDP by Industrial Origin	362.4	403.8	451.8	486.2	529.5	593.5	717.1	896.4
010	Agriculture	101.8	125.9	135.9	154.6	176.2	196.1	229.6	254.2
011	Mining								
012	Manufacturing	160.7	177.0	199.7	204.8	216.2	237.6	278.9	344.9
013	Electricity, gas and water								
014	Construction	13.8	14.4	19.6	20.7	22.1	27.1	31.7	41.8
015	Trade	26.6	22.0	21.4	25.6	19.9	23.1	41.2	87.8
016	Transport and communications	17.3	18.4	20.5	21.1	23.7	26.5	32.7	40.7
017	Finance								
018	Public administration								
019	Others	42.2	46.1	54.7	59.4	71.4	83.1	103.0	127.0
020	Net factor income from abroad	–	–	–	-0.2	0.7	2.3	3.6	2.5
021	GNP	362.4	403.8	451.8	486.0	530.2	595.7	720.7	898.9
022	Expenditure on GDP	362.4	403.8	451.8	486.2	529.5	593.5	717.1	896.4
023	Private consumption	175.9	200.5	231.7	260.4	286.8	318.3	367.5	458.9
024	Government consumption	48.0	61.4	65.9	70.5	77.0	83.8	102.0	118.4
025	Gross fixed capital formation	107.4	115.1	131.8	125.3	149.3	170.9	212.6	264.1
026	Increase in stocks	30.4	32.3	27.2	32.8	26.7	29.6	34.3	74.5
027	Net exports of goods and services	-1.1	-2.0	-1.5	1.1	9.1	5.1	0.1	-36.7
028	Statistical discrepancy	1.8	-3.6	-3.4	-4.0	-19.4	-14.1	0.7	17.2
	At Constant 1990 Prices								
029	GDP by Industrial Origin	...	...	...	...	...	...	...	...
030	Agriculture	...	...	...	...	...	...	...	...
031	Mining								
032	Manufacturing	...	...	...	...	...	...	...	...
033	Electricity, gas and water								
034	Construction	...	...	...	...	...	...	...	...
035	Trade	...	...	...	...	...	...	...	...
036	Transport and communications	...	...	...	...	...	...	...	...
037	Finance								
038	Public administration								
039	Others	...	...	...	...	...	...	...	...
040	Net factor income from abroad	...	...	...	...	...	...	...	...
041	GNP	...	...	...	...	...	...	...	...
042	Expenditure on GDP	...	...	...	...	...	...	...	...
043	Private consumption	...	...	...	...	...	...	...	...
044	Government consumption	...	...	...	...	...	...	...	...
045	Gross fixed capital formation	...	...	...	...	...	...	...	...
046	Increase in stocks	...	...	...	...	...	...	...	...
047	Exports of goods and services	...	...	...	...	...	...	...	...
048	Less: Imports of goods and services	...	...	...	...	...	...	...	...
049	Statistical discrepancy	...	...	...	...	...	...	...	...

	1986	1987	1988	1989	1990	1991	1992	1993	1994	1995	
As of 1 July											
	1066.8	1084.0	1101.6	1118.7	1135.2	1150.8	1165.0	1178.4	1191.8	1204.9 *	001
Year ending 31 December											
	515.46	530.60	546.30	557.07	571.23	587.17	597.96	606.40	619.46	...	002
	512.82	527.83	543.34	553.29	567.40	583.65	594.32	602.20	614.70	...	003
	312.54	316.63	322.49	332.25	341.17	349.65	347.95	339.66	333.86	...	004
	89.80	93.43	96.61	95.68	96.98	99.47	102.19	104.67	107.74	...	005
	110.48	117.77	124.24	125.36	129.25	134.53	144.18	157.87	173.10	...	006
	2.64	2.77	2.96	3.78	3.83	3.52	3.64	4.20	4.76	...	007
	2.0	2.0	2.0	2.6	2.5	2.3	2.3	2.6	2.8	...	008
Calendar year											
	1020.2	1196.3	1492.8	1690.9	1854.8	2161.8	2663.8	3463.4	4658.5	5773.4	009
	276.4	320.4	383.1	422.8	501.7	528.9	580.0	688.2	945.7	1136.5	010
											011
	396.7	458.6	577.7	648.4	685.8	808.7	1028.5	1414.4	1935.9	2471.8	012
											013
	52.6	66.6	81.0	79.4	85.9	101.5	141.5	228.5	301.2	355.6	014
	94.3	115.9	161.8	168.7	142.0	208.7	273.5	309.1	407.6	509.4	015
	47.6	54.5	66.1	78.6	114.8	141.0	168.2	212.3	264.9	323.7	016
											017
											018
	152.6	180.3	223.1	293.0	324.6	373.0	472.1	610.9	803.2	976.4	019
	0.9	-0.8	-0.6	0.9	5.1	4.5	1.4	-7.4	-8.9	-8.4	020
	1021.1	1195.5	1492.2	1691.8	1859.8	2166.3	2665.2	3456.1	4649.6	5765.0	021
	1020.2	1196.3	1492.8	1690.9	1854.8	2161.8	2663.8	3463.4	4658.5	5773.4	022
	517.5	596.1	763.3	852.4	911.3	1031.6	1246.0	1568.2	2123.0	2634.3	023
	136.7	149.0	172.7	203.3	225.2	283.0	349.2	450.0	598.6	697.3	024
	309.8	374.2	462.4	433.9	473.2	594.0	831.7	1298.0	1685.6	2000.1	025
	74.8	58.0	87.1	175.6	171.2	157.7	131.9	201.8	173.6	278.7	026
	-25.5	1.2	-15.1	-18.6	51.0	61.8	27.6	-67.9	63.4	157.9	027
	6.9	17.8	22.4	44.4	22.8	33.7	77.4	13.4	14.3	5.1	028
	...	...	...	...	...	...	...	...	...	...	029
	...	...	...	...	...	...	...	...	...	...	030
											031
	...	...	...	...	...	...	...	...	...	...	032
											033
											034
	...	...	...	...	...	...	...	...	...	...	035
	...	...	...	...	...	...	...	...	...	...	036
	...	...	...	...	...	...	...	...	...	...	037
											038
	...	...	...	...	...	...	...	...	...	...	039
	...	...	...	...	...	...	...	...	...	...	040
	...	...	...	...	...	...	...	...	...	...	041
	...	...	...	...	...	...	...	...	...	...	042
	...	...	...	...	...	...	...	...	...	...	043
	...	...	...	...	...	...	...	...	...	...	044
	...	...	...	...	...	...	...	...	...	...	045
											046
	...	...	...	...	...	...	...	...	...	...	047
	...	...	...	...	...	...	...	...	...	...	048
	...	...	...	...	...	...	...	...	...	...	049

Item	1978	1979	1980	1981	1982	1983	1984	1985
Investment Financing, at current prices								
050 Gross domestic capital formation	137.8	147.4	159.0	158.1	176.0	200.5	246.9	338.6
051 Gross national saving	138.5	141.9	154.1	155.0	166.4	193.7	251.2	321.6
052 Gross domestic saving	138.5	141.9	154.1	155.2	165.7	191.4	247.6	319.1
053 Net factor income from abroad	–	–	–	-0.2	0.7	2.3	3.6	2.5
054 Foreign saving	-0.7	5.6	4.9	3.1	9.6	6.8	-4.4	17.1
055 Net transfers from abroad	...	...	...	...	...	...	...	...
056 Net borrowing from abroad	...	...	...	...	...	...	...	...
Per Capita GDP, Yuan								
057 Current prices	379	417	460	489	525	580	692	853
058 Constant 1990 prices	...	...	...	...	...	...	...	...
PRODUCTION								**Thousand metric tons;**
Agriculture								
059 1.Rice	136930	143750	139910	143955	161600	168865	178255	168569
060 2.Wheat	53842	62733	55210	59640	68470	81390	87815	85805
061 3.Maize	55950	60040	62600	59210	60560	68210	73410	63826
062 4.Sugarcane	21116	21508	22807	29668	36882	31141	39519	51549
063 5.Sweet potatoes, yams & potatoes	31740	28460	28730	25970	27050	29250	28480	26040
064 6.Soya beans	7570	7460	7940	9341	9030	9760	9330	10500
065 7.Beetroots	2702	3106	6305	6360	6712	9182	8284	8919
Mining								
066 1.Crude petroleum	93640	106150	105950	101220	102120	106070	114610	124900
067 2.Iron ore, Fe content	34790	36730	38020	34170	35510	37380	40010	43840
068 3.Coal	618000	635000	620000	622000	666000	715000	789000	872000
Manufacturing								
069 1.Cement	65236	73896	79857	82897	95196	108250	123020	145950
070 2.Crude steel	31780	34480	37120	35600	37164	40020	43470	46790
071 3.Phosphate fertilizers	1033	1817	2308	2508	2537	2666	2360	1760
072 4.Nitrogenous fertilizers	7639	8821	9993	9857	10219	11094	12210	11438
Production Indexes								**Period**
073 Agriculture, 1979-81 = 100	92.0	99.0	100.0	106.0	118.0	121.3	132.8	130.3
074 Mining, 1978 = 100	100.0	102.0	101.0	104.0	108.0	119.0	128.0	135.4
075 Manufacturing, 1980 = 100	94.3	99.9	100.0	91.7	105.6	124.5	148.7	176.9
ENERGY								**Annual**
Crude petroleum, Mn m.t.								
076 Production	104	106	106	101	102	106	115	125
077 Exports	11	13	12	14	15	15	22	30
078 Imports	1	0	0	–	0	–	–	–
079 Consumption	93	93	93	88	88	91	93	95
Coal, Mn m.t.								
080 Production	433	445	620	622	666	715	789	872
081 Exports	3	4	6	7	65	7	7	8
082 Imports	2	2	2	2	2	2	2	2
083 Consumption	433	444	610	606	649	687	750	816
Natural gas, Bn cu. m.								
084 Production	14	15	14	13	12	12	12	13
085 Consumption	14	15	14	13	12	12	12	13
Electricity, Bn kWh								
086 Production	257	282	301	309	328	351	377	411
087 Exports	...	...	...	...	...	...	0	0
088 Imports	...	0	–	0	0	0	0	1
089 Consumption	257	282	301	310	328	352	378	412
PRICE INDEXES								**Period**
090 Consumer (National), 1985 = 100	...	...	...	...	...	...	...	100.0
091 Consumer (Urban), 1985 = 100	74.5	75.9	81.6	83.6	85.2	87.0	89.3	100.0
092 Retail, 1978 = 100	100.0	102.0	108.1	110.7	112.8	114.5	117.7	128.1
093 Implicit GDP deflator, 1990 = 100	...	...	...	...	...	...	...	...

1986	1987	1988	1989	1990	1991	1992	1993	1994	1995	
384.6	432.2	549.5	609.5	644.4	751.7	963.6	1499.8	1859.2	2278.8	050
366.9	450.4	556.2	636.2	723.3	851.7	1070.0	1437.9	1928.0	2433.4	051
366.0	451.2	556.8	635.3	718.3	847.2	1068.6	1445.3	1936.9	2441.8	052
0.9	-0.8	-0.6	0.9	5.1	4.5	1.4	-7.4	-8.9	-8.4	053
17.8	-18.2	-6.7	-26.7	-78.9	-100.0	-106.4	61.9	-68.8	-154.6	054
...	...	...	...	...	...	...	...	...	...	055
...	...	...	...	...	...	...	...	...	...	056
956	1104	1355	1512	1634	1879	2287	2939	3909	4792 *	057
...	...	...	...	...	...	...	...	...	...	058

Calendar year

172224	174260	169110	180130	189331	183813	186222	177702	175933	185000 *	059
90040	85900	85430	90807	98229	95953	101587	106390	99297	102000 *	060
70856	79240	77351	78930	96819	98773	95383	102704	99275	112000 *	061
50219	47363	49064	48795	57620	67898	73011	64194	60927	64400 *	062
25337	28200	26970	27304	27430	27160	28442	31811	30254	32000 *	063
11614	12470	11650	10227	11000	9710	12520	19504	20956	17800 *	064
8306	8140	12810	9243	14525	16289	15069	12048	12526	13600 *	065
130690	134140	137050	137640	138310	140992	142100	145240	146080	...	066
50640	54324	56405	58200	62380	88489	195938	234730	...	...	067
894000	928000	980000	1054000	1080000	1087000	1116000	1150000	1240000	...	068
166060	186250	210136	210295	209710	252610	308220	367880	421180	...	069
52200	56280	59430	61590	66350	71000	80940	89560	92610	...	070
2340	3384	3692	3728	4114	4597	4622	4190	5044	...	071
11592	13423	13656	14240	14636	15101	15705	15256	17363	...	072

averages

133.8	140.5	143.2	146.1	159.3	166.7	171.4	179.4	188.2	191.9	073
142.1	...	...	...	...	...	...	...	...	...	074
137.5	232.5	243.5	258.5	...	...	...	...	...	...	075

values

131	134	137	138	138	141	142	145	146	149	076
29	27	26	24	24	29	22	19	18	...	077
0	–	1	3	3	12	11	15	12	...	078
102	107	112	116	118	124	132	138	140	...	079
894	928	980	1054	1080	1087	1116	1150	1210	1298	080
10	14	16	15	17	20	20	20	24	...	081
2	2	2	2	2	1	1	1	1	...	082
869	928	994	1034	1055	1104	1141	1209	1285	...	083
14	14	14	15	15	16	16	17	17	18	084
14	14	14	15	15	16	16	17	17	...	085
450	497	545	585	621	678	754	838	928	1000	086
0	0	0	0	0	0	0	0	4	...	087
1	1	2	2	2	3	5	5	2	...	088
451	499	547	587	623	680	759	843	926	...	089

averages

106.5	114.3	135.8	160.2	165.2	170.8	181.7	208.4	258.6	...	090
107.0	116.4	140.5	163.3	165.4	173.8	188.8	219.2	274.1	...	091
135.8	145.7	172.7	203.4	207.7	213.7	225.2	254.9	310.2	...	092
...	...	...	...	...	...	...	...	...	...	093

Item	1978	1979	1980	1981	1982	1983	1984	1985
MONEY AND BANKING [e]								**Billion Yuan;**
094 Money supply (M1)	58.04	92.15	114.88	134.52	148.84	174.89	244.94	301.73
095 Currency in circulation	21.20	...	...	...	...	...	...	98.78
096 Demand deposits	36.84	...	...	...	...	...	...	202.95
097 Quasi-money	30.93	40.63	52.23	63.25	77.73	96.39	114.91	185.76
098 Money supply (M2)	88.97	132.78	167.11	197.77	226.57	271.28	359.85	487.49
099 Foreign assets (net)	0.54	-1.64	-2.78	2.67	16.14	23.95	27.03	21.91
100 Domestic credit	139.31	198.11	242.25	273.99	304.67	343.70	451.45	592.95
101 Claims on govt. sector (net)	-45.69	-5.85	0.82	-2.48	-0.56	0.59	9.49	-9.33
102 Claims on private sector	185.00	203.96	241.43	276.47	305.23	343.11	441.96	602.28
103 Claims on other financial insts.								
104 Other items	-50.88	-63.69	-72.36	-78.89	-94.24	-96.37	-118.63	-127.37
GOVERNMENT FINANCE								**Billion Yuan;**
Central Government [f]								
105 Current revenue	112.11	110.33	108.52	108.96	112.40	124.90	150.19	186.64
106 Taxes	51.93	53.78	57.17	62.99	70.00	77.56	94.74	204.08
107 Non-taxes	60.18	56.55	51.35	45.97	42.40	47.34	55.45	-17.44
108 Current expenditure	111.10	127.39	121.27	111.50	115.33	129.25	154.64	184.48
109 Current surplus/deficit	1.01	-17.06	-12.75	-2.54	-2.93	-4.35	-4.45	2.16
110 Capital receipts	...	...	...	...	...	...	...	...
111 Capital expenditure	45.19	51.47	41.94	33.06	30.92	38.28	48.89	58.38
112 Capital account surplus/deficit	-45.19	-51.47	-41.94	-33.06	-30.92	-38.28	-48.89	-58.38
113 Net lending	...	-3.53	-4.30	-7.31	-8.39	-7.94	-7.73	-8.99
114 Overall surplus/deficit	-44.18	-72.06	-58.99	-42.91	-42.24	-50.57	-61.07	-65.21
Financing								
115 Domestic borrowing	...	...	...	...	4.38	4.16	4.25	6.06
116 Foreign borrowing	0.15	3.64	4.30	7.31	4.00	3.78	3.48	2.92
117 Foreign grants	...	...	...	...	...	...	...	...
118 Use of cash balances	44.03	68.42	54.69	35.60	33.86	42.63	53.34	56.23
Expenditure by Function, Central Govt.								
119 Total	111.10	127.39	121.27	111.50	115.33	129.25	156.44	182.23
120 General public services	4.91	5.69	6.68	7.09	8.16	10.22	13.73	14.36
121 Defence	16.78	22.27	19.38	16.80	17.64	17.71	18.08	19.15
122 Education								
123 Health	14.70	17.52	19.90	21.15	24.30	28.25	33.21	40.84
124 Social security & welfare	1.89	2.21	2.03	2.17	2.14	2.40	2.52	3.12
125 Housing & community amenities	...	...	...	...	...	...	...	...
126 Economic services	70.78	76.16	67.08	54.44	54.32	63.52	78.47	89.50
127 Agriculture	7.70	9.01	8.21	7.37	7.99	8.67	9.60	10.10
128 Industry								
129 Electricity, gas & water								
130 Transport and communications	1.78	2.10	2.28	2.37	2.38	2.79	3.07	3.52
131 Other economic services	61.30	65.05	56.59	44.70	43.95	52.06	65.80	75.88
132 Others	2.04	3.54	6.20	9.85	8.77	7.15	10.43	15.26
EXTERNAL TRADE								**Million US dollars;**
133 Exports, fob	9745	13658	18119	22007	22321	22226	26139	27350
134 Imports, cif	10893	15675	20017	22014	19285	21390	27410	42253
135 Trade balance	-1148	-2017	-1898	-7	3036	836	-1271	-14903
Exports, by SITC section								
136 Food and live animals	2316	2701	2985	2924	2908	2853	3232	3803
137 Beverage and tobacco	71	86	78	60	97	104	110	105
138 Crude materials excl. fuels	1417	1804	1711	1948	1653	1892	2421	2653
139 Mineral fuels, etc.	1345	2654	4280	5228	5314	4666	6027	7132
140 Animal, vegetable oil & fats	67	70	60	88	78	105	144	135
141 Chemicals	234	424	1120	1342	1196	1251	1364	1358
142 Basic manufactures	444	609	3999	4706	4302	4365	5054	4493
143 Machines, transport equipment	332	464	843	1087	1263	1221	1493	772

	1986	1987	1988	1989	1990	1991	1992	1993	1994	1995	
As of end of period											
	385.90	457.40	548.74	583.42	700.95	898.78	1171.43	1424.42	2153.99	2557.83	094
	121.84	145.46	213.40	234.40	264.44	317.78	433.63	...	...	...	095
	264.06	311.94	335.34	349.02	436.51	581.00	737.80	...	...	...	096
	248.96	338.34	411.47	555.89	767.24	961.11	1261.30	1583.15	2538.04	3514.67	097
	634.86	795.74	960.21	1139.31	1468.19	1859.89	2432.73	3007.57	4692.03	6072.50	098
	10.59	29.20	33.81	40.42	103.79	145.58	168.52	168.53	506.45	638.50	099
	794.18	970.87	1153.64	1349.79	1668.92	2002.67	2449.92	2986.11	4310.37	5293.60	100
	5.86	20.80	30.54	24.66	42.07	58.20	101.05	109.48	133.26	132.34	101
	788.32	950.07	1123.10	1325.13	1626.85	1944.47	2348.87	2876.63	4177.11	5161.26	102
											103
	-169.91	-204.33	-227.24	-250.90	-304.52	-288.36	-185.71	-147.07	-124.79	140.40	104
Calendar year											
	226.03	236.89	262.80	291.90	331.30	361.10	312.15	409.30	500.50	...	105
	209.07	214.00	239.10	273.10	282.30	299.00	312.20	404.00	487.10	...	106
	16.96	22.89	23.70	18.80	49.00	62.10	-0.05	5.30	13.40	...	107
	233.08	182.10	207.40	240.20	272.70	307.37	274.30	332.80	420.70	...	108
	-7.05	54.79	55.40	51.70	58.60	53.73	37.85	76.50	79.80	...	109
	...	...	...	...	...	...	...	...	...	...	110
	67.18	62.80	63.30	61.30	72.60	74.00	...	...	...	...	111
	-67.18	-62.80	-63.30	-61.30	-72.60	-74.00	...	...	...	...	112
	-13.80	...	...	...	...	...	...	...	...	...	113
	-88.03	-8.01	-7.90	-9.60	-14.00	-20.27	-23.70	-20.00	-57.40	...	114
	6.25	6.31	13.10	5.50	19.70	28.13	46.01	38.13	...	...	115
	7.57	10.65	13.00	16.50	17.80	18.01	20.89	35.79	...	...	116
	...	...	...	...	...	...	...	...	...	...	117
	74.21	-8.95	-18.20	-12.40	-23.50	-25.87	-43.20	-53.92	...	...	118
	223.17	238.40	272.27	301.50	284.23	345.42	...	...	...	...	119
	18.24	19.54	23.94	28.48	33.35	37.58	46.34	58.58	...	...	120
	20.10	20.98	21.80	25.15	29.03	33.03	37.79	42.58	...	...	121
											122
	48.51	50.58	58.12	66.84	73.76	84.97	79.30	95.80	...	...	123
	3.60	3.70	4.20	4.96	5.50	6.73	6.65	7.53	...	...	124
	8.00	8.50	10.10	...	...	...	...	...	...	...	125
	123.47	126.00	139.70	143.53	154.62	160.86	182.10	214.40	...	...	126
	12.40	13.40	15.90	19.71	22.18	24.36	26.90	...	...	...	127
											128
											129
	3.66	3.31	3.90	4.50	4.69	5.24	6.46	...	...	...	130
	107.41	109.29	119.90	119.32	127.75	131.26	148.74	...	...	...	131
	1.25	9.10	14.41	32.54	...	22.26	...	...	...	...	132
Calendar year											
	30942	39437	47516	52538	62091	71843	84940	91744	121006	148770	133
	42904	43216	55268	59140	53345	63791	80585	103959	115614	132078	134
	-11962	-3779	-7752	-6602	8746	8052	4355	-12215	5392	16692	135
	4448	4781	5890	6145	6609	7226	8309	8399	10015	9954	136
	119	175	235	314	342	529	720	902	1002	1369	137
	2908	3650	4257	4212	3537	3486	3143	3052	4127	4374	138
	3683	4544	3950	4321	5237	4754	4692	4109	4069	5335	139
	114	81	74	86	161	150	139	205	495	454	140
	1733	2235	2897	3201	3730	3818	4348	4623	6236	9094	141
	5886	8570	10489	10897	12576	14456	16136	16392	23218	32243	142
	1094	1741	2769	3874	5588	7149	13220	15281	21895	31391	143

Item	1978	1979	1980	1981	1982	1983	1984	1985
144 Misc. manufactured goods	3519	4846	2836	3725	3705	3804	4697	3486
145 Unclassified goods	–	–	207	899	1805	1965	1597	3413
Exports, by principal commodity								
146 1. Crude petroleum	958	1750	2690	3355	3216	2899	4201	5236
147 2. Cotton yarn & cloth	636	767	854	926	836	1075	1502	1289
148 3. Cereals	309	352	399	275	199	191	419	1040
149 4. Aquatic products	258	348	365	359	315	278	305	275
150 5. Coal	100	177	258	344	358	306	291	314
Imports, by SITC section								
151 Food and live animals	...	2264	2927	3622	4201	3122	2331	1553
152 Beverage and tobacco	...	22	36	213	130	46	116	206
153 Crude materials excl. fuels	...	1849	3554	4027	3012	2459	2542	3236
154 Mineral fuels, etc.	...	99	203	83	183	111	139	172
155 Animal, vegetable oil & fats	...	188	239	99	108	70	80	122
156 Chemicals	...	1627	2909	2606	2936	3183	4237	4469
157 Basic manufactures	...	4862	4154	4035	3906	6289	7318	11898
158 Machines, transport equipment	...	4053	5119	5866	3204	3988	7245	16239
159 Misc. manufactured goods	...	711	542	558	486	782	1182	1902
160 Unclassified goods	...	–	334	905	1119	1340	2220	2456
Direction of Trade								*Million US dollars;*
161 Exports, Total	9745.0	13657.0	18136.0	21473.0	21863.0	22094.0	24822.0	27325.0
162 1. Hong Kong	2532.6	3328.3	4353.2	5262.7	5180.6	5796.7	6586.1	7148.1
163 2. United States	270.7	595.0	982.6	1505.1	1764.7	1713.0	2312.5	2336.2
164 3. Japan	1718.7	2764.1	4032.2	4746.6	4806.4	4517.0	5155.0	6091.4
165 4. Germany	329.5	459.2	710.5	834.9	773.2	859.1	764.1	745.7
166 5. Korea, Rep. of	–	–	–	–	–	–	–	–
167 6. Singapore	247.9	296.5	420.9	657.5	647.8	566.9	1208.7	2063.2
168 7. United Kingdom	370.4	478.9	563.7	412.5	307.9	600.5	329.1	357.5
169 8. Russia	...	...	...	...	...	...	...	...
170 9. Netherlands	92.2	136.9	196.8	458.9	293.7	326.1	317.1	327.0
171 10. Italy	165.5	302.8	351.1	258.2	236.2	232.3	302.5	294.4
172 Imports, Total	10915.0	15675.0	19501.0	21628.0	18919.0	21311.0	25951.0	42478.0
173 1. Japan	3105.2	3944.0	5168.9	6183.0	3901.7	5495.2	8056.9	15178.4
174 2. United States	721.1	1856.6	3830.2	4682.4	4304.6	2753.0	3837.1	5198.7
175 3. Hong Kong	74.7	214.4	569.8	1236.3	1314.2	1709.8	2830.2	4762.1
176 4. Germany	1030.1	1739.4	1332.9	1336.5	966.8	1208.5	1258.5	2447.4
177 5. Korea, Rep. of	–	–	–	–	–	–	–	–
178 6. Russia	...	...	...	...	...	...	...	...
179 7. Italy	190.9	308.7	248.8	344.4	320.0	303.1	432.5	902.7
180 8. Singapore	46.3	104.7	189.8	113.1	103.1	113.7	140.8	240.7
181 9. Australia	715.1	985.2	1063.0	558.9	914.0	613.1	896.7	1124.0
182 10. France	247.1	406.2	314.7	394.7	231.1	639.1	357.1	717.8
Trade Indexes								*1980 = 100;*
Unit value index								
183 Exports	53.3	74.7	100.0	121.5	123.2	122.7	144.3	150.9
184 Imports	55.7	80.2	100.0	109.9	96.3	106.8	136.9	211.0
185 Terms of Trade	95.7	93.1	100.0	110.6	127.9	114.9	105.4	71.5
BALANCE OF PAYMENTS								*Million US dollars;*
186 Merchandise exports, fob	9607	13658	18492	22027	21125	20707	23905	25108
187 Merchandise imports, fob	-10745	-15619	-21243	-20292	-16876	-18717	-23891	-38231
188 Trade balance	-1138	-1961	-2751	1735	4249	1990	14	-13123
189 Other goods, services and income	-168	-270	-294	-206	939	1739	1574	1463
190 Credit	999	1693	2409	3130	3604	4028	4819	4533
191 Debit	-1167	-1963	-2703	-3336	-2665	-2289	-3245	-3070

1986	1987	1988	1989	1990	1991	1992	1993	1994	1995	
4948	6273	8268	10755	12686	16620	34233	38781	49937	54549	144
6009	7387	8687	8733	11625	13655	0	0	12	7	145
2392	3141	2580	2750	3402	2889	2774	2409	2000	2239	146
1695	2060	1999	2025	1993	2199	2448	2645	3193	3988	147
875	539	562	992	544	1075	1547	1473	1532	76	148
478	703	933	985	1316	1181	1366	1254	1815	2087	149
400	476	515	554	654	748	743	702	771	1011	150
1625	2443	3476	4192	3335	2799	3146	2206	3137	6131	151
172	263	346	202	157	200	238	245	68	393	152
3143	3321	5090	4835	4107	5003	5775	5438	7437	10158	153
504	539	787	1650	1272	2113	3570	5819	4035	5127	154
205	349	369	875	982	719	525	502	1809	2601	155
3771	5008	9139	7556	6648	9277	11157	9704	12130	17300	156
11192	9730	10410	12335	8906	10493	19274	28527	28084	28772	157
16781	14607	16697	18207	16845	19601	31312	45023	51467	52638	158
1877	1878	1982	2073	2103	2439	5588	6495	6768	8265	159
3634	5078	6972	7215	8990	11147	0	0	679	693	160
Calendar year										
31357.0	39444.0	47646.0	52916.0	62876.0	71940.0	85492.0	91611.0	120822.0	148755.0	161
9776.3	13764.2	18239.2	21915.9	27162.6	32137.6	37511.3	22067.5	32365.4	36003.5	162
2632.7	3030.4	3398.7	4413.6	5313.9	6198.0	8598.8	16976.5	21421.4	24743.9	163
5078.6	6391.8	8046.4	8394.7	9210.4	10251.8	11699.3	15782.3	21489.8	28466.4	164
1011.2	1223.2	1491.0	1608.7	2062.1	2355.6	2446.5	3970.7	4762.1	5672.2	165
–	–	–	–	432.7	2178.7	2437.6	2860.0	4376.0	6687.9	166
1216.5	1322.8	1493.6	1692.1	2015.6	2014.2	2030.8	2244.5	2563.0	3499.7	167
1437.4	532.0	659.2	635.1	663.7	727.6	922.7	1928.5	2414.4	2790.8	168
...	...	...	...	...	...	2336.8	2691.5	1577.9	1674.2	169
462.8	606.2	749.1	759.4	942.8	1062.7	1200.2	1608.8	2271.9	3232.7	170
363.1	570.3	746.0	714.9	872.6	932.0	1095.5	1305.8	1590.9	2067.5	171
43244.0	43218.0	55344.0	59131.0	53915.0	63855.0	81843.0	103552.0	115629.0	132007.0	172
12463.2	10087.2	11062.1	10533.9	7655.9	10031.7	13685.6	23302.5	26318.9	29007.3	173
4718.2	4835.6	6633.0	7863.6	6591.0	8010.3	8902.7	10632.8	13976.7	16123.2	174
5572.0	8437.0	12004.7	12540.4	14565.0	17543.3	20538.7	10501.1	9487.8	8598.9	175
3626.5	3129.4	3450.4	3379.0	2980.0	3048.6	4022.9	6055.9	7136.0	8034.7	176
–	–	–	–	236.4	1066.1	2623.0	5360.0	7318.2	10287.6	177
...	...	...	...	...	...	3512.0	4985.9	3466.0	3798.8	178
1141.4	1248.1	1552.0	1835.4	1086.9	1458.3	1748.2	2738.0	3067.8	3116.2	179
552.8	617.6	1018.4	1498.9	849.5	1062.5	1237.5	2647.0	2481.4	3398.2	180
1403.1	1325.4	1112.6	1472.3	1361.3	1556.4	1671.3	1945.0	2447.8	2584.6	181
742.0	899.2	986.7	1420.3	1673.7	1571.9	1498.9	1645.0	1939.9	2648.7	182
Period averages										
170.8	217.7	262.2	289.9	342.7	396.5	...	...	...	...	183
214.3	215.9	276.1	295.4	266.5	318.6	...	...	...	...	184
79.7	100.8	95.0	98.1	128.6	124.5	...	...	...	...	185
Calendar year										
25756	34734	41054	43220	51519	58919	69568	75659	102561	...	186
-34896	-36395	-46369	-48840	-42354	-50176	-64385	-86313	-95271	...	187
-9140	-1661	-5315	-5620	9165	8743	5183	-10654	7290	...	188
1727	1737	1094	922	2558	3698	63	-2127	-717	...	189
4927	5413	6327	6497	8872	10698	14844	15583	22357	...	190
-3200	-3676	-5233	-5575	-6314	-7000	-14781	-17710	-23074	...	191

	Item	1978	1979	1980	1981	1982	1983	1984	1985
192	Unrequited transfers [g]	528	626	570	575	494	519	452	249
193	Private	597	656	640	467	...	...	...	...
194	Official	-69	-30	-70	108	...	...	...	...
195	Current balance [g]	-778	-1605	-2475	2104	5682	4248	2040	-11411
196	Capital account [g]	...	...	...	...	-8	-8	-10	-6
197	Direct investment	...	...	57	265	386	543	1124	1030
198	Portfolio investment	...	...	...	-9	21	-621	-1638	3027
199	Other long-term capital	830	822	1711	-50				
200	Other short-term capital	-241	1554	76	-959	-69	-148	-489	4914
201	Net errors and omissions	...	...	...	...	293	128	-889	6
202	Overall balance	-189	771	-631	1351	6305	4142	138	-2440
203	Allocations of SDRs	...	...	145	155	...	...	...	...
204	Monetary movement	189	-771	486	-1506	-6305	-4142	-138	2440
	INTERNATIONAL RESERVES								*Million US dollars;*
205	Total [h]	2141	2744	3116	5574	11840	15451	17801	13214
206	Gold, national valuation	584	590	571	516	491	464	435	486
207	Foreign exchange [h]	1557	2154	2262	4783	11135	14476	16705	11913
208	Reserve position in the Fund	...	...	191	–	–	176	255	332
209	SDRs	...	...	92	275	214	335	406	483
	EXCHANGE RATES								*Yuan per*
210	End of period	1.5771	1.4962	1.5303	1.7455	1.9227	1.9809	2.7957	3.2015
211	Average of period	1.6836	1.5550	1.4984	1.7045	1.8925	1.9757	2.3200	2.9367
	EXTERNAL INDEBTEDNESS								*Million US dollars;*
212	Total outstanding & disbursed	623	2183	4504	5798	8358	9609	12082	16696
213	Long-term	623	2183	4504	4914	5220	5301	6179	9937
214	Public and publicly guaranteed	623	2183	4504	4914	5220	5301	6179	9937
215	Private non-guaranteed	0	0	0	0	0	0	0	0
216	Short-term	0	0	0	0	2300	3984	5600	6419
217	Use of IMF credit	0	0	0	884	838	324	303	340
	Debt service								*Transactions*
218	Principal repayments on LT debt	0	0	612	1204	1302	1389	1287	1297
219	Interest on long-term debt	0	61	318	518	541	523	610	586
220	Interest on short-term debt	0	0	0	0	248	277	386	594
	Average terms of new commitments								
221	Interest (%)	6.6	7.7	10.3	8.1	6.8	7.5	7.4	7.4
222	Maturity (years)	10.7	8.3	11.0	13.2	18.7	16.7	18.1	11.8
223	Grace period (years)	1.5	1.9	3.3	3.7	5.6	4.5	4.8	4.1
224	Grant element (%)	13.5	8.3	4.4	14.6	25.6	17.4	18.1	13.5

Footnotes:

a   Refers to labor force within the working age range 16-50 for men and 16-45 for women, excluding military personnel, prisoners and the disabled. This series excludes unemployed rural laborers also.

b   Refers to social labor force that generates income including total staff and workers, employees in urban private enterprises, urban individual laborers, rural laborers and other social laborers.

c   Includes those in mining, manufacturing, water supply, electricity generation and supply, steam, hot water and gas sectors.

d   Refers to urban unemployment only.

e   Refers to consolidated data from the People's Bank of China, the specialized banks, and the rural credit cooperatives except data before the fourth quarter of 1985 which excluded the rural credit cooperatives and the People's Construction Bank of China.

f   Refers to consolidated central and local governments.

g   Unrequited transfers consist of current and capital transfers from 1978-1981. From 1982 onwards, capital transfers are classified as a separate account (capital account) from the current account balance.

h   Foreign exchange comprises the foreign exchange holdings of the People's Bank of China and the Bank of China. Beginning July 1992, foreign exchange holdings of the Bank of China are excluded.

1986	1987	1988	1989	1990	1991	1992	1993	1994	1995	
329	138	128	308	155	642	942	1079	-41	...	192
...	...	...	...	...	...	...	...	...	...	193
...	...	...	...	...	...	...	...	...	...	194
-7084	214	-4093	-4390	11878	13083	6188	-11702	6532	...	195
50	86	291	73	119	189	213	93	376		196
1425	1669	2344	2613	2657	3453	7156	23115	31787	...	197
1568	1051	876	-180	-241	235	-57	3049	3543	...	198
							...	...	...	199
2951	3281	3913	1290	839	4344	-7349	-2690	-2685	...	200
-958	-1518	-957	115	-3205	-6767	-8211	-10096	-9100	...	201
-2048	4783	2374	-479	12047	14537	-2060	1769	30453	...	202
									...	203
2048	-4783	-2374	479	-12047	-14537	2060	-1769	-30453	...	204

As of end of period

1986	1987	1988	1989	1990	1991	1992	1993	1994	1995	
11994	16934	19135	18547	30209	44308	21230	22999	53560	76037	205
541	629	594	587	623	634	610	612	646	660	206
10514	15236	17548	17022	28594	42664	19443	21199	51620	73579	207
370	429	407	398	430	433	758	704	755	1216	208
569	640	586	540	562	577	419	484	539	582	209

US dollar

1986	1987	1988	1989	1990	1991	1992	1993	1994	1995	
3.7221	3.7221	3.7221	4.7221	5.2221	5.4342	5.7518	5.8000	8.4462	8.3174	210
3.4528	3.7221	3.7221	3.7651	4.7832	5.3234	5.5146	5.7620	8.6187	8.3514	211

As of end of year

1986	1987	1988	1989	1990	1991	1992	1993	1994	1995	
23719	35340	42439	44933	52750	59779	69508	84178	100536	...	212
16571	25963	32620	37118	45515	49479	58663	70632	85137	...	213
16571	25963	32620	37118	45515	49479	58462	70076	84554	...	214
0	0	0	0	0	0	200	556	583	...	215
6076	8221	8806	6907	6766	10300	10846	13546	15399	...	216
1072	1155	1013	908	469	0	0	0	0	...	217

during the year

1986	1987	1988	1989	1990	1991	1992	1993	1994	1995	
1874	1956	2285	2365	3319	4123	5213	6729	6343	8992 *	218
645	1125	1611	2511	2534	2953	2708	2630	3844	4657 *	219
417	640	534	628	547	707	697	809	948	...	220
6.4	6.6	7.2	7.3	7.5	6.1	6.2	5.2	5.7	...	221
14.8	15.4	14.9	18.0	16.6	18.4	14.9	14.0	16.1	...	222
4.5	4.0	3.7	4.6	3.9	4.8	3.5	3.9	4.8	...	223
19.7	19.1	15.5	17.2	15.6	25.1	19.3	23.5	24.5	...	224

Item	1978	1979	1980	1981	1982	1983	1984	1985
								Thousand;
001 **POPULATION**	18.5	18.2	17.9	17.5	17.4	17.4	17.0	17.2
								Thousand;
002 **LABOR FORCE** [a]	...	...	...	...	...	...	...	...
003 Employed [b]	...	3.9	3.6	5.8	3.7	3.6	3.6	4.2
004 Agriculture	...	0.3	0.2	1.7	0.2	0.2	0.2	0.2
005 Manufacturing								
006 Mining	...	0.4	0.4	0.4	0.4	0.4	0.3	0.5
007 Others	...	3.2	3.0	3.7	3.1	3.0	3.1	3.5
008 Unemployed	...	...	...	...	...	...	...	...
009 Unemployment rate, %	...	...	...	...	...	...	...	...
NATIONAL ACCOUNTS [c]								*Thousand New Zealand dollars;*
At Current Market Prices								
010 GDP by Industrial Origin	...	...	...	...	32457	35683	44846	55089
011 Agriculture	...	...	...	...	6667	6567	7413	8200
012 Mining	...	...	...	...	95	47	93	74
013 Manufacturing	...	...	...	...	997	1585	2220	2449
014 Electricity, gas and water	...	...	...	...	47	137	420	56
015 Construction	...	...	...	...	833	864	928	1406
016 Trade	...	...	...	...	8460	8872	11717	15508
017 Transport and communications	...	...	...	...	3291	3455	4682	5754
018 Finance	...	...	...	...	813	622	1082	2079
019 Public administration	...	...	...	...	9176	10892	13077	15761
020 Others	...	...	...	...	2078	2642	3214	3802
021 Net factor income from abroad	...	...	...	...	...	...	...	...
022 GNP	...	...	...	...	...	...	...	...
At Constant 1990 Prices								
023 GDP by Industrial Origin	...	...	...	...	69728	70049	79028	85954
024 Agriculture	...	...	...	...	17285	16819	17272	17627
025 Mining	...	...	...	...	186	84	151	106
026 Manufacturing	...	...	...	...	1921	2759	3511	3449
027 Electricity, gas and water	...	...	...	...	99	260	720	84
028 Construction	...	...	...	...	1622	1529	1502	1995
029 Trade	...	...	...	...	16999	16801	20027	23233
030 Transport and communications	...	...	...	...	7461	6854	8354	8918
031 Finance	...	...	...	...	2317	1618	2474	3896
032 Public administration	...	...	...	...	16713	17066	18415	20370
033 Others	...	...	...	...	5125	6259	6602	6276
034 Net factor income from abroad	...	...	...	...	...	...	...	...
035 GNP	...	...	...	...	...	...	...	...
Per Capita GDP, New Zealand $								
036 Current prices	...	...	...	...	1865	2051	2638	3203
037 Constant *1990* prices	...	...	...	...	4007	4026	4649	4997
ENERGY								*Annual*
Electricity, *Mn kWh*								
038 Production	10	13	12	11	10	10	11	12
039 Consumption	10	13	12	11	10	10	11	12
PRICE INDEXES								*Period*
040 Consumer(Rarotonga), *1975 = 100*I	165.6	184.2	209.5	254.1	285.9	307.4	343.9	387.2
June 1989 = 100								
041 Food	166.0	185.0	208.0	254.0	284.0	301.0	338.0	373.0
042 Implicit GDP deflator *1990 = 100*	...	...	...	...	46.5	50.9	56.7	64.1

	1986	1987	1988	1989	1990	1991	1992	1993	1994	1995	
As of 1 July											
	17.1	17.7	17.7	17.9	18.4	18.5	18.6	19.2	19.6	20.2	001
Calendar year											
	...	...	...	...	...	...	...	...	...	...	002
	4.3	...	...	4.8	4.9	6.6	...	6.3	...	...	003
	0.2	...	...	0.3	0.3	0.8	...	0.4	...	...	004
										...	005
	0.5	...	...	0.4	0.4	0.3	...	0.3	...	...	006
	3.6	...	...	4.2	4.3	5.5	...	5.6	...	...	007
	...	...	...	...	...	...	...	...	...	...	008
	...	...	...	...	...	...	...	...	...	...	009
Calendar year											
	67095	76505	88964	102422	106891	116732	126871	137009	147148	157286	010
	8965	9793	14281	19747	18891	21136	22971	24807	26643	28478	011
	47	41	106	11	404	148	161	174	187	200	012
	3332	4033	4033	3271	3046	4841	5261	5681	6102	6522	013
	715	1151	865	975	1086	1315	1429	1543	1657	1771	014
	2742	3937	3706	3448	2485	4566	4963	5360	5756	6153	015
	16077	18061	19460	20791	23409	26570	28877	31185	33493	35800	016
	7962	8658	8357	12068	12652	13377	14539	15701	16863	18025	017
	4654	5095	9051	11525	12679	11175	12145	13116	14086	15057	018
	18540	22027	25187	26871	28242	28027	30461	32895	35329	37763	019
	4061	3709	3918	3715	3997	5577	6064	6547	7032	7517	020
	...	...	...	...	...	...	...	...	...	...	021
	...	...	...	...	...	...	...	...	...	...	022
	91843	91947	98444	105073	106891	109095	111290	113231	114959	116510	023
	17437	14858	18091	19010	18891	19753	20150	20502	20815	21095	024
	61	49	117	12	404	139	141	144	146	148	025
	4273	4745	4440	3432	3046	4524	4615	4695	4767	4831	026
	964	1401	969	1029	1086	1229	1253	1275	1295	1312	027
	3490	4597	4067	3628	2485	4268	4354	4429	4497	4558	028
	21599	21938	21772	21900	23409	24831	25331	25773	26166	26519	029
	10971	10692	9431	12750	12652	12502	12754	12976	13174	13352	030
	7351	6886	10709	12331	12679	10443	10654	10839	11005	11153	031
	20081	21737	24939	27079	28242	26193	26720	27186	27601	27973	032
	5616	5044	3909	3902	3997	5213	5318	5412	5493	5569	033
	...	...	...	...	...	...	...	...	...	...	034
	...	...	...	...	...	...	...	...	...	...	035
	3924	4322	5026	5722	5809	6310	6821	7136	7508	7786	036
	5371	5195	5562	5870	5809	5897	5983	5897	5865	5767	037
values											
	13	14	14	15	16	16	17	19	19	19	038
	13	14	14	15	16	16	17	19	...	...	039
averages											
	425.7	471.8	510.8	100.8	106.1	112.3	116.2	124.7	128.0	129.1	040
	412.6	456.7	494.2	101.4	105.3	107.6	111.4	119.0	121.3	120.9	041
	73.1	83.2	90.4	97.5	100.0	107.0	114.0	121.0	128.0	135.0	042

	Item	1978	1979	1980	1981	1982	1983	1984	1985
	GOVERNMENT FINANCE							*Thousand New Zealand dollars;*	
	Central government								
043	Current revenue	12991	13862	15887	19436	21182	24873	29437	33966
044	Taxes	3359	4140	5456	6551	7008	8494	9922	11636
045	Non-taxes	9632	9722	10431	12885	14174	16379	19515	22330
046	Current expenditure	12488	13830	15232	18156	20712	24372	27922	33012
047	Current surplus/deficit	503	32	655	1280	470	501	1515	954
048	Capital receipts	–	–	–	–	–	–	–	–
049	Capital expenditure	788	871	1182	595	722	501	1400	1101
050	Capital account surplus/deficit	-788	-871	-1182	-595	-722	-501	-1400	-1101
051	Overall surplus/deficit	-285	-839	-527	685	-252	–	115	-147
	Financing								
052	Domestic borrowing	...	...	...	...	...	...	...	...
053	Foreign borrowing	...	...	...	...	...	...	...	...
054	Foreign grants	...	...	...	...	...	...	...	...
055	Use of cash balance	...	...	...	...	...	...	...	...
	EXTERNAL TRADE							*Thousand New Zealand dollars;*	
056	Exports, fob [d]	2428	3779	4190	5015	4980	4890	6515	6223
057	Imports, cif	18226	22459	23610	28731	26854	35085	36168	49663
058	Trade balance	-15798	-18680	-19420	-23716	-21874	-30195	-29653	-43440
	Exports, by SITC section [d]								
059	Food & live animals	1494	1160	1067	2234	2083	1654	1908	2294
060	Beverage & tobacco	–	797	902	–	–	–	–	–
061	Crude materials excl. fuels	216	960	505	694	640	465	1653	1161
062	Mineral fuels, etc.	–	–	–	–	–	–	–	–
063	Animal, vegetable oil & fats	–	–	–	–	–	–	–	33
064	Chemicals	–	–	–	–	–	–	3	–
065	Basic manufactures	–	113	338	–	37	85	111	17
066	Machines, transport equipment	–	–	–	–	–	40	27	–
067	Misc. manufactured goods	717	696	1292	2087	2016	2646	2813	2510
068	Unclassified goods	–	53	85	–	204	–	–	208
	Exports, by principal commodity [d]								
069	1. Clothing	698	696	1292	2038	1950	2586	2718	2307
070	2. Fruit - fresh & canned	1550	1957	1970	2006	1595	1144	1548	1661
071	3. Copra	188	960	504	348	433	315	1013	628
	Imports, by SITC section								
072	Food & live animals	3978	4716	5270	6009	5714	6917	7729	10260
073	Beverage & tobacco	1107	1201	1531	1415	1329	1666	2033	2871
074	Crude materials excl. fuels	409	383	509	632	999	537	770	978
075	Mineral fuels, etc.	1329	1771	2428	5345	2256	5900	3447	6287
076	Animal, vegetable oil & fats	80	76	98	140	112	120	181	263
077	Chemicals	1022	1814	1430	1686	1851	1730	2459	3303
078	Basic manufactures	3540	5027	4718	5343	5760	6509	7512	9784
079	Machines, transport equipment	4391	4847	4382	3690	5265	6800	6937	9143
080	Misc. manufactured goods	2265	2544	3122	4392	3530	3872	4901	6600
081	Unclassified goods	105	80	122	79	38	1034	199	174
	EXCHANGE RATES							*New Zealand dollars*	
082	End of period	0.9376	1.0140	1.0392	1.2130	1.3652	1.5277	2.0938	2.0060
083	Average of period	0.9644	0.9785	1.0267	1.1528	1.3326	1.4968	1.7640	2.0234

Footnotes:

a   Figures for 1981 are census data which included approximately 2000 workers (workers on agricultural holdings, workers on commission basis and unpaid family workers) who are not usually included in the employment surveys.

b   The Employment Survey for 1983 covers wage and salary workers on the main island (Rarotonga) only while the other employment surveys cover all wage and salary earners from all islands.

	1986	1987	1988	1989	1990	1991	1992	1993	1994	1995	
Fiscal year beginning 1 April											
	41837	47068	56943	55080	60253	79745	67507	72940	96861	78793 *	043
	15991	19591	28939	29126	32942	40037	45841	...	...	52851 *	044
	25846	27477	28004	25954	27311	39708	21666	...	...	25942 *	045
	40559	45332	54593	55829	58205	76918	63787	70788	95728	75401 *	046
	1278	1736	2350	-749	2048	2827	3719	2152	1133	3392 *	047
	–	–	–	–	–	–	–	–	–	– *	048
	1349	1925	1348	1233	1947	2647	3859	4052	6256	8217 *	049
	-1349	-1925	-1348	-1233	-1947	-2647	-3859	-4052	-6256	-8217 *	050
	-71	-189	1002	-1982	101	180	-140	-1900	-5123	-4825 *	051
											052
	...	...	...	...	...	...	...	...	...	...	053
	...	...	...	...	...	...	...	...	...	...	054
	...	...	...	...	...	...	...	...	...	...	055
Calendar year											
	9233	12039	6627	4667	8172	9428	6030	7155	6963	6959	056
	50309	56982	64526	73078	86331	94505	109163	124249	142911	160832	057
	-41076	-44943	-57899	-68411	-78159	-85077	-103133	-117094	-135948	-153873	058
	1773	1676	2532	1891	2083	1588	1849	1894	1571	2233	059
	–	–	–	1	23	15	2	–	–	–	060
	932	1229	545	1113	566	416	228	206	220	99	061
	–	–	–	–	2	2	4	10	18	16	062
	–	–	–	–	–	1	–	3	–	1	063
	25	12	10	26	3	2	14	27	9	1	064
	49	72	12	504	4370	6634	3186	3833	4189	3910	065
	364	532	426	286	599	56	78	173	152	9	066
	5917	8435	2965	644	526	714	669	907	774	687	067
	–	–	137	202	–	–	–	102	29	3	068
	5635	8081	2936	578	334	53	16	33	258	347	069
	1282	1049	2065	1456	1400	1358	1622	1720	916	965	070
	206	64	–	–	–	–	–	2	–	–	071
	10285	11862	13318	15079	12361	19525	22553	25682	29526	33228	072
	3090	3341	3826	4370	3803	5614	6495	7380	8489	9553	073
	1097	1192	1342	1548	2908	1985	2303	2609	3001	3377	074
	6020	6490	7750	8617	2684	11189	12872	14649	16878	18978	075
	326	320	374	425	170	529	611	708	800	918	076
	3766	3967	4536	5235	9590	6691	7754	8797	10132	11403	077
	9849	11406	12757	14462	25647	18731	21636	24639	28339	31893	078
	8723	10440	11628	13074	20227	17011	19638	22390	25738	28965	079
	7084	7770	8821	10086	8871	12975	15002	17047	19622	22082	080
	69	194	174	182	71	255	299	348	386	435	081
per US dollar											
	1.9102	1.5209	1.5916	1.6745	1.7013	1.8481	1.9444	1.7895	1.5564	1.5307	082
	1.9132	1.6946	1.5244	1.6708	1.6750	1.7265	1.8584	1.8495	1.6844	1.5235	083

c   From 1990-94, national accounts estimates were based on turnover tax.
d   Prior to 1985, exports to Nauru were excluded.

	Item	1978	1979	1980	1981	1982	1983	1984	1985
001	**POPULATION**	607	621	634	646	658	672	686	*Thousand;* 697
	LABOR FORCE								*Thousand;*
002	Employed [a]	76.6	78.5	80.5	81.4	78.3	80.1	78.6	81.1
003	Agriculture	2.8	2.3	2.6	2.5	2.3	2.5	2.2	2.6
004	Mining	0.8	0.7	1.1	1.1	1.1	1.2	1.2	1.2
005	Manufacturing	13.5	13.9	15.4	14.2	13.5	14.7	14.2	14.1
006	Others	59.5	61.6	61.4	63.6	61.4	61.7	61.0	63.2
007	Unemployed	...	...	...	...	14.6	16.0	16.8	18.6
008	Unemployment rate, %	...	...	...	...	...	6.9	7.4	7.9
	NATIONAL ACCOUNTS *At Current Factor Cost*								*Million Fiji dollars;*
009	GDP by Industrial Origin	642.9	779.3	901.0	953.6	1020.5	1031.7	1151.7	1177.7
010	Agriculture	141.1	168.0	199.5	189.7	206.8	189.9	220.2	215.7
011	Mining	0.6	1.4	-2.5	0.7	6.1	6.5	0.9	13.9
012	Manufacturing	70.8	98.5	107.6	100.1	108.9	94.4	112.5	111.3
013	Electricity, gas and water	7.2	10.8	14.8	20.0	22.0	27.2	41.7	40.4
014	Construction	47.5	57.2	73.4	81.8	80.6	75.3	61.3	63.9
015	Trade	112.9	143.9	162.4	188.3	180.8	183.3	203.7	210.0
016	Transport and communications	61.1	67.4	80.4	86.2	90.3	98.4	108.5	121.7
017	Finance	86.5	100.6	112.4	126.3	138.9	140.7	153.9	165.9
018	Public administration [b]	132.2	151.9	184.0	205.8	227.5	255.0	281.4	271.3
019	Others					7.1	7.7	8.3	10.0
020	Less: Imputed service charges	17.0	20.4	31.0	45.3	48.6	46.8	40.5	46.6
021	Indirect taxes less subsidies	59.2	72.8	82.7	102.4	92.9	110.4	123.6	138.8
022	GDP at current market prices	702.1	852.1	983.7	1056.0	1113.4	1142.1	1275.3	1316.5
023	Net factor income from abroad	-4.5	-12.5	-14.6	-9.2	-33.8	-28.2	-30.3	-36.3
024	GNP at current market prices	697.6	839.6	969.1	1046.8	1079.6	1113.9	1245.0	1280.2
	At Current Market Prices								
025	Expenditure on GDP	702.1	852.1	983.7	1056.1	1113.4	1142.2	1275.3	1316.5
026	Private consumption	458.2	519.6	574.7	660.0	684.7	748.2	794.1	838.1
027	Government consumption	115.1	143.9	156.7	173.1	203.8	231.6	244.9	252.4
028	Gross fixed capital formation	149.8	197.3	249.8	280.5	262.6	239.2	218.0	239.1
029	Increase in stocks	27.8	59.6	63.4	81.7	21.9	2.3	23.3	12.2
030	Exports of goods and services	299.5	385.8	477.5	454.4	481.3	498.1	546.2	583.6
031	Less: Imports of goods and services	330.5	432.1	510.8	606.6	552.6	560.1	559.8	588.6
032	Statistical discrepancy	-17.8	-22.0	-27.5	13.0	11.7	-17.1	8.7	-20.3
	At Constant 1977 Factor Cost								
033	GDP by Industrial Origin	616.6	690.9	679.3	719.9	712.2	683.9	741.3	703.7
034	Agriculture	139.5	163.4	152.8	172.6	175.6	143.8	180.9	156.2
035	Mining	0.4	0.4	0.3	0.4	0.6	0.6	0.7	0.8
036	Manufacturing	74.3	87.7	80.7	88.9	86.5	77.7	91.0	79.3
037	Electricity, gas and water	6.1	6.5	6.5	6.8	7.0	7.4	8.0	8.4
038	Construction	44.5	50.7	59.7	60.5	53.4	50.9	39.8	38.1
039	Trade	108.7	124.9	117.3	125.5	113.0	122.3	122.0	124.8
040	Transport and communications	57.6	66.9	66.8	70.6	77.6	78.0	87.7	90.3
041	Finance	80.2	83.1	84.3	87.9	90.8	93.7	95.8	97.6
042	Public administration [b]	121.3	122.9	124.1	125.3	126.6	129.8	136.3	130.1
043	Others	0.6	2.8	5.2	1.4	1.4	1.3	1.5	1.5
044	Less: Imputed service charges	16.6	18.4	18.5	20.0	20.3	21.6	22.3	23.3
045	GDP at *1977* market prices	...	...	...	...	...	...	...	...
046	Net factor income from abroad	...	...	...	...	...	...	...	...
047	GNP at *1977* market prices	...	...	...	...	...	...	...	...

	1986	1987	1988	1989	1990	1991	1992	1993	1994	1995	
As of July 1											
	714	721	719	724 *	732 *	742 *	753 *	765 *	779 *	793 *	001
Midyear											
	79.9	78.2	77.5	88.2	89.0	91.5	92.5	94.3	95.3	97.3	002
	2.2	2.0	2.0	2.1	2.3	2.6	2.2	2.0	2.3	2.3	003
	1.2	1.4	1.5	1.5	1.4	1.1	1.4	1.9	1.9	2.1	004
	14.0	13.9	14.0	19.7	21.1	23.4	21.2	23.5	23.7	25.3	005
	62.5	60.9	60.0	64.9	64.2	64.4	67.7	66.9	67.4	67.6	006
	18.0	23.0	23.4	15.1	16.2	15.2	14.2	15.8	16.5	...	007
	7.5	9.3	9.2	6.1	6.4	5.9	5.4	5.9	6.0	...	008
Calendar year											
	1326.1	1329.2	1433.3	1661.4	1810.9 *	1938.3 *	2098.3 *	2224.2 *	2338.2 *	...	009
	277.1	306.2	279.9	325.5	...	...	...	...	...	...	010
	17.5	31.2	62.1	55.6	...	...	...	...	...	...	011
	136.6	157.3	137.2	174.6	...	...	...	...	...	...	012
	48.2	44.0	51.9	55.0	...	...	...	...	...	...	013
	64.0	49.6	59.5	66.3	...	...	...	...	...	...	014
	223.5	208.8	282.2	379.1	...	...	...	...	...	...	015
	131.7	132.8	163.5	169.2	...	...	...	...	...	...	016
	181.9	182.0	197.0	216.2	...	...	...	...	...	...	017
	299.7	276.2	273.4	305.2	...	...	...	...	...	...	018
	10.4	11.1	11.7	12.5	...	...	...	...	...	...	019
	64.5	70.0	85.2	97.9							020
	135.6	136.0	154.3	199.2	234.4 *	234.0 *	282.9 *	333.6 *	398.7 *	...	021
	1461.7	1465.2	1587.6	1860.6	2045.3 *	2172.3 *	2381.2 *	2557.8 *	2736.9 *	...	022
	-34.3	-47.9	-35.2	-36.3	-37.7	-30.1	-40.6	-15.5	-68.1	...	023
	1427.4	1417.3	1552.4	1824.3	2007.6	2142.2	2340.6	2542.3	2668.8	...	024
	1461.7	1465.3	1587.6	1860.6	2045.3 *	2172.3 *	2381.2 *	2557.8 *	2736.9 *	...	025
	873.3	959.7	1093.5	1210.2	1366.0 *	1484.0 *	1580.1 *	1688.8 *	1786.2 *	...	026
	252.6	255.1	263.4	296.1	339.6 *	396.5 *	449.0 *	513.9 *	454.2 *	...	027
	215.4	229.9	191.5	231.8	321.9 *	266.9 *	280.5 *	344.0 *	292.8 *	...	028
	51.1	4.5	12.6	24.5	35.0 *	26.0 *	30.0 *	40.0 *	40.0 *	...	029
	609.0	663.9	894.8	1162.9	1310.1 *	1279.0 *	1316.1 *	1424.6 *	1611.0 *	...	030
	577.0	616.3	814.6	1058.9	1329.7 *	1235.5 *	1258.6 *	1486.5 *	1573.7 *	...	031
	37.4	-31.5	-53.7	-6.0	2.4 *	-44.6 *	-15.9 *	33.0 *	126.4 *	...	032
	760.5	711.5	726.8	820.5	849.4	853.8	880.9	896.7	936.9	...	033
	186.0	173.8	170.0	189.6	181.9	179.4	184.9	191.2	207.5	...	034
	1.3	1.3	1.9	1.9	1.8	1.2	1.6	1.7	1.5	...	035
	94.6	83.9	83.2	92.8	99.1	103.7	102.9	108.0	116.7	...	036
	9.0	8.9	9.6	10.1	10.6	11.0	12.0	12.3	13.3	...	037
	38.7	29.1	29.2	35.5	29.7	34.2	42.2	29.6	32.3	...	038
	136.0	117.1	130.3	160.7	183.4	172.6	168.9	183.4	193.5	...	039
	89.8	87.7	94.6	112.7	121.1	124.1	135.9	136.5	142.3	...	040
	98.4	95.6	96.4	99.4	106.2	107.5	110.2	113.4	116.6	...	041
	129.0	134.8	132.9	140.6	142.5	147.2	150.3	150.0	144.1	...	042
	1.5	1.4	1.4	1.6	1.7	1.7	1.7	1.8	1.8	...	043
	23.7	22.0	22.6	24.4	28.6	28.7	29.8	31.1	32.7	...	044
	...	...	...	...	...	...	...	...	...	...	045
	...	...	...	...	...	...	...	...	...	...	046
	...	...	...	...	...	...	...	...	...	...	047

Item	1978	1979	1980	1981	1982	1983	1984	1985
Investment Financing, at current prices								
048 Gross domestic capital formation	177.6	256.9	313.2	362.2	284.5	241.5	241.2	251.3
049 Gross national saving	124.4	176.1	237.7	213.8	191.1	134.2	206.0	189.7
050 Gross domestic saving	128.9	188.6	252.3	223.0	224.9	162.4	236.3	226.0
051 Net factor income from abroad	-4.5	-12.5	-14.6	-9.2	-33.8	-28.2	-30.3	-36.3
Per Capita GDP, Fiji dollars								
052 Current market prices	1157	1372	1552	1635	1692	1700	1859	1889
053 Constant *1977* factor cost	1016	1113	1071	1114	1082	1018	1081	1010
PRODUCTION								*Thousand metric tons;*
Agriculture								
054 1. Sugarcane [c]	2849	4058	3360	3931	4075	2202	4290	3042
055 2. Paddy rice	16	19	18	17	20	16	22	28
056 3. Fish	6	7	7	11	11	11	11	10
057 4. Copra	26	22	23	21	22	24	25	21
058 5. Chicken	2	3	3	3	3	4	4	4
Manufacturing								
059 1. Gold, kg.	873	923	774	960	1423	1248	1509	1865
060 2. Silver, kg.	327	326	208	260	576	405	473	459
061 3. Sugar [c]	347	473	397	470	486	275	480	341
062 4. Cement	87	87	83	92	88	110	98	93
063 5. Flour	16	19	19	20	21	23	22	24
064 6. Soap	5	6	6	6	6	7	7	6
065 7. Coconut oil	16	15	15	14	15	16	16	13
Production indexes								*Period*
066 Agriculture, *1979-81 = 100*	82.5	103.7	93.2	103.2	107.8	79.5	117.8	97.2
067 Mining, *1986 = 100*	30.6	32.3	27.1	33.6	49.8	43.7	52.8	65.3
068 Manufacturing, *1986 = 100*	74.7	73.7	81.2	89.4	88.3	79.1	93.8	83.6
ENERGY								*Annual*
Coal, *'000 m.t.*								
069 Imports	25	23	21	18	23	18	22	16
070 Consumption	25	23	21	18	23	18	22	16
Electricity, *Mn kWh*								
071 Production	284	305	306	321	331	327	369	395
072 Consumption	284	305	306	321	331	327	369	395
PRICE INDEXES								*Period*
073 Consumer, *1985	1993 = 100*	58.1	62.6	71.7	79.7	85.2	91.0	95.8	100.0
074 Food	55.2	58.6	67.5	76.2	83.3	88.2	92.3	100.0
075 Non-food	60.7	64.8	73.9	81.7	86.6	92.4	96.7	100.0
076 Implicit GDP deflator, *1977 = 100* [d]	104.3	112.8	132.6	132.5	143.3	150.9	155.4	167.4
MONEY AND BANKING [e]								*Million Fiji dollars;*
077 Money supply (M1)	103	117	105	126	131	142	142	146
078 Currency in circulation [f]	39	45	44	49	53	59	61	62
079 Demand deposits	64	72	61	77	78	83	81	85
080 Quasi-money	152	189	238	239	264	302	348	356
081 Money supply (M2)	255	306	343	364	395	444	490	502
082 Foreign assets (net) [g]	105	109	134	120	106	108	118	131
083 Domestic credit	172	224	232	279	334	382	413	442
084 Claims on govt. sector (net)	24	30	22	20	39	33	29	32
085 Claims on private sector	127	168	189	233	246	275	325	350
086 Claims on other financial insts. [h]	21	26	21	26	49	73	59	60
087 Other items	-22	-27	-23	-35	-45	-46	-40	-70

	1986	1987	1988	1989	1990	1991	1992	1993	1994	1995	
	266.5	234.4	204.1	256.3	356.9	292.9	310.5	384.0	332.8	...	048
	301.6	202.6	195.4	318.0	302.0	261.7	311.5	339.6	428.4	...	049
	335.9	250.5	230.6	354.3	339.7	291.8	352.1	355.1	496.5	...	050
	-34.3	-47.9	-35.2	-36.3	-37.7	-30.1	-40.6	-15.5	-68.1	...	051
	2047	2032	2208	2570	2794	2928	3162	3344	3513	...	052
	1065	987	1011	1133	1160	1151	1170	1172	1203	...	053
Calendar year											
	4109	2960	3185	4099	4016	3380	3533	3704	4064	...	054
	25	23	32	32	32	29	22	22	18	17	055
	10	12	13	13	13	14	14	14	16	...	056
	23	13	11	13	19	15	16	11	8	...	057
	4	4	4	5	5	6	6	6	8	...	058
	2856	2864	4272	4221	4116	2743	3701	3784	3440	...	059
	774	814	988	1055	779	477	1258	1112	1386	...	060
	502	401	363	461	408	389	426	443	517	...	061
	92	59	44	58	78	79	84	80	94	...	062
	25	26	26	28	25	27	28	33	38	...	063
	7	7	8	6	7	7	7	7	7	...	064
	14	8	7	8	12	9	9	6	5	...	065
averages											
	116.2	93.8	97.5	115.0	120.0	107.0	112.9	114.1	121.0	119.9	066
	100.0	100.3	149.6	147.8	144.1	96.1	129.6	132.5	...	...	067
	100.0	88.9	95.1	104.3	111.9	115.0	117.1	123.9	130.0	...	068
values											
	15	16	17	13	19	18	20	...	...	...	069
	15	16	17	13	19	18	20	...	...	...	070
	406	394	413	437	446	474	470	480	520	...	071
	406	394	413	437	446	474	470	480	520	...	072
averages											
	101.8	107.6	120.3	127.7	138.1	147.1	154.3	162.3 I	100.8	103.0	073
	98.2	104.2	123.4	135.8	146.9	149.3	148.7	158.8 I	100.5	101.2	074
	103.3	110.0	118.7	123.5	133.6	146.0	157.2	164.1 I	101.0	104.0	075
	174.4	186.8	197.2	202.5	213.2	227.0	238.2	248.0	249.6	...	076
As of end of period											
	178	173	279	276	274	293	337	386	368	413 *	077
	63	65	68	78	86	91	103	112	116	...	078
	115	108	212	198	188	202	234	274	252	...	079
	409	435	454	534	734	871	991	1028	1088	1112 *	080
	587	608	733	809	1007	1164	1328	1413	1456	1525 *	081
	190	195	328	332	392	410	499	442	422	514 *	082
	472	541	501	662	781	961	1081	1208	1257	1271 *	083
	48	81	19	53	29	61	82	69	31	21 *	084
	368	394	411	541	676	803	880	994	1081	1112 *	085
	56	66	70	68	75	98	118	144	145	138 *	086
	-75	-128	-96	-184	-165	-208	-252	-236	-223	-260 *	087

	Item	1978	1979	1980	1981	1982	1983	1984	1985
	Deposit Money Banks								
088	Demand deposits	63	70	59	75	75	80	79	82
089	Savings deposits	66	75	80	83	88	99	102	107
090	Time deposits	87	115	158	156	176	203	246	249
091	Domestic credits outstanding	136	174	196	...	...	...	...	...
	GOVERNMENT FINANCE								*Million Fiji dollars;*
	Central Government								
092	Current revenue	161.6	198.7	232.6	259.5	258.3	288.6	325.6	338.9
093	Taxes	132.5	155.5	178.6	206.4	202.9	229.8	266.9	271.4
094	Non-taxes	29.1	43.2	54.0	53.1	55.4	58.8	58.7	67.5
095	Current expenditure	170.3	189.0	223.1	234.1	272.6	310.2	344.4	349.3
096	Current surplus/deficit	-8.7	9.7	9.5	25.4	-14.3	-21.6	-18.8	-10.4
097	Capital receipts	–	6.4	2.0	0.6	2.4	0.4	4.5	5.5
098	Capital expenditure	49.5	56.9	63.0	87.9	80.5	50.7	49.3	53.2
099	Capital account surplus/deficit	-49.5	-50.5	-61.0	-87.3	-78.1	-50.3	-44.8	-47.7
100	Underline account	–	–	-2.2	-4.5	-5.9	–	–	–
101	Overall surplus/deficit	-58.2	-40.8	-53.7	-66.4	-98.3	-71.9	-63.6	-58.1
	Financing								
102	Domestic borrowing	29.0	25.3	19.2	23.1	65.7	53.0	60.3	55.8
103	Foreign borrowing	10.8	17.1	30.5	34.5	23.6	12.1	18.6	14.1
104	Foreign grants	–	–	3.9	6.9	9.0	6.4	10.0	6.1
105	Use of cash balances	18.4	-1.6	0.1	1.9	0.0	0.4	-25.3	-17.9
	Expenditure by Function, Central Govt.								
106	Total	107.0	135.2	145.7	161.2	192.5	218.0	230.8	232.2
107	General public services	22.9	25.5	28.8	31.4	38.3	51.4	48.5	60.3
108	Defence	5.6	7.8	8.4	8.9	13.9	14.2	15.3	15.2
109	Education	31.5	43.4	46.8	52.8	60.1	67.4	74.0	69.6
110	Health	14.4	16.0	18.6	21.4	25.5	29.0	32.3	30.6
111	Social security & welfare	0.8	1.1	1.1	1.0	1.0	1.0	1.2	1.1
112	Housing & community amenities	0.4	1.5	1.1	0.9	0.9	1.2	1.6	1.8
113	Economic services	31.5	39.9	40.8	44.6	52.7	53.5	57.6	53.4
114	Agriculture	2.3	4.9	4.6	5.3	7.8	6.4	6.5	7.0
115	Industry	9.2	7.5	7.9	8.1	9.3	9.6	10.8	10.5
116	Electricity, gas & water	2.4	...	0.2	0.1	0.2	0.3	0.3	0.3
117	Transport & communications	10.3	13.5	13.5	13.9	13.7	15.8	16.9	15.7
118	Other economic services [i]	7.3	14.0	14.6	17.1	21.8	21.4	23.1	19.9
119	Others	0.1	–	0.2	0.2	0.2	0.3	0.3	0.3
	EXTERNAL TRADE								*Thousand Fiji dollars;*
120	Exports, fob	166493	215042	305558	268965	267556	245014	280140	271427
121	Imports, cif	299996	392862	458753	539907	475591	493184	486982	507993
122	Trade balance	-133503	-177820	-153195	-270942	-208035	-248170	-206842	-236566
	Exports, by SITC section								
123	Food & live animals	101248	142259	201580	165541	148301	138938	142530	141286
124	Beverage & tobacco	280	103	85	75	95	241	218	343
125	Crude materials excl. fuels	2063	2529	5025	2722	2521	2881	5816	4659
126	Mineral fuels, etc.	0	0	0	1	0	1	0	2
127	Animal, vegetable oil & fats	13206	11691	6543	6376	6200	10626	18555	7705
128	Chemicals	924	740	752	773	1149	1749	1836	2064
129	Basic manufactures	2254	2256	1915	2861	4748	4280	6010	7406
130	Machines, transport equipment	366	69	69	1242	54	43	95	1809
131	Misc. manufactured goods	634	789	595	752	925	1206	1744	3067
132	Unclassified goods	5339	7149	13090	13389	17205	17910	21064	22288
133	Re-exports	40179	47457	75904	75233	86358	67139	82272	80797

1986	1987	1988	1989	1990	1991	1992	1993	1994	1995	
111	105	207	188	179	194	228	263	239	283 *	088
119	143	183	198	245	242	265	299	307	...	089
288	292	271	336	488	629	725	728	781	...	090
...	...	...	...	...	...	...	...	...	...	091

Fiscal year ending 31 December

348.2	341.2	389.6	461.7	538.2	563.8	550.6	642.7	685.7	683.8 *	092
270.1	260.7	291.2	373.2	441.5	449.7	444.6	525.4	560.6	533.3 *	093
78.1	80.5	98.4	88.5	96.7	114.1	105.9	117.2	125.1	150.5 *	094
371.0	393.9	434.5	454.0	500.7	551.0	600.6	678.7	650.3	692.2 *	095
-22.8	-52.7	-44.9	7.7	37.5	12.8	-50.0	-36.0	35.4	-8.4 *	096
5.0	13.6	28.1	6.6	18.3	12.5	22.5	13.0	10.3	9.9 *	097
56.2	49.5	63.5	91.9	88.6	107.8	104.6	90.4	112.3	94.2 *	098
-51.2	-35.9	-35.4	-85.3	-70.3	-95.3	-82.1	-77.4	-102.0	-84.3 *	099
-27.9	–	–	-35.3	-15.2	–	–	–	–	–	100
-101.9	-88.6	-80.3	-112.9	-48.0	-82.5	-132.1	-113.4	-66.6	-92.7 *	101
63.3	88.7	130.5	50.0	18.0	50.6	62.0	76.8	54.6	76.8 *	102
17.1	7.9	11.3	34.0	21.7	21.6	11.3	20.6	25.7	25.7 *	103
7.6	11.4	21.9	11.8	11.8	7.3	7.2	9.9	4.9	5.1 *	104
13.9	-19.4	-83.4	17.1	-3.5	3.0	51.6	6.1	-18.6	-14.9 *	105
234.4	236.8	210.2	223.9	264.7	282.8	338.4	427.2	457.1	...	106
48.3	49.2	40.7	50.5	78.7	63.6	97.3	94.6	106.1	110.5	107
15.4	26.3	27.9	25.2	25.8	31.1	32.9	36.3	37.1	34.8	108
69.9	68.6	62.8	69.6	69.5	82.6	95.0	137.5	142.9	147.7	109
31.8	31.3	27.5	27.4	31.3	37.8	43.7	50.5	56.9	61.7	110
0.9	0.8	0.6	0.8	0.8	0.8	1.0	4.0	4.9	5.0	111
2.1	2.0	2.0	1.8	2.3	1.0	0.8	3.1	2.7	2.9	112
65.8	58.4	48.6	48.4	56.0	65.1	65.5	98.2	102.0	...	113
16.1	8.9	7.3	6.2	7.4	15.6	9.5	18.9	18.3	18.1	114
13.5	12.6	12.3	12.9	14.2	14.4	16.8	17.9	20.8	...	115
6.2	5.3	4.6	2.0	4.3	6.8	14.3	23.4	28.8	...	116
15.5	14.7	12.4	12.3	13.3	14.9	13.1	18.0	16.0	...	117
14.5	17.0	11.9	15.0	16.9	13.4	11.8	20.0	18.1	...	118
0.3	0.3	0.2	0.3	0.3	0.8	2.2	3.0	4.5	...	119

Calendar year

312443	408604	533246	658617	731865	664599	666976	692402	800495	869941	120
493598	465106	658821	860436	1112901	961767	947110	1109807	1209852	1218933	121
-181155	-56502	-125575	-201819	-381036	-297168	-280134	-417405	-409357	-348992	122
174006	237354	277674	306628	307608	305529	300203	305885	351711	395642	123
582	707	309	387	515	460	365	258	614	453	124
6014	13855	22693	31288	37269	30484	33809	35724	36721	51310	125
0	0	1	2	13	16	13	4	8	18	126
4300	3246	4412	5561	5370	2591	6145	4001	4072	4375	127
2176	3007	3435	4078	4940	4143	4696	4536	5686	5428	128
8352	11118	16757	19606	25216	18790	19264	20642	27434	32492	129
251	256	797	857	1659	2822	2027	3582	4457	4984	130
6445	10238	33242	105145	124812	140946	125568	145213	161462	208712	131
39739	54311	89954	78887	78028	49004	62688	68544	64876	61067	132
70578	74513	83972	106178	146435	109814	112198	104013	143454	105460	133

	Item	1978	1979	1980	1981	1982	1983	1984	1985
	Exports, by principal commodity								
134	1. Sugar	83273	116962	174175	131561	125076	111935	109955	111828
135	2. Gold	4952	6492	12410	11872	15579	16864	20497	21821
136	3. Molasses	4534	7363	11989	9620	5082	3171	6678	6486
137	4. Coconut oil	8941	11683	6528	6355	6165	10579	18467	7636
138	5. Cement	577	236	145	69	10	127	395	714
	Imports, by SITC section								
139	Food & live animals	59965	61838	64934	76589	70764	78098	74736	80057
140	Beverage & tobacco	3731	4818	3851	4522	4030	3623	3560	4299
141	Crude materials excl. fuels	2500	4062	3315	4437	3686	5194	3508	3303
142	Mineral fuels etc.	47314	72424	105711	138501	136873	114753	107051	115365
143	Animal, vegetable oil & fats	4629	5152	5111	5899	5174	6840	9371	10478
144	Chemicals	22265	27489	30546	37329	34999	39063	44286	38835
145	Basic manufactures	57586	75146	85567	89038	78933	91480	90984	100782
146	Machines, transport equipment	58425	88313	103741	117933	82010	93040	86512	91625
147	Misc. manufactured goods	33403	40905	39611	47647	46585	47416	51256	50050
148	Unclassified goods	10178	12715	16366	18012	12537	13677	15718	13199
	Direction of Trade								*Million US dollars;*
149	Exports, Total	203.4	258.7	358.3	311.4	283.6	240.0	255.8	229.8
150	1. Australia	22.1	23.6	26.3	23.1	30.7	27.6	35.2	31.2
151	2. United Kingdom	82.0	95.0	90.4	77.3	63.2	59.2	73.4	68.4
152	3. United States	19.9	38.7	37.3	31.7	27.1	20.0	25.5	11.2
153	4. Japan	1.8	3.4	27.5	22.9	5.5	5.9	6.5	6.9
154	5. New Zealand	17.8	24.6	37.8	25.3	27.3	11.8	10.0	10.7
155	6. Malaysia	6.4	6.0	27.6	25.8	15.1	20.0	21.2	17.5
156	7. Canada	6.3	8.4	24.9	12.4	6.8	5.9	4.7	4.8
157	8. Tonga	5.4	5.9	9.0	13.3	9.9	9.0	8.2	8.2
158	9. American Samoa	1.8	2.0	2.2	2.3	2.1	2.6	3.8	4.5
159	10. Western Samoa	7.6	7.5	7.8	7.3	8.0	9.5	9.1	7.7
160	Imports, Total	356.2	469.7	559.3	631.5	509.2	484.3	449.8	441.5
161	1. Australia	105.9	165.5	171.5	227.2	198.7	185.6	156.2	149.0
162	2. New Zealand	55.2	70.5	81.9	87.7	79.9	79.2	72.5	75.1
163	3. United States	16.5	26.7	38.0	44.6	18.7	18.8	18.2	18.0
164	4. Singapore	24.9	22.9	61.2	44.8	46.8	20.0	24.8	21.4
165	5. Japan	56.5	66.9	79.3	101.0	71.6	81.5	72.8	66.5
166	6. Hong Kong	9.2	10.0	8.5	10.3	8.4	7.5	8.0	7.8
167	7. China, People's Rep. of	–	7.5	9.6	12.0	10.3	10.5	11.4	9.8
168	8. Thailand	2.0	1.8	1.7	2.3	1.9	2.0	2.1	1.7
169	9. United Kingdom	33.0	41.7	40.8	34.7	21.2	24.5	22.8	29.3
170	10. Malaysia	0.7	1.0	1.0	1.0	0.9	0.9	1.3	3.7
	Trade Indexes								*1977 = 100;*
	Quantum index								
171	Exports	97.3	124.7	128.4	120.7	126.2	107.5	118.5	129.0
172	Imports	97.9	116.8	99.0	120.7	100.1	113.0	109.0	100.8
	Unit value index								
173	Exports	107.9	106.9	143.7	126.5	123.9	131.0	129.6	116.7
174	Imports	108.3	123.5	147.8	157.7	161.3	158.2	162.8	160.8
175	Terms of trade	144.9	148.0	250.6	182.5	129.7	131.8	113.4	94.2
	BALANCE OF PAYMENTS [j]								*Million US dollars;*
176	Merchandise exports, fob	179	243	341	282	253	222	250	213
177	Merchandise imports, fob	-302	-412	-491	-546	-441	-429	-423	-393
178	Trade balance	-123	-169	-150	-264	-188	-207	-173	-180
179	Other goods, services & income	80	99	72	79	81	118	130	144
180	Credit	185	233	256	287	292	300	322	...

	1986	1987	1988	1989	1990	1991	1992	1993	1994	1995	
	133716	186158	198347	228286	223669	220400	221281	230688	252183	276112	134
	38632	50557	81519	76197	75832	46612	60723	66746	62607	58598	135
	7913	10559	11375	9781	6436	13300	1311	9991	13602	21301	136
	4162	3022	3423	5270	4919	2338	5718	3662	3787	3899	137
	199	291	462	2060	3347	1865	528	360	197	1283	138
	77701	82447	110838	124468	142881	141444	136192	166939	165889	182314	139
	3464	3452	5047	6511	8169	7888	8133	9863	10489	13182	140
	2928	3272	4311	7699	7552	7864	7198	6423	7023	9106	141
	82101	75725	88603	109839	157113	146326	133487	132710	137252	137470	142
	5867	7939	11578	9643	11228	10087	11329	13138	12679	16487	143
	41311	40077	66084	78167	81577	72525	78634	82142	89521	92835	144
	103156	103485	155017	205987	244245	245175	239342	251559	278999	336961	145
	116214	90162	138893	222013	341565	216265	233473	306255	377204	277783	146
	44495	40958	57357	84953	106582	104005	90150	126590	118476	139333	147
	16361	17589	21093	11156	11989	10188	9172	14188	12320	13462	148

Calendar year

	1986	1987	1988	1989	1990	1991	1992	1993	1994	1995	
	275.8	328.5	365.1	387.0	497.7	450.6	418.0	506.4	595.4	653.0	149
	47.1	58.4	81.2	74.3	87.9	70.9	37.7	107.5	121.2	142.2	150
	96.0	111.6	106.8	97.1	113.9	116.7	132.5	118.9	101.6	114.7	151
	13.0	17.9	11.2	20.0	41.8	50.9	59.7	68.1	94.0	81.6	152
	4.8	9.9	18.6	26.0	29.5	25.7	22.5	29.9	54.1	51.5	153
	18.5	18.9	27.8	44.9	58.2	40.2	24.8	22.1	27.5	30.0	154
	–	24.3	15.2	24.8	–	–	27.1	22.3	29.0	26.8	155
	4.4	4.5	13.2	11.1	10.8	15.0	11.8	18.2	21.9	21.5	156
	–	9.4	10.2	11.5	–	–	13.7	16.3	18.6	21.6	157
	–	5.6	6.0	6.3	–	–	8.9	10.5	12.0	13.9	158
	–	4.3	5.4	5.3	–	–	8.2	8.9	8.9	10.3	159
	435.7	373.9	461.5	661.0	755.2	652.1	630.3	634.8	769.4	756.8	160
	148.1	107.4	135.6	195.5	209.8	205.1	202.2	245.1	277.0	339.0	161
	73.3	63.3	87.3	109.6	123.0	119.4	106.1	130.1	129.7	131.5	162
	20.7	19.7	22.4	32.5	98.6	28.3	55.1	29.5	129.8	35.7	163
	14.6	42.5	19.4	38.3	44.0	40.4	40.2	38.2	51.1	59.3	164
	63.0	45.4	47.1	87.7	83.4	74.1	65.0	58.9	51.1	46.4	165
	7.5	7.5	15.2	19.6	22.0	23.8	20.2	25.3	21.7	24.2	166
	9.3	9.6	12.7	20.5	21.4	18.9	21.3	17.6	16.6	17.3	167
	2.5	4.2	5.5	9.9	13.1	15.3	11.5	13.0	13.8	15.3	168
	18.0	16.6	16.8	18.3	22.8	19.5	19.8	13.7	10.4	11.3	169
	0.0	1.4	3.1	4.5	0.0	0.0	5.7	7.2	7.0	9.3	170

Period averages

	1986	1987	1988	1989	1990	1991	1992	1993	1994	1995	
	118.7	120.8	...	...	...	...	...	...	...	...	171
	99.2	92.1	...	...	...	...	...	...	...	...	172
	156.7	214.2	223.7	...	...	...	...	...	...	...	173
	148.5	181.9	174.2	...	...	...	...	...	...	...	174
	95.6	100.0	142.8	136.0	129.8	147.3	155.9	...	...	...	175

Calendar year

	1986	1987	1988	1989	1990	1991	1992	1993	1994	1995	
	248	313	351	420	416	361	349	368	485	494	176
	-369	-325	-399	-489	-642	-549	-539	-653	-726	-726	177
	-121	-12	-48	-69	-226	-188	-190	-285	-241	-233	178
	117	15	55	67	133	118	122	142	124	156	179
	...	238	273	445	466	479	506	544	599	654	180

Item	1978	1979	1980	1981	1982	1983	1984	1985
181 Debit	-105	-134	-184	-208	-211	-182	-192	...
182 Unrequited transfer	-2	4	32	17	17	25	16	23
183 Private	-4	-9	-2	-9	-3	-2	-4	-11
184 Official	2	13	34	26	20	27	20	34
185 Current balance	-45	-66	-46	-168	-90	-64	-27	-13
186 Direct investment	-11	3	-3	38	36	32	20	1
187 Portfolio investment	-3	23	60	–	–	–	–	8
188 Other long-term capital	12	11	31	95	41	40	12	2
189 Other short-term capital [k]	–	–	-13	–	–	1	3	...
190 Net errors & omissions	28	37	6	16	-15	-12	5	-2
191 Overall balance	-19	8	35	-19	-28	-3	13	-4
192 Allocation of SDRs	–	–	3	–	–	–	–	–
193 Monetary movements	19	-8	-38	19	28	3	-13	4
INTERNATIONAL RESERVES								*Million US dollars;*
194 Total	135.1	137.0	168.0	135.5	127.4	116.2	117.8	131.3
195 Gold, national valuation	0.4	0.5	0.5	0.5	0.4	0.4	0.4	0.4
196 Foreign exchange	128.9	128.4	157.2	123.6	116.9	107.4	103.6	116.6
197 Reserve position in the Fund	4.1	4.0	6.8	6.2	6.0	8.2	7.7	8.6
198 SDRs	1.7	4.1	3.5	5.3	4.1	0.3	6.2	5.7
EXCHANGE RATES								*Fiji dollars*
199 End of period	0.8197	0.8409	0.7911	0.8767	0.9473	1.0462	1.1430	1.1204
200 Average of period	0.8468	0.8357	0.8180	0.8546	0.9324	1.0170	1.0826	1.1536
EXTERNAL INDEBTEDNESS								*Million US dollars;*
201 Total outstanding & disbursed	103.1	141.7	281.2	372.2	401.9	437.4	413.3	443.8
202 Long-term	84.6	109.9	244.9	333.2	365.0	397.3	378.1	410.3
203 Public and publicly guaranteed	84.6	109.9	180.0	237.5	265.4	292.3	279.3	302.3
204 Private non-guaranteed	–	–	64.9	95.7	99.6	105.0	98.8	108.0
205 Short-term	10.0	23.2	36.3	39.0	22.0	26.0	22.0	19.0
206 Use of IMF credit	8.5	8.6	–	–	14.9	14.1	13.2	14.5
Debt service								*Transactions*
207 Principal repayment on LT debt	12.0	7.6	11.1	9.6	11.8	14.6	26.7	31.0
208 Interest on long-term debt	6.3	6.3	9.6	16.5	22.4	22.8	24.3	24.6
209 Interest on short-term debt	2.1	4.3	6.3	4.6	2.3	2.4	1.9	1.6
Average terms of commitment								
210 Interest (%)	7.3	10.5	8.1	10.8	12.3	10.7	9.1	7.1
211 Maturity (years)	16.3	16.5	14.4	12.2	14.0	12.0	10.3	13.7
212 Grace period (years)	3.7	4.9	3.7	5.2	4.3	4.0	3.0	4.8
213 Grant element (%)	15.0	3.1	9.5	-3.9	-13.0	0.2	7.0	18.8

Footnotes:

a   Consists of salaried personnel and wage earners.
b   Refers to community, social and personal services.
c   Figures relate to season, not calendar year.
d   At factor cost.
e   Data are as of the last Wednesday of the year.
f   Refers to notes and coins issued less local currency held with commercial banks.
g   Refers to total foreign assets of commercial banks, the Reserve Bank of Fiji, and Central Government less foreign liabilities of commercial banks and the Reserve Bank of Fiji.
h   Refers to official entities.
i   Residual.
j   Data from 1990 were reported in Fiji dollars and were converted using the average exchange rate to US dollar.
k   Includes net trade credit.

1986	1987	1988	1989	1990	1991	1992	1993	1994	1995	
...	-223	-218	-378	-333	-362	-383	-402	-475	-498	181
9	-9	30	12	46	72	78	70	58	80	182
-5	-19	-4	-14	-22	-25	-16	-11	-24	-25	183
15	10	34	27	69	96	94	81	82	104	184
6	-5	37	10	-46	1	10	-73	-58	3	185
30	8	45	19	68	-4	70	54	69	49	186
-31	–	–	–	–	–	–	–	–	–	187
-9	-25	7	-39	}						188
3	-21	-2	-39	-17	-4	-22	-59	-48	0	189
19	18	18	-3	40	22	6	37	30	–	190
18	-25	105	-53	44	15	65	-40	-8	52	191
–	–	–	–	...	...	...	...	...	...	192
-18	25	-105	53	-44	-15	-65	40	8	-52	193

As of end of period

1986	1987	1988	1989	1990	1991	1992	1993	1994	1995	
171.5	132.6	233.8	211.9	261.1	271.7	317.2	269.8	273.5	349.4	194
0.5	0.4	0.4	0.3	0.3	0.3	0.3	0.3	0.3	0.3	195
154.3	107.0	202.5	180.3	227.2	248.5	294.3	247.2	247.8	322.8	196
9.6	11.2	10.6	10.4	10.1	9.7	14.3	13.7	14.6	14.9	197
7.1	14.0	20.3	20.9	23.5	13.3	8.2	8.6	10.8	11.4	198

per US dollar

1986	1987	1988	1989	1990	1991	1992	1993	1994	1995	
1.1453	1.4405	1.4049	1.4939	1.4592	1.4728	1.5645	1.5408	1.4091	1.4294	199
1.1329	1.2439	1.4303	1.4833	1.4809	1.4756	1.5030	1.5418	1.4641	1.4063	200

As of end of year

1986	1987	1988	1989	1990	1991	1992	1993	1994	1995	
441.2	468.3	472.1	414.2	412.6	360.5	338.6	330.0	298.7	...	201
413.3	440.1	436.7	399.4	400.6	349.1	308.1	283.3	282.7	...	202
311.8	336.4	335.7	301.6	305.9	270.7	226.8	199.3	195.2	...	203
101.5	103.7	101.0	97.8	94.7	78.4	81.3	84.0	87.5	...	204
20.0	21.5	31.4	14.0	12.0	11.4	30.5	46.7	16.0	...	205
7.9	6.7	4.0	0.8	–	–	–	–	–	...	206

during the year

1986	1987	1988	1989	1990	1991	1992	1993	1994	1995	
31.4	36.6	36.7	55.0	72.2	73.2	59.9	56.9	59.6 *	...	207
25.2	26.1	24.9	31.9	31.3	28.4	23.0	19.4	19.2 *	...	208
1.3	2.0	3.0	1.0	1.5	1.2	1.3	1.9	1.9 *	...	209
6.7	–	6.5	6.2	6.6	2.9	–	6.9	–	...	210
16.1	11.7	15.5	14.6	24.7	11.9	–	20.5	–	...	211
4.1	4.7	3.4	4.2	5.1	3.6	–	4.6	–	...	212
15.8	53.7	17.5	20.6	22.9	36.0	–	19.6	–	...	213

Item	1978	1979	1980	1981	1982	1983	1984	1985
								Million;
001 **POPULATION** [a]	4.67	4.93	5.06	5.18	5.26	5.35	5.40	5.46
								Million;
002 **LABOR FORCE** [b]	2.02	2.14	2.32	2.50	2.50	2.54	2.61	2.63
003 Employed	1.94	2.08	2.24	2.40	2.41	2.43	2.51	2.54
004 Agriculture	...	0.03	0.03	0.05	0.03	0.03	0.03	0.04
005 Manufacturing	0.82	0.90	0.94	0.99	0.90	0.88	0.93	0.92
006 Mining	...	...	...	...	...	...	...	...
007 Others	1.12	1.15	1.26	1.36	1.48	1.52	1.55	1.58
008 Unemployed	0.06	0.06	0.09	0.10	0.09	0.11	0.10	0.08
009 Unemployment rate, %	2.8	2.9	3.8	3.9	3.6	4.5	3.9	3.2
NATIONAL ACCOUNTS [c]								*Million Hong Kong dollars;*
At Current Factor Cost								
010 GDP by Industrial Origin	75408	99216 |	134451	164711	183206	201515	239789	253874
011 Agriculture	856	991 |	1102	1128	1240	1225	1245	1211
012 Mining	144	161 |	213	253	308	316	299	356
013 Manufacturing	18325	24718 |	31806	37557	38070	46242	58329	56192
014 Electricity, gas and water	1085	1267 |	1703	2229	3243	4739	5687	6665
015 Construction	4760	6184 |	8929	12385	13371	12885	12917	12679
016 Trade	16275	21767 |	28762	33449	36602	41204	55503	57943
017 Transport and communications	5444	7279 |	9922	12202	14069	16529	18680	20629
018 Finance	13131	19585 |	30938	39361	41197	35563	37454	40739
019 Public administration	10308	12648 |	16248	21320	27880	32163	37003	42511
020 Others	5080	4616 |	4828	4827	7226	10649	12672	14949
021 Indirect taxes less subsidies	3523	4061 |	5966	7010	6813	8273	9493	12464
022 GDP at current market prices	78931	103277 |	140417	171721	190019	209788	249282	266338
023 Net factor income from abroad	...	...	...	...	...	...	...	...
024 GNP at current market prices	...	...	...	...	...	...	...	...
At Current Market Prices								
025 Expenditure on GDP	85206	111754	141796	170750	192488	212673	256493	271655
026 Private consumption	54466	67172	84660	101829	117902	136840	156223	167483
027 Government consumption	5436	6755	8720	12226	14566	16359	18056	19787
028 Gross fixed capital formation	22578	33521	46011	56300	58820	52966	57332	57280
029 Change in stocks	2067	3256	3745	3953	1403	4329	5803	1469
030 Net export of goods and services	659	1050	-1340	-3558	-203	2179	19079	25636
031 Statistical discrepancy [d]	-6275	-8477	-1379	971	-2469	-2885	-7211	-5317
At Constant 1990 Prices								
032 Expenditure on GDP	252826	281954	310499	339044	348364	368171	404872	406619
033 Private consumption	142758	156307	174813	188031	197945	213146	225373	234956
034 Government consumption	19607	21685	23330	28437	29995	31813	33068	33977
035 Gross fixed capital formation	74274	85346	102107	111488	113487	103953	106567	106413
036 Change in stocks	4388	5991	6026	6112	1907	5184	6444	1655
037 Net export of goods and services	14659	15269	7394	9533	10846	17023	32198	31481
038 Statistical discrepancy	-2860	-2644	-3171	-4557	-5816	-2948	1222	-1863
Investment Financing, at current prices								
039 Gross domestic capital formation	24645	36777	49756	60253	60223	57295	63135	58749
040 Gross national saving	...	...	...	...	...	...	...	...
041 Gross domestic saving	25304	37827	48416	56695	60020	59474	82214	84385
042 Net factor income from abroad	...	...	...	...	...	...	...	...
Per Capita GDP, Hong Kong dollars								
043 Current prices	18255	22670	28006	32942	36563	39788	47517	49788
044 Constant *1990* prices	54167	57195	61326	65410	66172	68880	75005	74524

1986	1987	1988	1989	1990	1991	1992	1993	1994	1995	
As of 1 July										
5.52	5.58	5.63	5.69	5.70	5.75	5.81	5.92	6.06	6.19	001
Calendar year										
2.70	2.73	2.76	2.75	2.75	2.80	2.79	2.87	2.97	3.07	002
2.62	2.68	2.73	2.72	2.71	2.75	2.74	2.82	2.92	2.97	003
0.04	0.04	0.03	0.03	0.02	0.02	0.02	0.02	0.02	0.02	004
0.92	0.92	0.87	0.81	0.75	0.72	0.65	0.60	0.57	0.55	005
...	...		...		...	...	...			006
1.66	1.72	1.82	1.88	1.94	2.01	2.07	2.20	2.33	2.41	007
0.08	0.05	0.04	0.03	0.04	0.05	0.05	0.06	0.06	0.10	008
2.8	1.7	1.4	1.1	1.3	1.8	2.0	2.0	1.9	3.2	009
Calendar year										
296008	366795	438255	498936	559446	631514	732120	830169	953328	...	010
1308	1334	1417	1386	1432	1441	1468	1612	1596	...	011
346	257	229	224	210	222	205	197	249	...	012
66836	80713	90035	96170	98352	97223	99764	92582	88539	...	013
8385	9691	10199	10860	12612	13521	15637	17591	22168	...	014
14253	17024	20658	25738	30220	34659	37337	43089	49863	...	015
66020	89249	109793	124749	140722	163284	190760	224462	257798	...	016
24192	31693	40005	44654	52927	60604	71227	78993	92926	...	017
50306	65707	82813	97297	113127	143296	178923	214550	248750	...	018
47406	53011	61002	70124	81328	94293	110703	130408	148905	...	019
16956	18116	22104	27734	28516	22971	26096	26685	42534	...	020
15212	20445	21451	25391	29614	36323	48777	53278	55792	...	021
311220	387240	459706	524327	589060	667837	780897	883447	1009120	...	022
...	...	...	...	...	...	...	...	...	...	023
...	...	...	...	...	...	...	...	...	...	024
312561	384488	455022	523861	582549	668512	779335	897463	1016567	1111391	025
189159	219315	254682	287677	330459	391098	451670	514239	590991	653671	026
22887	25722	30008	36253	43283	51470	64070	72620	83316	95263	027
67758	91712	116129	136204	153776	177729	213808	245182	297238	322410	028
6183	9746	14132	3463	5728	4098	8187	2299	28004	65283	029
26574	37993	40071	60264	49303	44117	41600	63123	17018	-25236	030
-1341	2752	4684	466	6511	-675	1562	-14016	-7447	...	031
450411	508763	549302	563368	582549	612016	650347	690223	727505	760773	032
253618	279138	302329	312682	330459	359019	386519	415618	441874	447667	033
36185	37598	39005	41035	43283	46617	52789	53935	55841	58247	034
112995	129040	137455	142204	153776	168059	183480	190259	216963	230762	035
7095	10464	14317	3376	5728	4081	8453	2224	24311	52515	036
40518	52523	56196	64071	49303	34240	19106	28187	-11484	-28418	037
–	–	–	–	–	–	–	–	–	–	038
73941	101458	130261	139667	159504	181827	221995	247481	325242	387693	039
...	...	...	...	...	...	...	...	...	...	040
100515	139451	170332	199931	208807	225944	263595	310604	342260	362457	041
...	...	...	...	...	...	...	...	...	...	042
56576	68898	80855	92128	102121	116166	134102	151624	167712	179552	043
81528	91168	97609	99076	102121	106349	111907	116611	120023	122908	044

	Item	1978	1979	1980	1981	1982	1983	1984	1985
	PRODUCTION							*Thousand metric tons;*	
	Agriculture								
045	1. Vegetable (fresh,frozen,etc.)	175	192	195	176	155	153	159	151
046	2. Chicken	28	30	29	33	34	30	27	27
047	3. Fresh fruits and nuts	3	1	3	5	5	5	2	1
	Mining								
048	1. Feldspar	3	1	3	0	2	5	23	27
049	2. Kaolin	26	3	1	8	0	1	0	10
	Manufacturing								
050	1. Cigarettes, *Mn*	...	...	4234	5250	5116	6577	8681	12496
051	2. Manufactured gas, *teracalorie*	598	722	842	963	1160	1415	1650	1906
052	3. Cement	1236	1279	1489	1517	1436	1717	1847	1835
053	4. Woven cotton fabrics, *Mn sq. m.*	654	717	661	616	566	642	659	639
	Production Indexes								*Period*
054	Agriculture, *1979-81 = 100*	86.4	103.7	89.8	106.5	78.4	74.7	78.8	104.5
055	Manufacturing, *1986 = 100*	...	...	...	...	69	78	91	87
	ENERGY								*Annual*
	Coal, *'000 m.t.*								
056	Production	...	...	...	...	...	...	...	...
057	Exports	0	0	0	0	0	0	0	0
058	Imports [e]	8	6	3	57	1455	3418	4462	5523
059	Consumption [f]	8	6	3	57	1455	3418	4462	5523
	Electricity, *Mn kWh*								
060	Production	10373	11391	12649	13309	14506	16489	17923	19235
061	Exports	0	252	308	236	272	368	740	1050
062	Imports	0	0	0	0	0	0	0	0
063	Consumption	9109	9879	10922	11561	12436	14035	15046	15928
	Retail prices, *HK $/litre*								
064	Gasoline, leaded	1.41	1.69	2.27	2.61	3.17	4.32	4.58	4.75
065	Diesel	1.07	1.33	2.04	2.24	2.32	3.03	3.31	3.35
	PRICE INDEXES							*October 1989-September 1990 = 100;*	
066	Consumer [g]	36.5	40.8	47.1	53.7	59.4	65.2	70.6	72.8
067	Food	37.2	41.2	47.2	54.9	61.3	66.6	71.1	71.4
068	Wholesale	...	...	...	...	...	...	...	...
069	Implicit GDP deflator, *1990 = 100*	33.7	39.6	45.7	50.4	55.3	57.8	63.4	66.8
	MONEY AND BANKING							*Million Hong Kong dollars;*	
070	Money supply (M1) [h]	20110	20851	24198	25193	27484	30895	36791	45266
071	Currency in circulation	6543	7285	8367	9826	11441	12713	13273	16857
072	Demand deposits	13567	13566	15831	15367	16043	18182	23518	28409
073	Quasi-money	46362	54419	72042	91562	179203	226789	277290	344973
074	Money supply (M2) [i]	66472	75270	96240	116755	206687	257684	314081	390239
	Deposit Money Banks								
075	Demand deposits	13567	13566	15831	15367	16043	18182	23518	28409
076	Savings deposits	24850	33258	42808	52852	69590	71156	81150	98765
077	Time deposits	21512	21161	28114	36239	104626	150535	191436	240050
078	Domestic credits outstanding	62839	83005	124535	161799	208702	255165	286277	312942
	Interest Rates								*Per cent;*
	On deposits								
079	Savings	2.5	7.6	8.2	11.4	8.2	6.5	6.8	3.1
080	Time: 6 months	3.2	8.3	9.5	14.4	10.9	9.2	8.2	4.1
081	12 months	4.3	9.9	11.0	13.9	10.4	9.4	8.1	4.5
	On loans & discounts [j]								
082	Commercial bills	5.9	12.7	13.6	17.5	14.2	12.3	12.5	8.2

	1986	1987	1988	1989	1990	1991	1992	1993	1994	1995	
Calendar year											
	158	141	132	131	112	105	95	91	89	88	045
	32	32	28	26	25	24	21	21	19	18	046
	2	2	2	3	4	4	3	4	5	5	047
	35	23	11	5	4	0	0	0	0	...	048
	1	0	0	0	0	0	0	0	0	...	049
	11841	15309	18089	19601	23132	32721	36513	25759	...	...	050
	2160	2528	2925	3265	3596	3878	4349	4585	4950	...	051
	2236	2226	2189	2141	1808	1677	1643	1712	1927	1913	052
	759	851	804	818	818	753	806	755	691	...	053
averages											
	50.0	56.0	117.0	117.0	123.0	120.0	73.0	76.0	79.5	80.4	054
	100	116	123	124	123	124	126	125	125	...	055
values											
	...	...	...	...	...	...	...	...	...	...	056
	0	0	0	0	0	0	0	0	0	0	057
	6393	8010	9266	9928	8931	9635	10215	11830	8451	9109	058
	6393	8010	9266	9928	8931	9635	10215	11830	8451	9109	059
	21412	23753	25508	27361	28938	31807	35076	35948	26741	27916	060
	1208	1362	1440	1770	1797	3061	4963	4500	1758	1483	061
	0	0	0	0	0	0	0	446	8253	7546	062
	17664	19618	21009	22386	23834	25317	26153	27725	29182	29855	063
	4.37	4.51	4.62	5.10	6.40	7.57	7.75	8.14	8.61	9.25	064
	2.93	3.18	3.25	3.57	4.45	4.88	4.99	5.27	5.50	5.83	065
Period averages											
	74.9	79.0	84.9	93.5	102.6	114.5	125.2	135.9	146.9	159.7	066
	72.3	75.7	83.0	93.2	102.5	114.1	124.1	133.1	141.6	151.8	067
	...	...	...	...	...	...	...	...	...	...	068
	69.4	75.6	82.8	93.0	100.0	109.2	119.8	130.0	139.7	146.1	069
As of end of period											
	56093	81902	88834	94858	107509	128497	155557	187608	185334	189651	070
	19294	24764	29876	34192	37694	42608	52172	63353	67783	71335	071
	36799	57138	58958	60666	69815	85889	103385	124255	117551	118316	072
	462037	595140	735814	893978	1102541	1242532	1363220	1573354	1803141	2075026	073
	518130	677042	824648	988836	1210050	1371029	1518777	1760962	1988475	2265277	074
	36799	57138	58958	60666	69815	85889	103385	124255	11751	118316	075
	125476	181109	175529	193186	231672	314052	353878	422282	400506	439397	076
	329078	403439	544502	683802	853632	911491	992126	1129408	1366274	1594478	077
	390747	666072	866480	1173005	1679576	2117205	2331386	2713505	3101237	3552064	078
Period averages											
	2.4	2.1	3.3	5.8	5.9	4.7	2.3	1.5	2.5	4.2	079
	3.6	3.5	4.6	7.3	7.4	6.2	3.8	3.0	4.4	6.0	080
	4.3	4.2	5.4	8.0	8.2	7.0	4.6	3.8	5.1	6.3	081
	7.1	6.6	7.9	10.5	10.5	9.4	7.3	6.5	7.3	8.9	082

	Item	1978	1979	1980	1981	1982	1983	1984	1985
	GOVERNMENT FINANCE							*Million Hong Kong dollars;*	
	Central Government								
083	Current revenue	10146	13473	18952	24014	24883	27251	30581	36461
084	Taxes	7497	9721	13382	16514	17140	18933	21838	27658
085	Non-taxes	2649	3752	5570	7500	7743	8318	8743	8803
086	Current expenditure	7308	8865	11919	16295	20498	22876	25991	29166
087	Current surplus/deficit	2838	4608	7033	7719	4385	4375	4590	7295
088	Capital receipts	2411	3323	11339	10299	6215	5562	7929	7233
089	Capital expenditure	3782	5007	11674	11483	14099	12469	10095	11679
090	Capital investment fund	853	1363	3336	5646	3292	3305	2616	3959
091	Capital account surplus/deficit	-2224	-3047	-3671	-6830	-11176	-10212	-4782	-8405
092	Overall surplus/deficit [k]	614	1561	3362	889	-6791	-5837	-192	-1110
	Expenditure by Function, Central Govt.								
093	Total	12122	15620	22057	29385	35684	38596	39882	43444
094	General public services [l]	1478	2088	2424	3274	4800	5438	5922	6797
095	Defence	587	642	1591	1499	1471	1558	1523	1493
096	Education	1949	2438	3382	4172	5105	5758	6951	7558
097	Health	947	1230	1664	2160	2665	2956	3312	3767
098	Social security & welfare	586	764	968	1318	1805	2048	2357	2608
099	Housing & community amenities [m]	2087	3374	5048	5738	7247	8293	8222	8722
100	Economic services	3456	3740	5242	8919	9254	9083	7995	8380
101	Agriculture	36	43	53	88	106	100	82	76
102	Industry	231	289	455	568	536	459	464	538
103	Electricity, gas & water	386	470	697	1263	1413	1342	1240	1318
104	Transport and communications [n]	2514	2598	3614	6477	6581	6494	5466	5561
105	Other economic services [o]	289	340	423	523	618	688	743	887
106	Others [p]	1032	1344	1738	2305	3337	3462	3600	4119
	EXTERNAL TRADE							*Million Hong Kong dollars;*	
107	Exports, fob [q]	53907	75934	98243	122163	127386	160698	221440	235152
108	Imports, cif	63055	85835	111650	138375	142891	175442	223368	231420
109	Trade balance	-9148	-9901	-13407	-16212	-15505	-14744	-1928	3732
	Exports, by SITC section [q]								
110	Food & live animals	711	844	813	1018	1150	1360	1372	1346
111	Beverage & tobacco	55	73	114	191	191	404	655	1116
112	Crude materials excl. fuels	412	650	1108	985	835	1880	1920	1493
113	Mineral fuels, etc.	0	50	89	99	107	160	312	443
114	Animal, vegetable oil & fats	3	5	10	8	8	10	11	9
115	Chemicals	345	432	542	755	785	1016	1312	1278
116	Basic manufactures	4635	6509	7732	8606	8313	11069	13884	12911
117	Machines, transport equipment	6403	9314	12375	15043	15074	23328	33300	28782
118	Misc. manufactured goods	27815	37525	44814	53381	55996	64400	84041	80862
119	Unclassified goods	331	510	574	338	574	777	1129	1642
120	Re-exports	13197	20022	30072	41739	44353	56294	83504	105270
	Exports, by principal commodity								
121	1. Articles of apparel & clothing accessories	15709	20131	23258	28288	28824	34365	46714	44912
122	2. Electrical machinery, apparatus and appliances, and electrical parts	2109	3235	4490	5812	6055	8203	11479	10037
123	3. Textile yarn, fabrics & made-up articles	2869	4065	4535	5302	5052	7084	8631	7823
124	4. Parts and accessories suitable for use with office machines and automatic data processing machines	713	851	15328	2197	1774	3963	6694	5383
125	5. Watches & clocks	2734	4354	6288	7104	7168	8259	8875	9088
126	6. Telecommunication equipment	316	475	633	1001	1476	3900	5003	4641

1986	1987	1988	1989	1990	1991	1992	1993	1994	1995	
Fiscal year beginning 1 April										
41894	53555	64302	73430	81401	99973	119255	139758	60785	151408	083
31731	41216	48295	53879	61122	77937	95788	112604	30567	119371	084
10163	12339	16007	19551	20279	22036	23467	27154	30218	32037	085
32423	35729	41260	50106	60378	70773	81593	93191	106022	121253	086
9471	17826	23042	23324	21023	29200	37662	46567	-45237	30155	087
6709	7320	8356	8999	8123	14725	16056	26844	27880	29318	088
10280	12646	15331	18973	18964	19624	25678	42013	39548	40388	089
2133	3371	2952	2287	6214	1794	6061	12234	18585	21550	090
-5704	-8697	-9927	-12261	-17055	-6693	-15683	-27403	-30253	-32620	091
3767	9129	13115	11063	3968	22507	21979	19164	10843	-2465	092
47930	53636	64799	81945	95198	108422	123493	155207	165950	195245	093
7099	7932	7827	9470	12579	15052	16367	21654	21305	27105	094
1564	1640	1640	1539	1657	1744	2009	1708	1476	1060	095
8769	9634	11355	13030	16074	18895	21639	25409	28878	33780	096
4467	5123	5672	7307	9287	11164	13636	18458	19322	23852	097
2858	3184	3804	4762	5811	6913	7837	9170	10948	14558	098
8927	10640	14396	18040	20732	21706	22723	27696	32916	37948	099
9349	10426	12299	18020	17152	20115	25005	35498	33606	36679	100
99	137	104	177	274	223	508	525	184	238	101
590	606	965	1162	1414	1521	1808	6722	1991	2276	102
1607	1786	2073	2826	3046	3410	3624	4300	4977	5569	103
6134	6989	8326	12880	11297	13609	17241	22071	24837	26352	104
919	908	831	975	1121	1352	1824	1880	1617	2244	105
4897	5057	7806	9777	11906	12833	14277	15614	17499	20263	106
Calendar year										
276530	378034	493069	570509	639874	765886	924953	1046250	1170014	1344128	107
275957	377947	498798	562781	642530	778982	955295	1072597	1250709	1491121	108
573	87	-5729	7728	-2656	-13096	-30342	-26347	-80695	-146993	109
1620	1730	2016	2097	2341	2530	2640	2498	2883	2934	110
1146	1531	2086	2340	3350	2990	3016	2897	2968	2878	111
1235	1912	2207	2356	2155	1958	1919	1674	1818	2429	112
463	502	521	669	780	1277	2091	1941	834	731	113
10	18	71	97	84	76	113	113	128	247	114
1502	2512	4208	5347	6651	7482	7686	7765	8418	9178	115
17042	24157	25844	26996	26695	27859	28316	28009	26455	25711	116
33306	43155	55104	56235	56124	59550	61437	61697	62211	68149	117
95783	117208	123087	125180	124806	123883	122526	112342	112472	115304	118
1877	2529	2519	2786	2890	3440	4381	4090	3906	4097	119
122546	182780	275405	346405	413999	534841	690829	823224	947921	1112470	120
										121
52162	65321	67309	71874	72165	75525	77156	71857	73086	73801	
										122
11214	14501	17498	17888	17293	19380	20138	22668	24815	31889	
10955	16005	15551	16814	16906	17595	17226	16180	15038	14030	123
										124
4565	5487	7676	8777	10355	12372	15239	13810	13483	13297	
11323	13393	16588	16344	18319	17037	15476	13161	13196	13620	125
5887	7998	11092	11840	12683	11519	10991	12095	10990	10065	126

	Item	1978	1979	1980	1981	1982	1983	1984	1985
	Imports, by SITC section								
127	Food & live animals	8207	9646	11558	13993	16172	18911	20134	19965
128	Beverage & tobacco	989	1353	1583	2060	2327	2672	3241	3852
129	Crude materials excl. fuels	3756	4312	5267	5616	5581	7345	9310	8990
130	Mineral fuels, etc.	3122	4906	7882	10966	11477	11657	12263	10826
131	Animal, vegetable oil & fats	279	355	376	427	436	596	688	731
132	Chemicals	4606	6819	7934	9059	9486	12942	15523	16236
133	Basic manufactures	20498	26931	33720	40149	39734	49500	63844	64621
134	Machines, transport equipment	12467	18609	25133	32298	32029	39424	57741	59427
135	Misc. manufactured goods	8884	12525	17628	23179	24978	31783	39715	45400
136	Unclassified goods	247	379	569	628	671	612	909	1372
	Direction of Trade								*Million US dollars;*
137	Exports, Total	11495	15154	19720	21816	20893	21949	28314	30182
138	1. China, People's Rep. of	63	382	1249	1965	1939	2495	5031	7857
139	2. United States	3491	4144	5157	6056	6040	7069	9405	9301
140	3. Japan	882	1026	909	1022	941	966	1251	1279
141	4. Germany	989	1358	1615	1372	1265	1203	1355	1226
142	5. United Kingdom	856	1267	1527	1540	1284	1269	1467	1255
143	6. Singapore	532	642	863	890	918	926	913	850
144	7. Korea, Rep. of	155	205	227	288	319	380	493	544
145	8. Canada	286	355	394	472	490	604	698	715
146	9. Netherlands	222	307	350	322	309	329	365	340
147	10. France	139	239	334	327	298	278	313	311
148	Imports, Total	13443	17135	22399	24768	23444	24005	28558	29701
149	1. China, People's Rep. of	2250	3021	4401	5272	5397	5847	7131	7568
150	2. Japan	3072	3858	5142	5756	5176	5516	6730	6848
151	3. United States	1605	2068	2653	2589	2538	2638	3121	2815
152	4. Singapore	687	961	1481	1901	1679	1430	1564	1448
153	5. Korea, Rep. of	383	505	775	985	748	690	932	1065
154	6. Germany	442	554	579	606	575	625	705	856
155	7. United Kingdom	634	866	1094	1125	1128	1027	1113	1084
156	8. Italy	204	266	275	330	335	318	380	460
157	9. Malaysia	136	185	213	201	187	186	203	173
158	10. Thailand	220	264	317	329	325	324	281	295
	Trade Indexes [r]								*1990 = 100;*
	Quantum index								
159	Exports [q]	18	22	26	29	29	33	40	42
160	Imports	22	25	30	33	33	36	41	43
	Unit value index								
161	Exports [q]	46	53	58	63	68	75	85	85
162	Imports	46	54	58	65	68	77	85	83
163	Terms of trade	100	100	100	98	99	98	99	103
	EXCHANGE RATES								*Hong Kong dollar*
164	End of period	4.803	4.948	5.130	5.675	6.495	7.780	7.823	7.811
165	Average of period	4.685	5.003	4.976	5.593	6.072	7.273	7.818	7.791
	EXTERNAL INDEBTEDNESS [s]								*Million US dollars;*
166	Total outstanding & disbursed	...	...	...	...	5685	6580	6924	8554
167	Long-term	...	...	...	...	3287	3560	3913	5168
168	Public and publicly guaranteed	215	330	485	309	...	...	...	...
169	Private non-guaranteed	...	...	...	...	...	...	...	...
170	Short-term	...	...	443	555	2398	3020	3011	3386
171	Use of IMF credit	...	...	0	0	—	—	—	—

1986	1987	1988	1989	1990	1991	1992	1993	1994	1995	
22481	25530	31303	32922	35588	39496	43469	43235	50776	58195	127
3944	5460	7652	9836	13611	16152	19203	18108	19178	18995	128
9865	14806	17042	17632	15701	19718	20450	18926	23816	32398	129
8860	9472	9520	13482	15654	16331	18930	19493	24378	28660	130
684	672	786	1041	1236	1228	1133	1244	3007	4253	131
21226	30679	44659	43627	47802	60806	67627	66836	84122	111777	132
80241	107542	131760	145879	158293	182443	207778	220253	259536	305588	133
66247	98184	143685	156204	179383	227440	307002	377482	443633	553915	134
60876	83541	110013	139358	172376	212468	265599	303058	337549	372394	135
1533	2061	2380	2801	2887	2899	4103	3961	4714	4946	136

Calendar year

1986	1987	1988	1989	1990	1991	1992	1993	1994	1995	
35438	48473	63182	73113	82143	98578	119532	135005	151393	173546	137
7551	11291	17029	18817	20332	26736	35412	43684	49669	57861	138
11108	13511	15689	18505	19817	22391	27583	31159	35179	37851	139
1651	2470	3696	4525	4680	5307	6262	6959	8436	10596	140
1755	2615	3177	3693	5315	6613	6338	7080	7042	7491	141
1590	2202	2811	3020	3287	3651	4281	4564	4866	5584	142
1032	1329	1784	2158	2615	2688	3130	3683	4214	4944	143
831	1270	1670	1915	1907	2111	1938	2262	2415	2804	144
832	1046	1246	1501	1527	1739	2083	2248	2377	2633	145
463	734	1049	1114	1396	1605	1894	2133	2370	2825	146
451	717	930	1047	1289	1641	1835	2013	2133	2666	147
35360	48463	63900	72149	82482	100274	123430	138596	161770	192764	148
10462	15049	19938	25213	30313	37758	45785	51987	60864	69737	149
7228	9221	11915	11950	13269	16397	21473	23015	25238	28602	150
2980	4141	5302	5933	6653	7576	9128	10271	11565	14882	151
1395	1841	2365	2854	3353	4057	5050	6184	8018	10089	152
1406	2175	3364	3265	3614	4497	5705	6234	7454	9472	153
1030	1304	1672	1742	1904	2142	2831	3221	3709	4142	154
1198	1502	1655	1662	1812	2129	2483	2771	3287	3936	155
566	791	1032	1269	1392	1509	1916	2311	2948	3573	156
263	474	796	865	1053	1269	1657	2050	2609	3723	157
385	530	768	873	1046	1323	1526	1682	2225	2728	158

Period averages

1986	1987	1988	1989	1990	1991	1992	1993	1994	1995	
49	65	83	91	100	117	141	160	176	197	159
49	65	82	90	100	119	146	164	187	213	160
87	90	93	97	100	103	103	103	105	108	161
87	90	94	98	100	102	102	102	104	1110	162
100	99	98	100	100	101	101	102	100	99	163

per US dollar

1986	1987	1988	1989	1990	1991	1992	1993	1994	1995	
7.795	7.760	7.808	7.807	7.801	7.781	7.741	7.726	7.738	7.732	164
7.803	7.798	7.806	7.800	7.789	7.771	7.741	7.736	7.728	7.736	165

As of end of year

1986	1987	1988	1989	1990	1991	1992	1993	1994	1995	
11784	12069	11864	12135	12570	13455	14091	17841	20444	...	166
7623	7971	7389	7348	6788	7181	7625	10492	12274	...	167
...	...	...	...	...	...	...	...	...	...	168
...	...	...	...	...	...	...	...	...	...	169
4161	4098	4475	4787	5778	6274	6466	7349	8171	...	170
–	–	–	–	–	...	...	...	...	...	171

	Item	1978	1979	1980	1981	1982	1983	1984	1985
	Debt service								*Transactions*
172	Principal repayments on LT debt	79	10	36	155 I	317	412	603	565
173	Interest on long-term debt	14	10	45	37 I	212	273	312	305
174	Interest on short-term debt	...	...	...	...	285	271	317	262
	Average terms of new commitments								
175	Interest (%)	8.4	10.0	7.9	7.9	7.8	9.5	12.5	...
176	Maturity (years)	10.2	10.8	13.5	11.8	12.3	15.5	4.1	...
177	Grace period (years)	5.4	4.6	3.5	3.7	3.6	4.5	1.2	...
178	Grant element (%)	7.1	-1.1	10.2	9.8	10.3	13.5	-5.9	...

Footnotes:

a   Population estimates for 1986-1992 have been revised based on 1991 Census.

b   Figures of 1978-1980 are based on the results of Labour Force Surveys. Figures for 1981 are obtained from the 1981 Census while those for 1982 onwards are from the General Household Surveys.

c   Figures before 1980 are not comparable with those of 1980 onwards. The former are income-based estimates whereas the latter are production-based estimates.

d   Computed as the difference between production-based GDP and expenditure-based GDP estimates.

e   Refers to steam coal and other coal and anthracite only.

f   Refers to retained imports of steam coal and other coal anthracite only.

g   Based on Consumer Price Index (A) which refers to 50% of urban households spending between HK$2,500 and HK$9,999 a month in 1989/90.

h   Refers to notes and coins with the public, plus customers' demand deposit with the licensed banks.

i   Refers to M1 plus customers' saving and time deposits with licensed banks, plus negotiable certificates of deposit issued by licensed banks and held outside the monetary sector.

j   Refer to the Hong Kong and Shanghai Banking Corporation Limited's quoted best lending rate.

k   Includes the consolidated account (i.e. General Revenue account and fund accounts).

l   Include "Support of public services", "Information & Broadcasting" and "Coordination of External Matters".

m   Include "Housing", "Recreation, Culture & Amenities"," District and Community Relations" and "Environment".

n   Include "Transport", "Air & Sea Communications", "Posts, Telecommunications & Power" and "Land & Buildings".

o   Include "Monetary Affairs", "Travel and Tourism", "Public Safety" and "Employment".

p   Include "Internal Security other than Defence", "Immigration", "Legal Administration", "Judicial Administration" and "Anti-Corruption".

q   For exports, data refer to total exports (i.e., domestic exports and re-exports). As from 1992 onwards, the system of commodity classification for trade statistics is the Standard International Trade Classification (SITC) Revision 3. Thus, the 1992 statistics may not be strictly comparable with those of earlier periods, except for 1991 data which have been recompiled in terms of SITC Revision 3 to facilitate comparison with statistics from 1992 onwards.

r   In the trade indexes for 1987 onwards, the specification price indices for toys and knitted outer garments are newly incorporated, hence series are strictly not directly comparable with those for early years. Also, the quantum indices for 1991 onwards are not strictly comparable to those for earlier years due to adoption of a new method of compiling quantum indices.

s   Break in series shows data are not comparable due to different sources used.

1986	1987	1988	1989	1990	1991	1992	1993	1994	1995	
during the year										
872	600	658	1108	755	645	...	...	...	...	172
313	431	444	960	528	463	...	...	...	...	173
256	282	338	412	435	359	...	...	...	...	174
...	...	...	...	...	...	...	...	...	...	175
...	...	...	...	...	...	...	...	...	...	176
...	...	...	...	...	...	...	...	...	...	177
...	...	...	...	...	...	...	...	...	...	178

	Item	1978	1979	1980	1981	1982	1983	1984	1985
001	**POPULATION** [a]	644.33	658.73	673.39	688.32	703.57	719.09	734.87	*Million;* 750.91
	LABOR FORCE								*Million;*
002	Employed (organised sectors only)	21.61	21.88	22.83	23.33	23.80	24.14	24.60	25.01
003	Agriculture	1.28	1.25	1.36	1.30	1.32	1.32	1.31	1.36
004	Manufacturing	5.68	5.85	6.04	6.23	6.28	6.22	6.24	6.29
005	Mining	0.89	0.90	0.95	0.94	0.98	1.02	1.08	1.08
006	Others	13.76	13.88	14.48	14.86	15.22	15.58	15.96	16.28
007	Unemployed [b]	12.68	14.33	16.20	17.84	19.75	21.95	23.55	26.27
008	Unemployment rate, %	...	...	...	...	...	...	...	...
	NATIONAL ACCOUNTS *At Current Factor Cost*								*Billion Rupees;*
009	GDP by Industrial Origin	938.8	1024.4	1224.3	1432.2	1594.0	1867.2	2085.3	2338.0
010	Agriculture	358.5	370.9	466.5	526.8	561.5	675.0	719.5	772.2
011	Mining	12.2	15.2	18.9	35.4	43.9	49.1	54.6	62.0
012	Manufacturing	169.2	193.8	216.4	252.6	280.7	330.4	372.4	417.8
013	Electricity, gas and water	15.5	17.9	20.7	24.1	28.5	33.6	40.5	48.9
014	Construction	46.6	47.0	61.1	69.9	80.8	94.2	111.0	129.5
015	Trade	101.4	119.5	147.1	180.3	199.7	229.9	266.9	310.5
016	Transport and communications	48.7	53.7	57.2	70.4	86.0	102.8	118.7	141.0
017	Finance	88.8	96.9	107.9	125.4	141.6	155.9	176.0	198.8
018	Public administration	44.1	50.0	57.9	66.6	79.6	92.4	108.4	125.1
019	Others	53.8	59.7	70.4	80.7	91.7	103.9	117.4	132.2
020	Indirect taxes less subsidies	103.1	119.1	135.9	165.4	187.4	208.7	228.1	284.4
021	GDP at current market prices	1041.9	1143.5	1360.1	1597.6	1781.4	2075.9	2313.4	2622.4
022	Net factor income from abroad	-1.6	1.5	3.4	0.4	-6.3	-9.4	-14.2	-14.3
023	GNP at current market prices	1040.3	1145.0	1363.6	1598.0	1775.1	2066.5	2299.2	2608.1
	At Current Market Prices								
024	Expenditure on GDP	1041.9	1143.5	1360.1	1597.6	1781.4	2075.9	2313.4	2622.4
025	Private consumption	746.5	807.9	981.3	1127.1	1241.1	1459.6	1614.6	1768.5
026	Government consumption	97.2	111.7	130.8	153.6	182.7	211.4	243.5	291.7
027	Gross fixed capital formation	188.8	213.1	262.8	314.6	357.7	399.9	455.7	542.6
028	Increase in stocks	43.4	48.4	21.8	85.6	50.2	30.7	32.2	83.7
029	Exports of goods and services	71.2	83.4	90.3	102.6	115.6	131.4	158.5	149.5
030	Less: Imports of goods and services	74.2	100.9	136.0	148.1	157.4	176.8	194.8	217.5
031	Statistical discrepancy	-31.0	-20.1	9.2	-37.8	-8.6	19.6	3.9	4.0
	At Constant 1980/81 Factor Cost								
032	GDP by Industrial Origin	1202.1	1142.4	1224.3	1298.9	1339.2	1448.7	1504.3	1565.7
033	Agriculture	473.8	413.2	466.5	494.1	488.0	540.8	540.6	542.2
034	Mining	16.6	16.8	18.9	21.4	23.9	24.5	24.9	26.2
035	Manufacturing	220.2	216.0	216.4	233.8	249.1	273.8	291.5	303.2
036	Electricity, gas and water	19.4	19.6	20.7	22.6	24.1	25.9	28.6	31.0
037	Construction	57.0	54.0	61.1	64.5	61.5	65.8	68.3	71.8
038	Trade	144.5	139.9	147.1	156.7	165.5	174.2	181.7	196.5
039	Transport and communications	50.8	53.6	57.2	60.1	62.8	66.9	73.0	79.5
040	Finance	104.9	105.9	107.9	112.8	121.1	128.6	137.1	147.1
041	Public administration	50.8	54.4	57.9	59.3	65.5	67.7	74.5	80.2
042	Others	64.1	69.0	70.4	73.6	77.7	80.5	84.1	88.0
043	Indirect taxes less subsidies	141.3	133.3	135.9	150.1	164.6	166.8	170.6	200.8
044	GDP at *1980/81* market prices	1343.4	1275.7	1360.1	1449.0	1503.8	1615.5	1674.9	1766.5
045	Net factor income from abroad	-2.0	1.4	3.4	0.4	-6.2	-10.0	-11.8	-12.0
046	GNP at *1980/81* market prices	1341.4	1277.1	1363.6	1449.4	1497.6	1605.5	1663.1	1754.5
	At Constant 1980/81 Market Prices								
047	Expenditure on GDP	1343.4	1275.7	1360.1	1449.0	1503.8	1615.5	1674.9	1766.5
048	Private consumption	933.1	903.6	981.3	1038.5	1070.7	1150.6	1194.6	1240.5
049	Government consumption	117.1	124.2	130.8	136.6	150.8	157.5	169.8	189.2
050	Gross fixed capital formation	244.0	236.9	262.8	280.8	293.0	296.3	307.8	329.7

1986	1987	1988	1989	1990	1991	1992	1993	1994	1995	
As of 1 July										
767.20	783.73	800.50	817.49	834.70	851.66	867.82	883.91	899.95	916.46 *	001
As of December			**As of 31 March**							
25.31	25.62	25.95	26.28 I	26.35	26.73	27.06	...	...	...	002
1.40	1.41	1.43	1.45 I	1.43	1.45	1.48	...	...	...	003
6.26	6.26	6.23	6.31 I	6.34	6.33	6.43	...	...	...	004
1.06	1.03	1.06	1.06 I	1.07	1.10	1.09	...	...	...	005
16.58	16.92	17.22	17.46 I	17.51	17.85	18.06	...	...	...	006
30.13	30.25	30.05	32.78 I	34.63	36.30	36.76	...	...	...	007
...	...	...	...	...	...	...	...	...	...	008
Fiscal year beginning 1 April										
2600.3	2948.5	3527.1	4086.6	4778.0	5527.7	6301.8	7231.0	8541.0	9622.8 *	009
824.1	923.8	1140.7	1270.5	1480.0	...	...	...	...	...	010
68.0	70.8	92.1	103.1	117.9	...	...	...	...	...	011
461.7	528.7	628.6	770.8	891.6	...	...	...	...	...	012
55.7	62.7	73.2	87.2	104.6	...	...	...	...	...	013
152.2	176.1	206.8	235.9	286.2	...	...	...	...	...	014
345.5	384.3	452.2	529.1	618.7	...	...	...	...	...	015
165.4	199.4	238.7	277.3	339.1	...	...	...	...	...	016
223.1	247.6	282.6	335.8	389.0	...	...	...	...	...	017
149.3	179.5	208.6	241.3	271.1	...	...	...	...	...	018
155.4	175.7	203.5	235.7	279.8	...	...	...	...	...	019
329.2	383.5	430.8	481.6	577.2	640.3	751.5	779.3	915.1	1342.2 *	020
2929.5	3332.0	3957.8	4568.2	5355.2	6168.0	7053.3	8010.3	9456.2	10965.0 *	021
-18.1	-26.2	-45.0	-57.3	-75.4	...	-118.1	-146.0	-145.9	-164.6 *	022
2911.4	3305.8	3912.9	4510.9	5279.7	...	6935.2	7864.3	9310.2	10800.4 *	023
2929.5	3332.0	3957.8	4568.2	5355.2	6168.0	7053.3	8010.3	9456.2	10965.0 *	024
1986.0	2225.5	2574.2	2882.4	3303.7	...	4301.8	4894.0	5633.4	6771.5 *	025
346.3	408.4	473.3	542.0	617.8	...	786.0	896.8	1012.5	1429.3 *	026
620.5	721.9	856.7	1027.8	1240.0	1365.0	1587.4	1722.5	2130.6	2048.4 *	027
93.9	26.9	113.9	80.2	133.9	35.7	108.1	-12.4	58.6	247.8 *	028
165.4	202.8	259.1	346.1	406.4	...	673.1	891.4	} 621.1	1353.4 *	029
223.6	252.6	320.1	402.1	487.0	...	730.0	880.0		1486.3 *	030
-59.0	-1.0	0.8	91.9	140.4	...	326.9	498.1		600.9 *	031
1632.7	1703.2	1884.6	2014.5	2122.8	2139.8	2248.9	2360.6	2510.1	2592.8 *	032
532.8	534.8	622.1	632.6	656.5 }	684.8	680.2	702.3	736.9	737.3 *	033
29.8	30.8	35.4	38.0	42.1		44.1	45.9	47.9 }		034
324.4	348.2	378.7	422.9	448.6		449.9	469.3	511.5	772.9 *	035
34.2	36.9	40.8	45.1	48.0 }	585.1	57.0	61.1	66.0		036
75.4	77.8	83.8	88.1	98.3		103.8	106.2	113.6		037
208.5	218.0	233.9	252.3	265.8 }	386.1	286.5	310.3	334.8		038
84.8	92.3	98.0	106.6	111.6		124.3	131.4	142.3		039
159.2	168.7	184.2	204.0	217.2	239.7	246.9	267.9	279.4	1082.7 *	040
88.1	97.0	103.4	112.1	113.3 }	244.1	121.7	125.0	128.8		041
95.5	98.7	104.3	112.8	121.3		134.5	141.3	149.0		042
219.8	237.6	248.8	259.1	279.9	...	290.9	278.1	294.9	399.9 *	043
1852.5	1940.9	2133.5	2273.7	2402.6	...	2539.8	2638.7	2805.0	2992.7 *	044
-17.4	-22.0	-32.3	-33.7	-37.7	...	-47.8	-59.8	-54.0	-50.6 *	045
1835.1	1918.8	2101.1	2240.0	2364.9	...	2492.0	2578.9	2751.0	2942.2 *	046
1852.5	1940.9	2133.5	2273.7	2402.6	...	2539.8	2638.7	2805.0	2992.7 *	047
1302.6	1351.3	1434.7	1497.4	...	...	...	...	...	...	048
208.5	226.6	238.7	252.1	...	...	...	...	...	...	049
360.0	399.5	428.0	465.1	...	...	...	...	...	...	050

	Item	1978	1979	1980	1981	1982	1983	1984	1985
051	Increase in stocks	59.9	56.8	21.8	78.1	46.9	26.1	24.7	64.8
052	Exports of goods and services			90.3					
053	Less: Imports of goods and services	-10.7	-45.8	136.0	-85.0	-57.6	-15.0	-22.0	-57.7
054	Statistical discrepancy			9.2					
	Investment Financing, at current prices								
055	Gross domestic capital formation	232.2	261.5	284.5	400.2	407.9	430.6	487.9	626.3
056	Gross national saving	196.6	225.4	251.5	317.3	351.3	395.5	441.1	547.9
057	Gross domestic saving	198.2	223.9	248.0	316.9	357.6	404.9	455.3	562.2
058	Net factor income from abroad	-1.6	1.5	3.4	0.4	-6.3	-9.4	-14.2	-14.3
059	Foreign saving	-9.9	13.0	20.9	26.1	25.7	25.2	32.9	62.3
060	Net transfer from abroad	3.0	3.4	4.4	2.9	2.7	2.6	4.4	3.1
061	Net borrowing from abroad	-12.9	9.6	16.5	23.2	23.0	22.6	28.5	59.2
	Per Capita GNP, Rupees								
062	Current prices	1615	1738	2025	2322	2523	2874	3129	3473
063	Constant *1980/81* prices	2082	1939	2025	2106	2129	2233	2263	2336
	PRODUCTION								*Thousand metric tons;*
	Agriculture [c]								
064	1. Sugar cane	151655	128833	154248	186358	189506	174076	170319	170648
065	2. Rice, paddy	80609	63476	80312	79883	70772	90048	87553	95818
066	3. Wheat	35508	31830	36313	37452	42794	45476	44069	47052
067	4. Potatoes	10133	8327	9668	9912	9956	12152	12571	10423
068	5. Sorghum	11436	11648	10431	12062	10753	11919	11402	10197
069	6. Pulses	12183	8572	10627	11507	11857	12893	11963	13361
070	7. Cotton (lint)	1353	1300	1192	1340	1281	1086	1446	1484
071	8. Jute & jute-like fibres	1500	1433	1469	1507	1291	1390	1402	2276
	Mining								
072	1. Iron ore	39288	39859	42168	41618	42752	39036	43140	44964
073	2. Dolomite	2003	2179	2064	2068	2198	2232	2352	2268
074	3. Manganese ore	1619	1771	1632	1532	1491	1212	1176	1284
	Manufacturing								
075	1. Cement	19625	18270	18660	29291	27000	25422	29568	33036
076	2. Sugar	6522	5614	4896	5148	8436	7871	6123	6756
077	3. Finished steel	6492	6156	5767	6761	6701	6196	6564	7924
078	4. Paper & paper board	986	1047	1199	1205	1236	1138	1452	1813
079	5. Jute manufactures	1173	2179	1233	1366	1294	1335	1154	1277
080	6. Tea	565	552	568	560	562	576	639	657
	Production Indexes								*Period*
081	Agriculture, *1979-81 = 100*	100.7	95.8	97.7	106.4	104.5	117.2	120.7	123.7
082	Mining, *1980/81 = 100* [d]	99.3	103.4	100.0	117.7	132.3	147.8	160.8	167.5
083	Manufacturing, *1980/81 = 100* [d]	99.3	99.3	100.0	107.9	109.4	115.6	124.8	136.9
	ENERGY								*Annual*
	Crude petroleum, *'000 m.t.*								
084	Production	11271	12839	9399	14925	19734	25148	27933	29860
085	Exports	...	...	0	0	4391	4723	6760	2044
086	Imports	14892	15382	15976	15528	17327	15552	14620	14811
087	Consumption	25626	28153	25075	29528	32107	34534	35235	41226
	Coal, *'000 m.t.*								
088	Production	101541	103454	109102	122453	128504	133349	144820	149710
089	Exports	446	78	117	166	180	80	97	215
090	Imports	0	890	310	620	1240	539	429	1817
091	Consumption	100122	103896	112748	119550	126344	36696	140230	152510
	Natural gas, *Mn cu. m.*								
092	Production	2770	3084	2077	3486	4661	5768	6820	7908
093	Exports	...	...	...	...	...	...	...	...
094	Imports	...	...	...	...	...	...	...	...
095	Consumption	1669	1993	1241	1857	2682	3206	3989	4685

	1986	1987	1988	1989	1990	1991	1992	1993	1994	1995	
	39.3	21.3	82.7	44.4	...	...	...	...	...	...	051
					...	...	...	...	...	...	052
	-57.9	-57.9	-50.6	14.7	...	...	...	...	...	...	053
											054
	714.4	748.8	970.5	1107.9	1373.9	1400.7	1695.5	1710.1	2189.2	2296.2 *	055
	579.1	671.9	865.4	1086.5	1358.2	...	1847.4	2073.5	2664.3	2599.6 *	056
	597.2	698.1	910.3	1143.8	1433.7	...	1965.5	2219.5	2810.3	2764.2 *	057
	-18.1	-26.2	-45.0	-57.3	-75.4	...	-118.1	-146.0	-145.9	-164.6 *	058
	63.6	68.2	123.0	122.8	182.0	52.4	...	...	...	...	059
	5.3	5.3	7.2	9.0	8.3	10.5	...	...	...	...	060
	58.3	62.9	115.8	113.8	173.7	41.9	...	...	...	...	061
	3795	4218	4888	5518	6325	...	7992	8897	10345	11785 *	062
	2392	2448	2625	2740	2833	...	2872	2918	3057	3210 *	063

Fiscal year beginning 1 April

	1986	1987	1988	1989	1990	1991	1992	1993	1994	1995	
	186090	196737	203037	225569	241046	253995	228033	227059	258400 *	...	064
	90779	85339	106639	110311	111517	112042	109301	118464	...	...	065
	44323	46169	54110	49850	55135	55690	57210	59131	65500 *	...	066
	12740	14046	14857	14771	15206	16388	16230	18037	...	...	067
	9185	12196	10170	12898	11681	8099	12957	...	...	...	068
	11707	10963	13849	12858	14265	12014	12815	13100	14100 *	...	069
	1174	1085	1486	1942	1671	1651	1938	1821	...	...	070
	1553	1220	1415	1492	1661	1051	1546	1527	...	...	071
	52260	50928	49911	55437	55591	58534	57147	58338	60744	...	072
	2172	2208	2261	2509	2648	2949	3225	3509	3120	...	073
	1272	1308	1386	1457	1492	1640	1903	1677	1728	...	074
	34983	36936	42708	45048	46609	52014	53937	57035	62952	...	075
	8508	8760	9576	9420	11810	12989	12531	9968	12612	...	076
	9706	10638	11118	10531	9584	10179	10129	14354	11994	...	077
	1871	1998	2071	2209	2433	2467	2563	2746	3158	...	078
	1394	1192	1388	1301	1342	1162	1126	1341	1162	...	079
	622	680	700	706	719	727	727	798	737	...	080

averages

	1986	1987	1988	1989	1990	1991	1992	1993	1994	1995	
	123.4	121.8	136.7	146.5	147.4	152.3	159.1	162.7	166.9	169.0	081
	177.9	184.6	199.1	211.6	218.7	226.3	226.0	232.0	246.0	...	082
	149.7	161.5	175.6	190.7	207.8	206.2	210.7	223.5	243.7	...	083

values

	1986	1987	1988	1989	1990	1991	1992	1993	1994	1995	
	31157	30142	31580	33685	33311	31007	27874	26508	30896	...	084
	...	...	...	...	...	...	...	...	...	...	085
	14481	17977	17712	18919	20793	21813	29977	30309	27895	...	086
	44940	47440	47896	51974	51671	50954	54254	53509	56314	...	087
	163371	177345	189018	198659	202194	226862	233883	246041	25178	...	088
	144	170	203	105	108	69	119	99	107	...	089
	2354	2037	3397	4183	4916	5200	6538	5889	7940	...	090
	162980	165890	187743	201390	219270	229313	237175	250294	261244	...	091
	9464	10906	12784	15926	17990	18649	18372	18121	19422	...	092
	...	...	...	...	...	...	...	...	...	...	093
	...	...	...	...	...	...	...	...	...	...	094
	6655	7662	8832	11070	12427	13982	13917	16282	17268	...	095

	Item	1978	1979	1980	1981	1982	1983	1984	1985
	Electricity, *Mn kWh* [d]								
096	Production	110130	112820	119260	131125	140299	150994	169205	183390
097	Exports	50	40	42	94	78	89	111	107
098	Imports	6	6	5	5	6	4	6	16
099	Consumption [e]	110086	112786	119223	131036	140227	150909	169100	183299
	Retail prices, *Rs/litre* [f]								
100	Gasoline, premium	3.39	4.04	4.41	5.11	6.07	6.07	5.99	6.12
101	Diesel	1.34	1.34	1.58	2.28	3.02	3.02	3.19	3.22
	PRICE INDEXES								*Period*
	Consumer (Industrial workers, Delhi)								
102	*1982 = 100*	...	...	...	...	...	...	...	...
103	Food	...	...	...	...	...	...	...	...
104	Non-food	...	...	...	...	...	...	...	...
	Consumer (Industrial workers, India)								
105	*1960 = 100\ 1982 = 100*	329.0	350.0	390.0	441.0	475.0	532.0	576.0	608.0
106	Food	346.0	362.0	406.0	465.0	498.0	564.0	604.0	626.0
107	Non-food	...	...	...	...	...	...	...	...
108	Wholesale, *1981/82 = 100*	66.5	74.2	89.1	100.0	104.3 [g]	110.8	118.5	124.0
109	Implicit GDP deflator, *1980/81 = 100*	77.6	89.6	100.0	110.3	118.5	128.5	138.1	148.5
	MONEY AND BANKING								*Billion Rupees;*
110	Money supply (M1)	172.9	200.0	234.2	249.4	285.3	334.0	399.1	440.9
111	Currency in circulation	102.3	116.5	134.3	144.7	166.6	196.0	226.7	250.6
112	Demand deposits	70.6	83.5	99.9	104.7	118.7	138.0	172.4	190.3
113	Quasi-money	228.2	272.3	323.5	378.1	446.5	531.3	630.2	753.0
114	Money supply (M2)	401.1	472.3	557.7	627.5	731.8	865.3	1029.3	1193.9
115	Foreign assets (net)	53.4	53.4	47.3	27.7	18.3	16.5	31.3	38.7
116	Domestic credit	414.6	510.3	623.6	740.9	864.2	1013.7	1212.9	1411.2
117	Claims on govt. sector (net)	159.3	200.2	257.2	306.3	352.6	406.4	503.4	583.2
118	Claims on private sector	255.3	310.1	366.4	434.6	511.6	607.3	709.5	828.0
119	Claims on other financial insts.								
120	Other items	-66.9	-91.4	-113.2	-141.1	-150.6	-164.9	-214.9	-256.0
	Deposit Money Banks								
121	Demand deposits [h]	50.6	60.6	68.8	80.6	87.2	104.0	118.1	148.1
122	Savings deposits	–	–	–	–	–	–	–	–
123	Time deposits [h]	179.2	219.0	260.0	311.7	364.4	425.5	506.6	597.3
124	Domestic credits outstanding [h]	162.3	193.0	231.1	272.7	320.9	383.6	444.0	523.4
	Interest Rates								*Per cent;*
	On deposits								
125	Savings	4.50	4.50	5.00	5.00	5.00	5.00	5.00	5.00
126	Time: 6 months	4.50	4.50	4.50	4.50	6.00	6.00	6.00	6.00
127	12 months	6.00	6.00	7.00	7.50	8.00	8.00	8.00	8.00
	On loans and discounts								
128	Commercial bills [i]	13.00-16.00	13.00-15.00	13.00-15.00	13.00-15.00	18.00-19.50	18.00-19.50	17.50-18.00	17.50-18.00
129	Export credit [j]	11.00	11.00	11.00	12.50-17.50	12.50-17.50	12.50-17.50	12.00-16.00	12.00-16.50
130	Other commercial [k]	15.00	15.00	18.00	19.50	19.50	19.50	18.00	18.00
	GOVERNMENT FINANCE [l]								*Billion Rupees;*
	Central Government								
131	Current revenue	110.17	110.27	124.56	152.55	177.92	202.12	239.90	286.93
132	Taxes	85.68	85.68	93.88	115.73	130.56	154.76	176.90	...
133	Non-taxes	24.49	24.59	30.68	36.82	47.36	47.36	63.00	...
134	Current expenditure	114.77	123.34	154.77	163.79	200.90	242.63	291.29	360.84
135	Current surplus/deficit	-4.60	-13.07	-30.21	-11.24	-22.98	-40.51	-51.39	-73.91
136	Capital receipts	42.48	28.85	53.94	55.06	73.58	102.96	120.76	128.57
137	Capital expenditure	18.88	21.39	30.50	37.87	41.14	49.03	65.95	69.55
138	Capital account surplus/deficit	23.60	7.46	23.44	17.19	32.44	53.92	54.81	59.02

	1986	1987	1988	1989	1990	1991	1992	1993	1994	1995	
	201279	218983	241308	268664	289439	315631	332713	356263	384139 *	...	096
	67	30	97	105	62	53	146	173		...	097
	170	885	1297	1402	1440	1506	1352	1199	...	...	098
	201382	219838	242508	269961	290817	317084	333919	357289	...	...	099
	7.00	7.43	7.43	8.50	9.84	12.23	14.62	15.71	16.78	...	100
	3.39	3.50	3.50	3.50	4.08	5.05	5.05	6.17	6.98	...	101

averages

	1986	1987	1988	1989	1990	1991	1992	1993	1994	1995	
	...	...	...	180.3	194.6	218.4	246.7	272.1	298.6	326.7	102
	...	...	...	190.1	210.1	243.3	269.7	302.6	337.0	...	103
	...	...	...	...	...	...	...	...	...	...	104
	661.0	719.2	774.7 [g]	170.9	186.3	212.1	237.1	252.2	277.9	306.3	105
	685.0	750.0	807.0 [g]	175.3	190.7	222.3	250.8	265.2	296.1	...	106
	...	...	...	...	...	...	...	...	...	...	107
	130.9	140.0	152.2	162.5	177.2	201.4	224.7	242.1	271.4	292.4 *	108
	158.1	171.7	185.5	200.9	222.9	...	277.7	303.6	337.1	366.4 *	109

As of end of period

	1986	1987	1988	1989	1990	1991	1992	1993	1994	1995	
	515.1	585.6	667.8	810.6	928.9	1148.4	1144.1	1240.6	1507.8	...	110
	283.8	335.6	383.3	463.0	530.5	611.0	611.0	682.7	823.0	...	111
	231.3	250.0	284.5	347.6	398.4	537.4	533.1	557.9	684.8	...	112
	901.2	1057.2	1267.1	1498.9	1729.4	2026.4	2026.4	2427.6	2836.3	...	113
	1416.3	1642.8	1934.9	2309.5	2658.3	3174.8	3170.5	3668.2	4344.1	...	114
	48.2	56.7	68.0	68.2	105.8	218.7	212.3	244.4	526.3	...	115
	1667.6	1918.6	2243.6	2688.5	3119.6	3462.6	3462.5	3963.7	4416.9	...	116
	720.2	843.7	964.8	1171.5	1401.9	1582.6	1582.6	1762.4	2039.2	...	117
	947.4	1074.9	1278.8	1517.0	1717.7	1880.0	1879.9	2201.3	2377.7	...	118
											119
	-299.5	-332.5	-376.6	-447.2	-567.1	-506.5	-504.3	-539.9	-599.1	...	120
	163.0	199.6	211.3	246.7	301.9	348.2	474.0	489.3	586.7	...	121
	–	–	–	–	–	–	–	–	–	...	122
	715.9	856.8	1002.7	1208.3	1429.6	1648.2	1923.3	2302.4	2706.5	...	123
	599.5	674.7	754.4	918.8	1097.8	1255.8	1367.1	1642.1	1773.2	...	124

As of end of period

	1986	1987	1988	1989	1990	1991	1992	1993	1994	1995	
	5.00	5.00	5.00	5.00	5.00	5.00	5.00	6.00	5.00	...	125
	8.00	8.00	8.00	8.00	8.00	8.00	11.00	11.00	10.00	...	126
	8.50	8.50	9.00	9.00	9.00	9.00	11.00	10.00	11.00	...	127
	17.00-17.50	17.00-17.50	15.50	15.50	15.50	16.50	15.50-19.00	18.00	14.90	...	128
	12.00-16.50	9.50-16.50	9.50-15.50	7.50-15.50	7.50-15.50	7.50-15.50	15.00-24.00	3.00-22.00	3.00-21.00	...	129
	17.50	17.50	16.50	16.00	16.00	16.00	19.00	17.00	15.00	...	130

Fiscal year beginning 1 April

	1986	1987	1988	1989	1990	1991	1992	1993	1994	1995	
	343.32	385.00	451.40	538.60	570.65	681.52	766.53	794.12	898.56 *	...	131
	...	...	...	...	...	...	...	...	...	...	132
	...	...	...	...	...	...	...	...	...	...	133
	439.06	513.01	601.44	709.40	809.56	904.02	1019.35	1215.94	1310.90 *	...	134
	-95.74	-128.01	-150.04	-170.80	-238.91	-222.50	-252.82	-421.82	-412.34 *	...	135
	112.99	129.37	149.85	201.66	279.20	255.97	271.83	511.09	516.36 *	...	136
	76.48	61.22	63.67	73.96	74.04	63.59	78.31	64.05	69.81 *	...	137
	36.51	68.15	86.18	127.70	205.16	192.38	193.52	447.04	446.55 *	...	138

	Item	1978	1979	1980	1981	1982	1983	1984	1985
139	Net lending	56.66	42.20	56.50	62.48	97.68	86.05	101.73	107.69
140	Overall surplus/deficit	-37.66	-47.81	-63.27	-56.53	-88.22	-72.63	-98.31	-122.58
	Financing								
141	Domestic borrowing	6.43	45.89	53.33	38.34	109.29	41.28	41.76	50.09
142	Foreign borrowing	3.84	5.84	7.98	10.29	13.54	14.37	15.16	14.49
143	Foreign grants	2.23	3.13	3.73	3.20	2.99	2.81	3.94	4.85
144	Use of cash balances	25.16	-7.05	-1.77	4.70	-37.60	14.17	37.45	53.15
	EXTERNAL TRADE								*Million Rupees;*
145	Exports, fob [m]	57260	64184	67107	78059	88033	97708	117437	108946
146	Imports, cif	68106	91426	125491	136075	142927	158315	171342	196057
147	Trade balance	-10846	-27242	-58384	-58016	-54894	-60607	-53905	-87112
	Exports, by SITC section								
148	Food & live animals	14476	17033	17051	19192	18967	20651	24390	25061
149	Beverage & tobacco	1170	1157	1414	2364	2488	1787	1793	1704
150	Crude materials excl. fuels	5126	6666	8136	7747	8168	8910	9997	11190
151	Mineral fuels, etc.	198	212	278	2249	12404	15900	18229	6550
152	Animal, vegetable oil & fats	179	524	193	200	260	450	583	486
153	Chemicals	1555	2084	2346	3754	3482	3270	4777	3910
154	Basic manufactures	23399	23976	23143	25797	26359	29524	36066	37064
155	Machines, transport equipment	3965	4473	5260	6174	5801	5182	6551	6767
156	Misc. manufactured goods	6883	7737	8686	10385	9776	11438	14532	15626
157	Unclassified goods	129	162	158	127	176	179	130	114
	Exports, by principal commodity								
158	1. Non-metallic mineral manufactures	7558	5678	6460	8110	9878	12505	11969	14531
159	2. Textile yarn, fabrics, articles, etc.	6807	9777	10164	10299	9497	9482	13912	12544
160	3. Clothing	4556	4990	5653	6576	6047	7409	9833	11057
	4. Coffee, tea, cocoa, spices								
161	& manufactures	6344	6810	7517	6427	6530	8172	11850	11783
162	5. Leather manufactures, n.e.s.	3277	4856	3371	3693	3600	4289	6271	6467
	Imports, by SITC section	68106	91426	125492	136076	142926	158315	171343	196577
163	Food & live animals	2453	2799	3802	6901	6396	10402	7337	8780
164	Beverage & tobacco	7	6	8	12	12	31	16	36
165	Crude materials excl. fuels	5780	5333	5654	8433	7670	9533	11234	15024
166	Mineral fuels, etc.	16869	33319	52930	52302	57584	48634	54640	52130
167	Animal, vegetable oil & fats	5524	4554	7088	6880	4477	7982	10078	7702
168	Chemicals	8365	9688	13246	13239	9889	14065	24311	28728
169	Basic manufactures	14772	19714	22420	25978	28218	31967	29700	37811
170	Machines, transport equipment	12599	13827	18208	19807	25727	31735	30271	40840
171	Misc. manufactured goods	1475	1889	2116	2487	2909	3899	3671	5006
172	Unclassified goods	262	297	22	37	44	67	86	520
	Direction of Trade								*Million US dollars;*
173	Exports, Total	6626.4	7745.6	8440.5	6827.0	8271.8	7858.1	8230.8	8265.4
174	1. United States	900.9	915.2	967.0	769.1	979.0	1296.1	1450.7	1563.3
175	2. Japan	628.0	823.8	775.8	557.1	909.6	834.2	826.7	920.6
176	3. Germany	304.7	422.8	494.3	327.7	368.4	373.6	416.1	401.5
177	4. United Kingdom	558.3	650.2	528.8	385.1	449.8	461.2	538.0	433.2
178	5. Hong Kong	126.1	118.9	165.7	61.7	185.2	185.8	161.9	153.8
179	6. United Arab Emirates	164.9	163.1	184.8	191.2	224.4	213.4	200.3	217.1
180	7. Belgium-Luxembourg	280.6	212.5	201.7	76.6	206.3	239.2	166.8	169.4
181	8. Singapore	87.7	98.5	126.8	94.8	126.0	129.2	124.7	103.0
182	9. Italy	145.7	247.6	213.5	153.5	150.9	151.1	179.8	168.5
183	10. France	204.5	232.6	204.0	133.3	165.3	146.1	155.6	161.6

1986	1987	1988	1989	1990	1991	1992	1993	1994	1995	
100.04	94.11	105.44	168.90	196.34	177.22	162.97	204.19	187.65 *	...	139
-159.27	-153.97	-169.30	-212.00	-230.09	-207.34	-222.27	-178.97	-153.44 *	...	140
									...	
52.11	56.71	82.28	72.59	78.96	75.10	36.76	37.00	37.00 *	...	141
20.19	34.18	24.60	25.95	31.81	54.21	53.19	38.37	42.79 *	...	142
4.36	4.92	6.00	7.54	5.85	9.48	9.20	13.00	13.65 *	...	143
82.61	58.16	56.42	105.92	113.47	68.55	123.12	90.60	60.00 *	...	144

Fiscal year beginning 1 April

1986	1987	1988	1989	1990	1991	1992	1993	1994	1995	
124519	156740	202315	276815	325533	440418	536883	696558	826741	...	145
200958	222440	282352	354118	431929	478508	633745	731010	899707	...	146
-76439	-65700	-80037	-77303	-106396	-38090	-96862	-34452	-72966	...	147
27794	29090	31687	40984	50912	73112	83807	112603	...	...	148
1866	1370	1285	1797	2753	4166	5159	5073	...	...	149
11858	11990	16225	25085	31565	20298	22995	33544	...	...	150
4176	6570	5186	7396	9480	10407	15198	15537	...	...	151
318	210	123	700	876	1782	1644	3286	...	...	152
4849	8020	12172	20300	25487	37856	36690	49392	...	...	153
45287	62180	86839	109081	187340	249038	316016	405911	...	...	154
8185	10140	14637	20417	24140	33377	43863	56956	...	...	155
19513	26960	806	1047	1840	1868	2549	3921	...	...	156
320	210	3371	4114	4491	6017	8143	10335	...	...	157
20374	26649	44726	54008	53926	70087	92922	131330	...	...	158
14058	15841	16632	20709	27292	32358	56970	67778	...	...	159
14038	18199	21020	32269	40134	54220	69309	81119	...	...	160
11533	11765	9109	15390	15408	18466	16460	20535	...	...	161
7312	2773	3780	6532	9351	13402	36404	35111	...	...	162
200957	222440	282352	354118	431929	478508	633743	731010			
7502	8650	14914	10304	10931	10316	21645	20120	...	...	163
30	60	91	135	117	80	112	187	...	...	164
16246	18610	26626	23418	23675	11278	36069	35929	...	...	165
30294	42850	48143	69004	117884	143161	187054	198412	...	...	166
6563	9700	7632	2505	3643	3421	2870	3460	...	...	167
26366	23340	37633	42333	46956	64168	81038	84110	...	...	168
43570	48030	69185	111044	114607	132151	161321	185020	...	...	169
62785	64050	67613	76844	86840	75151	104294	149849	...	...	170
6725	7150	9643	17868	26060	36899	37815	51884	...	...	171
876	–	872	663	1216	1883	1525	2039	...	...	172

Calendar year

1986	1987	1988	1989	1990	1991	1992	1993	1994	1995	
9135.3	10797.8	13192.6	15839.0	17812.9	17872.3	18498.0	20258.2	24195.0	31052.8	173
1777.7	2114.0	2513.1	4423.5	2693.7	2922.3	3533.2	3885.1	4660.5	5634.2	174
1017.3	1198.5	1420.6	2136.7	1656.0	1654.0	1522.8	1656.5	1923.5	2651.6	175
524.9	742.8	909.7	1227.0	1351.9	1271.1	1441.5	1526.5	1585.9	2196.9	176
512.4	708.4	849.1	1201.0	1109.0	1136.7	1333.2	1265.2	1532.9	2080.3	177
280.7	347.3	456.8	826.9	545.0	615.4	721.4	1145.1	1349.9	1703.9	178
223.4	241.8	278.7	...	454.7	737.9	479.5	725.6	1210.4	1331.4	179
238.4	342.7	502.9	463.5	699.2	668.2	693.9	804.4	912.2	1030.8	180
172.9	188.3	218.0	370.8	308.3	386.5	515.1	727.4	738.0	856.0	181
198.6	350.0	405.5	569.5	499.3	580.7	655.0	570.9	767.8	1197.3	182
198.8	256.4	305.0	523.7	421.7	421.2	490.6	484.9	544.9	997.9	183

	Item	1978	1979	1980	1981	1982	1983	1984	1985
184	Imports, Total	7819.7	9898.6	14822.2	14549.8	15634.8	13892.7	15115.3	16329.0
185	1. United States	928.4	1044.3	1865.2	1370.1	1562.2	1704.1	1481.7	1769.9
186	2. Germany	703.5	790.0	836.4	910.7	996.5	884.3	1166.7	1257.5
187	3. Japan	603.0	760.7	815.1	880.4	1179.4	1265.1	1085.1	1363.6
188	4. Belgium-Luxembourg	397.4	329.4	373.5	545.0	608.1	517.6	725.1	786.4
189	5. Saudi Arabia	246.2	406.4	520.6	721.3	1719.6	969.6	1014.7	842.7
190	6. United Kingdom	637.9	904.2	953.5	790.7	976.2	927.4	1001.9	927.2
191	7. Kuwait	122.5	178.8	337.0	378.6	297.6	260.8	353.4	229.6
192	8. United Arab Emirates	109.6	220.3	378.3	598.3	409.3	229.8	284.9	482.4
193	9. Australia	88.7	190.4	210.2	174.5	405.9	183.4	58.3	411.8
194	10. Singapore	99.6	109.7	475.2	463.1	438.3	348.7	445.3	321.4
	Trade Indexes								*1978/79 = 100;*
	Quantum index								
195	Exports	100.0	106.2	108.0	110.1	117.0	113.0	121.0	111.0
196	Imports	100.0	116.4	138.0	150.6	155.0	189.0	156.0	182.0
	Unit value index								
197	Exports	100.0	105.4	109.0	124.1	132.0	151.0	170.0	171.0
198	Imports	100.0	114.1	134.0	133.1	136.0	124.0	162.0	159.0
199	Terms of trade (net)	100.0	92.4	81.3	93.2	97.1	121.8	104.9	107.5
	BALANCE OF PAYMENTS								*Million US dollars;*
200	Merchandise exports, fob	6518	7597	8303	8437	9226	9770	10192	9465
201	Merchandise imports, fob	-7402	-9819	-13947	-14149	-14046	-13868	-14216	-15081
202	Trade balance	-884	-2222	-5644	-5711	-4820	-4098	-4025	-5616
203	Other goods, services and income	-50	227	525	7	-620	-917	-1088	-1338
204	Credit	1997	2832	4029	3769	3541	3770	3719	3912
205	Debit	-2047	-2605	-3504	-3762	-4161	-4687	-4807	-5250
206	Unrequited transfer	1618	2042	3333	3006	2917	3062	2770	2776
207	Private	1147	1424	2743	2281	2599	2650	2278	2456
208	Official	471	618	590	725	318	412	492	320
209	Current balance	683	48	-1785	-2698	-2524	-1953	-2343	-4177
210	Direct investment	–	–	–	–	–	–	–	–
211	Portfolio investment	–	–	–	–	–	–	–	–
212	Other long-term capital $\Big\}$	805	482	483	845	456	2051	3044	3281
213	Other short-term capital								
214	Net errors and omissions	431	301	-361	-325	369	-850	368	500
215	Overall balance	1920	832	-1663	-2178	-1698	-752	1070	-397
216	Allocation of SDRs	–	–	–	–	–	–	–	–
217	Monetary movements	-1920	-832	1663	2178	1698	752	-1070	397
	INTERNATIONAL RESERVES								*Million US dollars;*
218	Total	6694	7717	7227	4941	4549	5153	6026	6623
219	Gold, national valuation	268	284	284	248	234	215	184	203
220	Foreign exchange	6042	6731	6043	3764	3539	4318	5034	5549
221	Reserve position in the Fund	90	213	420	384	402	510	477	535
222	SDRs	294	489	480	545	374	110	331	336
	EXCHANGE RATES								*Rupees*
223	End of period	8.188	7.907	7.930	9.099	9.634	10.493	12.451	12.166
224	Average of period	8.193	8.126	7.863	8.659	9.455	10.099	11.363	12.369
	EXTERNAL INDEBTEDNESS								*Million US dollars;*
225	Total outstanding and disbursed	16466	17898	20582	22609	27438	32004	33826	40971
226	Long-term	15815	17200	18334	19459	21595	23953	25698	31781
227	Public and publicly guaranteed	15467	16865	17998	18586	20566	22768	24357	30284
228	Private non-guaranteed	348	335	336	873	1029	1185	1341	1497
229	Short-term	651	698	1271	1597	2397	3338	3672	4358
230	Use of IMF credit	0	0	977	1553	3446	4713	4456	4832

	1986	1987	1988	1989	1990	1991	1992	1993	1994	1995	
	15051.4	16839.7	19034.5	19296.9	23989.7	19509.4	23226.5	21225.5	25477.5	34187.5	184
	1429.8	1503.1	1855.8	2309.5	2634.8	1891.2	2258.3	2170.7	2431.7	3604.8	185
	1365.4	1583.4	1740.7	1472.7	1835.7	1551.3	1907.1	1587.4	1899.2	2834.3	186
	1931.2	1741.7	1874.5	1493.7	1800.8	1364.3	1504.2	1376.5	1839.9	2797.2	187
	813.4	1008.2	1219.0	1508.5	1928.6	1394.6	1785.6	1922.7	1217.6	1351.6	188
	639.9	601.1	900.3	895.6	1475.2	1109.3	1649.5	1600.7	1512.9	1634.0	189
	1176.5	1447.2	1660.2	1650.1	1664.5	1185.5	1393.1	1458.6	1470.6	2837.2	190
	242.2	375.4	367.8	575.4	421.2	215.0	965.0	1065.5	1385.5	...	191
	341.5	527.0	532.7	793.2	963.7	993.8	727.1	657.8	1307.1	1411.6	192
	332.1	342.8	425.0	432.7	756.8	560.8	826.3	685.8	841.0	894.4	193
	252.6	309.9	365.6	491.6	689.1	311.1	688.6	593.1	720.0	835.2	194

Period averages [d]

	121.0	140.0	152.0	174.9	194.1	208.6	222.9	257.0	293.0	...	195
	212.0	205.0	224.0	227.8	237.7	228.0	280.0	329.0	532.0	...	196
	179.0	195.0	232.0	276.6	292.5	369.5	421.5	474.0	495.0	...	197
	139.0	160.0	186.0	228.4	267.7	309.1	333.4	327.0	249.0	...	198
	128.8	121.9	124.7	121.1	109.3	119.5	126.4	145.0	198.8	...	199

Calendar year

	10248	11884	13510	16144	18286	18095	20019	...	...	...	200
	-15686	-17661	-20091	-22254	-23437	-21087	-22150	...	...	...	201
	-5438	-5777	-6581	-6110	-5151	-2992	-2130	...	...	...	202
	-1780	-2421	-3319	-3566	-4521	-4759	-5311	...	...	...	203
	3746	3813	4218	4586	5061	5157	5303	...	...	...	204
	-5526	-6234	-7537	-8152	-9582	-9916	-10614	...	...	...	205
	2622	3006	2752	3070	2836	3723	3335	...	...	...	206
	2223	2636	2295	2567	2337	...	...	...	...	...	207
	399	370	457	503	499	...	...	...	...	...	208
	-4598	-5192	-7148	-6606	-6836	-4028	-4107	...	...	...	209
	–	–	–	–	–	–	–	...	...	...	210
								...	...	...	211
	3992	5734	7243	7212	5528	3485	4131	...	...	...	212
								...	...	...	213
	197	-409	-112	-369	-633	343	1104	...	...	...	214
	-409	133	-16	237	-1941	-200	1128	...	...	...	215
	–	–	–	–	–	–	–	...	...	...	216
	409	-133	16	-237	1941	200	-1128	...	...	...	217

As of end of period

	6605	6666	5083	4019	5188	6794	8665	13524	23053	21591	218
	209	213	183	161	3667	3168	2908	3325	3355	3669	219
	5444	5603	4148	3105	1205	3580	5461	9807	19386	17467	220
	596	691	656	640	–	–	292	292	310	316	221
	356	159	96	113	316	46	4	100	2	139	222

per US dollar

	13.122	12.877	14.949	17.035	18.073	25.834	26.200	31.380	31.380	35.180	223
	12.611	12.962	13.917	16.226	17.504	22.742	25.918	30.493	31.374	32.427	224

As of end of fiscal year

	48278	55727	58443	73389	81983	83947	89822	92104	98990	...	225
	38564	46032	49512	64322	70816	73426	78684	83438	89589	...	226
	37176	44379	48039	62771	69328	71881	77479	81668	87880	...	227
	1388	1652	1473	1551	1488	1545	1205	1770	1709	...	228
	4946	5673	6358	7501	8544	7070	6340	3626	5089	...	229
	4768	4023	2573	1566	2623	3451	4798	5041	4312	...	230

	Item	1978	1979	1980	1981	1982	1983	1984	1985
									Transactions
	Debt service								
231	Principal repayments on LT debt	667	712	755	747	933	1084	1092	1310
232	Interest on long-term debt	379	395	503	561	738	916	972	1273
233	Interest on short-term debt	0	73	134	197	227	261	389	326
	Average terms of new commitments								
234	Interest (%)	1.9	4.0	5.6	5.0	7.1	6.8	6.9	6.2
235	Maturity (years)	44.4	36.6	33.3	34.0	26.0	24.5	27.3	26.4
236	Grace period (years)	9.2	8.0	8.6	9.7	9.0	10.6	10.1	10.7
237	Grant element (%)	71.4	54.6	43.2	43.8	23.9	25.4	25.8	29.3

Footnotes:

a   Data prior to 1992 have been interpolated using the census growth rates between 1971-81 and 1981-91. For 1992-94, data are projections based on the census population for 1991. ADB staff estimate for 1995.

b   Refers to applicants currently registered at employment exchanges.

c   Relates to agricultural year beginning 1 July of the year stated.

d   Period averages for the fiscal year beginning 1 April.

e   Includes electricity consumed in auxiliary stations and losses in transmission and distribution system.

f   Refers to prices quoted for New Delhi only as of 1 January of each year up to 1986 and as of 1 April of each year therefater.

g   Refers to average for January-September only.

h   Refers to scheduled commercial banks and state cooperative banks.

i   Discount rates up to 1986 refer to the rates charged by the biggest bank in the country. From 1987 onwards, rates refer to those charged by scheduled commercial banks.

j   Refers to average of varying rates depending on the type and period of credit.

k   Refers to ceiling rate on general credit as prescribed by Reserve Bank of India (RBI). With effect from October 10, 1988, the RBI has prescribed a minimum lending rate of 16% on general credit.

l   Revised estimates for FY 1993/94 and budget estimates for FY 1994/95.

m   Includes re-exports.

1986	1987	1988	1989	1990	1991	1992	1993	1994	1995	
during the fiscal year										
2291	1894	1949	1964	2397	2569	2949	4169	4814	...	231
1662	1992	2123	3307	3733	3445	3370	3512	3831	...	232
356	429	437	570	899	826	399	367	469	...	233
6.1	5.7	6.5	5.8	5.8	5.8	5.3	4.7	4.6	...	234
22.3	24.8	22.4	21.3	25.7	20.9	25.0	25.4	27.3	...	235
11.0	10.4	11.3	9.2	12.7	7.6	11.9	10.8	12.5	...	236
26.6	32.2	25.7	28.7	33.9	32.2	34.2	39.7	43.6	...	237

Item	1978	1979	1980	1981	1982	1983	1984	1985
								Million;
001 **POPULATION** [a]	141.4	144.7	148.0	151.3	154.7	158.1	161.6	164.6
								Thousand;
002 **LABOR FORCE** [b]	53097	52730	52421	60762	59599	58993	61362	63826
003 Employed	51780	51004	51553	59123	57803	57811	60084	62458
004 Agriculture	31545	32661	28834	36336	31593	32014	33079	34142
005 Manufacturing	3856	5464	4680	4727	6022	5339	5565	5796
006 Mining	-	238	387	326	391	405	411	416
007 Others	16379	12641	17652	17734	19797	20053	21029	22104
008 Unemployed	1317	1726	868	1639	1796	1182	1278	1368
009 Unemployment Rate	2.5	3.3	1.7	2.7	3.0	2.0	2.0	2.1
NATIONAL ACCOUNTS [c] *At Current Market Prices*								*Billion Rupiah;*
010 GDP by Industrial Origin	22746	32025	45446	58127	62476	77623	89885	96997
011 Agriculture	6706	8996	11290	13698	15062	17765	20420	22513
012 Mining	4358	6980	11673	13218	12153	16107	16938	13571
013 Manufacturing	2420	3311	5288	7067	7482	9896	13113	15503
014 Electricity, gas and water	118	149	225	292	341	314	354	396
015 Construction	1242	1790	2524	3500	3769	4597	4757	5302
016 Trade	3450	4775	6391	8781	9947	11419	13435	15417
017 Transport and communications	1032	1422	1965	2370	3164	4098	5051	6100
018 Finance [d]	1066	1569	1952	2900	3514	4714	5631	6271
019 Public administration	1685	2200	3142	4203	4706	5712	6470	7925
020 Others	668	835	996	2099	2339	3001	3718	3999
021 Net factor income from abroad	-892	-1484	-2011	-1930	-1980	-3283	-4183	-3941
022 GNP	21854	30541	43435	56197	60496	74340	85702	93056
023 Expenditure on GDP	22746	32025	45446	58127	62476	77623	89885	96997
024 Private consumption [e]	15185	19514	27503	32293	37924	47063	54067	57201
025 Government consumption	2659	3733	4688	6452	7209	8077	9122	10893
026 Gross fixed capital formation	4671	6704	9485	14135	15822	19468	20136	22367
027 Increase in stocks	...	...	...	3190	1583	2794	3406	4837
028 Exports of goods and services	4974	9629	13849	16177	15103	19847	22999	21534
029 Less: Imports of goods and services	4742	7555	10080	14119	15186	19626	19845	19835
030 Statistical discrepancy	–	–	–	–	20	–	–	–
At Constant 1973 | 1983 | 1993 Prices								
031 GDP by Industrial Origin	9567	10165	11169	12055	12325 |	77623	83037	85082
032 Agriculture	3135	3256	3425	3594	3670 |	17765	18513	19300
033 Mining	1049	1047	1035	1069	940 |	16107	17120	15480
034 Manufacturing	1236	1395	1705	1878	1901 |	9896	12079	13431
035 Electricity, gas and water	57	69	78	90	106 |	314	324	361
036 Construction	529	563	639	720	758 |	4597	4394	4508
037 Trade	1530	1681	1852	2043	2159 |	11419	11811	12399
038 Transport and communications	514	560	609	677	717 |	4098	4443	4487
039 Finance [d]	452	486	544	590	636 |	4714	5241	5481
040 Public administration	768	805	972	1076	1115 |	5712	5997	6455
041 Others	297	304	311	319	326 |	3001	3117	3180
042 Net factor income from abroad	-508	-649	-759	-674	-653 |	-3283	-3822	-3846
043 GNP	9059	9516	10411	11381	11673 |	74340	79216	81236
044 Expenditure on GDP	9567	10165	11169	12055	12325 |	77623	83037	85082
045 Private consumption [e]	6880	7866	8868	10350	10698 |	47063	48942	49448
046 Government consumption	1228	1345	1490	1641	1776 |	8077	8353	8991
047 Gross fixed capital formation	2333	2436	2896	3219	3637 |	19468	18297	19616
048 Increase in stocks	...	...	...	...	... |	2794	4452	6641
049 Exports of goods and services	1824	1822	1719	1678	1444 |	19847	21145	19495
050 Less: Imports of goods and services	2699	3304	3803	4833	5229 |	19626	18151	19109
051 Statistical discrepancy	–	–	–	–	– |	–	–	–

1986	1987	1988	1989	1990	1991	1992	1993	1994	1995	
As of 1 July										
168.4	172.0	175.6	179.1	179.2	182.9	186.0	189.1	192.2	195.3	001
Calendar year										
70193	72245	74596	75508	77803	78455	80704	81446	81200	...	002
68338	70403	72518	73425	75851	76423	78518	79200	79900	...	003
37644	38722	40558	41284	42378	41206	42153	40072	40600	...	004
5606	5818	5997	7335	7693	7946	8255	8784	9100	...	005
...	...	...	449	528	565	525	653	600	...	006
25088	25863	25963	24357	25252	26706	27585	29691	29600	...	007
1855	1842	2078	2083	1952	2032	2186	2246	1300	...	008
2.6	2.5	2.8	2.8	2.5	2.6	2.7	2.8	1.6	...	009
Calendar year										
102683	124817 I	149669	179582	210866	249969	282395	329776	379212 *	445401 *	010
24871	29116 I	33651	38894	40930	45636	52746	58963	65992 *	76557 *	011
11503	17267 I	18200	22921	25634	31953	30587	31497	33507 *	37631 *	012
17185	21150 I	29484	35441	43569	53379	62016	73556	88992 *	108164 *	013
647	747 I	873	1508	1489	1898	2472	3290	3913 *	4809 *	014
5314	6087 I	7219	8991	11795	13762	16878	22513	28017 *	34339 *	015
17122	21048 I	25345	30415	35824	41981	47144	55298	62207 *	73126 *	016
6407	7443 I	9884	10936	13362	16968	19714	23249	26989 *	30202 *	017
7013	8144 I	9006	12196	16403	20835	23994	28048	34506 *	39891 *	018
8307	8912 I	9846	11574	14322	15218	17399	22458	22755 *	26555 *	019
4315	4903 I	6161	6706	7538	8339	9447	10903	12335 *	14127 *	020
-4193	-6022 I	-6922	-8074	-9616	-10913	-12542	-12553	-14279 *	-19583 *	021
98490	118795 I	142748	171508	201251	239056	269853	317223	364933 *	425818 *	022
102683	124817 I	149669	179582	210866	249969	282395	329776	379212 *	445401 *	023
63355	71989 I	89722	100234	124184	145540	157910	183531	213257 *	249370 *	024
11329	11764 I	12756	15698	18649	20785	24731	29757	31014 *	36576 *	025
24782	30980 I	38356	47706	59758	67488	72774	86667	105381 *	128105 *	026
4243	8166 I	4815	10773	5032	12541	18737	22908	24588 *	40263 *	027
20010	29874 I	35585	43614	53289	63865	78723	85296	96847 *	113357 *	028
21036	27956 I	31566	38443	50046	60249	70481	78383	91874 *	122270 *	029
–	– I	–	–	–	–	–	–	– *	– *	030
90081	94518 I	221407	241521	263262	286765	307474	329776	354442 *	383051 *	031
19799	20224 I	49073	51476	53056	54583	58002	58963	59287 *	61637 *	032
16309	16366 I	23241	24832	26628	29969	30461	31497	33262 *	35145 *	033
14678	16235 I	43516	48426	54211	59941	66042	73556	82726 *	91929 *	034
430	495 I	1850	2100	2508	2720	2961	3290	3707 *	4281 *	035
4609	4803 I	11499	13022	15226	17487	19664	22513	25858 *	29191 *	036
13399	14356 I	33963	37714	41725	46669	50344	55298	59351 *	63945 *	037
4668	4939 I	15272	16917	18474	20040	21618	23249	25066 *	27148 *	038
6028	6313 I	15574	18317	21479	24309	26164	28048	30901 *	34369 *	039
6862	7366 I	18734	19832	20738	21380	22012	22458	22752 *	23046 *	040
3299	3422 I	8685	8885	9218	9670	10207	10903	11533 *	12360 *	041
-3802	-4248 I	-9429	-10091	-11397	-12508	-13351	-12553	-12965 *	-16756 *	042
86278	90270 I	211978	231430	251865	274257	294123	317223	341477 *	366295 *	043
90081	94518 I	221407	241521	263262	286765	307474	329776	354442 *	383051 *	044
50530	52200 I	123144	132330	155094	167455	172640	183531	194185 *	206322 *	045
9241	9226 I	23080	25458	26689	28094	29702	29757	30443 *	31476 *	046
21422	22597 I	52116	59891	69519	78488	81302	86667	98589 *	111282 *	047
6333	5049 I	12650	12846	11133	9884	16125	22908	27996 *	48778 *	048
22460	25745 I	53950	59566	59808	71702	82605	85296	92981 *	97011 *	049
19906	20299 I	43533	48570	58981	68856	74900	78383	89752 *	111817 *	050
–	– I	–	–	–	–	–	–	– *	– *	051

Item	1978	1979	1980	1981	1982	1983	1984	1985
Investment Financing, at current prices								
052 Gross domestic capital formation [f]	4671	6704	9485	17324	17406	22261	23543	27204
053 Gross national saving	4010	7294	11244	17452	15364	19199	22514	24962
054 Gross domestic saving	4903	8778	13255	19382	17343	22483	26697	28902
055 Net factor income from abroad	-892	-1484	-2011	-1930	-1980	-3283	-4183	-3941
Per Capita, GNP, '000 Rupiah								
056 Current prices	155	211	293	371	391	470	530	565
057 Constant *1973Ι 1983Ι 1993* prices	64	66	70	75 Ι	75	470	490	493
PRODUCTION								*Thousand metric tons;*
Agriculture								
058 1. Rice, paddy	25771	26283	29652	32774	33584	35303	38136	39033
059 2. Cassava	12902	13751	13726	13301	12988	12103	14167	14057
060 3. Maize	4029	3606	3991	4509	3235	5087	5288	4330
061 4. Palm oil	525	560	691	752	834	891	1080	1159
062 5. Copra	732	1596	1630	1765	1587	1590	1738	1895
063 6. Sugar cane	1126	1275	1188	1194	1609	1572	1500	1767
064 7. Bananas	1378	1622	1977	2508	2036	1781	1992	1909
065 8. Sweet potatoes	2083	2194	2074	2094	1676	2213	2157	2161
066 9. Soya beans	617	680	653	704	521	536	769	870
067 10. Peanuts	446	424	470	475	437	460	535	528
Mining								
068 1. Copper Ore Concentrates	180.9	188.8	186.1	188.5	223.7	205.0	190.3	232.4
069 2. Nickel Ore	1206.7	1551.9	1537.4	1543.2	1640.9	1278.0	1066.8	955.6
070 3. Tin Ore Concentrates	27.4	29.4	32.5	35.4	33.8	26.6	23.2	21.8
Manufacturing								
071 1. Cement	3648.9	4431.5	5817.8	6844.2	7417.6	8095.1	8893.2	9939.7
072 2. Fertilizer	2108.7	1651.0	2745.9	2813.8	2809.1	3201.5	4005.4	5264.0
073 3. Paper	69.6	74.4	78.2	78.4	77.6	70.2	84.6	96.7
Production Indexes								**Period**
074 Agriculture, *1979-81 = 100*	88.0	92.8	100.8	106.4	105.5	114.4	122.8	126.1
075 Manufacturing, *1983Ι 1993 = 100*	63.8	69.0	84.7	93.0	93.4	100.0	104.8	112.6
ENERGY								*Annual*
Crude Petroleum, *'000 m.t.*								
076 Production	80258	78072	77610	78848	65818	66128	68518	67710
077 Exports	69560	60418	50887	50130	56070	51313	45779	39185
078 Imports	2467	3530	5187	2676	4183	3371	5533	3655
079 Consumption	22280	24700	26182	26315	24642	25051	21145	20908
Coal, *'000 m.t.*								
080 Production	264	279	304	350	481	486	1085	1942
081 Exports	32	60	112	157	211	424	882	1080
082 Imports	3	4	5	5	3	1	–	662
083 Consumption	189	223	237	273	313	268	66	1358
Natural Gas, *terajoules*								
084 Production	353433	481932	607205	652150	646348	773139	940480	937377
085 Exports	198618	325532	449011	422980	443760	423583	757150	792202
086 Imports	–	–	–	–	–	–	–	–
087 Consumption	154815	156400	158194	189170	202588	229409	253330	250500
Electricity, *Mn kWh*								
088 Production	5811	7291	8730	9885	12144	15232	18432	20939
089 Consumption	5811	7291	8730	9885	12144	15232	18432	20939
Retail Prices, *Rp/litre*								
090 Gasoline, premium	70	100	150	240	240	320	350	385
091 Diesel	22	30	45	75	75	125	200	220

1986	1987		1988	1989	1990	1991	1992	1993	1994	1995	
29025	39146	I	43171	58479	64790	80028	91512	109576	129968 *	168368 *	052
23806	35043	I	40269	55576	58417	72731	87212	103936	120663 *	139873 *	053
27999	41065	I	47191	63650	68033	83644	99754	116489	134941 *	159455 *	054
-4193	-6022	I	-6922	-8074	-9616	-10913	-12542	-12553	-14279 *	-19583 *	055
585	691	I	813	957	1123	1307	1450	1677	1899 *	2181 *	056
512	525	I	1207	1292	1405	1499	1581	1677	1777 *	1876 *	057

Calendar year

39727	40078	41676	44726	45179	44688	48240	48181	46641 *	49860 *	058
13312	14356	15471	17117	15830	15954	16516	17285	15729 *	15312 *	059
5920	5156	6652	6193	6734	6256	7995	6460	6869 *	8223 *	060
1351	1381	1609	1860	2097	1844	2186	2288	1930 *	2477 *	061
1975	2099	2144	2221	2332	2478	2511	2515	...	...	062
2013	2086	2004	2071	2173	2233	2345	2336	2421 *	2015 *	063
2079	2100	1860	2192	2411	2472	2651	2876	3134 *	...	064
2091	2013	2159	2224	1971	2039	2171	2088	1845 *	2138 *	065
1227	1161	1270	1315	1487	1555	1870	1709	1565 *	1689 *	066
642	533	589	620	651	652	739	639	632 *	758 *	067
251.2	258.8	293.7	324.6	437.3	656.5	906.7	928.2	1065.5	...	068
1533.1	1860.5	1733.2	2020.9	2217.4	2300.3	2511.6	1975.8	2302.0	...	069
24.9	26.2	29.6	31.3	30.4	30.4	28.2	28.6	30.6	...	070
11322.3	11860.6	12001.2	15659.4	15783.0	16153.4	17279.8	18990.0	21907.3	...	071
5713.9	6476.4	6302.5	6692.9	7012.1	6568.2	6577.2	6944.2	6641.0	...	072
110.5	121.5	948.2	1149.0	1339.7	1644.0	2222.6	2489.3	2736.9	...	073

averages

134.7	136.2	143.8	148.5	157.7	160.8	171.3	174.2		171.6	175.3	074
128.4	143.5	164.2	184.1	209.4	232.3	257.9	286.7	I	117.6	...	075

values

71012	64625	66212	69323	73071	79605	75642	76712	...	...	076
44454	39134	36654	39147	47487	53175	49234	46990	...	...	077
3794	3928	4310	4643	6351	5636	8349	...	...	...	078
20593	21982	23071	24588	27801	30097	32719	...	...	...	079
2572	1887	3669	8711	10532	14143	23120	27585	28601	...	080
999	893	1307	2197	4196	6667	16299	18172	21436	...	081
1272	2077	1035	1299	621	673	454	...	...	...	082
3011	3071	3036	5213	5674	6074	7099	7832	7510	...	083
1119657	1079657	1219657	1462449	1578536	1819419	2021655	...	...	...	084
808135	826291	853383	887971	1087516	1170920	1091923	...	...	...	085
–	–	–	–	–	–	–	...	...	...	086
276522	263366	307700	484478	500320	573499	804732	...	...	...	087
23583	22305	25622	29570	34868	38737	41934	46719	...	...	088
23583	17076	19993	23937	27741	31481	34979	38962	...	...	089
385	385	385	385	450	550	700	700	700	...	090
200	200	200	200	235	285	285	380	380	...	091

Item	1978	1979	1980	1981	1982	1983	1984	1985
PRICE INDEXES								*Period*
092 Consumer (Jakarta I 17 cities I 27 cities), [g] Sep 66\ Apr77-Mar 78\ Apr 88-Mar 89 = 100	2146.0 I	132.4	156.3	175.5	192.1	214.7	237.2	248.4
093 Food	2458.0 I	130.6	152.8	175.4	185.8	202.8	222.8	228.2
094 Wholesale, *1983 = 100*	37.5	54.8	71.3	79.2	84.6	100.0	111.9	116.2
095 Implicit GDP deflator *1973\ 1983\ 1993 = 100*	237.8	315.1	406.9	482.2	506.9 I	100.0	108.2	114.0
MONEY AND BANKING								*Billion Rupiah;*
096 Money supply (M1)	2488	3385	4995	6485	7121	7569	8581	10104
097 Currency in circulation	1240	1552	2153	2557	2934	3333	3712	4440
098 Demand deposits	1248	1833	2842	3928	4187	4236	4869	5664
099 Quasi-money	1321	1837	2696	3231	3954	7094	9356	13049
100 Money supply (M2)	3809	5222	7691	9716	11075	14663	17937	23153
101 Foreign assets (net)	1663	3318	6419	6811	5565	8837	12368	14119
102 Domestic credit	4046	4232	3979	5651	8846	9744	10345	13975
103 Claims on govt. sector (net)	1442	1073	-360	-443	534	-939	-3984	-3687
104 Claims on private sector	2604	3159	4339	6094	8312	10683	14329	17662
105 Claims on other financial insts.	–	–	–	–	–	–	–	–
106 Other items [h]	-1900	-2328	-2707	-2746	-3336	-3918	-4776	-4941
Deposit Money Banks								
107 Demand deposits	1193	1737	2795	3847	4134	4177	4817	5560
108 Savings deposits }	1054	1140	1481	2033	2491	4693	6387	9607
109 Time deposits }								
110 Domestic credits outstanding [i]	3621	4318	5658	7853	10622	13648	19079	22729
Interest Rates								*Per cent;*
On deposits								
111 Savings [j]	15	15	15	15	15	15	15	15
112 Time: 6 months [k]	6	6	6	6	6	20	18	17
113 12 months	9	9	9	9	9	18	19	19
GOVERNMENT FINANCE *Central Government*								*Billion Rupiah;*
114 Current revenue	4267	6697	10227	12213	12418	14433	15905	19253
115 Taxes	4075	6510	9911	11876	11983	13914	15218	17761
116 Non-taxes [l]	192	187	316	337	435	519	687	1492
117 Current expenditure	2744	4062	5800	6978	6996	8412	9429	11951
118 Current surplus/deficit	1523	2635	4427	5236	5421	6021	6476	7302
119 Capital receipts	–	–	–	–	–	–	–	–
120 Capital expenditure	2556	4014	5916	6940	7360	9899	9952	10873
121 Capital account surplus/deficit	-2556	-4014	-5916	-6940	-7360	-9899	-9952	-10873
122 Overall surplus/deficit	-1033	-1379	-1489	-1705	-1938	-3878	-3476	-3571
Financing								
123 Domestic borrowing	–	–	–	–	–	–	–	–
124 Foreign borrowing }	1035	1381	1494	1709	1940	3882	3478	3572
125 Foreign grants }								
126 Use of cash balances	-2	-2	-5	-5	-2	-4	-2	-1
Expenditure by Function, Central Govt.								
127 Total [m]	2555	4014	5916	6907	8165	9899	9952	10873
128 General public services [n]	107	201	309	330	437	676	414	660
129 Defense	159	330	479	566	477	526	702	590
130 Education	251	361	575	726	704	1032	1231	1413
131 Health }	79	142	218	286	259	279	320	398
132 Social security & welfare }								
133 Housing & community amenities [o]	350	494	739	866	963	1051	1121	1333
134 Economic services	1609	2486	3596	4133	5325	6335	6164	6479
135 Agriculture [p]	450	628	1077	1106	1929	1106	1929	1381
136 Industry	157	356	415	528	506	512	603	963
137 Electricity, gas & water [q]	319	377	507	828	1165	2299	1148	1673

1986	1987	1988	1989	1990	1991	1992	1993	1994	1995	
averages										
263.2	287.3	310.4	330.3 ǀ	112.7	123.0	132.3	145.1	157.4	172.3	092
248.3	275.1	310.7	335.6 ǀ	110.1	118.3	127.4	136.3	151.1	171.1	093
115.9	141.5	149.3	161.9	178.1	187.1	196.8	204.1	215.2	240.1	094
114.0	132.1 ǀ	67.6	74.4	80.1	87.2	91.8	100.0	107.0	116.3	095
As of end of period										
11677	12685	14392	20114	23819	26341	28779	36805	45374	52677	096
5338	5782	6246	7426	9094	9346	11478	14431	18634	20807	097
6339	6903	8146	12688	14725	16995	17301	22374	26740	31870	098
15984	21200	27606	38590	60811	72717	90274	108397	129138	169961	099
27661	33885	41998	58704	84630	99058	119053	145202	174512	222638	100
15989	18433	17884	18293	16122	23621	30634	29700	25272	32626	101
19243	27755	39730	62131	93142	112154	126611	159077	191751	233088	102
-2966	-699	207	476	-4322	-5573	-6373	-4137	-9308	-15345	103
22209	28454	39523	61655	97464	117727	132984	163214	201059	248433	104
–	–	–	–	–	–	–	–	–	–	105
-7571	-12303	-15616	-21720	-24634	-36717	-38192	-43575	-42511	-43076	106
6128	6676	8032	12513	14532	16752	16997	21987	26398	31530	107
11355	16230	20939	30518	46150	52632	67560	82953	98372	47146	108
									83745	109
27542	34837	46340	69614	105441	125790	141619	173494	210701	259027	110
Period averages										
15	15	15	15	15	15	15	15	15	15	111
15	18	18	18	20	23	18	13	13	16	112
16	18	18	19	19	23	19	14	13	15	113
Fiscal year beginning 1 April										
16141	20803	23004	28740	39546	41585	47452	52280	61370	66265 *	114
13984	18826	21435	26678	37431	39098	44459	48385	55373	59774 *	115
2157	1977	1569	2062	2115	2487	2993	3895	5997	6491 *	116
12641	14021	15035	18359	23145	22932	25853	29388	33045	37979 *	117
3500	6782	7969	10381	16401	18653	21599	22892	28325	28286 *	118
–	–	–	–	–	–	–	–	–	–	119
6716	11122	11399	12836	18191	20440	22756	24249	27551	29324 *	120
-6716	-11122	-11399	-12836	-18191	-20440	-22756	-24249	-27551	-29324 *	121
-3216	-4340	-3430	-2455	-1790	-1787	-1157	-1357	774	-1038 *	122
-1502	1824	-101	-4	-2	-2	-2	1808	-9	- *	123
4718	2516	3531	2459	1792	1789	1159	-451	-765	1038 *	124
										125
–	–	–	–	–	–	–	–	–	- *	126
8332	9477	12251	13834	19452	21764	24135	25661	29163	...	127
396	316	900	521	805	751	987	969	1159	...	128
554	514	555	720	996	1023	1204	1147	1155	...	129
1184	1181	1606	1507	2052	2417	3147	3064	3068	...	130
326	225	338	470	723	891	957	1146	1333	...	131
										132
1348	1407	1664	1948	2751	3404	4134	4497	6025	...	133
4524	5834	7188	8668	10125	11778	13706	14838	16423	...	134
1063	2137	1836	2523	2848	3152	3630	3722	3270	...	135
465	215	447	400	547	545	570	43	475	...	136
1176	1206	2074	1418	1874	2463	3333	3672	3871	...	137

	Item	1978	1979	1980	1981	1982	1983	1984	1985
138	Transport and communications [r]	413	466	780	806	876	1528	1428	1484
139	Other economic services [s]	270	659	817	865	849	890	1056	978
140	Others	–	–	–	–	–	–	–	–
	EXTERNAL TRADE								*Million US dollars;*
141	Exports, fob	11643	15590	23951	22260	22328	21146	21888	18587
142	Imports, cif	6691	7204	10835	13272	16859	16354	13882	10260
143	Trade Balance	4952	8386	13116	8988	5469	4792	8006	8327
	Exports, by SITC section								
144	Food & live animals	989	1208	1291	929	905	1093	1368	1383
145	Beverage & tobacco	55	58	61	54	42	48	44	49
146	Crude materials excl.fuels	1891	3064	3569	2208	1581	1650	1762	1403
147	Mineral fuels, etc.	7986	10166	17785	17764	18408	16153	16045	12757
148	Animal, vegetable oil & fats	214	222	285	129	133	149	175	414
149	Chemicals	55	64	84	64	61	119	170	210
150	Basic manufactures	332	571	615	777	817	1350	1565	1804
151	Machines, transport equipment	71	116	109	154	180	133	223	98
152	Misc. manufactured goods	31	81	120	121	141	213	372	437
153	Unclassified goods	19	40	32	60	60	238	164	31
	Exports, by principal commodity								
154	1. Petroleum and products	7438	8871	15595	18164	15493	13558	12477	9083
155	2. Plywood	...	...	56	161	270	509	668	825
156	3. Rubber	716	937	1165	854	608	849	955	718
157	4. Shrimp, fresh and frozen	162	201	181	163	181	194	196	202
158	5. Coffee	491	615	658	346	342	427	565	556
	Imports, by SITC section								
159	Food & live animals	1042	1038	1285	1356	1074	1135	676	556
160	Beverage & tobacco	27	21	42	45	51	28	29	21
161	Crude materials excl.fuels	295	368	491	565	609	676	883	729
162	Mineral fuels, etc.	583	797	1754	1727	3550	4150	2705	1288
163	Animal, vegetable oil & fats	65	31	9	29	13	12	52	36
164	Chemicals	756	1012	1255	1754	1804	1893	2137	1917
165	Basic manufactures	1263	1403	2053	2518	2732	2352	1885	1718
166	Machines, transport equipment	2434	2291	3634	4619	6260	5684	5037	3618
167	Misc. manufactured goods	198	215	285	325	376	359	379	331
168	Unclassified goods	28	28	27	334	390	65	99	46
	Direction of Trade								*Million US dollars;*
169	Exports, Total	11811	15579	21910	23876	22329	21147	21889	18597
170	1. Japan	4566	7189	10793	11416	11193	9678	10353	8594
171	2. United States	2962	3171	4303	4360	3546	4267	4505	4040
172	3. Korea, Rep. of	252	384	294	295	611	327	595	656
173	4. Germany	226	338	389	258	253	252	246	255
174	5. China, People's Rep. of	0	0	0	8	14	27	8	84
175	6. Hong Kong	43	99	152	147	145	182	261	348
176	7. United Kingdom	54	94	142	136	126	199	168	191
177	8. Malaysia	21	66	60	47	59	58	98	77
178	9. Netherlands	353	398	415	368	265	289	332	392
179	10. Australia	107	190	339	454	674	208	275	149
180	Imports, Total	6691	7227	10838	13272	16859	16352	13880	10275
181	1. Japan	2016	2101	3413	3989	4279	3793	3308	2644
182	2. United States	839	1053	1409	1795	2417	2534	2560	1721
183	3. Korea, Rep. of	99	117	234	489	304	388	214	205
184	4. Germany	587	453	685	905	1193	741	820	677
185	5. Australia	218	223	378	362	365	402	372	461
186	6. China, People's Rep. of	122	132	197	254	231	204	224	249
187	7. Hong Kong	142	102	139	68	87	65	86	52

1986	1987	1988	1989	1990	1991	1992	1993	1994	1995	
1131	1598	2012	3006	3744	3910	4538	5592	6390	...	138
689	678	819	1321	1112	1708	1635	1809	2417	...	139
–	–	–	–	2000	1500	–	–	...	...	140

Calendar year

1986	1987	1988	1989	1990	1991	1992	1993	1994	1995	
14805	17136	19219	22159	25675	29142	33967	36823	40053	45416	141
10718	12370	13248	16360	21837	25869	27280	28328	31983	40629	142
4087	4766	5971	5799	3838	3273	6687	8495	8070	4787	143
1774	1684	2001	2073	2286	2533	2464	2923	3558	3583	144
69	72	69	115	136	155	218	193	137	195	145
1473	1926	2661	1885	1725	1998	2259	2554	3235	5035	146
8310	8582	7723	8760	11241	11172	11275	10391	10524	11508	147
166	290	540	458	423	562	762	848	1374	1384	148
260	251	346	489	596	810	755	829	1010	1524	149
1984	3267	4281	6176	6102	7195	9183	9668	9470	10438	150
63	57	126	196	351	638	1318	2206	3048	3828	151
678	732	1154	1748	2690	3928	5575	7031	7550	7875	152
29	275	318	259	125	151	158	180	147	46	153
5501	6157	5042	6062	7404	6714	6619	5693	6005	6443	154
1002	1759	2074	2351	2726	2871	3230	4257	3716	3462	155
726	987	1212	1087	891	1025	1117	1107	1433	2233	156
285	352	499	541	671	759	757	872	1005	1032	157
818	535	550	482	369	363	217	320	697	596	158
610	624	642	911	852	1081	1274	1342	1897	3023	159
28	33	34	34	54	74	89	118	142	178	160
830	990	1205	1674	1885	2152	2409	2428	2728	3643	161
1107	1144	959	1253	1937	2320	2104	2156	2425	3007	162
18	97	177	151	25	41	149	101	104	105	163
1910	2326	2541	2873	3394	3434	3776	4045	4854	6251	164
1668	1785	2062	2638	3553	4139	4668	4841	5222	6669	165
4117	4819	5096	6182	9328	11631	11701	12158	13450	16290	166
389	469	451	634	797	980	1095	1133	1145	1426	167
41	83	81	10	12	17	15	6	16	37	168

Calendar year

1986	1987	1988	1989	1990	1991	1992	1993	1994	1995	
14810	17171	19389	21941	25681	29186	33977	36843	37311	43007	169
6644	7393	8088	9252	10923	10767	10761	11172	11526	12908	170
2902	3349	3138	3475	3365	3509	4419	5230	6297	7223	171
356	674	849	907	1363	1948	2083	2220	2584	3021	172
334	361	456	487	752	907	978	1178	1640	1760	173
139	343	492	534	834	1191	1396	1249	1432	1866	174
345	420	554	529	618	703	881	900	1165	1485	175
197	213	349	371	517	654	844	1005	1096	1292	176
82	94	184	210	253	342	488	586	835	1092	177
453	493	646	679	723	838	1100	1086	938	922	178
159	310	297	372	403	628	746	774	743	996	179
10726	12863	13489	16467	22008	25940	27283	28333	31195	39211	180
3128	3596	3427	3832	5455	6327	6014	6248	8460	10966	181
1482	1415	1734	2216	2520	3397	3822	3255	3249	3730	182
159	268	441	569	992	1439	1894	2103	2698	3267	183
719	836	908	918	1527	2067	2141	2072	2459	2946	184
414	463	579	944	1206	1378	1413	1399	1616	1911	185
337	408	410	537	653	835	752	936	1196	1582	186
94	104	133	179	273	232	229	247	883	1168	187

	Item	1978	1979	1980	1981	1982	1983	1984	1985
188	8. France	159	143	236	345	571	591	432	284
189	9. Malaysia	22	35	36	60	57	60	86	52
190	10. United Kingdom	208	202	261	547	445	364	297	300
	Trade Indexes							*1975 l 1983 = 100*	
	Quantum Index								
191	Exports	136.4	143.7	127.2　l	...	...	...	...	...
192	Imports	...	...	...	...	...	...	...	...
	Unit value index								
193	Exports	126.8	229.7	244.4　l	...	...	100.0	97.6	91.6
194	Imports	118.9	210.2	149.5　l	...	...	100.0	95.0	83.5
195	Terms of Trade	106.7	109.3	163.5　l	...	...	100.0	102.7	109.7
	BALANCE OF PAYMENTS							*Million US dollars;*	
196	Merchandise exports, fob	11035	15154	21795	23348	19747	18689	20754	18527
197	Merchandise imports, fob	-8386	-9245	-12624	-16542	-17854	-17726	-15047	-12705
198	Trade Balance	2649	5909	9171	6806	1893	963	5707	5822
199	Other goods, services and income	-4076	-4959	-6361	-7622	-7351	-7415	-7730	-7833
200	Credit	291	398	446	1530	1527	1177	1398	1612
201	Debit	-4368	-5357	-6807	-9152	-8878	-8592	-9128	-9445
202	Unrequited transfers	14	30	201	250	134	114	167	88
203	Official	14	30	201	250	134	104	114	27
204	Private	0	0	0	0	0	10	53	61
205	Current balance	-1413	980	3011	-566	-5324	-6338	-1856	-1923
206	Direct investment	279	226	180	133	225	292	222	310
207	Portfolio investment	103	60	46	47	315	368	-10	-35
208	Other long-term capital	1214	1034	1927	1971	4556	4663	2769	1605
209	Other short-term capital	121	-454	-820	-290	526	731	476	-98
210	Net errors and omissions	-133	-402	-1738	-1669	-2151	467	-620	651
211	Overall balance	171	1444	2606	-374	-1853	183	981	510
212	Allocation of SDRs	0	65	66	62	0	0	0	0
213	Monetary movements	-171	-1444	-2606	374	1853	-183	-981	-510
	INTERNATIONAL RESERVES							*Million US dollars;*	
214	Total	2663	4167	6500	6076	4196	4814	5720	5880
215	Gold, national valuation	37	105	1108	1062	1052	1096	947	906
216	Foreign exchange	2461	3795	5012	4521	2593	3639	4702	4838
217	Reserve position in the Fund	90	97	205	229	241	76	71	80
218	SDRs	75	170	175	264	311	4	1	56
	EXCHANGE RATES							*Rupiah per*	
219	End of period	625.0	627.0	626.8	644.0	692.5	994.0	1074.0	1125.0
220	Average of period	442.1	623.1	627.0	631.8	661.4	909.3	1025.9	1110.6
	EXTERNAL INDEBTEDNESS							*Million US dollars;*	
221	Total outstanding and disbursed	18053	18631	20944	22761	25134	30230	32020	36709
222	Long-term	16267	16523	18169	19487	21518	25146	26199	30614
223	Public and publicly guaranteed	13227	13383	15027	15908	18318	21493	22268	26777
224	Private non-guaranteed	3040	3140	3142	3579	3200	3652	3931	3837
225	Short-term	1786	2108	2775	3274	3616	4639	5408	6049
226	Use of IMF credit	...	...	...	...	...	445	413	46
	Debt Service							*Transactions*	
227	Principal repayments on LT debt	2113	2016	1633	1790	1942	1798	2266	3036
228	Interest on long-term debt	720	1049	1182	1428	1554	1583	2078	2041
229	Interest on short-term debt	...	...	270	280	360	351	469	342

1986	1987	1988	1989	1990	1991	1992	1993	1994	1995	
281	392	479	411	662	544	816	853	824	1139	188
50	139	300	371	290	407	525	517	760	1041	189
342	325	342	359	441	603	719	782	652	884	190
Period averages										
...	118.3	127.6	148.2	155.4	174.1	277.0	324.3	411.8	...	191
...	...	...	...	...	...	...	...	...	...	192
64.0	64.9	72.7	81.8	92.7	91.0	83.2	90.3	77.3	...	193
72.7	74.8	99.9	115.9	113.9	121.7	121.9	124.6	115.8	...	194
88.0	86.9	72.8	70.6	81.4	74.8	68.3	72.5	66.8	...	195
Calendar year										
14396	17206	19509	22974	26807	29635	33796	36607	40223	...	196
-11938	-12532	-13831	-16310	-21455	-24834	-26774	-28376	-32322	...	197
2458	4674	5678	6664	5352	4801	7022	8231	7901	...	198
-6628	-7029	-7329	-8111	-8758	-9323	-10373	-10874	-11310	...	199
1576	1626	1861	2437	2897	3739	4209	5149	6072	...	200
-8204	-8655	-9190	-10548	-11655	-13062	-14582	-16023	-17382	...	201
259	257	254	339	418	262	571	537	619	...	202
188	171	155	172	252	132	...	...	...	...	203
71	86	99	167	166	130	...	...	...	...	204
-3911	-2098	-1397	-1108	-2988	-4260	-2780	-2106	-2790	...	205
258	385	576	682	1093	1482	1777	2004	2109	...	206
268	-88	-98	-173	-93	-12	-88	1805	1100	...	207
2356	2214	1331	2507	3724 }	4227	4440	1963	630	...	208
1295	970	408	-98	-229 }					...	209
-1269	-753	-933	-1315	744	91	-1279	-3072	-265	...	210
-1003	630	-113	495	2251	1528	2070	594	784	...	211
0	0	0	0	0	0	0	0	0	...	212
1003	-630	113	-495	-2251	-1528	-2070	-594	-784	...	213
As of end of period										
5411	6911	6206	6498	8520	10250	11395	12355	13200	14787	214
1360	1319	1158	1044	1061	992	946	1092	1067	1079	215
3919	5483	4948	5357	7353	9151	10181	10988	11820	13306	216
89	103	97	95	103	104	267	274	312	401	217
43	6	3	1	3	4	0	0	0	1	218
US dollar										
1641.0	1650.0	1731.0	1797.0	1901.0	1992.0	2062.0	2110.0	2200.0	2308.0	219
1282.6	1643.8	1685.7	1770.1	1842.8	1950.3	2029.9	2087.1	2160.8	2248.6	220
As of end of year										
42922	52500	54095	59394	69955	79778	88296	89477	96500	...	221
36404	45424	46745	50811	58326	65298	70239	71490	79391	...	222
32626	40853	41200	44255	48065	52122	53958	57461	63848	...	223
3778	4571	5545	6556	10261	13176	16281	14029	15543	...	224
6466	6360	6727	7975	11135	14315	18057	17987	17109	...	225
51	716	623	608	494	166	–	–	–	...	226
during the year										
3287	4058	5240	5872	5774	6548	7830	9294	9318	...	227
2392	2604	2954	3345	3425	3749	3843	4134	4332	...	228
302	319	349	440	506	816	737	840	1142	...	229

	Item	1978	1979	1980	1981	1982	1983	1984	1985
	Average terms of new commitments								
230	Interest (%)	7.6	6.7	8.1	8.9	9.0	8.7	9.0	7.2
231	Maturity (years)	19.1	19.2	19.4	16.0	15.4	15.5	16.4	17.2
232	Grace period (years)	5.4	5.9	5.6	4.9	5.1	5.4	5.3	6.0
233	Grant element (%)	18.5	23.1	17.5	7.0	5.9	7.9	7.0	18.1

Footnotes:

a   Data are projections except for 1990, which is a census figure.

b   Data for 1978 and 1986-89 are as of 1 July while those for 1980 and 1985 are as of end of October of each year.

c   National accounts data from 1988 have been rebased to 1993 prices. In addition, there have been changes in the sectoral classification system and some refinements in the estimation procedures.

d   Includes ownership of dwelling.

e   Prior to 1983, item refers to "private consumption" plus "increase in stocks".

f   Prior to 1983, item refers to "gross fixed capital formation" only since "increase in stocks" cannot be disaggregated from "private consumption expenditure".

g   Prior to March 1979, data refer to cost of living in Jakarta with base year September 1966. Since March 1979, the Consumer Price Index (CPI) which was a composite of 17 cities with base year April 1977-March 1978 has been used as a measure of cost of living. Since April 1990, however, the CPI was revised to become a composite of 27 cities with a new base year April 1988-March 1989.

h   Includes import deposits and other items (net).

i   Refers to claims on public sector, private enterprises and individuals.

j   Relates to TABANAS (National Development Savings Scheme).

k   Relates to rates of deposit money banks.

l   Includes surplus on petroleum sales.

m   Refers to development expenditure only.

n   Refers to law and order, state apparatus and science, technology and research.

o   Refers to housing and human settlement, regional, rural and urban development, religion, information, press and social communication.

p   Refers to agriculture and irrigation, natural resources and environment.

q   Refers to mining and energy.

r   Refers to transportation and tourism.

s   Refers to trade and cooperatives, manpower and transmigration and development of business enterprises.

1986	1987	1988	1989	1990	1991	1992	1993	1994	1995	
6.7	5.8	5.3	6.1	6.1	6.2	5.9	5.5	4.9	...	230
15.6	19.6	20.6	20.2	20.7	19.1	18.1	18.5	20.3	...	231
6.0	6.7	6.8	6.4	6.0	5.5	5.2	5.1	6.2	...	232
19.4	29.0	33.1	27.5	28.0	25.4	26.3	28.7	33.4	...	233

	Item	1978	1979	1980	1981	1982	1983	1984	1985
									Million;
001	**POPULATION** [a]	...	...	...	15.10	15.28	15.46	15.65	15.83
									Million;
002	**LABOR FORCE**	...	...	...	...	...	...	...	...
003	Employed [b]	...	...	6.04	...	...	...	...	6.50
004	Agriculture and forestry	...	...	1.20	...	...	...	...	1.31
005	Industry	...	...	1.30	...	...	...	...	1.40
006	Others	...	...	3.54	...	...	...	...	3.79
007	Unemployed [c]	...	...	...	...	...	...	...	...
008	Unemployment rate, % [c]	...	...	...	...	...	...	...	...
	NATIONAL ACCOUNTS								*Billion Rubles I Billion Tenge;*
	At Current Market Prices								
009	NMP by Industrial Origin	...	...	20.57	...	...	...	...	23.15
010	Agriculture	...	...	5.34	...	...	...	...	6.82
011	Industry	...	...	6.67	...	...	...	...	7.63
012	Construction	...	...	3.09	...	...	...	...	3.73
013	Trade	...	...	1.07	...	...	...	...	1.21
014	Transport and communications	...	...	1.77	...	...	...	...	2.32
015	Others	...	...	2.63	...	...	...	...	1.46
016	GDP at current market prices	...	...	28.70	29.60	31.00	33.00	34.10	33.40
017	Net factor income from abroad	...	...	...	...	...	...	...	...
018	GNP	...	...	...	...	...	...	...	...
019	Expenditure on NMP	...	...	20.57	...	...	...	...	23.15
020	Private consumption	...	...	15.13	...	...	...	...	18.50
021	Government consumption	...	...	2.37	...	...	...	...	3.10
022	Gross fixed capital formation	...	...	4.20	...	...	...	...	5.30
023	Increase in stocks	...	...	2.00	...	...	...	...	4.60
024	Net exports of goods and services	...	...	-3.13	...	...	...	...	-8.30
025	Statistical discrepancy	...	...	–	...	...	...	...	-0.05
	At Constant 1993 Prices								*Billion Tenge;*
026	GDP by Industrial Origin	...	...	...	...	...	...	...	...
027	Agriculture	...	...	...	...	...	...	...	...
028	Mining	...	...	...	...	...	...	...	...
029	Manufacturing	...	...	...	...	...	...	...	...
030	Electricity, gas and water	...	...	...	...	...	...	...	...
031	Construction	...	...	...	...	...	...	...	...
032	Trade	...	...	...	...	...	...	...	...
033	Transport and communications	...	...	...	...	...	...	...	...
034	Finance	...	...	...	...	...	...	...	...
035	Public administration	...	...	...	...	...	...	...	...
036	Others	...	...	...	...	...	...	...	...
037	Expenditure on GDP	...	...	...	...	...	...	...	...
038	Private consumption	...	...	...	...	...	...	...	...
039	Government consumption	...	...	...	...	...	...	...	...
040	Gross fixed capital formation	...	...	...	...	...	...	...	...
041	Increase in stocks	...	...	...	...	...	...	...	...
042	Net export of goods and services	...	...	...	...	...	...	...	...
043	Statistical discrepancy	...	...	...	...	...	...	...	...
	Per Capita GDP								
044	Current prices, *Rubles I Tenge*	...	...	...	1961	2029	2134	2179	2110
045	Constant *1993* prices, *Tenge*	...	...	...	...	...	...	...	...

	1986	1987	1988	1989	1990	1991	1992	1993	1994	1995	
As of 1 July											
	16.02	16.23	16.43	16.61	16.74	16.88	16.98	16.96	16.81	16.61	001
Calendar year											
	...	...	...	...	...	7.72	7.57	6.96	7.12	...	002
	6.56	6.59	6.57	6.50	6.48	6.49	6.31	5.63	5.42	5.04	003
	1.30	1.30	1.29	1.22	1.22	1.21	1.17	1.12	1.20	1.23	004
	1.41	1.42	1.42	1.39	1.36	1.39	1.35	1.20	1.12	1.05	005
	3.85	3.86	3.86	3.89	3.90	3.89	3.78	3.31	3.09	2.76	006
	...	...	...	...	...	0.00	0.03	0.04	0.07	0.14	007
	...	...	...	...	...	0.05	0.45	0.58	0.98	...	008
Calendar year											
	24.27	24.20	26.72	28.00	33.36	66.83	840.42 I	20.08	334.89	680.34	009
	8.28	8.07	9.21	10.46	13.96	22.86	255.74 I	4.20	63.04	113.02	010
	6.68	6.92	6.76	5.66	7.00	24.76	390.25 I	8.30	116.64	242.09	011
	4.19	4.35	4.84	5.62	5.34	9.02	64.82 I	2.60	40.80	78.54	012
	1.30	1.12	1.34	1.48	1.60	2.68	29.77 I	3.30	75.53	159.83	013
	2.35	2.44	2.61	2.63	3.26	5.67	67.17 I	1.60	37.38	81.86	014
	1.47	1.31	1.96	2.14	2.20	1.84	32.67 I	0.08	1.50	5.00	015
	35.30	37.80	39.20	40.89	46.40	81.00	1213.62 I	26.84	447.72	992.50	016
	...	...	...	...	...	...	... I	...	...	...	017
	...	...	...	...	...	...	... I	...	...	...	018
	24.27	24.20	26.72	28.00	33.36	66.83	840.42 I	20.08	334.89	680.34	019
	18.70	19.11	20.40	22.19	24.44	47.63	579.33 I	14.58	234.92	...	020
	3.10	3.37	3.50	3.65	4.01	15.46	88.45 I	1.90	24.94	...	021
	5.70	6.04	5.10	5.33	5.59	5.14	242.73 I	8.10	85.34	...	022
	3.40	2.27	3.40	3.40	6.10	17.34	82.24 I	-2.90	10.90	...	023
	-6.60	-7.20	-5.70	-7.36	-7.76	-19.41	-161.35 I	-1.60	-21.21	...	024
	-0.03	0.61	0.02	0.79	0.97	0.66	9.01 I	–	–	...	025
Calendar year											
	...	...	...	...	42.50	36.20	30.80	26.84	20.00	18.22 *	026
	...	...	...	...	7.20	5.50	5.50	4.80	3.70	...	027
	...	...	...	...						...	028
	...	...	...	...	20.30	17.60	13.50	10.90	8.00	...	029
	...	...	...	...						...	030
	...	...	...	...						...	031
	...	...	...	...						...	032
	...	...	...	...	15.00	13.10	11.80	11.14	8.30	...	033
	...	...	...	...						...	034
	...	...	...	...						...	035
	...	...	...	...						...	036
	...	...	...	...	42.50	36.20	30.80	26.84	20.00	...	037
	...	...	...	...	...	...	...	...	...	...	038
	...	...	...	...	...	...	...	...	...	...	039
	...	...	...	...	...	...	...	...	...	...	040
	...	...	...	...	...	...	...	...	...	...	041
	...	...	...	...	...	...	...	...	...	...	042
	...	...	...	...	...	...	...	...	...	...	043
	2204	2329	2386	2462	2772	4799	71494 I	1582	26633	59753	044
	...	...	...	...	2539	2145	1814	1582	1190	1097 *	045

	Item	1978	1979	1980	1981	1982	1983	1984	1985
	PRODUCTION								*Thousand metric tons;*
	Agriculture								
046	1. Wheat	17845	22486	17548	14641	11566	13051	8537	14191
047	2. Barley	6365	7646	6036	5675	4539	6460	4187	5955
048	3. Potatoes	1728	1830	2238	1684	1895	1908	2078	2197
049	4. Sugar Beets	...	...	...	...	...	...	...	1750
050	5. Vegetables	1073	1216	1134	1204	1128	1169	1210	1085
	Mining								
051	1. Iron Ore	24909	25251	25763	25551	25415	24593	23972	22977
	Manufacturing								
052	1. Steel	6075	6088	5967	6069	5924	6123	6197	6155
053	2. Rolled Steel	...	...	...	...	...	...	...	4200
054	3. Sulphuric Acid	3343	3215	3293	3308	2966	3327	3173	3098
055	4. Sugar (Powder)	168	227	272	272	270	324	330	337
	Production Indexes								*Period*
056	Agriculture, *1979-81 = 100*	...	...	...	...	...	...	...	...
057	Mining, *1980 = 100*	101.5	101.8	100.0	101.5	102.5	104.8	107.0	110.3
058	Manufacturing, *1980 = 100*	104.6	104.6	100.0	104.6	105.9	111.3	115.8	120.1
	ENERGY								*Annual*
	Crude Petroleum, *'000 m.t.*								
059	Production	19203	18309	18538	18943	19136	19363	20348	21381
060	Exports	...	...	...	...	...	...	...	...
061	Imports	...	...	...	...	...	...	...	...
062	Consumption	...	...	...	...	...	...	...	...
	Coal, *'000 m.t.*								
063	Production	103354	106060	115169	115878	118260	122504	125440	130534
064	Exports	...	...	...	...	...	...	...	...
065	Imports	...	...	...	...	...	...	...	...
066	Consumption	...	...	...	...	...	...	...	...
	Natural gas, *Mn cu. m.*								
067	Production	...	...	...	...	...	...	...	5456
068	Exports	...	...	...	...	...	...	...	...
069	Imports	...	...	...	...	...	...	...	...
070	Consumption	...	...	...	...	...	...	...	...
	Electricity, *Mn kWh*								
071	Production	...	...	61500	...	...	...	...	81263
072	Exports	...	...	...	...	...	...	...	...
073	Imports	...	...	...	...	...	...	...	...
074	Consumption	...	...	72100	...	...	...	...	91800
	Retail prices, *Tenge/litre*								
075	Gasoline, leaded	...	...	...	...	...	...	...	...
076	Diesel	...	...	...	...	...	...	...	...
	PRICE INDEXES								*1992 = 100;*
077	Consumer	...	...	...	...	...	...	...	...
078	Food	...	...	...	...	...	...	...	...
079	Non-food	...	...	...	...	...	...	...	...
080	Wholesale	...	...	...	...	...	...	...	...
081	Implicit GDP deflator, *1993 = 100*	...	...	...	...	...	...	...	...
	MONEY AND BANKING								*Million Tenge;*
082	Money supply (M1)	...	...	...	...	...	...	...	...
083	Currency in circulation	...	...	...	...	...	...	...	...
084	Demand deposits	...	...	...	...	...	...	...	...
085	Quasi-money	...	...	...	...	...	...	...	...
086	Money supply (M2)	...	...	...	...	...	...	...	...
087	Foreign assets (net)	...	...	...	...	...	...	...	...
088	Domestic credit	...	...	...	...	...	...	...	...

	1986	1987	1988	1989	1990	1991	1992	1993	1994	1995	

Calendar year

16743	16108	12162	10784	16197	6889	18285	11585	9052	6490		046
7095	6929	5851	5309	8500	3085	8511	7149	5497	2208		047
2137	2066	2260	1783	2324	2143	2570	2296	2040	1720		048
1587	1662	1214	1094	1044	674	1160	843	433	371		049
1211	1190	1354	1254	1136	955	985	808	781	780		050
23630	24224	24342	23764	23846	21993	17671	13129	10521	15133		051
6496	6555	6766	6831	6753	6355	6063	4558	2969	3028		052
4600	4600	4900	5000	4900	4700	4400	...	...	...		053
3283	3440	3605	3455	3151	2815	2349	1179	681	694		054
342	349	314	377	319	307	213	164	97	108		055

averages

...	...	...	...	...	...	...	...	...	...		056
114.7	118.5	122.5	122.4	117.9	119.2	110.2	90.8	76.3	...		057
126.5	132.2	137.0	141.2	140.5	138.8	117.7	100.8	72.2	...		058

values

21581	21814	22248	21953	21676	22036	21934	19572	18544	17935		059
...	...	...	...	...	20800	20000	16900	9445	2638		060
...	...	...	...	...	12500	11400	8500	1836	56		061
...	...	...	...	...	18300	17100	14600	...	...		062
137237	141270	140714	135208	128000	126463	122384	107211	99811	79516		063
...	...	...	...	...	51200	44300	35400	22407	12951		064
...	...	...	...	...	5600	1000	1000	406	1193		065
...	...	...	...	...	84800	83200	77500	...	...		066
5824	6311	7134	6710	7114	7885	8113	6685	4490	4871 *		067
...	...	...	...	...	4200	3900	4000	...	...		068
...	...	...	...	...	12800	13400	11900	7173	9121		069
...	...	...	...	...	16500	17600	14700	...	...		070
85095	88490	88417	89657	87379	85984	82700	77444	65126	63737 *		071
...	...	...	...	...	12700	12000	8700	...	...		072
...	...	...	...	...	28200	26000	20400	13031	7393		073
95400	99700	101700	103700	104700	101200	96500	88900	...	...		074
...	...	...	...	...	...	...	1.33	7.54	18.30		075
...	...	...	...	...	...	...	...	...	...		076

Period averages

...	...	...	...	...	...	100	2265	28500	45695		077
...	...	...	...	...	...	...	2297	26548	42139		078
...	...	...	...	...	...	...	1796	20827	27800		079
...	...	...	...	...	...	...	1424	28787	40815		080
...	...	...	...	...	...	...	100	2239	5447 *		081

As of end of period

...	...	...	...	...	...	...	...	54827	77659		082
...	...	...	...	...	...	...	...	20255	28987		083
...	...	...	...	...	...	...	...	34572	48672		084
...	...	...	...	...	...	...	...	...	...		085
...	...	...	...	...	...	...	...	...	...		086
...	...	...	...	...	...	...	...	...	...		087
...	...	...	...	...	...	...	...	...	...		088

Item	1978	1979	1980	1981	1982	1983	1984	1985
089 Claims on govt. sector, net	...	...	...	...	...	...	...	...
090 Claims on private sector	...	...	...	...	...	...	...	...
091 Claims on other financial insts.	...	...	...	...	...	...	...	...
092 Other items	...	...	...	...	...	...	...	...
GOVERNMENT FINANCE								*Billion Rubles I Billion Tenge;*
Central Government								
093 Current revenue	...	...	...	...	...	...	...	10.43
094 Taxes	...	...	...	...	...	...	...	10.11
095 Non-taxes	...	...	...	...	...	...	...	0.32
096 Current expenditure [d]	...	...	...	...	...	...	...	11.52
097 Current surplus/deficit	...	...	...	...	...	...	...	-1.09
098 Capital receipts	...	...	...	...	...	...	...	...
099 Capital expenditure	...	...	...	...	...	...	...	...
100 Capital account surplus/deficit	...	...	...	...	...	...	...	...
101 Extrabudgetary funds & quasi-fiscal operations	...	...	...	...	...	...	...	...
102 Overall surplus/deficit	...	...	...	...	...	...	...	...
Financing								...
103 Domestic borrowing	...	...	...	...	...	...	...	...
104 Foreign borrowing	...	...	...	...	...	...	...	...
105 Foreign grants	...	...	...	...	...	...	...	...
106 Use of cash balances	...	...	...	...	...	...	...	...
EXTERNAL TRADE [e]								*Million US dollars;*
107 Exports, fob	...	...	...	...	...	...	...	...
108 Imports, cif	...	...	...	...	...	...	...	...
109 Trade balance	...	...	...	...	...	...	...	...
Direction of Trade [f]								*Million US dollars;*
110 Exports, Total	...	...	...	...	...	...	...	...
111 1. Russia	...	...	...	...	...	...	...	...
112 2. China, People's Rep. of	...	...	...	...	...	...	...	...
113 3. United Kingdom	...	...	...	...	...	...	...	...
114 4. Germany	...	...	...	...	...	...	...	...
115 5. Italy	...	...	...	...	...	...	...	...
116 6. Poland	...	...	...	...	...	...	...	...
117 7. United States	...	...	...	...	...	...	...	...
118 8. France	...	...	...	...	...	...	...	...
119 9. Turkey	...	...	...	...	...	...	...	...
120 10. Japan	...	...	...	...	...	...	...	...
121 Imports, cif Total	...	...	...	...	...	...	...	...
122 1. Russia	...	...	...	...	...	...	...	...
123 2. Germany	...	...	...	...	...	...	...	...
124 3. China, People's Rep. of	...	...	...	...	...	...	...	...
125 4. Turkey	...	...	...	...	...	...	...	...
126 5. United States	...	...	...	...	...	...	...	...
127 6. France	...	...	...	...	...	...	...	...
128 7. Italy	...	...	...	...	...	...	...	...
129 8. Netherlands	...	...	...	...	...	...	...	...
130 9. Japan	...	...	...	...	...	...	...	...
131 10. United Kingdom	...	...	...	...	...	...	...	...
BALANCE OF PAYMENTS								*Million US dollars;*
132 Merchandise exports, fob	...	...	...	...	...	...	...	...
133 Merchandise imports, fob	...	...	...	...	...	...	...	...
134 Trade balance	...	...	...	...	...	...	...	...
135 Other goods, services and income	...	...	...	...	...	...	...	...
136 Credit	...	...	...	...	...	...	...	...
137 Debit	...	...	...	...	...	...	...	...
138 Unrequited transfer	...	...	...	...	...	...	...	...
139 Private	...	...	...	...	...	...	...	...

1986	1987	1988	1989	1990	1991	1992	1993	1994	1995	
...	...	...	...	...	...	...	...	...	...	089
...	...	...	...	...	...	...	...	...	...	090
...	...	...	...	...	...	...	...	...	...	091
...	...	...	...	...	...	...	...	...	...	092

Fiscal year ending 31 December

1986	1987	1988	1989	1990	1991	1992	1993	1994	1995	
10.09	10.30	10.37	11.36	12.30	19.90	276.01 |	7.96	104.10	252.49	093
9.75	9.98	10.12	11.07	11.85	17.49	253.15 |	5.68	61.09	158.36	094
0.34	0.32	0.25	0.29	0.45	2.41	22.86 |	2.28	43.01	94.13	095
11.77	12.50	13.50	15.38	17.06	32.80	259.01 |	7.48	101.94	250.51	096
-1.68	-2.20	-3.13	-4.02	-4.76	-12.90	17.00 |	0.48	2.16	1.98	097
...	...	...	...	...	...	...	...	...	...	098
...	...	...	...	...	...	...	...	...	...	099
...	...	...	...	...	...	...	...	...	...	100
...	...	...	...	...	...	...	...	...	...	102
...	...	...	...	...	...	...	...	...	...	103
...	...	...	...	...	...	...	...	...	...	104
...	...	...	...	...	...	...	...	...	...	105
...	...	...	...	...	...	...	...	...	...	106

Calendar year

1986	1987	1988	1989	1990	1991	1992	1993	1994	1995	
...	...	...	...	1402	928	1451	1486 |	2691	4110	107
...	...	...	...	1490	584	566	472 |	4213	5320	108
...	...	...	...	-88	344	885	1014 |	-1522	-1210	109

Calendar year

1986	1987	1988	1989	1990	1991	1992	1993	1994	1995	
...	...	...	...	...	...	...	...	2691.0	4110.1	110
...	...	...	...	...	...	...	...	1832.4	2935.1	111
...	...	...	...	...	...	128.1	239.1	179.2	286.5	112
...	...	...	...	...	...	...	75.8	97.2	77.0	113
...	...	...	...	...	...	37.4	89.4	76.3	102.3	114
...	...	...	...	...	...	13.4	54.1	66.0	117.9	115
...	...	...	...	...	...	...	40.2	67.6	95.0	116
...	...	...	...	...	...	21.7	37.1	59.5	104.5	117
...	...	...	...	...	...	4.2	31.8	45.1	34.7	118
...	...	...	...	...	...	...	39.1	29.4	41.4	119
...	...	...	...	...	...	12.3	34.5	33.1	38.1	120
...	...	...	...	...	...	...	...	4212.7	5320.4	121
...	...	...	...	...	...	...	...	2516.8	3956.3	122
...	...	...	...	...	...	96.2	488.0	552.4	383.9	123
...	...	...	...	...	...	244.7	188.9	152.6	83.0	124
...	...	...	...	...	...	...	73.7	145.0	109.9	125
...	...	...	...	...	...	16.2	74.5	143.9	74.8	126
...	...	...	...	...	...	15.9	72.3	117.9	39.2	127
...	...	...	...	...	...	15.7	101.9	77.4	58.8	128
...	...	...	...	...	...	12.4	89.6	31.0	32.9	129
...	...	...	...	...	...	30.4	64.0	32.2	17.4	130
...	...	...	...	...	...	...	24.6	68.5	43.7	131

As of end of period

1986	1987	1988	1989	1990	1991	1992	1993	1994	1995	
...	...	...	...	...	...	...	3323.5	3283.9	5109.0	132
...	...	...	...	...	...	...	-4563.4	-4153.4	-5776.9	133
...	...	...	...	...	...	...	-1239.9	-869.5	-667.9	134
...	...	...	...	...	...	...	384.0	-68.0	-399.3	135
...	...	...	...	...	...	...	810.5	421.7	512.7	136
...	...	...	...	...	...	...	-426.5	-489.7	-912.0	137
...	...	...	...	...	...	...	72.5	96.8	60.5	138
...	...	...	...	...	...	...	–	–	–	139

	Item	1978	1979	1980	1981	1982	1983	1984	1985
140	Official	...	...	...	...	...	...	...	...
141	Current balance	...	...	...	...	...	...	...	...
142	Direct investment	...	...	...	...	...	...	...	...
143	Portfolio investment	...	...	...	...	...	...	...	...
144	Other long-term capital	...	...	...	...	...	...	...	...
145	Other short-term capital	...	...	...	...	...	...	...	...
146	Net errors and omissions	...	...	...	...	...	...	...	...
147	Overall balance	...	...	...	...	...	...	...	...
148	Allocations of SDRs	...	...	...	...	...	...	...	...
149	Monetary movement [g]	...	...	...	...	...	...	...	...
	INTERNATIONAL RESERVES							*Million US dollars;*	
150	Total [h]	...	...	...	...	...	...	...	...
151	Gold, national valuation	...	...	...	...	...	...	...	...
152	Foreign exchange	...	...	...	...	...	...	...	...
153	Reserve position in the Fund	...	...	...	...	...	...	...	...
154	SDRs	...	...	...	...	...	...	...	...
	EXCHANGE RATES [i]							*Rubles I Tenge*	
155	End of period	...	...	...	...	...	...	...	...
156	Average of period	...	...	...	...	...	...	...	...
	EXTERNAL INDEBTEDNESS							*Million US dollars;*	
157	Total outstanding & disbursed	...	...	...	...	...	...	...	...
158	Long-term	...	...	...	...	...	...	...	...
159	Public and publicly guaranteed	...	...	...	...	...	...	...	...
160	Private non-guaranteed	...	...	...	...	...	...	...	...
161	Short-term	...	...	...	...	...	...	...	...
162	Use of IMF credit	...	...	...	...	...	...	...	...
	Debt service							*Transactions*	
163	Principal repayments on LT debt	...	...	...	...	...	...	...	...
164	Interest on long-term debt	...	...	...	...	...	...	...	...
165	Interest on short-term debt	...	...	...	...	...	...	...	...
	Average terms of new commitments								
166	Interest (%)	...	...	...	...	...	...	...	...
167	Maturity (years)	...	...	...	...	...	...	...	...
168	Grace period (years)	...	...	...	...	...	...	...	...
169	Grant element (%)	...	...	...	...	...	...	...	...

Footnotes:

a   Mid-year estimates based on data for beginning of period.
b   Number of employees in national economy except those in cooperatives, collective farms, small and private enterprises and joint ventures.
c   Refers to registered unemployed only.
d   Refers to total expenditure including transfers to all Union Budget for 1985-91.
e   Excludes trade with other states of the former USSR for 1990-93.
f   The top ten trading partners listed do not include other states of the former USSR due to unavailability of data for earlier years.
g   Financing of the overall surplus/deficit.
h   Net reserves of the National Bank of Kazakstan.
i   The tenge was introduced as the official currency in mid-November 1993.

1986	1987	1988	1989	1990	1991	1992	1993	1994	1995	
...	...	...	...	...	...	...	72.5	96.8	60.5	140
...	...	...	...	...	...	...	-783.4	-840.7	-1006.7	141
...	...	...	...	...	...	...	1272.2	635.0	723.3	142
...	...	...	...	...	...	...	-0.2	12.6	30.0	143
										144
...	...	...	...	...	...	...	-2075.3 }	-1508.8 }	-789.7 }	145
...	...	...	...	...	...	...	-565.0	1176.4	703.4	146
...	...	...	...	...	...	...	-2151.7	-525.5	-339.7	147
...	...	...	...	...	...	...	–	–	–	148
...	...	...	...	...	...	...	2151.7	525.5	339.7	149

As of end of period

1986	1987	1988	1989	1990	1991	1992	1993	1994	1995	
...	...	...	...	...	...	...	581.0	907.0	982.0	150
...	...	...	...	...	...	...	...	...	...	151
...	...	...	...	...	...	...	...	...	...	152
...	...	...	...	...	...	...	...	...	...	153
...	...	...	...	...	...	...	...	...	...	154

per US dollar

1986	1987	1988	1989	1990	1991	1992	1993	1994	1995	
...	...	...	...	...	0.60	414.50 I	5.70	54.30	64.00	155
...	0.63	0.61	0.63	0.59	0.58	205.40 I	2.50	35.80	60.90	156

As of end of year

1986	1987	1988	1989	1990	1991	1992	1993	1994	1995	
...	...	...	...	...	...	35.0	1654.6	2704.2	...	157
...	...	...	...	...	...	25.8	1567.2	2200.8	...	158
...	...	...	...	...	...	25.8	1567.2	2200.8	...	159
...	...	...	...	...	...	–	–	–	...	160
...	...	...	...	...	...	9.2	2.4	214.3	...	161
...	...	...	...	...	...	–	85.0	289.1	...	162

during the year

1986	1987	1988	1989	1990	1991	1992	1993	1994	1995	
...	...	...	...	...	...	–	0.4	12.4	...	163
...	...	...	...	...	...	–	7.5	33.4	...	164
...	...	...	...	...	...	–	0.5	5.0	...	165
...	...	...	...	...	...	8.1	6.4	5.5	...	166
...	...	...	...	...	...	9.6	9.8	12.8	...	167
...	...	...	...	...	...	3.9	3.2	3.9	...	168
...	...	...	...	...	...	6.9	13.5	21.1	...	169

	Item	1978	1979	1980	1981	1982	1983	1984	1985
001	**POPULATION** [a]	56.2	56.1	56.7	58.0	59.5	61.0	62.4	*Thousand;* 64.0
002	**LABOR FORCE**	...	...	...	...	...	...	...	*Thousand;* ...
003	Employed [b]	6.63	...	...	...	...	...	...	6.99
004	Agriculture	0.50	...	...	...	...	...	...	0.48
005	Manufacturing	0.18	...	...	...	...	...	...	0.13
006	Mining	0.32	...	...	...	...	...	...	0.01
007	Others	5.63	...	...	...	...	...	...	6.36
008	Unemployed	...	...	...	...	...	...	...	...
009	Unemployment rate, %	...	...	...	...	...	...	...	...
	NATIONAL ACCOUNTS [c] *At Current Factor Cost*							*Thousand Australian dollars;*	
010	GDP by Industrial Origin	37200	36178	23430	25331	29300	31685	37758	31243
011	Agriculture	7300	6694	4860	6823	7681	8391	10385	8469
012	Mining	16800	15031	–	–	–	–	–	–
013	Manufacturing	700	494	494	535	572	649	670	705
014	Electricity, gas and water	600	473	289	356	358	595	763	797
015	Construction	3100	1214	1330	1480	1510	1417	1379	1607
016	Trade	2400	2533	3687	3884	4886	3902	4251	4439
017	Transport and communications	1000	2234	3908	3862	5600	5600	4683	5341
018	Finance	200	657	637	1207	1451	1409	1692	2310
019	Public administration	2600	6598	7938	7301	6599	7426	7680	7749
020	Others	2500	250	287	-117	643	2296	6255	-174
021	Indirect taxes less subsidies	2300	1949	1104	174	-59	986	1624	1312
022	GDP at current market prices	39500	38127	24534	25505	29241	32671	39382	32555
023	Net factor income from abroad	4500	5267	9079	8059	14904	17819	19976	27050
024	GNP at current market prices	44000	43394	33613	33564	44145	50490	59358	59605
	At Current Market Prices								
025	Expenditure on GDP	39500	38128	24533	25503	29241	32670	39382	32556
026	Private consumption	20263	21286	22711	23382	19349	20671	20895	22066
027	Government consumption	7624	11741	14521	14775	15795	15939	15377	16631
028	Gross fixed capital formation	8176	4762	6815	12583	17170	18810	16037	17477
029	Increase in stocks	–	812	1309	86	1343	575	-100	62
030	Exports of goods and services	21686	23366	5750	7597	2653	4327	12806	6435
031	Less: Imports of goods and services	18249	22721	27037	31260	34053	32850	34527	38395
032	Statistical discrepancy	–	-1118	464	-1660	6984	5198	8894	8280
	At Constant 1988 Factor Cost								
033	GDP by Industrial Origin	...	...	...	...	36928	38212	44472	35527
034	Agriculture	...	...	...	...	9354	9201	11512	9461
035	Mining	...	...	...	...	–	–	–	–
036	Manufacturing	...	...	...	...	784	837	819	825
037	Electricity, gas and water	...	...	...	...	490	767	933	933
038	Construction	...	...	...	...	2069	1826	1686	1882
039	Trade	...	...	...	...	6693	5028	5197	5198
040	Transport and communications	...	...	...	...	7671	7216	5725	6254
041	Finance	...	...	...	...	1893	1755	2033	2575
042	Public administration	...	...	...	...	7664	8625	8920	8525
043	Others	...	...	...	...	310	2957	7647	-126
044	Indirect taxes less subsidies	...	...	...	...	-517	1470	3107	1230
045	GDP at constant *1988* market prices	...	...	...	...	36411	39682	47579	36757
046	Net factor income from abroad	...	...	...	...	18564	21666	24110	30518
047	GNP at constant *1988* market prices	...	...	...	...	54975	61348	71689	67275
	Per Capita GDP, Australian dollars								
048	Current prices	703	679	433	439	492	535	631	508
049	Constant *1988* prices	...	...	...	...	612	650	762	574

1986	1987	1988	1989	1990	1991	1992	1993	1994	1995	
As of 1 July										
65.4	66.8	68.2	69.4	72.3	73.9 *	75.6 *	77.3 *	79.1 *	80.8 *	001
Calendar year										
...	...	...	...	...	...	...	...	...	...	002
...	...	...	...	10.97	...	...	...	...	...	003
...	...	...	...	2.58	...	...	...	...	...	004
...	...	...	...	0.62	...	...	...	...	...	005
...	...	...	...	0.00	...	...	...	...	...	006
...	...	...	...	7.77	...	...	...	...	...	007
...	...	...	...	...	...	...	...	...	...	008
...	...	...	...	...	...	...	...	...	...	009
Calendar year										
33606	34387	38476	38592	38869	40402	43847	...	...	...	010
9979	8634	12192	10923	9243	10017	11022	...	...	...	011
–	–	–	–	–	–	–	...	...	...	012
723	761	760	820	840	875	920	...	...	...	013
735	871	832	1129	1035	759	800	...	...	...	014
2227	1980	2200	2580	3220	2660	2300	...	...	...	015
4633	5000	5500	5556	5831	6331	6530	...	...	...	016
5727	5750	6100	6340	6630	6790	7130	...	...	...	017
2802	2880	2977	3160	3103	3210	3210	...	...	...	018
7679	8423	8612	9822	9941	11642	12175	...	...	...	019
-899	88	-697	-1738	-974	-1882	-240	...	...	...	020
679	1230	1204	2388	2344	3398	2413	...	...	...	021
34285	35617	39680	40980	41213	43800	46260	...	...	...	022
33548	26116	27190	28049	30802	40840	37812	...	...	...	023
67833	61733	66870	69029	72015	84640	84072	...	...	...	024
34285	35617	39680	40981	41212	43801	46260	...	...	...	025
22913	24040	24702	26744	27033	29587	31592	...	...	...	026
16615	17312	18135	19880	19231	23176	25039	...	...	...	027
22265	24700	23700	22560	33650	27700	25750	...	...	...	028
263	300	500	250	250	250	250	...	...	...	029
2904	3310	7146	6949	4236	4762	5798	...	...	...	030
41468	40774	45035	46596	53596	52537	52625	...	...	...	031
10793	6729	10532	11194	10408	10863	10456	...	...	...	032
35046	35197	38491	36884	37131	37299	38785	...	...	...	033
9155	8891	12207	10797	9910	11119	11294	...	...	...	034
		–					...	...	...	035
794	785	760	779	761	752	753	...	...	...	036
807	898	832	1072	938	652	655	...	...	...	037
2444	2041	2200	2451	2917	2285	1882	...	...	...	038
5086	5155	5500	5277	5281	5439	5344	...	...	...	039
6286	5928	6100	6021	6005	5833	5835	...	...	...	040
2819	2915	2977	3056	3120	3215	3293	...	...	...	041
8448	8423	8612	9078	9188	9791	10240	...	...	...	042
-793	161	-697	-1647	-989	-1787	-511	...	...	...	043
1000	549	1204	2198	1838	2395	1894	...	...	...	044
36046	35746	39695	39082	38969	39694	40679	...	...	...	045
35282	26235	27175	26723	29099	37042	33263	...	...	...	046
71328	61981	66870	65805	68068	76736	73942	...	...	...	047
524	533	582	591	570	592	612	...	...	...	048
551	535	582	563	539	537	538	...	...		049

Item	1978	1979	1980	1981	1982	1983	1984	1985
PRODUCTION								*Metric tons;*
Agriculture								
050 1. Copra	10426	8937	7527	11270	9889	6947	13388	8483
ENERGY								*Annual*
Electricity, *Mn kWh*								
051 Production	6	6	5	6	6	6	6	6
052 Consumption	6	6	5	6	6	6	6	6
PRICE INDEXES								*Period*
053 Consumer, *1975 = 100*[d]	133.0	142.3	165.2	178.0	187.8	199.6	210.4	219.9
054 Implicit GDP deflator, *1988 = 100*	...	...	...	...	80.3	82.3	82.8	88.6
MONEY AND BANKING								*Thousand Australian dollars;*
055 Money supply (M1)[e]	3724	4567	...	...	3800	4900	5000	4200
Deposit Money Banks								
056 Demand deposits	...	...	...	...	3400	4500	3600	2600
057 Savings deposits[f]	4772	5412	...	...	2700	2700	3100	3600
058 Time deposits	...	...	...	...	2400	4100	12800	22000
059 Domestic credits outstanding	438	597	...	...	4300	3600	800	1000
GOVERNMENT FINANCE								*Thousand Australian dollars;*
Central Government								
060 Current revenue	14462	17649	16769	17046 I	12742	13211	15783	17395
061 Taxes	11682	13727	6775	5672 I	4465	4605	4536	4968
062 Non-taxes	2780	3922	9994	11374 I	8277	8606	11247	12427
063 Current expenditure	13270	16687	14362	16253 I	15891	15922	15737	16781
064 Current surplus/deficit	1192	962	2407	793 I	-3149	-2711	46	614
065 Capital receipts	6131	5622	4615	4031 I	...	...	...	...
066 Capital expenditure	5719	3365	4803	5186 I	6300	7700	3796	28
067 Capital account surplus/deficit	412	2257	-188	-1155 I	-6300	-7700	-3796	-28
068 Overall surplus/deficit[g]	1604	3219	2219	-362 I	-9449	-10411	-3750	586
Financing								
069 Domestic borrowing	–	389	–	– I	...	...	...	...
070 Foreign borrowing	–	–	–	– I	...	...	...	...
071 Foreign grants	412	5233	4615	4031 I	9800	11200	3597	1485
072 Use of cash balances	-2016	-8841	-6834	-3669 I	-351	-789	153	-2071
EXTERNAL TRADE[h]								*Thousand Australian dollars;*
073 Exports, fob	21446	21309	2602	3577	2352	4003	12456	6058
074 Imports, fob	14115	15545	18263	22830	22772	19606	20877	21582
075 Trade balance	7331	5764	-15661	-19253	-20420	-15603	-8421	-15524
Exports, by SITC section								
076 Food & live animals	–	176	208	716	545	1521	1767	1052
077 Beverage & tobacco	–	–	–	–	–	–	–	–
078 Crude materials excl. fuels	18902	17953	–	–	–	–	–	–
079 Mineral fuels, etc.	–	-	–	–	–	–	–	–
080 Animal, vegetable oil & fats	2473	3684	2171	2638	1454	2158	6987	4718
081 Chemicals	–	–	–	–	–	–	–	–
082 Basic manufactures	–	–	–	–	–	–	–	–
083 Machines, transport equipment	–	–	–	–	–	–	–	–
084 Misc. manufactured goods	21	6	3	3	2	1	4	8
085 Unclassified goods	–	20	20	20	17	9	10	12
086 Re-exports	50	200	200	200	335	316	3687	265
Exports, by principal commodity								
087 1. Copra	2473	3684	2171	2638	1454	2158	6987	4718
088 2. Fish	...	151	189	701	515	1503	1718	1017

	1986	1987	1988	1989	1990	1991	1992	1993	1994	1995	
Calendar year											
	5911	6026	14406	9924	5602	8661	...	...	...	...	050
values											
	6	7	7	7	7	7	7	...	...	...	051
	6	7	7	7	7	7	7	...	...	...	052
averages											
	234.3	249.5	252.3	265.8	275.8	291.6	303.4	321.9	339.1	351.4	053
	95.1	99.6	100.0	104.9	105.8	110.3	113.7	...	...	...	054
As of end of period											
	5400	...	...	...	...	...	...	...	...	...	055
	3400	...	...	...	...	...	...	...	...	...	056
	4100	...	...	...	...	...	...	...	...	...	057
	21700	...	...	...	...	...	...	...	...	...	058
	1700	...	...	...	...	...	...	...	...	...	059
Fiscal year ending 31 December											
	13652	19084	18887	20267	23056	28053	33108	32468	32721	42200	060
	5649	7566	7365	8332	9220	10282	10179	11698	11811	12200	061
	8003	11518	11522	11935	13836	17771	22929	20770	20910	30000	062
	15415	16801	18295	21987	22034	24760	25712	26431	30852	48100	063
	-1763	2283	592	-1720	1022	3293	7396	6037	1869	-5900	064
	...	...	3	...	18	12	10	23	0		065
	900	716	523	259	351	535	736	1332	3279	22500	066
	-900	-716	-520	-259	-333	-523	-726	-1309	-3279	-22500	067
	-2663	1567	72	-1979	689	2770	6670	4728	-1410	-28400	068
	...	...	...	...	...	...	...	...	...	20000	069
	...	...	...	...	...	...	...	...	...	...	070
	...	...	...	...	...	...	...	...	...	...	071
	2663	-1567	-72	1979	-689	-2770	-6670	-4728	1410	8400	072
Calendar year											
	2496	2869	6670	6435	3681	3697	6513	5069	7110	...	073
	21452	25143	28185	28596	34446	33226	50530	40873	36115	...	074
	-18956	-22274	-21515	-22161	-30765	-29529	-44017	-35804	-29005	...	075
	1818	901	1639	2727	1719	977	767	...	...	...	076
	–	–	–	–	–	–	–	...	...	...	077
	–	–	–	–	–	–	–	...	...	...	078
	–	–	–	–	–	–	–	...	...	...	079
	459	1173	4203	3127	1023	1625	4350	...	...	...	080
	–	–	–	–	–	–	–	...	...	...	081
	–	–	–	–	–	–	–	...	...	...	082
	–	–	–	–	–	–	–	...	...	...	083
	3	3	–	4	3	1	8	...	...	...	084
	14	41	6	115	264	347	520	...	...	...	085
	202	751	823	462	672	748	868	...	...		086
	459	1173	4203	3127	1023	1625	4350	2348	4480	...	087
	1775	823	1606	2600	964	277	363	513	263	...	088

	Item	1978	1979	1980	1981	1982	1983	1984	1985
	Imports, by SITC section								
089	Food & live animals	3838	4696	5436	4961	5213	5138	5626	5975
090	Beverage & tobacco	890	1505	1303	1110	1174	1147	1130	1039
091	Crude materials excl. fuels	279	262	303	404	375	517	268	184
092	Mineral fuels, etc.	1476	2258	2504	3671	3441	2520	3088	3236
093	Animal, vegetable oil & fats	17	19	22	23	30	18	38	29
094	Chemicals	753	861	903	868	917	822	1090	1086
095	Basic manufactures	2715	1869	2601	2489	2843	3378	2169	2060
096	Machines, transport equipment	3624	2742	3328	7714	6276	4446	6062	6354
097	· Misc. manufactured goods	1418	1448	1632	1387	2356	1515	1314	1417
098	Unclassified goods	103	91	233	203	146	105	93	202
	Direction of Trade								***Million US dollars;***
099	Exports, Total	16.2	17.7	3.2	2.4	2.5	2.9	6.2	2.1
100	1. Japan	0.1	0.1	0.6	0.1	0.9	0.5	0.0	0.1
101	2. United States	0.0	0.0	0.0	0.0	0.0	0.0	0.0	0.0
102	3. France	0.0	0.0	0.0	0.0	0.0	0.0	0.0	0.0
103	4. Hong Kong	0.0	0.0	0.0	0.0	0.0	0.0	0.0	0.0
104	5. Bangladesh	0.0	0.0	0.0	0.0	0.0	0.0	0.2	0.0
105	6. Malaysia	0.0	0.0	0.0	0.0	0.0	0.0	0.0	0.0
106	7. Poland	0.0	0.0	0.0	0.0	0.0	0.0	0.0	0.0
107	8. Netherlands	0.0	0.0	0.0	0.8	0.0	0.0	0.0	0.0
108	9. Germany	0.0	0.0	0.0	0.0	0.0	0.0	0.0	0.5
109	10. Sweden	0.0	0.0	0.0	0.0	0.0	0.7	0.0	0.7
110	Imports, Total [i]	15.8	14.9	25.0	36.9	42.9	22.8	17.8	15.0
111	1. France	0.0	0.0	0.0	1.1	0.2	0.0	0.7	0.9
112	2. Australia	9.7	11.4	12.9	8.5	7.5	11.1	7.3	5.5
113	3. United States	0.0	0.0	0.0	0.0	0.0	0.0	0.0	0.0
114	4. Fiji	0.0	0.0	0.0	5.2	5.3	3.6	3.3	2.0
115	5. Japan	4.7	1.2	4.2	2.9	4.5	3.1	3.7	3.6
116	6. New Zealand	1.4	1.2	1.3	1.4	1.3	2.7	1.6	1.2
117	7. Denmark	0.0	0.0	0.0	0.0	0.0	0.0	0.1	0.0
118	8. Netherlands	0.0	0.0	0.0	0.0	0.0	0.0	0.0	0.0
119	9. Poland	0.0	0.0	0.0	0.0	0.0	0.0	0.0	0.0
120	10. Papua New Guinea	0.0	0.0	0.0	0.0	0.0	0.0	0.0	0.1
	BALANCE OF PAYMENTS								***Thousand US dollars;***
121	Merchandise exports, fob	24492	24594	2963	4137	2394	3612	10956	6058
122	Merchandise imports, fob	-16157	-17551	-20853	-26204	-23167	-17692	-18364	-21582
123	Trade balance [h]	8335	7043	-17890	-22067	-20773	-14080	-7408	-15524
124	Other goods, services and income	-6647	-671	-2507	-2758	3990	4421	5873	4700
125	Credit	...	8496	10369	14366	15847	16489	17999	21424
126	Debit	...	-9167	-12876	-17125	-11857	-12068	-12126	-16724
127	Unrequited transfer [j]	14613	10620	17093	20572	17330	16959	14028	8366
128	Private [j]	...	-112	-114	1379	407	361	352	10422
129	Official [j]	...	10732	17206	19193	16923	16598	13676	-2056
130	Current balance	16301	16992	-3305	-4252	547	7300	12493	-2458
131	Direct investment	426	...	...	...	...	...	...	...
132	Portfolio investment	–	...	...	...	...	...	...	...
133	Other long-term capital	–	...	...	...	...	...	...	9568
134	Other short-term capital	–	...	...	...	...	...	...	677
135	Net errors and omissions	...	...	5356	-919	1223	942	2967	-6818
136	Overall balance [k]	16727	14197	456	-2758	-1567	-5715	-13261	969
137	Allocation of SDRs	...	...	...	...	...	...	...	...
138	Monetary movements	-16727	-14197	-456	2758	1567	5715	13261	-969
	INTERNATIONAL RESERVES								***Million US dollars;***
139	Total [i]	72	74	80	75	80	87	74	94
140	Gold, national valuation	...	...	...	...	...	...	...	...
141	Foreign exchange	72	74	80	75	80	87	74	94

1986	1987	1988	1989	1990	1991	1992	1993	1994	1995	
5691	7783	8080	8669	9147	9953	10654	11923	11415	...	089
1236	1540	1588	1506	1530	2285	2534	2641	3153	...	090
338	266	574	451	954	503	626	891	751	...	091
2239	2671	2960	3201	3694	3631	3951	3032	3356	...	092
24	29	44	126	149	83	95	119	125	...	093
1142	1248	1371	2389	1754	1838	1746	2645	2323	...	094
4408	3633	3564	2949	4074	4113	4051	5016	4825	...	095
4251	5219	7661	6585	6566	8241	23885	10089	6271	...	096
1964	2460	2151	2406	6381	2382	2788	4290	3602	...	097
159	293	195	314	197	197	200	228	293	...	098

Calendar year

1986	1987	1988	1989	1990	1991	1992	1993	1994	1995	
1.7	2.1	11.8	5.7	3.1	6.6	3.1	6.4	7.0	9.3	099
0.1	0.1	0.0	0.0	0.4	0.0	0.0	0.0	2.3	2.2	100
0.0	0.0	1.8	1.3	0.3	0.6	0.4	1.7	1.2	1.5	101
0.0	0.0	0.0	0.0	0.0	0.0	0.0	0.0	0.0	1.9	102
0.0	0.0	0.0	0.0	0.0	0.0	0.0	0.5	0.9	0.8	103
0.0	0.0	0.0	0.0	0.0	0.0	1.9	0.5	0.6	0.6	104
0.0	0.0	0.0	0.0	0.0	0.0	0.0	1.2	0.5	0.5	105
0.0	0.0	0.0	0.0	0.0	0.0	0.0	0.3	0.4	0.5	106
0.0	0.0	0.0	0.1	0.2	0.0	0.0	0.1	0.1	0.6	107
0.5	0.3	2.7	3.4	0.8	0.4	0.1	1.2	0.6	0.0	108
0.3	0.4	0.4	0.0	0.3	0.1	0.4	0.4	0.2	0.2	109
18.6	16.0	23.9	39.8	43.2	53.1	110.9	93.0	98.8	86.0	110
0.7	0.8	0.1	0.0	0.1	0.2	28.5	22.8	27.3	43.0	111
9.9	8.3	9.9	8.8	10.6	10.7	11.4	12.0	16.1	14.5	112
0.0	0.0	3.7	17.1	21.0	30.1	39.1	33.8	25.9	2.6	113
2.0	2.1	2.5	4.4	0.0	0.0	6.1	7.2	8.2	9.5	114
3.9	1.7	2.6	3.6	5.0	5.3	12.4	4.4	7.4	1.8	115
1.5	1.2	0.9	1.4	2.5	2.6	2.0	2.3	2.5	3.2	116
0.0	0.0	0.0	0.1	0.0	0.0	0.8	1.3	2.5	2.8	117
0.0	0.0	0.0	0.0	0.0	0.0	1.5	1.9	2.2	2.1	118
0.0	0.0	0.0	0.0	0.0	0.0	0.0	1.5	1.3	1.5	119
0.0	0.0	0.0	0.0	0.0	0.6	0.6	0.8	0.9	1.0	120

Calendar year

1986	1987	1988	1989	1990	1991	1992	1993	1994	1995	
2496	2869	6670	6435	3681	3697	6513	5069	7110	6000	121
-21452	-25143	-28185	-28596	-34446	-33226	-50530	-42373	-36115	-36600	122
-18956	-22274	-21515	-22161	-30765	-29529	-44017	-37304	-29005	-30600	123
7228	6630	7835	7710	7105	18545	17823	15204	20779	12500	124
25889	27465	27988	29994	35180	43587	46158	46721	48640	30900	125
-18661	-20835	-20153	-22284	-28075	-25042	-28335	-31517	-27861	-18400	126
7798	10937	11330	12507	11891	16487	13761	16003	10047	23700	127
10371	13692	13877	15325	14278	19392	16943	18986	12247	6900	128
-2573	-2755	-2547	-2818	-2387	-2905	-3182	-2983	-2200	16800	129
-3930	-4707	-2350	-1944	-11769	5503	-12433	-6097	1821	5600	130
...	...	...	...	...	...	...	...	...	...	131
...	...	...	...	...	...	...	...	...	...	132
13381	9672	8560	9294	15973	7865	22337	8401	3478	...	133
-5510	-10746	-4597	-6849	-6447	-15160	-20341	-10971	-6546	...	134
-7504	-2572	-5351	-5975	-6417	-12372	-12183	1192	-6923	...	135
-3563	-8353	-3738	-5474	-8660	-14164	-22620	-7475	-8170	...	136
...	...	...	...	...	...	...	...	...	...	137
3563	8353	3738	5474	8660	14164	22620	7475	8170	...	138

As of end of period

1986	1987	1988	1989	1990	1991	1992	1993	1994	1995	
...	...	...	...	...	...	...	...	...	...	139
...	...	...	...	...	...	...	...	...	...	140
...	...	...	...	...	...	...	...	...	...	141

Item	1978	1979	1980	1981	1982	1983	1984	1985
142 Reserve position in the Fund	...	...	...	...	...	...	...	...
143 SDRs	...	...	...	...	...	...	...	...
EXCHANGE RATES								*Australian dollars*
144 End of period	0.8692	0.9046	0.8470	0.8866	1.0198	1.1086	1.2080	1.4686
145 Average of period	0.8736	0.8945	0.8776	0.8701	0.9829	1.1082	1.1369	1.4269
EXTERNAL INDEBTEDNESS								*Million US dollars;*
146 Total outstanding and disbursed	0.0	9.0	9.0	9.0	9.0	10.0	9.0	10.0
147 Long term	0.0	8.0	8.0	8.0	8.0	9.0	8.0	10.0
148 Public and publicly guaranteed	0.0	8.0	8.0	8.0	8.0	9.0	8.0	10.0
149 Private non-guaranteed	0.0	0.0	0.0	0.0	0.0	0.0	0.0	0.0
150 Short term	0.0	1.0	1.0	1.0	1.0	1.0	1.0	0.0
151 Use of IMF credit	0.0	0.0	0.0	0.0	0.0	0.0	0.0	0.0
Debt service								*Transactions*
152 Principal repayments on LT debt	0.0	0.0	0.0	0.0	0.0	0.0	0.0	0.0
153 Interest on long-term debt	0.0	0.0	0.0	0.0	0.0	0.0	0.0	1.0
154 Interest on short-term debt	0.0	0.0	0.0	0.0	0.0	0.0	0.0	0.0

Footnotes:

a   Figures for 1978, 1985 and 1990 represent census data. Growth rates calculated from adjusted 1980 and 1985 population figures are used to derive the intervening years estimates. A 2.3% growth rate was used for 1991-1995 for all the islands.

b   Refers to "formal sector employment" only. For 1990, data refer to the indigenous "cash employment" which includes cash earning activities, mostly at the household level.

c   The dramatic decline in national accounts estimates and in other economic variables during the period 1979-1980 was due to the phasing out of phosphate production. Data from 1982-1992 represent revised estimates.

d   Refers to local consumption pattern of urban Tarawa as reflected in the retail price index for 1978-1987.

e   M1 series is derived as the difference between M2 and quasi-money for 1982-1986.

f   Include time deposits for 1978-1979.

g   Includes net lending for 1985-1994.

h   Includes value of trade of the Gilbert Islands only. In 1979, the Gilbert Islands was officially renamed as Kiribati. Domestic export earnings beginning 1980 declined significantly due to the exhaustion of phosphate in Banaba Island.

i   Imports on direction of trade are on cif basis.

j   Private and official transfers represent credit and debit transactions from Government and other entities, respectively for 1985-1994.

k   Includes an increase in overseas holding of US$ 4,322,000 in 1978. Figures have been adjusted to include net errors and omissions from 1985-1994.

l   Refers to foreign exchange only.

	1986	1987	1988	1989	1990	1991	1992	1993	1994	1995	
	...	...	...	...	...	...	...	...	...	...	142
	...	...	...	...	...	...	...	...	...	...	143
per US dollar											
	1.5042	1.3841	1.1689	1.2615	1.2932	1.3161	1.4522	1.4769	1.2873	1.3423	144
	1.4905	1.4267	1.2752	1.2618	1.2799	1.2835	1.3600	1.4704	1.3667	1.3484	145
As of end of year											
	10.0	17.0	13.0	14.8	14.7	14.9	16.0	16.3	...	...	146
	10.0	12.0	13.0	13.5	14.2	14.2	14.5	15.5	...	...	147
	10.0	12.0	13.0	13.5	14.2	14.2	14.5	15.5	...	...	148
	0.0	0.0	0.0	0.0	0.0	0.0	0.0	0.0	...	...	149
	0.0	5.0	0.0	1.3	0.5	0.7	1.5	0.8	...	...	150
	0.0	0.0	0.0	0.0	0.0	0.0	0.0	0.0	...	...	151
during the year											
	1.0	0.0	0.0	0.0	0.0	0.0	0.0	0.0	...	...	152
	1.0	1.0	1.0	1.0	1.0	1.0	1.0	1.0	...	...	153
	0.0	0.0	0.0	0.0	0.0	0.0	0.0	0.0	...	...	154

	Item	1978	1979	1980	1981	1982	1983	1984	1985
									Million;
001	**POPULATION**	36.97	37.53	38.12	38.72	39.33	39.91	40.41	40.81
									Thousand;
002	**LABOR FORCE** [a]	13850	14142	14432	14683	15033	15119	14997	15592
003	Employed	13413	13602	13684	14023	14379	14506	14429	14970
004	Agriculture	5154	4866	4654	4801	4612	4315	3914	3733
005	Manufacturing	2986	3099	2955	2859	3033	3266	3348	3504
006	Mining	106	110	124	124	110	109	143	155
007	Others	5167	5527	5951	6239	6624	6816	7024	7578
008	Unemployed	437	540	748	660	654	613	568	622
009	Unemployment rate, %	3.2	3.8	5.2	4.5	4.4	4.1	3.8	4.0
	NATIONAL ACCOUNTS [a]								**Billion Won;**
	At Current Market Prices								
010	GDP by Industrial Origin	24327	31323	38041	47482	54443	63833	72645 I	82064
011	Agriculture	5019	6014	5677	7431	7989	8678	9392 I	10246
012	Mining	321	347	491	647	637	689	733 I	909
013	Manufacturing	6831	9032	11299	14199	15908	19106	22375 I	24080
014	Electricity, gas and water	318	524	752	1022	1208	1577	2000 I	2425
015	Construction	1873	2661	3186	3437	4211	5171	5739 I	6234
016	Trade	3270	4062	4842	6059	6898	7733	8872 I	11156
017	Transport and communications	1598	2167	2897	3874	4626	5166	5789 I	5955
018	Finance	1938	2712	4173	4592	4804	6313	7532 I	9477
019	Public administration	1669	2164	2910	3617	4347	4853	5232 I	5869
020	Others [b]	1492	1642	1814	2604	3815	4549	4980 I	5713
021	Net factor income from abroad	-326	-521	-1291	-1954	-2260	-2110	-2561 I	-2763
022	GNP	24002	30802	36750	45528	52182	61722	70084 I	79301
023	Expenditure on GDP	24327	31323	38041	47482	54443	63833	72645 I	82064
024	Private consumption	14786	19367	24585	30633	34554	38728	43201 I	48027
025	Government consumption	2530	3109	4387	5515	6255	6852	7263 I	8305
026	Gross fixed capital formation	7909	10576	12226	13276	15446	18669	20998 I	23435
027	Increase in stocks	132	702	-154	718	117	-308	668 I	849
028	Exports of goods and services	7227	8739	12944	17341	18770	22748	26126 I	27968
029	Less: Imports of goods and services	8063	10831	15774	19719	20174	23049	26039 I	26923
030	Statistical discrepancy	-193	-337	-171	-281	-525	192	428 I	403
	At Constant 1985 I 1990 Prices								
031	GDP by Industrial Origin	51289	55182	53989	57615	61821	69101	75606 I	111330
032	Agriculture	8846	9460	7657	8750	9401	10129	9977 I	15425
033	Mining	854	817	775	781	700	739	762 I	1067
034	Manufacturing	13166	14535	14426	15851	16914	19517	22901 I	28170
035	Electricity, gas and water	815	882	1026	1181	1248	1601	1998 I	1908
036	Construction	3975	4231	4158	3947	4678	5671	5987 I	11395
037	Trade	6651	6956	6637	7147	7701	8413	9084 I	13599
038	Transport and communications	3533	4132	4318	4534	4800	5223	5872 I	7185
039	Finance	4954	5272	5940	6071	6633	7443	8211 I	14369
040	Public administration	4729	4941	5168	5363	5543	5673	5738 I	10768
041	Others [b]	3767	3957	3884	3990	4203	4692	5076 I	7444
042	Net factor income from abroad	-643	-892	-1728	-2261	-2499	-2298	-2602 I	-3200
043	GNP	50646	54290	52261	55354	59322	66803	73004 I	108130
044	Expenditure on GDP	51289	55182	53989	57615	61821	69101	75606 I	111330
045	Private consumption	31885	34701	34366	36000	38337	41831	45006 I	61701
046	Government consumption	6322	6401	6875	7267	7339	7590	7702 I	12581
047	Gross fixed capital formation	16192	17807	15771	15126	16693	19662	21812 I	31018
048	Increase in stocks	890	2117	136	1082	774	169	984 I	1213
049	Exports of goods and services	15547	15859	17278	19890	20780	24776	26744 I	30882
050	Less: Imports of goods and services	19537	21778	20662	21871	22528	25233	27090 I	25718
051	Statistical discrepancy	-11	75	225	120	426	306	449 I	-347

1986	1987	1988	1989	1990	1991	1992	1993	1994	1995	
As of 1 July										
41.21	41.62	42.03	42.45	42.87	43.27	43.66	44.06	44.45	44.85	001
Calendar year										
16116	16873	17304	18023	18539	19048	19426	19803	20326	20797	002
15505	16354	16869	17560	18085	18612	18961	19253	19837	20377	003
3662	3580	3483	3438	3237	3064	2991	2828	2699	2541	004
3826	4416	4667	4882	4911	4994	4828	4652	4695	4773	005
187	186	140	90	79	67	63	52	40	27	006
7830	8172	8579	9150	9858	10487	11079	11721	12403	13037	007
611	519	435	463	454	436	465	550	489	419	008
3.8	3.1	2.5	2.6	2.4	2.3	2.4	2.8	2.4	2.0	009
Calendar year										
95738	112130	133134	149165	179539	215734	240392	267146	305970	351295	010
10685	11368	13585	14381	15592	16550	17806	18833	21498	23069	011
1034	1068	1088	992	1025	1142	929	899	1095	1109	012
29449	35174	42679	46253	52351	61527	66710	72162	82132	94485	013
3119	3420	3627	3732	3889	4507	5285	6195	7166	7893	014
6685	8151	10156	13358	20737	30035	32871	37006	41327	49636	015
13371	16016	18325	19822	23111	26420	28803	31188	35752	40086	016
6915	7960	9126	10328	12017	14357	16390	19112	22190	25945	017
11321	13717	17746	21302	26801	33052	39923	45481	52539	59268	018
6575	7527	8793	10788	13098	15898	18824	21232	24298	27505	019
6584	7731	8009	8209	10918	12246	12851	15039	17974	22299	020
-2829	-2403	-1763	-1223	-1277	-1494	-1688	-1628	-2198	-3011	021
92909	109727	131371	147942	178262	214240	238705	265518	303773	348284	022
95738	112130	133134	149165	179539	215734	240392	267146	305970	351295	023
52822	59031	67963	79424	96388	115043	129735	143722	164356	185899	024
9575	10843	12660	15237	18187	22170	26110	28746	32425	36387	025
26969	32587	39425	47625	66569	82947	87907	96219	109379	128659	026
505	841	1932	2539	-270	973	35	-2512	936	1724	027
36034	45051	51132	48829	53467	60735	69433	78163	92121	116603	028
30366	36356	40567	44785	54417	66050	71840	76971	94360	120214	029
197	133	589	296	-385	-84	-988	-220	1113	2237	030
124194	138500	154111	163952	179540	195935	205859	217699	236375	257535	031
16148	15163	16517	16350	15592	15661	16603	16123	16380	16832	032
1132	1140	1143	1100	1025	1028	916	879	918	887	033
33656	40236	45773	47714	52351	57108	60001	63015	69596	77075	034
2400	2674	2956	3299	3889	4194	4497	5080	5721	6272	035
11751	13250	14389	16503	20737	23800	23644	25635	26843	29475	036
15847	18166	20149	21060	23111	25076	26311	27438	29809	32096	037
7868	8872	9929	10875	12017	13380	14646	15838	17829	20450	038
16052	18495	21504	23975	26801	30123	33350	37500	41177	44187	039
11113	11475	11984	12535	13098	13577	14068	14464	14700	14831	040
8227	9029	9767	10541	10919	11988	11823	11729	13401	15430	041
-3157	-2587	-1882	-1268	-1278	-1476	-1628	-1537	-2042	-2801	042
121037	135913	152229	162684	178262	194459	204231	216162	234333	254734	043
124194	138500	154111	163952	179540	195935	205859	217699	236375	257535	044
66701	72132	78606	87109	96388	105526	112501	118883	127865	138015	045
13640	14474	15633	16970	18187	19725	21223	21869	22788	23433	046
34316	40142	45646	52885	66569	74973	74376	78279	87484	98374	047
545	665	2028	2894	-270	1147	153	-1891	1190	164	048
39078	47543	53507	51336	53467	59786	66351	73857	86040	106768	049
30329	36259	40954	47614	54417	64890	68208	72777	88519	108164	050
243	-197	-355	372	-384	-332	-537	-522	-473	-1055	051

	Item	1978	1979	1980	1981	1982	1983	1984	1985
	Investment Financing, at current prices								
052	Gross domestic capital formation	8041	11278	12071	13994	15563	18361	21666 I	24284
053	Gross national saving	6687	8326	7778	9380	11374	16142	19620 I	22969
054	Gross domestic saving	7012	8847	9070	11334	13634	18253	22181 I	25732
055	Net factor income from abroad	-326	-521	-1291	-1954	-2260	-2110	-2561 I	-2763
056	Foreign saving	1162	2614	4122	4332	3665	2411	2474 I	1715
057	Net transfer from abroad	645	602	924	1247	1689	1201	1376 I	957
058	Net borrowing from abroad	517	2012	3198	3085	1976	1210	1098 I	758
	Per Capita GNP, '000 Won								
059	Current prices	651	823	968	1181	1334	1554	1739 I	1952
060	Constant *1985* I *1990* prices	1370	1446	1371	1429	1508	1674	1807 I	2662
	PRODUCTION								*Thousand metric tons;*
	Agriculture, *crop year*								
061	1. Rice	5797	5565	3550	5063	5175	5404	5682	5626
062	2. Radish	2407	2082	1973	2016	1970	1568	1738	1586
063	3. Barley	555	584	354	329	278	333	353	346
064	4. Soybeans	293	257	216	257	233	226	254	234
065	5. Sweet potatoes	504	430	342	344	261	314	277	244
066	6. White potatoes	61	71	89	111	108	94	87	115
067	7. Corn	100	149	154	145	117	101	133	132
068	8. Wheat	36	42	92	57	66	112	18	11
	Mining								
069	1. Iron ore	587.5	458.7	545.2	554.8	553.4	591.3	553.6	625.1
070	2. Zinc ore	132.5	124.4	112.3	113.0	118.1	113.9	106.2	87.7
071	3. Lead ore	30.3	24.9	21.2	22.9	20.6	21.1	19.8	16.9
	Manufacturing								
072	1. Pig iron	2741.1	5062.5	5577.3	7928.3	8444.7	8024.4	8763.5	8832.7
073	2. Compound fertilizer	1658.0	1696.4	1438.5	1210.5	1667.1	1614.0	1860.6	1988.2
074	3. Wheat flour	1184.1	1241.9	1471.6	1438.8	1444.2	1475.9	1546.8	1611.6
075	4. Refined sugar	511.0	625.4	756.8	689.8	645.6	772.2	747.9	823.5
076	5. Steel ingot	3138.5	5199.9	5712.1	5890.9	5636.1	5061.7	5014.4	4885.0
077	6. Newsprint paper	163.2	173.9	213.1	236.4	213.0	207.4	216.1	244.0
078	7. Cotton yarn	189.2	244.5	265.0	245.1	271.9	271.3	274.7	258.6
079	8. Sulphuric acid	1461.4	1644.8	1701.7	1304.1	1596.0	1610.1	1974.8	2036.8
	Production Indexes								*Period*
080	Agriculture, *1979-81 = 100*	112.8	111.7	90.7	98.5	102.9	101.3	109.2	110.3
081	Mining, *1985 = 100* I *1990 = 100*	87.9	87.9 I	97.8	100.5	94.2	94.8	103.5	113.2
082	Manufacturing, *1985 = 100* I *1990 = 100*	54.4	61.0 I	31.9	36.2	38.2	44.5	51.4	53.5
	ENERGY								*Annual*
	Crude petroleum, *'000 m.t.*								
083	Production	–	–	–	–	–	–	–	–
084	Exports	–	–	–	–	–	–	–	–
085	Imports	22664	25247	24886	24880	24274	26250	27175	26989
086	Consumption	22713	25317	24982	24807	24655	26033	26478	26356
	Coal, *'000 m.t.*								
087	Production	18054	18208	18624	19865	20116	19861	21370	22543
088	Exports	–	–	–	–	–	–	–	–
089	Imports	2815	6366	7723	11538	11331	10989	13103	19961
090	Consumption	20122	23169	25862	28847	29368	31328	37003	40533
	Electricity, *Mn kWh*								
091	Production	31510	35600	37239	40207	43122	48850	53808	58007
092	Exports	–	–	–	–	–	–	–	–
093	Imports	–	–	–	–	–	–	–	–
094	Consumption	27326	31145	32734	35424	37880	42620	47051	50732

	1986	1987	1988	1989	1990	1991	1992	1993	1994	1995	
	27474	33428	41357	50164	66299	83920	87942	93707	110315	130383	052
	30512	39853	50748	53280	63687	77027	82859	93050	106991	125999	053
	33341	42256	52511	54503	64964	78521	84547	94678	109189	129010	054
	-2829	-2403	-1763	-1223	-1277	-1494	-1688	-1628	-2198	-3011	055
	-2841	-6291	-8803	-2820	2227	6810	4095	436	4667	...	056
	1179	1718	1408	522	616	401	589	739	754	-147	057
	-4020	-8009	-10210	-3342	1611	6409	3506	-30.3	3914	...	058
	2264	2647	3138	3498	4165	4957	5471	6031	6837	7769	059
	2949	3279	3636	3847	4165	4499	4681	4910	5266	5680	060

Calendar year

	5607	5493	6053	5898	5606	5384	5331	4750	5060	...	061
	1705	1536	1757	1842	1761	1558	1516	1601	1593	...	062
	249	264	281	259	224	198	183	191	156	...	063
	199	204	239	252	233	183	176	170	154	...	064
	212	168	174	184	134	117	98	87	77	...	065
	113	90	85	126	74	83	145	124	98	...	066
	113	127	106	121	120	75	92	82	89	...	067
	5	4	2	1	1	1	1	1	2	...	068
	563.2	565.0	666.0	677.1	650.4	563.1	583.2	648.5	545.5	476.0	069
	76.0	47.0	45.6	45.1	46.4	45.0	45.2	28.5	15.3	16.5	070
	19.5	26.3	25.8	25.9	20.3	17.2	17.5	–	–	–	071
	9016.7	10868.9	12577.8	14948.8	15333.7	18546.0	19238.1	21869.6	21169.3	22343.9	072
	1907.1	2026.4	2075.9	1984.9	1959.5	1926.7	2187.9	2365.5	2514.5	2453.6	073
	1596.3	1612.7	1692.3	1614.3	1615.8	1564.1	1553.0	1553.6	1591.4	1679.4	074
	828.1	894.5	909.7	976.4	1008.0	998.6	1076.5	1038.2	1140.5	1131.1	075
	4075.5	2646.0	2177.6	1272.2	863.7	1058.7	760.6	578.0	607.7	...	076
	272.6	299.2	377.7	442.7	531.9	569.0	602.2	742.3	867.2	956.9	077
	265.6	284.5	324.2	328.1	330.1	317.9	301.6	295.5	315.7	302.0	078
	1902.1	2038.3	2224.7	2234.7	2239.4	2232.2	2392.7	–	–	–	079

averages

	111.9	108.5	113.7	108.0	113.3	105.2	115.5	109.8	123.4	127.4	080
	121.2	122.7	122.7	109.7	100.0	99.8	85.9	79.9	78.7	73.6	081
	65.3	78.5	89.1	91.8	100.0	109.7	116.2	121.1	134.4	150.6	082

values

	–	–	–	–	–	–	–	–	–	–	083
	–	–	–	–	–	–	–	–	–	–	084
	31310	29418	33531	40312	41938	54475	69341	76309	78099	...	085
	27299	28649	34099	39052	48215	57809	70001	76855	84637	...	086
	24253	24274	24295	20785	17217	15058	11970	9443	7400	...	087
	–	–	–	–	–	–	–	–	–	...	088
	21012	21325	24620	25027	23969	29411	30106	34849	38825	...	089
	42879	43304	45906	44138	43407	42392	39814	41594	41987	...	090
	64695	73992	85462	94475	107670	118619	130963	144437	164993	136123	091
	–	–	–	–	–	–	–	–	–	–	092
	–	–	–	–	–	–	–	–	–	–	093
	56310	64169	74318	82192	94383	104374	115244	127734	146540	163270	094

Item	1978	1979	1980	1981	1982	1983	1984	1985
Retail prices, *Won/litre*								
095 Gasoline, premium	232	347	715	971	1060	904	890	890
096 Diesel	69	95	178	244	278	277	277	277
PRICE INDEXES								*1990 = 100*
097 Consumer (Seoul)	35.8	42.3	54.4	66.0	70.8	73.3	74.9	76.8
098 Food	36.0	40.9	52.1	67.0	68.6	69.3	70.2	78.8
099 Non-food	35.2	42.9	55.7	64.9	72.0	75.8	77.9	79.2
100 Wholesale	44.0	52.2	72.5	87.3	91.4	91.5	92.2	93.0
101 Implicit GDP deflator, *1985 = 100* | *1990 = 100*	47.4	56.8	70.5	82.4	88.1	92.4	96.1 |	73.7
MONEY AND BANKING								*Billion Won;*
102 Money supply (M1)	2714	3275	3807	3982	5799	6783	6821	7558
103 Currency in circulation	1364	1604	1856	2025	2574	2874	3109	3286
104 Demand deposits	1349	1671	1951	1957	3226	3909	3711	4272
105 Quasi-money	5215	6603	8728	11689	14105	16155	17885	21007
106 Money supply (M2)	7929	9878	12535	15671	19904	22938	24706	28565
107 Foreign assets (net)	727	237	-597	-2278	-4323	-5082	-6191	-7696
108 Domestic credit	8722	11826	16778	22016	27529	31847	36059	42561
109 Claims on govt. sector (net)	464	335	731	1742	2158	2013	1973	2013
110 Claims on private sector	8258	11491	16047	20273	25371	29834	34086	40548
111 Claims on other financial insts.	–	–	–	–	–	–	–	–
112 Other items	-1520	-2186	-3646	-4067	-3301	-3826	-5163	-6300
Deposit Money Banks								
113 Demand deposits	2633	3251	3845	5534	7530	8235	10618	10777
114 Savings deposits	3024	3900	4654	6214	7391	8604	9754	12874
115 Time deposits	2108	2631	3923	5286	6269	7068	7553	7372
116 Domestic credits outstanding	8722	11826	16778	22016	27529	31847	36059	42561
Interest Rates								*Per cent;*
On deposits								
117 Savings [c]	14.8	17.3	23.5	19.2	10.9	8.0	9.1	10.0
118 Time: 6 months	15.6	17.1	20.2	16.8	10.5	7.6	6.0	6.0
119 over 12 months	16.7	18.6	22.9	19.3	10.9	8.0	9.1	10.0
On loans and discounts								
120 Commercial bills [d]	16.9	18.5	22.9	19.3	12.3	10.0	10.0	10.0
121 Export credit	8.5	9.0	14.8	15.0	10.9	10.0	10.0	10.0
122 Other commercial [e]	16.9	18.5	22.9	19.3	12.2	10.0	10.6	11.5
GOVERNMENT FINANCE								*Billion Won;*
Central Government								
123 Current revenue	4084.2	5375.9	6736.7	8533.7	9874.8	11417.3	12510.4	13737.0
124 Taxes	3702.1	4837.4	5896.8	7364.4	8529.9	10207.4	11077.3	12105.1
125 Non-taxes	382.1	538.5	839.9	1169.3	1344.9	1209.9	1433.1	1631.9
126 Current expenditure	3196.6	4472.4	5641.1	6931.1	8296.3	9144.9	10212.8	11523.0
127 Current surplus/deficit	887.6	903.5	1095.6	1602.6	1578.5	2272.4	2297.6	2214.0
128 Capital receipts	23.5	69.5	96.5	71.1	108.4	120.2	92.9	185.0
129 Capital expenditure	585.3	751.6	920.9	1113.7	1818.7	1536.4	1661.8	1813.9
130 Capital account surplus/deficit	-561.8	-682.1	-824.4	-1042.6	-1710.3	-1416.2	-1568.9	-1628.9
131 Net lending	626.1	766.0	1120.0	2145.0	1524.2	1518.8	1570.0	1530.1
132 Overall surplus/deficit	-300.3	-544.6	-848.8	-1585.0	-1656.0	-662.6	-841.3	-945.0
Financing								
133 Domestic borrowing }	300.3	544.6	848.8	1585.0	1656.0	662.6	841.3	501.7
134 Foreign borrowing }								443.3
135 Foreign grants	–	–	–	–	–	–	–	–
136 Use of cash balances	–	–	–	–	–	–	–	–

1986	1987	1988	1989	1990	1991	1992	1993	1994	1995	
811	774	540	373	477	497	728	798	723	...	095
239	225	187	182	182	182	195	210	220	...	096

Period averages

1986	1987	1988	1989	1990	1991	1992	1993	1994	1995	
78.8	81.4	87.0	91.9	100.0	109.7	115.9	121.7	129.0	134.0	097
74.4	77.3	85.0	90.9	100.0	112.7	118.5	123.8	134.8	135.4	098
81.5	84.0	88.2	92.4	100.0	108.4	114.8	120.8	126.4	132.8	099
91.7	92.1	94.6	96.0	100.0	104.7	107.0	108.6	111.6	116.8	100
77.1	81.0	86.4	91.0	100.0	110.1	116.8	122.7	129.3	136.4	101

As of end of period

1986	1987	1988	1989	1990	1991	1992	1993	1994	1995	
8809	10107	12151	14329	15905	21752	24586	29041	32511	30921	102
3679	4443	5133	6140	7011	7913	8581	12109	13127	11989	103
5130	5665	7018	8189	8894	13839	16006	16932	19383	18932	104
25024	30172	36787	44309	52802	61993	71672	83178	100668	123025	105
33833	40279	48939	58638	68708	83746	96259	112219	133179	153945	106
-6128	-1605	7251	9104	10140	8076	12142	17539	20120	22600	107
49496	57041	64099	79089	96888	118186	131975	148193	175585	200295	108
4744	3818	903	-718	-1678	-343	-649	-1343	-4214	-13375	109
43581	49187	57338	70264	86655	106288	119224	133487	164399	191243	110
1171	4037	5858	9543	11912	12241	13400	16048	15400	17025	111
-9535	-15157	-22411	-29555	-38320	-42517	-47858	-53512	-62526	-68949	112
11335	16020	20970	23140	31620	37620	36519	33240	35065	31029	113
17149	21889	26038	29697	36620	43824	53474	63056	73552	74765	114
7442	7811	10477	14081	15814	17064	17253	19436	26574	25495	115
49486	57044	64089	79089	96888	118186	131975	148192	175585	200295	116

Period averages

1986	1987	1988	1989	1990	1991	1992	1993	1994	1995	
10.0	10.0	10.0	10.0	10.0	10.0	10.0	8.5-10.0	8.5-9.0	8.3-12.0	117
6.0	6.0	6.0	6.0	6.0	6.0	6.0	5.0	5.0	9.5-10.0	118
10.0	10.0	10.0	10.0	10.0	10.0	10.0	8.5	8.5-10.0	9.5-10.0	119
10.0	10.0	...	...	...	...	...	...	...	...	120
10.0	10.0	...	...	...	...	...	...	...	...	121
10.0	10.0	...	...	...	...	...	...	...	...	122

Fiscal year ending 31 December

1986	1987	1988	1989	1990	1991	1992	1993	1994	1995	
15721.5	18510.0	22557.8	25502.0	31332.3	35947.2	42870.5	49834.3	57365.2	...	123
13882.2	16689.7	20389.4	22393.6	28362.6	32195.6	37751.4	43547.8	50624.3	...	124
1839.3	1820.3	2168.4	3108.4	2969.7	3751.6	5119.1	6286.5	6740.9	...	125
12829.8	14324.8	16746.0	20024.9	24648.1	29967.6	35435.2	39062.2	45687.3	...	126
2891.7	4185.2	5811.8	5477.1	6684.2	5979.6	7435.3	10772.1	11677.9	...	127
118.9	147.9	332.2	460.2	757.0	870.4	935.2	916.5	1458.5	...	128
2119.0	2618.8	2707.7	3751.1	4355.9	5651.2	5340.8	5948.1	8264.6	...	129
-2000.1	-2470.9	-2375.5	-3290.9	-3598.9	-4780.8	-4405.6	-5031.6	-6806.1	...	130
977.9	1236.5	2008.6	1901.2	4292.2	4692.7	4217.4	4036.3	6473.3	...	131
-86.3	477.8	1427.7	285.0	-1206.9	-3493.9	-1187.7	1704.2	-1601.5	...	132
232.3	-488.8	-1296.3	315.2	1534.8	3775.9	1498.7	863.0	1932.4	...	133
-146.0	11.0	-711.8	-600.2	-327.9	-281.9	-310.9	-446.9	-330.9	...	134
–	–	–	–	–	–	–	–	–	...	135
–	–	580.4	–	–	–	–	–	–	...	136

167

	Item	1978	1979	1980	1981	1982	1983	1984	1985
	Expenditure by Function, Central Gov't.								
137	Total	4408.0	5990.0	7682.0	10189.8	11639.2	12200.2	13444.5	14867.0
138	General public services	419.1	547.5	655.5	907.7	1076.6	1236.9	1208.0	1400.7
139	Defence	1438.1	1597.4	2349.1	2849.0	3180.1	3402.4	3573.4	3957.9
140	Education	605.0	863.0	1124.4	1465.6	1980.5	2188.6	2258.1	2462.3
141	Health	68.3	56.8	78.3	103.4	140.6	180.4	172.9	191.9
142	Social security & welfare	189.2	283.0	437.9	496.5	991.5	568.9	670.0	779.0
143	Housing & community amenities	55.0	105.5	191.1	763.8	383.4	589.2	1061.5	718.5
144	Economic services	1154.9	1905.2	1996.7	2519.4	2513.7	2430.5	2564.9	3250.9
145	Agriculture	217.1	598.3	451.8	922.2	637.3	627.4	1038.9	1234.7
146	Industry	317.4	355.1	565.5	404.1	524.0	449.5	263.5	360.1
147	Electricity, gas & water	208.0	265.2	163.7	324.1	214.7	110.2	95.5	113.9
148	Transport and communications	92.3	212.9	285.7	344.0	487.0	360.2	659.3	951.5
149	Other economic services	320.1	473.7	530.0	525.0	650.7	883.2	507.7	590.7
150	Others	478.4	631.6	849.0	1084.4	1372.8	1603.3	1935.7	2105.8
	Provincial and Other Local Govts.								
151	Revenue [†]	1824.6	2568.8	3153.7	3884.1	4867.7	5894.7	6568.1	7193.7
152	Tax	445.7	599.0	767.8	914.4	1119.2	1397.2	1508.3	1654.6
153	Non-tax	435.4	595.9	635.8	778.3	987.7	1284.1	1508.5	1684.4
154	Subsidy/grants	869.7	1294.9	1682.8	2092.7	2659.2	3093.3	3425.1	3717.6
155	Expenditure	1740.9	2455.2	3206.1	4029.7	4760.9	5717.6	6474.8	7202.2
	EXTERNAL TRADE								*Million US dollars;*
156	Exports, fob	12711	15056	17505	21254	21853	24445	29245	30283
157	Imports, cif	14972	20339	22292	26131	24251	26192	30631	31136
158	Trade balance	-2261	-5283	-4787	-4877	-2398	-1747	-1386	-853
	Exports, by SITC section								
159	Food and live animals	933	1082	1153	1323	1081	1092	1149	1136
160	Beverage and tobacco	120	118	124	119	128	126	119	107
161	Crude materials excl. fuels	326	354	331	284	273	292	328	298
162	Mineral fuels, etc.	42	30	46	183	310	556	832	951
163	Animal, vegetable oil & fats	11	27	13	15	9	4	4	4
164	Chemicals	329	504	755	644	670	677	845	936
165	Basic manufactures	3796	4831	6252	7232	6650	6957	7378	7064
166	Machines, transport equipment	2711	3236	3555	4839	6153	7981	10462	11384
167	Misc. manufactured goods	4414	4854	5229	6501	6534	6721	8093	8372
168	Unclassified goods	30	21	47	114	47	38	34	32
	Exports, by principal commodity								
169	1. Woven fabrics other than cotton	776	873	1005	1268	1140	1234	1319	1326
170	2. Ships and boats other than warships	801	515	618	1411	2832	3735	4684	5040
171	3. Telecommunication equipment	208	274	248	282	289	466	458	529
172	4. Rubber tires and tubes	214	325	477	460	282	362	470	440
173	5. Cement	142	114	235	339	332	204	111	96
	Imports, by SITC section								
174	Food and live animals	931	1432	1797	2721	1561	1712	1622	1398
175	Beverage and tobacco	52	71	85	67	10	30	65	50
176	Crude materials excl. fuels	2398	3261	3632	3632	3361	3463	3939	3857
177	Mineral fuels, etc.	2460	3788	6660	7786	7607	6976	7296	7363
178	Animal, vegetable oil & fats	104	152	118	137	137	141	174	146
179	Chemicals	1282	1984	1800	2065	2051	2242	2709	2789
180	Basic manufactures	2231	2732	2450	2787	2630	3026	3788	3555
181	Machines, transport equipment	4996	6154	5001	6037	6011	7589	9817	10648
182	Misc. manufactured goods	508	718	687	760	788	915	1117	1233
183	Unclassified goods	9	48	62	140	95	99	106	97

1986	1987	1988	1989	1990	1991	1992	1993	1994	1995	
15926.7	18180.1	20881.4	25677.2	33296.2	40311.5	44993.3	51814.2	...	...	137
1597.4	1702.6	1884.7	2275.6	2823.9	3562.9	4397.1	5082.4	...	...	138
4375.7	4632.2	5266.3	5925.1	6673.2	7899.7	8703.5	9627.3	...	...	139
2712.5	3113.7	3695.8	4402.2	5648.8	5608.8	6491.9	7498.6	...	...	140
232.3	400.8	432.2	475.2	568.6	716.2	422.9	503.8	...	...	141
967.7	1132.9	1504.5	2046.5	2691.2	3438.2	4166.7	4800.9	...	...	142
615.2	663.4	1013.5	2216.5	3543.9	3918.9	3479.1	3729.7	...	...	143
2885.5	3212.1	4054.3	4854.1	6789.0	8332.8	8427.2	10893.6	...	...	144
1148.9	1436.6	2347.9	2752.8	3410.3	3754.8	3938.7	4851.9	...	...	145
427.0	315.1	191.0	324.2	680.0	146.0	143.6	1000.1	...	...	146
122.0	136.1	58.8	-506.9	206.2	241.0	203.2	201.3	...	...	147
750.6	873.6	115.3	196.6	468.1	408.0	1916.4	1931.6	...	...	148
437.0	450.7	1341.3	2087.4	2024.4	3783.0	2225.3	2908.7	...	...	149
2540.4	3322.4	3030.1	3482.0	4557.6	6834.0	8904.9	9677.9	...	...	150
8172.1	9970.9	11818.7	15558.7	20106.4	23120.1	27005.8	29627.4	...	...	151
1809.7	2192.3	3099.0	4973.3	6378.6	7883.8	8244.3	14045.8	...	...	152
1871.4	2298.6	2452.8	2825.2	4362.2	5207.7	7753.8	12092.7	...	...	153
4289.2	5312.5	5981.6	7295.1	9036.9	9746.7	10381.1	2037.4	...	...	154
7887.9	9081.2	10880.7	13781.0	18329.2	23377.3	30523.6	33066.7	...	...	155

Calendar year

1986	1987	1988	1989	1990	1991	1992	1993	1994	1995	
34715	47281	60696	62377	65016	71870	76632	82236	96013	125058	156
31584	41020	51811	61465	69844	81525	81775	83800	102348	135119	157
3131	6261	8885	912	-4828	-9655	-5143	-1564	-6335	-10061	158
1570	2089	2380	2213	2037	2158	2119	2060	2295	2656	159
95	90	131	114	123	116	77	72	102	147	160
338	452	692	902	991	989	1073	1160	1430	1790	161
649	748	584	687	697	1509	1742	1852	1746	2472	162
4	4	3	2	1	2	7	6	8	21	163
1068	1321	1879	2049	2512	3190	4454	4921	6339	8944	164
8173	10198	12645	13735	14357	16079	18491	20686	22949	27568	165
11661	16906	23458	23591	25545	29985	32556	36965	47067	65646	166
11094	15349	18732	18972	18573	17644	15875	14220	13504	13382	167
63	125	193	114	179	198	237	294	573	2433	168
1832	2400	2766	3151	3812	4734	5362	6062	7380	7579 *	169
1815	1138	1760	1788	2801	4129	4113	4061	4945	4898 *	170
837	1373	1598	1762	1981	2116	2337	2922	3687	3864 *	171
521	642	781	760	873	898	1053	1132	1233	1215 *	172
132	157	147	151	75	74	75	172	161	128 *	173
1422	1622	2299	3067	3247	3932	4097	4001	4761	5926	174
44	32	87	186	188	228	243	263	349	535	175
4291	5897	7754	8742	8651	8907	8321	8876	9404	11713	176
5052	6022	5986	7627	11023	12748	14636	15053	15415	19013	177
124	139	175	171	185	-246	269	259	324	393	178
3495	4594	6272	7144	7430	8282	7661	8228	9763	13156	179
4558	6250	7970	9672	10581	13462	11899	12070	15936	21270	180
10640	13813	18242	21106	23944	28251	28966	28417	37408	49437	181
1655	2132	2879	3555	4240	5098	5210	6148	8165	10803	182
305	520	147	195	355	373	472	486	824	2873	183

	Item	1978	1979	1980	1981	1982	1983	1984	1985
	Direction of Trade								**Million US dollars;**
184	Exports, Total	12594	15036	17439	21271	21827	24459	29259	30289
185	1. United States	4076	4389	4624	5688	6286	8262	10528	10789
186	2. Japan	2627	3353	3039	3503	3405	3383	4610	4546
187	3. Hong Kong	385	531	823	1155	905	817	1281	1565
188	4. China, People's Rep. of	0	0	0	0	0	0	0	0
189	5. Singapore	144	197	267	306	436	537	497	491
190	6. Germany	663	845	875	805	760	776	924	980
191	7. Indonesia	103	195	366	371	384	252	254	196
192	8. United Kingdom	393	542	573	705	1024	1003	955	913
193	9. Malaysia	48	86	184	164	234	226	253	449
194	10. Panama	91	128	144	207	353	227	540	746
195	Imports, Total	14975	20176	22063	26154	24250	26196	30628	31058
196	1. Japan	5982	6657	5858	6374	5305	6239	7640	7557
197	2. United States	3044	4603	4891	6050	5957	6278	6877	6554
198	3. China, People's Rep. of	0	0	0	0	0	0	0	0
199	4. Germany	491	844	637	672	680	651	795	956
200	5. Saudi Arabia	1281	1585	3318	3561	3213	2033	1420	719
201	6. Australia	464	599	680	910	913	971	1096	1120
202	7. Indonesia	408	592	485	385	683	387	653	669
203	8. Canada	204	326	378	531	485	444	638	632
204	9. Italy	78	134	119	121	122	167	205	219
205	10. Malaysia	228	383	472	643	610	777	1004	1235
	Trade Indexes								**1985 = 100 I 1990 = 100;**
	Quantum index								
206	Exports	50.1	49.6	55.2	64.9	69.2	80.4	93.0	100.0
207	Imports	63.5	71.1	64.6	71.9	72.0	81.7	94.3	100.0
	Unit value index								
208	Exports	83.9	100.3	104.7	108.1	104.4	100.4	103.9	100.0
209	Imports	75.4	92.1	110.9	116.9	108.2	103.1	104.4	100.0
210	Terms of trade	111.3	108.9	94.4	92.5	96.5	97.4	99.5	100.0
	BALANCE OF PAYMENTS								**Million US dollars;**
211	Merchandise exports, fob	12711	14705	17214	20671	20879	23204	26335	26442
212	Merchandise imports, fob	-14491	-19100	-21598	-24299	-23474	-24968	-27371	-26461
213	Trade balance	-1780	-4395	-4384	-3628	-2595	-1764	-1036	-19
214	Other goods, services and income	224	-195	-1386	-1519	-554	-434	-878	-1446
215	Credit	4450	4826	5363	6598	7476	7179	7316	6664
216	Debit	-4226	-5021	-6749	-8117	-8030	-7613	-8194	-8110
217	Unrequited transfer	471	439	449	501	499	592	541	578
218	Private	434	399	399	421	447	566	517	555
219	Official	37	40	50	80	52	26	24	23
220	Current balance	-1085	-4151	-5321	-4646	-2650	-1606	-1373	-887
221	Direct investment	100	126	96	105	101	101	171	250
222	Portfolio investment	42	43	46	104	44	196	411	988
223	Other long-term capital	2024	2494	1714	2633	1086	973	1485	-137
224	Other short-term capital	-1171	844	1945	-82	4	894	-758	-588
225	Net errors and omissions	-312	-329	-370	-411	-1296	-942	-894	-880
226	Overall balance	-402	-973	-1890	-2297	-2711	-384	-958	-1254
227	Allocation of SDRs	–	–	–	–	–	–	–	–
228	Monetary movements	402	973	1890	2297	2711	384	958	1254

	1986	1987	1988	1989	1990	1991	1992	1993	1994	1995	
Calendar year											
	34793	47303	60683	60496	65027	71870	76632	81736	96040	126495	184
	13920	18382	21478	20203	19446	18608	18090	18138	20553	24343	185
	5426	8437	12004	13167	12638	12356	11599	11564	13523	17014	186
	1691	2204	3561	3351	3780	4769	5909	6431	8015	10387	187
	0	0	0	0	0	1003	2654	5151	6203	9517	188
	532	928	1355	1499	1805	2702	3222	3109	4152	6580	189
	1242	2002	2368	2067	2849	3196	2877	3593	4313	5965	190
	179	241	402	626	1079	1350	1935	2095	2540	2969	191
	1034	1525	1951	1851	1750	1768	1830	1661	1783	2930	192
	219	300	410	512	708	1037	1136	1430	1652	2967	193
	494	517	567	461	547	0	1842	1081	1968	2626	194
	31734	41026	51812	60210	69858	81508	80602	80967	102348	135925	195
	10869	13657	15847	17167	18574	21120	19458	20016	25390	32845	196
	6548	8761	12706	15445	16946	18904	18287	17928	21579	30271	197
	0	0	0	0	0	3441	3725	3929	5463	7751	198
	1216	1799	2072	2554	3284	3698	3743	3955	5159	6680	199
	691	1117	831	1042	1733	3269	3797	3735	3965	5379	200
	1080	1279	1794	2227	2589	3009	3086	3347	3782	4919	201
	428	825	905	1116	1600	2052	2292	2588	2843	3324	202
	709	947	1195	1632	1465	1907	1574	1695	2005	2546	203
	310	537	637	839	1170	1431	1348	1398	1954	2410	204
	902	1086	1324	1471	1586	1869	1758	1947	1876	2475	205
Period averages											
	112.2	138.9 ǀ	93.4	94.3	100.0	109.9	119.1	127.2	146.1	181.3	206
	108.1	130.7 ǀ	76.9	88.2	100.0	116.7	119.0	126.7	153.9	186.4	207
	102.1	112.4 ǀ	100.1	101.7	100.0	100.6	99.0	99.4	101.1	106.2	208
	93.8	100.8 ǀ	96.5	99.8	100.0	100.0	98.4	94.7	95.2	103.7	209
	108.8	111.5 ǀ	103.7	101.9	100.0	100.6	100.6	105.0	106.2	102.4	210
Calendar year											
	33913	46244	59648	61409	63124	69582	75169	80950	93676	123242	211
	-29707	-38585	-48203	-56812	-65127	-76561	-77316	-79090	-96822	-127991	212
	4206	7659	11445	4597	-2004	-6980	-2146	1860	-3145	-4749	213
	-627	977	1267	211	-451	-1596	-2614	-1967	-1989	-3512	214
	8052	10010	11252	12642	14269	15529	16010	18253	22551	29898	215
	-8679	-9033	-9985	-12431	-14719	-17125	-18625	-20220	-24540	-33410	216
	1039	1217	1448	247	275	-152	232	491	604	-556	217
	1028	1199	1404	199	267	21	257	634	...	...	218
	11	18	44	48	8	-173	-25	-143			219
	4618	9853	14160	5055	-2179	-8727	-4529	384	-4531	-8817	220
	478	625	920	453	-105	-242	-497	-540	-1318	-1703	221
	403	339	180	-30	811	3193	5742	10725	6805	8916	222
	-2863	-6800	-3833	-3786	-159	1235	1988	-1285	374	-1638	223
	-393	-7	1336	60	3334	41	1110	-2021	3163	7960	224
	-544	1191	-589	701	-1976	760	1084	-721	-1672	-1639	225
	1699	5201	12175	2453	-274	-3740	4899	6542	2821	3080	226
	–	–	–	–	–	–	–	–	–	–	227
	-1699	-5201	-12175	-2453	274	3740	-4899	-6542	-2821	-3080	228

	Item	1978	1979	1980	1981	1982	1983	1984	1985
	INTERNATIONAL RESERVES								*Million US dollars;*
229	Total	4937.6	5708.8	6571.7	6889.9	6985.2	6908.7	7649.7	7748.7
230	Gold, national valuation	29.7	30.6	30.8	32.2	30.9	31.0	31.1	31.4
231	Foreign exchange	2735.5	2909.5	2912.3	2618.7	2743.6	2229.5	2723.3	2828.8
232	Reserve position in the Fund	13.6	24.8	–	–	–	54.2	–	0.8
233	SDRs	14.9	24.9	12.6	63.0	63.7	63.1	30.3	39.8
234	Other banks' assets [g]	2144.0	2719.0	3616.0	4176.0	4147.0	4531.0	4865.0	4848.0
	EXCHANGE RATES								*Won per*
235	End of period	484.00	484.00	659.90	700.50	748.80	795.50	827.40	890.20
236	Average of period	484.00	484.00	607.43	681.03	731.08	775.75	805.98	870.02
	EXTERNAL INDEBTEDNESS								*Million US dollars;*
237	Total outstanding and disbursed	17301	22886	29480	32989	37329	40419	42099	47133
238	Long-term	12514	15583	18236	21517	23643	26951	29107	34893
239	Public and publicly guaranteed	11317	13766	15933	18361	20191	22176	23833	28279
240	Private non-guaranteed	1197	1817	2303	3156	3452	4775	5274	6614
241	Short-term	4525	7165	10561	10226	12427	12115	11425	10732
242	Use of IMF credit	262	138	683	1246	1259	1354	1567	1508
	Debt service								*Transactions*
243	Principal repayments on LT debt	1262	1724	1554	2015	2141	2665	2850	4452
244	Interest on long-term debt	794	1123	1637	2031	2439	2280	2510	2778
245	Interest on short-term debt	–	–	1210	1769	1604	1330	1400	1300
	Average terms of new commitments								
246	Interest (%)	8.7	10.4	11.3	12.1	11.3	9.5	9.5	8.5
247	Maturity (years)	14.8	3.4	15.3	15.0	13.9	13.6	12.5	11.8
248	Grace period (years)	4.1	3.4	3.9	4.4	4.2	4.1	4.6	5.3
249	Grant element (%)	7.3	-1.1	-3.6	-7.6	-6.0	2.9	2.9	7.5

Footnotes:

a   Details may not add up to total due to rounding.
b   Include community, social and personal services, private non-profit services to households, and import duties.
c   Refer to installment savings deposit.
d   Relate to superior enterprises.
e   Refer to loans whose maturity is up to one year.
f   Includes capital revenue.
g   Beginning 1988, data include claims of foreign banks' branches on nonresidents.

	1986	1987	1988	1989	1990	1991	1992	1993	1994	1995	
As of end of period											
	8043.1	9193.3	20891.3	23113.2	24356.6	24438.3	30058.2	36472.5	42699.0	57029.0	229
	31.5	31.6	31.6	31.6	31.6	32.2	32.6	33.3	33.6	34.4	230
	3301.1	3566.3	12340.1	14977.8	14459.2	13306.0	16639.9	19704.2	21120.3	30414.1	231
	0.8	1.0	0.9	234.2	319.4	365.3	438.7	465.9	530.8	651.8	232
	17.7	16.4	5.7	1.6	14.4	29.8	42.0	58.1	76.3	97.7	233
	4692.0	5578.0	8513.0	7868.0	9532.0	10705.0	12905.0	16211.0	20938.0	25831.0	234
US dollar											
	861.40	792.30	684.10	679.60	716.40	760.80	788.40	808.10	788.70	774.70	235
	881.45	822.57	731.47	671.46	707.76	733.35	780.65	802.67	803.45	771.27	236
As of end of year											
	46724	39808	35716	32799	34987	39733	44157	47203	54543	...	237
	35920	29993	25936	22999	24187	28533	32237	35003	40653	...	238
	29351	23890	20024	17038	18787	22481	24051	24567	27103	...	239
	6569	6103	5912	5961	5400	6052	8186	10436	13550	...	240
	9256	9291	9780	9800	10800	11200	11920	12200	13890	...	241
	1549	525	–	–	–	–	–	–	–	...	242
during the year											
	7096	13826	7001	5956	4,993	3369	4238	6270	4818	4993 *	243
	2863	2407	2052	1938	2,534	1707	1984	2115	2256	2534 *	244
	860	676	850	870	913	975	751	788	848	...	245
	7.6	7.1	7.6	8.2	7.9	7.7	7.1	5.7	6.0	...	246
	13.2	14.1	19.7	19.7	17.6	11.3	13.0	10.1	11.8	...	247
	4.0	4.8	4.0	2.5	5.3	3.9	5.1	4.6	6.9	...	248
	11.8	15.9	14.9	8.9	13.2	9.4	15.3	17.0	20.7	...	249

	Item	1978	1979	1980	1981	1982	1983	1984	1985
001	**POPULATION**	...	...	3.58	...	...	...	...	*Million;* 3.95
002	**LABOR FORCE**	...	...	...	...	...	...	...	*Thousand;* ...
003	Employed	...	...	1425	...	...	...	...	1614
004	Agriculture	...	...	456	...	...	...	...	529
005	Industry [a]	...	...	398	...	...	...	...	441
006	Others	...	...	571	...	...	...	...	644
007	Unemployed	...	...	...	...	...	...	...	...
008	Unemployment rate, %	...	...	...	...	...	...	...	...
	NATIONAL ACCOUNTS **At Current Market Prices**								*Million Soms;*
009	NMP by Industrial Origin	...	...	...	...	...	...	...	...
010	Agriculture	...	...	...	...	...	...	...	...
011	Industry	...	...	...	...	...	...	...	...
012	Construction	...	...	...	...	...	...	...	...
013	Trade	...	...	...	...	...	...	...	...
014	Transport and communications	...	...	...	...	...	...	...	...
015	Finance	...	...	...	...	...	...	...	...
016	Public administration ⎫	...	...	...	...	...	...	...	...
017	Others ⎬	...	...	...	...	...	...	...	...
018	Indirect taxes less subsidies	...	...	...	...	...	...	...	...
019	GDP at current market prices	...	...	...	...	...	...	...	...
020	Net factor income from abroad	...	...	...	...	...	...	...	...
021	GNP at current market prices	...	...	...	...	...	...	...	...
022	Expenditure on GDP	...	...	...	...	...	...	...	...
023	Private consumption	...	...	...	...	...	...	...	...
024	Government consumption	...	...	...	...	...	...	...	...
025	Gross fixed capital formation	...	...	...	...	...	...	...	...
026	Increase in stocks	...	...	...	...	...	...	...	...
027	Exports of goods & services	...	...	...	...	...	...	...	...
028	Less: Imports of goods & services	...	...	...	...	...	...	...	...
029	Statistical discrepancy	...	...	...	...	...	...	...	...
	At Constant 1990 Prices								
030	NMP by Industrial Origin	...	...	...	...	...	...	...	...
031	Agriculture	...	...	...	...	...	...	...	...
032	Industry	...	...	...	...	...	...	...	...
033	Construction	...	...	...	...	...	...	...	...
034	Trade	...	...	...	...	...	...	...	...
035	Transport and communications	...	...	...	...	...	...	...	...
036	Finance	...	...	...	...	...	...	...	...
037	Public administration ⎫	...	...	...	...	...	...	...	...
038	Others ⎬	...	...	...	...	...	...	...	...
039	Indirect taxes less subsidies	...	...	...	...	...	...	...	...
040	GDP at constant market prices	...	...	...	...	...	...	...	...
041	Net factor income from abroad	...	...	...	...	...	...	...	...
042	GNP at current market prices	...	...	...	...	...	...	...	...
043	Expenditure on GDP	...	...	...	...	...	...	...	...
044	Private consumption	...	...	...	...	...	...	...	...
045	Government consumption	...	...	...	...	...	...	...	...
046	Gross fixed capital formation	...	...	...	...	...	...	...	...
047	Increase in stocks	...	...	...	...	...	...	...	...
048	Exports of goods & services	...	...	...	...	...	...	...	...
049	Less: Imports of goods & services	...	...	...	...	...	...	...	...
050	Statistical discrepancy	...	...	...	...	...	...	...	...

	1986	1987	1988	1989	1990	1991	1992	1993	1994	1995	
As of 1 July	4.03	4.11	4.18	4.25	4.34	4.39	4.45	4.49	4.47	4.48 *	001
Year ending 31 December											
	...	...	...	...	...	...	...	...	...	...	002
	1651	1703	1716	1739	1748	1754	1836	1681	1645	...	003
	539	577	577	577	572	623	700	669	686	...	004
	451	457	462	486	487	466	414	359	342	...	005
	661	669	677	676	689	665	722	653	617	...	006
	...	...	...	...	...	...	...	...	...	...	007
	...	...	...	...	...	...	...	...	...	...	008
Calendar year											
	...	...	...	...	41.7	88.2	707.4	5106.1	11279.2	14436.7	009
	...	...	...	...	14.0	32.6	276.3	2090.6	4601.3	6289.6	010
	...	...	...	...	11.3	25.4	238.3	1344.5	2461.7	2425.5	011
	...	...	...	...	3.3	5.9	29.1	289.6	408.9	1029.9	012
	...	...	...	...	1.7	3.9	26.1	349.9	1162.4	1469.1	013
	...	...	...	...	2.4	3.5	21.2	208.4	547.4		014
	...	...	...	...	0.3	1.2	12.5	253.9	576.9	3222.6	015
	...	...	...	...							016
	...	...	...	...	8.7	15.8	104.0	569.4	1520.7		017
	...	...	...	...	1.1	4.3	33.9	248.6	740.1	1169.4	018
	...	...	...	...	42.8	92.6	741.3	5354.7	12019.2	15606.1	019
	...	...	...	...	...	...	...	...	...	...	020
	...	...	...	...	...	...	...	...	...	...	021
	...	...	...	...	42.8	92.6	741.3	5354.7	12019.2	15606.1	022
	...	...	...	...	30.5	59.3	524.2	4053.1	7899.9	10507.4	023
	...	...	...	...	10.7	20.2	158.4	1086.2	2431.8	3525.7	024
	...	...	...	...	9.9	16.2	108.1	714.6	1492.7	3465.9	025
	...	...	...	...	0.5	-1.9	39.6	-89.8	920.9	-1015.5	026
	...	...	...	...	12.5	32.7	263.8	1795.5	4019.9	4110.5	027
	...	...	...	...	21.2	33.9	352.8	2204.8	4745.9	5005.3	028
	...	...	...	...	–	–	–	–	–	17.4	029
	...	...	...	...	41.7	38.4	33.1	28.0	22.3	21.0	030
	...	...	...	...	14.0	12.8	12.4	11.3	10.3	10.1	031
	...	...	...	...	11.3	11.3	8.4	6.5	4.1	3.1	032
	...	...	...	...	3.3	2.2	1.6	1.3	0.7	1.3	033
	...	...	...	...	1.7	1.5	0.7	0.6	0.6	0.6	034
	...	...	...	...	2.4	2.4	1.8	1.1	0.9		035
	...	...	...	...	0.3	0.3	0.4	0.4	0.4	6.0	036
	...	...	...	...							037
	...	...	...	...	8.7	7.9	7.8	6.8	5.2		038
	...	...	...	...	1.1	1.0	0.9	0.7	0.6	0.5	039
	...	...	...	...	42.8	39.4	34.0	28.7	22.9	21.5	040
	...	...	...	...	...	...	...	...	...	...	041
	...	...	...	...	...	...	...	...	...	...	042
	...	...	...	...	42.8	39.4	34.0	28.7	22.9	21.5	043
	...	...	...	...	30.5	25.2	22.4 *	20.3 *	14.1 *	...	044
	...	...	...	...	10.7	9.2	7.6 *	6.1 *	4.7 *	...	045
	...	...	...	...	9.9	9.3	6.1 *	4.7 *	3.4 *	...	046
	...	...	...	...	0.5	-0.0	2.0 *	0.8 *	3.2 *	...	047
	...	...	...	...	12.5	11.0	6.0 *	7.4 *	8.1 *	...	048
	...	...	...	...	21.2	15.3	10.0 *	10.7 *	10.6 *	...	049
	...	...	...	...	–	–	– *	– *	– *	...	050

	Item	1978	1979	1980	1981	1982	1983	1984	1985
	Per Capita GDP, Soms								
051	Current prices	...	...	...	...	...	...	...	...
052	Constant *1990* prices	...	...	...	...	...	...	...	...
	PRODUCTION								***Thousand metric tons;***
	Agriculture								
053	1. Wheat	748	767	594	717	364	585	493	524
054	2. Barley	536	564	483	556	309	585	393	553
055	3. Potatoes	236	227	293	297	336	309	297	307
056	4. Maize	203	194	216	256	273	322	310	381
057	5. Vegetables	316	361	400	426	368	458	499	445
058	6. Meat	153	154	159	163	165	170	173	169
059	7. Milk	641	668	682	684	694	706	731	771
	Production Indexes								***Period***
060	Agriculture, *1985 = 100*	91	92	93	96	90	101	103	100
061	Industry, *1985 = 100*	...	...	125	120	116	110	104	100
	ENERGY								***Annual***
	Coal, *'000 m.t.*								
062	Production	...	...	...	...	...	...	...	...
063	Exports	...	...	...	...	...	...	...	...
064	Imports	...	...	...	...	...	...	...	...
065	Consumption	...	...	...	...	...	...	...	...
	Electricity, *Mn kWh*								
066	Production	...	...	9172	10365	11416	10754	11161	10472
067	Exports	...	...	...	...	...	...	...	...
068	Imports	...	...	...	...	...	...	...	...
069	Consumption	...	...	5645	5699	5982	6116	6615	6901
	PRICE INDEXES								***Period***
070	Consumer, *1990 = 100*	...	...	...	...	...	...	...	...
071	Food	...	...	...	...	...	...	...	...
072	Non-food	...	...	...	...	...	...	...	...
073	Wholesale	...	...	...	...	...	...	...	...
074	Implicit GDP deflator, *1990 = 100*	...	...	...	...	...	...	...	...
	MONEY AND BANKING								***Million Soms;***
075	Money supply (M1)	...	...	...	...	...	...	...	...
076	Currency in circulation	...	...	...	...	...	...	...	...
077	Demand deposits	...	...	...	...	...	...	...	...
078	Quasi-money	...	...	...	...	...	...	...	...
079	Money supply (M2)	...	...	...	...	...	...	...	...
080	Foreign assets (net)	...	...	...	...	...	...	...	...
081	Domestic credit	...	...	...	...	...	...	...	...
082	Claims on govt. sector (net)	...	...	...	...	...	...	...	...
083	Claims on private sector	...	...	...	...	...	...	...	...
084	Claims on other financial insts.	...	...	...	...	...	...	...	...
085	Other items	...	...	...	...	...	...	...	...
	Deposit Money Banks								
086	Demand deposits	...	...	...	...	...	...	...	...
087	Savings deposits	...	...	...	...	...	...	...	...
088	Time deposits	...	...	...	...	...	...	...	...
089	Domestic credits outstanding	...	...	...	...	...	...	...	...

1986	1987	1988	1989	1990	1991	1992	1993	1994	1995	
...	...	...	...	9.9	21.1	166.5	1191.7	2690.5	3482.6	051
...	...	...	...	9.9	9.0	7.6	6.4	5.1	4.8	052

Calendar year

1986	1987	1988	1989	1990	1991	1992	1993	1994	1995	
586	746	578	609	510	465	679	885	608	677	053
589	669	649	568	631	596	621	510	310	173	054
329	287	332	324	365	326	362	308	311	432	055
430	460	497	452	406	364	281	184	129	121	056
512	491	553	585	487	399	404	259	266	318	057
193	204	223	241	254	230	228	214	197	176	058
909	998	1063	1202	1185	1131	961	946	872	864	059

averages

1986	1987	1988	1989	1990	1991	1992	1993	1994	1995	
108	110	114	117	118	107	101	91	74	65	060
104	106	113	119	118	118	87	65	46	...	061

values

1986	1987	1988	1989	1990	1991	1992	1993	1994	1995	
...	...	...	...	...	...	...	...	...	...	062
...	...	...	...	...	...	...	...	...	...	063
...	...	...	...	...	...	1339	...	...	...	064
...	...	...	...	...	...	2465	...	...	...	065
11394	9348	14230	15116	13370	14171	11892	11091	12791	...	066
...	...	...	...	...	...	...	...	...	...	067
...	...	...	...	...	...	...	...	...	...	068
7086	7335	7559	8065	8357	8814	8616	8467	8189	...	069

averages

1986	1987	1988	1989	1990	1991	1992	1993	1994	1995	
...	...	...	...	100.0	185.8	1766.7	23112.5	87382.5	124833.0	070
...	...	...	...	...	...	...	...	...	...	071
...	...	...	...	...	...	...	...	...	...	072
...	...	...	...	...	...	...	...	...	...	073
...	...	...	...	100.0	234.7	2182.1	18657.5	52417.1	72518.9	074

As of end of period

1986	1987	1988	1989	1990	1991	1992	1993	1994	1995	
...	...	...	...	...	13.5	89.5	600.1	1391.9	2441.7	075
...	...	...	...	...	13.5	89.5	398.4	1002.3	1940.8	076
...	...	...	...	...			201.7	389.6	500.9	077
...	...	...	...	...	34.0 }	161.4 }	102.1	137.3	272.8	078
...	...	...	...	...	47.5	250.9	702.2	1529.2	2714.5	079
...	...	...	...	...	13.9	-38.4	-579.7	-181.0	-245.6	080
...	...	...	...	...	41.6	443.4	1358.5	1976.3	3519.7	081
...	...	...	...	...	-3.7	99.7	559.1	939.5	...	082
...	...	...	...	...	0.0	69.3	799.4	1036.8	...	083
...	...	...	...	...	45.3	274.4	0.0	0.0	...	084
...	...	...	...	...	-8.0	-154.1	-76.6	-266.1	-559.6	085
...	...	...	...	...	...	...	...	...	500.9	086
...	...	...	...	...	...	...	...	...	188.7	087
...	...	...	...	...	...	...	...	...	84.0	088
...	...	...	...	...	...	...	...	...	...	089

Item	1978	1979	1980	1981	1982	1983	1984	1985
Interest Rates								*Period*
On deposits								
090 Savings	...	...	...	...	...	...	...	...
091 Time: 6 months	...	...	...	...	...	...	...	...
092 12 months	...	...	...	...	...	...	...	...
On loans & discounts								
093 Commercial bills	...	...	...	...	...	...	...	...
GOVERNMENT FINANCE [b]					*Billion Rubles until 1992 I Million Soms thereafter;*			
Central Government								
094 Current revenue	...	...	...	...	...	...	...	...
095 Taxes	...	...	...	...	...	...	...	...
096 Non-taxes	...	...	...	...	...	...	...	...
097 Current expenditure	...	...	...	...	...	...	...	...
098 Current surplus/deficit	...	...	...	...	...	...	...	...
099 Capital receipts [c]	...	...	...	...	...	...	...	...
100 Capital expenditure	...	...	...	...	...	...	...	...
101 Capital account surplus/deficit	...	...	...	...	...	...	...	...
102 Net lending	...	...	...	...	...	...	...	...
103 Overall surplus/deficit	...	...	...	...	...	...	...	...
Financing								
104 Domestic borrowing	...	...	...	...	...	...	...	...
105 Foreign borrowing	...	...	...	...	...	...	...	...
106 Foreign grants	...	...	...	...	...	...	...	...
107 Use of cash balances	...	...	...	...	...	...	...	...
Expenditure by Function, Central Govt.								
108 Total	...	...	...	...	...	...	...	...
109 General public services	...	...	...	...	...	...	...	...
110 Defence	...	...	...	...	...	...	...	...
111 Education	...	...	...	...	...	...	...	...
112 Health	...	...	...	...	...	...	...	...
113 Social security & welfare	...	...	...	...	...	...	...	...
114 Housing & community amenities	...	...	...	...	...	...	...	...
115 Economic services	...	...	...	...	...	...	...	...
116 Agriculture	...	...	...	...	...	...	...	...
117 Industry	...	...	...	...	...	...	...	...
118 Electricity, gas & water	...	...	...	...	...	...	...	...
119 Transport and communications	...	...	...	...	...	...	...	...
120 Other economic services	...	...	...	...	...	...	...	...
121 Others	...	...	...	...	...	...	...	...
EXTERNAL TRADE							*Million US dollars;*	
122 Exports, fob	...	...	...	...	...	...	...	...
123 Imports, cif	...	...	...	...	...	...	...	...
124 Trade balance	...	...	...	...	...	...	...	...
Exports, by SITC section								
125 Food & live animals	...	...	...	...	...	...	...	...
126 Beverage & tobacco	...	...	...	...	...	...	...	...
127 Crude materials excl. fuels	...	...	...	...	...	...	...	...
128 Mineral fuels, etc.	...	...	...	...	...	...	...	...
129 Animal, vegetable oil & fats	...	...	...	...	...	...	...	...
130 Chemicals	...	...	...	...	...	...	...	...
131 Basic manufactures	...	...	...	...	...	...	...	...
132 Machines, transport equipment	...	...	...	...	...	...	...	...
133 Misc. manufactured goods	...	...	...	...	...	...	...	...
134 Unclassified goods	...	...	...	...	...	...	...	...

1986	1987	1988	1989	1990	1991	1992		1993	1994	1995	
averages											
...	...	...	...	...	...	...		...	...	...	090
...	...	...	...	...	...	...		...	...	...	091
...	...	...	...	...	...	...		...	...	...	092
...	...	...	...	...	...	...		...	...	...	093
Fiscal year ending 31 December											
...	2.0	2.0	2.3	2.3	3.5	25.5	I	859.9	2005.1	2615.7	094
...	1.8	1.8	2.1	2.2	2.7	22.4	I	721.3	...	2430.1	095
...	0.2	0.2	0.2	0.1	0.8	3.1	I	138.6	...	185.6	096
...	1.9	2.1	2.3	2.7	4.5	38.0	I	1153.3	2725.9	4170.9	097
...	0.1	-0.1	0.0	-0.4	-1.1	-12.5	I	-293.4	-720.8	-1555.2	098
...	0.4	0.6	0.5	0.9	1.9	0.0	I	–	–	55.2	099
...	0.3	0.4	0.4	0.5	0.2	2.3	I	102.3	200.8	408.9	100
...	0.1	0.2	0.2	0.4	1.7	-2.3	I	-102.3	-200.8	-353.7	101
...	...	...	...	...	...	12.1	I	...	...	...	102
...	0.2	0.1	0.2	0.0	0.7	-26.8	I	-395.7	-921.6	-1908.9	103
...	...	...	...	...	...	...	I	420.1	572.8 *	921.0 *	104
...	...	...	...	...	...	...	I	353.2	878.2 *	815.9 *	105
...	...	...	...	...	...	...	I	}	}	}	106
...	...	...	...	...	...	...	I	-377.6	-529.4 *	172.0 *	107
...	2.2	2.5	2.7	3.2	4.9	40.3	I	1255.6	2926.7	4579.8	108
...	0.0	0.0	0.0	0.0	0.2	2.1	I	80.7	310.6	757.3	109
...	–	–	–	–	–	1.1	I	38.8	105.4	153.4	110
...	0.6	0.6	0.7	0.7	1.2	8.0	I	244.0	798.5	1222.0	111
...	0.2	0.2	0.3	0.3	0.6	4.3	I	138.2	421.7	614.4	112
...	0.3	0.3	0.4	0.4	1.0	5.1	I	118.3	370.0	914.0	113
...	0.1	0.1	0.1	0.1	0.2	2.0	I	68.9	131.1	188.0	114
...	0.8	1.1	1.1	1.5	1.4	9.1	I	249.9	256.2	387.4	115
...	0.3	0.4	0.4	0.6	0.5	4.9	I	117.7	86.3	160.4	116
...	0.0	0.0	0.0	0.0	0.0	0.2	I	0.2	26.6	95.8	117
...	–	–	–	–	–	0.5	I	25.7	28.9	1.2	118
...	0.1	0.1	0.1	0.1	0.1	0.9	I	31.3	65.6	72.7	119
...	0.4	0.6	0.6	0.8	0.8	2.6	I	75.0	48.8	57.3	120
...	0.2	0.2	0.1	0.2	0.3	8.6	I	316.8	533.2	343.3	121
Calendar year											
...	...	...	...	...	...	257.9		339.6	340.0 *	408.9 *	122
...	...	...	...	...	...	331.6		502.9	398.3 *	537.4 *	123
...	...	...	...	...	...	-73.7		-163.3	-58.3 *	-128.5 *	124
...	...	...	...	...	...	...		...	...	...	125
...	...	...	...	...	...	...		...	...	...	126
...	...	...	...	...	...	...		...	...	...	127
...	...	...	...	...	...	...		...	...	...	128
...	...	...	...	...	...	...		...	...	...	129
...	...	...	...	...	...	...		...	...	...	130
...	...	...	...	...	...	...		...	...	...	131
...	...	...	...	...	...	...		...	...	...	132
...	...	...	...	...	...	...		...	...	...	133
...	...	...	...	...	...	...		...	...	...	134

Item	1978	1979	1980	1981	1982	1983	1984	1985
Imports, by SITC section								
135 Food & live animals	...	...	...	...	...	...	...	...
136 Beverage & tobacco	...	...	...	...	...	...	...	...
137 Crude materials excl. fuels	...	...	...	...	...	...	...	...
138 Mineral fuels, etc.	...	...	...	...	...	...	...	...
139 Animal, vegetable oil & fats	...	...	...	...	...	...	...	...
140 Chemicals	...	...	...	...	...	...	...	...
141 Basic manufactures	...	...	...	...	...	...	...	...
142 Machines, transport equipment	...	...	...	...	...	...	...	...
143 Misc. manufactured goods	...	...	...	...	...	...	...	...
144 Unclassified goods	...	...	...	...	...	...	...	...
Direction of Trade					*Million Rubles until 1992 I Million Soms thereafter;*			
145 Exports, Total	...	...	...	...	...	...	...	...
146 1. Kazakstan	...	...	...	...	...	...	...	...
147 2. Russian Federation	...	...	...	...	...	...	...	...
148 3. Uzbekistan	...	...	...	...	...	...	...	...
149 4. Ukraine	...	...	...	...	...	...	...	...
150 5. Turkmenistan	...	...	...	...	...	...	...	...
151 6. Belarus	...	...	...	...	...	...	...	...
152 7. Tajikistan	...	...	...	...	...	...	...	...
153 8. Azerbaijan	...	...	...	...	...	...	...	...
154 9. Moldova	...	...	...	...	...	...	...	...
155 10. Armenia	...	...	...	...	...	...	...	...
156 Imports, Total	...	...	...	...	...	...	...	...
157 1. Russian Federation	...	...	...	...	...	...	...	...
158 2. Kazakstan	...	...	...	...	...	...	...	...
159 3. Uzbekistan	...	...	...	...	...	...	...	...
160 4. Turkmenistan	...	...	...	...	...	...	...	...
161 5. Ukraine	...	...	...	...	...	...	...	...
162 6. Belarus	...	...	...	...	...	...	...	...
163 7. Tajikistan	...	...	...	...	...	...	...	...
164 8. Azerbaijan	...	...	...	...	...	...	...	...
165 9. Moldova	...	...	...	...	...	...	...	...
166 10. Armenia	...	...	...	...	...	...	...	...
Trade Indexes								*Period*
Quantum index								
167 Exports	...	...	...	...	...	...	...	...
168 Imports	...	...	...	...	...	...	...	...
Unit value index								
169 Exports	...	...	...	...	...	...	...	...
170 Imports	...	...	...	...	...	...	...	...
171 Terms of trade	...	...	...	...	...	...	...	...
BALANCE OF PAYMENTS								*Million US dollars;*
172 Merchandise exports, fob	...	...	...	...	...	...	...	...
173 Merchandise imports, cif	...	...	...	...	...	...	...	...
174 Trade balance	...	...	...	...	...	...	...	...
175 Other goods, services and income	...	...	...	...	...	...	...	...
176 Credit	...	...	...	...	...	...	...	...
177 Debit	...	...	...	...	...	...	...	...
178 Unrequited transfers	...	...	...	...	...	...	...	...
179 Private	...	...	...	...	...	...	...	...
180 Official	...	...	...	...	...	...	...	...
181 Current balance	...	...	...	...	...	...	...	...
182 Direct investment	...	...	...	...	...	...	...	...

1986	1987	1988	1989	1990	1991	1992		1993	1994	1995	
...	...	...	...	...	...	...		...	...	...	135
...	...	...	...	...	...	...		...	...	...	136
...	...	...	...	...	...	...		...	...	...	137
...	...	...	...	...	...	...		...	...	...	138
...	...	...	...	...	...	...		...	...	...	139
...	...	...	...	...	...	...		...	...	...	140
...	...	...	...	...	...	...		...	...	...	141
...	...	...	...	...	...	...		...	...	...	142
...	...	...	...	...	...	...		...	...	...	143
...	...	...	...	...	...	...		...	...	...	144

Calendar year

1986	1987	1988	1989	1990	1991	1992		1993	1994	1995	
...	...	2596.7	2600.6	2501.0	6546.3	52785.7	I	1767.4	2427.9	2909.8	145
...	...	...	...	...	848.8	10358.4	I	362.4	1040.7	721.7	146
...	...	...	...	...	2792.7	18096.7	I	572.7	632.0	1134.1	147
...	...	...	...	...	718.7	4794.3	I	119.8	476.3	753.9	148
...	...	...	...	...	600.3	8008.2	I	71.0	97.4	90.9	149
...	...	...	...	...	278.1	1126.6	I	44.1	81.6	23.8	150
...	...	...	...	...	205.0	1385.8	I	24.4	40.9	54.2	151
...	...	...	...	...	274.7	647.9	I	31.1	32.9	89.5	152
...	...	...	...	...	119.1	397.0	I	18.0	17.8	23.2	153
...	...	...	...	...	56.7	263.3	I	5.4	5.2	10.6	154
...	...	...	...	...	98.2	109.9	I	0.3	1.1	0.4	155
...	...	3743.3	4295.8	4243.9	6916.0	70586.2	I	2204.6	2247.0	3675.9	156
...	...	...	...	...	2702.2	32987.7	I	798.0	751.5	1240.4	157
...	...	...	...	...	779.8	15583.1	I	489.2	628.4	1215.5	158
...	...	...	...	...	817.1	6136.3	I	293.2	678.1	809.5	159
...	...	...	...	...	109.3	4105.4	I	36.1	107.8	202.0	160
...	...	...	...	...	389.3	5478.1	I	34.5	32.2	53.6	161
...	...	...	...	...	223.0	1033.4	I	15.6	27.5	54.7	162
...	...	...	...	...	81.5	461.7	I	7.5	11.4	52.3	163
...	...	...	...	...	80.0	327.1	I	10.8	6.8	35.3	164
...	...	...	...	...	62.8	349.0	I	2.5	0.7	2.5	165
...	...	...	...	...	45.3	95.1	I	1.9	0.1	6.5	166

averages

1986	1987	1988	1989	1990	1991	1992	1993	1994	1995	
...	...	...	...	...	...	...	...	...	...	167
...	...	...	...	...	...	...	...	...	...	168
...	...	...	...	...	...	...	...	...	...	169
...	...	...	...	...	...	...	...	...	...	170
...	...	...	...	...	...	...	...	...	...	171

Calendar year

1986	1987	1988	1989	1990	1991	1992	1993	1994	1995	
...	...	...	...	...	...	257.9	339.6	340.0 *	408.9 *	172
...	...	...	...	...	...	331.6	502.9	398.3 *	537.4 *	173
...	...	...	...	...	...	-73.7	-163.3	-58.3 *	-128.5 *	174
...	...	...	...	...	...	-13.0	-8.7	-26.7 *	-62.4 *	175
...	...	...	...	...	...	...	...	...	...	176
...	...	...	...	...	...	...	...	...	...	177
...	...	...	...	...	...	13.0	29.0	15.6 *	57.9 *	178
...	...	...	...	...	...	...	-85.9	-46.0 *	-20.1 *	179
...	...	...	...	...	...	...	114.9	61.6 *	78.0 *	180
...	...	...	...	...	...	-73.7	-143.0	-69.4 *	-133.0 *	181
...	...	...	...	...	...	...	10.0	...	...	182

	Item	1978	1979	1980	1981	1982	1983	1984	1985
183	Portfolio investment	...	...	...	...	...	...	...	...
184	Other long-term capital	...	...	...	...	...	...	...	...
185	Other short-term capital	...	...	...	...	...	...	...	...
186	Net errors and omissions	...	...	...	...	...	...	...	...
187	Overall balance	...	...	...	...	...	...	...	...
188	Allocations of SDRs	...	...	...	...	...	...	...	...
189	Monetary movement	...	...	...	...	...	...	...	...
	INTERNATIONAL RESERVES								*Million US dollars;*
190	Total [d]	...	...	...	...	...	...	...	...
191	Gold, national valuation	...	...	...	...	...	...	...	...
192	Foreign exchange	...	...	...	...	...	...	...	...
193	Reserve position in the Fund	...	...	...	...	...	...	...	...
194	SDRs	...	...	...	...	...	...	...	...
	EXCHANGE RATES [e]								*Rubles I Soms*
195	End of period	...	...	...	...	...	...	...	...
196	Average of period	...	...	...	...	...	...	...	...
	EXTERNAL INDEBTEDNESS								*Million US dollars;*
197	Total outstanding & disbursed	...	...	...	...	...	...	...	...
198	Long-term	...	...	...	...	...	...	...	...
199	Public and publicly guaranteed	...	...	...	...	...	...	...	...
200	Private non-guaranteed	...	...	...	...	...	...	...	...
201	Short-term	...	...	...	...	...	...	...	...
202	Use of IMF credit	...	...	...	...	...	...	...	...
	Debt service								*Transactions*
203	Principal repayments on LT debt	...	...	...	...	...	...	...	...
204	Interest on long-term debt	...	...	...	...	...	...	...	...
205	Interest on short-term debt	...	...	...	...	...	...	...	...
	Average terms of new commitments								
206	Interest (%)	...	...	...	...	...	...	...	...
207	Maturity (years)	...	...	...	...	...	...	...	...
208	Grace period (years)	...	...	...	...	...	...	...	...
209	Grant element (%)	...	...	...	...	...	...	...	...

Footnotes:

a   Includes mining, manufacturing and construction.
b   Refers to consolidated government operations.
c   Refer to privatization proceeds, recurring grants and union grants.
d   Refers to gross official reserves.
e   Som was introduced in 15 May 1993 as the sole legal tender in the country; 1993 average data covers only the last three quarters.

1986	1987	1988	1989	1990	1991	1992	1993	1994	1995	
...	...	...	...	...	...	-7.0	-9.5	...	...	183
...	...	...	...	...	...	4.0	71.4	...	...	184
...	...	...	...	...	...	...	...	...	...	185
...	...	...	...	...	...	33.7	-47.2	...	...	186
...	...	...	...	...	...	-43.0	-118.3	23.9 *	-72.4 *	187
...	...	...	...	...	...	...	...	...	...	188
...	...	...	...	...	...	...	...	...	...	189

As of end of period

...	...	...	...	...	...	...	63.4	97.9 *	78.0 *	190
...	...	...	...	...	...	...	...	...	...	191
...	...	...	...	...	...	...	...	...	...	192
...	...	...	...	...	...	...	...	...	...	193
...	...	...	...	...	...	...	...	...	...	194

per US dollar

...	...	...	...	...	...	414.5 |	8.0	10.7	11.0	195
...	...	...	...	...	...	192.8 |	5.8	10.8	10.8	196

As of end of year

...	...	...	...	...	...	0.6	309.0	441.3	...	197
...	...	...	...	...	...	0.6	248.8	350.9	...	198
...	...	...	...	...	...	0.6	248.8	350.9	...	199
...	...	...	...	...	...	–	–	–	...	200
...	...	...	...	...	...	–	–	12.6	...	201
...	...	...	...	...	...	–	60.2	77.8	...	202

during the year

...	...	...	...	...	...	–	–	–	46.8 *	203
...	...	...	...	...	...	–	0.3	13.1	22.7 *	204
...	...	...	...	...	...	–	–	–	...	205
...	...	...	...	...	...	3.5	4.5	1.6	...	206
...	...	...	...	...	...	4.1	21.6	34.3	...	207
...	...	...	...	...	...	4.0	6.6	10.0	...	208
...	...	...	...	...	...	20.5	37.6	71.2	...	209

Item	1978	1979	1980	1981	1982	1983	1984	1985
								Million;
001 **POPULATION**	3.58	3.63	3.20	3.26	3.33	3.42	3.53	3.62
NATIONAL ACCOUNTS *At Current Factor Cost*								*Million Kips;*
002 GDP by Industrial Origin	...	...	...	...	...	...	...	84282
003 Agriculture	...	...	...	...	...	...	...	45437
004 Mining	...	...	...	...	...	...	...	313
005 Manufacturing	...	...	...	...	...	...	...	8392
006 Electricity, gas and water	...	...	...	...	...	...	...	4823
007 Construction	...	...	...	...	...	...	...	1405
008 Trade	...	...	...	...	...	...	...	10878
009 Transport and communications	...	...	...	...	...	...	...	7714
010 Finance	...	...	...	...	...	...	...	1290
011 Public administration	...	...	...	...	...	...	...	2520
012 Others	...	...	...	...	...	...	...	1509
013 Indirect taxes less subsidies	...	...	...	...	...	...	...	124
014 GDP at current market prices	...	...	...	6083	10874	20174	29109 I	84406
015 Net factor income from abroad	...	...	...	...	...	...	...	...
016 GNP	...	...	...	...	...	...	...	...
At Constant 1986 I 1990 Factor Cost								
017 NMP I GDP by Industrial Origin	...	...	...	37940	40629	42531	45579 I	492756
018 Agriculture	...	...	...	30825	31324	32292	34638 I	312689
019 Mining	...	...	...					942
020 Manufacturing	...	...	...	3156	3440	3569	3785 I	37532
021 Electricity, gas and water	...	...	...					9337
022 Construction	...	...	...	583	1023	1378	1613 I	11450
023 Trade	...	...	...	2423	3923	4293	4478 I	31974
024 Transport and communications	...	...	...	637	575	642	687 I	22245
025 Finance	...	...	...					10128
026 Public administration	...	...	...	316	344	357	378 I	38306
027 Others	...	...	...					18153
028 Indirect taxes less subsidies	...	...	...	12330	13202	13822	14813 I	4478
029 GDP at *1986* I *1990* market prices	...	...	...	50270	53831	56353	60392 I	497234
030 Net factor income from abroad	...	...	...	...	...	...	...	...
031 GNP at *1986* I *1990* market prices	...	...	...	...	...	...	...	...
Per Capita GDP, Kips								
032 Current prices	...	...	...	1865	3265	5899	8246 I	23317
033 Constant *1986* I *1990* prices	...	...	...	15416	16166	16477	17108 I	137357
PRODUCTION *Agriculture, crop year*								*Thousand metric tons;*
034 1. Rice	724	867	1053	1155	1092	1101	1322	1395
035 2. Sweet potatoes	22	25	28	29	30	35	97	100
036 3. Cassava	55	60	68	70	72	74	95	100
037 4. Maize	30	32	28	33	35	32	34	36
038 5. Potatoes	28	31	34	35	40	44	46	49
Mining								
039 1. Tin concentrates, *m.t.*	600	600	600 I	256	302	360	430	520
Production Index								*Period*
040 Agriculture, *1979-81 = 100*	75	88	101	111	111	114	127	134
041 Mining	...	...	...	...	...	...	...	...
042 Manufacturing	...	...	...	...	...	...	...	...

1986	1987	1988	1989	1990	1991	1992	1993	1994	1995	
As of 1 July										
3.72	3.83	3.94	4.05	4.14	4.25	4.36	4.47	4.59	4.71	001
Calendar year										
124158	160558	223758	424195	607317	712022	834200	934922	1089176	1365462 *	002
69989	91927	135048	258246	371835	414461	492904	538001	621966	763675 *	003
252	222	530	1049	896	936	1161	1684	2345	2679 *	004
14024	14520	15794	37575	60462	88939	106890	122315	139670	182548 *	005
4491	3028	2855	3745	8839	9840	9751	12581	17320	17814 *	006
3431	4536	7469	12499	17908	20119	23746	29307	36651	52365 *	007
15850	16950	16466	33878	41968	52369	61580	77546	89286	113813 *	008
7860	16769	18259	29902	31687	36442	42784	46895	56194	62092 *	009
2444	5277	7124	10030	6939	7036	8608	10357	11967	15428 *	010
4760	5135	11250	19590	35633	36715	37265	44000	56000	68000 *	011
1056	2195	8965	17682	31150	45165	49511	52236	57777	87048 *	012
146	320	4846	7127	5364	9976	10150	16000	18577	29587 *	013
124304	160878	228604	431322	612681	721998	844350	950922	1107753	1395049 *	014
...	...	...	...	...	...	...	...	...	...	015
...	...	...	...	...	...	...	...	...	...	016
516706	511433	501842	566042	607317	627974	672163	707101	763990	817120 *	017
328654	324824	311286	342206	371835	365347	395537	406233	439980	461641 *	018
1159	936	817	976	896	825	932	1272	1659	1620 *	019
42887	40047	37526	52340	60462	78400	85776	92358	98798	110350 *	020
8946	6013	5656	7433	8839	8674	7825	9499	12252	10769 *	021
15537	10562	12174	15091	17908	17735	19055	22129	25926	31654 *	022
34941	35358	31943	41177	41968	46163	49415	58553	63158	68800 *	023
26365	33661	33702	36181	31687	32124	34333	35409	36920	37535 *	024
10625	12103	11762	4004	6939	6202	6908	7820	8465	9326 *	025
38316	38344	38306	39378	35633	31888	31034	30967	28923	27619 *	026
9276	9585	18670	27257	31150	40616	41348	42861	47909	57806 *	027
4636	4317	4436	8129	5364	9186	9635	14718	16668	19262 *	028
521342	515750	506278	574172	612681	637160	681798	721819	780657	836382 *	029
...	...	...	...	...	...	...	...	...	...	030
...	...	...	...	...	...	...	...	...	...	031
33415	42005	58021	106499	147991	169882	193658	212734	241340	303272 *	032
140146	134660	128497	141770	147991	149920	156376	161480	170078	181822 *	033
Calendar year										
1449	1207	1003	1404	1491	1223	1502	1251	1653	1418 *	034
115	120	187	160	218	132	105	113	119	...	035
85	88	90	62	65	66	67	68	68	...	036
42	36	51	44	67	69	59	48	77	48 *	037
51	53	55	28	30	33	35	34	34	...	038
559	501	246	384	342	349	346	308	810	687	039
averages										
136	129	122	146	156	138	154	146	171	167	040
...	...	...	...	...	...	...	...	...	...	041
...	...	...	...	...	...	...	...	...	...	042

Item	1978	1979	1980	1981	1982	1983	1984	1985
ENERGY								*Annual*
Coal, *'000 m.t.*								
043 Production	0	0	0	1	...	...	...	1
044 Exports	0	0	0	0	...	...	...	...
045 Imports	...	...	...	...	...	...	...	...
046 Consumption	0	0	0	1	...	...	...	...
Electricity, *Mn kWh*								
047 Production	510	1088	975	1150	1200	1075	990	919
048 Exports	221	788	766	740	752	701	710	716
049 Imports	-	-	8	9	13	25	22	14
050 Consumption	289	300	217	419	461	399	302	217
PRICE INDEXES								*Period*
051 Consumer, *Jun 1979 Dec 1987 = 100* [a]	67.0	105.0	170.0	209.0	296.0	389.0	594.0	982.0	
052 Food	...	...	...	...	...	...	...	...
053 Non-food	...	...	...	...	...	...	...	...
054 Implicit GDP deflator, *1986 1990 = 100*	...	...	...	12.1	20.2	35.8	48.2		17.0
MONEY AND BANKING								*Million Kips;*
055 Money supply (M1)	...	...	...	785	1205	1668	1655	2226
056 Currency in circulation	...	...	...	169	236	320	450	635
057 Demand deposits	...	...	...	616	969	1348	1205	1591
058 Quasi-money	...	...	...	20	17	27	37	54
059 Money supply(M2)	...	...	...	805	1222	1695	1692	2280
060 Foreign assets (net)	...	...	...	...	...	...	...	147
061 Domestic credit	...	...	...	...	...	...	...	2717
062 Claims on govt. sector (net)	...	...	...	...	...	...	...	2467
063 Claims on private sector	...	...	...	...	...	...	...	250
064 Claims on other financial insts.	...	...	...	...	...	...	...	–
065 Other items	...	...	...	...	...	...	...	-584
GOVERNMENT FINANCE								*Million Kips;*
Central Government								
066 Current revenue	106	268	748	989	2755	3496	4947	10299
067 Taxes	55	48	98	396	775	1056	1669	1397
068 Non-taxes	51	220	650	593	1980	2440	3278	8902
069 Current expenditure	384	394	1028	1028	2259	2946	4126	9454
070 Current surplus/deficit	-278	-126	-280	-39	496	551	821	845
071 Capital receipts	–	–	–	–	–	–	–	–
072 Capital expenditure	189	242	749	928	3216	3750	4258	10184
073 Capital account surplus/deficit	-189	-242	-749	-928	-3216	-3750	-4258	-10184
074 Overall surplus/deficit	-467	-368	-1029	-967	-2720	-3200	-3437	-9339
Financing								
075 Domestic borrowing (net)	36	14	-4	–	–	–	–	-164
076 Foreign borrowing	–	–	–	967	2720	3200	3437	7537
077 Foreign grants	431	354	1033	–	–	–	–	1965
078 Use of cash balances	–	–	–	–	–	–	–	–
Expenditure by Function, Central Gov't.								
079 Total	...	...	...	...	...	...	...	10184
080 General public services [b]	...	...	...	...	...	...	...	496
081 Defence	...	...	...	...	...	...	...	...
082 Education	...	...	...	...	...	...	...	265
083 Health	...	...	...	...	...	...	...	601
084 Social security & welfare	...	...	...	...	...	...	...	...
085 Housing & community amenities	...	...	...	...	...	...	...	...
086 Economic services	...	...	...	...	...	...	...	7311
087 Agriculture	...	...	...	...	...	...	...	1549
088 Industry [c]	...	...	...	...	...	...	...	1556

	1986	1987	1988	1989	1990	1991	1992	1993	1994	1995	
values											
	2	1	1	1	3	...	...	...	...	...	043
	...	...	...	...	...	...	...	...	...	...	044
	...	...	...	...	...	...	...	...	...	...	045
	...	...	...	...	...	...	...	...	...	...	046
	880	577	536	708	844	828	753	919	1197	1044	047
	683	378	374	469	607	562	462	356	829	705	048
	19	18	16	13	26	35	40	48	58	43	049
	216	217	178	252	263	192	...	...	...	...	050
averages											
	...	...	106.6	170.3	231.4	262.1	287.9	309.0	329.7	414.3	051
	...	...	104.3	171.0	222.9	247.0	276.0	265.6	273.0	334.2	052
	...	...	110.4	169.1	245.3	286.6	307.1	364.0	413.0	481.2	053
	23.8	31.2	45.2	75.0	100.0	113.3	123.8	131.7	141.9	166.8	054
As of end of period											
	3781	6888	12104	25127	25090	28226	35145	52238	61343	67177	055
	1047	2091	3486	16842	18570	19217	22827	33241	38610	41955	056
	2734	4797	8618	8285	6520	9009	12318	18997	22733	25222	057
	95	8954	9611	15987	19251	23087	41319	73609	104645	126089	058
	3876	15842	21715	41114	44341	51313	76464	125847	165988	193266	059
	238	-1914	386	20054	21571	22657	36649	72909	58710	78000	060
	4329	20164	27634	26710	31073	40845	56093	74693	128874	157173	061
	3560	4723	3909	-14340	-14556	-877	571	-9544	12642	651	062
	769	110	870	4403	5899	21301	37683	65912	98802	128856	063
	–	15331	22855	36647	39730	20421	17839	18325	17430	27666	064
	-691	-2408	-6305	-5650	-8303	-12189	-16278	-21755	-21596	-41907	065
Calendar year											
	18503	20108	28531	35556	60960	74672	90456	111840	164592	220310	066
	1755	1970	21474	27421	37644	54355	63513	85854	103616	140670	067
	16748	18138	7057	8135	23316	20317	26943	25986	60976	79640	068
	14804	16025	28038	39936	69864	81956	92424	104805	303616	363742	069
	3699	4083	493	-4380	-8904	-7284	-1968	7035	-139024	-143432	070
	–	–	–	–	–	–	–	–	...	...	071
	11732	13480	47006	66455	73583	69123	82217	65745	153000	188500	072
	-11732	-13480	-47006	-66455	-73583	-69123	-82217	-65745	-153000	-188500	073
	-8033	-9397	-46513	-70835	-82487	-76407	-84185	-58710	...	...	074
	-211	-222	242	-14539	5107	19278	16808	15810	...	...	075
	6591	8413	33641	68497	60340	29552	38948	27940	...	...	076
	1653	1207	12630	16877	22960	32550	39946	31370	67283 *	52520 *	077
	–	–	–	–	-5920	-4973	-11517	-16410	...	...	078
	11732	13480	141940	141940	143440	151080	174640	170510	265870	303310	079
	654	720	39940	39940	69860	81960	92420	104930	126300	160310	080
	...	...	...	...	...	...	...	...	...	...	081
	780	1139	2169	2885	3146	1560	2000	1950	2790	1810	082
	714	805	1435	258	851	1000	780	940	1150	1610	083
	...	...	...	...	...	280	...	...	...	600	084
	...	...	...	...	...	1010	2400	2450	3510	4950	085
	8134	9056	36962	52784	56357	...	...	...	...	...	086
	1993	2086	7669	5689	8696	1470	3740	2850	4450	4660	087
	1208	1276	10122	22472	18535	740	1230	1260	1570	1570	088

Item	1978	1979	1980	1981	1982	1983	1984	1985
089 Electricity, gas & water	...	...	...	...	...	...	...	...
090 Transport and communications	...	...	...	...	...	...	...	3717
091 Other economic services [d]	...	...	...	...	...	...	...	489
092 Others	...	...	...	...	...	...	...	1511
EXTERNAL TRADE								*Million US dollars;*
093 Exports, fob	8	19	28	23	40	41	44	54
094 Imports, cif	74	70	92	110	132	150	162	193
095 Trade balance	-66	-51	-64	-87	-92	-109	-118	-139
Exports, by principal commodity								
096 1. Wood products [e]	3	9	6	8	4	3	5	11
097 2. Electricity	...	...	...	11	24	24	25	26
098 3. Green coffee	1	4	0	3	8	9	9	9
099 4. Tin	1	0	1	2	1	1	1	1
Direction of Trade								*Million US dollars;*
100 Exports, Total	10.8	16.2	21.3	15.1	24.2	24.0	11.4	16.6
101 1. Turkey	2.5	2.4	1.7	0.0	0.0	0.0	1.2	0.0
102 2. Thailand	0.0	0.0	0.6	0.7	1.5	1.1	0.9	1.1
103 3. Japan	0.0	0.1	0.3	3.5	1.1	2.3	0.6	1.1
104 4. France	4.0	8.3	5.4	0.0	0.0	0.0	0.0	0.1
105 5. Germany	–	–	–	0.0	0.0	0.0	0.0	0.0
106 6. Netherlands	–	0.0	0.0	0.0	0.0	0.0	0.0	0.0
107 7. Viet Nam	1.1	1.9	0.9	0.0	0.0	0.0	0.0	0.0
108 8. United States	–	0.0	0.0	1.0	1.5	2.5	2.0	0.5
109 9. China, People's Rep. of	–	–	–	7.7	6.2	4.2	4.8	8.6
110 10. Italy	–	–	0.0	0.0	0.1	0.0	0.0	0.0
111 Imports, Total	62.3	73.6	111.4	72.1	76.1	26.1	40.5	52.8
112 1. Thailand	19.5	34.9	48.9	29.3	36.8	12.7	19.1	21.7
113 2. Turkey	5.2	10.1	13.8	0.0	0.0	0.0	0.0	0.0
114 3. China, People's Rep. of	–	–	–	0.9	0.0	0.0	0.0	0.0
115 4. Japan	1.7	2.2	6.7	9.9	10.9	4.9	5.6	13.1
116 5. Viet Nam	4.0	0.9	8.8	0.0	0.0	0.1	0.1	0.1
117 6. Australia	1.3	0.7	2.6	0.1	0.1	0.1	0.1	0.0
118 7. Singapore	3.2	0.6	1.8	14.6	13.2	0.2	6.9	10.9
119 8. France	4.8	5.9	1.7	8.7	5.1	1.9	0.7	1.5
120 9. Germany	1.5	1.5	0.2	0.3	2.1	1.9	0.6	0.4
121 10. Sweden	4.0	1.7	3.1	2.2	2.5	0.0	0.7	1.1
BALANCE OF PAYMENTS								*Million US dollars;*
122 Merchandise exports, fob	10.0	19.4	28.2	23.1	40.0	40.8	43.8	53.6
123 Merchandise imports, cif	-74.0	-70.3	-92.3	-109.5	-132.2	-149.6	-161.9	-193.2
124 Trade balance	-64.0	-50.9	-64.1	-86.4	-92.2	-108.8	-118.1	-139.6
125 Other goods, services and income	-22.0	-21.1	-2.3	-6.3	-7.1	-12.5	-9.8	-7.1
126 Credit	6.0	...	...	...	...	...	15.1	21.3
127 Debit	-28.0	...	...	...	...	...	-24.9	-28.4
128 Unrequited transfer [f]	93.0	80.7	–	23.5	31.0	25.4	44.9	53.1
129 Private	...	...	–	–	0.2	0.3	2.8	3.5
130 Official	...	...	–	23.5	30.8	25.1	42.1	49.6
131 Current balance	...	...	-66.4	-69.2	-68.3	-95.9	-83.0	-93.6
132 Direct investment	...	...	...	...	...	...	–	–
133 Portfolio investment	...	...	...	...	...	...	–	–
134 Other long-term capital	...	...	46.7	51.4	60.2	76.5	30.3	47.7
135 Other short-term capital	...	...	...	...	...	...	53.4	50.2
136 Net errors and omissions	1.0	-2.0	8.6	13.2	3.8	31.1	-3.2	19.1
137 Overall balance	8.0	6.7	-11.1	-4.6	-4.3	11.7	-2.5	23.4
138 Allocation of SDRs	...	...	...	...	...	...	–	–
139 Monetary movements	...	...	...	...	...	...	2.5	-23.4

1986	1987	1988	1989	1990	1991	1992	1993	1994	1995	
									...	089
4491	4886	17495	24540	29126	4500	4670	9280	15190	15820	090
442	808	1676	83	...	...	...	...	...	1000	091
1450	1760	4915	10450	5726	...	...	...	...	...	092

Calendar year

1986	1987	1988	1989	1990	1991	1992	1993	1994	1995	
55	64	58	63	79	97	133	241	300	347	093
186	216	149	194	185	210	244	432	654	587	094
-131	-152	-91	-131	-106	-113	-111	-191	354	-240	095
8	33	30	21	26	42	43	66	96	88	096
30	14	11	15	19	21	17	20	25	24	097
12	10	7	9	9	3	2	4	3	4	098
3	2	2	2	1	1	1	2	1	1	099

Calendar year

1986	1987	1988	1989	1990	1991	1992	1993	1994	1995	
14.1	23.3	55.9	95.4	64.4	82.1	104.3	154.1	353.5	268.1	100
0.0	0.0	0.0	27.3	0.0	0.0	0.0	0.0	160.0	23.9	101
1.2	5.4	20.4	39.7	40.3	42.7	37.3	57.4	62.8	68.9	102
1.3	1.4	6.2	7.2	4.6	4.0	10.9	10.6	28.1	26.9	103
0.2	2.1	0.1	0.2	2.5	8.1	12.1	16.8	18.0	26.3	104
0.0	0.0	0.0	0.2	1.7	8.6	5.3	12.2	18.6	20.1	105
0.0	0.0	0.0	0.0	0.2	1.7	5.7	14.4	10.1	14.1	106
0.0	0.0	0.0	2.5	3.5	3.0	7.0	8.3	9.5	11.0	107
0.3	0.9	2.9	0.8	0.1	2.0	5.8	8.4	8.6	9.5	108
8.8	9.6	16.1	11.4	5.9	2.0	3.4	3.2	4.0	5.9	109
0.1	0.0	0.5	0.4	0.3	0.9	1.3	2.7	2.1	3.3	110
58.6	79.8	102.0	128.7	148.6	154.3	258.4	357.2	642.1	637.1	111
32.9	40.9	56.4	70.2	72.3	84.3	133.1	192.5	320.7	380.8	112
0.0	0.0	0.0	6.4	0.0	0.0	0.0	0.0	91.5	2.5	113
0.0	0.7	3.3	4.9	15.9	12.3	30.6	40.8	39.6	52.5	114
14.4	17.1	21.8	26.8	21.6	23.5	30.8	40.8	37.2	31.7	115
0.1	0.1	0.2	3.0	17.6	4.0	17.6	20.9	23.9	27.7	116
0.1	0.1	0.5	0.5	1.2	0.4	15.8	11.6	31.1	23.0	117
0.0	0.0	0.0	0.0	0.0	0.0	4.7	11.0	30.5	35.4	118
1.2	0.7	1.1	1.8	3.1	3.3	3.3	4.0	21.2	26.4	119
0.8	2.1	0.8	1.9	1.0	0.9	1.4	4.5	8.2	7.9	120
1.4	2.3	1.0	2.2	3.0	0.3	0.8	6.6	5.9	6.6	121

Calendar year

1986	1987	1988	1989	1990	1991	1992	1993	1994	1995	
55.0	64.3	57.9	63.3	78.7	96.6	132.6	240.5	300.4	347.9	122
-185.7	-216.2	-149.4	-193.8	-185.4	-209.7	-244.4	-431.9	-564.1	-587.2	123
-130.7	-151.9	-91.5	-130.5	-106.7	-113.1	-111.8	-191.4	-263.7	-239.3	124
6.5	7.2	-12.5	-12.4	-5.4	61.3	17.4	20.0	14.1	5.6	125
24.4	26.3	18.2	23.3	25.9	41.1	67.0	95.3	93.9	100.7	126
-17.9	-19.1	-30.7	-35.7	-31.3	-34.8	-49.6	-75.3	-79.8	-95.1	127
34.2	25.4	29.1	24.2	28.6	93.0	69.3	111.0	130.9	119.3	128
3.7	3.5	6.7	8.3	10.9	10.4	8.6	9.5	9.5	13.4	129
30.5	21.9	22.4	15.9	17.7	82.6	60.7	101.5	121.4	105.9	130
-90.0	-119.3	-74.9	-118.7	-83.5	-19.2	-35.8	-53.0	-100.0	-100.7	131
–	–	2.0	4.0	6.0	8.0	9.0	47.6	42.4	77.2	132
–	–	–	–	–	1.1	1.2	3.3	1.0	6.7	133
45.4	56.4	58.7	42.8	45.0	35.1	62.1	69.5	55.7	109.2	134
58.7	55.0	38.1	83.2	58.5	51.6	-10.3	-49.6	-36.8	-30.4	135
-2.4	-0.2	-25.0	0.8	0.6	-75.6	-21.0	-44.8	65.5	-63.5	136
11.7	-8.1	-1.1	12.1	26.6	1.0	5.2	-27.0	27.8	-1.5	137
–	–	–	–	–	–	–	–	–	–	138
-11.7	8.1	1.1	-12.1	-26.6	-1.0	-5.2	27.0	-27.8	1.5	139

	Item	1978	1979	1980	1981	1982	1983	1984	1985
	INTERNATIONAL RESERVES [g]							*Million US dollars;*	
140	Total	21.5	26.1	14.0	13.3	8.3	19.4	11.2	25.9
141	Gold, national valuation	...	...	...	...	...	...	0.6	0.6
142	Foreign exchange [h]	...	...	...	...	...	...	10.6	25.3
143	Reserve position in the Fund	...	...	...	...	...	...	...	...
144	SDRs	...	...	...	...	...	...	–	–
	EXCHANGE RATES [i]							*Kips*	
145	End of period	4.00	10.00	10.00	30.00	35.00	35.00	35.00	95.00
146	Period average	4.20	5.71	10.22	20.00	35.00	35.00	35.00	45.00
	EXTERNAL INDEBTEDNESS							*Million US dollars;*	
147	Total outstanding and disbursed	255	308	350	390	428	450	518	618
148	Long-term	248	295	333	374	413	436	505	606
149	Public and publicly guaranteed	248	295	333	374	413	436	505	606
150	Private non-guaranteed	–	–	–	–	–	–	–	–
151	Short-term	1	1	1	1	2	1	1	2
152	Use of IMF credit	7	12	16	15	14	13	11	10
	Debt service							*Transactions*	
153	Principal repayments on LT debt	9	11	1	1	3	3	5	4
154	Interest on long-term debt	2	2	1	1	1	1	1	1
155	Interest on short-term debt	–	–	–	–	–	–	–	–
	Average terms of new commitments								
156	Interest (%)	0.2	0.1	0.2	0.1	0.1	0.2	0.2	0.2
157	Maturity (years)	31.5	31.9	33.0	29.3	33.1	31.7	32.3	31.3
158	Grace period (years)	25.5	25.1	25.6	26.7	25.3	26.2	25.4	26.8
159	Grant element (%)	90.2	91.1	91.1	90.8	91.5	91.2	90.0	91.7

Footnotes:

a   Relates to end-of-year data for 1978-1985.
b   Include public works only.
c   Includes mining and energy.
d   Relate to trade and cooperatives only.
e   Includes timber.
f   Refers to capital and net transfers for 1978-1979.
g   Data from 1989 onward are based on IMF,IFS to allow data comparability across countries.
h   Data prior to 1991 refer to the midpoint between the buying and selling rates quoted by state-owned commercial banks. Beginning 1991, data refer to the midpoint between the buying and selling rates quoted by the Bank of Lao P.D.R.
i   A unified market related exchange rate was adopted in September 1987. The official buying rate is quoted from 1987 onward as the official rate.

	1986	1987	1988	1989	1990	1991	1992	1993	1994	1995	
As of end of period											
	32.4	21.2	16.7	2.0	2.4	29.3	40.9	63.6	61.5	92.7	140
	0.6	0.6	0.6	0.6	0.6	0.6	0.6	0.6	0.6	0.6	141
	31.8	20.6	16.1	1.4	1.8 I	28.2	39.5	60.3	50.0	78.0	142
	...	...	...	...	...	...	...	...	...	...	143
	–	–	–	0.0	0.0	0.5	0.8	2.6	10.9	14.1	144
per US dollar											
	95.00	367.50	452.50	713.50	695.50	711.50	717.00	718.00	719.00	923.00	145
	95.00	175.12	392.01	583.02	708.57	702.80	716.08	716.25	717.67	804.69	146
As of end of year											
	868	1161	1330	1473	1768	1875	1917	1985	2080	...	147
	857	1151	1323	1463	1758	1850	1887	1948	2080	...	148
	857	1151	1323	1463	1758	1850	1887	1948	2080	...	149
	–	–	–	–	–	–	–	–	–	...	150
	3	4	5	1	2	4	2	1	...	...	151
	9	6	3	8	8	21	28	36	47	...	152
during the year											
	4	5	5	13	6	12	9	8	8	14 *	153
	2	2	2	3	3	4	4	6	6	7 *	154
	–	–	0	0	0	0	0	0	0	0 *	155
	0.1	0.4	0.2	0.4	0.9	0.6	0.9	0.9	0.5	...	156
	25.1	34.2	35.0	34.6	39.9	36.9	39.8	39.5	39.7	...	157
	15.7	21.9	23.6	20.1	10.0	15.8	10.2	10.0	10.2	...	158
	79.7	88.1	90.4	86.9	79.0	83.8	79.6	78.5	82.6	...	159

	Item	1978	1979	1980	1981	1982	1983	1984	1985
001	**POPULATION**	13.13	13.28	13.76	14.13	14.51	14.89	15.27	*Million;* 15.68
002	**LABOR FORCE**	4802	4955	5122	5312	5500	5727	5907	*Thousand;* 6039
003	Employed	4542	4700	4835	5061	5247	5429	5565	5625
004	Agriculture	1968	1999	1800	1782	1730	1711	1724	1760
005	Manufacturing	665	707	749	789	816	841	879	855
006	Mining	80	81	62	59	55	50	47	44
007	Others	1829	1913	2224	2431	2646	2828	2915	2965
008	Unemployed	260	255	287	251	253	298	342	417
009	Unemployment rate, %	5.4	5.2	5.6	4.7	4.6	5.2	5.8	6.9
	NATIONAL ACCOUNTS *At Current Market Prices*								*Million Ringgit;*
010	GDP by Industrial Origin	37886	46424	53308	57613	62579	69941	79550	77470
011	Net factor income from abroad	-1700	-2070	-1918	-2011	-2889	-4411	-5368	-5508
012	GNP	36186	44354	51390	55602	59690	65530	74182	71962
013	Expenditure on GDP	37886	46424	53308	57613	62579	69941	79550	77470
014	Private consumption	19584	22406	26946	30594	33226	36458	39594	40283
015	Government consumption	6090	6475	8811	10425	11469	11015	11741	11844
016	Gross fixed capital formation	9381	12250	16597	20759	22745	25213	25391	23124
017	Increase in stocks	723	1173	-380	-602	593	1253	1306	-1757
018	Exports of goods and services	18585	26004	30676	30154	31846	35795	43171	42537
019	Less: Imports of goods and services	16477	21884	29342	33717	37300	39793	41653	38561
020	Statistical discrepancy	–	–	–	–	–	–	–	–
	At Constant 1978 prices								
021	GDP by Industrial Origin	37886	41428	44512	47602	50430	53582	57741	57093
022	Agriculture	9513	10060	10190	10684	11375	11302	11623	11854
023	Mining	3912	4586	4487	4289	4617	5342	6073	5985
024	Manufacturing	7189	8004	8742	9155	9668	10429	11711	11263
025	Electricity, gas and water	530	584	640	689	721	798	890	948
026	Construction	1572	1761	2066	2367	2598	2867	2988	2738
027	Trade	4156	4669	5384	5694	6104	6583	7107	6911
028	Transport and communications	1867	2107	2543	2847	2984	3138	3464	3630
029	Finance	3177	3434	3686	3953	4231	4570	4892	5094
030	Public administration	4106	4375	4563	5649	6027	6328	6817	6957
031	Others	1864	1848	2213	2275	2105	2225	2176	1712
032	Net factor income from abroad	-1700	-1934	-1562	-1427	-2136	-3424	-4228	-4255
033	GNP	36186	39494	42950	46175	48294	50158	53513	52838
034	Expenditure on GDP	37886	41428	44512	47602	50430	53582	57741	57093
035	Private consumption	19584	21698	24445	25686	26531	27376	29142	29242
036	Government consumption	6090	6195	7750	8784	9552	9989	9500	9417
037	Gross fixed capital formation	9381	11170	13931	16450	17767	19193	19761	17888
038	Increase in stocks	723	285	-319	-498	478	445	952	-1262
039	Exports of goods and services	18585	21924	22619	22431	24826	27889	31733	31875
040	Less: Imports of goods and services	16477	19844	23914	25251	28724	31310	33347	30067
041	Statistical discrepancy	–	–	–	–	–	–	–	–
	Investment Financing, at current prices								
042	Gross domestic capital formation	10104	13423	16217	20157	23338	26466	26697	21367
043	Gross national saving	10512	15473	15633	14583	14995	18057	22847	19835
044	Gross domestic saving	12212	17543	17551	16594	17884	22468	28215	25343
045	Net factor income from abroad	-1700	-2070	-1918	-2011	-2889	-4411	-5368	-5508
	Per Capita GNP, Ringgit								
046	Current prices	2756	3340	3734	3935	4114	4401	4858	4589
047	Constant *1978* prices	2756	2974	3120	3268	3328	3369	3504	3369

	1986	1987	1988	1989	1990	1991	1992	1993	1994	1995	
As of 1 July	16.11	16.53	16.94	17.35	17.76	18.18	18.62	19.06	19.49	20.10	001
Calendar year	6222	6457	6658	6850	7042	7204	7370	7627	7846	8060	002
	5707	5984	6176	6390	6686	6891	7096	7396	7618	7832	003
	1807	1846	1889	1833	1738	1680	1585	1577	1518	1480	004
	861	929	987	1171	1333	1470	1639	1742	1878	1997	005
	37	33	29	33	37	36	36	37	38	39	006
	3002	3176	3271	3353	3578	3705	3836	4040	4185	4316	007
	516	473	482	460	356	313	274	231	228	228	008
	8.3	7.3	7.2	6.7	5.1	4.3	3.7	3.0	2.9	2.8	009
Calendar year	71594	79625	90861	102451	115701	129381	146737	161779	185692	213653 *	010
	-4780	-4946	-5084	-5903	-5064	-6800	-8006	-8256	-9328	-11265 *	011
	66814	74679	85777	96548	110637	122581	138731	153523	176364	202388 *	012
	71594	79625	90861	102451	115701	129381	146737	161779	185692	213653 *	013
	36499	37685	44856	52165	60903	69609	76046	82913	91968	108246 *	014
	12127	12239	13015	14808	16209	18412	19340	21606	23936	25959 *	015
	18865	18280	21922	30063	37490	46181	50697	57356	71457	85463 *	016
	-261	175	1647	-967	-1335	125	-1393	-584	315	1255 *	017
	40305	50838	61165	74889	88354	104740	114153	132423	166515	204043 *	018
	35941	39592	51744	68507	85920	109686	112106	131935	168499	211313 *	019
	–	–	–	–	–	–	–	–	–	–	020
	57751	60863	66218	72297	79329	86149	92866	100617	109915	120489 *	021
	12348	13216	13933	14768	14826	14828	15531	16205	16047	16721 *	022
	6368	6408	6803	7383	7757	7944	8075	8039	8241	8851 *	023
	12111	13734	16151	18444	21340	24307	26859	30324	34782	39895 *	024
	1027	1109	1211	1344	1526	1697	1931	2176	2474	2820 *	025
	2354	2077	2133	2380	2832	3240	3619	4023	4589	5287 *	026
	6147	6423	6988	7687	8807	10068	11190	12428	13427	14635 *	027
	3851	4055	4412	4839	5487	6079	6481	6921	7776	8787 *	028
	5071	5483	6088	6771	7759	8733	9644	10650	11713	12884 *	029
	7253	7543	7734	8073	8446	8768	9201	10073	11022	11463 *	030
	1221	815	765	608	549	485	335	-222	-156	-854 *	031
	-3596	-3699	-3701	-4085	-3425	-4638	-5199	-5320	-5915	-6806 *	032
	54155	57164	62517	68212	75904	81511	87667	95297	104000	113683 *	033
	57751	60863	66218	72297	79329	86149	92866	100617	109915	120489 *	034
	26315	26857	31189	35128	39728	43507	45401	47788	51121	58135 *	035
	9536	9676	10153	10929	11512	12943	13464	14903	16372	17565 *	036
	14601	13954	16084	21212	25872	31352	33877	37912	45613	53747 *	037
	-211	62	1133	-731	-1103	75	-1017	-400	186	712 *	038
	35632	40819	45577	53800	62990	72535	76303	87426	105455	125458 *	039
	28122	30505	37918	48041	59670	74263	75162	87012	108832	135128 *	040
	–	–	–	–	–	–	–	–	–	–	041
	18604	18455	23569	29096	35155	46306	49304	56772	71772	86718 *	042
	18188	24755	27906	29575	33525	34560	43345	49004	60460	68183 *	043
	22968	29701	32990	35478	38589	41360	51351	57260	69788	79448 *	044
	-4780	-4946	-5084	-5903	-5064	-6800	-8006	-8256	-9328	-11265 *	045
	4147	4518	5063	5564	6229	6743	7394	7993	8975	10069 *	046
	3362	3459	3690	3931	4273	4484	4673	4962	5293	5656 *	047

Item	1978	1979	1980	1981	1982	1983	1984	1985
PRODUCTION								*Thousand metric tons;*
Agriculture								
048 1. Palm oil	1786	2188	2576	2825	3514	3018	3716	4133
049 2. Palm kernels	368	475	557	590	911	837	1046	1213
050 3. Rubber [a]	1583	1570	1530	1510	1474	1564	1531	1470
051 4. Rice [b]	979	1351	1318	1303	1213	1130	1012	1175
052 5. Copra [c]	113	125	117	120	105	104	94	97
053 6. Coconut oil [a]	66	68	64	68	62	58	49	44
054 7. Saw logs, *'000 cu.m.*	28683	28709	27916	30653	32824	32784	31089	30957
055 8. Sawn timber, *'000 cu.m.*	5905	5954	6237	5994	6185	7141	5749	5575
Mining								
056 1. Bauxite	615.1	386.5	920.3	700.9	589.0	501.8	680.4	492.0
057 2. Iron ore	320.0	350.5	371.1	532.4	340.3	113.7	193.8	181.7
058 3. Tin-in-concentrates	62.7	63.0	61.4	59.9	52.3	41.4	41.3	36.9
Manufacturing [d]								
059 1. Cement	2196.5	2265.2	2349.0	2833.0	3123.0	3231.0	3469.0	3128.0 I
060 2. Iron and steel bars and rods	...	...	...	...	265.5	306.4	543.0	323.4 I
061 3. Prepared animal feed	444.8	457.3	548.6	564.6	485.7	559.5	626.7	640.1 I
062 4. Refined sugar	...	...	...	...	477.5	583.8	603.2	591.2 I
063 5. Kerosene	...	...	...	...	158.5	407.2	568.5	446.6 I
064 6. Liquefied petroleum gas	...	...	...	...	76.3	93.1	138.7	305.8 I
065 7. Sweetened condensed milk	99.4	107.9	113.4	106.4	110.8	113.8	117.4	129.5 I
066 8. Galvanized iron sheets	...	...	...	...	48.8	52.3	51.0	51.0 I
067 9. Soap and soap compound	42.8	49.1	49.0	50.3	33.2	35.3	33.5	42.3 I
Production Indexes								*Period*
068 Agriculture, *1979-81 = 100*	89.1	95.6	100.5	104.4	114.7	113.3	122.5	134.6
069 Mining [d], *1988 = 100*	51.5	52.0	50.6	49.7	52.4	65.7	82.4	82.8
070 Manufacturing [d], *1988 = 100*	47.7	52.1	56.5	58.3	61.6	65.7	73.1	68.6
ENERGY								*Annual*
Crude petroleum, *'000 m.t.*								
071 Production	10554	13845	13245	12360	15543	18372	21371	21202
072 Exports	9153	12034	11227	10143	11974	14224	16497	16701
073 Imports	4225	4426	3961	3552	2540	3701	2554	2252
074 Consumption	4790	5200	5725	5668	5308	7588	7349	6941
Coal, *'000 m.t.*								
075 Production	...	...	...	...	...	...	...	...
076 Exports	...	...	...	...	...	...	...	...
077 Imports	14	24	49	108	107	361	385	476
078 Consumption	14	24	49	108	107	361	385	476
Natural gas, *terajoules*								
079 Production	39373	43664	10291	9158	12863	116232	226062	305557
080 Exports	...	...	...	0	0	101169	192589	236731
081 Imports	21200	23400	...	...	...	...	...	...
082 Consumption	60573	67064	10291	9158	12863	15063	33473	68826
Electricity, *Mn kWh*								
083 Production	7963	8795	8974	10895	11498	12655	13651	14995
084 Exports	...	...	...	0	5	18	0	0
085 Imports	...	...	...	74	68	61	79	56
086 Consumption	7963	8795	8974	10969	11561	12698	13730	15051
Retail prices, *Ringgit/litre*								
087 Gasoline, premium [e]	0.753	0.760	0.903	1.057	1.073	1.050	1.067	1.120
088 Diesel [f]	...	0.274	0.342	0.440	0.462 I	0.466	0.577	0.573
PRICE INDEXES								*Period*
089 Consumer (Malaysia), *1994 = 100*	37.0	57.9	61.8	67.8	71.7	74.4	77.0	77.3
090 Food	56.8	58.2	60.9	67.9	68.5	73.6	76.1	74.3
091 Non-food	64.0	66.7	72.2	78.4	85.2	86.6	89.7	91.6

	1986	1987	1988	1989	1990	1991	1992	1993	1994	1995	
Calendar year											
	4544	4533	5030	6057	6095	6141	6374	7404	7220	7814 *	048
	1337	1315	1465	1794	1845	1785	1874	2266	2204	...	049
	1539	1581	1660	1419	1291	1256	1173	1074	1101	1200 *	050
	1116	1105	1148	1186	1269	1377	1333	1263	1010	...	051
	78	66	63	68	64	47	40	35	...	...	052
	38	33	38	39	40	30	37	39	36	...	053
	29869	36149	37727	40812	40101	39860	43511	37260	35671	...	054
	5278	6037	6551	8418	8725	8803	9458	9224	8704	...	055
	566.2	482.1	360.8	355.2	398.2	376.4	330.6	68.8	161.9	...	056
	208.0	161.3	131.8	105.8	293.2	355.3	314.8	222.8	243.2	...	057
	28.1	30.4	28.9	32.0	28.5	20.7	14.3	10.4	6.5	5.0	058
	3569.0	3316.0	3775.0	4794.0	5881.0	7451.0	8366.0	8797.0	9928.0	10713.0	059
	296.0	449.7	610.3	970.5	1114.1	1293.4	1858.2	1913.1	2310.3	2462.2	060
	849.1	921.7	1080.0	1090.5	1165.8	1331.4	1302.2	1294.5	1288.0	1408.3	061
	674.0	737.8	733.8	829.6	800.9	895.4	951.0	957.4	1551.0	1052.5	062
	941.3	911.3	880.3	921.0	858.6	890.0	915.7	1065.5	1067.2	1877.0	063
	394.2	409.2	453.2	489.8	544.1	482.3	565.2	955.5	1210.1	1317.3	064
	126.9	135.0	145.0	147.1	135.6	147.8	170.1	181.3	212.5	200.2	065
	50.1	68.3	104.1	99.6	111.5	142.6	126.3	141.7	203.6	279.4	066
	48.5	50.6	63.3	67.0	79.9	88.1	101.7	104.5	135.8	124.1	067
averages											
	143.8	151.8	163.6	176.9	184.2	197.8	204.2	223.6	219.4	225.9	068
	92.4	93.0	100.0	107.5	113.1	118.9	122.1	123.6	128.1	139.8	069
	75.0	84.8	100.0	114.2	132.1	150.4	166.2	187.6	215.2	246.4	070
values											
	23853	23604	25749	27950	29556	30765	31292	30583	31115	...	071
	18792	17999	19899	21323	22110	22595	22527	...	...	...	072
	1933	1563	1508	1019	1004	1084	1138	...	...	...	073
	7769	7653	7352	7733	8653	9436	9568	...	...	...	074
	...	...	23	114	105	180	190	264	174	...	075
	...	...	23	17	42	97	90	...	...	...	076
	380	520	342	1590	2060	2009	2075	...	...	...	077
	380	520	342	1687	1956	2185	2205	...	...	...	078
	369490	477101	473461	494255	502372	625834	782950	...	...	...	079
	284008	324302	342418	354133	363422	477844	490000	...	...	...	080
											081
	89164	174765	131043	140122	138950	147990	292950	...	...	...	082
	16099	17387	19314	21473	22979	28362	31949	35579	40059	...	083
	78	29	70	232	162	151	95	112	50	...	084
	3	0	0	12	104	128	75	140	102	...	085
	16024	17358	19244	21253	22921	28339	27375	30199	35083	...	086
	0.969	0.934	0.946	1.025	1.075	1.130	1.130	1.130	1.128	1.105	087
	0.479	0.462	0.479	0.519	0.594	0.658	0.658	0.650	0.658	0.660	088
averages											
	77.9	78.4	80.4	82.6	85.2	88.9	93.1	96.4	100.0	103.4	089
	74.5	74.1	76.9	79.7	83.1	87.2	92.8	95.0	100.0	104.9	090
	92.5	93.8	95.4	97.6	100.0	104.1	93.3	97.2	100.0	102.6	091

	Item	1978	1979	1980	1981	1982	1983	1984	1985
092	Producer, *1978 = 100*	100.0	111.6	122.3	127.0	123.9	126.6	131.0	128.2
093	Implicit GDP deflator, *1978 = 100*	100.0	112.1	119.8	121.0	124.1	130.5	137.8	135.7
	MONEY AND BANKING								*Million Ringgit;*
094	Money supply (M1)	7242.8	8487.0	9761.4	11014.5	12476.7	13432.3	13356.7	13578.9
095	Currency in circulation	3578.4	4094.2	4757.9	5099.7	5727.0	6025.3	5974.4	6220.2
096	Demand deposits	3664.4	4392.8	5003.5	5914.8	6749.7	7407.0	7382.3	7358.7
097	Quasi-money	10223.7	13219.4	18230.4	21758.2	25423.2	28831.8	34376.5	36833.3
098	Money supply (M2)	17466.5	21706.4	27991.8	32772.7	37899.9	42264.1	47733.2	50412.2
099	Foreign assets (net)	6677.8	9529.8	9354.9	8202.4	8297.2	7926.0	6120.2	9111.1
100	Domestic credit	12861.1	14331.1	21825.1	28412.8	34149.0	40919.2	48964.3	52188.5
101	Claims on govt. sector (net)	1016.9	-732.0	628.9	2316.4	3986.2	3701.7	5070.4	2374.7
102	Claims on private sector	11844.2	15063.1	21196.2	26096.4	30162.8	37217.5	43893.9	49813.8
103	Claims on other financial insts.	...	...	...	...	...	...	...	...
104	Other items	-2072.4	-2154.5	-3188.2	-3842.5	-4546.3	-6581.1	-7351.3	-10887.4
	Deposit Money Banks								
105	Demand deposits	3801.9	4548.9	5326.2	6234.8	7223.5	8062.5	8088.3	7950.4
106	Savings deposits	2972.1	3566.5	4183.3	4214.2	4674.2	5630.3	5534.2	6245.9
107	Time deposits	7926.3	11025.9	13816.8	17657.5	21145.2	23431.4	28952.9	31656.9
108	Domestic credits outstanding [g]	12288.4	15384.6	21031.1	25521.4	29665.6	36781.8	43504.3	48981.7
	Interest Rates [h]								*Per cent;*
	On deposits								
109	Savings	5.00	5.00	5.25	6.33	6.58	6.25	6.50	6.65
110	Time: 6 months	5.75	5.75	6.54	9.67	9.94	8.25	9.52	9.06
111	12 months	6.50	6.75	7.42	9.92	10.42	8.75	9.64	9.27
	GOVERNMENT FINANCE [i]								*Million Ringgit;*
	Central Government								
112	Current revenue	8841	10505	13926	15806	16690	18608	20805	21115
113	Taxes	7567	8997	12060	12594	12590	15263	16474	16700
114	Non-taxes	1274	1508	1866	3212	4100	3345	4331	4415
115	Current expenditure	7391	7890	10292	13686	15922	16124	17506	18766
116	Current surplus/deficit	1450	2615	3634	2120	768	2484	3299	2349
117	Capital receipts	–	–	–	–	–	–	–	–
118	Capital expenditure	3699	4150	7338	11135	11189	9417	8074	6756
119	Capital account surplus/deficit	-3699	-4150	-7338	-11135	-11189	-9417	-8074	-6756
120	Overall surplus/deficit	-2249	-1535	-3704	-9015	-10421	-6933	-4775	-4407
	Financing								
121	Domestic borrowing (net)	1164	2508	2311	4072	6047	4502	3156	3591
122	Foreign borrowing (net)	541	679	310	3419	4893	4569	3093	956
123	Special receipts	3	2	1	236	1	4	46	12
124	Use of cash balances	541	-1654	1082	1288	-520	-2142	-1520	-152
	Expenditure by Function, Central Govt.								
125	Total [j]	11172	12172	17763	25044	27407	25794	25913	25908
126	General public services [k]	1061	1172	1739	2030	2493	2484	2479	2978
127	Defense	2183	2547	3389	4693	5140	4712	4331	3906
128	Education	2043	2257	2786	3517	4073	3897	4192	4341
129	Health	611	666	777	973	1066	992	1057	1119
130	Social security & welfare [l]	541	582	968	1182	1306	1229	1289	1362
131	Housing & community amenities	294	419	295	1231	1658	552	908	976
132	Economic services	3220	3182	5726	8205	7965	7466	6895	6029
133	Agriculture	964	1086	1540	2005	2250	1994	1893	2204
134	Industry	731	478	1718	3532	1796	1522	1067	838
135	Electricity, gas & water	339	406	665	748	856	1027	1132	788
136	Transport & communications	1177	1203	1795	1907	3055	2915	2794	2187
137	Other economic services	10	10	7	14	9	8	9	12
138	Others [m]	1219	1348	2081	3213	3706	4462	4763	5198

1986	1987	1988	1989	1990	1991	1992	1993	1994	1995	
120.3	124.7	133.9	139.0	140.2	145.9	147.5	149.6	156.9	165.8	092
124.0	130.8	137.2	141.7	145.8	150.2	158.0	160.8	168.9	177.3	093

As of end of period

13957.0	15768.2	17839.8	21248.7	24240.5	26903.0	30395.1	41792.3	46470.9	51923.9	094
6580.5	7358.4	8376.7	9174.1	10059.2	11044.5	12142.1	13533.8	15921.9	17479.1	095
7376.5	8409.8	9463.1	12074.6	14181.3	15858.5	18253.0	28258.5	30549.8	34444.8	096
42139.8	44003.5	46232.3	53144.1	59662.4	69189.5	84085.8	98007.7	113894.7	146949.4	097
56096.8	59771.7	64072.1	74392.8	83902.9	96092.5	114480.9	139800.0	160365.6	198873.3	098
14243.8	19457.1	20540.0	23150.1	26442.9	25125.7	33727.9	55462.5	61816.1	58510.6	099
57509.3	60597.8	65465.2	75528.7	91012.9	106906.5	114168.5	129786.3	144902.1	185777.8	100
3938.7	6436.2	6371.6	4358.7	3649.0	1730.4	189.6	1156.6	-3587.1	-5590.6	101
53570.6	54161.6	59093.6	71170.0	87363.9	105176.1	113978.9	128629.7	148489.2	191368.4	102
										103
...	...	...	...	...	...	...	...	...	...	
-15656.3	-20283.2	-21933.1	-24286.0	-33552.9	-35939.7	-33415.5	-45448.8	-46352.6	-45425.1	104

7598.2	9017.3	10032.9	12762.1	15024.8	16650.5	19068.4	29280.0	31777.4	36300.5	105
7161.9	10226.0	11825.1	12943.0	13428.2	13101.6	14584.2	18199.4	21680.3	23482.6	106
33717.7	30427.0	30810.3	34180.4	33806.1	46490.8	59004.0	71604.5	77755.1	102209.6	107
52328.7	52180.7	56837.6	67141.7	80758.0	97206.1	105720.1	117235.5	134151.0	175007.4	108

Period averages

6.00	4.04	3.50	3.50	3.49	3.47	3.28	3.25	3.25	3.27	109
7.17	3.97	3.57	4.58	6.38	7.30	7.99	6.97	5.10	6.18	110
7.42	4.50	4.24	5.08	6.57	7.41	8.03	6.97	5.42	6.55	111

Fiscal year ending 31 December

19518	18143	21967	25273	29521	34053	39250	41691	49446	50935	112
14682	12474	14708	16674	21244	25831	28772	31900	37487	41670	113
4836	5669	7259	8599	8277	8222	10478	9791	11959	9283	114
20075	20185	21212	22982	25026	28296	32075	32217	35064	36573	115
-557	-2042	755	2291	4495	5757	7175	9474	14382	14380	116
–	–	–	–	–	–	–	–	–	–	117
6949	4111	4045	5701	7932	8397	8418	9120	11302	12520	118
-6949	-4111	-4045	-5701	-7932	-8397	-8418	-9120	-11302	-12520	119
-7506	-6153	-3290	-3410	-3437	-2640	-1243	354	637	1860	120
4930	8693	7854	2474	3793	3157	1479	375	1751	...	121
1348	-2438	-3095	-1060	-815	117	-3169	-3135	-2073	-1635	122
111										123
1117	-102	-1469	1996	459	-634	2933	2406	-315	...	124
27299	24926	26444	30678	35715	37840	41763	42340	46011	50624	125
3367	3291	3299	3499	4153	4981	4639	5373	5978	...	126
3788	3574	3700	4381	4866	6269	6960	7478	7702	8892	127
4807	4649	4980	5649	6688	6897	7848	8217	9673	10603	128
1217	1126	1208	1461	1776	2052	2407	2421	2327	2772	129
1536	1429	1659	1960	2213	2963	3452	3596	4805	...	130
1048	79	58	182	42	51	113	70	359	483	131
6189	4825	5364	6500	9147	7091	8638	7536	8118	...	132
2044	1798	1869	2051	2306	2548	2787	2489	2428	2495	133
839	942	1287	1426	3322	1384	1717	1191	1316	1842	134
638	651	656	993	820	700	715	610	790	707	135
2659	1425	1543	2022	2689	2450	3401	3228	3550	4192	136
8	9	10	8	11	8	18	18	34	...	137
5349	5954	6178	7046	6830	7538	7707	7649	7049	...	138

	Item	1978	1979	1980	1981	1982	1983	1984	1985
	EXTERNAL TRADE								*Million Ringgit;*
139	Exports, fob	17074	24222	28172	27109	28108	32771	38647	38017
140	Imports, cif	13646	17161	23451	26604	29023	30795	32926	30438
141	Trade balance	3428	7061	4721	506	-915	1976	5721	7579
	Exports, by SITC section [n]								
142	Food & live animals	872	1082	1013	1135	1153	1273	1480	1662
143	Beverage & tobacco	16	21	29	30	22	28	28	26
144	Crude materials excl. fuels	6360	9025	9105	7710	7583	8262	8121	7248
145	Mineral fuels, etc.	2343	4346	6898	7147	7981	9301	11435	12051
146	Animal, vegetable oil & fats	2106	3016	3131	3376	3256	3829	5868	4845
147	Chemicals	102	131	172	192	236	294	427	428
148	Basic manufactures	2825	3315	3691	3281	2626	3035	2555	3095
149	Machines, transport equipment	1816	2535	3238	3325	4335	5653	7323	7059
150	Misc. manufactured goods	496	604	738	700	754	902	1196	1391
151	Unclassified goods	138	147	156	215	163	195	214	212
	Exports, by principal commodity [o]								
152	1. Petroleum, crude & partly refined	2247	4214	6709	6921	7694	7871	8737	8698
153	2. Saw logs & sawn timber	2528	4211	3962	3595	4547	4157	3982	3908
154	3. Palm oil	1871	2471	2603	2836	2742	2995	4546	3963
155	4. Rubber	3601	4482	4618	3713	2655	3664	3672	3672
156	5. Tin	2022	2316	2505	2138	1484	1718	1162	1648
	Imports, by SITC section [n]								
157	Food & live animals	1979	2052	2444	2942	2999	2985	3227	3064
158	Beverage & tobacco	185	185	221	255	248	250	213	229
159	Crude materials excl. fuels	726	850	1053	1191	1132	1187	1158	1036
160	Mineral fuels, etc.	1470	2077	3554	4579	4390	4242	3332	3722
161	Animal, vegetable oil & fats	26	30	30	35	37	56	120	81
162	Chemicals	1218	1747	2022	2096	2145	2425	2636	2640
163	Basic manufactures	2237	2920	3849	4277	4916	4882	5086	4419
164	Machines, transport equipment	4950	6374	9105	9884	11548	13171	15129	13262
165	Misc. manufactured goods	722	791	975	1077	1354	1396	1716	1674
166	Unclassified goods	135	135	197	268	255	202	310	312
	Direction of Trade								*Million US dollars;*
167	Exports, Total	7412.6	11076.6	12960.3	11772.9	12043.5	14127.5	16563.0	15407.6
168	1. Singapore	1197.3	1933.0	2479.8	2683.2	3005.2	3181.9	3380.5	2991.1
169	2. United States	1378.7	1913.2	2118.9	1537.9	1399.4	1863.8	2231.0	1969.6
170	3. Japan	1605.3	2594.5	2957.7	2489.0	2449.1	2782.3	3769.7	3783.6
171	4. Hong Kong	115.0	187.7	243.5	237.3	230.9	244.8	234.9	207.1
172	5. United Kingdom	356.4	431.2	357.6	346.4	329.8	384.4	420.7	397.1
173	6. Thailand	99.8	148.7	188.4	195.9	440.6	578.4	464.9	527.2
174	7. Germany	267.8	405.1	467.3	344.5	339.6	454.2	504.6	405.0
175	8. Korea, Rep. of	131.7	213.1	262.2	429.2	441.4	661.1	828.6	905.9
176	9. China, People's Rep. of	110.3	181.9	217.0	88.4	110.4	156.7	164.7	161.1
177	10. Netherlands	418.6	620.4	777.7	699.7	723.4	771.8	670.4	898.5
178	Imports, Total	5928.5	7841.9	10821.3	11580.6	12408.9	13240.8	14056.9	12301.3
179	1. Japan	1371.6	1756.9	2470.6	2828.8	3101.4	3361.7	3691.7	2833.3
180	2. United States	824.1	1173.1	1632.3	1688.2	2181.4	2127.3	2295.0	1881.2
181	3. Singapore	505.8	723.0	1264.9	1513.4	1781.9	1844.5	1838.8	1947.8
182	4. Germany	365.0	465.8	586.1	517.8	524.0	682.5	591.9	550.0
183	5. United Kingdom	439.7	501.2	585.8	527.5	507.4	469.2	505.8	485.9
184	6. Korea, Rep. of	57.8	113.6	202.1	165.1	260.0	238.9	252.2	275.9
185	7. Australia	382.2	475.5	593.6	639.3	563.6	541.8	565.6	499.0
186	8. Thailand	250.0	281.9	320.3	395.1	460.4	397.7	481.4	435.4
187	9. China, People's Rep. of	221.1	222.6	253.5	274.5	276.9	269.5	285.3	250.8
188	10. France	86.3	154.8	205.1	212.8	161.8	339.9	342.3	283.7

1986	1987	1988	1989	1990	1991	1992	1993	1994	1995	
Calendar year										
35319	45225	55260	67825	79646	94497	103882	121226	153680	...	139
27921	31934	43293	60858	79119	100831	102510	117405	155920	...	140
7397	13291	11967	6967	527	-6334	1372	3821	-2240	...	141
1965	2458	2851	3130	3391	3652	3718	3975	4479	...	142
37	57	83	80	95	169	191	185	211	...	143
7868	10583	12418	12667	11468	11140	11081	10984	11508	8328	144
8006	8911	8731	11003	14595	14659	13418	12484	11144	8316	145
3610	4168	5763	6198	5680	6227	6875	7241	10485	8436	146
605	736	1221	1233	1298	1667	2123	2651	4085	3691	147
2587	3710	4488	5721	6320	7360	8831	11610	13910	10599	148
9010	11701	15666	21987	28418	38866	45410	58751	82162	63509	149
1500	2619	3830	5621	7943	10320	11426	12524	14609	10016	150
133	283	210	186	438	438	809	821	1087	1710	151
5401	6290	6116	7893	10639	10196	9122	7926	6546	3935	152
4178	5926	5850	7262	7106	7108	7339	7460	6875	3673	153
3020	3292	4540	4691	4411	5045	5413	5773	8348	6020	154
3183	3915	5256	3949	3028	2690	2357	2132	2927	2556	155
650	839	910	1161	902	684	721	489	507	315	156
2914	2965	3826	4609	4551	5139	5436	5816	6668	...	157
210	192	208	237	293	424	398	391	430	...	158
1017	1286	1816	2495	2548	2810	2630	3264	3765	3015	159
2388	2381	2318	2908	4021	4253	4243	4247	3995	2805	160
69	205	267	270	218	395	331	404	559	310	161
2687	3281	4782	5419	6691	7663	8103	8848	10609	9129	162
4038	4952	7167	9990	12421	15924	16270	17705	21638	17244	163
12579	14400	19522	29180	39585	54165	55711	65439	93719	75564	164
1701	1954	2467	3271	4434	5650	5868	6521	8425	6002	165
321	317	921	2480	4357	4409	3520	4770	6112	6397	166
Calendar year										
13976.8	17934.3	21095.4	25049.3	29420.1	34405.0	40709.0	47128.1	58748.2	73640.6	167
2366.1	3263.1	4080.6	4948.4	6752.8	8019.5	9391.2	10228.1	12167.3	14889.9	168
2297.4	2972.2	3663.2	4684.0	4986.1	5808.1	7594.3	9580.3	12447.7	15216.4	169
3256.9	3503.8	3577.2	4016.4	4505.5	5458.4	5400.7	6113.1	7010.1	9333.9	170
310.7	505.5	715.9	770.1	933.6	1151.8	1549.5	1941.5	2714.8	3798.3	171
481.0	573.9	738.2	942.7	1159.7	1503.0	1642.7	1983.8	2228.9	2937.1	172
360.9	511.4	416.6	615.4	1032.7	1097.5	1490.2	1695.0	2217.7	2785.0	173
501.1	615.9	723.4	892.6	1148.7	1244.3	1636.1	1722.4	1944.8	2363.5	174
721.8	951.9	1009.7	1253.9	1359.5	1514.2	1389.0	1613.8	1645.8	2072.8	175
163.3	279.5	415.0	480.9	619.2	638.8	772.1	1203.9	1932.7	1996.8	176
473.1	619.4	638.9	895.0	774.6	828.2	991.0	1146.6	1352.3	1723.9	177
10828.0	12701.4	16567.4	22588.5	29169.7	36749.4	39926.9	45616.3	59554.6	76998.9	178
2220.6	2750.3	3816.5	5437.8	7055.3	9581.7	10378.7	12532.5	15906.7	20866.4	179
2033.9	2376.0	2925.0	3802.8	4944.2	5625.8	6330.6	7724.6	9899.8	12448.2	180
1629.8	1873.7	2186.0	3058.7	4308.0	5700.5	6268.6	6954.7	8385.9	9664.3	181
486.7	538.5	646.6	856.8	1267.5	1593.1	1684.4	1743.2	2496.2	3482.4	182
492.0	545.6	812.3	1215.2	1600.3	1697.5	1360.5	1426.0	1904.7	2188.1	183
245.3	333.8	429.7	563.1	742.1	1072.1	1212.8	1390.7	1898.2	3184.2	184
458.4	526.9	686.9	858.5	1004.7	1175.0	1061.2	1292.9	1766.8	2052.7	185
429.1	442.8	504.2	677.7	702.4	891.5	994.0	1133.8	1473.5	2005.2	186
281.5	374.4	482.4	609.3	560.8	802.5	975.1	1096.1	1363.1	1746.8	187
229.4	204.0	256.5	276.0	437.6	467.0	524.6	651.6	1569.2	2236.2	188

Item	1978	1979	1980	1981	1982	1983	1984	1985
Trade Indexes (Peninsular Malaysia) [p]								*1970 = 100;*
Quantum index								
189 Exports	173.7	209.0	229.9	221.3	235.0	268.4	292.6	298.9
190 Imports	177.3	211.2	256.2	252.6	287.7	322.0	365.8	336.3
Unit value index								
191 Exports	199.4	230.7	254.3	238.1	213.0	225.6	228.2	211.0
192 Imports	208.1	223.2	267.6	306.3	304.9	291.9	283.3	280.4
193 Terms of trade	95.8	103.4	95.0	77.7	69.9	77.3	80.6	75.2
BALANCE OF PAYMENTS								*Million US dollars;*
194 Merchandise exports, fob	7311	10994	12868	11675	11966	13683	16407	15133
195 Merchandise imports, fob	-5718	-7838	-10462	-11780	-12719	-13251	-13426	-11556
196 Trade balance	1593	3157	2406	-105	-753	432	2981	3577
197 Other goods, services and income	-1441	-2219	-2670	-2305	-2816	-3920	-4614	-4184
198 Credit	1075	1425	1968	2204	2332	2534	2660	2643
199 Debit	-2516	-3644	-4638	-4509	-5148	-6454	-7274	-6827
200 Unrequited transfers	-45	-8	-20	-34	-32	-9	-39	-6
201 Private	-68	-36	-43	-55	-53	-35	-63	-46
202 Official	23	28	23	21	21	26	24	40
203 Current balance	108	929	-285	-2444	-3601	-3497	-1672	-613
204 Direct investment	500	573	934	1265	1397	1260	797	695
205 Portfolio investment [q]	79	194	-11	1131	1804	1409	1003	335
206 Other long-term capital	111	158	98	178	409	1298	999	673
207 Other short-term capital	-63	-724	414	42	140	-113	-123	350
208 Net errors and omissions	-455	-329	-682	-646	-412	-381	-872	-148
209 Overall balance	279	802	468	-474	-263	-24	132	1292
210 Allocation of SDRs	–	34	35	32	–	–	–	–
211 Monetary movements	-279	-836	-503	442	263	24	-132	-1292
INTERNATIONAL RESERVES								*Million US dollars;*
212 Total	3329	4013	4492	4193	3858	3869	3803	5002
213 Gold, national valuation	86	98	104	95	90	85	80	90
214 Foreign exchange	3123	3711	4114	3816	3509	3509	3470	4621
215 Reserve position in the Fund	70	89	149	136	129	167	156	175
216 SDRs	50	115	125	146	130	108	97	116
EXCHANGE RATES								*Ringgit per*
217 End of period	2.2060	2.1890	2.2224	2.2423	2.3213	2.3383	2.4250	2.4265
218 Average of period	2.3160	2.1884	2.1769	2.3041	2.3354	2.3213	2.3436	2.4830
EXTERNAL INDEBTEDNESS								*Million US dollars;*
219 Total outstanding and disbursed	4167	4955	6611	9180	13354	17550	18733	20269
220 Long-term	3356	4081	5256	7335	11357	14193	15945	17466
221 Public and publicly guaranteed	2543	3083	4008	5698	8159	11462	13170	14506
222 Private non-guaranteed	814	998	1248	1637	3198	2732	2775	2960
223 Short-term	811	874	1355	1624	1723	3027	2531	2685
224 Use of IMF credit	0	0	0	221	274	330	258	118
								Transactions
Debt service								
225 Principal repayments on LT debt	864	475	345	434	594	690	1133	3635
226 Interest on long-term debt	189	344	338	515	725	935	1272	1437
227 Interest on short-term debt	105	99	251	194	191	179	204	152

	1986	1987	1988	1989	1990	1991	1992	1993	1994	1995	
Period averages											
	357.0	418.5	...	...	...	...	...	...	...	...	189
	331.4	392.3	...	...	...	...	...	...	...	...	190
	178.3	193.6	...	...	...	...	...	...	...	...	191
	247.1	250.0	...	...	...	...	...	...	...	...	192
	72.2	77.4	...	...	...	...	...	...	...	...	193
Calendar year											
	13547	17754	20852	24667	28636	33533	39613	45990	56589	72255	194
	-10301	-11919	-15306	-20754	-26014	-33006	-36233	-42792	-54851	-72004	195
	3246	5835	5546	3913	2622	527	3380	3198	1738	251	196
	-3405	-3338	-3887	-4206	-3595	-4798	-5719	-6216	-6048	-7525	197
	2638	3229	3597	4185	5877	5978	6808	7460	9205	10833	198
	-6043	-6567	-7484	-8390	-9472	-10776	-12526	-13677	-15254	-18357	199
	37	138	151	81	54	37	132	149	120	160	200
	-19	-25	70	-17	3	29	65	70	48	...	201
	56	163	81	97	51	8	67	80	71	...	202
	-122	2635	1810	-212	-918	-4234	-2207	-2869	-4191	-7113	203
	489	423	719	1668	2332	3998	5183	5006	4347	3993	204
	599	-948	-966	-155	-1048	-242	1129	380	183	2224	205
	223	-32	-982	-515							206
	-18	-989	-1113	577	501	1867	4694	5412	-3020	293	207
	512	58	110	-132	1115	-144	32	3430	-468	-1154	208
	1683	1147	-422	1230	1982	1246	6573	11359	-3148	-1758	209
	–	–	–	–	=	–	–	–	–	–	210
	-1683	-1147	422	-1230	-1982	-1246	-6573	-11359	3148	1758	211
As of end of period											
	6127	7552	6637	7892	9871	11003	17342	27364	25545	27845	212
	100	117	111	109	117	118	115	115	122	...	213
	5697	7055	6134	7393	9327	10421	16784	26814	24888	...	214
	195	217	231	223	233	257	330	315	400	678	215
	135	163	161	167	194	207	113	121	135	151	216
US dollar											
	2.6030	2.4928	2.7153	2.7033	2.7015	2.7240	2.6120	2.7015	2.5600	2.5420	217
	2.5814	2.5196	2.6188	2.7088	2.7049	2.7501	2.5474	2.5741	2.6243	2.5044	218
As of end of year											
	21880	22839	18567	16278	16080	17811	19959	23335	24767	...	219
	19168	20494	16972	14005	14173	15737	16320	16384	18578	...	220
	16277	17884	14632	12628	12684	14014	13469	13863	13751	...	221
	2891	2610	2340	1377	1489	1723	2851	2521	4827	...	222
	2712	2345	1595	2273	1906	2074	3639	6951	...	...	223
	0	0	0	0	0	0	0	0	...	...	224
during the year											
	1900	2792	4422	3016	2342	1801	1937	2940	1388	...	225
	1295	1471	1461	1123	1060	1053	987	1004	994	1074 *	226
	202	190	174	199	169	188	176	284	394	...	227

Item	1978	1979	1980	1981	1982	1983	1984	1985
Average terms of new commitments								
228 Interest (%)	8.6	8.0	11.2	12.2	11.6	9.4	8.8	8.7
229 Maturity (years)	11.5	13.8	13.8	13.9	11.4	11.1	16.2	21.5
231 Grace period (years)	4.6	5.5	5.4	5.2	5.4	6.3	9.7	18.3
232 Grant element (%)	6.6	11.7	-6.6	-12.7	-8.3	2.5	6.6	9.3

Footnotes:

a   Production for Sabah and Sarawak were estimated from exports.

b   Based on a conversion rate of 65 percent from paddy to milled rice. Production data on paddy are available on a crop year basis only. e.g., the figure for 1978 relates to crop year 1977/78; harvesting of the main crop is normally centered during the period November 1977-March 1978.

c   Relates to Peninsular Malaysia only for 1991-1993.

d   Relates to Peninsular Malaysia only prior to 1986 and to the whole of Malaysia thereafter.

e   Refer to average prices for Peninsular Malaysia only for 1978.

f   Refer to average prices for Sabah and Sarawak only prior to 1983.

g   Refers to loans and advances.

h   Refer to average of six months only for 1989, 9 months for 1990 and eight months for 1993.

i   Refers to federal government finance. Data for 1995 are estimates given by the Ministry of Finance which may change in the future.

j   Refers to federal government current and development expenditures including loans to State Government, statutory authorities and public corporations with substantial government participation.

k   Refers to general administration including grants to States, subscription to international organizations and expenditure of State Reserve Fund and Welfare Services Fund but excluding loan disbursements.

l   Refers to pensions and outlays in welfare services, sports, labor, local government and housing that cannot be disaggregated from the current expenditure account.

m   Refers to contributions to statutory funds, public debt charges and other transfer payments.

n   Data for 1995 refer up to August only.

o   Data for 1995 refer up to July only.

p   Compilation of the series has been discontinued since January 1988.

q   Relates to the sum of portfolio investment and other long-term capital from 1990 onwards.

1986	1987	1988	1989	1990	1991	1992	1993	1994	1995	
6.9	6.5	5.2	7.6	5.9	7.4	5.8	5.2	6.8	...	228
14.4	14.8	17.5	12.1	18.5	13.3	20.9	11.4	17.8	...	229
5.2	6.7	6.7	7.2	6.9	6.5	4.0	4.9	2.8	...	231
17.7	21.1	31.4	14.8	29.2	14.5	27.3	23.2	17.0	...	232

	Item	1978	1979	1980	1981	1982	1983	1984	1985
									Thousand;
001	**POPULATION**	148	152	158	161	167	172	178	180
									Thousand;
002	**LABOR FORCE**	...	...	...	...	...	...	...	52.26
003	Employed	...	...	66.30	...	...	...	...	51.42
004	Agriculture	...	...	35.90	...	...	...	...	15.44
005	Manufacturing	...	...	14.50	...	...	...	...	11.56
006	Mining	...	...	...	...	...	...	...	0.64
007	Others	...	...	15.90	...	...	...	...	23.78
008	Unemployed	...	...	...	...	...	...	...	0.84
009	Unemployment Rate, %	...	...	...	...	...	...	...	1.61
	NATIONAL ACCOUNTS								
	At Current Market Prices								*Million Rufiyaa;*
010	Expenditure on GDP	...	...	320.6	338.1	343.7	407.7	527.5	600.3
011	Private consumption	...	...	267.0	344.0	366.3	385.0	336.0	...
012	Government consumption	...	...	39.0	49.5	60.9	75.8	99.0	...
013	Gross fixed capital formation	...	...	76.0	98.5	105.5	115.2	165.0	...
014	Increase in stocks	...	...	...	...	...	...	...	...
015	Exports of goods and services	...	...	58.5	64.5	68.6	94.5	125.1	...
016	Less: Imports of goods and services	...	...	185.5	194.6	275.1	361.9	363.1	...
017	Statistical discrepancy	...	...	...	...	...	...	...	...
	At Constant 1984 I 1985 Prices								
018	GDP by Industrial origin	...	...	...	368.5	357.4	415.5	527.5 I	600.3
019	Agriculture	...	...	...	150.2	140.8	145.6	157.3 I	69.5
020	Mining	...	...	...	9.0	9.6	10.4	11.1 I	11.7
021	Manufacturing	...	...	...	19.3	26.0	29.8	32.1 I	33.5
022	Electricity, gas and water								
023	Construction	...	...	...	28.5	33.4	34.4	40.8 I	49.0
024	Trade	...	...	...	36.6	49.5	69.4	87.7 I	97.2
025	Transport and communications	...	...	...	43.0	-16.3	-11.2	12.1 I	13.9
026	Public administration	...	...	...	18.6	32.2	37.6	42.8 I	45.8
027	Others [a]	...	...	...	63.3	82.2	99.5	143.6 I	279.7
028	Net factor income from abroad	...	...	...	...	-74.5	-41.3	-135.5 I	-140.0
029	GNP	...	...	...	...	282.9	374.2	392.0 I	460.3
030	Expenditure on GDP	...	...	...	368.5	357.4	415.5	527.5 I	600.3
031	Private consumption	...	...	...	346.6	366.3	384.8	336.0 I	498.7
032	Government consumption	...	...	...	45.0	60.9	72.0	99.0 I	111.0
033	Gross fixed capital formation	...	...	...	102.8	105.5	112.1	165.0 I	233.6
034	Increase in stocks	...	...	...	...	...	...	... I	...
035	Exports of goods and services	...	...	...	70.3	71.3	96.4	124.1 I	163.1
036	Less: Imports of goods and services	...	...	...	212.1	286.1	369.1	363.1 I	340.0
037	Statistical discrepancy	...	...	...	...	...	...	... I	
	Per Capita GDP, Rufiyaa								
038	Current prices	...	...	2035	2101	2063	2366	2963	3333
039	Constant *1984 I 1985* prices	...	...	...	2290	2145	2411	2963 I	3333
	PRODUCTION								*Metric tons;*
	Fishery								
040	1. Skipjack	13800	17900	23600	20900	15600	19700	32000	42600
041	2. Yellowfin tuna	3700	4300	4200	5300	4000	6200	7100	6100
042	3. Other marine fishes	5600	3000	4200	5500	6700	7000	11000	8200
	Production Indexes								*Period*
043	Agriculture, *1979-81 = 100*	96.1	89.1	106.1	105.8	110.2	118.1	119.9	122.1
044	Mining	...	...	...	...	...	...	...	...
045	Manufacturing	...	...	...	...	...	...	...	...

	1986	1987	1988	1989	1990	1991	1992	1993	1994	1995	
As of 1 July											
	190	196	203	209	213	223	230	238	245	253	001
Calendar year											
	...	...	...	...	56.44	...	...	...	...	...	002
	...	...	...	...	55.95	...	...	...	...	...	003
	...	...	...	...	14.11	...	...	...	...	...	004
	...	...	...	...	8.44	...	...	...	...	...	005
	...	...	...	...	0.50	...	...	...	...	...	006
	...	...	...	...	32.90	...	...	...	...	...	007
	...	...	...	...	0.49	...	...	...	...	...	008
	...	...	...	...	0.87	...	...	...	...	...	009
Calendar year											
	711.2	867.0	987.4	1148.1	1393.5	1686.5	2028.7	2380.4	2789.7	3188.9	010
	...	...	...	...	...	...	...	...	...	...	011
	...	...	...	...	...	...	...	...	...	...	012
	...	...	...	...	...	...	...	...	...	...	013
	...	...	...	...	...	...	...	...	...	...	014
	...	...	...	...	...	...	...	...	...	...	015
	...	...	...	...	...	...	...	...	...	...	016
	...	...	...	...	...	...	...	...	...	...	017
	651.9	709.7	771.6	843.2	980.0	1054.8	1121.1	1190.2	1268.6	1359.5	018
	76.0	77.9	79.9	82.2	87.1	90.4	93.8	97.5	101.2	104.5	019
	12.4	13.2	14.0	14.9	17.9	19.3	20.3	21.3	22.3	23.4	020
	36.1	39.7	43.6	48.2	55.6	61.2	66.5	72.8	78.6	84.6	021
											022
	52.8	58.1	63.9	70.5	83.9	92.4	101.7	110.2	115.9	126.7	023
	103.6	115.5	128.8	144.1	166.8	183.5	202.8	226.8	242.7	262.1	024
	33.7	37.1	40.8	45.0	57.0	66.3	71.7	77.5	84.1	91.4	025
	55.5	60.5	66.0	72.2	90.1	94.1	99.8	109.3	114.8	121.2	026
	281.7	307.7	334.6	366.1	421.6	447.6	464.5	474.8	509.0	545.6	027
	-154.4	-166.4	-208.6	-228.8	-273.1	-321.6	...	...	...	...	028
	497.5	543.3	563.0	614.4	706.9	733.2	...	...	...	...	029
	651.9	709.7	771.6	843.2	980.0	1054.8	1121.1	1190.2	1268.6	1359.5	030
	515.1	443.7	425.9	494.2	517.5	658.0	...	...	...	...	031
	128.8	193.7	214.1	280.2	351.4	446.0	...	...	...	...	032
	238.2	429.2	442.5	552.1	629.0	941.0	...	...	...	...	033
	...	...	...	...	...	...	...	...	...	...	034
	169.3	239.2	285.5	323.1	418.9	...	...	...	...	...	035
	284.6	610.3	685.1	822.8	1096.2	...	...	...	...	...	036
	...	...	...	...	...	...	...	...	...	...	037
	3739	4410	4864	5483	6535	7553	8789	9986	11345	12589	038
	3427	3610	3801	4027	4596	4724	4857	4993	5159	5367	039
Calendar year											
	45500	42100	58600	58100	59900	58900	58600	58700	69400	...	040
	5300	6600	6500	6100	5300	7700	8700	10100	13100	...	041
	5600	5000	3400	3400	6000	9600	8600	11400	14400	...	042
averages											
	118.3	118.9	120.5	125.5	127.9	127.7	128.3	128.7	124.6	124.6	043
	...	...	...	...	...	...	...	...	...	...	044
	...	...	...	...	...	...	...	...	...	...	045

	Item	1978	1979	1980	1981	1982	1983	1984	1985
	ENERGY								*Annual*
	Electricity, *Mn kWh*								
046	Production	2	3	4	5	8	7	9	10
047	Consumption	2	3	4	5	8	7	9	10
	Retail Prices,								
048	Gasoline, *premium*	3.5	5.5	6.5	6.0	5.0	3.7	4.0	5.2
049	Diesel	1.5	2.5	3.5	3.0	2.9	2.8	2.9	3.0
	PRICE INDEXES								*Period*
050	Consumer (country), *1981 = 100*	...	...	...	...	...	...	...	130.1
051	Implicit GDP deflator, *1984 = 100\ 1985 = 100*	...	...	...	91.8	96.2	98.1	100.0	100.0
	MONEY AND BANKING								*Million Rufiyaa;*
052	Money supply (M1)	37.5	53.4	80.7	109.3	92.8	88.8	113.9	163.7
053	Currency in circulation	17.5	23.1	27.5	32.4	41.7	50.3	56.8	68.5
054	Demand deposits	20.0	30.3	53.2	76.9	51.1	38.5	57.1	95.2
055	Quasi-money	29.3	37.0	62.2	48.5	47.8	49.3	68.9	72.5
056	Money supply (M2)	66.8	90.4	142.9	157.8	140.6	138.1	182.8	236.2
057	Foreign assets (net)	18.3	14.8	10.4	-55.0	-81.6	-135.0	-169.6	-193.3
058	Domestic credit	46.4	79.8	151.7	219.5	274.8	327.7	389.9	496.0
059	Claims on govt. sector (net)	32.7	59.2	94.5	129.3	162.5	157.3	132.1	218.2
060	Claims on private sector	13.7	17.6	16.5	51.2	97.9	126.5	187.1	184.0
061	Claims on other financial insts.	–	3.0	40.7	39.0	14.4	43.9	70.7	93.7
062	Other items	2.1	-4.2	-19.2	-6.7	-52.6	-54.6	-37.5	-66.5
	Deposit Money Banks								
063	Demand deposits [b]	3.9	6.2	7.3	6.3	14.3	18.6	29.4	26.2
064	Time and Savings deposits [c]	29.3	37.0	62.2	48.0	47.1	49.2	68.7	72.4
065	Domestic credits outstanding	13.7	20.6	57.1	112.6	145.9	189.3	252.8	273.4
	Interest Rates								*Percent;*
	On deposits								
066	Savings	...	...	...	4.0	6.0	6.0	6.0	6.0
067	Time: 6-12 months \ 12 months	...	...	...	6.7	8.0	9.0-11.0	7.0-9.0	9.0
	On loans & discounts								
068	Private	...	...	...	23.0	20.0-21.0	17.0-19.0	17.0	15.0-20.0
069	Public	...	...	...	18.5	15.0	12.4	13.0	10.0-15.0
	GOVERNMENT FINANCE								*Million Rufiyaa;*
	Central Government								
070	Current revenue	11.7	17.1	45.1	70.5	95.0	115.8	134.9	159.6
071	Taxes	3.1	6.9	16.5	23.3	42.1	51.6	71.1	90.7
072	Non-taxes	8.6	10.2	28.6	47.2	52.9	64.2	63.8	68.9
073	Current expenditure	15.3	27.2	39.4	52.3	92.8	95.2	102.9	120.9
074	Current surplus/deficit	-3.6	-10.1	5.7	18.2	2.2	20.6	32.0	38.7
075	Capital receipts	–	0.5	0.8	3.0	4.4	1.0	0.2	6.3
076	Capital expenditure	25.9	25.7	99.8	55.9	50.6	105.7	98.5	80.6
077	Capital account surplus/deficit	-25.9	-25.2	-99.0	-52.9	-46.2	-104.7	-98.3	-74.3
078	Net lending	–	–	–	–	–	–	–	–
079	Overall surplus/deficit	-29.5	-35.3	-93.3	-34.7	-44.0	-84.1	-66.3	-35.6
	Financing								
080	Domestic borrowing	...	17.5	34.3	0.1	7.7	35.3	14.6	28.6
081	Foreign borrowing	...	9.9	47.5	26.3	12.9	36.4	16.5	-2.7
082	Foreign grants	...	7.9	11.5	8.3	23.4	12.4	35.2	9.7
083	Use of cash balances	...	–	–	–	–	–	–	–
	Expenditure by Function, Central Govt.								
084	Total	...	...	...	...	143.4	200.9	201.4	201.5
085	General public services	...	...	...	...	27.8	45.6	52.0	46.2
086	Defence	...	...	...	...	14.1	18.8	25.1	23.6

1986	1987	1988	1989	1990	1991	1992	1993	1994	1995	
values										
12	15	17	20	24	35	38	37	42	51	046
12	15	17	20	24	28	30	...	...	...	047
5.3	6.5	5.1	5.1	5.3	6.0	7.5	5.5	...	...	048
2.7	2.7	2.7	2.7	3.3	3.3	3.8	3.4	...	...	049
averages										
143.4	157.3	167.5	179.5	186.0	213.4	249.3	299.6	...	...	050
109.1	122.2	128.0	136.2	142.2	159.9	181.0	200.0	219.9	234.6	051
As of end of period										
188.8	198.5	221.7	263.1	312.9	402.1	463.9	694.5	850.9	899.1	052
92.0	116.5	140.1	158.3	206.7	253.5	300.9	330.4	382.3	405.8	053
96.8	81.9	81.6	104.8	106.1	148.6	163.0	364.1	468.6	493.2	054
107.1	132.8	157.0	190.3	225.3	270.2	295.5	340.8	434.8	586.9	055
295.9	331.3	378.7	453.5	538.2	672.2	759.4	1035.3	1285.6	1486.0	056
-125.3	-55.0	70.5	38.8	62.5	184.2	190.0	33.5	131.3	311.5	057
499.6	493.6	417.2	574.5	680.0	790.6	904.2	1369.5	1563.2	1661.9	058
226.3	199.5	136.3	167.5	265.2	340.5	484.2	784.2	901.3	837.4	059
181.5	180.6	159.2	195.6	255.3	247.8	256.8	398.5	518.5	655.1	060
91.8	113.5	121.7	211.5	159.5	202.2	163.2	186.8	143.4	169.4	061
-78.3	-107.3	-109.0	-159.9	-204.3	-302.5	-334.7	-367.7	-408.9	-487.4	062
39.5	51.2	57.3	67.0	68.2	113.0	117.0	281.1	356.1	393.7	063
107.0	132.2	156.3	189.8	224.7	269.5	293.9	340.1	429.3	569.9	064
272.3	285.2	267.7	389.5	416.0	418.1	421.1	579.8	655.7	816.1	065
Period averages										
6.0	3.5-4.5	3.5-4.5	2.0-4.5	2.0-4.5	2.0-4.5	3.0-5.0	5.0	5.0-6.5	5.0-6.5	066
9.0-11.0	5.5-7.0	5.5-7.0	5.0-7.5	3.0-7.0 I	3.5-9.0	5.0-9.0	5.0	5.0-6.5	...	067
15.0-20.0	7.0-15.0	7.0-15.0	7.0-15.0	7.0-15.0	12.0	10.0	11.0	12.0-14.0	12.0-14.0	068
8.5-10.5	7.0-20.0	7.0-20.0	7.0-20.0	7.0-20.0	9.5	7.5	11.0	12.0-14.0	12.0-14.0	069
Fiscal year ending 31 December										
196.8	284.5	335.0	428.4	498.1	614.5	732.9	834.6	998.4	1188.0 *	070
104.4	161.7	205.0	266.2	293.8	374.2	460.6	493.7	548.6	647.6 *	071
92.4	122.8	130.0	162.2	204.3	240.3	272.3	340.9	449.8	540.4 *	072
138.9	176.8	211.0	279.6	376.4	483.0	576.7	666.5	691.9	940.1 *	073
57.9	107.7	124.0	148.8	121.7	131.5	156.2	168.1	306.5	247.9 *	074
0.7	6.7	2.4	2.2	5.5	3.8	4.0	1.0	2.0	1.8 *	075
169.7	166.9	186.1	344.2	362.0	572.3	629.6	722.2	668.9	725.8 *	076
-169.0	-160.2	-183.7	-342.0	-356.5	-568.5	-625.6	-721.2	-666.9	-724.0 *	077
2.4	12.6	8.7	10.4	8.8	13.1	22.3	-2.1	-7.3	-11.6 *	078
-113.5	-65.1	-68.4	-203.6	-243.6	-450.1	-491.7	-551.0	-353.1	-464.5 *	079
16.2	-25.7	-28.9	-5.6	85.1	96.4	173.3	362.1	90.3	28.9 *	080
31.0	1.3	-4.0	43.5	73.5	127.5	167.0	35.6	100.2	210.7 *	081
66.3	89.5	101.3	165.7	85.0	226.2	151.4	153.3	162.6	224.9 *	082
–	–	–	–	–	–	–	–	–	– *	083
311.0	356.3	405.8	634.2	747.2	1068.4	1228.6	1386.6	1353.5	1654.3 *	084
57.7	66.6	78.7	88.3	126.6	179.4	256.6	347.2	351.4	301.0 *	085
30.1	35.0	39.9	96.8	127.7	120.0	140.6	179.6	174.8	234.4 *	086

	Item	1978	1979	1980	1981	1982	1983	1984	1985
087	Education	...	...	...	...	12.1	15.0	19.6	22.4
088	Health	...	...	...	...	8.3	7.6	9.1	10.8
089	Social security & welfare	...	...	...	...	27.5	14.8	7.5	6.9
090	Housing & community amenities	...	...	...	...	13.0	33.0	35.1	36.6
091	Economic services	...	...	...	...	35.4	60.7	45.1	40.1
092	Agriculture	...	...	...	...	13.1	36.0	16.4	12.9
093	Industry	...	...	...	...	1.1	0.9	0.8	0.8
094	Electricity, gas & water	...	...	...	...	–	–	–	–
095	Transport and communications	...	...	...	...	20.4	22.7	25.8	25.0
096	Other economic services	...	...	...	...	0.8	1.1	2.1	1.4
097	Others	...	...	...	...	5.2	5.4	7.9	14.9
	EXTERNAL TRADE [d]							*Million US dollars;*	
098	Exports, fob	7.2	10.7	12.8	15.8	17.3	19.8	23.1	25.5
099	Imports, fob	14.8	21.7	44.0	41.7	46.0	57.6	61.0	58.0
100	Trade Balance	-7.6	-11.0	-31.2	-25.9	-28.7	-37.8	-37.9	-32.5
	Exports, by principal commodity								
101	1. Fresh skipjack	2540	3288	4763	5240	3563	3891	6656	8805
102	2. Dry skipjack	210	62	82	23	88	735	679	1313
103	3. Dry salted fish	670	859	1610	1366	1763	1267	1048	3151
	Direction of Trade							*Million US dollars;*	
104	Exports, Total	5.2	5.7	7.9	9.4	11.9	13.3	13.1	23.0
105	1. Sri Lanka	0.2	0.9	1.7	1.8	1.6	1.6	1.7	4.5
106	2. United Kingdom	0.1	0.1	0.6	0.0	0.0	0.0	0.0	0.0
107	3. United States	–	–	–	0.0	0.0	0.0	0.0	5.6
108	4. Germany	–	–	–	0.6	0.0	0.4	1.2	0.9
109	5. Japan	2.1	2.9	2.4	2.6	2.8	0.8	0.6	2.3
110	6. Thailand	–	–	–	1.1	3.4	4.8	7.3	6.8
111	7. Hong Kong	–	0.2	–	0.0	0.2	0.0	0.0	0.1
112	8. Netherlands	–	–	–	0.0	0.0	0.0	0.0	0.0
113	9. Singapore	–	–	–	1.3	3.3	4.2	0.6	0.3
114	10. Canada	–	–	–	0.0	0.0	0.0	0.0	1.8
115	Imports, Total	10.5	12.2	20.1	38.5	68.6	66.2	70.8	70.1
116	1. Singapore	–	–	–	17.5	30.8	40.1	34.8	31.1
117	2. India	1.4	2.5	3.2	0.6	3.2	1.5	1.7	0.8
118	3. Sri Lanka	0.8	1.3	1.3	2.2	19.6	5.0	4.3	5.7
119	4. United Arab Emirates	–	–	–	–	–	–	–	–
120	5. Thailand	0.8	0.0	–	0.0	0.3	1.1	0.4	1.8
121	6. Malaysia	0.1	0.1	0.1	0.3	1.0	1.2	1.0	1.0
122	7. Japan	3.7	1.7	4.3	3.7	2.5	7.4	11.2	13.1
123	8. United Kingdom	0.7	0.5	2.9	2.6	1.2	1.1	1.0	2.0
124	9. Hong Kong	–	0.1	0.0	0.6	2.6	2.1	1.3	3.9
125	10. Germany	0.2	1.8	2.9	2.9	1.1	0.8	0.9	2.4
	Trade Indexes							*1987 = 100;*	
	Unit value index								
126	Exports	...	...	...	...	...	...	...	...
127	Imports	...	...	...	...	...	...	...	...
128	Terms of Trade	...	...	...	...	...	...	...	...
	BALANCE OF PAYMENTS [d]							*Million US dollars;*	
129	Merchandise exports, fob [e]	7.2	10.7	12.8	15.8	17.3	19.8	23.1	25.5
130	Merchandise imports, fob [f]	-14.8	-21.7	-44.0	-41.7	-46.0	-57.6	-61.0	-58.0
131	Trade Balance	-7.6	-11.0	-31.2	-25.9	-28.7	-37.8	-37.9	-32.5
132	Other goods, services and income	4.2	4.5	6.6	3.3	6.3	8.5	15.0	25.4
133	Credit [e]	5.6	31.1	52.4	58.7	59.7	57.5	61.8	65.9
134	Debit [g]	-1.4	-26.6	-45.8	-55.4	-53.4	-49.0	-46.8	-40.5
135	Unrequited transfers	5.0	1.7	2.4	2.4	3.3	5.1	6.6	1.6

	1986	1987	1988	1989	1990	1991	1992	1993	1994	1995	
	23.8	31.0	39.9	101.3	78.8	176.2	166.8	212.6	212.2	229.2 *	087
	12.4	34.9	50.9	42.0	114.2	130.4	104.6	99.0	128.8	160.1 *	088
	7.5	12.2	16.4	18.0	13.8	21.0	17.1	23.7	43.5	41.7 *	089
	29.1	13.9	58.1	79.0	36.8	45.0	48.5	73.0	56.2	89.0 *	090
	138.1	134.2	98.0	189.8	228.0	361.9	450.6	422.6	337.8	515.7 *	091
	56.0	46.7	26.6	20.6	13.0	53.7	81.6	123.3	120.1	181.5 *	092
	1.2	1.4	1.9	1.9	2.2	2.0	4.8	8.9	9.5	13.6 *	093
	3.4	6.7	0.6	1.3	26.8	20.6	12.0	18.1	30.6	39.6 *	094
	75.9	77.2	66.2	160.4	179.0	277.1	342.6	261.8	164.6	257.3 *	095
	1.6	2.2	2.7	5.6	7.0	8.5	9.6	10.5	13.0	23.7 *	096
	12.3	28.5	23.9	19.0	21.3	34.5	43.8	28.9	48.8	83.2 *	097

Calendar year

	31.2	39.8	54.3	63.7	78.0	76.2	65.1	52.7	75.4	85.0	098
	63.0	66.5	87.3	111.3	121.2	141.8	167.9	177.8	195.1	235.8	099
	-31.8	-26.7	-33.0	-47.6	-43.2	-65.6	-102.8	-125.0	-119.6	-150.8	100

	9922	8452	13043	14180	13928	7773	3405	7380	6679	...	101
	2282	1886	2875	3962	4038	6118	6919	6402	6865	...	102
	2378	2807	844	1330	2261	3399	2546	2699	3443	...	103

Calendar year

	24.5	30.8	40.2	44.7	52.1	53.7	39.7	34.6	47.9	61.6	104
	4.7	5.1	4.0	5.9	7.2	10.3	10.2	10.5	11.8	13.7	105
	0.4	0.6	4.1	8.4	9.8	13.3	11.7	8.4	11.4	13.3	106
	8.1	10.8	9.3	8.8	12.6	12.4	5.5	3.9	8.6	12.4	107
	0.5	3.0	1.5	3.0	3.2	3.5	4.9	2.1	5.4	5.6	108
	0.9	1.1	0.6	1.0	4.5	2.1	1.3	1.4	2.5	3.8	109
	8.9	6.8	12.8	13.4	8.7	5.9	2.6	4.8	4.4	3.1	110
	0.1	0.2	0.8	0.9	1.5	1.0	0.4	0.4	1.2	2.4	111
	0.1	0.3	0.9	0.1	0.4	1.1	0.3	0.1	0.4	1.4	112
	0.4	0.8	4.5	1.6	2.6	2.7	2.2	1.2	1.1	1.2	113
	0.6	1.2	0.7	0.7	1.1	0.9	0.1	0.1	0.2	0.0	114

	78.4	98.1	122.0	143.0	137.9	161.8	190.5	192.7	221.7	274.7	115
	40.0	49.0	69.6	79.3	82.5	92.0	110.2	99.2	104.2	120.9	116
	2.0	2.5	3.3	7.0	6.6	11.2	13.9	16.4	24.5	28.4	117
	6.5	7.1	8.8	6.4	9.6	11.0	12.3	12.8	14.0	16.2	118
	–	0.0	0.0	–	0.7	3.2	3.9	11.1	12.8	13.8	119
	1.7	3.8	8.4	8.6	4.2	4.8	6.2	6.5	6.3	13.2	120
	1.1	0.9	1.0	2.4	2.2	2.5	4.7	4.3	6.1	9.1	121
	7.8	14.4	11.8	9.5	4.5	6.5	7.3	7.4	6.9	8.3	122
	2.2	4.8	3.3	6.0	3.4	9.3	7.4	5.6	5.5	7.4	123
	3.3	6.7	5.4	4.8	4.1	5.9	5.1	5.8	7.9	7.2	124
	4.4	3.3	4.0	7.6	11.9	2.9	3.5	3.8	4.3	4.9	125

Period averages

	...	...	...	...	...	125.8	116.9	97.8	...	...	126
	...	...	...	...	...	115.9	117.9	116.7	...	...	127
	...	...	...	...	...	108.5	99.2	83.8	...	...	128

Calendar year

	31.2	39.8	54.3	63.7	78.0	76.2	65.1	52.7	75.4	85.0	129
	-63.0	-66.5	-87.3	-111.3	-121.2	-141.8	-167.9	-177.8	-195.1	-235.8	130
	-31.8	-26.7	-33.0	-47.6	-43.2	-65.6	-102.8	-125.0	-119.6	-150.8	131
	23.7	27.4	35.4	45.1	49.2	51.1	87.7	84.4	114.4	137.8	132
	66.8	72.7	75.6	90.3	105.7	111.9	157.1	163.7	201.2	237.7	133
	-43.1	-45.3	-40.1	-45.2	-56.5	-60.8	-69.4	-79.2	-86.8	-100.0	134
	7.8	7.3	6.5	13.2	3.8	5.5	-4.6	-13.2	-5.9	-3.5	135

	Item	1978	1979	1980	1981	1982	1983	1984	1985
136	Private	0.0	0.0	-0.2	-0.3	-1.3	0.5	-0.9	-2.0
137	Official [h]	5.0	1.7	2.6	2.7	4.6	4.6	7.5	3.6
138	Current balance	1.6	-4.8	-22.2	-20.2	-19.1	-24.2	-16.3	-5.5
139	Direct investment	–	–	–	–	–	–	–	–
140	Portfolio investment	–	–	–	–	–	–	–	–
141	Other long-term capital	2.4	2.8	18.1	11.5	4.5	2.9	-3.2	-3.2
142	Other short-term capital [i]	-2.5	5.1	-2.2	10.5	12.5	3.8	4.7	-1.1
143	Net errors and omissions [i]	-1.3	-3.1	6.3	-2.9	8.2	13.7	9.5	11.3
144	Overall balance	0.2	–	–	-1.1	6.1	-3.8	-5.3	1.5
145	Allocation of SDRs	–	–	–	0.1	–	–	–	–
146	Monetary movements	-0.2	–	–	1.1	-6.1	3.8	5.3	-1.5
	INTERNATIONAL RESERVES								*Million US dollars;*
147	Total	0.57	0.71	0.95	1.21	8.45	4.58	5.17	4.63
148	Gold, national valuation [j]	–	–	–	0.06	0.04	0.04	0.04	0.04
149	Foreign exchange [k]	0.35	0.37	0.49	0.61	7.91	4.07	5.12	4.57
150	Reserve position in the Fund	0.22	0.22	0.38	0.35	0.33	0.47	–	–
151	SDRs	–	0.12	0.08	0.19	0.17	–	0.01	0.02
	EXCHANGE RATES								*Rufiyaa per*
152	End of period	8.625	7.550	7.550	7.550	7.050	7.050	7.050	7.129
153	Average of period	8.969	7.489	7.550	7.550	7.174	7.050	7.050	7.098
	EXTERNAL INDEBTEDNESS								*Million US dollars;*
154	Total outstanding and disbursed	8.9	12.8	25.8	38.9	65.2	77.2	82.9	83.0
155	Long-term	3.9	6.8	24.8	36.9	42.2	48.2	49.9	49.0
156	Public and publicly guaranteed	3.9	6.8	24.8	36.9	42.2	48.2	49.9	49.0
157	Private non-guaranteed	–	–	–	–	–	–	–	–
158	Short-term	5.0	6.0	1.0	2.0	23.0	29.0	33.0	34.0
159	Use of IMF credit	–	–	–	–	–	–	–	–
	Debt Service								*Transactions*
160	Principal repayments on LT debt	–	–	–	0.2	0.7	2.6	14.1	6.6
161	Interest on long-term debt	–	0.1	0.3	0.4	0.8	1.6	2.0	1.8
162	Interest on short-term debt	0.7	0.5	0.3	1.9	2.5	3.2	3.1	1.8
	Average terms of new commitments								
163	Interest (%)	2.2	0.7	2.9	3.1	7.0	7.2	8.6	5.8
164	Maturity (years)	18.5	42.7	14.7	16.5	11.3	23.4	18.1	24.7
165	Grace period (years)	4.8	9.1	4.4	5.5	3.2	4.1	3.4	5.8
166	Grant element (%)	50.4	77.8	41.1	44.3	19.6	28.5	21.8	33.7

Footnotes:

a   Include finance.
b   Until 1984, these include current deposits, call deposits and other sight deposits in both Rufiyaa and foreign currency, and demand deposits of non-residents. Beginning 1985, these refer to Rufiyaa demand deposits only, excluding government deposits and deposits of non-residents.
c   Refer to time and saving and all foreign currency deposits, excluding government deposits and deposits of non-residents from 1985 onward.
d   Data relating to the period prior to 1986 are not directly comparable with data from 1986 onward due to changes in coverage and compilation methodology. External trade figures have been changed to reflect BOP trade account figures.
e   Jet fuel has been removed from services receipts and included in re-exports.
f   Government imports have been adjusted upward in 1993.
g   Service payments have been increased to reflect 15 percent of loan disbursements as consultancy and other service related from 1993 onward. This estimate of 15 percent will be revised to reflect actual figures from the Department of External Resources (DER).
h   The source of official transfers has been changed from the Ministry of Finance and Treasury (MOFT) to the Department of External Resources (DER) from 1994 onward, as DER includes more components of grant aid than MOFT.
i   Private capital movements have been separated from net errors/omissions from 1992 onward.
j   Calculated on the basis of cost of acquisition as given in the accounts of the monetary authority.
k   Relates to holdings of the Treasury and the State Trading Organization until June 1981 and to the holdings of the Monetary Authority thereafter.

	1986	1987	1988	1989	1990	1991	1992	1993	1994	1995	
	-1.5	-2.4	-5.0	-5.1	-7.4	-16.6	-18.9	-26.5	-22.2	-26.6	136
	9.3	9.7	11.5	18.3	11.2	22.1	14.3	13.3	16.3	23.0	137
	-0.3	8.1	9.0	10.7	9.8	-9.0	-19.7	-53.8	-11.1	-16.5	138
	–	–	–	–	–	–	–	–	–	–	139
	–	–	–	–	–	–	–	–	–	–	140
	-3.4	-0.3	-2.2	1.0	5.1	11.6	17.1	3.8	8.2	22.6	141
	–	–	–	–	–	–	17.5	20.7	13.1	33.9	142
	7.0	3.7	7.3	-15.8	-13.3	8.8	-13.8	13.4	-2.1	-24.6	143
	3.3	11.5	14.1	-4.1	1.6	11.4	1.1	-15.9	8.1	15.3	144
	–	–	–	–	–	–	–	–	–	–	145
	-3.3	-11.5	-14.1	4.1	-1.6	-11.4	-1.1	15.9	-8.1	-15.3	146
As of end of period											
	6.95	8.23	21.63	24.81	24.42	23.51	28.23	26.19	31.26	47.95	147
	0.04	0.04	0.04	0.04	0.04	0.04	0.04	0.04	0.04	–	148
	6.89	8.18	21.56	24.74	24.35	23.44	26.97	24.91	29.89	46.57	149
	–	–	–	–	–	–	1.21	1.21	1.28	1.31	150
	0.02	0.01	0.03	0.03	0.03	0.03	0.01	0.03	0.05	0.07	151
US dollar											
	7.244	9.395	8.525	9.205	9.620	10.320	10.535	11.105	11.770	11.770	152
	7.151	9.223	8.785	9.041	9.552	10.253	10.569	10.957	11.586	11.770	153
As of end of period											
	68.7	72.9	71.3	66.8	78.0	81.2	97.1	114.7	126.7	...	154
	58.7	61.9	59.3	54.4	64.0	78.0	92.7	111.7	125.7	...	155
	58.7	61.9	59.3	54.4	64.0	78.0	92.7	111.7	125.7	...	156
	–	–	–	–	–	–	–	–	–	...	157
	10.0	11.0	12.0	12.4	14.0	3.2	4.4	3.0	1.0	...	158
	–	–	–	–	–	–	–	–	–	...	159
during the year											
	9.1	4.9	6.9	7.4	5.9	5.4	5.2	5.8	6.4	7.3 *	160
	2.2	1.6	1.8	1.4	1.4	1.5	1.5	2.4	2.9	3.8 *	161
	0.7	0.9	1.1	1.1	1.5	0.7	0.3	0.3	0.1	...	162
	5.2	1.3	7.1	3.5	0.8	9.9	1.5	3.4	4.7	...	163
	21.4	28.3	11.4	27.7	37.5	6.8	27.0	17.7	13.9	...	164
	1.1	6.8	3.0	6.8	9.2	1.2	6.9	6.8	3.7	...	165
	28.0	64.4	16.7	52.8	77.7	-0.3	62.7	41.2	30.8	...	166

Item	1978	1979	1980	1981	1982	1983	1984	1985
								Thousand;
001 **POPULATION** [a]	29.20	30.40	31.68	32.94	34.30	35.71	37.18	38.71
								Thousand;
002 **LABOR FORCE**	...	...	7.309	...	...	...	...	...
003 Employed	...	...	6.598	...	...	...	...	...
004 Agriculture [b]	...	...	3.044	...	...	...	...	...
005 Manufacturing	...	...	0.114	...	...	...	...	...
006 Mining	...	...	...	...	...	...	...	...
007 Others	...	...	3.440	...	...	...	...	...
008 Unemployed	...	...	0.711	...	...	...	...	...
009 Unemployment rate, %	...	...	9.728	...	...	...	...	...
NATIONAL ACCOUNTS [c] *At Current Market Prices*								**Thousand US dollars;**
010 GDP	...	...	...	27152	30564	36543	39513	38406
At Constant 1991 Prices								
011 GDP	...	...	...	...	37487	43612	44786	43628
Per Capita GDP, US dollars								
012 Current prices	...	...	...	824	891	1023	1063	992
013 Constant *1991* prices	...	...	...	...	1093	1221	1205	1127
PRODUCTION Agriculture								**Short tons** [d]**;**
014 1. Copra	5876	6488	6257	5760	5773	6491	4483	4301
015 2. Taro	...	...	...	...	...	...	...	...
016 3. Pandanus	...	...	...	...	...	...	...	...
017 4. Breadfruit	...	...	...	...	...	...	...	...
018 5. Banana	...	...	...	...	...	...	...	...
019 6. Sweet potatoes	...	...	...	...	...	...	...	...
020 7. Vegetables	...	...	...	...	...	...	...	...
021 8. Papaya	...	...	...	...	...	...	...	...
ENERGY Electricity, *'000 kWh*								*Annual*
022 Production [e]	...	...	...	...	...	...	...	...
023 Exports	...	...	...	...	...	...	...	...
024 Imports	...	...	...	...	...	...	...	...
025 Consumption [e]	...	...	...	...	...	...	...	...
PRICE INDEXES								*Period*
026 Consumer (Majuro), *4th Qtr 1982 = 100*	...	...	...	...	...	102.8	108.2	108.0
027 Food	...	...	...	...	...	104.5	108.2	105.6
028 Non-food	...	...	...	...	...	100.5	108.2	111.2
029 Implicit GDP deflator, *1991 = 100*	...	...	...	...	81.5	83.8	88.2	88.0
GOVERNMENT FINANCE *Central Government*								*Million US dollars;*
030 Current revenue	...	...	...	...	...	...	...	...
031 Taxes	...	...	...	...	...	...	...	...
032 Non-taxes	...	...	...	...	...	...	...	...
033 Current expenditure	...	...	...	...	...	...	...	...
034 Current surpus/deficit	...	...	...	...	...	...	...	...
035 Capital receipts	...	...	...	...	...	...	...	...

	1986	1987	1988	1989	1990	1991	1992	1993	1994	1995	
As of 30 June											
	40.29	41.93	42.69	44.41	46.19	48.04	49.97	51.98	53.75	55.58	001
For the Census year											
	...	...	11.488	...	...	...	...	...	...	...	002
	...	...	10.056	...	...	...	...	...	...	...	003
	...	...	2.178	...	...	...	...	...	...	...	004
	...	...	0.946	...	...	...	...	...	...	...	005
	...	...	0.002	...	...	...	...	...	...	...	006
	...	...	6.930	...	...	...	...	...	...	...	007
	...	...	1.432	...	...	...	...	...	...	...	008
	...	...	12.465	...	...	...	...	...	...	...	009
Fiscal year ending 30 September											
	49007	55130	61874	63721	68691	72219	79709	87059	94596	105239	010
	53419	60453	66157	66713	71410	72219	72246	75180	72296	80146	011
	1216	1315	1449	1435	1487	1503	1595	1675	1760	1894	012
	1326	1442	1550	1502	1546	1503	1446	1446	1345	1442	013
Calendar year											
	6815	5405	5475	5805	5159	4213	5861	4627	4836	7728	014
	...	...	...	1203	1190	1450	1120	...	...	...	015
	...	...	...	889	890	920	659	...	...	...	016
	...	...	...	654	660	710	507	...	...	...	017
	...	...	...	237	250	290	265	...	...	...	018
	...	...	...	159	175	200	125	...	...	...	019
	...	...	...	71	116	150	109	...	...	...	020
	...	...	...	47	50	70	22	...	...	...	021
values											
	...	35717	38072	38911	42912	45759	48252	53303	57891	61668	022
	...	...	...	...	...	...	...	...	...	...	023
	...	...	...	...	...	...	...	...	...	...	024
	...	35717	38072	38911	42912	45759	48252	53303	57891	61668	025
averages											
	112.5	111.9	114.7	117.2	118.0	122.7	135.3	142.0	150.1	161.0	026
	108.0	104.8	109.7	114.7	118.5	122.6	132.1	135.5	137.5	142.6	027
	118.7	121.4	121.5	120.5	117.3	122.7	139.8	151.0	167.3	186.2	028
	91.7	91.2	93.5	95.5	96.2	100.0	110.3	115.8	130.8	131.3	029
Fiscal year ending 30 September											
	14.3	15.9	18.9	21.6	24.1	23.7	22.6	24.5 *	27.6 *	...	030
	10.8	11.0	11.3	13.7	13.8	14.7	16.7	17.4 *	18.2 *	...	031
	3.6	4.9	7.5	7.9	10.3	9.0	5.9	7.1 *	9.4 *	...	032
	39.2	45.7	44.0	46.8	51.3	58.6	62.8	59.0 *	65.0 *	...	033
	-24.9	-29.8	-25.1	-25.2	-27.2	-34.9	-40.2	-34.6 *	-37.4 *	...	034
	–	–	–	–	–	–	–	–	–	...	035

Item	1978	1979	1980	1981	1982	1983	1984	1985
036 Capital expenditure	...	...	...	...	...	...	...	...
037　Capital account surplus/deficit	...	...	...	...	...	...	...	...
038 Net lending	...	...	...	...	...	...	...	...
039 Overall surplus/deficit	...	...	...	...	...	...	...	...
Financing								
040　Domestic borrowing	...	...	...	...	...	...	...	...
041　Foreign borrowing	...	...	...	...	...	...	...	...
042　Foreign grants	...	...	...	...	...	...	...	...
043　Use of cash balances	...	...	...	...	...	...	...	...
EXTERNAL TRADE								*Thousand US dollars;*
044 Exports, fob	...	3397	2577	2968	2225	3143	5522	2691
045 Imports, fob I cif [f]	10791	14238	17155	22208	18777	17503	22608	29176
046　Trade balance	...	-10841	-14578	-19240	-16552	-14360	-17086	-26485
Exports, by principal commodity								
047　1. Crude coconut oil	...	2993	1832	2253	1766	2794	5202	2417
048　2. Chilled fish	...	...	...	...	–	–	...	...
049　3. Frozen fish	...	...	...	...	–	–	...	...
050　4. Pet fish	...	62	50	73	60	58	49	37
051　5. Copra cake	...	84	462	341	304	320	241	195
052　6. Handicraft	...	258	233	301	95	29	30	33
Imports, fob I cif, by SITC section [f]								
053　Food & live animals	3809	4221	4678	5183	5215	...	...	...
054　Beverage & tobacco	1146	1475	1792	2234	1884	...	...	...
055　Crude materials excl. fuels	98	235	342	407	192	...	...	...
056　Mineral fuels, etc.	1553	2086	2718	3317	3684	...	...	...
057　Animal, vegetable oil & fats	4	19	22	23	33	...	...	...
058　Chemicals	525	611	657	703	681	...	...	...
059　Basic manufactures	1651	2252	2976	3548	1525	...	...	...
060　Machines, transport equipment	998	1676	2013	4274	1966	...	...	...
061　Misc. manufactured goods	1007	1663	1957	2519	1031	...	...	...
062　Unclassified goods	–	–	–	–	2566	...	...	...
Direction of Trade								*Thousand US dollars;*
063 Imports, Total, fob I cif [f]								
064　1. United States	...	...	...	...	...	...	16266	20942
065　2. Japan	...	...	...	...	...	...	5098	6097
066　3. Australia	...	...	...	...	...	...	66	1370
067　4. Hong Kong	...	...	...	...	...	...	259	311
068　5. New Zealand	...	...	...	...	...	...	85	163
069　6. Taipei, China	...	...	...	...	...	...	200	108
070　7. Fiji	...	...	...	...	...	...	...	...
071　8. Philippines	...	...	...	...	...	...	23	41
BALANCE OF PAYMENTS [h]								*Thousand US dollars;*
072 Merchandise exports, fob	...	...	...	...	...	...	...	...
073 Merchandise imports, fob	...	...	...	...	...	...	...	...
074　Trade balance	...	...	...	...	...	...	...	...
075 Other goods, services and income	...	...	...	...	...	...	...	...
076　Credit	...	...	...	...	...	...	...	...
077　Debit	...	...	...	...	...	...	...	...
078 Unrequited transfer	...	...	...	...	...	...	...	...
079　Private	...	...	...	...	...	...	...	...
080　Official	...	...	...	...	...	...	...	...

	1986	1987	1988	1989	1990	1991	1992	1993	1994	1995	
	1.7	11.8	14.0	18.7	19.8	13.9	16.8	17.9 *	14.4 *	...	036
	-1.7	-11.8	-14.0	-18.7	-19.8	-13.9	-16.8	-17.9 *	-14.4 *	...	037
	–	–	2.3	-2.3	3.9	3.9	7.5	–	–	...	038
	-26.6	-41.6	-41.4	-41.6	-50.9	-52.7	-64.5	-52.5 *	-51.8 *	...	039
	...	...	...	...	...	...	...	...	...	...	040
											041
	23.8	53.8	53.4	45.9	52.3	45.3	43.0	40.5 *	43.5 *	...	042
	...	...	...	...	...	...	...	...	...		043
Calendar year											
	1159	1918	2108	2489	1719	2890	9201	7660	22170	23071	044
	30571	33541	33764 I	44389 g	55591	56442	61839	61082	70398	75055	045
	-29412	-31623	-31656 I	-41900	-53872	-53552	-52638	-53422	-48228	-51984	046
	974	1654	1743	1679	1148	1396	1137	2142	1952	3147	047
	...	...	1	–	1069	1725	1548	1309	10414	12671	048
	...	16	8	8	32	6822	5744	3640	4687	...	049
	31	8	8	–	268	709	483	383	297	349	050
	128	38	6	99	94	18	109	168	163	201	051
	26	31	1	–	2	4	4	5	19	20	052
	9079	9557	11499 I	...	13615	13717	15132	17757	19861	18056	053
	3424	3612	3254 I	...	3801	5575	3347	4129	4038	3133	054
	428	451	607 I	...	3217	3677	4014	5160	5036	5119	055
	5350	5643	3618 I	...	2738	6288	8524	8528	15323	22520	056
	31	32	18 I	...	319	109	101	167	266	331	057
	1253	1322	681 I	...	2117	1508	1938	2701	2356	1915	058
	4249	4482	1866 I	...	10851	5463	7500	5265	5953	4873	059
	3760	3966	3636 I	...	10916	9172	11153	10495	8716	9599	060
	2996	3161	4108 I	...	8017	10932	976	1379	1882	1724	061
	–	1315	4477 I	...	–	–	9154	5501	6967	7785	062
Calendar year											063
	22168	23713	25502 I	34852	41613	47248	49163	49135	59923	49296	064
	5945	6641	5929 I	6488	8335	5446	7652	5906	4169	5571	065
	1579	2080	1052 I	...	1148	895	2106	1058	1332	1410	066
	382	436	522 I	700	1573	482	836	664	1466	1259	067
	204	268	31 I	736	761	247	1328	709	511	1059	068
	180	201	388 I	196	261	98	233	269	767	622	069
	...	...	... I	452	1133	821	115	198	447	612	070
	23	34	168 I	40	115	241	154	127	269	43	071
Fiscal year ending 30 September											
	1540	1728	2061	2217	2513	...	...	...	...	...	072
	-37476	-40670	-41798	-47088	-53457	...	...	...	...	...	073
	-35936	-38942	-39738	-44871	-50944	...	...	...	...	...	074
	-3651	8807	695	10815	7481	...	...	...	...	...	075
	8726	23792	18265	30702	32630	...	...	...	...	...	076
	-12377	-14984	-17570	-19887	-25149	...	...	...	...	...	077
	35429	63191	69751	66849	69798	...	...	...	...	...	078
	5471	7238	6464	4859	5677	...	...	...	...	...	079
	29959	55953	63287	61989	64120	...	...	...	...	...	080

Item		1978	1979	1980	1981	1982	1983	1984	1985
081	Current balance	...	...	...	...	...	...	...	...
082	Direct investment								
083	Portfolio investment	...	...	...	...	...	...	...	...
084	Other long-term capital								
085	Other short-term capital								
086	Net errors and omissions	...	...	...	...	...	...	...	...
087	Overall balance	...	...	...	...	...	...	...	...
088	Allocation of SDRs	...	...	...	...	...	...	...	...
089	Monetary movements	...	...	...	...	...	...	...	...

090 **EXCHANGE RATES** [i]

Footnotes:

a   For 1978-1993, estimates of mid-year population are based on the 1973 and 1988 censuses. For 1994-95, estimates are based on the 1994 Household Survey of Population and Housing.

b   Data for 1980 includes forestry, fisheries and mining.

c   The Office of Planning and Statistics, with the assistance from ESCAP and Forum Secretariat, has estimated the GDP for 1981-90 based on the income approach while those for 1991-95 were calculated based on the value added approach. All data for this section are provisional.

d   A short ton is approximately equal to 0.9 metric ton.

e   Refers to Majuro only.

f   Import values are on f.o.b. basis up to 1988. For 1979-1988, imports exclude government imports and tax-exempted goods.

g   For 1989, imports, c.i.f. figure was estimated based on three months of complete registration.

h   Balance of payments is presented on a fiscal year basis as nontrade data are derived from budget. Merchandise trade data which are compiled and published on a calendar year basis are converted to a fiscal year basis by Marshall Islands authorities. All data under this section are provisional.

i   The unit of currency of Marshall Islands is US dollar.

1986	1987	1988	1989	1990	1991	1992	1993	1994	1995	
-4158	33056	30708	32792	26335	...	...	...	...	...	081
										082
-6500	11700	-6500	13500	-9467	...	...	...	...	...	083
										084
										085
...	...	...	...	...	...	...	...	...	...	086
-10658	44756	24208	46292	16868	...	...	...	...	...	087
...	...	...	...	...	...	...	...	...	...	088
...	...	...	...	...	...	...	...	...	...	089
										090

Item	1978	1979	1980	1981	1982	1983	1984	1985
								Thousand;
001 **POPULATION**	...	...	73.162[a]	...	...	...	...	91.01
								Thousand;
002 **LABOR FORCE**	...	...	...	...	...	...	...	...
003 Employed	...	...	...	...	...	...	...	...
004 Agriculture	...	...	...	...	...	...	...	...
005 Manufacturing	...	...	...	...	...	...	...	...
006 Mining	...	...	...	...	...	...	...	...
007 Others	...	...	...	...	...	...	...	...
008 Unemployed	...	...	...	...	...	...	...	...
009 Unemployment rate, %	...	...	...	...	...	...	...	...
NATIONAL ACCOUNTS								*Million US dollars;*
At Current Factor Cost								
010 GDP by Industrial Origin	...	...	...	...	...	100.8	...	...
011 Agriculture	...	...	...	...	...	44.9	...	...
012 Mining	...	...	...	...	...	–	...	...
013 Manufacturing	...	...	...	...	...	0.4	...	...
014 Electricity, gas and water	...	...	...	...	...	1.0	...	...
015 Construction	...	...	...	...	...	1.0	...	...
016 Trade	...	...	...	...	...	13.7	...	...
017 Transport and communications	...	...	...	...	...	1.5	...	...
018 Finance	...	...	...	...	...	0.6	...	...
019 Public administration	...	...	...	...	...	31.5	...	...
020 Others	...	...	...	...	...	6.2	...	...
021 Indirect taxes less subsidies	...	...	...	...	...	5.7	...	...
022 GDP at current market prices	...	...	...	...	...	106.5	...	...
023 Net factor income from abroad	...	...	...	...	...	4.5	...	...
024 GNP at current market prices	...	...	...	...	...	111.0	...	...
At Current Market Prices								
025 Expenditure on GDP	...	...	...	...	...	106.5	...	...
026 Private consumption	...	...	...	...	...	89.4	...	...
027 Government consumption	...	...	...	...	...	62.1	...	...
028 Gross fixed capital formation	...	...	...	...	...	37.8	...	...
029 Increase in stocks	...	...	...	...	...	2.4	...	...
030 Exports of goods and services	...	...	...	...	...	3.6	...	...
031 Less: Imports of goods and services	...	...	...	...	...	89.8	...	...
032 Statistical discrepancy	...	...	...	...	...	1.0	...	...
At Constant 1983 I 1995 Prices								
033 GDP by Industrial Origin	...	...	...	...	...	106.5	...	... I
034 Agriculture	...	...	...	...	...	...	...	...
035 Mining	...	...	...	...	...	...	...	...
036 Manufacturing	...	...	...	...	...	...	...	...
037 Electricity, gas and water	...	...	...	...	...	...	...	...
038 Construction	...	...	...	...	...	...	...	...
039 Trade	...	...	...	...	...	...	...	...
040 Transport and communications	...	...	...	...	...	...	...	...
041 Finance	...	...	...	...	...	...	...	...
042 Public administration	...	...	...	...	...	...	...	...
043 Others	...	...	...	...	...	...	...	...
044 Net factor income from abroad	...	...	...	...	...	4.5	...	...
045 GNP	...	...	...	...	...	111.0	...	...
Per Capita GDP, US dollars								
046 Current prices	...	...	...	...	...	...	...	...
047 Constant *1995* prices	...	...	...	...	...	...	...	...

1986	1987	1988	1989	1990	1991	1992	1993	1994	1995	
As of 1 July										
92.93	94.88	96.89	98.69	100.52	101.51	102.49	103.48	104.72	105.99 *	001
Calendar year										
...	...	...	...	30.64	...	...	...	...	...	002
...	...	...	...	26.50	...	...	...	...	...	003
...	...	...	...	12.72	...	...	...	...	...	004
...	...	...	...	1.59	...	...	...	...	...	005
...	...	...	...	–	...	...	...	...	...	006
...	...	...	...	12.19	...	...	...	...	...	007
...	...	...	...	4.14	...	...	...	...	...	008
...	...	...	...	13.51	...	...	...	...	...	009
Calendar year										
117.6	124.8	144.1	147.1	149.0	159.8	165.6	183.0	193.7	204.3 *	010
...	...	...	...	...	...	...	...	...	...	011
...	...	...	...	...	...	...	...	...	...	012
...	...	...	...	...	...	...	...	...	...	013
...	...	...	...	...	...	...	...	...	...	014
...	...	...	...	...	...	...	...	...	...	015
...	...	...	...	...	...	...	...	...	...	016
...	...	...	...	...	...	...	...	...	...	017
...	...	...	...	...	...	...	...	...	...	018
...	...	...	...	...	...	...	...	...	...	019
...	...	...	...	...	...	...	...	...	...	020
4.9	5.0	7.3	8.3	5.7	8.2	8.5	12.0	11.8	11.5 *	021
122.5	129.8	151.4	155.4	154.7	168.0	174.1	195.0	205.5	215.8 *	022
...	...	...	...	...	...	...	...	...	...	023
...	...	...	...	...	...	...	...	...	...	024
122.5	129.8	151.4	155.4	154.7	168.0	174.1	195.0	205.5	215.8 *	025
...	...	...	...	...	...	...	...	...	...	026
...	...	...	...	...	...	...	...	...	...	027
...	...	...	...	...	...	...	...	...	...	028
...	...	...	...	...	...	...	...	...	...	029
...	...	...	...	...	...	...	...	...	...	030
...	...	...	...	...	...	...	...	...	...	031
...	...	...	...	...	...	...	...	...	...	032
178.9	182.0	204.9	201.3	193.5	202.2	199.5	210.9	213.7	215.8 *	033
...	...	...	...	...	...	...	...	...	...	034
...	...	...	...	...	...	...	...	...	...	035
...	...	...	...	...	...	...	...	...	...	036
...	...	...	...	...	...	...	...	...	...	037
...	...	...	...	...	...	...	...	...	...	038
...	...	...	...	...	...	...	...	...	...	039
...	...	...	...	...	...	...	...	...	...	040
...	...	...	...	...	...	...	...	...	...	041
...	...	...	...	...	...	...	...	...	...	042
...	...	...	...	...	...	...	...	...	...	043
...	...	...	...	...	...	...	...	...	...	044
...	...	...	...	...	...	...	...	...	...	045
1318	1368	1563	1575	1539	1655	1699	1885	1962	2036 *	046
1925	1919	2114	2040	1925	1992	1947	2038	2041	2036 *	047

Item	1978	1979	1980	1981	1982	1983	1984	1985
PRODUCTION							*Thousand metric tons;*	
Agriculture, *crop year*								
048 1. Copra (*'000 short tons*)	...	8.5	6.0	4.0	3.2	4.5	3.0	5.8
GOVERNMENT FINANCE							*Million US dollars;*	
Central Government								
049 Current revenue	...	...	...	...	...	...	...	...
050 Taxes	...	...	...	...	...	...	...	...
051 Non-taxes [b]	...	...	...	...	...	...	...	...
052 Current expenditure [c]	...	...	...	...	...	...	...	...
053 Current surplus/deficit	...	...	...	...	...	...	...	...
054 Capital receipts	...	...	...	...	...	...	...	...
055 Capital expenditure	...	...	...	...	...	...	...	...
056 Capital account surplus/deficit	...	...	...	...	...	...	...	...
057 Net lending	...	...	...	...	...	...	...	...
058 Overall surplus/deficit	...	...	...	...	...	...	...	...
Financing								
059 Domestic borrowing (net)	...	...	...	...	...	...	...	...
060 Foreign borrowing (net)	...	...	...	...	...	...	...	...
061 Foreign grants	...	...	...	...	...	...	...	...
062 Use of cash balances [d]	...	...	...	...	...	...	...	...
EXTERNAL TRADE							*Thousand US dollars;*	
063 Exports, fob [e]	1612	3478	3219	2427	2088	1632	2202	2562
064 Imports, fob [f]	22352	25772	28729	38569	43404	48877	38155	41415
065 Trade balance	-20740	-22294	-25510	-36142	-41316	-47245	-35953	-38853
Exports, by principal commodity								
066 1. Trochus shells/meat	...	...	...	...	...	...	334	10
067 2. Copra	...	...	...	...	...	...	1326	1968
068 3. Fish	...	...	...	...	...	...	58	37
069 4. Bananas	...	...	...	...	...	...	30	39
Imports, by SITC section								
070 Food and live animals	...	...	...	...	...	...	13123	14178
071 Beverage and tobacco	...	...	...	...	...	...	4255	5117
072 Crude materials excl. fuels	...	...	...	...	...	...	853	358
073 Mineral fuels, etc. [f]	...	...	...	...	...	...	22	1
074 Animal, vegetable oil & fats	...	...	...	...	...	...	85	38
075 Chemicals	...	...	...	...	...	...	2470	2347
076 Basic manufactures	...	...	...	...	...	...	4700	5550
077 Machines, transport equipment	...	...	...	...	...	...	7341	6578
078 Misc. manufactured goods	...	...	...	...	...	...	4103	6075
079 Unclassified goods	...	...	...	...	...	...	1203	1172
Direction of Trade							*Thousand US dollars;*	
080 Exports, Total	...	...	...	...	...	...	...	...
081 1. Japan	...	...	...	...	...	...	...	...
082 2. United States	...	...	...	...	...	...	...	...
083 3. Marshall Islands	...	...	...	...	...	...	...	...
084 Imports, Total	...	...	...	...	...	...	...	...
085 1. United States	...	...	...	...	...	...	...	...
086 2. Japan	...	...	...	...	...	...	...	...
087 3. Australia	...	...	...	...	...	...	...	...
BALANCE OF PAYMENTS							*Million US dollars;*	
088 Merchandise exports, fob	...	...	...	...	...	3.6	...	...
089 Merchandise imports, fob	...	...	...	...	...	-54.4	...	...
090 Trade balance	...	...	...	...	...	-50.8	...	...

1986	1987	1988	1989	1990	1991	1992	1993	1994	1995	
Calendar year										
1.3	0.7	2.0	1.1	2.3	1.0	...	...	...	...	048
Fiscal year ending 31 December I 30 September										
...	...	28.4	41.5	43.5 I	48.2	54.1	60.5	55.5	51.9 *	049
...	...	12.4	13.4	13.8 I	16.7	17.6	20.5	20.0	20.9 *	050
...	...	16.0	28.1	29.7 I	31.5	36.5	40.0	35.5	31.0 *	051
...	...	96.0	96.2	101.5 I	122.6	124.8	137.7	135.0	134.6 *	052
...	...	-67.6	-54.8	-58.0 I	-74.4	-70.7	-77.2	-79.5	-82.7 *	053
...	...	–	–	– I	–	–	–	–	– *	054
...	...	19.5	29.6	26.3 I	46.3	31.3	31.0	33.7	33.3 *	055
...	...	-19.5	-29.6	-26.3 I	-46.3	-31.3	-31.0	-33.7	-33.3 *	056
...	...	–	–	– I	7.0	-0.9	-2.3	0.0	0.0 *	057
...	...	-87.1	-84.4	-84.3 I	-127.7	-101.1	-105.9	-113.2	-116.0 *	058
...	...	–	–	– I	–	–	–	–	– *	059
...	...	–	–	– I	–	–	–	–	– *	060
...	...	136.7	114.4	118.5 I	118.9	100.4	102.5	103.9	106.9 *	061
...	...	-49.6	-30.0	-34.2 I	8.8	0.7	3.4	9.3	9.1 *	062
Calendar year										
1198	938	2744	2286	3688	11027	...	...	...	...	063
44213	41890	67701	72725	83880	88631	...	...	...	...	064
-43015	-40951	-64958	-70439	-80192	-77604	...	...	...	...	065
263	25	764	–	628	428	...	...	...	...	066
307	136	587	590	346	1041	...	...	...	...	067
98	127	416	501	1836	8628	...	...	...	...	068
37	44	57	88	117	136	...	...	...	...	069
15134	13116	16390	17319	20309	23795	...	...	...	...	070
5130	5201	11659	7394	8874	8549	...	...	...	...	071
156	61	338	182	225	134	...	...	...	...	072
6	5	4063	7182	14485	11692	...	...	...	...	073
15	41	45	25	61	0	...	...	...	...	074
3556	2976	3544	3308	3798	3661	...	...	...	...	075
6257	6680	9868	12237	11500	12757	...	...	...	...	076
6261	6641	9163	11691	12543	12509	...	...	...	...	077
7097	6091	9996	6848	7925	8218	...	...	...	...	078
602	1077	2636	6538	4160	7315	...	...	...	...	079
Calendar year										
...	...	2289	...	...	10532	...	...	...	...	080
...	...	1332	...	...	9280	...	...	...	...	081
...	...	788	...	...	1116	...	...	...	...	082
...	...	125	...	...	38	...	...	...	...	083
...	41890	67701	72725	83880	88631	...	...	...	...	084
...	24757	44631	47305	60492	62188	...	...	...	...	085
...	11714	14873	17063	16516	17078	...	...	...	...	086
...	2760	2666	2185	2201	3316	...	...	...	...	087
Calendar year										
0.9	0.7	2.3	1.8	3.2	...	...	...	...	...	088
-54.8	-53.8	-77.0	-79.0	-91.2	...	...	...	...	...	089
-53.9	-53.1	-74.7	-77.2	-88.0	...	...	...	...	...	090

	Item	1978	1979	1980	1981	1982	1983	1984	1985
091	Other goods, services and income	...	...	...	...	...	-1.3	...	...
092	Credit	...	...	...	...	...	–	...	...
093	Debit	...	...	...	...	...	-1.3	...	...
094	Unrequited transfer	...	...	...	...	...	79.3	...	...
095	Private	...	...	...	...	...	-2.8	...	...
096	Official	...	...	...	...	...	82.1	...	...
097	Current balance	...	...	...	...	...	27.2	...	...
098	Direct investment	...	...	...	...	...	...	...	...
099	Portfolio investment	...	...	...	...	...	...	...	...
100	Other long-term capital	...	...	...	...	...	...	...	...
101	Other short-term capital	...	...	...	...	...	...	...	...
102	Net errors and omissions	...	...	...	...	...	...	...	...
103	Overall balance	...	...	...	...	...	...	...	...
104	Allocation of SDRs	...	...	...	...	...	...	...	...
105	Monetary movements	...	...	...	...	...	...	...	...

Footnotes:

a   Census estimate.
b   Include fishing rights fees.
c   Includes adjustment for transfers to states from 1991 to 1995.
d   Includes net change in deferred payments from 1991 to 1995.
e   Include estimated purchases of handicrafts, souvenirs and gifts from 1984 to 1991.
f   Exclude petroleum products imported through Mobil Oil Micronesia from 1984 to 1987.

1986	1987	1988	1989	1990	1991	1992	1993	1994	1995	
-7.2	-5.1	-6.2	4.6	5.1	...	...	...	...	...	091
9.7	11.2	17.2	28.8	31.6	...	...	...	...	...	092
-16.9	-16.3	-23.4	-24.2	-26.5	...	...	...	...	...	093
86.0	130.9	139.5	124.7	129.5	...	...	...	...	...	094
7.9	7.9	8.4	9.0	9.5	...	...	...	...	...	095
78.1	123.0	131.1	115.7	120.0	...	...	...	...	...	096
24.9	72.7	58.6	52.1	46.6	...	...	...	...	...	097
–	–	–	–		...	...	...	...	...	098
–	–	–	–		...	...	...	...	...	099
–	–	–	–	23.6	...	...	...	...	...	100
–	–	–	–		...	...	...	...	...	101
–	–	–	–		...	...	...	...	...	102
24.9	72.7	58.6	52.1	70.2	...	...	...	...	...	103
...	...	...	...	...	...	...	...	...	...	104
...	...	...	...	...	...	...	...	...	...	105

	Item	1978	1979	1980	1981	1982	1983	1984	1985
001	POPULATION [a]	1.57	1.61	1.66	1.70	1.74	1.79	1.83	*Million;* 1.88
002	LABOR FORCE [b]	...	...	...	...	...	...	...	*Thousand;* 778.7
003	Employed	480.5	495.2	516.0	518.0	523.2	543.0	550.3	589.5
004	Agriculture	196.8	199.2	202.1	195.4	196.3	195.9	189.6	199.7
005	Industry	74.3	77.7	85.4	85.0	92.5	96.8	100.9	108.7
006	Others	209.4	218.3	228.5	237.6	234.4	250.3	259.8	281.1
007	Unemployed	...	...	...	...	...	...	...	...
008	Unemployment rate, %	...	...	...	...	...	...	...	...
	NATIONAL ACCOUNTS *At Current Factor Cost*								*Million Tugriks;*
009	GDP by Industrial Origin	...	...	7550.7	8267.1	9082.7	9674.8	9927.1	10346.9
010	Agriculture	...	...	1043.1	1224.2	1441.2	1561.9	1503.6	1501.6
011	Mining								
012	Manufacturing } [c]	...	...	2084.2	2258.2	2608.7	2887.6	3032.7	3182.2
013	Electricity, gas & water								
014	Construction	...	...	399.7	402.8	411.9	416.1	434.9	452.3
015	Trade	...	...	2066.8	2256.5	2354.6	2454.4	2489.7	2574.2
016	Transport & communications	...	...	855.5	951.7	1039.6	1092.4	1157.6	1259.9
017	Finance								
018	Public administration } [d]	...	...	1101.4	1173.7	1226.7	1262.4	1308.6	1376.7
019	Others								
020	Subsidies at current prices	...	...	-795.6	-841.4	-877.6	-912.5	-931.4	-975.0
021	GDP at current market prices	...	...	6755.1	7425.7	8205.1	8762.3	8995.7	9371.9
022	Net factor income from abroad	...	...	-1037.4	-1073.9	-1098.9	-1131.5	-1168.3	-1216.6
023	GNP	...	...	5717.7	6351.8	7106.2	7630.8	7827.4	8155.3
	At Current Market Prices								
024	Expenditure on GDP	...	...	6755.1	7425.7	8205.1	8762.3	8995.7	9371.9
025	Private consumption }	...	...	5694.5	6200.5	6514.8	6887.2	7232.5	7572.5
026	Government consumption								
027	Gross fixed capital formation }	...	...	3276.2	4670.8	5177.4	4565.2	4668.8	5285.8
028	Increase in stocks								
029	Net exports of goods and services	...	...	-1830.6	-2651.0	-2322.0	-2304.5	-2347.9	-2886.5
030	Statistical discrepancy	...	...	-385.0	-794.5	-1165.1	-385.5	-557.7	-599.8
	At Constant 1993 Market Prices								
031	GDP by Industrial Origin	...	...	124149.4	134523.2	145739.2	154246.2	163392.2	172737.2
032	Agriculture	...	...	40927.9	45116.9	50962.7	51732.0	51107.4	55717.7
033	Mining								
034	Manufacturing } [c]	...	...	36629.3	39715.2	43520.6	48104.0	53692.6	56398.3
035	Electricity, gas & water								
036	Construction	...	...	5129.1	5112.9	5117.0	5243.1	5610.2	5812.0
037	Trade	...	...	21563.9	23502.8	24081.2	25844.2	27949.9	28388.3
038	Transport & communications	...	...	9641.7	10348.0	11012.6	11880.8	12951.8	13945.3
039	Finance								
040	Public administration } [d]	...	...	10257.5	10727.4	11045.1	11442.1	12080.3	12475.6
041	Others								
044	Net factor income from abroad	...	...	-20225.8	-20889.2	-21310.8	-21909.3	-24290.8	-23502.0
045	GNP	...	...	103923.6	113634.0	124428.4	132336.9	139101.4	149235.2
046	Expenditure on GDP	...	...	124149.4	134523.2	145739.2	154246.2	163392.2	172737.2
047	Private consumption	...	...	...	...	...	...	...	...
048	Government consumption	...	...	...	...	...	...	...	...
049	Gross fixed capital formation	...	...	...	...	...	...	...	...
050	Increase in stocks	...	...	...	...	...	...	...	...
051	Net exports of goods and services	...	...	...	...	...	...	...	...
052	Statistical discrepancy	...	...	...	...	...	...	...	...

	1986	1987	1988	1989	1990	1991	1992	1993	1994	1995	
As of 1 July											
	1.92	1.97	2.02	2.07	2.12	2.17	2.20	2.23	2.26	2.29	001
Calendar year											
	806.8	833.6	863.0	903.7	946.7	1003.6	1059.9	1080.9	1089.3	1103.1	002
	643.1	665.4	743.3	764.1	783.6	795.7	806.0	772.8	786.5	794.7	003
	235.2	236.6	243.8	244.3	256.1	274.9	294.2	302.2	336.6	354.3	004
	102.7	108.1	118.0	123.1	131.6	132.2	133.9	124.1	100.9	108.1	005
	305.2	320.7	381.5	396.7	395.9	388.6	377.9	346.5	349.0	332.3	006
	...	21.4	28.9	30.0	45.7	55.4	54.0	71.9	74.9	45.1	007
	...	3.1	3.7	3.8	5.5	6.5	6.3	8.5	8.7	5.4	008
Calendar year											
	10158.1	10618.3	11241.3	12081.9	11822.8	20343.9	48847.2	171869.1	301986.3	...	009
	1805.9	1707.4	1824.5	2046.4	2008.2	3234.5	15008.8	59755.1	105050.7	...	010
										...	011
	3144.8	3308.2	3461.2	3826.7	3909.7	5917.3	15181.2	52327.8	95442.9	...	012
										...	013
	511.9	596.6	675.0	697.7	561.1	791.8	995.7	2724.6	6225.5	...	014
	1929.0	2104.2	2201.8	2405.1	2363.4	5433.8	7770.5	29637.9	40895.5	...	015
	1272.7	1306.6	1356.0	1347.5	1315.4	1117.1	2258.0	7817.6	17296.2	...	016
										...	017
	1493.8	1595.3	1722.8	1758.5	1665.0	3849.4	7633.0	19606.1	37075.5	...	018
										...	019
	-848.1	-908.7	-940.3	-1351.0	-1357.8	-1434.3	-1549.2	-5650.0	-18723.3	...	020
	9310.0	9709.6	10301.0	10730.9	10465.0	18909.6	47298.0	166219.1	283263.0	391103.4	021
	-1257.9	-1358.9	-1287.9	-1186.0	-1169.7	-985.6	-1599.0	-11579.0	-11029.9	-15890.6	022
	8052.1	8350.7	9013.1	9544.9	9295.3	17924.0	45699.0	154640.1	272233.1	375212.8	023
	9310.0	9709.6	10301.0	10730.9	10465.0	18909.6	47298.0	166219.1	283263.0	391103.4	024
	8034.5	8418.2	8879.5	9303.7	9627.8	17188.8	35993.8	145607.9	251254.3	328945.6	025
											026
	5343.9	4437.3	4336.7	4936.2	3579.0	6731.8	13858.3	46042.7	70249.2	96709.1	027
											028
	-3565.7	-2961.4	-2832.8	-2661.3	-2197.7	-4330.3	-1986.5	-8477.2	-15862.7	27097.3	029
	-502.7	-184.5	-82.4	-847.7	-544.2	-680.7	-567.6	-16954.4	-22377.8	-61648.6	030
	188929.1	195461.4	205439.6	214027.7	208641.9	189349.2	171365.4	166219.1	170042.3	180775.4	031
	63861.0	58304.2	60287.0	64908.9	64045.4	61235.4	59958.1	58335.0	59910.9	62453.5	032
											033
	58570.2	62587.3	65578.4	69111.4	69336.5	60701.1	54812.1	51307.8	52174.9	59913.8	034
											035
	6540.7	8095.4	9141.1	9476.0	7144.3	5967.0	3250.9	2724.6	3010.9	3329.3	036
	30382.0	34475.5	36430.1	37651.3	37134.4	32594.3	25205.1	26536.6	26532.8	26564.4	037
	15917.4	16887.0	17976.0	17037.6	16091.2	9851.9	8094.4	7713.7	7539.1	7449.4	038
											039
	13657.8	15112.0	16027.0	15842.5	14890.1	18999.5	20044.8	19601.4	20873.7	21065.0	040
											041
	-24217.1	-26230.7	-24698.4	-22545.0	-21839.5	-8429.9	-4442.0	-11579.0	-10608.4	-10978.3	044
	164712.0	169230.7	180741.2	191482.7	186802.4	180919.3	166923.4	154640.1	159433.9	169797.1	045
	188929.1	195461.4	205439.6	214027.7	208641.9	189349.2	171365.4	166219.1	170042.3	180775.4	046
	...	...	...	...	...	...	...	...	...	...	047
	...	...	...	...	...	...	...	...	...	...	048
	...	...	...	...	...	...	...	...	...	...	049
	...	...	...	...	...	...	...	...	...	...	050
	...	...	...	...	...	...	...	...	...	...	051
	...	...	...	...	...	...	...	...	...	...	052

	Item	1978	1979	1980	1981	1982	1983	1984	1985
	Investment Financing, at current prices								
053	Gross domestic capital formation	...	...	3276.2	4670.8	5177.4	4565.2	4668.8	5285.8
054	Gross national saving	...	...	23.2	151.3	591.4	743.6	594.9	582.8
055	Gross domestic saving	...	...	1060.6	1225.2	1690.3	1875.1	1763.2	1799.4
056	Net factor income from abroad	...	...	-1037.4	-1073.9	-1098.9	-1131.5	-1168.3	-1216.6
057	Foreign saving	...	...	3253.0	4519.5	4586.0	3821.6	4073.9	4703.0
058	Net transfer from abroad	...	...	...	...	...	...	...	...
059	Net borrowing from abroad	...	...	...	...	...	...	...	...
	Per Capita GNP, Tugrik								
060	Current prices	...	...	3444	3736	4084	4263	4277	4338
061	Constant 1993 prices	...	...	62605	66844	71511	73931	76012	79380
	PRODUCTION								*Thousand metric tons;*
	Agriculture								
062	1. Wheat	299	263	230	296	440	648	460	689
063	2. Milk, Mn liters	232	240	219	221	233	235	252	262
064	3. Potatoes	49	72	38	40	75	98	126	114
065	4. Barley	51	59	35	33	68	89	87	132
066	5. Vegetables and melons	26	24	26	29	36	34	35	41
067	6. Oats	25	37	19	13	34	57	38	53
	Mining								
068	1. Lignite and brown coal	3478	3734	3984	3957	4520	4566	4973	6035
069	2. Coal	320	380	392	346	401	408	458	480
070	3. Salt	15	14	9	14	15	14	13	19
	Manufacturing								
071	1. Cement	166	185	178	106	179	165	141	151
072	2. Meat	58	60	57	67	67	64	67	61
073	3. Sawnwood (coniferous), '000 cu.m.	527	577	559	579	647	683	702	686
074	4. Wheat flour	112	141	83	125	120	150	185	176
	Production Indexes								*Period*
075	Agriculture, 1979-81 = 100	102.2	102.3	97.7	100.0	104.1	107.9	104.2	106.7
076	Mining	...	...	...	...	...	...	...	...
077	Manufacturing	...	...	...	...	...	...	...	...
	ENERGY								*Annual*
	Coal, '000 m.t.								
078	Production	...	...	4376	4303	4921	4975	5425	6523
079	Exports	...	...	0	0	259	201	300	225
080	Imports	...	...	2	34	1	2	12	–
081	Consumption [e]	...	...	4378	4337	4663	4776	5137	6298
	Electricity, Mn kWh								
082	Production	...	...	1566	1563	1518	1768	2264	2843
083	Exports	...	...	–	–	–	–	–	–
084	Imports	...	...	263	478	774	694	417	153
085	Consumption [e]	...	...	1829	2041	2292	2462	2681	2996
	Retail Prices, Tug/litre								
086	Gasoline, premium	...	...	0.90	...	...	...	...	...
087	Diesel	...	...	0.54	...	...	...	...	...
	PRICE INDEXES								*Period*
088	Consumer, 1978 = 100\ Jan91 = 100	...	...	100.1	100.0	102.5	102.5	102.5	103.1
089	Implicit GDP deflator, 1993 = 100	...	...	5.44	5.52	5.63	5.68	5.51	5.43
	MONEY AND BANKING								*Million Tugriks;*
090	Money supply (M1)	...	...	2113.6	...	...	...	...	3951.5
091	Currency in circulation	...	...	377.0	...	...	...	...	408.0

	1986	1987	1988	1989	1990	1991	1992	1993	1994	1995	
	5343.9	4437.3	4336.7	4936.2	3579.0	6731.8	13858.3	46042.7	70249.2	96709.1	053
	17.6	-67.5	133.6	241.2	-332.5	735.2	9705.2	9032.2	20978.8	46267.2	054
	1275.5	1291.4	1421.5	1427.2	837.2	1720.8	11304.2	20611.2	32008.7	62157.8	055
	-1257.9	-1358.9	-1287.9	-1186.0	-1169.7	-985.6	-1599.0	-11579.0	-11029.9	-15890.6	056
	5326.3	4504.8	4203.1	4695.0	3911.5	5996.6	4153.1	37010.5	49270.4	50441.9	057
	...	...	...	...	...	...	...	...	...	...	058
	...	...	...	...	...	...	...	...	...	...	059
	4194	4239	4462	4611	4385	8260	20772	69345	120457	163848	060
	85788	85904	89476	92504	88114	83373	75874	69345	70546	3538	061
Calendar year											
	664	543	672	687	596	538	453	450	322	257	062
	290	290	292	310	307	302	299	284	312	343	063
	133	148	103	156	131	97	79	60	54	52	064
	146	102	100	108	89	48	35	22	6	4	065
	47	48	55	59	42	23	16	23	23	27	066
	50	38	37	38	30	7	4	6	2	0	067
	6567	7110	7916	7352	6562	4837	4290	4040	3655	3581	068
	497	655	690	692	595	2200	1957	1569	1355	1290	069
	21	16	13	13	6	1	0	0	1	1	070
	425	541	502	513	441	227	133	82	86	109	071
	62	63	59	58	54	47	25	17	11	11	072
	624	581	541	553	509	270	125	84	50	61	073
	186	194	196	200	190	174	182	176	127	196	074
averages	113.2	108.7	107.5	115.6	115.3	118.0	101.9	96.5	97.8	98.2	075
	...	...	...	...	...	...	...	...	...	...	076
	...	...	...	...	...	...	...	...	...	...	077
values											
	7065	7765	8606	8045	7157	7037	6247	5617	5158	5020	078
	300	611	1041	776	490	121	88	–	–	–	079
	–	–	73	77	73	–	–	–	–	–	080
	6765	7154	7638	7346	6740	6916	6159	5617	5158	5020	081
	3170	3349	3544	3568	3348	3229	2929	2582	2715	2629	082
	–	–	–	–	–	–	–	–	–	–	083
	87	70	75	158	228	84	102	197	215	381	084
	3257	3419	3619	3726	3576	3313	3031	2779	2930	3010	085
	1.25	1.25	1.25	1.25	1.25	10.50	52.00	...	...	...	086
	1.13	1.13	1.13	1.13	1.13	1.13	50.00	...	...	...	087
averages	102.1	102.1	102.1	102.1	102.1	143.3	363.7	1339.8	2513.0	3939.7	088
	4.93	4.97	5.01	5.01	5.02	9.99	27.60	100.00	166.58	216.35	089
As of end of period											
	2738.1	2835.2	3021.7	3506.0	4750.0	7313.7	7640.2	18548.4	32871.2	42636.5	090
	439.9	490.0	526.1	581.1	742.7	2003.0	2896.4	10786.1	21804.8	29755.7	091

Item	1978	1979	1980	1981	1982	1983	1984	1985
092 Demand deposits	...	...	1736.6	...	...	...	...	3543.5
093 Quasi-money	...	...	479.3	...	...	...	...	901.1
094 Money supply (M2)	...	...	2592.9	...	...	...	...	4852.6
095 Foreign assets (net)	...	...	109.8	...	...	...	...	189.2
096 Domestic credit	...	...	3572.6	...	...	...	...	5687.0
097 Claims on govt. sector (net) [f]	...	...	3189.5	...	...	...	...	5404.4
098 Claims on private sector	...	...	383.1	...	...	...	...	282.6
099 Claims on other financial insts. [g]	...	...	...	...	...	...	...	–
100 Other items	...	...	-1089.5	...	...	...	...	-1023.6
Interest Rates								**Per cent;**
On deposits								
101 Savings	...	...	...	...	...	...	...	6.0
102 Time: 12 months	...	...	...	...	...	...	...	8.0
GOVERNMENT FINANCE								**Million Tugriks;**
Central Government								
103 Current revenue	2834.3	3167.9	3452.6	3720.3	4182.5	4477.7	4680.4	4918.0
104 Taxes [h]	2577.1	2846.3	3129.2	3368.8	3793.4	4096.1	4272.8	4415.4
105 Non-taxes [h]	257.2	321.6	323.4	351.5	389.1	381.6	407.6	502.6
106 Current expenditure	2828.3	3182.7	3392.4	3696.4	4094.7	4330.1	4606.3	4765.4
107 Current surplus/deficit	6.0	-14.8	60.2	23.9	87.8	147.6	74.1	152.6
108 Capital receipts	...	...	...	...	...	...	...	...
109 Capital expenditure [i]	432.7	573.4	651.6	573.5	662.0	795.6	776.8	935.5
110 Capital account surplus/deficit	-432.7	-573.4	-651.6	-573.5	-662.0	-795.6	-776.8	-935.5
111 Net lending [j]	...	...	...	...	...	...	...	...
112 Overall surplus/deficit	-426.7	-588.2	-591.4	-549.6	-574.2	-648.0	-702.7	-782.9
Financing								
113 Domestic borrowing	...	...	...	...	...	...	...	...
114 Foreign borrowing	589.7	643.9	620.7	649.0	647.0	678.3	750.5	823.0
115 Foreign grants	...	...	...	...	...	...	...	...
116 Use of cash balances [k]	-163.0	-55.7	-29.3	-99.4	-72.8	-30.3	-47.8	-40.1
Expenditure by Function, Central Govt.								
117 Total [l]	2408.7	2751.8	2934.3	3215.2	3591.0	3774.5	4027.7	4157.7
118 General public services	455.0	512.2	581.6	621.6	641.5	664.5	691.6	712.6
119 Defence } [m]								
120 Education								
121 Health } [n]								
122 Social security & welfare	1249.4	1397.4	1494.9	1612.2	1723.7	1819.3	1903.5	1999.4
123 Housing & community amenities }								
124 Economic services	590.9	642.5	608.1	656.3	849.9	821.1	985.7	932.8
125 Agriculture	...	...	...	...	...	...	...	...
126 Industry	...	...	...	...	...	...	...	...
127 Electricity, gas & water	...	...	...	...	...	...	...	...
128 Transport and communications	...	...	...	...	...	...	...	...
129 Other economic services	...	...	...	...	...	...	...	...
130 Others	113.4	199.7	249.7	325.1	375.9	469.6	446.9	512.9
EXTERNAL TRADE								**Million US dollars;**
131 Exports, fob	180.8	212.2	402.8	468.8	561.7	609.8	674.4	689.3
132 Imports, cif	225.3	246.8	547.8	703.7	790.8	928.1	975.2	1095.5
133 Trade balance	-44.5	-34.6	-145.0	-234.9	-229.1	-318.3	-300.8	-406.2
Direction of Trade								**Million US dollars;**
134 Exports, Total	180.8	212.2	402.8	468.8	561.7	609.8	674.4	689.3
135 1. Russia [o]	...	...	319.6	...	...	...	...	530.7
136 2. China, People's Rep. of	...	...	3.8	...	...	...	...	2.7
137 3. Japan	...	...	0.8	...	...	...	...	7.6
138 4. Kazakstan	...	...	...	...	...	...	...	...
139 5. Switzerland	...	...	–	...	...	...	...	6.6

	1986	1987	1988	1989	1990	1991	1992	1993	1994	1995	
	2298.2	2345.2	2495.6	2924.9	4007.3	5310.7	4743.8	7762.3	11066.4	12880.8	092
	1461.8	1539.2	1752.5	1577.9	883.2	2601.1	5412.1	24215.8	43905.8	59408.1	093
	4199.9	4374.4	4774.2	5083.9	5633.2	9914.8	13052.3	42764.2	76777.0	102044.6	094
	-358.0	-197.1	38.9	267.0	-331.6	495.4	-27.0	23395.7	29699.3	51709.7	095
	5520.3	5433.0	5786.1	5902.7	6988.6	10971.2	16078.2	24460.3	49190.3	45494.7	096
	5223.2	5127.1	5397.2	5512.0	6472.8	7895.9	9152.5	14601.0	8420.2	-6344.5	097
	297.1	305.9	388.9	391.0	515.8	3075.3	6925.7	9859.3	40638.0	51653.5	098
	–	–	–	–	–	–	–	–	132.1	185.7	099
	-962.4	-861.5	-1050.8	-1085.8	-1023.8	-1551.8	-2998.9	-5091.8	-2112.6	4840.2	100

As of end of period

	1986	1987	1988	1989	1990	1991	1992	1993	1994	1995	
	3.0	3.0	3.0	3.0	3.0	4.0	10-52	24-100	10-64	12-43	101
	4.0	4.0	4.0	4.0	4.0	6.0	50-70	70-153	50-101	12.5-101	102

Calendar year

	1986	1987	1988	1989	1990	1991	1992	1993	1994	1995	
	4360.6	4540.4	4680.7	5209.0	5289.0	6055.2	11289.6	51816.4	82194.0	127512.7	103
	3860.7	4047.2	4210.5	4836.0	4262.0	5145.8	10231.0	49810.1	67596.4	109269.5	104
	499.9	493.2	470.2	373.0	1027.0	909.4	1058.6	2006.3	14597.6	18243.2	105
	4924.8	5116.0	5226.9	5383.0	5435.0	9778.0	13401.0	41553.3	74676.2	105536.2	106
	-564.2	-575.6	-546.2	-174.0	-146.0	-3722.8	-2111.4	10263.1	7517.8	21976.5	107
	...	...	...	3.0	6.0	9.9	11.6	–	672.1	3751.2	108
	1131.4	1292.6	1514.8	1630.0	1276.0	1019.0	4497.0	8269.9	10550.6	22559.3	109
	-1131.4	-1292.6	-1514.8	-1627.0	-1270.0	-1009.1	-4485.4	-8269.9	-9878.5	-18808.1	110
						-1867.7	-5537.1	11838.7	16099.3	19635.1	111
	-1695.6	-1868.2	-2061.0	-1801.0	-1416.0	2864.2	-1059.7	-9845.5	-18460.0	-16466.7	112
				193.0	318.0	...	...	...	...	...	113
	...	...	...	1608.0	1098.0	...	...	...	...	...	114
	1750.5	1901.3	2066.8			432.1	615.2	3026.9	3265.3	5010.5	115
	-54.9	-33.1	-5.8	–	–	-3296.3	444.5	6818.6	15194.7	11456.2	116
	4316.5	4488.8	4547.2	4735.8	4828.5	8929.3	12360.9	61661.9	101326.1	147730.6	117
	790.2	792.5	813.2	777.0	680.6	910.1	888.3	3615.1	8392.5	12540.8	118
						991.0	1794.8	6424.9	11249.9	17073.9	119
						2049.0	3273.2	9595.6	16439.0	23415.3	120
						1109.7	1944.4	6329.7	11609.9	17754.4	121
	2095.3	2228.6	2371.6	2445.7	2612.1	1050.2	1577.5	5717.8	13459.2	21887.3	122
						631.3	898.3	3370.8	5337.2	6358.1	123
	718.2	664.7	583.2	699.2	649.5	1860.1	1692.2	12332.0	26776.8	34395.0	124
	...	...	...	...	...	282.0	639.2	1539.3	2182.7	2791.3	125
	...	...	...	...	...	544.2	389.1	1139.1	9829.1	14330.6 *	126
	...	...	...	...	...	422.3	131.3	3348.0	7522.2	10597.0	127
	...	...	...	...	...	414.6	324.3	1276.3	4576.2	3593.4	128
	...	...	...	...	...	197.0	208.3	5029.3	2666.6	3082.7	129
	712.8	803.0	779.2	813.9	886.3	327.9	292.2	14276.0	8061.6	14305.8 *	130

Calendar year

	1986	1987	1988	1989	1990	1991	1992	1993	1994	1995	
	716.0	717.9	739.1	721.5	660.7	348.0	388.4	382.6	367.5	511.6	131
	1839.7	1104.6	1113.6	963.0	924.0	360.9	418.3	379.0	258.4	388.7	132
	-1123.7	-386.7	-374.5	-241.5	-263.3	-12.9	-29.9	3.6	109.1	122.9	133

Calendar year

	1986	1987	1988	1989	1990	1991	1992	1993	1994	1995	
	716.0	717.9	739.1	721.5	660.7	348.0	388.4	382.6	367.5	511.6	134
	563.3	559.7	558.7	528.4	517.5	235.2	219.7	201.4	103.8	66.9	135
	3.3	3.7	3.1	4.2	11.3	52.8	69.4	120.2	73.2	73.2	136
	6.3	8.4	21.9	24.5	7.6	11.7	18.7	17.1	45.0	95.6	137
							...	...	52.1	77.7	138
	8.4	8.4	8.4	7.9	1.2	1.0	16.4	10.4	22.4	67.6	139

	Item	1978	1979	1980	1981	1982	1983	1984	1985
140	6. Korea, Rep. of	...	...	–	...	...	...	...	–
141	7. Italy	...	...	0.3	...	...	...	...	0.9
142	8. United States	...	...	0.1	...	...	...	...	0.1
143	9. United Kingdom	...	...	2.8	...	...	...	...	2.8
144	10. Germany	...	...	14.7	...	...	...	...	24.3
145	Imports, Total	225.3	246.8	547.8	703.7	790.8	928.1	975.2	1095.5
146	1. Russia [o]	...	...	469.8	...	...	...	...	951.6
147	2. China, People's Rep. of	...	...	3.6	...	...	...	...	4.9
148	3. Japan	...	...	0.7	...	...	...	...	1.8
149	4. United States	...	...	–	...	...	...	...	–
150	5. Hong Kong	...	...	–	...	...	...	...	–
151	6. Germany	...	...	14.3	...	...	...	...	29.7
152	7. Korea, Rep. of	...	...	–	...	...	...	...	–
153	8. Singapore	...	...	–	...	...	...	...	–
154	9. Switzerland	...	...	2.0	...	...	...	...	1.3
155	10. Czechoslovakia I Czech Rep.	...	...	19.1	...	...	...	...	29.0

Trade Indexes
Unit value index *1980 = 100;*

				1980	1981	1982	1983	1984	1985
156	Exports	...	...	100	106	116	111	118	125
157	Imports	...	...	100	107	124	127	143	146
158	Terms of Trade	...	...	100	99	94	87	83	86

BALANCE OF PAYMENTS [p]
Million US dollars;

				1980	1981	1982	1983	1984	1985
159	Merchandise exports, fob	...	...	402.26	437.42	518.43	558.56	594.31	568.30
160	Merchandise imports [q]	...	...	-676.46	-767.97	-888.75	-1011.01	-935.37	-1006.09
161	Trade balance	...	...	-274.21	-330.54	-370.32	-452.44	-341.06	-437.79
162	Turnkey projects	...	...	-184.98	-470.14	-463.38	-355.81	-369.03	-363.26
163	Services balance	...	...	-31.20	-5.22	-12.40	-19.18	-27.32	-14.48
164	Receipts	...	...	40.80	38.58	49.49	56.41	53.43	71.89
165	Expenditures	...	...	-72.00	-43.79	-61.89	-75.59	-80.75	-86.36
166	Unrequited transfers	...	...	146.38	-0.10	-0.14	-0.09	-0.09	-0.14
167	Private	...	...	-0.08	-0.10	-0.14	-0.09	-0.09	-0.14
168	Official	...	...	146.45	–	–	–	–	–
169	Current balance	...	...	-344.01	-806.00	-846.23	-827.53	-737.49	-815.68
170	Direct investment	...	...	...	...	...	...	...	...
171	Portfolio investment	...	...	...	...	...	...	...	...
172	Other long-term capital [r]	...	...	417.80	805.63	859.02	742.97	743.43	755.93
173	Other short-term capital [s]	...	...	–	0.68	7.69	0.88	-0.23	3.61
174	Net errors and omissions	...	...	-73.88	-0.33	-16.96	80.60	10.40	86.95
175	Overall balance	...	...	-0.10	-0.02	3.51	-3.07	16.11	30.82
176	Allocation of SDRs	...	...	...	...	...	...	...	...
177	Monetary movements	...	...	0.10	0.02	-3.51	3.07	-16.11	-30.82

INTERNATIONAL RESERVES
Million US dollars;

				1980	1981	1982	1983	1984	1985
178	Total	...	...	20.10	21.20	24.50	20.80	35.00	58.70
179	Gold, national valuation [t]	...	...	11.00	12.60	13.10	13.50	12.90	18.00
180	Foreign exchange	...	...	9.10	8.60	11.40	7.30	22.10	40.70
181	Reserve position in the Fund	...	...	0.00	0.00	0.00	0.00	0.00	0.00
182	SDRs	...	...	0.00	0.00	0.00	0.00	0.00	0.00

EXCHANGE RATES [u]
Tugriks per

				1980	1981	1982	1983	1984	1985
183	End of period	...	...	2.96	3.11	3.31	3.41	3.79	3.40
184	Average of period	...	...	2.90	3.19	3.24	3.30	3.54	3.71

EXTERNAL INDEBTEDNESS
Million US dollars;

				1980	1981	1982	1983	1984	1985
185	Total outstanding and disbursed	...	...	...	...	...	...	...	2.8
186	Long-term	...	...	...	...	...	...	...	2.8

1986	1987	1988	1989	1990	1991	1992	1993	1994	1995	
–	–	–	–	–	0.5	1.6	1.3	19.1	25.5	140
0.1	0.3	0.1	1.8	5.5	4.7	8.8	10.5	8.7	11.3	141
0.1	0.1	1.5	0.1	0.9	0.3	4.4	4.3	12.4	29.9	142
2.8	3.9	1.6	4.9	3.0	1.9	3.8	1.2	5.1	19.4	143
24.6	24.5	22.5	22.5	13.7	10.2	12.1	3.0	2.4	6.5	144
1839.7	1104.6	1113.6	963.0	924.0	360.9	418.3	379.0	258.4	388.7	145
988.8	963.6	957.2	797.2	716.2	238.3	214.3	221.6	148.8	202.0	146
9.6	15.8	12.9	19.9	22.3	16.3	57.6	65.9	23.9	39.4	147
3.4	2.7	5.0	6.9	9.8	2.8	40.1	20.8	16.7	44.5	148
–	–	–	–	–	1.3	1.8	17.2	11.4	14.1	149
–	–	0.1	–	2.7	0.8	9.6	10.3	10.7	5.9	150
27.3	25.8	24.9	25.9	37.4	12.5	22.1	6.7	10.0	14.8	151
–	–	–	–	0.9	7.3	8.1	4.3	14.9	20.3	152
–	–	0.2	0.4	0.7	0.9	6.4	3.7	3.6	7.0	153
3.4	1.3	3.4	4.1	5.9	6.6	5.1	2.3	3.5	0.6	154
27.2	20.9	33.1	20.7	34.0	9.7	5.4	0.6	3.3	8.3	155

Period averages

1986	1987	1988	1989	1990	1991	1992	1993	1994	1995	
117	122	127	122	122	...	...	...	...	...	156
154	159	162	147	143	...	...	...	...	...	157
76	77	78	83	85	...	...	...	...	...	158

Calendar year

1986	1987	1988	1989	1990	1991	1992	1993	1994	1995	
742.66	818.80	815.80	795.80	444.80	346.50	355.80	365.80	367.00	...	159
-1331.61	-1362.10	-1393.60	-1911.80	-1023.60	-501.20	-400.00	-374.50	-344.80	...	160
-588.95	-543.30	-577.80	-1116.00	-578.80	-154.70	-44.20	-8.70	22.20	...	161
-512.13	-469.50	-385.20	...	...	...	...	...	...	...	162
37.67	20.10	11.60	-124.40	-72.60	-5.80	-25.40	-31.10	-22.10	...	163
84.43	...	...	...	53.10	26.50	35.20	26.80	4.30	...	164
-46.76	...	...	...	-125.70	-32.30	-60.60	-57.90	-26.40	...	165
-0.20	-0.30	0.00	–	7.40	41.60	35.20	70.90	76.77	...	166
-0.20	...	...	–	–	–	-2.70	-0.10	0.20	...	167
–	...	...	–	7.40	41.60	37.90	71.00	76.57	...	168
-1063.61	-993.00	951.40	-1240.00	-644.00	-118.90	-34.40	31.10	76.87	...	169
...	...	...	–	–	–	2.00	7.70	6.98	...	170
...	...	...	...	...	...	...	...	...	...	171
1053.91	1115.80	1083.80	1228.40	516.70	130.30	86.30	21.30	11.46	...	172
6.06	-20.00	-75.20	-33.30	66.80	-23.40	-57.60	-38.60	-51.04	...	173
25.62	-68.40	-52.30	51.20	7.20	-80.10	-8.90	5.20	-34.97	...	174
21.98	34.40	4.90	5.90	-53.20	-92.10	-12.60	26.70	9.30	...	175
...	...	...	...	...	...	...	...	...	...	176
-21.98	-34.40	-4.90	-5.90	53.20	92.10	12.60	-26.70	-9.30	...	177

End of period

1986	1987	1988	1989	1990	1991	1992	1993	1994	1995	
71.50	146.90	150.00	279.10	145.50	125.64	40.54	65.05	92.39	151.53	178
18.00	18.50	19.70	19.00	22.90	49.70	24.20	5.31	11.00	34.50	179
53.50	128.40	130.30	260.10	122.60	75.90	16.32	59.70	78.49	114.50	180
0.00	0.00	0.00	0.00	0.00	0.00	0.01	0.01	0.01	0.01	181
0.00	0.00	0.00	0.00	0.00	0.04	0.01	0.03	2.89	2.52	182

US dollar

1986	1987	1988	1989	1990	1991	1992	1993	1994	1995	
3.06	2.84	3.00	3.00	5.63	40.00	40.00	396.51	414.09	473.62	183
3.18	2.89	2.89	3.00	5.63	24.92	40.00	...	412.72	448.61	184

As of end of year

1986	1987	1988	1989	1990	1991	1992	1993	1994	1995	
6.5	8.3	7.5	7.7	25.3	190.1	350.3	374.6	443.0	...	185
6.5	8.3	7.5	7.7	25.3	173.8	272.2	328.3	382.4	...	186

Item	1978	1979	1980	1981	1982	1983	1984	1985
187 Public and publicly guaranteed	...	...	...	...	...	...	...	2.8
188 Private non-guaranteed	...	...	...	...	...	...	...	...
189 Short-term	...	...	...	...	...	...	...	...
190 Use of IMF credit	...	...	...	...	...	...	...	...
Debt Service								*Transactions*
191 Principal repayments on LT debt	...	...	...	...	...	...	...	...
192 Interest on long-term debt	...	...	...	...	...	...	...	...
193 Interest on short-term debt	...	...	...	...	...	...	...	...
Average terms of new commitments								
194 Interest (%)	...	...	...	...	...	...	...	3.0
195 Maturity (years)	...	...	...	...	...	...	...	12.5
196 Grace period (years)	...	...	...	...	...	...	...	3.0
197 Grant element (%)	...	...	...	...	...	...	...	34.9

FOOTNOTES:

a   Mid-year estimates based on start-of-year values.

b   Total labor force consists of economically active population in working age and working people who are outside the working age. By definition, the working age for female is 16-54 years and 16-59 years for male.

c   Collectively referred to as Industry in Mongolia State Statistical Office publications.

d   Refers to services and others in Mongolia State Statistical Office publications.

e   Includes net stocks.

f   Includes state enterprises.

g   Residual for domestic credit.

h   Social security contribution is classified as non-tax revenue before 1991. Thereafter, it is included as tax revenue.

i   Includes net lending for 1989-92.

j   Refers to the balance between total expenditure and the sum of current and capital expenditures for 1991-92. Refers to net lending and foreign amortization for 1993-95.

k   Balancing item for financing of the overall surplus/deficit.

l   Total for expenditure by function for 1978-90 refers only to current expenditures less the amount of "wages and salaries" which cannot be allocated to each of the functions.

m   Defence includes public order and safety for 1991-95.

n   Includes recreation, culture, arts and sports for 1991-95.

o   USSR for 1980, 1985-90, CIS for 1991-93.

p   Prior to 1989 conversion of BOP data from transferable ruble to US dollars was done using official cross rates

q   For trade with the former CMEA areas, imports are in cif; for trade under bilateral clearing arrangements and with convertible currency areas, imports are both in fob and cif bases. For 1989-95, imports are in cif.

r   Refers to medium/long-term capital based on BOP with the former CMEA areas and under bilateral clearing arrangements and disbursements and amortization of capital not classified whether long-term or short-term for BOP with convertible currency areas.

s   Includes other short-term capital, non-residents' bank deposits and International Bank for Economic Cooperation (IBEC) balance.

t   Latest valuation of gold is at 4300 tugriks per gram on June 6, 1993.

u   In May 1993, in accordance with the Government's decision, Mongolia adopted a free market exchange rate. From 1993, data refers to the midpoint of the average buying and selling rates that are freely determined on the basis of market transactions between commercial banks and the non-bank public.

1986	1987	1988	1989	1990	1991	1992	1993	1994	1995	
6.5	8.3	7.5	7.7	25.3	173.8	272.2	328.3	382.4	...	187
...	...	...	...	...	–	–	–	–	...	188
...	...	...	...	...	0.2	59.2	14.7	5.3	...	189
...	...	...	...	...	16.1	18.9	31.6	55.3	...	190
during the year										
...	...	0.8	0.8	1.2	0.9	56.1	10.3	30.0	...	191
...	...	0.1	0.2	0.2	0.1	9.4	6.1	7.9	...	192
...	...	...	...	...	...	0.7	2.3	0.9	...	193
...	...	...	...	6.2	1.9	5.4	1.1	0.9	...	194
...	...	8.3	...	5.7	24.4	8.5	34.8	39.8	...	195
...	...	1.7	...	2.2	7.3	3.4	9.8	10.3	...	196
...	...	36.7	...	11.4	57.3	21.3	75.1	79.5	...	197

Item	1978	1979	1980	1981	1982	1983	1984	1985
001 **POPULATION** [a]	31.85	32.45	33.11	33.78	34.46	35.66	36.36	*Million;* 37.07
002 **LABOR FORCE**	13.36	13.65	14.01	14.41	14.85	14.93	15.20	*Million;* 15.47
003 Employed	12.94	13.21	13.52	13.79	14.19	14.50	14.79	15.13
004 Agriculture	8.70	8.86	9.03	9.21	9.40	9.59	9.77	9.96
005 Manufacturing	0.97	1.01	1.06	1.10	1.15	1.20	1.23	1.29
006 Mining	0.07	0.07	0.07	0.07	0.09	0.09	0.09	0.09
007 Others	3.20	3.27	3.36	3.41	3.55	3.62	3.70	3.79
008 Unemployed	0.42	0.44	0.49	0.62	0.66	0.43	0.41	0.34
009 Unemployment rate, %	3.14	3.22	3.50	4.30	4.44	2.88	2.70	2.20
NATIONAL ACCOUNTS *At Current Market Prices*								*Million Kyats;*
010 GDP by Industrial Origin	31800	35333	38609	42879	46811	49823	53597	55989
011 Agriculture	14058	16203	17970	20330	22319	23711	25795	26983
012 Mining	316	410	427	430	501	504	545	534
013 Manufacturing	3172	3363	3683	4009	4350	4775	5280	5561
014 Electricity, gas and water	98	126	135	167	210	227	263	278
015 Construction	419	503	647	692	833	872	946	945
016 Trade	9283	9670	10121	10714	11512	12273	12886	13389
017 Transport and communications	960	1215	1357	1612	1834	1985	2106	2218
018 Finance	564	648	829	1039	1096	1172	1254	1332
019 Public administration	1687	1766	1837	2032	2215	2266	2397	2568
020 Others	1243	1429	1603	1855	1941	2038	2125	2182
021 Net factor income from abroad	-93	-145	-160	-168	-347	-510	-517	-581
022 GNP	31707	35188	38449	42711	46464	49313	53080	55408
023 Expenditure on GDP	31800	35333	38609	42879	46811	49823	53597	55989
024 Private consumption	27404	29088	31775	35218	39747	42685	47395	49532
025 Government consumption								
026 Gross fixed capital formation	5364	7389	7228	8635	10044	9057	8477	8650
027 Increase in stocks	414	487	1065	1206	331	-95	-367	44
028 Exports of goods and services	1842	2679	3176	3432	3003	3373	3133	2566
029 Less: Imports of goods and services	3224	4310	4635	5611	6314	5197	5041	4802
030 Statistical discrepancy	–	–	–	–	–	–	–	–
At Constant 1985/86 Prices								
031 GDP by Industrial Origin	39261	41112	44362	47157	49714	51878	54437	55989
032 Agriculture	18197	19166	21262	22904	24307	25443	26424	26983
033 Mining	340	396	382	399	432	446	513	534
034 Manufacturing	3839	3965	4237	4529	4770	4968	5403	5561
035 Electricity, gas and water	119	131	150	181	212	229	264	278
036 Construction	518	621	674	783	836	879	953	945
037 Trade	10597	10843	11256	11493	11892	12358	12910	13389
038 Transport and communications	1345	1464	1560	1759	1937	2046	2166	2218
039 Finance	694	789	988	1080	1116	1175	1256	1332
040 Public administration	1827	1908	1975	2100	2243	2284	2412	2568
041 Others	1785	1829	1878	1929	1969	2050	2136	2182
042 Net factor income from abroad	-66	-105	-91	-91	-184	-270	-274	-308
043 GNP	39195	41007	44271	47066	49530	51608	54163	55681
044 Expenditure on GDP	39261	41112	44362	47157	49714	51878	54437	55989
045 Private consumption	33465	34621	37481	39802	42879	44916	48523	49532
046 Government consumption								
047 Gross fixed capital formation	6763	8056	7880	8963	10178	9142	8546	8650
048 Increase in stocks	511	566	1224	1326	355	-108	-383	44
049 Exports of goods and services	2194	2658	2800	2888	2729	3153	2819	2566
050 Less: Imports of goods and services	3672	4789	5022	5822	6427	5225	5067	4802
051 Statistical discrepancy	–	–	–	–	–	–	–	–

	1986	1987	1988	1989	1990	1991	1992	1993	1994	1995	
Mid-fiscal year											
	37.80	38.54	39.29	40.03	40.79	41.55	42.33	43.12	43.92	44.74	001
Fiscal year beginning 1 April											
	15.68	15.61	...	...	16.53	16.95	18.98	19.47	19.98	20.49	002
	15.41	15.40	15.14	15.22	15.74	16.01	16.47	16.82	17.23	17.59	003
	9.95	10.00	10.02	10.08	10.32	10.52	10.78	10.97	11.12	11.27	004
	1.17	1.15	1.09	1.14	1.13	1.12	1.20	1.25	1.41	1.48	005
	0.08	0.08	0.08	0.08	0.08	0.08	0.08	0.09	0.11	0.12	006
	4.21	4.17	3.95	3.92	4.21	4.29	4.41	4.51	4.59	4.72	007
	0.27	0.21	...	...	0.69	0.71	0.79	0.81	0.83	0.85	008
	1.72	1.35	...	...	4.17	4.19	4.16	4.16	4.15	4.15	009
Fiscal year beginning 1 April											
	59028	68698	76243	124666	151941	186802	249395	351333	436427	475158	010
	29633	37990	43739	71069	86999	109888	150902	221986	273270	295200	011
	483	478	512	988	1036	1158	1305	1705	2041	2784	012
	5450	5338	5723	10731	11824	13059	17278	22426	29935	34325	013
	289	289	321	435	386	318	463	649	1178	1680	014
	976	970	833	1538	2763	3863	4507	5211	7450	8026	015
	13526	14581	15849	27156	34542	41640	56456	76949	97504	106595	016
	2311	2459	2240	3346	4045	4967	5604	6414	7738	8238	017
	1421	1498	1538	222	270	318	367	516	694	788	018
	2673	2770	2997	5747	6024	6413	6692	8528	9385	9995	019
	2266	2326	2491	3434	4052	5178	5823	6949	7233	7527	020
	-658	-520	-261	-305	47	-291	-153	-429	-375	-272	021
	58370	68178	75982	124361	151988	186511	249242	350904	436052	474886	022
	59028	68698	76243	124666	151941	186802	249395	351333	436427	475158	023
	53067	63168	67754	113726	134188	160610	217384	312559	388026	417321	024
											025
	8617	8683	7296	11827	22318	27571	31184	37258	48378	52237	026
	-1139	-742	2467	-325	-1995	1032	2601	5211	4368	9562	027
	2419	1655	2169	2834	2953	2926	3590	4228	4773	5562	028
	3936	4066	3443	3395	5523	5337	5365	7923	9117	9525	029
	–	–	–	–	–	–	–	–	–	–	030
	55397	53178	47141	48883	50260	49933	54757	58001	61950	66716	031
	27120	25819	22595	23589	24022	23451	25914	27013	28665	30746	032
	498	430	343	448	443	492	590	719	810	960	033
	5123	4870	4094	4555	4560	4376	4850	5323	5799	6556	034
	289	301	283	323	340	363	475	588	601	626	035
	947	898	688	913	1240	1452	1615	1804	1979	2094	036
	12820	11993	10558	11118	11385	11104	12087	12697	13638	14721	037
	2259	2328	1989	2188	2267	2438	2730	2957	3107	3264	038
	1421	1498	1604	229	268	316	363	498	670	760	039
	2659	2746	2787	3287	3426	3574	3678	3859	4046	4250	040
	2261	2296	2199	2232	2310	2368	2454	2543	2636	2739	041
	-571	-442	-222	-205	-195	-69	-34 *	-25 *	-27 *	...	042
	54826	52736	46919	48678	50065	49864	54723 *	57976 *	61923 *	...	043
	55397	53178	47141	48883	50260	49933	54757	58001	61950	66716	044
	49053	47629	41065	41826	42199	40315	43543	46755	49632	53079	045
											046
	8272	7556	5399	6453	8852	9188	9250	10236	11936	12889	047
	-1083	-578	1024	-77	-618	353	412	212	393	500	048
	3068	2496	2762	3528	4038	3926	5381	6229	6062	6593	049
	3913	3924	3109	2846	4213	3848	3830	5431	6074	6346	050
	–	–	–	–	–	–	–	–	–	–	051

Item	1978	1979	1980	1981	1982	1983	1984	1985
Investment Financing, at current prices								
052 Gross domestic capital formation	5778	7876	8293	9840	10375	8962	8110	8693
053 Gross national saving	4303	6100	6675	7493	6717	6628	5685	5876
054 Gross domestic saving	4396	6245	6835	7661	7064	7138	6202	6457
055 Net factor income from abroad	-93	-145	-160	-168	-347	-510	-517	-581
056 Foreign saving	1475	1776	1619	2347	3658	2334	2425	2817
Per Capita GNP, Kyats								
057 Current prices	996	1084	1161	1264	1348	1383	1460	1495
058 Constant *1985/86* prices	1231	1264	1337	1393	1437	1447	1490	1502
PRODUCTION								***Thousand metric tons;***
Agriculture								
059 1. Paddy	10528	10283	13107	13923	14146	14062	14030	14091
060 2. Sugarcane	1841	1438	2003	2693	3660	3605	3708	3792
061 3. Groundnut	390	337	431	564	541	523	656	551
062 4. Sesamum	209	108	155	177	195	204	249	245
063 5. Maize (seeds)	77	125	163	203	235	305	299	294
064 6. Gram	96	38	101	153	124	171	136	168
065 7. Cotton	52	49	63	94	96	102	124	98
066 8. Jute	96	95	97	32	63	54	51	49
Mining								
067 1. Zinc concentrates	4.9	5.5	7.4	6.5	10.0	8.4	9.5	8.1
068 2. Dolomite, *'000 long tons*	1.9	2.2	3.8	4.2	1.3	4.6	2.9	1.1
069 3. Refined lead	4.9	6.2	6.0	6.6	7.8	7.6	7.0	9.5
Manufacturing [b]								
070 1. Cement	254.0	390.6	385.3	317.4	344.2	334.7	311.2	430.2
071 2. Fertilizer	125.0	126.0	134.0	129.0	110.0	117.0	124.0	273.0
072 3. Bricks & tiles, *Mn pcs.*	41.8	40.3	43.0	45.9	41.2	42.2	45.2	38.5
073 4. Salt	303.8	258.1	82.3	85.3	75.2	99.6	81.3	93.6
074 5. Sugar	38.3	37.0	41.5	47.4	41.3	47.1	61.7	59.5
075 6. Paper	13.4	12.8	13.4	18.4	17.8	18.5	18.3	20.5
076 7. Cotton	14.4	13.5	14.5	14.2	19.3	17.1	21.1	13.8
077 8. Aluminum ware, *Mn lbs.*	1.6	1.8	1.1	1.5	2.6	2.2	1.1	1.1
Production Indexes								***Period***
078 Agriculture, *1979-81 = 100*	92.4	93.7	99.3	107.3	116.9	122.6	130.6	138.4
079 Mining, *1969/70* | *1985/86 = 100*	150.0	171.5	167.7	178.0	182.3	188.5	223.6 |	100.0
080 Manufacturing, *1969/70* | *1985/86 = 100*	122.2	126.5	135.6	145.5	152.0	157.7	167.9 |	100.0
ENERGY								***Annual***
Crude petroleum, *'000 m.t.*								
081 Production	1413	1514	1559	1431	1478	1438	1585	1451
082 Exports	0	40	53	0	0	0	0	0
083 Imports	0	0	0	0	0	0	0	0
084 Consumption	1230	1274	1315	1350	1368	1438	1585	1451
Coal, *'000 m.t.* [b]								
085 Production	21	14	11	14	31	30	42	43
086 Imports	210	200	210	215	200	180	30	40
087 Consumption	231	212	224	226	218	210	72	83
Natural gas, *terajoules*								
088 Production	10648	11279	13293	16394	16440	20100	26980	36420
089 Consumption	10648	11279	13293	16394	16440	20100	26980	36420
Electricity, *Mn kWh* [b]								
090 Production	977	1081	1228	1394	1552	1675	1890	2119
091 Consumption	1243	1340	1340	1517	1715	1675	1890	2119
Retail prices, *Kyats/litre* [c]								
092 Gasoline, premium	0.77	0.77	0.77	0.77	0.77	0.77	0.77	0.77
093 Diesel	0.55	0.55	0.55	0.55	0.55	0.55	0.55	0.55

1986	1987	1988	1989	1990	1991	1992	1993	1994	1995	
7479	7941	9763	11501	20323	28603	33786	42469	52745	61800	052
5303	5010	8228	10635	17800	25901	31858	38345	48026	57565	053
5961	5530	8489	10940	17753	26192	32011	38774	48401	57837	054
-658	-520	-261	-305	47	-291	-153	-429	-375	-272	055
2176	2931	1535	866	2523	2702	1928	4124	4719	4235	056
1544	1769	1934	3107	3726	4489	5888	8139	9928	10614	057
1450	1368	1194	1216	1227	1200	1293 *	1345 *	1410 *	...	058

Fiscal year beginning 1 April

13904	13420	12956	13586	13748	12993	14603	16495	17908	19259 *	059
3379	3510	2309	2163	2072	2392	3356	2804	2320	3132 *	060
535	511	431	451	465	372	426	425	493	560 *	061
196	167	143	204	212	168	233	220	299	345 *	062
281	220	190	191	184	188	205	201	280	212 *	063
151	162	72	100	102	110	99	59	76	104 *	064
79	71	59	62	61	62	68	42	85	211 *	065
46	41	46	33	24	22	38	27	34	43 *	066
8.5	5.1	6.1	4.3	4.5	2.8	3.0	2.4	8.7	2.0	067
0.6	1.1	1.5	0.5	3.2	2.9	2.1	1.3	4.2	3.5	068
5.3	4.0	3.7	3.9	1.7	2.2	2.2	1.6	1.8	1.8	069
442.9	389.6	349.0	441.3	420.2	449.8	471.9	406.5	477.1	525.2	070
319.0	273.0	244.0	192.0	153.0	110.0	97.0	171.0	149.4	139.2	071
49.5	51.7	50.3	60.9	60.7	62.2	55.3	62.8	58.7	62.9	072
52.8	65.0	67.1	67.1	27.4	47.8	47.8	59.9	59.9	82.5	073
55.2	50.5	27.4	31.7	28.6	35.7	50.2	47.6	48.4	41.5	074
15.7	9.1	7.6	15.1	11.3	12.1	13.4	14.5	14.5	16.7	075
10.9	9.7	8.3	6.9	9.3	5.3	3.3	3.7	4.1	4.9	076
0.7	–	0.2	0.3	0.3	0.3	0.3	0.3	0.0	...	077

averages

140.2	138.8	130.5	116.7	118.3	119.5	124.9	137.3	149.7	159.9	078
97.6	81.2	64.1	86.7	85.9	95.4	116.4	147.6	164.3	...	079
164.8	167.0	77.5	86.1	86.6	83.8	93.7	102.1	111.0	...	080

values

1430	979	762	889	825	700	750	...	...	...	081
0	0	2	10	12	5	6	...	...	...	082
0	0	120	1	125	30	33	...	...	...	083
1430	979	880	880	938	725	777	...	...	...	084
43	39	27	44	31	37	34	32	36	38	085
40	40	0	0	0	0	0	...	...	...	086
83	79	23	47	35	35	34	...	...	...	087
42310	43567	44745	...	...	...	...	...	...	...	088
42310	43567	44745	...	...	...	...	...	...	...	089
2245	2320	2226	2494	2546	2631	2852	3326	3554	3876	090
2245	2320	2226	2494	2622	2650	2674	3326	3127	...	091
0.77	0.77	3.52	3.52	3.52	3.52	3.52	3.52	4.34	...	092
0.55	0.55	2.31	2.31	2.31	2.31	2.31	2.31	3.18	...	093

	Item	1978	1979	1980	1981	1982	1983	1984	1985
	PRICE INDEXES								*Period*
094	Consumer (Yangon), *1978\ 1986 = 100*	100.0	106.1	107.2	107.5	112.0	118.3	124.0	132.5 I
095	Food, *1986 = 100*[d]	...	...	...	...	...	...	...	...
096	Non-food, *1986 = 100*[e]	...	...	...	...	...	...	...	...
097	Wholesale, *1978 = 100*[e]	100.0	101.7	105.6	98.4	100.8	104.5	107.5	...
098	Implicit GDP deflator, *1985/86 = 100*	81.0	85.9	87.0	90.9	94.2	96.0	98.5	100.0
	MONEY AND BANKING								*Million Kyats;*
099	Money supply (M1)	6357	7064	7916	9157	9844	11128	12830	11612
100	Currency in circulation	5783	6448	7289	8410	9045	10165	11768	10505
101	Demand deposits	574	616	627	747	799	963	1062	1107
102	Quasi-money	953	1481	2015	2853	3721	4574	5638	6533
103	Money supply (M2)	7310	8545	9931	12010	13565	15702	18468	18145
104	Foreign assets (net)	98	888	1489	1272	235	23	-110	-863
105	Domestic credit	8766	10015	11720	13551	16495	19174	22300	25817
106	Claims on govt. sector (net)	6405	8008	9591	11013	14027	16549	19909	23069
107	Claims on private sector	2361	2007	2129	2538	2468	2625	2391	2748
108	Claims on other financial insts.	...	...	...	...	...	...	...	...
109	Other items	-1554	-2358	-3278	-2813	-3165	-3495	-3722	-6809
	Deposit Money Banks								
110	Demand deposits [f]	574	616	627	747	799	963	1062	1107
111	Savings deposits	759	1118	1429	1939	2434	2930	3610	4233
	GOVERNMENT FINANCE								*Million Kyats;*
	Central Government [g]								
112	Current revenue	4765	5490	6263	7226	7343	7479	7908	7703
113	Taxes	3183	3608	3711	4257	4602	4602	4601	4622
114	Non-taxes	1582	1882	2552	2969	2741	2877	3307	3081
115	Current expenditure	3292	3439	3842	4340	4514	4622	4540	5140
116	Current surplus/deficit	1473	2051	2421	2886	2829	2857	3368	2563
117	Capital receipts	1	3	5	3	2	2	2	3
118	Capital expenditure	682	952	1219	1291	1940	1919	1841	2052
119	Capital account surplus/deficit	-681	-949	-1214	-1288	-1938	-1917	-1839	-2049
120	Net lending	...	...	...	...	...	...	...	...
121	Overall surplus/deficit	792	1102	1207	1598	891	940	1529	514
	Financing								
122	Domestic borrowing	...	...	...	...	...	...	...	...
123	Foreign borrowing								
124	Foreign grants	596	788	922	854	1114	912	998	1292
125	Use of cash balances	-1388	-1890	-2129	-2452	-2005	-1852	-2527	-1806
	EXTERNAL TRADE								*Million Kyats;*
126	Exports, fob	2066	2588	2733 I	3453	3036	3420	3195	2654
127	Imports, cif	3235	3783	4882 I	5611	6314	5197	5041	4802
128	Trade balance	-1169	-1195	-2149 I	-2158	-3278	-1778	-1847	-2148
	Exports, by SITC section								
129	Food and live animals	677	1122	1406 I	1958	1648	1787	1440	1157
130	Beverage and tobacco	...	...	... I	7	1	...	...	0
131	Crude materials excl. fuels	774	1200	927 I	1130	1166	1250	1396	1220
132	Mineral fuels, etc.	65	105	145 I	127	23	85	55	16
133	Animal, vegetable oil & fats	–	–	– I	–	–	–	–	–
134	Chemicals	12	1	– I	3	4	24	6	27
135	Basic manufactures	522	134	203 I	176	123	211	211	104
136	Machines, transport equipment	–	–	– I	–	–	–	–	–
137	Misc. manufactured goods	–	3	2 I	8	10	17	14	11
138	Unclassified goods	–	–	– I	24	29	13	12	31
139	Re-exports	16	23	50 I	20	32	33	61	88

	1986	1987	1988	1989	1990	1991	1992	1993	1994	1995	
averages											
	100.0	123.9	144.8	184.2	216.6	286.5	349.3	460.0	571.5	715.4	094
	100.0	126.7	152.9	196.4	234.2	322.0	394.4	547.7	658.4	828.8	095
	100.0	118.9	129.7	161.4	184.0	220.9	265.8	299.0	410.2	505.3	096
	...	...	...	...	...	...	...	...	...	...	097
	106.6	129.2	161.7	255.0	302.3	374.1	455.5	605.7	704.5	712.2	098
As of end of period											
	16404	9713	15931	21536	32333	43737	60200	74982	98323	131800	099
	15218	8299	14659	19926	29211	39289	54429	68663	90659	119329	100
	1186	1414	1272	1610	3122	4448	5771	6319	7664	12471	101
	7415	8413	7584	9406	11406	13609	17573	23636	33737	54952	102
	23819	18126	23515	30942	43739	57346	77773	98618	132060	186752	103
	-433	-236	...	...	...	...	...	...	...	...	104
	30437	34491	...	...	...	...	...	...	...	...	105
	27432	31498	...	...	...	...	...	...	...	...	106
	3005	2993	...	...	...	...	...	...	...	...	107
	...	...	...	...	...	...	...	...	...	...	108
	-6185	-16129	...	...	...	...	...	...	...	...	109
	1115	1414	1277	1610	3122	4448	5771	6319	7664	12471	110
	4902	5727	5013	6838	8744	10794	14158	19630	28465	...	111
Fiscal year beginning 1 April											
	7284	7053	6257	8934	14539	15704	20102	26327	27227	27694 *	112
	4375	4373	3426	5312	9417	10480	12563	17036	16427	15660 *	113
	2909	2680	2831	3622	5122	5224	7539	9291	10800	12034 *	114
	5525	5381	5925	12284	12841	14573	16420	20089	23821	24621 *	115
	1759	1672	332	-3350	1698	1131	3682	6238	3406	3073 *	116
	6	5	18	2097	45	100	892	1198	711	707 *	117
	2328	2159	1633	2751	6050	8198	9757	12304	16760	16057 *	118
	-2322	-2154	-1615	-654	-6005	-8098	-8865	-11106	-16049	-15350 *	119
	...	...	...	...	...	...	...	...	...		120
	-563	-482	-1283	-4004	-4307	-6967	-5183	-4868	-12643	-12277 *	121
	2250	3679	6680	4202	...	...	...	...	...	...	122
											123
	984	1050	1276	-274	...	...	...	...	...	...	124
	-2671	-4247	-6673	76	4307	6967	5183	4868	12643	12277 *	125
*CY 1978-1980	FY 1981/82 onwards*											
	2514	1679	2193	2847	2962	2932	3655	4228	5405	...	126
	3936	4066	3443	3395	5523	5337	5365	7923	8332	...	127
	-1422	-2387	-1250	-549	-2561	-2405	-1710	-3696	-2927	...	128
	873	501	182	571	867	857	1316	1460	2737	...	129
	...	...	...	...	11	3	0	0	0	...	130
	1276	884	769	968	1271	1244	1219	1555	1524	...	131
	23	28	40	47	8	7	8	9	50	...	132
	–	–	–	–	–	–	–	–	1	...	133
	57	68	46	33	9	1	1	2	2	...	134
	161	144	111	117	205	64	280	199	247	...	135
	–	12	2	1	–	1	1	21	24	...	136
	21	14	12	24	17	69	119	247	367	...	137
	7	4	1006	1073	565	681	646	736	453	...	138
	96	24	24	13	9	6	65	0	0	...	139

	Item	1978	1979	1980	1981	1982	1983	1984	1985
	Exports, by principal commodity								
140	1. Teak and other hardwood	577	870	732	772	804	909	1062	1046
141	2. Pulses and beans	...	...	...	249	264	213	215	238
142	3. Rice and rice products	514	917	1218	1509	1143	1397	1024	763
143	4. Raw rubber	60	74	82	81	60	62	58	56
144	5. Base metals and ores	84	190	130	265	280	301	313	114
145	6. Oilcakes	44	52	46	41	47	58	35	32
	Imports, by SITC section								
146	Food and live animals	51	73	71	94	157	136	93	63
147	Beverage and tobacco	1	–	–	2	14	10	4	3
148	Crude materials excl. fuels	10	16	30	32	74	62	30	23
149	Mineral fuels, etc.	108	63	160	114	163	52	164	100
150	Animal, vegetable oil & fats	76	97	121	172	110	48	249	78
151	Chemicals	288	337	451	836	764	484	577	484
152	Basic manufactures	697	770	948	1177	1238	1008	1207	1194
153	Machines, transport equipment	1873	2270	2876	2849	3459	3098	2436	2452
154	Misc. manufactured goods	121	141	211	296	289	280	268	402
155	Unclassified goods	10	16	14	39	46	19	13	4
	Direction of Trade								_Million US dollars;_
156	Exports, Total	309.0	389.0	415.0	446.1	391.0	378.1	300.6	302.8
157	1. China, People's Rep. of	1.0	8.4	4.9	5.5	4.8	4.6	3.7	3.7
158	2. Singapore	30.1	55.5	59.2	43.4	38.0	36.8	29.2	29.4
159	3. India	1.6	1.9	5.7	10.2	8.9	8.6	6.9	6.9
160	4. Japan	27.8	40.1	41.3	37.3	32.7	31.7	25.2	25.3
161	5. United States	28.2	4.2	2.0	3.4	3.0	2.9	2.3	2.3
162	6. Hong Kong	29.6	46.7	31.4	40.8	35.7	34.6	27.5	27.7
163	7. Malaysia	8.5	15.2	11.6	9.9	8.6	8.4	6.6	6.7
164	8. Pakistan	6.3	4.3	1.9	8.5	7.4	7.2	5.7	5.8
165	9. United Kingdom	9.0	10.0	11.3	7.8	6.8	6.6	5.2	5.3
166	10. Indonesia	26.1	41.1	39.2	31.2	27.3	26.4	21.0	21.2
167	Imports, Total	475.2	572.7	785.5	823.0	408.7	267.8	238.9	282.6
168	1. Singapore	28.6	18.7	47.7	48.1	23.9	15.6	14.0	16.5
169	2. China, People's Rep. of	17.0	20.5	29.3	26.0	12.9	8.5	7.5	8.9
170	3. Malaysia	6.5	9.4	14.9	21.4	10.6	7.0	6.2	7.3
171	4. Japan	183.5	259.4	342.9	321.1	159.5	104.5	93.2	110.3
172	5. Thailand	1.4	1.5	1.3	4.5	2.2	1.5	1.3	1.5
173	6. Hong Kong	1.6	1.7	4.2	5.1	2.5	1.7	1.5	1.8
174	7. Indonesia	0.1	0.1	0.2	0.2	0.1	0.1	0.0	0.1
175	8. Germany	36.7	53.4	58.2	55.1	27.4	17.9	16.0	18.9
176	9. France	5.9	20.1	7.6	20.3	10.1	6.6	5.9	7.0
177	10. United Kingdom	44.9	52.6	68.8	74.5	37.0	24.3	21.6	25.6
	Trade Indexes								_1985/86 = 100;_
	Quantum index								
178	Exports	79.0	119.0	133.0	108.2	108.4	129.1	106.9	100.0
179	Imports	76.0	95.0	106.0	106.0	103.4	90.6	111.5	100.0
	Unit Value Index								
180	Exports	...	...	...	135.2	109.8	110.8	115.7	100.0
181	Imports	...	...	...	97.7	98.2	98.8	99.5	100.0
182	Terms of Trade	...	...	...	138.4	111.8	112.2	116.3	100.0

1986	1987	1988	1989	1990	1991	1992	1993	1994	1995	
1079	745	661	891	999	931	949	1241	1061	...	140
183	131	52	123	515	429	667	724	799		141
523	254	54	266	172	251	249	268	1166	...	142
47	31	13	8	3	34	71	91	122	...	143
155	117	70	68	72	48	27	29	61	...	144
25	21	6	15	11	8	17	26	12	...	145
2	10	12	27	105	192	145	164	463	...	146
0	0	1	2	10	12	16	36	34	...	147
4	13	9	18	29	11	19	26	50	...	148
77	36	57	114	239	185	86	328	284	...	149
59	40	35	73	434	384	397	529	805	...	150
461	290	222	374	312	384	615	1053	607	...	151
765	872	510	371	674	622	861	1354	1457	...	152
2390	2578	1447	1208	2045	1721	1486	2491	2653	...	153
157	205	113	138	206	163	164	314	356	...	154
21	22	1038	1070	1469	1663	1576	1628	1623	...	155

Calendar year

1986	1987	1988	1989	1990	1991	1992	1993	1994	1995	
287.7	218.6	147.4	214.5	417.1	553.8	723.6	889.0	951.7	1150.3	156
3.5	2.7	1.8	2.6	33.3	96.3	119.3	149.7	129.8	136.0	157
28.0	21.2	14.3	20.9	46.2	81.0	98.4	101.3	127.6	148.0	158
6.6	5.0	3.4	4.9	44.2	46.6	94.6	106.5	109.5	127.0	159
24.1	18.3	12.3	18.0	28.4	44.9	43.0	65.0	68.8	85.5	160
2.2	1.7	1.1	1.6	9.4	26.6	37.8	45.6	66.0	80.7	161
26.3	20.0	13.5	19.6	22.9	33.7	44.6	56.1	50.0	58.4	162
6.4	4.8	3.3	4.7	8.6	15.6	17.1	52.4	25.0	35.9	163
5.5	4.2	2.8	4.1	3.8	5.0	29.5	23.7	10.7	28.0	164
5.0	3.8	2.6	3.7	4.7	4.4	8.0	12.4	19.3	14.8	165
20.1	15.3	10.3	15.0	10.1	2.6	10.0	13.8	16.7	18.4	166
304.4	268.4	244.0	194.3	667.7	1068.2	1057.9	1247.8	1590.1	2173.3	167
17.8	15.7	14.2	11.3	119.2	295.8	288.6	368.0	430.3	499.1	168
9.6	8.5	7.7	6.1	137.7	314.8	284.9	357.2	406.0	679.6	169
7.9	7.0	6.3	5.1	31.6	73.7	98.6	114.3	243.5	273.4	170
118.8	104.7	95.2	75.8	110.8	90.8	106.1	110.0	74.6	173.4	171
1.7	1.5	1.3	1.1	19.8	4.2	0.0	0.0	98.3	125.1	172
1.9	1.7	1.5	1.2	8.6	14.7	16.6	44.7	48.8	69.3	173
0.1	0.1	0.0	0.0	3.2	7.3	15.6	43.7	46.0	49.7	174
20.4	18.0	16.3	13.0	31.9	37.8	22.5	38.7	29.4	34.7	175
7.5	6.6	6.0	4.8	15.2	9.2	5.5	7.0	50.1	53.8	176
27.6	24.3	22.1	17.6	25.7	16.0	17.6	31.9	21.9	23.8	177

Period averages

1986	1987	1988	1989	1990	1991	1992	1993	1994	1995	
104.8	76.7	46.4	59.9	63.8	61.2	144.5	172.2	157.0	...	178
83.6	83.8	50.8	59.4	83.8	87.5	80.5	113.1	99.7	...	179
82.5	68.1	83.4	96.4	97.7	91.1	73.8	68.9	91.3	...	180
100.6	103.6	112.2	119.0	131.1	138.7	140.1	145.9	163.2	...	181
82.0	65.7	74.3	81.0	74.5	65.7	52.7	47.2	55.9	...	182

	Item	1978	1979	1980	1981	1982	1983	1984	1985
	BALANCE OF PAYMENTS								*Million US dollars;*
183	Merchandise exports, fob	272	362	429	533	423	375	364	311
184	Merchandise imports, fob	-495	-732	-788	-863	-913	-728	-565	-513
185	Trade balance	-223	-369	-360	-330	-490	-353	-200	-202
186	Other goods, services and income	-19	-47	-68	-68	-75	-79	-85	-84
187	Credit	31	49	66	93	95	68	67	69
188	Debit	-50	-97	-134	-161	-170	-147	-152	-153
189	Unrequited transfers [h]	27	58	80	84	67	82	68	81
190	Private	...	...	...	...	...	...	...	...
191	Official	...	...	...	...	...	...	...	...
192	Current balance [h]	-215	-359	-348	-314	-498	-350	-217	-205
193	Capital account [h]	–	–	–	–	–	–	–	–
194	Direct investment	–	–	–	–	–	–	–	–
195	Portfolio investment	–	–	–	–	–	–	–	–
196	Other long-term capital	184	429	371	318	340	246	194	149
197	Other short-term capital								
198	Net errors and omissions	-32	-13	8	-33	30	80	15	42
199	Overall balance	-64	57	31	-29	-128	-24	-9	-15
200	Allocation of SDRs	–	–	–	–	–	–	–	–
201	Monetary movements	64	-57	-31	29	128	24	9	15
	INTERNATIONAL RESERVES								*Million US dollars;*
202	Total	107.3	214.9	271.8	239.2	114.0	98.6	70.7	43.6
203	Gold, national valuation	10.9	11.6	11.2	10.2	9.7	9.2	8.6	9.7
204	Foreign exchange	92.6	197.1	253.7	215.8	88.8	82.0	55.3	33.9
205	Reserve position in the Fund	–	–	–	10.5	14.3	7.2	6.7	–
206	SDRs	3.8	6.2	6.9	2.7	1.2	0.2	0.1	–
	EXCHANGE RATES								*Kyats*
207	End of period	6.6028	6.5186	6.7572	7.3970	7.7775	8.2231	8.7512	7.8420
208	Average of period	6.8844	6.6538	6.5983	7.2807	7.7903	8.0355	8.3855	8.4749
	EXTERNAL INDEBTEDNESS								*Million US dollars;*
209	Total outstanding and disbursed	953.4	1280.7	1499.2	1714.4	2043.2	2323.2	2332.9	3090.8
210	Long-term	822.5	1126.9	1389.6	1579.7	1897.8	2166.2	2196.5	2896.6
211	Public and publicly guaranteed	822.5	1126.9	1389.6	1579.7	1897.8	2166.2	2196.5	2896.6
212	Private non-guaranteed	–	–	–	–	–	–	–	–
213	Short-term	8.0	26.0	4.0	15.0	13.0	11.0	15.0	86.0
214	Use of IMF credit	122.9	127.8	105.6	119.7	132.4	146.0	121.4	108.2
	Debt service								*Transactions*
215	Principal repayments on LT debt	27.8	60.3	66.3	83.1	67.7	85.5	92.3	118.1
216	Interest on long-term debt	19.3	33.8	45.3	53.2	51.8	63.4	62.1	69.9
217	Interest on short-term debt	1.2	2.3	3.3	1.5	1.6	4.2	3.2	3.6
	Average terms of new commitments								
218	Interest (%)	3.3	2.7	3.5	3.9	3.3	1.5	2.5	3.2
219	Maturity (years)	26.2	28.5	29.0	26.1	29.7	39.3	28.9	29.6
220	Grace period (years)	7.1	9.1	7.3	7.3	8.2	10.0	7.7	8.0
221	Grant element (%)	51.8	58.4	52.2	46.6	55.1	72.0	58.0	54.2

Footnotes:

a   Population estimates were based on 1983 census and the 1991 Myanmar Population Changes and Fertility Survey from 1993/94 onwards.
b   Based on CSO compilations from relevant agencies.
c   New prices of gasoline and diesel were set on 20 October 1988.
d   Includes beverages.
e   Refers to agricultural products only.
f   Excludes government deposits.
g   Current and capital expenditures include special accounts (except foreign loans account) and representative bodies.
h   Refers to current transfers only. Capital transfers have been classified as separate account (capital account) from the current account balance.

	1986	1987	1988	1989	1990	1991	1992	1993	1994	1995	
Calendar year											
	331	220	166	223	223	248	...	...	...	...	183
	-621	-453	-370	-304	-524	-302	...	...	...	...	184
	-290	-233	-205	-82	-302	-53	...	...	...	...	185
	-97	-54	-64	-42	-169	-270	...	...	...	...	186
	71	75	50	59	96	57	...	...	...	...	187
	-168	-129	-114	-101	-264	-327	...	...	...	...	188
	94	107	92	56	39	55	...	...	...	...	189
	...	...	...	...	...	...	...	...	...	...	190
	...	...	...	...	...	...	...	...	...	...	191
	-293	-180	-177	-68	-431	-267	...	...	...	...	192
	–	–	–	84	233	–	...	...	...	...	193
	–	–	–	8	161	238	...	...	...	...	194
	–	–	–	–	–	–	...	...	...	...	195
	274	203	140	74	25	37	...	...	...	...	196
							...	...	...	...	197
	69	15	117	53	21	-54	...	...	...	...	198
	49	38	80	151	9	-46	...	...	...	...	199
	–	–	–	–	–	–	...	...	...	...	200
	-49	-38	-80	-151	-9	46	...	...	...	...	201
As of end of period											
	43.9	39.7	89.2	275.0	325.3	271.0	292.2	315.0	434.8	573.2	202
	10.8	12.5	11.8	11.6	12.5	12.6	12.1	12.1	12.8	12.0	203
	33.1	27.1	77.3	262.8	312.0	258.2	280.1	302.6	421.9	561.1	204
	–	–	–	–	–	–	–	–	–	–	205
	–	0.1	0.1	0.6	0.8	0.2	–	0.3	0.1	0.1	206
per US dollar											
	7.0395	6.1097	6.4104	6.4942	6.0804	6.0137	6.2411	6.2456	5.9030	5.7810	207
	7.3304	6.6535	6.3945	6.7049	6.3386	6.2837	6.1045	6.1570	5.9749	5.9170	208
As of end of fiscal year											
	3792.2	4387.4	4414.2	4171.2	4673.1	4852.6	5326.6	5730.3	6502.0	...	209
	3617.8	4245.1	4220.2	4044.9	4444.1	4556.7	4974.0	5366.7	6098.6	...	210
	3617.8	4245.1	4220.2	4044.9	4444.1	4556.7	4974.0	5366.7	6098.6	...	211
	–	–	–	–	–	–	–	–	–	...	212
	101.9	112.9	186.5	124.7	229.0	295.9	352.6	363.6	403.4	...	213
	72.5	29.4	7.5	1.6	–	–	–	–	–	...	214
during the fiscal year											
	144.7	101.2	66.9	120.7	44.9	28.9	26.4	17.9	52.0	293.1 *	215
	89.3	69.6	39.2	69.4	12.8	48.9	26.0	86.7	120.2	86.7 *	216
	5.1	5.7	2.5	1.0	1.7	2.3	1.8	0.5	0.8	...	217
	2.7	1.6	0.0	0.0	1.5	0.0	1.5	2.3	0.0	...	218
	33.0	30.8	0.0	20.0	16.7	19.1	7.8	6.2	0.0	...	219
	9.1	9.1	0.0	8.0	5.2	10.2	1.5	1.0	0.0	...	220
	60.0	64.2	0.0	72.0	53.3	74.3	29.6	22.7	0.0	...	221

	Item	1978	1979	1980	1981	1982	1983	1984	1985
001	**POPULATION**	13.89	14.26	14.63	15.02	15.34	15.66	15.99	*Million;* 16.32
	NATIONAL ACCOUNTS *At Current Factor Cost*								*Million Rupees;*
002	GDP by Industrial Origin [a]	18421	24692	21886	23689	29037	31644	37004	44016
003	Agriculture	11616	13365	13520	15510	17715	19082	22570	22761
004	Mining	20	34	42	58	66	85	111	193
005	Manufacturing	794	848	936	1049	1243	1460	1816	2511
006	Electricity, gas and water	42	48	60	67	82	127	158	184
007	Construction	1338	4200	1570	197	2342	2377	2576	3761
008	Trade	707	724	889	953	1068	1199	1520	4561
009	Transport and communications	1093	2520	1541	1889	1992	2129	2468	2679
010	Finance	1534	1613	1833	2077	2366	2594	2937	3987
011	Public administration [b]	1277	1340	1495	1889	2163	2591	2848	3803
012	Others	–	–	–	–	–	–	–	–
013	Less: Imputed value of banking service	–	–	–	–	–	–	–	425
014	Indirect taxes less subsidies	1306	1436	1465	1841	1951	2177	2286	2571
015	GDP at market I producers' prices	19727	26128	23351	25530	30988	33821	39290 I	46587
016	Net factor income from abroad	291	390	494	587	615	697	625	661
017	GNP at current market prices	20018	26518	23845	26117	31603	34518	39915	47248
	At Current Market Prices								
018	Expenditure on GDP	19727	26128	23351	25530	30988	33821	39290	46587
019	Private consumption	15721	17741	19195	22411	25272	27458	31860	35977
020	Government consumption	1471	1889	1565	1922	2638	3416	3644	4371
021	Gross fixed capital formation	3294	3263	3681	4299	5465	6576	6907	9386
022	Increase in stocks	213	251	589	509	-151	52	444	798
023	Exports of goods and services	2086	2618	2695	3523	3592	3455	4196	5372
024	Less: Imports of goods and services	3053	3547	4374	5357	5828	7196	7661	9317
025	Statistical discrepancy	-5	3913	–	-1777	–	60	-100	–
	At Constant 1974/75 Market Prices I 1984/85 Factor Cost								
026	GDP by Industrial Origin [a]	18607	19048	18606	20158	20920	20297	22262 I	44016
027	Agriculture	11141	11480	10933	12066	12616	12478	13668 I	22761
028	Mining							I	193
029	Manufacturing							I	2511
030	Electricity, gas and water							I	184
031	Construction							I	3761
032	Trade							I	4561
033	Transport and communications	7466	7568	7673	8092	8304	7819	8594 I	2679
034	Finance							I	3987
035	Public administration [b]							I	3803
036	Others							I	–
037	Less: Imputed value of banking service	–	–	–	–	–	–	– I	425
038	Indirect taxes less subsidies	...	...	...	...	...	...	... I	2571
039	GDP at market I producers' prices	18607	19048	18606	20158	20920	20297	22262 I	46587
040	Net factor income from abroad	...	...	...	...	...	...	...	...
041	GNP	...	...	...	...	...	...	...	...
	Investment Financing, at current prices								
042	Gross domestic capital formation	3507	3514	4270	4808	5314	6628	7351	10184
043	Gross national saving	3211	7467	3929	2735	4921	5017	5909	7003
044	Gross domestic saving	2535	6498	2591	1197	3078	2947	3786	6239
045	Net factor income from abroad	291	390	494	587	615	697	625	661
046	Net current transfer from abroad	385	579	844	951	1228	1373	1498	103
	Per Capita GDP, Rupees								
047	Current prices	1421	1833	1596	1699	2020	2160	2457	2854
048	Constant *1974/75* I *1984/85* market prices	1340	1336	1271	1342	1364	1296	1392 I	2854

	1986	1987	1988	1989	1990	1991	1992	1993	1994	1995	
As of 1 July											
	16.67	17.02	17.37	17.74	18.11	18.49	19.02	19.54	20.07 *	20.60 *	001
Fiscal year ending 15 July											
	52727	60373	72215	84513	97748	113838	141997	161684	186486	205209 *	002
	27136	30623	36755	42572	50470	55368	65156	70090	81621	87072 *	003
	228	257	317	421	449	575	795	921	1092	1248 *	004
	3253	3740	4615	4857	5956	7894	12822	14618	17227	18827 *	005
	327	396	441	466	523	815	1238	1437	1778	1923 *	006
	4550	5162	6303	8231	8943	11078	14769	17318	19621	22432 *	007
	5622	6821	8118	9052	10507	12902	16563	19260	21870	24115 *	008
	3088	3600	4250	4732	5724	6560	8558	10819	12625	15252 *	009
	4728	5669	6681	8032	9269	10944	13241	15684	18122	20673 *	010
	4282	4873	5691	7469	7861	9991	11788	15115	17003	18930 *	011
	–	–	–	–	–	–	–	–	–	–	012
	487	768	956	1319	1954	2289	2933	3578	4473	5323 *	013
	3007	3492	4692	4758	5668	6532	7487	9702	12930	16809 *	014
	55734	63864	76906	89269	103416	120371	149485	171386	199416	222018 *	015
	709	1203	1575	1541	1934	2147	2715	3231	3862	...	016
	56443	65067	78481	90810	105350	122518	152200	174617	203278	...	017
	55734	63864	76906	89269	103416	120371	149485	171386	199416	222018 *	018
	44782	50746	62407	70172	86314	97771	121370	136664	156489	...	019
	5065	5797	6895	8947	8959	11085	11908	14900	18129	...	020
	9431	11825	13414	16392	17002	22780	29277	33928	38339	...	021
	1168	1073	1823	3023	2074	2294	2342	2375	2612	...	022
	6506	7555	8717	9897	10887	14226	23909	30948	47671	...	023
	11218	13132	16350	19162	21820	27785	39321	47429	63824	...	024
	–	–	–	–	–	–	–	–	–	...	025
	46086	46831	50098	52696	55051	58590	61266	63187	67658	69070 *	026
	23376	23213	24735	26260	27774	28372	28070	27896	29910	29706 *	027
	207	207	231	263	249	271	293	300	318	331 *	028
	2892	2959	3128	2907	3192	3756	4958	5266	5834	5909 *	029
	225	261	283	266	343	461	493	447	473	498 *	030
	4058	4121	4602	5226	5120	5532	5962	6250	6662	6937 *	031
	4869	5216	5463	5514	5641	6289	6658	7085	7471	7785 *	032
	2813	2972	3086	3125	3460	3916	4256	4615	4986	5410 *	033
	4107	4319	4514	4815	5137	5654	5951	6298	6697	7108 *	034
	3964	4160	4720	5142	5235	5516	5890	6427	6931	7191 *	035
	–	–	–	–	–	–	–	–	–	–	036
	426	596	663	822	1100	1178	1265	1399	1624	1805 *	037
	2628	2709	3255	2967	3192	3362	3230	3497	3789	4547 *	038
	48714	49540	53353	55662	58243	61952	64496	66684	71447	73617 *	039
	...	...	...	...	...	...	...	...	...	...	040
	...	...	...	...	...	...	...	...	...	...	041
	10599	12898	15237	19415	19076	25074	31619	36303	40951	...	042
	6773	8690	9335	11807	10249	13880	19404	23634	29155	...	043
	5887	7321	7604	10150	8143	11515	16207	19822	24798	...	044
	709	1203	1575	1541	1934	2147	2715	3231	3862	...	045
	177	166	156	116	172	218	482	581	495	...	046
	3344	3753	4426	5032	5710	6510	7861	8771	9938	10780	047
	2923	2911	3071	3138	3216	3350	3392	3413	3560	3574 *	048

	Item	1978	1979	1980	1981	1982	1983	1984	1985
	PRODUCTION								*Thousand metric tons;*
	Agriculture								
049	1. Rice (paddy)	2282	2339	2060	2464	2560	1833	2757	2837
050	2. Sugar cane	387	370	385	480	590	616	509	425
051	3. Maize	740	743	576	743	752	718	761	1024
052	4. Wheat	411	415	440	477	526	657	634	625
053	5. Potato	272	279	278	281	321	373	383	504
054	6. Millet	130	133	119	122	122	121	115	179
055	7. Barley	22	23	23	23	23	21	22	25
056	8. Jute	56	66	68	59	43	39	25	33
	Manufacturing								
057	1. Cement	38.1	21.0	29.2	32.3	30.1	37.0	39.2	31.5
058	2. Iron goods	3.6	4.5	6.0	5.1	7.3	11.7	12.4	15.3
059	3. Sugar	26.5	27.2	14.2	12.0	20.8	22.4	17.5	11.0
060	4. Soap	1.3	1.1	1.2	2.6	3.0	5.1	5.6	7.7
061	5. Jute goods	16.3	15.5	14.8	16.3	15.5	19.6	21.3	20.0
062	6. Tea	0.4	0.3	0.4	0.5	0.6	0.7	0.8	1.0
063	7. Straw board	0.7	1.4	1.0	1.6	1.2	0.7	0.4	0.9
064	8. Fertilizer	17.5	18.5	21.0	22.5	23.8	31.3	37.3	42.8
	Production indexes								*Period*
065	1. Agriculture, *1979-81 = 100*	98	94	102	105	98	116	116	117
066	2. Mining	...	...	...	...	...	...	...	...
067	3. Manufacturing, *1974/75\ 1986/87 = 100*	138	135	143	143	160	191	208	204
	ENERGY								*Annual*
	Coal, *'000 m.t.*								
068	Imports	...	...	...	...	...	...	...	...
069	Consumption	...	...	31	32	35	36	86	69
	Electricity, *Mn kWh*								
070	Production	179	201	216	216	252	323	357	384
071	Exports	6	6	5	4	5	5	10	11
072	Imports	14	17	18	19	23	24	25	38
073	Consumption	132	149	161	165	185	232	245	287
	Retail prices, *US $/litre*								
074	Gasoline, premium	0.58	0.58	0.69	0.75	0.70	0.63	0.57	0.58
075	Diesel	0.28	0.28	0.38	0.46	0.43	0.39	0.36	0.40
	PRICE INDEXES [c]								*Period*
076	Consumer (National urban), *1983/84 = 100*	58.0	60.0	65.8	74.6	82.4	94.1	100.0	104.1
077	Food	57.7	58.6	65.0	73.8	81.9	95.0	100.0	101.3
078	Non-food	58.1	62.5	67.3	76.2	83.4	92.2	100.0	109.9
079	Implicit GDP deflator, *1974/75\ 1984/85 = 100*	106.0	137.2	125.5	126.6	148.1	166.6	176.5 |	100.0
	MONEY AND BANKING								*Million Rupees;*
080	Money Supply (M1)	2060.6	2504.9	2830.4	3207.8	3611.5	4348.9	4931.5	5480.0
081	Currency in circulation	1351.9	1615.2	1799.3	2065.7	2436.7	2752.0	3273.4	3737.3
082	Demand deposits	708.7	889.7	1031.1	1142.1	1174.8	1596.9	1658.1	1742.7
083	Quasi-money	1711.5	2006.5	2454.9	3099.9	3846.5	4873.5	5523.7	6816.6
084	Money supply (M2)	3772.1	4511.4	5285.3	6307.7	7458.0	9222.4	10455.2	12296.6
085	Foreign assets (net)	1783.3	2288.0	2231.9	2214.5	3097.4	2611.4	2539.8	1897.6
086	Domestic credit	2905.3	3540.8	4305.8	5161.4	6043.1	8490.9	9824.5	12550.9
087	Claims on govt. sector (net)	965.5	1129.3	1258.3	1262.7	2061.5	4089.6	5028.7	6492.1
088	Claims on private sector	1071.1	1331.6	1916.5	2498.1	2638.2	2699.1	3174.0	4036.6
089	Claims on other financial insts. [d]	868.7	1079.9	1131.0	1400.6	1343.4	1702.2	1621.8	2022.2
090	Other items [e]	-916.5	-1317.4	-1252.4	-1068.2	-1682.5	-1879.9	-1909.1	-2151.9
	Deposit Money Banks								
091	Demand deposits	694.1	880.0	853.5	1019.6	1033.7	1379.0	1507.1	1667.9
092	Savings deposits	361.1	454.5	571.2	716.6	877.4	1068.7	1333.9	1776.3
093	Time deposits	1350.6	1477.7	1814.9	2228.3	2789.8	3417.9	3912.3	4693.7
094	Domestic credits outstanding [f]	2077.2	2582.7	3169.2	3928.0	4223.3	5152.4	5770.5	7507.2

	1986	1987	1988	1989	1990	1991	1992	1993	1994	1995	
Fiscal year ending 15 July											
	2892	2494	2999	3302	3409	3498	3223	2712	3493 *	2928 *	049
	587	828	819	904	997	1106	1291	1366	1431 *	1501 *	050
	1039	1021	1003	1122	1201	1228	1205	1291	1210 *	1273 *	051
	677	743	740	828	855	836	779	765	873 *	914 *	052
	412	438	582	629	877	746	733	733	780 *	840 *	053
	179	178	181	196	230	231	229	237	274 *	268 *	054
	24	26	25	27	27	28	28	28	29 *	30 *	055
	61	23	15	18	16	16	19	10	11 *	11 *	056
	96.0	151.6	215.0	217.7	101.2	135.9	237.3	247.9	315.5	410.0 *	057
	28.4	34.5	25.6	34.8	36.3	45.6	59.7	60.3	71.0	95.0 *	058
	15.2	24.6	30.0	24.2	31.9	44.5	55.4	64.4	34.0	48.3 *	059
	9.2	11.5	12.3	14.9	11.9	20.1	20.9	23.0	20.6	21.7 *	060
	16.4	18.3	17.2	17.0	7.5	11.2	17.6	18.2	19.3	17.4 *	061
	1.1	1.1	1.3	1.2	1.4	1.2	1.5	1.6	2.0	2.0 *	062
	0.9	0.5	0.8	0.3	0.5	0.4	0.3	0.6	0.7	0.8 *	063
	43.4	45.0	54.2	56.8	67.3	72.7	80.8	...	...	...	064
averages											
	115	126	141	153	159	159	152	163	168	175	065
	...	...	...	...	...	...	...	...	...	...	066
	243 I	100	107	102	101	130	142	144	150	164	067
values											
	17	91	84	76	12	81	111	...	...	...	068
	46	74	76	70	21	58	63	...	...	...	069
	431	539	560	559	713	873	926	881	933	1007 *	070
	22	21	16	18	23	81	85	46	71	42 *	071
	58	33	68	114	61	34	55	82	102	110 *	072
	320	382	449	479	525	589	652	663	695	787 *	073
	0.51	0.59	0.59	0.51	0.65	0.58	0.65	0.59 *	0.58 *	0.52 *	074
	0.35	0.30	0.34	0.30	0.31	0.23	0.27	0.24 *	0.24 *	0.21 *	075
averages											
	120.6	136.6	151.7	161.3	179.9	197.6	239.1	260.4	283.7	305.4	076
	120.1	138.3	155.1	165.9	181.9	200.4	249.2	265.4	289.5	310.7 *	077
	121.7	133.3	145.3	153.7	177.2	193.4	222.4	252.4	274.8	297.0 *	078
	114.4	128.9	144.1	160.4	177.6	194.3	231.8	257.0	279.1	301.6 *	079
As of fiscal year ending 15 July											
	7029.3	8120.2	9596.6	11775.4	14223.0	16283.6	19457.7	23833.0	28510.4 *	32046.2 *	080
	4842.9	5746.1	6374.6	7946.6	9718.2	11654.5	13639.7	16313.0	19659.7 *	22501.0 *	081
	2186.4	2374.1	3222.0	3828.8	4504.8	4629.1	5818.0	7520.0	8850.7 *	9545.2 *	082
	8129.7	9378.0	11826.0	14829.7	17329.4	21428.9	26212.9	34489.5	41266.7 *	47772.6 *	083
	15159.0	17498.2	21422.6	26605.1	31552.4	37712.5	45670.6	58322.5	69777.1 *	79818.9 *	084
	2600.0	3059.9	5573.6	6203.5	9338.9	16151.7	20792.4	29125.0	36218.1 *	37181.6 *	085
	15322.9	17803.1	20469.3	26584.3	29661.6	34491.4	41609.1	49404.9	57828.1 *	71877.8 *	086
	7495.7	8712.3	9259.0	12345.1	13940.2	16821.4	19001.6	23446.2	23482.0 *	25191.2 *	087
	5167.9	6279.7	8308.7	11241.0	12893.2	15582.4	19799.2	23919.4	32317.4 *	44928.3 *	088
	2659.3	2811.1	2901.6	2998.2	2828.2	2087.6	2808.3	2039.3	2028.7 *	1758.3 *	089
	-2763.9	-3364.8	-4620.3	-6182.7	-7448.1	-12930.6	-16730.9	-20207.4	-24269.1 *	-29240.6 *	090
	2090.8	2353.9	2986.2	3924.0	4293.7	4782.4	6451.2	8302.1	10156.8	10882.0 *	091
	2255.7	2672.2	3338.8	4321.8	5218.2	6671.5	8634.9	12923.3	17460.7	22144.0 *	092
	5632.5	6386.2	8036.4	10044.7	11761.5	14382.6	17326.4	21414.7	23358.7	24553.2 *	093
	8997.6	10730.1	13523.5	17264.5	18917.1	24410.5	31794.8	36221.6	43650.9	55079.0 *	094

KEY INDICATORS OF DEVELOPING ASIAN AND PACIFIC COUNTRIES

	Item	1978	1979	1980	1981	1982	1983	1984	1985
	Interest Rates [g]								**Per cent;**
	On deposits								
095	Savings	8.00	8.00	8.00	8.00	8.38	8.50	8.69	8.50
096	Time: 6 months	9.00	9.00	9.00	9.00	9.38	9.50	9.63	9.50
097	12 months	12.00	12.00	12.00	12.00	12.38	12.50	12.63	12.50
	GOVERNMENT FINANCE								**Million Rupees;**
	Central Government								
098	Current revenue	1582.0	1811.9	1880.0	2419.2	2679.5	2841.6	3409.3	3916.6
099	Taxes	1243.9	1476.6	1527.6	2035.7	2211.5	2420.7	2737.0	3150.8
100	Non-taxes	338.1	335.3	352.4	383.5	468.0	420.9	672.3	765.8
101	Current expenditure [h]	822.6	985.1	1067.2	1274.9	1530.6	1903.5	2106.3	2731.5
102	Current surplus/deficit	759.4	826.8	812.8	1144.3	1148.9	938.1	1303.0	1185.1
103	Capital receipts	...	...	...	...	...	...	...	...
104	Capital expenditure	1808.0	1978.8	2308.6	2731.1	3726.9	4982.1	5163.8	5488.7
105	Capital account surplus/deficit	-1808.0	-1978.8	-2308.6	-2731.1	-3726.9	-4982.1	-5163.8	-5488.7
106	Net Lending	...	...	...	...	...	...	...	...
107	Overall surplus/deficit	-1048.6	-1152.0	-1495.8	-1586.8	-2578.0	-4044.0	-3860.8	-4303.6
	Financing								
108	Domestic borrowing (net)	216.2	166.6	108.1	194.8	432.0	953.9	1465.8	1694.4
109	Foreign borrowing (net) [i]	361.3	367.0	511.9	662.2	694.2	938.3	1615.4	1685.7
110	Foreign grants	466.6	599.2	805.6	868.9	993.3	1090.1	876.6	923.4
111	Use of cash balances	4.5	19.2	70.2	-139.1	458.5	1061.7	-97.0	0.1
	Expenditure by Function, Central Govt.								
112	Total [j]	2630.5	2963.9	3375.8	4006.0	5257.5	6885.6	7270.1	8220.1
113	General public services	252.3	296.1	323.9	418.2	469.7	583.8	615.1	686.5
114	Defence	167.9	192.2	223.0	258.9	282.8	392.4	453.6	507.9
115	Education	270.3	315.3	330.6	384.2	519.1	734.0	815.8	805.6
116	Health	137.8	150.7	129.9	162.9	233.3	318.6	317.6	394.2
117	Social security & welfare	60.0	73.8	63.7	68.6	165.2	215.3	138.9	152.1
118	Housing & community amenities [k]	161.1	184.9	122.2	188.8	413.3	635.3	626.4	619.2
119	Economic services	1392.1	1500.4	1919.0	2211.1	2686.6	3452.7	3757.1	3816.4
120	Agriculture	471.9	565.6	547.6	705.2	1100.7	1491.7	1439.1	1751.4
121	Industry	118.3	74.1	116.0	126.1	269.9	377.1	655.7	352.2
122	Electricity, gas & water	248.8	267.0	498.2	657.8	387.7	451.0	660.5	513.2
123	Transport and communications	538.1	563.8	740.9	704.3	878.5	985.7	958.4	1149.5
124	Other economic services	15.0	29.9	16.3	17.7	49.8	147.2	43.4	50.1
125	Others [l]	189.0	250.5	263.5	313.3	487.5	553.5	545.6	1238.2
	EXTERNAL TRADE								**Million Rupees;**
126	Exports, fob	1046	1297	1151	1609	1492	1132	1704	2741
127	Imports, cif	2470	2885	3480	4428	4930	6314	6514	7742
128	Trade balance	-1423	-1588	-2330	-2820	-3439	-5182	-4810	-5002
	Exports, by SITC section								
129	Food and live animals	405	489	307	589	736	328	584	992
130	Beverage and Tobacco	11	14	3	15	18	13	5	5
131	Crude materials incl. fuels	441	492	470	562	397	336	373	487
132	Mineral fuels, etc.	0	1	1	0	1	1	3	1
133	Animal, vegetable oil & fats	6	17	20	38	44	42	68	57
134	Chemicals	4	1	1	4	2	2	6	1
135	Basic manufactures	123	229	292	254	225	357	582	649
136	Machines, transport equipment	3	3	3	2	9	8	24	34
137	Misc. manufactured goods	51	52	54	143	58	45	58	513
138	Unclassified goods	1	0	1	2	1	0	1	1
	Exports, by principal commodity								
139	1. Carpets	24	46	55	65	84	138	265	249
140	2. Garments	6	9	8	13	14	10	21	471
141	3. Pulses	0	20	82	40	58	3	6	109

	1986	1987	1988	1989	1990	1991	1992	1993	1994	1995	
Period averages											
	8.50	8.50	9.25	9.00	9.00	8.75	9.50	...	...	...	095
	8.75	8.50	8.80	8.88	9.50	9.50	10.00	...	...	...	096
	12.50	12.50	12.50	12.50	11.50	11.50	11.50	11.80	11.00	11.00	097
Fiscal year ending 15 July											
	4644.5	5975.1	7350.4	7776.8	9287.5	10729.9	13512.7	15148.4	19580.7	24567.4 *	098
	3659.4	4372.4	5752.9	6287.2	7283.9	8176.3	9875.6	11662.5	15371.4	19653.8 *	099
	985.1	1602.7	1597.5	1489.6	2003.6	2553.6	3637.1	3485.9	4209.3	4913.6 *	100
	3241.1	3773.0	4224.6	5142.4	5869.9	6835.1	8698.4	9886.2	10511.0	16648.0 *	101
	1403.4	2202.1	3125.8	2634.4	3417.6	3894.8	4814.3	5262.2	9069.7	7919.4 *	102
											103
	6213.1	7378.0	9428.0	12328.7	12997.5	15979.5	16512.8	19413.6	21188.2	19365.1 *	104
	-6213.1	-7378.0	-9428.0	-12328.7	-12997.5	-15979.5	-16512.8	-19413.6	-21188.2	-19365.1 *	105
	...	...	...	...	...	...	...	...	...	...	106
	-4809.7	-5175.9	-6302.2	-9694.3	-9579.9	-12084.7	-11698.5	-14151.4	-12118.5	-11445.7 *	107
	1221.1	1544.7	1030.0	1184.5	2049.5	4402.7	1814.0	1275.0	1390.0	951.2 *	108
	2340.6	2455.2	3518.3	5277.8	5257.8	5667.7	5874.7	5668.0	7695.4	6948.1 *	109
	1172.9	1285.1	2076.8	1680.6	1975.4	2164.8	1643.8	3793.0	2393.6	2876.7 *	110
	75.1	-109.1	-322.9	1551.4	297.2	-150.5	2366.0	3415.4	639.5	669.7 *	111
	9454.4	11151.0	13652.8	17470.6	18867.6	22814.8	25211.2	29299.8	31699.2	36013.1	112
	873.5	1045.2	1129.4	1364.6	1504.4	1907.0	2445.0	2750.2	2908.1	3217.5	113
	606.2	712.4	768.3	898.7	1027.2	1151.4	1489.0	1723.6	1877.4	1917.6	114
	1087.0	1278.8	1489.3	1741.7	1799.5	2082.3	2867.8	4150.2	4564.0	5020.6	115
	405.9	491.7	589.3	867.1	690.4	660.6	918.1	1061.0	1065.6	1765.8	116
	189.3	265.2	296.8	473.8	1261.5	890.2	826.5	1030.8	1200.5	1064.2	117
	608.9	628.5	722.3	974.5	1082.6	868.9	1753.8	2492.0	2093.6	3527.9	118
	4646.9	5454.6	7041.5	8592.6	8624.4	12268.2	11612.0	12697.6	14446.7	13530.0	119
	2189.4	2078.8	2398.7	3386.8	3124.6	3309.5	4600.2	5271.8	6819.3	6217.7	120
	404.3	385.2	618.5	569.9	1065.1	1766.6	2448.2	1109.6	670.5	417.4	121
	1036.3	1239.2	1924.7	2003.4	2087.6	1363.1	1414.4	2229.1	2312.2	1689.8	122
	971.4	1330.9	1929.5	2479.5	2031.4	2300.5	2903.5	3732.5	4244.3	4875.6	123
	45.5	420.5	170.1	153.0	315.7	3528.5	245.7	354.6	400.4	329.5	124
	1036.7	1274.6	1615.9	2557.6	2877.6	2986.2	3299.0	3394.4	3543.3	5969.5	125
Fiscal year ending 15 July											
	3078	3192	4115	4295	5156	7388	13706	17267	19293 *	17899 *	126
	9341	10905	13870	16254	18325	23226	31940	39206	51571 *	65526 *	127
	-6263	-7714	-9755	-11958	-13169	-15839	-18234	-21939	-32278 *	-47628 *	128
	836	704	804	578	616	987	1942	1863	1163 *	1631 *	129
	0	4	10	7	4	11	13	13	13 *	25 *	130
	413	491	514	250	239	312	437	532	433 *	518 *	131
	0	0	1	–	–	–	–	0	–	–	132
	61	117	172	100	20	202	160	176	138 *	263 *	133
	3	2	13	26	11	18	20	29	212 *	303 *	134
	900	1010	1602	1983	2693	4312	7557	10298	10913 *	9263 *	135
	39	3	1	6	0	0	0	1	6 *	37 *	136
	827	862	997	1347	1573	1546	3576	4352	6415 *	5859 *	137
	0	0	3	–	–	–	–	1	–	–	138
	376	628	1224	1634	2319	3733	7048	9594	9534 *	7716 *	139
	804	611	917	1118	1399	1350	3255	3930	5943 *	5130 *	140
	262	135	127	98	212	247	1159	1049	347 *	454 *	141

Item	1978	1979	1980	1981	1982	1983	1984	1985
142 4. Jute goods	63	133	123	39	83	180	212	260
143 5. Raw jute and jute cuttings	170	164	140	159	124	104	38	44
Imports, by SITC section								
144 Food and live animals	323	292	413	601	619	925	728	783
145 Beverage and tobacco	44	36	26	25	36	63	72	79
146 Crude materials incl. fuels	53	61	101	116	143	206	266	425
147 Mineral fuels, etc.	250	232	410	584	579	702	749	919
148 Animal, vegetable oil & fats	31	22	26	93	64	66	79	123
149 Chemicals	255	298	397	527	599	646	698	908
150 Basic manufactures	819	1085	1090	1259	1556	1937	1802	2377
151 Machines, transport equipment	483	575	720	803	892	1181	1651	1671
152 Misc. manufactured goods	201	275	288	408	430	584	466	451
153 Unclassified goods	10	9	10	14	12	4	2	7
Direction of Trade								*Million US dollars;*
154 Exports, Total	47.9	68.1	63.2	83.3	71.0	76.8	83.3	134.8
155 1. Germany	4.1	7.4	8.5	9.4	10.6	17.4	18.2	14.3
156 2. United States	4.1	5.6	5.8	2.2	1.8	5.7	7.6	47.6
157 3. India	13.5	17.3	19.0	40.5	42.2	37.7	39.8	45.9
158 4. Switzerland	0.0	1.0	0.3	0.6	0.6	0.9	1.5	1.6
159 5. United Kingdom	2.5	3.1	4.8	4.4	6.1	8.4	6.9	10.9
160 6. Austria	0.0	0.0	0.1	0.0	0.0	0.0	0.3	0.2
161 7. Belgium-Luxembourg	1.3	0.6	0.4	0.4	0.0	0.0	0.1	0.3
162 8. Italy	0.6	1.7	1.9	0.0	0.0	0.0	0.0	0.0
163 9. France	3.2	2.4	1.3	2.4	1.0	1.4	1.3	1.7
164 10. Canada	0.0	0.0	0.0	0.0	0.0	0.1	0.1	0.7
165 Imports, Total	160.4	163.5	218.7	214.0	225.4	240.2	266.6	295.2
166 1. Thailand	1.4	0.6	0.8	2.1	2.0	3.1	3.7	3.9
167 2. India	76.7	84.7	104.0	87.4	56.2	67.7	104.5	89.9
168 3. Singapore	2.8	3.2	6.2	9.1	9.5	10.3	6.5	12.8
169 4. Japan	36.3	24.3	42.6	48.6	59.5	46.6	43.1	67.7
170 5. Hong Kong	5.5	6.2	4.9	4.4	5.3	7.0	4.5	5.4
171 6. China, People's Rep. of	0.0	0.0	0.0	11.1	23.2	28.1	11.9	19.1
172 7. New Zealand	0.4	0.1	0.3	0.5	0.4	0.2	1.4	0.8
173 8. Germany	4.2	5.9	6.5	7.8	11.2	7.9	9.5	13.9
174 9. Bangladesh	...	...	...	0.2	0.1	3.1	16.1	5.6
175 10. United Kingdom	...	...	...	3.5	9.0	8.5	9.8	11.7
BALANCE OF PAYMENTS [m]								*Million US dollars;*
176 Merchandise exports, fob	89.4	110.3	102.1	144.2	87.6	101.5	130.1	161.3
177 Merchandise imports, fob	-220.5	-251.4	-328.0	-362.4	-406.3	-468.3	-402.9	-444.0
178 Trade balance	-131.1	-141.1	-225.9	-218.2	-318.7	-366.8	-272.8	-282.7
179 Other goods, services and income	47.6	48.5	78.9	72.5	90.8	88.7	59.9	42.5
180 Credit	105.9	125.6	169.5	169.7	178.2	179.1	164.4	162.1
181 Debit	-58.3	-77.1	-90.6	-97.2	-87.4	-90.4	-104.4	-119.6
182 Unrequited transfer	57.8	81.2	108.2	126.6	142.6	132.5	117.7	118.7
183 Private	19.7	26.1	33.6	38.3	34.0	39.1	34.8	37.7
184 Official	38.1	55.1	74.6	88.3	108.6	93.4	82.9	81.0
185 Current balance	-25.7	-11.4	-38.8	-19.1	-85.4	-145.6	-95.2	-121.6
186 Direct investment	...	...	...	...	...	...	...	...
187 Portfolio investment	...	...	...	...	...	...	...	...
188 Other long-term capital	17.2	30.3	41.4	61.4	60.6	62.4	73.3 }	25.8
189 Other short-term capital	-23.7	3.8	-19.2	-0.5	2.1	45.4	-11.8 }	
190 Net errors and omissions	10.5	4.8	3.5	9.2	24.4	30.1	12.8	2.3
191 Overall balance	-21.7	27.5	-13.1	51.0	1.7	-7.6	-20.9	-93.5
192 Allocation of SDRs	...	2.6	2.6	2.4	...	...	...	...
193 Monetary movements	21.7	-30.1	10.5	-53.4	-1.7	7.6	20.9	93.5

	1986	1987	1988	1989	1990	1991	1992	1993	1994	1995	
	167	164	189	134	5	272	191	176	242 *	231 *	142
	2	15	53	47	118	6	1	44	40 *	85 *	143
	971	1029	1524	1323	1608	1821	2948	3025	4085 *	5149 *	144
	113	144	172	197	227	257	288	469	368 *	603 *	145
	393	657	1037	1183	1571	2013	3416	3977	3122 *	3916 *	146
	1054	930	1050	1117	1516	2278	3645	3834	4837 *	4704 *	147
	102	176	353	343	476	742	802	1085	1457 *	2055 *	148
	1170	1288	1495	1533	2824	3051	4615	5265	5541 *	7583 *	149
	2760	3227	3359	4671	5065	5951	8600	11633	19147 *	25392 *	150
	2135	2784	4144	4847	3790	5991	5893	7702	10038 *	12939 *	151
	637	664	729	1037	1248	1121	1548	2186	2885 *	3171 *	152
	7	7	7	5	1	2	187	30	91 *	15 *	153
Calendar year											
	134.3	147.6	226.6	183.4	216.1	257.3	352.4	364.0	347.2	329.5	154
	22.1	38.4	63.8	65.3	80.6	115.1	153.6	179.2	148.3	145.3	155
	34.1	34.3	55.6	49.7	45.8	60.6	81.0	100.4	117.3	100.0	156
	36.8	37.2	32.3	3.0	13.7	17.5	20.8	17.1	12.6	14.7	157
	3.2	6.0	7.8	11.2	12.7	13.4	21.3	15.0	14.5	11.0	158
	9.4	12.5	15.4	12.3	11.5	7.2	9.4	8.8	9.6	7.0	159
	0.0	0.7	1.0	3.3	3.3	3.8	5.2	6.1	6.5	7.7	160
	1.2	2.2	1.2	2.9	9.3	5.5	7.1	5.8	6.5	7.3	161
	0.0	0.0	0.0	2.6	4.7	5.4	4.7	4.2	5.0	7.7	162
	2.8	3.1	3.9	4.4	6.1	5.1	5.5	4.3	5.0	7.0	163
	0.6	0.6	1.2	1.3	2.0	1.8	3.9	4.5	3.6	3.6	164
	313.9	466.0	534.0	429.2	452.0	500.0	476.5	527.7	601.5	750.9	165
	6.4	28.3	57.7	38.3	10.5	17.1	26.4	70.1	109.5	156.2	166
	90.3	80.1	90.2	35.6	43.5	85.0	80.1	83.0	93.0	107.8	167
	19.3	35.2	49.5	66.9	76.0	60.3	57.2	62.5	75.3	87.3	168
	72.8	87.8	68.2	78.6	64.8	107.7	65.5	74.9	72.6	66.5	169
	8.7	11.1	13.4	15.4	25.2	28.7	34.0	41.3	52.3	81.8	170
	23.2	22.4	24.0	29.6	46.3	35.4	38.6	36.9	44.3	58.7	171
	2.0	11.1	18.2	20.7	25.3	35.7	39.0	48.8	25.0	37.1	172
	11.7	16.2	53.4	14.8	18.6	11.7	22.9	13.0	16.1	27.6	173
	11.1	5.6	5.1	11.4	8.1	12.7	0.3	7.7	14.7	16.0	174
	7.7	16.2	10.1	14.3	8.0	10.2	12.1	19.6	15.9	14.0	175
Calendar year											
	142.6	162.2	193.8	161.2	217.9	274.5	376.3	397.0	368.7	319.4 *	176
	-436.5	-512.4	-664.9	-568.1	-666.6	-756.9	-752.1	-858.6	-1158.9	-1264.2 *	177
	-293.9	-350.2	-471.1	-407.0	-448.7	-482.4	-375.8	-461.6	-790.2	-944.8 *	178
	63.6	86.6	74.8	66.1	51.0	66.7	65.5	86.6	286.4	405.5 *	179
	181.0	224.5	240.0	224.3	229.5	266.8	307.3	362.1	613.8	667.4 *	180
	-117.4	-137.9	-165.2	-158.2	-178.5	-200.1	-241.8	-275.5	-327.4	-261.9 *	181
	111.1	140.3	124.9	97.5	108.6	111.2	128.9	152.5	152.0	214.5 *	182
	41.3	67.2	60.1	48.5	60.4	53.7	45.7	74.3	...	79.6 *	183
	69.8	73.1	64.8	49.0	48.2	57.5	83.2	78.2	...	134.9 *	184
	-119.2	-123.3	-271.5	-243.3	-289.2	-304.4	-181.3	-222.5	-351.9	-324.8 *	185
	...	...	...	...	...	...	...	...	...	...	186
	...	...	...	...	...	...	...	...	...	...	187
	87.4	190.7	252.7	196.1	304.5	457.1	335.9	283.5	403.0	85.5 *	188
											189
	-0.8	-3.6	12.5	5.2	4.9	10.7	0.8	4.6	11.4	222.1 *	190
	-32.5	63.8	-6.3	-42.1	20.2	163.4	155.4	65.6	62.5	-17.2 *	191
	...	...	...	...	...	...	...	...	...	...	192
	32.5	-63.8	6.3	42.1	-20.2	-163.4	-155.4	-65.6	-62.5	17.2 *	193

	Item	1978	1979	1980	1981	1982	1983	1984	1985
	INTERNATIONAL RESERVES								*Million US dollars;*
194	Total	151.3	165.5	189.1	208.3	205.7	139.8	88.4	62.4
195	Gold, national valuation	6.2	6.3	6.4	6.4	6.4	6.4	6.4	6.4
196	Foreign exchange	140.4	153.8	176.0	195.3	192.1	127.2	76.3	49.7
197	Reserve position in the Fund	3.1	3.1	6.6	6.6	6.3	6.0	5.6	6.3
198	SDRs	1.6	2.3	0.1	...	0.9	0.2	0.1	0.0
	EXCHANGE RATES								*Rupees per*
199	End of period	12.000	12.000	12.000	13.200	14.300	15.200	18.000	20.700
200	Average of period	12.111	12.000	12.000	12.336	13.244	14.545	16.459	18.246
	EXTERNAL INDEBTEDNESS								*Million US dollars;*
201	Total outstanding and disbursed	112.6	146.3	204.5	278.5	352.8	452.2	470.0	589.5
202	Long-term	79.4	109.9	155.9	218.7	283.3	348.8	430.5	544.7
203	Public and publicly guaranteed	79.4	109.9	155.9	218.7	283.3	348.8	430.5	544.7
204	Private non-guaranteed	...	...	...	...	...	...	...	...
205	Short term	16.0	12.0	7.0	22.0	39.0	80.0	24.0	23.0
206	Use of IMF credit	17.2	24.4	41.6	37.8	30.5	23.4	15.5	21.8
	Debt service								*Transactions*
207	Principal repayments on LT debt	1.7	1.8	2.1	2.2	2.6	3.8	4.1	5.9
208	Interest on long-term debt	1.1	1.5	1.8	2.5	3.1	4.1	5.3	7.5
209	Interest on short-term debt	1.7	1.4	2.4	4.6	5.7	5.3	2.2	1.7
	Average terms of new commitments								
210	Interest(%)	0.9	1.2	0.8	1.3	2.0	1.7	1.8	1.6
211	Maturity (years)	45.1	43.2	45.9	39.8	38.7	38.2	39.3	42.1
212	Grace period (years)	10.0	9.0	10.1	9.2	9.6	9.4	8.2	8.8
213	Grant element (%)	80.1	75.6	81.2	73.7	69.6	71.7	69.0	73.1

Footnotes:

a   From 1985, total GDP by factor cost is net of imputed value of banking services.
b   Refers to community and social services.
c   Refers to period average for fiscal year.
d   Refers to claims on financial and non-financial government enterprises.
e   Refers to net capital and other items.
f   Refers to loans and advances.
g   Refers to minimum interest rates.
h   Refers to regular expenditure, excluding repayment of loan principal.
i   Refers to net foreign borrowing minus repayment of loan principal.
j   Refers to regular and development expenditure, excluding repayment of loan principal.
k   Refers to expenditure for drinking water and local development.
l   Refers to miscellaneous expenditures less pension, allowances and gratuity, plus loans and advances and payment of loan interest.
m   For 1995, data refer to the first eleven months only.

	1986	1987	1988	1989	1990	1991	1992	1993	1994	1995	
As of end of period											
	93.2	184.6	226.7	218.0	301.8	403.5	474.0	646.7	700.1	592.8	194
	6.4	6.4	6.4	6.4	6.5	6.5	6.5	6.5	6.5	6.4	195
	79.7	170.0	212.5	203.9	287.0	388.7	459.4	632.3	685.1	577.9	196
	7.0	8.1	7.7	7.5	8.1	8.2	7.9	7.9	8.4	8.5	197
	0.1	0.1	0.1	0.2	0.2	0.1	0.2	0.0	0.1	0.0	198
US dollar											
	22.000	21.600	25.200	28.600	30.400	42.700	43.200	49.240	49.880	56.000	199
	21.230	21.819	23.289	27.189	29.369	37.255	42.718	48.607	49.398	51.890	200
As of end of year											
	754.6	1000.3	1178.0	1368.5	1640.0	1771.4	1801.9	2003.8	2319.8	...	201
	709.7	936.3	1099.7	1294.9	1571.8	1707.5	1752.8	1933.9	2202.2	...	202
	709.7	936.3	1099.7	1294.9	1571.8	1707.5	1752.8	1933.9	2202.2	...	203
	...	...	...	...	...	...	...	...	...	...	204
	21.4	21.0	25.6	21.2	24.3	25.4	5.5	20.7	62.6	...	205
	23.5	43.0	52.7	52.4	43.9	38.5	43.6	49.2	55.0	...	206
during the year											
	12.2	15.0	21.8	25.3	29.2	31.2	37.6	40.5	44.2	...	207
	10.5	14.9	19.9	25.5	25.7	26.9	28.2	27.5	30.2	...	208
	1.2	1.6	2.2	1.9	2.1	2.6	0.8	0.7	2.3	...	209
	1.8	3.1	1.0	1.0	0.9	1.0	0.9	1.0	0.8	...	210
	39.9	32.4	38.8	38.5	39.3	38.4	39.7	39.7	39.6	...	211
	9.0	8.1	9.9	10.0	10.3	9.7	10.2	10.2	10.1	...	212
	71.7	58.9	77.2	77.8	78.9	77.8	79.5	78.5	80.5	...	213

	Item	1978	1979	1980	1981	1982	1983	1984	1985
001	**POPULATION**	77.75	80.13	82.58	85.12	87.76	90.48	93.29	*Million;* 96.18
002	**LABOR FORCE**	22.94	24.85	25.62	26.41	27.22	27.32	28.16	*Million;* 28.43
003	Employed	22.55	23.97	24.71	25.47	26.26	26.25	27.06	27.37
004	Agriculture	12.36	12.62	13.01	13.41	13.82	13.84	14.27	13.84
005	Manufacturing	3.07	3.48	3.59	3.70	3.81	3.53	3.63	3.74
006	Mining	0.03	0.03	0.03	0.03	0.04	0.03	0.03	0.05
007	Others	7.09	7.84	8.08	8.33	8.59	8.85	9.13	9.74
008	Unemployed	0.39	0.88	0.91	0.94	0.96	1.07	1.10	1.06
009	Unemployment rate, %	1.7	3.5	3.6	3.6	3.5	3.9	3.9	3.7
	NATIONAL ACCOUNTS *At Current Factor Cost*								*Billion Rupees;*
010	GDP by Industrial Origin	159.8	178.0	210.3 I	247.8	292.2	328.4	374.3	425.1
011	Agriculture	50.6	54.1	62.2 I	76.4	92.2	99.4	104.6	121.3
012	Mining	1.3	1.5	2.2 I	1.1	1.2	1.3	1.6	2.1
013	Manufacturing	24.0	27.5	33.6 I	37.4	44.2	50.2	60.4	67.6
014	Electricity, gas and water	2.4	3.4	4.8 I	5.9	6.4	7.3	8.3	8.7
015	Construction	8.7	9.7	11.9 I	11.6	13.2	13.7	14.7	17.1
016	Trade	25.0	28.3	33.7 I	37.3	44.2	50.0	58.2	67.6
017	Transport and communications	11.3	13.2	15.5 I	23.9	27.4	31.1	35.2	38.2
018	Finance	9.9	11.2	12.5 I	16.8	20.4	25.1	31.0	35.0
019	Public administration	13.2	13.9	16.3 I	19.3	21.5	26.5	33.1	36.7
020	Others	13.6	15.3	17.7 I	18.1	21.5	23.9	27.3	30.8
021	Indirect taxes less subsidies	16.5	17.1	23.9 I	30.4	32.0	36.0	45.5	47.1
022	GDP at current market prices	176.3	195.1	234.2 I	278.2	324.2	364.4	419.8	472.2
023	Net factor income from abroad	12.1	14.5	18.3 I	22.7	25.3	39.4	39.6	38.3
024	GNP at current market prices	188.5	209.6	252.5 I	300.9	349.5	403.8	459.4	510.5
	At Current Market Prices								
025	Expenditure on GDP	176.3	195.1	234.2 I	278.2	324.2	364.4	419.8	472.2
026	Private consumption	141.7	161.0	192.4 I	224.1	263.7	291.9	336.7	385.3
027	Government consumption	19.1	20.3	23.5 I	28.3	33.5	41.6	50.7	57.1
028	Gross fixed capital formation	30.5	33.1	41.3 I	47.7	54.6	61.8	69.2	77.9
029	Increase in stocks	1.0	1.8	2.0 I	4.5	7.9	6.7	7.5	8.6
030	Exports of goods and services	16.6	21.5	29.5 I	35.7	33.0	44.4	47.8	49.9
031	Less: Imports of goods and services	32.6	42.5	54.6 I	62.1	68.5	82.0	92.2	106.7
032	Statistical discrepancy	–	–	– I	–	–	–	–	–
	At Constant 1959/60 I 1980/81 Factor Cost								
033	GDP by Industrial Origin	45.7	48.2	51.7 I	247.8	266.6	284.7	296.0	321.8
034	Agriculture	14.4	14.8	15.8 I	76.4	80.0	83.5	79.5	88.2
035	Mining	0.2	0.2	0.3 I	1.1	1.2	1.2	1.2	1.3
036	Manufacturing	7.4	8.0	8.8 I	37.4	42.6	45.6	49.2	53.2
037	Electricity, gas and water	1.2	1.4	1.5 I	5.9	6.0	6.4	7.3	7.5
038	Construction	2.2	2.4	2.6 I	11.6	12.2	11.9	12.0	13.2
039	Trade	6.5	6.9	7.4 I	37.3	41.0	44.4	46.4	51.9
040	Transport and communications	3.0	3.3	3.5 I	23.9	25.9	28.0	30.3	32.7
041	Finance	2.7	2.9	2.9 I	16.8	18.8	21.6	25.0	26.6
042	Public administration	4.7	4.9	5.2 I	19.3	19.5	21.5	23.2	23.9
043	Others	3.3	3.5	3.7 I	18.1	19.3	20.6	21.9	23.3
044	Indirect taxes less subsidies	4.2	4.1	5.1 I	30.4	29.8	31.8	36.5	35.9
045	GDP at *1959/60* I *1980/81* market prices	49.9	52.3	56.9 I	278.2	296.4	316.5	332.5	357.7
046	Net factor income from abroad	2.7	3.1	3.2 I	22.7	22.9	33.0	31.6	28.8
047	GNP at *1959/60* I *1980/81* market prices	52.6	55.4	60.0 I	300.9	319.3	349.5	364.1	386.6
	At Constant 1959/60 I 1980/81 Market Prices								
048	Expenditure on GDP	49.9	52.3	56.9 I	278.2	296.4	316.5	332.5	357.7
049	Private consumption	39.9	43.6	47.2 I	224.1	234.2	243.7	258.7	281.2
050	Government consumption	5.9	6.1	6.4 I	28.3	30.7	36.3	40.7	43.5

	1986	1987	1988	1989	1990	1991	1992	1993	1994	1995	
As of 1 July	99.16	102.24	105.41	108.68	112.05	115.52	119.11	122.80	126.61	129.80	001
Fiscal year ending 30 June											
	28.47	30.06	30.38	31.38	32.30	32.31	33.48	34.22	35.30	36.19	002
	27.44	29.14	29.43	30.40	31.29	30.28	31.52	32.60	33.59	34.44	003
	14.82	14.35	15.05	15.57	16.00	14.37	15.21	15.50	16.81	17.23	004
	3.61	4.08	3.74	3.85	3.97	3.70	3.87	3.55	3.37	3.46	005
	0.07	0.07	0.04	0.05	0.05	0.05	0.08	0.03	0.03	0.03	006
	8.94	10.64	10.60	10.93	11.27	12.16	12.36	13.52	13.38	13.72	007
	1.03	0.92	0.95	0.98	1.01	2.03	1.96	1.62	1.71	1.75	008
	3.6	3.1	3.1	3.1	3.1	6.3	5.9	4.7	4.8	4.8	009
Fiscal year ending 30 June											
	466.3	515.4	601.0	683.1	759.9	908.4	1077.9	1200.1	1412.5	1671.7	010
	128.8	135.3	156.4	184.1	197.4	233.1	282.4	297.8	357.9	434.9	011
	3.3	3.7	4.8	4.9	5.4	6.4	7.1	7.4	8.7	9.0	012
	75.9	85.8	100.9	113.5	132.3	158.8	186.8	207.3	246.9	286.7	013
	10.6	11.8	15.7	17.1	21.5	30.6	36.6	38.6	40.9	51.5	014
	19.0	22.5	25.1	27.7	32.1	38.2	43.8	49.8	55.2	61.0	015
	72.7	80.9	100.6	115.8	129.1	152.0	178.0	195.3	229.3	273.8	016
	41.2	44.6	51.0	54.3	60.5	77.7	101.0	127.5	149.3	166.9	017
	38.3	41.8	46.3	50.3	55.6	66.6	76.9	89.1	109.0	125.6	018
	42.1	51.0	57.3	65.2	69.1	76.5	85.5	94.6	105.3	130.7	019
	34.4	38.0	42.9	50.2	56.9	68.4	79.9	92.7	110.0	131.6	020
	48.2	57.1	74.4	86.6	96.1	112.2	133.4	141.5	158.7	193.9	021
	514.5	572.5	675.4	769.7	855.9	1020.6	1211.4	1341.6	1571.2	1865.6	022
	41.4	36.4	29.1	28.0	36.9	23.9	12.5	10.0	4.0	15.0	023
	555.9	608.9	704.5	797.8	892.8	1044.5	1223.9	1351.6	1575.2	1880.6	024
	514.5	572.5	675.4	769.7	855.9	1020.6	1211.4	1341.6	1571.2	1865.6	025
	392.5	415.7	486.6	543.3	611.0	697.4	850.0	971.0	1119.7	1364.5	026
	65.7	77.5	104.8	129.2	129.6	145.6	155.6	174.7	189.1	207.8	027
	87.5	100.0	111.3	133.2	148.1	177.6	225.4	256.6	280.9	320.9	028
	9.0	9.5	10.4	12.4	14.0	15.8	18.7	21.1	24.6	28.2	029
	63.3	79.1	93.6	108.3	126.6	172.8	209.2	217.4	254.2	306.2	030
	103.5	109.3	131.2	156.6	173.3	188.7	247.4	299.1	297.3	362.1	031
	–	–	–	–	–	–	–	–	–	–	032
	342.2	362.1	385.4	403.9	422.5	446.0	480.4	491.3	513.5	536.2	033
	93.4	96.5	99.1	105.9	109.1	114.5	125.4	118.6	125.0	132.3	034
	1.7	1.8	2.0	2.1	2.3	2.5	2.6	2.6	2.8	2.7	035
	57.2	61.5	67.6	70.3	74.3	79.0	85.3	89.4	94.7	97.5	036
	8.4	9.2	10.7	12.1	13.9	15.4	16.8	17.9	18.5	20.5	037
	14.0	15.8	16.6	16.9	17.5	18.5	19.6	20.7	21.0	21.3	038
	55.4	58.7	63.9	67.3	69.7	73.4	78.8	81.1	83.3	86.7	039
	34.3	36.8	39.3	37.7	40.2	42.7	47.2	50.3	52.2	53.6	040
	27.8	28.9	30.3	31.7	32.9	34.2	35.9	38.7	41.0	42.9	041
	25.2	26.5	27.7	29.9	30.7	31.7	32.5	33.3	33.8	34.8	042
	24.9	26.5	28.2	30.1	32.0	34.1	36.3	38.7	41.2	43.9	043
	35.2	39.7	47.0	49.9	51.6	54.0	58.7	58.1	56.7	59.5	044
	377.4	401.8	432.4	453.9	474.1	500.0	539.1	549.4	570.2	595.7	045
	31.3	26.6	17.1	14.9	17.2	9.5	4.9	3.7	1.3	4.3	046
	408.7	428.3	449.5	468.8	491.3	509.4	544.1	553.1	571.5	600.0	047
	377.4	401.8	432.4	453.9	474.1	500.0	539.1	549.4	570.2	595.7	048
	278.2	288.0	317.3	319.9	334.3	331.5	376.2	384.3	392.9	429.5	049
	47.8	54.2	56.5	68.1	65.9	65.6	60.4	71.1	68.7	63.9	050

	Item	1978	1979	1980	1981	1982	1983	1984	1985
051	Gross fixed capital formation	6.9	6.7	6.9	47.7	52.3	57.5	60.4	66.6
052	Increase in stocks	0.3	0.4	0.4	4.5	7.3	5.9	6.0	6.6
053	Exports of goods and services	3.2	3.4	4.2	35.7	33.6	41.8	40.3	40.1
054	Less: Imports of goods and services	6.3	7.9	8.3	62.1	61.8	68.7	73.7	80.2
055	Statistical discrepancy	–	–	–	–	–	–	–	–
	Investment Financing, at current prices								
056	Gross domestic capital formation	31.5	34.9	43.3	52.2	62.4	68.5	76.7	86.5
057	Gross national saving	27.6	28.3	36.6	48.5	52.3	70.2	71.9	68.0
058	Gross domestic saving	15.5	13.8	18.3	25.8	27.0	30.8	32.3	29.7
059	Net factor income from abroad	12.1	14.5	18.3	22.7	25.3	39.4	39.6	38.3
060	Foreign saving	3.9	6.6	6.7	3.7	10.1	-1.7	4.8	18.5
061	Net transfer from abroad	...	...	...	...	...	...	...	...
062	Net borrowing from abroad	...	...	...	...	...	...	...	...
	Per Capita GNP, Rupees								
063	Current prices	2460	2655	3103	3589	4043	4531	5000	5389
064	Constant *1959/60* *1980/81* prices	687	702	738	3589	3693	3921	3963	4081
	PRODUCTION								*Thousand metric tons;*
	Agriculture								
065	1. Sugarcane	30077	27326	27498	32359	36580	32534	34287	32140
066	2. Wheat	8367	9950	10857	11475	11304	12414	10882	11703
067	3. Rice	2950	3272	3216	3123	3430	3445	3340	3315
068	4. Cotton	575	473	728	714	748	824	495	1009
069	5. Maize	821	799	875	970	930	1005	1014	1028
070	6. Gram	614	538	313	337	294	491	522	524
071	7. Jowar	284	252	249	230	225	222	222	230
072	8. Bajra	318	317	277	214	272	220	256	284
	Mining								
073	1. Lime stone	4029	3298	2798	3464	3682	4232	4696	4634
074	2. Rock salt	435	486	495	514	534	548	581	573
075	3. Gypsum	356	234	368	554	303	341	339	400
	Manufacturing								
076	1. Cement	3224	3023	3343	3538	3657	3938	4503	4732
077	2. Cycle tubes (rubber), *'000 units*	5020	4154	5147	5425	5449	5226	6173	7040
078	3. Urea	595	621	641	963	1224	1832	1798	1815
079	4. Sugar	861	607	586	851	1301	1127	1147	1306
080	5. Cotton yarn	298	328	363	375	430	448	432	432
081	6. Vegetable products	360	422	452	505	531	513	595	640
082	7. Cotton cloth, *Mn sq. m.*	391	339	342	308	325	336	297	272
083	8. Mild steel products	315	362	421	495	551	637	654	718
	Production Indexes								*Period*
084	Agriculture, *1979-81 = 100*	89	96	99	105	109	108	117	123
085	Mining, *1975-76* *1980-81 = 100*[a]	124	129	140	153	110	118	122	147
086	Manufacturing, *1980-81 = 100*[b]	75	80	90	100	116	123	133	143
	ENERGY								*Annual*
	Crude petroleum, *'000 bbl*								
087	Production	3578	3752	3649	3583	3963	4738	4884	9525
	Coal, *'000 m.t.*								
088	Production	1279	1261	1504	1597	1765	1855	1926	2168
	Natural gas, *Mn cu. m.*								
089	Production	5826	6300	7537	8623	9301	9826	9811	10250
090	Consumption	5826	6300	7537	8623	9301	9826	9511	10250

1986	1987	1988	1989	1990	1991	1992	1993	1994	1995	
69.8	73.0	72.0	77.3	81.3	82.3	91.6	96.4	95.5	98.3	051
6.6	6.6	6.6	7.1	7.5	7.6	8.7	8.7	8.8	8.7	052
53.3	59.9	57.1	65.0	65.7	87.7	99.8	101.1	104.3	99.2	053
78.3	79.8	77.1	83.5	80.6	74.6	97.7	112.1	100.1	103.9	054
–	–	–	–	–	–	–	–	–	–	055
96.5	109.5	121.7	145.6	162.1	193.4	244.1	277.7	305.5	349.1	056
97.7	115.7	113.2	125.2	152.3	201.5	218.3	205.9	266.4	308.3	057
56.3	79.3	84.1	97.2	115.4	177.6	205.8	195.9	262.4	293.3	058
41.4	36.4	29.1	28.0	36.9	23.9	12.5	10.0	4.0	15.0	059
-1.2	-6.2	8.5	20.4	9.8	-8.0	25.8	71.8	39.1	40.8	060
...	...	...	...	...	...	...	...	...	...	061
...	...	...	...	...	...	...	...	...	...	062
5692	6046	6786	7453	8090	9189	10454	11208	12688	14720	063
4185	4254	4330	4380	4451	4482	4647	4587	4603	4697	064

Fiscal year ending 30 June

1986	1987	1988	1989	1990	1991	1992	1993	1994	1995	
27856	29926	33029	36976	35494	35989	38865	38059	44427	47168	065
13923	12016	12675	14419	14316	14565	15684	16157	15213	17002	066
2919	3486	3241	3200	3220	3261	3243	3116	3995	3447	067
1217	1320	1469	1426	1456	1638	2181	1540	1368	1479	068
1009	1111	1127	1204	1179	1185	1203	1184	1213	1318	069
586	583	372	456	562	531	513	347	411	559	070
219	236	181	248	262	239	225	238	212	263	071
258	233	135	201	204	196	139	203	138	228	072
6313	6885	7610	7249	7736	9009	8528	9015	9125	9839	073
619	503	502	620	735	736	833	895	916	890	074
381	412	404	426	491	468	471	533	666	624	075
5773	6508	7072	7125	7488	7762	8321	8558	8100	7913	076
6121	6307	5748	6157	5501	5468	5757	5612	6191	5146	077
1820	1993	1985	2009	2109	2050	1898	2306	3104	3000	078
1116	1286	1771	1858	1857	1934	2322	2397	2922	3001	079
482	586	685	758	912	1041	1171	1219	1310	1370	080
612	609	697	624	683	656	639	725	671	678	081
253	238	282	270	295	293	308	325	315	322	082
732	782	870	...	...	...	...	...	...	...	083

averages

1986	1987	1988	1989	1990	1991	1992	1993	1994	1995	
134	135	141	150	155	167	166	171	181	190	084
183	187	212	218	250	275	278	278	275	270	085
154	165	179	183	192	203	219	228	237	238	086

values

1986	1987	1988	1989	1990	1991	1992	1993	1994	1995	
14366	15005	16309	17074	19473	23486	22394	21885	20662	...	087
2115	2157	2727	2619	2751	2872	3073	3078	3214	...	088
10769	11161	12383	12900	14094	15021	15597	16524	17768	...	089
...	...	...	...	...	...	...	...	...	...	090

	Item	1978	1979	1980	1981	1982	1983	1984	1985
	Electricity, *Mn kWh*								
091	Production	12161	12965	14978	16219	18161	20291	22492	23671
092	Consumption	...	...	10415	11392	12952	14432	16140	18158
	PRICE INDEXES [a]								*Period*
093	Consumer (General), *1980/81| 1990/91 = 100*	75.4	80.4	89.0	100.0	111.1	116.3	124.8	131.8
094	Wholesale, *1980/81 = 100*	73.8	78.7	88.4	100.0	107.4	113.1	124.4	130.9
095	Implicit GDP deflator, *1959/60| 1980/81 = 100*	353.2	372.9	411.8 |	100.0	109.4	115.1	126.3	132.0
	MONEY AND BANKING								*Billion rupees;*
096	Money supply (M1)	47.2	56.8	66.7	72.3	87.3	100.6	105.8	123.1
097	Currency in circulation	21.0	26.4	32.5	34.5	41.2	46.4	52.0	58.7
098	Demand deposits	26.2	30.4	34.2	37.8	46.1	54.2	53.8	64.4
099	Quasi-money	23.4	27.3	30.7	36.3	44.9	59.3	61.5	68.9
100	Money supply (M2)	70.6	84.1	97.3	108.6	132.2	159.9	167.4	192.0
101	Foreign assets (net)	1.5	4.3	8.9	2.8	-0.7	12.7	-3.6	-10.9
102	Domestic credit	80.2	96.5	111.5	127.0	157.1	179.9	206.7	242.8
103	Claims on govt. sector (net)	39.7	47.4	55.3	59.1	75.7	82.4	92.5	96.2
104	Claims on private sector	40.5	49.1	56.2	67.9	81.4	97.5	114.2	146.6
105	Claims on other financial insts.	–	–	–	–	–	–	–	–
106	Other items	-11.1	-16.7	-23.1	-21.2	-24.2	-32.7	-35.7	-39.9
	Deposit Money Banks								
107	Demand deposits	29.5	33.9	39.3	43.5	50.9	63.3	65.9	71.9
108	Savings deposits	22.0	25.3	28.6	34.2	41.8	52.6	57.3	64.2
109	Time deposits	25.1	29.0	32.1	38.9	46.9	62.0	66.0	82.4
110	Loans and advances	37.1	44.3	53.4	62.1	76.6	92.8	104.3	125.6
	Interest Rates								*Per cent;*
	On deposits [c]								
111	Savings	7.58	7.57	7.59	7.59	7.62	7.62	7.62	7.64
112	Time: 6 months	8.83	8.91	8.99	9.97	9.30	9.36	9.64	7.88
113	12 months	10.04	10.06	10.15	10.61	9.88	9.84	9.80	9.26
	GOVERNMENT FINANCE								*Million Rupees;*
	Central Government								
114	Current revenue	21969	25725	39732	37721	53839	61467	74855	80042
115	Taxes	16555	19339	32507	27881	43003	49029	53646	55963
116	Non-taxes [d]	5414	6386	7225	9840	10836	12438	21209	24079
117	Current expenditure	22782	29852	34845	39216	44544	57738	71945	83769
118	Current surplus/deficit	-813	-4127	4887	-1495	9295	3729	2910	-3727
119	Capital receipts	3547	4129	7626	6464	–	–	–	–
120	Capital expenditure	16041	19294	23744	21882	26469	29383	28057	33050
121	Capital account surplus/deficit	-12494	-15165	-16118	-15418	-26469	-29383	-28057	-33050
122	Net lending	–	–	–	–	–	–	–	–
123	Overall surplus/deficit	-13307	-19292	-11231	-16913	-17174	-25654	-25147	-36777
	Financing								
124	Domestic borrowing	4868	9326	10926	3417	6313	14368	12280	12873
125	Foreign borrowing	6402	9096	1826	9756	5345	5162	5001	5169
126	Foreign grants	1082	858	4456	1384	–	–	–	–
127	Use of cash balances	955	12	-5977	2356	5516	6124	7866	18735
	EXTERNAL TRADE								*Million Rupees;*
128	Exports, fob	13248	17078	23715	29565	26684	34675	37627	38517
129	Imports, cif	27817	36390	46932	53548	59490	68164	76718	89800
130	Trade balance	-14569	-19312	-23217	-23983	-32806	-33489	-39091	-51283
	Exports, by SITC section								
131	Food and live animals	3382	4598	5781	7294	6001	6238	8769	6187
132	Beverage and tobacco	137	102	81	55	106	123	146	161
133	Crude materials excl. fuels	1642	1371	4152	5911	3768	4837	2916	5684
134	Mineral fuels, etc.	626	608	1765	1676	2082	988	544	525

1986	1987	1988	1989	1990	1991	1992	1993	1994	1995	
26455	29326	34237	35562	37999	41390	46224	48911	49889	...	091
20107	22453	25650	26967	...	...	...	...	...	...	092

averages

1986	1987	1988	1989	1990	1991	1992	1993	1994	1995	
137.6	142.5	151.5	167.2	177.3	199.8 I	110.6	121.5	135.1	167.4	093
137.0	143.8	158.2	173.5	186.2	208.0	227.3	243.4	280.0	325.6	094
136.3	142.5	156.2	169.6	180.5	204.1	224.7	244.2	275.6	313.2	095

As of end of period

1986	1987	1988	1989	1990	1991	1992	1993	1994	1995	
145.3	173.1	189.8	217.1	260.6	284.1	354.4	387.1	435.4	491.0	096
71.6	81.9	92.1	105.3	125.4	142.9	162.3	177.9	195.8	234.0	097
73.7	91.2	97.7	111.8	135.2	141.2	192.1	209.2	239.6	257.0	098
77.6	86.3	89.5	83.0	82.6	127.4	201.8	231.2	279.0	322.0	099
222.8	259.4	279.3	300.1	343.2	411.5	556.2	618.4	714.4	813.0	100
-11.7	-8.5	-8.7	-23.9	-15.0	-23.9	-12.4	-10.3	40.3	-15.0	101
282.9	328.8	357.7	394.8	430.4	511.6	654.1	725.7	799.3	941.2	102
110.6	147.8	154.3	175.2	191.5	249.7	332.7	355.5	376.7	434.7	103
172.3	181.0	203.4	219.6	238.9	261.9	321.4	370.2	422.6	506.5	104
–	–	–	–	–	–	–	–	–	–	105
-48.4	-60.9	-69.7	-70.8	-72.2	-76.2	-85.5	-97.0	-125.2	-113.2	106
82.5	99.5	105.5	124.4	144.8	182.4	217.6	246.7	296.7	321.2 *	107
77.7	88.6	94.0	107.4	124.9	157.4	205.2	232.2	272.1	292.1 *	108
99.2	111.0	117.8	134.1	161.6	203.6	258.2	302.4	361.8	401.2 *	109
149.0	153.3	169.2	201.1	219.7	251.3	318.2	370.5	418.3	462.9 *	110

Period averages

1986	1987	1988	1989	1990	1991	1992	1993	1994	1995	
6.99	6.93	6.59	6.62	6.94	6.93	7.67	8.05	7.85	7.57 *	111
8.03	7.82	8.64	8.92	9.00	8.96	10.34	10.80	10.58	10.35 *	112
9.16	8.49	8.81	9.03	9.38	9.26	10.80	11.40	11.62	11.17 *	113

Fiscal year ending 30 June

1986	1987	1988	1989	1990	1991	1992	1993	1994	1995	
92819	105692	122810	144297	165585	171777	231504	241128	293257	364323	114
72423	82927	93456	110338	119435	129640	164308	178391	217607	297819	115
20396	22765	29354	33959	46150	42137	67196	62737	75650	66504	116
94686	116242	133645	153066	165595	195676	230120	272457	310014	346168	117
-1867	-10550	-10835	-8769	-10	-23899	1384	-31329	-16757	18155	118
–	–	–	–	–	–	–	–	–	–	119
39777	36160	46728	48110	56050	65293	91354	76196	74084	90000	120
-39777	-36160	-46728	-48110	-56050	-65293	-91354	-76196	-74084	-90000	121
–	–	–	–	–	–	–	–	–	–	122
-41644	-46710	-57563	-56879	-56060	-89192	-89970	-107525	-90841	-71845	123
26962	27371	30931	37865	29581	23724	-515	19972	55402	26097	124
8584	8424	12691	18195	22945	22101	18022	24334	25210	30595	125
–	–	–	–	–	–	–	–	–	–	126
6098	10915	13941	819	3534	43367	72463	63219	10229	15153	127

Fiscal year ending 30 June

1986	1987	1988	1989	1990	1991	1992	1993	1994	1995	
50363	65007	79353	91058	107672	139430	172883	177912	206309	252264	128
90979	92552	112617	135900	148891	171175	229959	258691	258365	320934	129
-40616	-27545	-33264	-44842	-41218	-31745	-57076	-80779	-52056	-68670	130
8607	8918	11049	10565	10320	13130	17211	16821	18538	28404	131
201	225	321	24	212	116	271	172	134	185	132
9579	9173	12917	20507	12921	13254	16944	10683	7197	7364	133
519	444	481	649	1028	2261	2071	2137	1621	2520	134

	Item	1978	1979	1980	1981	1982	1983	1984	1985
135	Animal, vegetable oil & fats	1	1	2	12	0	6	0	0
136	Chemicals	146	131	191	225	161	302	782	1474
137	Basic manufactures	5613	8328	9257	11285	11049	17436	17956	17440
138	Machines, transport equipment	209	302	303	252	270	431	374	527
139	Misc. manufactured goods	1143	1391	1789	2173	2563	3621	5331	5538
140	Unclassified goods	82	92	89	396	270	460	519	442
141	Re-exports	267	154	305	286	415	233	289	537
	Exports, by principal commodity								
142	1. Cotton yarn and thread	1130	2014	2108	2150	2159	3308	3047	4046
143	2. Cotton cloth	1741	2135	2416	2390	2949	3579	4856	4638
144	3. Rice	2408	3380	4179	5602	4128	3683	5688	3340
145	4. Leather	636	1247	1264	892	1152	1195	1972	2325
146	5. Raw cotton	1102	655	3321	5203	2938	3897	1772	4368
	Imports, by SITC section								
147	Food and live animals	3415	5376	3558	3616	3948	4491	5317	7960
148	Beverage and tobacco	18	20	25	25	19	27	28	28
149	Crude materials excl. fuels	1757	2141	2248	3883	3409	3739	5146	5253
150	Mineral fuels, etc.	4978	5328	10761	15354	18543	20910	19656	22489
151	Animal, vegetable oil & fats	1830	3280	2576	3137	3980	4167	7200	7895
152	Chemicals	3345	5347	5778	7349	5307	7508	8538	10049
153	Basic manufactures	4473	5754	7652	7403	9180	8896	9515	10161
154	Machines, transport equipment	7375	8424	13297	11591	13703	16815	19526	23730
155	Misc. manufactured goods	589	693	1020	1159	1385	1557	1707	2098
156	Unclassified goods	34	25	14	26	8	42	75	116
157	Re-imports	2	2	3	4	8	13	11	21
	Direction of Trade								*Million US dollars;*
158	Exports, Total	1490.3	2055.8	2617.9	2880.8	2401.6	3074.9	2558.7	2738.4
159	1. United States	98.9	119.1	139.3	197.3	169.1	192.3	262.6	274.4
160	2. Germany	89.6	116.3	142.8	115.0	100.6	136.6	138.0	148.7
161	3. United Kingdom	99.2	130.2	111.1	132.3	132.9	135.1	156.6	147.9
162	4. Japan	152.4	167.8	203.6	201.5	213.1	245.2	236.2	308.9
163	5. Hong Kong	124.5	142.3	169.8	93.3	117.9	95.5	37.0	83.4
164	6. United Arab Emirates	49.6	112.1	134.6	169.6	155.3	284.6	136.7	126.8
165	7. France	33.8	55.6	60.3	63.8	52.9	55.6	66.7	65.4
166	8. Saudi Arabia	72.7	110.6	141.8	190.1	197.6	264.4	189.2	180.2
167	9. Netherlands	30.4	33.7	40.2	38.0	28.8	27.4	36.2	42.4
168	10. Korea, Rep. of	11.5	6.9	15.7	7.1	8.9	19.8	20.2	46.3
169	Imports, Total	3285.2	4060.7	5349.5	5630.4	5459.5	5326.0	5852.2	5888.4
170	1. Japan	317.4	512.0	548.7	655.0	692.9	769.9	865.3	741.2
171	2. United States	494.3	517.0	751.8	470.7	538.0	505.5	636.5	821.8
172	3. Germany	217.2	218.9	241.9	305.0	313.0	358.2	329.3	374.3
173	4. Malaysia	67.5	83.2	164.6	166.0	142.6	175.2	322.2	256.8
174	5. Saudi Arabia	301.2	217.3	513.2	815.0	713.7	693.8	564.5	578.5
175	6. United Kingdom	213.9	284.4	302.6	328.1	381.2	321.4	382.9	360.3
176	7. Kuwait	198.3	327.7	507.5	456.8	602.6	364.8	490.9	482.1
177	8. China, People's Rep. of	83.4	123.2	167.8	180.3	149.3	146.8	143.6	144.5
178	9. Korea, Rep. of	51.7	80.3	73.1	107.2	103.9	98.3	84.0	83.7
179	10. France	105.8	100.8	215.9	216.2	85.3	111.9	104.0	81.9
	Trade Indexes								*1980/81 = 100;*
	Quantum index								
180	Exports	66.8	88.2	105.8	100.0	90.7	112.6	106.5	109.6
181	Imports	74.8	88.4	94.5	100.0	129.0	114.0	119.2	138.8
	Unit value index								
182	Exports	70.2	87.4	94.4	100.0	98.4	106.2	118.8	124.3
183	Imports	64.7	67.2	82.2	100.0	110.8	119.4	125.2	133.0

1986	1987	1988	1989	1990	1991	1992	1993	1994	1995	
0	2	5	0	1	–	0	1	1	15	135
990	166	291	328	593	491	691	820	913	1689	136
21348	31747	39002	41429	56981	76952	91066	98428	118716	142798	137
356	301	133	225	371	412	858	651	572	505	138
7727	12243	14046	16133	23767	31412	42087	46833	57336	67076	139
265	137	200	321	274	252	528	482	470	617	140
771	1652	908	875	1203	1149	1156	884	811	1091	141
4572	8766	9597	11704	17917	26751	29263	29308	38197	47250	142
5083	5931	8539	8947	12000	15199	20372	22430	24788	33373	143
5527	5139	6404	5966	5144	7848	10340	8214	7319	14026	144
2900	4079	5041	4702	6002	6184	5991	5769	6772	8401	145
8290	7676	10758	18032	9550	9553	12944	7001	2383	1424	146
9851	9035	7671	14147	17200	13736	18010	23067	18128	25657	147
31	36	37	34	50	80	95	77	90	282	148
4941	5650	8141	9375	9558	10582	15010	13945	17003	25679	149
17630	14806	19226	19596	25898	39215	36063	41864	46406	55237	150
6874	5003	8977	9663	9571	10433	11491	16668	16667	33273	151
11663	15773	17612	21317	25287	27903	36493	38781	45065	48975	152
10039	11484	13914	17214	17597	17395	23806	22250	25291	29853	153
27247	27543	32869	39961	39816	46567	82654	95350	81966	92234	154
2583	2995	3769	4132	3682	4828	5960	6364	6333	7427	155
86	105	334	399	193	373	308	278	1299	2273	156
32	121	66	59	37	61	69	47	117	44	157

Calendar year

3383.0	4168.2	4509.3	4660.1	5587.2	6494.3	7269.0	6700.9	7332.2	8107.8	158
365.7	462.6	506.9	583.7	695.1	742.0	932.6	974.4	1158.6	1275.1	159
220.1	296.3	313.5	318.4	475.9	543.1	509.2	551.1	541.1	568.5	160
216.0	290.5	308.3	298.5	413.8	450.9	504.8	489.4	563.1	534.2	161
330.4	476.6	515.8	489.3	456.7	520.5	557.1	485.3	536.6	536.6	162
89.7	102.0	193.1	232.9	278.2	387.0	572.4	367.7	567.2	603.3	163
145.4	155.7	184.5	180.7	184.4	233.4	362.8	429.8	397.7	348.9	164
114.6	133.0	139.8	154.4	222.6	252.5	292.1	288.8	269.4	267.1	165
262.7	229.1	174.8	100.3	163.4	256.5	315.6	259.0	207.8	229.0	166
67.0	76.8	93.7	83.0	112.4	127.5	177.5	189.5	228.4	241.7	167
90.0	112.1	135.8	144.5	166.3	265.2	169.5	167.0	210.0	259.6	168
5367.1	5818.5	6588.3	7106.8	7382.9	8431.3	9374.8	9492.2	8884.4	11555.1	169
874.5	925.8	971.7	927.7	877.0	1245.5	1331.2	1487.3	832.0	1281.0	170
705.5	547.0	855.6	1094.9	946.3	942.9	980.3	879.2	868.7	1059.2	171
466.8	468.5	500.6	515.6	544.8	671.7	726.9	678.2	700.5	712.7	172
178.8	188.3	259.9	240.3	245.0	381.8	418.6	480.8	658.3	1005.8	173
308.2	291.0	290.3	327.6	461.2	382.1	497.2	506.1	488.0	545.6	174
364.1	408.5	418.3	393.7	359.6	432.1	550.7	452.9	474.2	565.5	175
283.0	481.5	454.2	727.3	440.3	35.5	177.3	353.3	566.5	579.0	176
162.0	232.1	248.1	321.8	337.5	357.4	421.1	422.7	421.1	612.0	177
105.3	142.9	210.7	211.7	203.7	272.1	344.3	446.8	286.9	355.1	178
125.2	159.8	275.1	165.0	165.6	424.5	303.7	352.5	361.2	259.1	179

Period averages [a]

159.5	214.3	179.4	206.1	181.2	208.6	234.5	219.7	234.8	266.7	180
139.8	133.8	148.6	159.5	148.3	146.5	172.1	194.8	174.5	192.2	181
118.7	132.1	163.9	168.0	192.9	197.1	209.6	214.9	243.8	308.5	182
132.2	136.9	170.2	187.5	215.0	252.8	253.3	266.7	297.1	348.4	183

	Item	1978	1979	1980	1981	1982	1983	1984	1985
184	Terms of trade	108.5	130.1	114.8	100.0	88.8	88.9	94.9	93.5
	BALANCE OF PAYMENTS							*Million US dollars;*	
185	Merchandise exports, fob	1282	1644	2341	2798	2319	2627	2669	2457
186	Merchandise imports, fob	-2751	-3816	-4857	-5563	-5768	-5616	-5993	-6009
187	Trade balance	-1469	-2172	-2516	-2765	-3449	-2989	-3324	-3552
188	Other goods, services and income	-357	-436	-519	-501	-497	-603	-717	-815
189	Credit	403	512	666	759	864	910	975	941
190	Debit	-760	-948	-1185	-1260	-1361	-1513	-1692	-1756
191	Unrequited transfer	1338	1624	2163	2517	2830	3414	3353	3087
192	Private	1226	1496	1895	2242	2412	3081	3044	2687
193	Official	112	128	268	275	418	333	309	400
194	Current balance	-488	-984	-872	-749	-1116	-178	-688	-1280
195	Direct investment	34	34	68	71	122	26	43	77
196	Portfolio investment	–	–	–	–	–	–	–	23
197	Other long-term capital	665	572	1133	519	397	610	375	359
198	Other short-term capital	128	174	69	206	31	226	187	-165
199	Net errors and omissions	-24	-19	15	-39	-14	14	-6	-31
200	Overall balance	315	-225	413	8	-580	698	-89	-1017
201	Allocation of SDRs	–	38	59	37	–	–	–	–
202	Monetary movements	-315	187	-472	-45	580	-698	89	1017
	INTERNATIONAL RESERVES							*Million US dollars;*	
203	Total	740	941	1684	1507	1526	2729	1669	1412
204	Gold, national valuation	332	728	1188	786	557	756	633	605
205	Foreign exchange	368	168	467	665	853	1879	912	781
206	Reserve position in the Fund	–	–	–	–	65	93	87	0
207	SDRs	40	45	29	56	51	1	37	26
	EXCHANGE RATES							*Rupees per*	
208	End of period	9.900	9.900	9.900	9.900	12.840	13.500	15.360	15.980
209	Average of period	9.900	9.900	9.900	9.900	11.847	13.117	14.046	15.928
	EXTERNAL INDEBTEDNESS							*Million US dollars;*	
210	Total outstanding and disbursed	8329	8919	9931	1547	11640	11940	12141	13371
211	Long-term	7478	7905	8519	8620	9502	9530	9769	10606
212	Public and publicly guaranteed	7457	7889	8501	8595	9463	9497	9743	10580
213	Private non-guaranteed	21	16	18	25	39	34	26	26
214	Short-term	210	441	737	903	720	797	932	1310
215	Use of IMF credit	642	573	674	1024	1419	1613	1440	1455
	Debt service							*Transactions*	
216	Principal repayments on LT debt	217	308	353	364	337	789	607	734
217	Interest on long-term debt	183	214	248	202	254	316	316	310
218	Interest on short-term debt	–	–	87	89	86	67	68	72
	Average terms of new commitments								
219	Interest (%)	2.7	3.3	4.4	7.6	7.4	5.4	4.7	5.6
220	Maturity (years)	36.1	31.3	30.0	23.4	23.8	28.6	27.3	27.0
221	Grace period (years)	8.4	6.5	6.6	6.1	5.9	6.5	7.0	6.6
222	Grant element (%)	61.7	55.2	47.8	33.6	30.5	39.1	44.7	34.8

Footnotes:

a   Period averages of fiscal year.
b   Indices after 1987 are based on 96 items only due to non-availability of data for 10 items as a result of the withdrawal of excise duty starting July 1988. Data are period averages of fiscal year.
c   As of end of December.
d   Includes surplus of autonomous bodies from 1982 onward.

1986	1987	1988	1989	1990	1991	1992	1993	1994	1995	
89.8	96.5	96.3	89.6	89.7	78.0	82.7	80.6	82.1	88.5	184

Fiscal year ending 30 June

3191	3938	4396	4775	5368	6364	6762	6782	6685	7884	185
-5971	-6249	-7080	-7328	-8077	-8621	-8998	-10049	-8685	-10137	186
-2780	-2311	-2684	-2553	-2709	-2257	-2236	-3267	-2000	-2253	187
-1016	-1094	-1444	-1485	-1716	-1958	-2224	-2748	-2355	-2546	188
933	1082	944	1323	1515	1591	1581	1628	1720	1942	189
-1949	-2176	-2388	-2808	-3231	-3549	-3805	-4376	-4075	-4488	190
3151	2851	2724	2720	2780	2963	3114	2327	2390	2397	191
2676	2437	2096	2207	2269	2338	...	...	...	...	192
475	414	628	513	511	625	...	...	...	...	193
-645	-554	-1404	-1318	-1645	-1252	-1346	-3688	-1965	-2402	194
106	121	173	165	242	260	343	310	360		195
83	121	126	17	86	92	272	270	339		196
473	118	944	1264	1052	1123	1935	1939	1854	2969	197
-183	-33	415	-81	64	-157	-1040	554	918		198
-42	22	15	105	-129	-69	-34	26	79	-109	199
-208	-205	269	152	-330	-3	130	-589	1585	458	200
–	–	–	–	–	–	–	–	–	–	201
208	205	-269	-152	330	3	-130	589	-1585	-458	202

As of end of period

1363	1365	1215	1236	985	1237	1531	1889	3721	2454	203
654	863	820	716	689	710	681	692	792	721	204
696	486	388	519	295	519	850	1196	2929	1718	205
0	0	0	0	0	0	0	0	0	0	206
13	16	7	1	1	7	0	1	0	15	207

US dollar

17.250	17.450	18.650	21.420	21.900	24.720	25.700	30.120	30.800	34.250	208
16.648	17.399	18.003	20.541	21.707	23.801	25.083	28.107	30.567	31.643	209

As of end of year

14868	16707	16984	18346	20661	23046	24194	26173	29579	...	210
11811	13505	14001	14642	16640	17845	18672	20552	23165	...	211
11782	13450	13907	14505	16503	17730	18551	20429	22993	...	212
30	56	93	138	138	114	121	123	172	...	213
1863	2280	2429	2771	3185	4134	4394	4500	4856	...	214
1194	922	554	933	836	1068	1127	1122	1557	...	215

during the year

698	760	850	825	916	967	1200	1272	2055	...	216
356	397	435	455	521	586	631	691	801	...	217
129	147	190	233	254	323	339	387	466	...	218

5.6	4.8	5.3	5.0	5.3	5.7	4.4	3.6	4.3	...	219
26.9	25.6	23.7	23.6	22.5	20.4	18.5	20.2	23.0	...	220
6.8	7.0	6.2	6.6	6.1	5.4	6.6	5.7	6.4	...	221
34.7	39.1	36.8	39.5	34.9	31.4	36.2	40.6	42.3	...	222

	Item	1978	1979	1980	1981	1982	1983	1984	1985
001	**POPULATION** [a]	2.87	2.93	3.01	3.07	3.14	3.20	3.27	*Million;* 3.33
	NATIONAL ACCOUNTS *At Current Purchasers' Value*								*Million Kina;*
002	GDP by Industrial Origin	1413.3	1632.5	1708.1	1681.2	1749.1	2145.5	2282.2	2402.6
003	Agriculture	497.5	552.8	565.7	561.4	567.2	714.2	832.6	799.8
004	Mining	147.6	247.2	225.7	133.7	140.4	225.1	150.3	239.2
005	Manufacturing	134.0	152.2	162.3	166.6	164.6	213.4	249.8	261.5
006	Electricity, gas and water	17.0	20.8	6.3	19.9	19.4	30.9	45.1	45.4
007	Construction	52.4	54.6	64.2	70.5	82.0	123.6	111.0	94.0
008	Trade	130.9	145.5	135.2	140.3	142.4	218.0	224.4	237.5
009	Transport and communications	79.0	83.5	78.1	97.6	72.9	87.7	103.0	120.0
010	Finance	65.8	80.9	139.4	126.1	172.3	143.2	155.5	165.1
011	Public administration	106.5	106.5	125.7	143.0	144.5	360.6	378.7	409.7
012	Others	182.6	188.5	205.5	222.1	243.4	28.8	31.8	30.4
013	Net factor income from abroad	...	-39.6	-58.7	-43.0	-42.4	-119.4	-72.4	-88.5
014	GNP	...	1592.9	1649.4	1638.2	1706.7	2026.1	2209.8	2314.1
015	Expenditure on GDP	1413.3	1632.5	1708.1	1681.2	1749.1	2145.5	2282.2	2402.6
016	Private consumption	788.6	890.5	1051.3	1104.2	1117.9	1385.6	1445.7	1599.9
017	Government consumption	353.3	371.4	411.2	454.4	468.1	498.8	531.8	572.4
018	Gross fixed capital formation	268.5	326.2	394.2	450.7	576.7	636.9	547.5	446.8
019	Increase in stocks	27.8	57.1	36.4	7.4	-14.2	-6.2	71.5	33.8
020	Exports of goods and services	579.3	742.5	737.6	642.9	644.3	775.5	904.7	1020.9
021	Less: Imports of goods and services	627.5	744.3	910.8	987.6	1058.2	1145.2	1219.0	1271.2
022	Statistical discrepancy	23.3	-10.9	-11.8	9.2	14.5	0.1	–	–
	Constant 1977 | 1983 Purchasers' Value								
023	GDP by Industrial Origin	...	...	...	...	...	...	...	...
024	Agriculture	...	...	...	...	...	...	...	...
025	Mining	...	...	...	...	...	...	...	...
026	Manufacturing	...	...	...	...	...	...	...	...
027	Electricity, gas and water	...	...	...	...	...	...	...	...
028	Construction	...	...	...	...	...	...	...	...
029	Trade	...	...	...	...	...	...	...	...
030	Transport and communications	...	...	...	...	...	...	...	...
031	Finance	...	...	...	...	...	...	...	...
032	Public administration	...	...	...	...	...	...	...	...
033	Others	...	...	...	...	...	...	...	...
034	Net factor income from abroad	...	...	...	...	...	...	...	...
035	GNP	...	...	...	...	...	...	...	...
036	Expenditure on GDP	1409.7	1435.2	1402.2	1398.3	1396.4 |	2145.5	2117.4	2200.7
037	Private consumption	728.6	764.5	794.1	768.8	744.5 |	1385.6	1362.6	1469.0
038	Government consumption	343.4	349.6	337.8	324.8	313.7 |	498.8	502.2	520.4
039	Gross fixed capital formation	260.4	300.9	339.3	347.8	400.1 |	636.9	513.6	390.7
040	Increase in stocks	27.8	52.6	29.2	5.3	-10.2 |	-6.2	63.6	24.3
041	Exports of goods and services	639.1	637.4	635.3	669.6	670.5 |	775.5	799.9	897.9
042	Less: Imports of goods and services	613.3	660.6	723.5	724.7	732.1 |	1145.2	1124.5	1101.6
043	Statistical discrepancy	23.7	-9.2	-10.0	6.7	9.9 |	0.1	0.0	–
	Investment Financing at current PV								
044	Gross domestic capital formation	296.3	383.3	430.6	458.1	562.5	630.7	619.0	480.6
045	Gross national saving [b]	...	415.4	259.3	181.0	228.6	155.5	303.7	272.6
046	Gross domestic saving	274.0	455.0	318.0	224.0	271.0	274.9	376.1	230.5
047	Net factor income from abroad	...	-39.6	-58.7	-43.0	-42.4	-119.4	-72.4	-88.5
048	Foreign saving	22.3	-71.7	112.6	234.1	291.5	355.8	242.9	250.1
	Per Capita GNP, Kina								
049	Current purchasers' value	...	544	548	534	544	633	676	695
050	Constant *1977 | 1983* PV [c]	491	490	466	455	445 |	670	648	661

1986	1987	1988	1989	1990	1991	1992	1993	1994	1995	
As of 1 July										
3.40	3.47	3.54	3.61	3.69	3.76	3.84	3.92	4.00	4.08	001
Calendar year										
2572.4	2854.4	3169.9	3045.7	3076.1	3605.5	4139.6	5016.0	5282.0	...	002
828.0	852.4	924.0	856.3	891.2	936.5	1021.0	...	...	...	003
329.8	490.0	609.5	352.7	452.2	612.9	924.5	...	...	...	004
256.3	268.9	294.3	336.9	275.8	345.1	390.3	...	...	...	005
40.0	43.6	46.1	49.0	52.3	59.2	65.1	...	...	...	006
103.7	101.8	133.2	161.3	155.1	224.0	210.6	...	...	...	007
259.5	285.7	307.7	328.2	296.8	358.5	387.1	...	...	...	008
130.5	141.0	151.9	163.5	190.9	243.0	233.6	...	...	...	009
145.8	157.7	171.8	172.9	130.8	147.6	42.8	...	...	...	010
431.1	460.0	484.6	543.4	551.3	588.2	649.6	...	...	...	011
47.7	53.3	46.8	81.5	79.7	90.5	215.0	...	...	...	012
-72.1	-130.5	-122.1	-115.0	-117.9	-117.9	-208.3	-95.2	...	...	013
2500.3	2723.9	3047.8	2930.7	2958.2	3487.6	3931.3	4920.8	...	...	014
2572.4	2854.4	3169.9	3045.7	3076.1	3605.5	4139.6	5016.0	5282.0	...	015
1673.6	1814.9	1919.4	1962.0	1816.3	2165.9	2396.4	2532.0	...	...	016
591.1	639.7	662.9	744.9	763.9	808.1	929.5	1017.8	...	...	017
539.2	551.2	737.0	790.7	772.9	1010.1	984.1	943.0	...	...	018
-31.5	34.1	125.5	-83.4	-21.0	-22.0	0.0	0.0	...	...	019
1121.0	1232.1	1371.1	1238.0	1249.7	1523.9	1870.0	2516.0	...	...	020
1321.0	1417.8	1646.0	1606.5	1505.7	1880.5	2040.4	1992.8	...	...	021
–	–	–	–	–	–	–	–	...	...	022
2324.5	2388.9	2458.4	2423.2	2350.8	2574.8	2878.7	3355.0	3382.4	...	023
710.7	748.7	775.0	785.7	803.1	781.9	829.2	907.0	972.4	...	024
364.5	354.4	363.5	225.8	277.3	393.4	613.7	995.8		...	025
220.4	222.3	230.9	250.3	193.3	223.9	241.9	245.8	1328.9	...	026
34.2	36.0	36.0	36.6	36.6	38.6	40.2	39.4		...	027
90.3	84.5	105.0	119.1	108.9	144.8	133.2	116.0		...	028
248.0	272.9	277.7	298.6	264.5	296.0	309.8	322.2		...	029
112.1	116.5	119.1	121.4	133.7	157.9	147.5	158.7		...	030
127.2	131.3	137.0	126.3	99.8	24.7	28.4	28.0	1081.1	...	031
377.8	379.0	379.1	395.3	384.7	382.4	401.6	424.3		...	032
39.3	43.3	35.1	64.1	48.9	131.2	133.2	117.8		...	033
...	...	...	...	...	...	...	...	...	...	034
...	...	...	...	...	...	...	...	...	...	035
2324.5	2388.9	2458.4	2423.4	2350.8	2574.8	2878.7	3355.0	3382.4	...	036
1452.1	1500.0	1504.5	1486.4	1286.9	1434.7	1547.1	...	...	...	037
510.9	526.5	517.5	548.5	533.1	527.1	580.1	...	...	...	038
458.8	452.9	572.1	586.6	533.1	652.8	612.4	...	...	...	039
-23.7	25.1	102.2	-73.9	-17.2	-18.3	0.0	...	...	...	040
1005.7	995.5	981.3	972.5	928.1	1075.0	1305.7	...	...	...	041
1079.2	1111.1	1219.3	1096.6	913.1	1096.5	1166.6	...	...	...	042
–	–	–	–	–	–	–	...	...	...	043
507.7	585.4	862.5	707.3	751.9	988.1	984.1	943.0	...	...	044
404.7	413.5	581.1	395.3	664.0	737.1	947.1	...	...	...	045
346.8	454.0	622.7	436.9	668.9	608.0	969.4	...	...	...	046
-72.1	-130.5	-122.1	-115.0	-117.9	-117.9	-208.3	-95.2	...	...	047
160.9	131.4	239.8	270.4	83.0	380.1	14.7	...	...	...	048
735	785	861	812	802	928	1024	1255	...	...	049
684	688	694	671	637	685	750	856	846	...	050

KEY INDICATORS OF DEVELOPING ASIAN AND PACIFIC COUNTRIES

Item	1978	1979	1980	1981	1982	1983	1984	1985
PRODUCTION								*Thousand metric tons;*
Agriculture								
051 1. Sweet potatoes	430	436	440	450	455	460	464	469
052 2. Copra	146	160	146	144	148	134	153	176
053 3. Coffee	46	44	55	51	41	54	46	47
054 4. Cocoa	32	30	26	32	29	29	28	32
055 5. Rubber	3	4	5	5	4	4	3	4
056 6. Peanuts	3	4	5	1	1	1	1	1
057 7. Sorghum	4	4	4	4	4	4	2	2
058 8. Rice	1	1	1	0	0	1	1	1
Mining								
059 1. Copper	193	172	142	164	173	181	163	169
060 2. Gold [d], *m.t.*	24	21	15	18	19	19	19	32
Manufacturing								
1. Wood products,								
061 except furniture, *'000 cu. m.*	1186	1186	1464	1307	2005	1872	1861	1878
Production Indexes								*Period*
062 Agriculture, *1979-81 = 100*	94.6	96.1	101.0	103.0	103.5	106.8	109.8	114.0
063 Mining	...	...	...	...	...	...	...	...
064 Manufacturing	...	...	...	...	...	...	...	...
ENERGY								*Annual*
Electricity, *Mn kWh*								
065 Production	1187	1215	1252	1244	1287	1436	1491	1545
066 Consumption	1187	1215	1252	1244	1287	1436	1491	1545
PRICE INDEXES								*1977 = 100;*
067 Consumer (Port Moresby)	106.5	114.0	127.9	140.6	146.1	168.3	171.9	176.8
068 Food	104.0	108.8	127.1	137.2	143.9	153.2	161.0	167.2
069 Implicit GDP deflator, *1977│ 1983 = 100*	100.3	113.7	121.8	120.2	125.3 │	100.0	107.8	109.2
MONEY AND BANKING								*Million Kina;*
070 Money supply (M1)	174.0	193.5	199.2	193.2	187.6	205.2	248.6	239.2
071 Currency in circulation [e]	61.5	67.9	70.5	73.4	72.4	79.9	91.5	94.3
072 Demand deposits [f]	112.5	125.6	128.7	119.8	115.2	125.3	157.1	145.0
073 Quasi-money	133.9	169.4	183.5	219.6	246.9	362.2	420.6	494.3
074 Money supply (M2)	307.9	362.9	382.7	412.8	434.5	567.4	669.2	733.5
075 Foreign assets (net) [g]	265.0	353.9	298.1	221.8	205.0	321.1	354.1	397.5
076 Domestic credit	207.8	264.0	255.0	332.9	362.9	329.6	395.3	416.7
077 Claims on govt. sector (net) [h]	13.3	35.0	-8.1	43.5	71.2	0.3	-1.4	16.1
078 Claims on private sector [i]	194.5	229.0	306.1	321.6	354.6	406.1	498.7	597.6
079 Claims on other financial insts.	...	...	-43.0	-32.2	-62.9	-76.8	-102.0	-197.0
080 Other items [j]	-164.9	-255.0	-170.4	-141.9	-133.4	-83.3	-80.2	-80.7
Deposit Money Banks								
081 Demand deposits [k]	126.7	143.1	143.9	135.5	131.8	137.9	167.4	154.4
082 Savings deposits [l]	64.0	76.2	84.0	89.6	97.4	113.6	135.0	137.2
083 Time deposits	114.0	190.4	166.2	183.5	199.2	275.0	290.2	366.4
084 Domestic credits outstanding [m]	185.4	211.3	266.8	308.0	343.2	394.9	488.6	587.0
Interest Rates								*Per cent;*
On deposits								
085 Savings	...	...	5.8	8.0	6.5	6.0	6.0	3.0-6.0
086 Time: 6 months	...	...	6.8	10.0	8.0	6.0-8.0	6.0-8.0	8.3-12.0
087 12 months	...	...	7.5	10.8	8.6	6.5-9.0	6.5-9.0	8.3-12.0
On loans and discounts								
088 Commercial bills [n]	...	...	...	...	...	10.75	10.75	13.00

	1986	1987	1988	1989	1990	1991	1992	1993	1994	1995	
Calendar year											
	470	471	510	460	460	470	475	480	484	...	051
	158	149	136	134	117	87	117	126	100	...	052
	45	63	62	71	67	58	50	62	66	...	053
	32	34	36	47	40	34	41 *	37 *	27	...	054
	6	6	5	4	4	3	3 *	3 *	...	...	055
	1	1	1	1	1	1	1 *	1 *	...	...	056
	2	2	1	1	1	1	1	1	1	...	057
	1	1	1	1	1	1	1	1	1	1	058
	181	210	222	209	197	192	188	192	207	235	059
	37	35	35	31	34	58	67	59	56	55	060
	2141	2480	2480	2480	2480	2480	...	...	...	...	061
averages											
	110.2	118.0	122.0	129.0	129.3	127.9	132.0	136.0	135.1	135.9	062
	...	...	...	...	...	...	...	...	...	...	063
	...	...	...	...	...	...	...	...	...	...	064
values											
	1676	1797	1745	1775	1790	1790	...	...	...	...	065
	1676	1797	1745	1775	1790	1790	...	...	...	...	066
Period averages											
	189.0	196.3	208.4	214.8	230.8	247.9	259.0	269.3	279.8	...	067
	171.4	175.5	182.3	189.4	207.5	223.6	230.9	236.5	240.9	...	068
	110.7	119.5	128.9	125.7	130.9	140.0	143.8	149.5	156.2	...	069
As of end of period											
	251.6	280.9	322.8	352.0	353.3	458.0	509.1	527.5	571.3	633.7	070
	95.7	106.4	115.2	122.0	134.8	137.4	141.2	160.5	166.2	181.8	071
	155.9	174.5	207.6	230.0	218.5	320.6	367.9	367.0	405.1	451.9	072
	588.4	596.9	649.1	682.9	726.3	813.1	922.0	1097.8	1093.4	1212.1	073
	840.0	877.8	971.9	1034.9	1079.6	1271.1	1431.1	1625.3	1664.7	1845.8	074
	414.0	408.3	329.6	259.0	243.8	179.4	142.3	177.7	109.4	291.3	075
	515.2	534.7	655.2	778.5	837.8	1093.2	1289.4	1448.7	1555.3	1556.4	076
	30.6	10.0	47.7	69.6	135.9	248.8	380.8	506.3	488.1	574.6	077
	677.7	748.6	857.3	939.7	954.7	1077.7	1124.8	1128.5	1262.6	1198.1	078
	-193.1	-223.9	-249.8	-230.8	-252.8	-233.3	-216.2	-186.1	-195.4	-216.3	079
	-89.2	-65.2	-12.9	-2.6	-2.0	-1.5	-0.6	-1.1	0.0	-1.9	080
	163.1	181.9	201.5	218.6	210.5	285.9	299.3	368.2	405.1	451.9	081
	146.3	158.9	173.9	188.4	200.8	208.2	222.8	252.7	269.9	272.6	082
	446.4	440.4	478.6	499.3	543.6	622.0	715.8	722.6	676.4	833.2	083
	657.4	706.9	780.9	854.7	870.2	976.8	1021.9	1056.5	1193.5	1133.3	084
Period averages											
	3.0-7.0	3.0-7.0	3.5-7.0	3.5-7.0	3.5-7.0	3.5-7.0	3.0-5.8	3.5-4.3	3.5-5.0	3.5-4.5	085
	7.0-9.0	8.0-9.5	8.0-10.3	8.0-10.8	9.0-10.8	9.0-11.3	5.5-7.3	4.3-5.5	4.5-5.8	6.8-8.3	086
	7.0-8.8	8.3-9.5	8.5-10.3	8.5-10.8	9.8-11.3	10.5-11.3	6.0-7.8	5.0-5.8	4.5-6.0	7.3-9.0	087
	11.00	11.50	11.50	11.75	11.75	11.75	9.75	7.75	8.00	7.00	088

	Item	1978	1979	1980	1981	1982	1983	1984	1985
	GOVERNMENT FINANCE								*Million Kina;*
	Central Government								
089	Current revenue	274	283	344	372	369	404	492	489
090	Taxes	206	206	240	331	322	352	429	431
091	Non-taxes	68	77	104	41	47	52	63	58
092	Current expenditure	414	481	507	546	572	610	649	708
093	Current surplus/deficit	-140	-198	-163	-174	-203	-206	-157	-219
094	Capital receipts	–	–	–	–	1	0	5	1
095	Capital expenditure	56	59	90	74	61	69	84	56
096	Capital account surplus/deficit	-56	-59	-90	-74	-60	-69	-79	-55
097	Net lending	–	–	–	–	20	32	16	1
098	Overall surplus/deficit	-196	-257	-253	-248	-284	-307	-253	-275
	Financing								
099	Domestic borrowing	16	48	31	10	21	-22	-27	44
100	Foreign borrowing	5	24	47	77	77	117	49	16
101	Foreign grants [o]	172	176	175	184	187	213	232	216
102	Use of cash balances	3	9	0	-23	-1	-0	-0	0
	Expenditure by Function, Central Govt. [p]								*Million Kina;*
103	Total	...	404.1	501.0	568.0 I	633.9	679.3	733.6	755.0
104	General public services	...	...	129.0	120.0 I	130.5	138.7	157.7	169.7
105	Defense	...	18.0	25.0	26.0 I	25.8	28.4	35.0	34.3
106	Education	...	...	89.0	103.0 I	107.9	109.4	141.9	129.2
107	Health	...	...	48.0	55.0 I	59.5	61.9	66.7	73.0
108	Social security & welfare	...	76.9	1.0	1.0 I	3.3	2.4	2.7	3.0
109	Housing & community amenities	...	...	17.0	15.0 I	15.9	13.2	10.3	14.0
110	Economic services	...	88.4	94.0	99.0 I	142.0	133.4	155.3	141.6
111	Agriculture	...	...	30.0	34.0 I	38.5	35.9	43.0	38.1
112	Industry	...	...	4.0	– I	22.3	20.5	18.9	21.2
113	Electricity, gas & water	...	...	6.0	6.0 I	8.1	7.2	5.8	3.2
114	Transport and communications	...	...	31.0	42.0 I	54.0	57.6	70.4	60.7
115	Other economic services	...	...	23.0	17.0 I	19.1	12.2	17.2	18.4
116	Others	...	220.8	98.0	149.0 I	149.0	191.9	164.0	190.2
	EXTERNAL TRADE								*Million Kina;*
117	Exports, fob	504	628	640	565	570	683	805	913
118	Imports, cif	478	562	685	737	751	823	866	875
119	Trade balance	26	66	-45	-172	-181	-140	-61	38
	Exports, by SITC section								
120	Food and live animals	205	218	208	145	126	160	216	212
121	Beverage and tobacco	–	–	–	1	–	2	2	3
122	Crude materials excl. fuels	261	360	388	360	376	448	435	410
123	Mineral fuels, etc.	0	–	–	–	–	–	–	5
124	Animal, vegetable oil & fats	23	35	29	27	34	44	104	83
125	Chemicals	0	0	1	1	1	–	–	–
126	Basic manufactures	10	9	3	5	4	2	3	4
127	Machines, transport equipment	–	–	–	7	11	8	1	10
128	Misc. manufactured goods	0	0	1	1	–	1	9	1
129	Unclassified goods	5	6	10	18	18	18	35	185
	Exports, by principal commodity								
130	1. Copper	123	184	139	135	123	161	136	164
131	2. Gold	104	163	172	159	172	201	183	319
132	3. Coffee beans	107	125	119	74	78	95	111	118
133	4. Forest products	25	38	46	44	62	55	82	67
134	5. Cocoa	63	62	47	34	32	41	67	63
	Imports, by SITC section								
135	Food and live animals	...	...	133	136	139	135	155	154
136	Beverage and tobacco	...	...	9	8	8	8	11	10
137	Crude materials excl. fuels	...	...	2	4	4	5	6	7

1986	1987	1988	1989	1990	1991	1992	1993	1994	1995	
Calendar year										
577	626	692	807	777	901	920	1128	1213	1399	089
462	519	602	689	618	639	772	967	1024	1222	090
115	107	90	118	159	261	148	161	189	177	091
757	774	803	881	954	1077	1222	1443	1451	1538	092
-180	-148	-111	-73	-177	-176	-302	-315	-238	-139	093
1	1	1	–	1	1	1	1	31	93	094
80	71	70	106	113	197	126	146	190	233	095
-79	-70	-68	-106	-112	-196	-125	-145	-159	-140	096
28	18	39	45	40	8	-11	5	-8	5	097
-287	-237	-218	-225	-329	-380	-416	-465	-420	-282	098
13	43	38	34	33	144	256	204	252	-18	099
69	9	-10	1	14	-57	39	46	-9	-56	100
205	184	190	190	222	312	196	182	178	192	101
0	0	0	0	60	-18	-75	33	0	164	102
Calendar year										
795.7	829.1	873.1	985.9	1066.9	1275.6	1350.7	1588.8	1581.1	...	103
173.6	187.7	198.2	212.9	219.4	211.9	251.0	295.6	328.6	...	104
36.4	38.5	40.1	45.6	65.8	50.1	56.5	66.6	52.7	...	105
127.3	134.2	172.0	194.8	224.3	221.0	200.4	236.1	278.1	...	106
77.5	81.0	81.7	96.3	90.7	109.3	106.3	125.3	140.3	...	107
3.1	4.4	4.5	11.4	10.3	12.1	10.0	11.8	10.4	...	108
11.1	10.0	11.4	10.7	11.4	5.8	8.3	9.8	56.0	...	109
166.1	179.6	183.4	207.1	227.3	300.4	290.6	339.9	408.4	...	110
47.4	52.3	50.3	63.2	77.0	75.8	91.5	107.8	129.5	...	111
24.3	19.3	17.4	11.5	14.2	22.8	18.9	19.9	23.9	...	112
3.8	3.4	3.4	26.1	29.2	34.7	34.0	40.0	48.1	...	113
75.4	76.0	83.4	75.2	81.7	108.4	96.0	113.1	135.9	...	114
15.2	28.6	28.8	31.1	25.2	58.7	50.2	59.1	71.0	...	115
200.6	193.7	181.8	207.1	217.7	365.0	427.6	503.7	306.6	...	116
Calendar year										
1014	1061	1210	1206	1149	1550	2006	2478	2682	3420	117
900	1014	1133	1261	1092	1336	1275	1110	1336	1620	118
114	47	77	-55	57	214	607	1437	1346	1800	119
286	214	182	208	160	132	130	147	...	...	120
1	1	0	1	1	1	–	1	...	...	121
447	653	831	818	605	676	701	938	...	...	122
3	3	2	1	2	3	361	724	...	...	123
40	40	52	54	42	58	90	88	...	...	124
–	–	2	2	1	1	–	–	...	...	125
2	2	5	11	21	19	17	13	...	...	126
5	4	16	31	68	122	91	59	...	...	127
1	1	1	2	10	26	8	5	...	...	128
229	143	119	78	238	512	608	503	...	...	129
156	282	447	345	349	324	314	256	367	...	130
399	423	405	317	393	667	746	682	702	...	131
209	135	114	140	103	80	68	89	205	...	132
75	111	98	96	80	90	148	410	494	...	133
56	56	46	45	30	34	34	32	29	...	134
162	171	182	191	195	...	...	...	...	...	135
8	12	15	15	15	...	...	...	...	...	136
7	8	9	8	9	...	...	...	...	...	137

	Item	1978	1979	1980	1981	1982	1983	1984	1985
138	Mineral fuels, etc.	...	...	118	158	146	167	156	154
139	Animal, vegetable oil & fats	...	...	2	2	2	3	4	3
140	Chemicals	...	...	37	45	39	61	68	65
141	Basic manufactures	...	...	92	105	119	129	140	134
142	Machines, transport equipment	...	...	206	215	230	223	244	262
143	Misc. manufactured goods	...	...	53	54	54	58	70	75
144	Unclassified goods	...	...	33	10	10	34	12	11
	Direction of Trade							*Million US dollars;*	
145	Exports, Total	715.1	883.3	1133.2	839.3	773.0	822.2	893.8	917.6
146	1. Australia	68.9	77.9	162.2	97.3	78.4	74.0	85.7	101.9
147	2. Japan	218.8	301.0	422.0	316.4	253.3	282.3	254.8	202.6
148	3. Germany	179.1	216.8	281.6	180.4	201.2	205.7	183.3	268.8
149	4. China, People's Rep. of	17.8	18.6	19.4	7.6	20.9	34.6	28.3	17.7
150	5. United States	62.5	51.4	52.7	40.4	14.7	18.2	30.2	36.4
151	6. United Kingdom	42.6	53.8	43.6	42.8	44.4	48.1	100.7	71.3
152	7. Philippines	5.1	5.9	5.3	4.5	7.3	4.8	1.2	2.4
153	8. New Zealand	5.7	6.0	6.3	6.3	6.7	7.4	9.8	8.5
154	9. Malaysia	0.0	0.0	0.1	5.5	4.0	2.6	8.1	0.1
155	10. Hong Kong	1.3	3.1	5.2	2.3	4.9	4.4	1.5	0.7
156	Imports, cif Total	666.1	823.1 I	923.5	1001.8	1017.9	974.5	844.9	788.2
157	1. Australia	322.8	416.1 I	376.8	375.7	419.2	385.7	344.8	327.0
158	2. Japan	132.5	134.5 I	166.6	165.9	146.1	149.9	135.2	138.3
159	3. Singapore	73.9	117.4 I	140.9	183.7	149.4	130.6	102.8	80.9
160	4. New Zealand	35.5	35.9 I	37.4	51.3	55.1	48.5	45.7	44.4
161	5. United States	24.8	31.5 I	60.0	76.4	86.9	96.7	75.9	66.7
162	6. Malaysia	2.3	3.1 I	3.4	4.1	3.6	3.7	3.5	3.6
163	7. Hong Kong	18.6	21.1 I	20.6	20.3	20.7	19.4	19.9	18.5
164	8. Indonesia	21.6	24.3 I	0.1	0.3	0.1	1.5	0.5	0.6
165	9. Thailand	4.1	2.3 I	1.2	1.1	1.3	2.2	0.9	1.2
166	10. United Kingdom	0.0	0.0 I	38.6	42.6	46.1	37.7	30.1	23.8
	Trade Indexes							*1981 = 100;*	
	Unit value index								
167	Exports [q]	161.4	218.5	227.1	185.7 I	101.4	115.9	131.5	129.3
168	Imports	...	...	...	...	...	115.5	126.3	134.4
169	Terms of Trade	...	...	...	...	...	100.3	104.1	96.2
	BALANCE OF PAYMENTS							*Million US dollars;*	
170	Merchandise exports, fob	714	1009	985	840	770	820	914	921
171	Merchandise imports, fob	-688	-783	-1021	-1096	-1018	-975	-963	-875
172	Trade balance	26	226	-36	-256	-247	-155	-49	47
173	Other goods, services and income	-247	-305	-438	-419	-374	-380	-440	-331
174	Credit	74	91	103	132	155	134	115	120
175	Debit	-321	-396	-541	-551	-529	-514	-555	-450
176	Unrequited transfer	166	156	161	154	138	159	167	130
177	Private	-88	-96	-106	-126	-123	-97	-95	-89
178	Official	254	252	267	281	261	257	262	218
179	Current balance	-55	78	-312	-521	-483	-376	-322	-155
180	Direct investment	34	41	60	86	84	138	113	82
181	Portfolio investment	-13	-3	–	-2	–	–	–	–
182	Other long-term capital	-63	6	41	308	397	208	125	38
183	Other short-term capital	56	-9	-4	25	-2	6	19	3
184	Net errors and omissions	37	-4	133	53	-33	121	113	29
185	Overall balance	-4	109	-84	-51	-36	97	49	-1
186	Allocation of SDRs	–	4	4	4	–	–	–	–
187	Monetary movements	4	-113	80	47	36	-97	-49	1

1986	1987	1988	1989	1990	1991	1992	1993	1994	1995	
93	112	98	64	30	...	...	...	...	...	138
3	4	3	3	5	...	...	...	...	...	139
82	85	84	79	82	...	...	...	...	...	140
149	181	206	253	223	...	...	...	...	...	141
308	340	425	525	423	...	...	...	...	...	142
76	88	99	110	96	...	...	...	...	...	143
12	13	12	13	14	...	...	...	...	...	144

Calendar year

1986	1987	1988	1989	1990	1991	1992	1993	1994	1995	
1047.5	1186.1	1442.9	1434.2	1265.5	1407.2	1981.2	2217.6	2378.8	2579.1	145
147.2	93.0	96.0	153.0	328.5	560.8	817.2	903.7	822.1	866.8	146
274.0	341.3	598.4	542.1	351.4	318.6	367.0	606.1	661.1	605.1	147
361.9	319.9	314.7	340.4	201.2	115.9	150.9	138.8	193.8	280.3	148
19.3	26.2	1.2	1.1	2.5	4.2	88.8	95.4	125.3	70.7	149
33.7	24.6	38.2	27.2	30.1	27.9	63.1	97.2	107.2	63.0	150
47.4	55.5	73.4	65.8	54.2	61.3	65.8	73.1	79.3	132.4	151
0.2	30.6	84.2	31.5	53.7	69.4	51.7	67.0	64.4	72.3	152
9.5	5.4	4.7	5.7	11.6	4.2	10.3	14.3	75.9	46.7	153
0.4	0.6	1.0	1.9	1.0	2.3	9.1	19.0	46.4	31.3	154
0.8	9.4	15.7	7.1	2.7	7.7	3.2	23.5	31.3	38.8	155
844.4	1088.9	1307.2	1467.3	1195.7	1461.9	1481.8	1526.7	1674.2	1658.5	156
341.3	476.3	585.2	611.6	559.6	684.6	606.5	610.8	693.5	673.4	157
149.6	204.8	235.7	233.4	159.3	163.4	166.7	188.8	179.5	121.3	158
52.7	72.1	74.7	102.5	101.7	145.8	163.8	154.7	170.3	197.6	159
37.8	41.5	46.2	48.5	40.3	54.8	50.1	63.1	58.5	50.3	160
80.6	88.8	120.7	169.0	115.3	95.9	71.4	50.5	65.2	49.7	161
3.1	5.0	5.7	11.5	9.2	20.7	24.2	50.5	32.8	32.7	162
15.5	24.0	26.5	33.6	19.6	30.6	33.3	35.3	39.0	29.6	163
1.7	4.6	4.2	7.7	11.6	10.1	32.2	23.6	24.7	26.7	164
5.0	4.2	5.0	8.6	8.0	16.0	16.3	22.3	24.7	22.1	165
28.7	31.2	36.8	43.9	28.1	27.8	11.5	16.3	13.9	15.2	166

Period averages

1986	1987	1988	1989	1990	1991	1992	1993	1994	1995	
135.9	148.8	170.6	171.6	178.9	157.5	...	...	...	...	167
141.3	147.3	155.9	...	...	...	...	...	...	...	168
96.2	101.0	109.4	...	...	...	...	...	...	...	169

Calendar year

1986	1987	1988	1989	1990	1991	1992	1993	1994	1995	
1031	1244	1475	1319	1174	1483	1951	2505	2651	...	170
-929	-1130	-1385	-1341	-1107	-1404	-1322	-1135	-1325	...	171
102	114	91	-23	67	79	629	1370	1326	...	172
-341	-429	-520	-419	-301	-489	-725	-866	...	...	173
164	155	241	255	312	374	389	338	...	...	174
-505	-584	-761	-674	-612	-863	-1114	-1205	...	...	175
134	100	93	87	118	260	192	43	...	...	176
-79	-105	-125	-131	-107	-64	-63	-130	...	...	177
213	204	218	217	226	324	255	173	...	...	178
-105	-215	-337	-355	-115	-151	97	546	...	...	179
100	115	120	221	156	203	291	1	...	...	180
–	–	–	–	–	–	–	–	...	...	181
44	52	91	31	84	-140	-407	-548	...	...	182
-9	9	35	13	-23	0	-35	-110	...	...	183
-26	40	38	32	-79	2	-18	29	...	...	184
3	2	-54	-59	23	-86	-72	-81	...	...	185
–	–	–	–	–	–	–	–	...	...	186
-3	-2	54	59	-23	86	72	81	...	...	187

	Item	1978	1979	1980	1981	1982	1983	1984	1985
	INTERNATIONAL RESERVES								*Million US dollars;*
188	Total	412.7	514.7	438.2	412.1	467.4	452.7	447.0	453.5
189	Gold, national valuation	7.9	11.1	14.7	15.9	14.5	12.5	11.7	10.9
190	Foreign exchange	404.2	499.4	418.6	357.6	418.6	416.8	425.1	430.2
191	Reserve position in the Fund	0.0	3.1	4.8	0.1	0.1	5.6	5.2	5.9
192	SDRs	0.6	1.1	–	38.5	34.2	17.8	4.9	6.5
	EXCHANGE RATES								*Kina per*
193	End of period	0.6882	0.6902	0.6439	0.6805	0.7479	0.8755	0.9414	1.0125
194	Average of period	0.7084	0.7116	0.6704	0.6724	0.7375	0.8341	0.8942	1.0000
	EXTERNAL INDEBTEDNESS								*Million US dollars;*
195	Total outstanding & disbursed	583.3	608.6	718.9	1184.5	1627.6	1867.6	2029.4	2112.1
196	Long-term	500.3	556.7	624.0	947.4	1374.4	1733.0	1850.5	1937.2
197	Public and publicly guaranteed	368.1	393.2	485.4	609.5	721.1	912.9	960.5	1069.3
198	Private non-guaranteed	132.2	163.5	138.6	337.9	653.3	820.1	890.0	867.9
199	Short-term	53.0	28.0	64.0	162.0	182.0	67.0	145.0	146.0
200	Use of IMF credit	30.0	23.9	30.9	75.1	71.2	67.6	33.9	28.9
									Transactions
	Debt service								
201	Principal repayments on LT debt	83.0	50.3	71.6	81.6	115.6	155.5	219.1	190.8
202	Interest on long-term debt	35.9	37.2	51.7	71.2	102.1	117.1	146.6	131.7
203	Interest on short-term debt	5.0	6.7	19.1	25.7	12.0	10.8	13.5	8.3
	Average terms of new commitments								
204	Interest (%)	2.8	9.3	11.2	12.6	13.0	7.1	6.4	8.4
205	Maturity (years)	33.4	14.8	17.7	17.0	14.3	14.2	22.2	12.0
206	Grace period (years)	8.2	5.2	4.8	6.5	5.6	4.2	7.0	4.6
207	Grant element (%)	58.6	10.6	1.1	-9.4	-14.6	14.5	27.8	8.1

Footnotes:

a   Data for 1981-95 are mid-year estimates based on the intercensal growth rates from the 1980 and 1990 censuses. Estimates for the entire country were computed using census data that exclude North Solomon.
b   Includes net current transfers.
c   Refers to per capita GDP.
d   Refers to quantity exported including alluvial gold.
e   Refers to currency held by the public.
f   Refer mainly to non-interest bearing deposits with BPNG and commercial banks, and bills payable in PNG commercial banks and staff accounts.
g   Includes commercial bank borrowings in foreign currency.
h   Net credit to government differs from net domestic borrowing due to reporting period ending last Wednesday of the year rather than at end of year, inclusion of balances of Mineral Resources Stabilisation Fund rather than budgetted drawdowns, and valuation of treasury bills at factor cost rather than at face value.
i   Includes lending in foreign currency undertaken by commercial banks and bank deposits at non-bank institutions.
j   Relates to the value of deposits of Commercial Stabilization Funds with BPNG.
k   Refers to deposits not bearing interest.
l   Refers to deposits bearing interest (savings passbook accounts).
m   Relates to loans, advances and bills denominated in kina.
n   Refers to the minimum rate for fully drawn loans.
o   Data are all in Australian aid.
p   Data before 1982 are in fiscal year ending 30 June.
q   For 1978-81, the base year is 1972/73 = 100.

	1986	1987	1988	1989	1990	1991	1992	1993	1994	1995	
As of end of period											
	436.5	447.9	404.6	395.5	414.1	334.1	249.7	152.6	107.2	...	188
	11.1	11.1	11.1	11.1	11.1	11.1	11.1	11.1	11.1	...	189
	415.6	422.3	380.1	371.7	403.0	323.0	238.4	141.3	95.9	...	190
	6.6	9.9	9.4	9.2	–	–	0.1	0.1	0.1	0.1	191
	3.2	4.7	4.1	3.5	–	0.0	0.1	0.1	0.1	0.7	192
US dollar											
	0.9612	0.8784	0.8264	0.8596	0.9530	0.9526	0.9875	0.9814	1.1786	...	193
	0.9713	0.9081	0.8667	0.8558	0.9554	0.9520	0.9646	0.9784	1.0050	...	194
As of end of year											
	1984.0	2276.0	2249.9	2305.7	2571.4	2733.5	3740.0	3223.8	2878.5	...	195
	1906.9	2159.0	2108.9	2138.0	2438.8	2554.9	3268.9	2915.8	2763.9	...	196
	1232.9	1429.7	1252.9	1314.2	1501.1	1590.4	1543.2	1571.5	1622.2	...	197
	674.0	729.3	856.0	823.8	938.2	964.4	1725.7	1344.3	1141.7	...	198
	62.0	105.0	134.9	164.7	71.6	117.3	412.2	263.9	...	...	199
	15.1	12.0	6.1	3.0	61.0	61.3	58.9	44.1	15.6	...	200
during the year											
	168.9	187.8	315.6	343.0	392.4	362.6	479.4	681.6	...	...	201
	132.4	153.3	164.5	157.7	156.1	132.9	160.4	140.1	140	122.8 *	202
	3.5	9.1	12.7	12.4	5.7	7.0	15.9	22.0	...	...	203
	6.3	4.0	5.6	6.3	6.1	4.5	2.9	4.8	6.1	...	204
	15.9	19.9	15.6	14.4	15.8	24.5	28.8	19.6	7.5	...	205
	4.2	5.8	4.7	4.6	4.7	7.5	9.0	4.6	1.5	...	206
	20.5	35.3	25.8	23.9	22.0	42.5	57.4	31.3	11.4	...	207

Item	1978	1979	1980	1981	1982	1983	1984	1985
								Million;
001 **POPULATION**	45.8	47.0	48.3	49.5	50.8	52.1	53.4	54.7
								Thousand;
002 **LABOR FORCE** [a]	16809	16945	17308	18422	18473	20311	20969	21318
003 Employed	16118	16267	16434	17452	17371	19212	19673	19801
004 Agriculture	8422	7743	8453	8928	8920	9880	9740	9698
005 Manufacturing	1742	...	1814	1807	1741	1887	1931	1922
006 Mining	61	...	94	80	74	102	138	128
007 Others	5893	...	6073	6637	6636	7343	7864	8053
008 Unemployed	691	678	874	970	1102	1099	1296	1517
009 Unemployment rate, %	4.1	4.0	5.0	5.3	6.0	5.4	6.2	7.1
NATIONAL ACCOUNTS								
At Current Market Prices								*Billion Pesos;*
010 GDP by Industrial Origin	167.2	202.9	243.7	281.6	317.2	369.1	524.5	571.9
011 Agriculture	47.2	55.7	61.2	70.1	74.1	82.5	129.8	140.6
012 Mining	2.5	4.2	5.5	5.2	4.9	6.2	8.1	11.9
013 Manufacturing	43.5	51.0	62.7	71.8	79.6	89.5	129.2	143.9
014 Electricity, gas and water	2.3	2.9	3.8	4.9	6.6	9.0	12.8	15.8
015 Construction	13.4	17.9	22.6	28.4	32.1	40.2	48.7	29.0
016 Trade	18.7	23.7	29.7	33.3	39.7	46.7	70.8	82.8
017 Transport and communications	6.8	8.5	11.3	13.3	14.7	17.8	28.1	31.7
018 Finance	5.7	7.3	9.5	9.3	10.8	13.5	16.3	17.1
019 Public administration	9.0	10.2	12.0	14.6	16.7	18.0	22.9	27.9
020 Others	18.2	21.5	25.5	30.8	38.1	45.7	57.7	71.3
021 Net factor income from abroad	-0.7	0.6	-0.5	-1.1	-3.6	-5.8	-16.0	-15.8
022 GNP	166.6	203.5	243.3	280.5	313.5	363.3	508.5	556.1
023 Expenditure on GDP	167.2	202.9	243.7	281.6	317.2	369.1	524.5	571.9
024 Private consumption	105.0	129.4	156.8	181.5	208.1	237.5	362.3	420.8
025 Government consumption	16.8	19.0	22.1	24.7	28.9	30.6	36.9	43.5
026 Gross fixed capital formation	42.4	51.2	66.3	78.1	87.3	110.2	121.0	94.2
027 Increase in stocks	9.0	11.4	4.5	-0.8	1.1	-0.9	-14.3	-12.1
028 Exports of goods and services	34.6	43.7	57.5	67.1	64.5	78.8	126.0	137.3
029 Less: Imports of goods and services	41.7	54.0	69.4	76.5	82.9	103.6	131.5	125.2
030 Statistical discrepancy	1.1	2.2	5.9	7.5	10.1	16.7	24.1	13.3
At Constant 1985 Prices								
031 GDP by Industrial Origin	549.0	579.9	609.8	630.6	653.5	665.7	617.0	571.9
032 Agriculture	133.5	137.7	143.3	148.5	149.6	144.6	143.2	140.6
033 Mining	7.3	8.2	9.1	9.4	9.2	9.2	9.0	11.9
034 Manufacturing	154.3	161.5	168.3	171.6	174.3	173.8	156.2	143.9
035 Electricity, gas and water	10.1	11.4	12.4	14.2	17.4	15.8	16.9	15.8
036 Construction	47.7	54.2	57.3	63.4	64.1	70.2	56.0	29.0
037 Trade	69.4	74.8	79.3	79.5	86.3	89.7	83.6	82.8
038 Transport and communications	27.2	28.0	29.2	30.6	31.4	32.6	32.1	31.7
039 Finance	19.4	21.5	24.0	20.8	21.9	25.0	20.1	17.1
040 Public administration	22.9	24.0	25.4	27.1	28.2	27.8	27.8	27.9
041 Others	57.1	58.4	61.6	65.6	71.0	77.0	72.1	71.3
042 Net factor income from abroad	-2.2	1.8	-1.2	-2.3	-7.3	-9.8	-18.9	-15.8
043 GNP	546.8	581.7	608.6	628.3	646.2	656.0	598.0	556.1
044 Expenditure on GDP	549.0	579.9	609.8	630.6	653.5	665.7	617.0	571.9
045 Private consumption	362.7	380.3	397.4	408.0	422.1	424.6	425.8	420.8
046 Government consumption	46.6	48.4	50.2	48.7	52.3	49.9	44.0	43.5
047 Gross fixed capital formation	134.9	139.8	150.7	169.0	177.6	192.6	137.5	94.2
048 Increase in stocks	25.4	27.5	10.4	-3.4	1.9	-1.6	-17.1	-12.1
049 Exports of goods and services	106.1	110.7	154.7	169.4	151.3	156.5	163.6	137.3
050 Less: Imports of goods and services	129.2	150.1	179.5	178.1	182.4	176.8	145.9	125.2
051 Statistical discrepancy	2.5	23.4	25.8	17.0	30.6	20.5	9.1	13.3

	1986	1987	1988	1989	1990	1991	1992	1993	1994	1995	
As of 1 July											
	56.0	57.4	58.7	60.1	62.0	63.7	65.3	67.0	68.6	70.3	001
Calendar year											
	22067	22880	23451	23859	24525	25246	26180	26822	27483	28012	002
	20595	20795	21497	21849	22532	22979	23917	24443	25166	25672	003
	10289	9940	9920	9852	10185	10403	10869	11194	11249	11425	004
	1905	2059	2238	2298	2188	2391	2546	2455	2582	2527	005
	150	146	157	154	133	150	143	130	101	88	006
	8251	8650	9182	9545	10026	10035	10359	10664	11234	11635	007
	1472	2085	1954	2010	1993	2267	2263	2379	2317	2340	008
	6.7	9.1	8.3	8.4	8.1	9.0	8.6	8.9	8.4	8.4	009
Calendar year											
	608.9	682.8	799.2	925.4	1077.2	1248.0	1351.6	1474.5	1693.9	1905.3	010
	145.8	163.9	183.5	210.0	236.0	261.9	294.9	318.5	372.9	413.0	011
	14.1	14.4	15.3	15.4	16.7	17.5	16.3	16.6	16.5	18.2	012
	150.0	169.6	204.8	230.2	267.5	315.9	326.8	349.6	393.8	436.7	013
	16.6	14.0	18.1	20.1	22.3	29.1	32.7	36.4	44.9	49.4	014
	29.8	37.1	42.8	57.3	64.9	62.0	68.0	79.3	95.5	106.6	015
	87.8	96.5	114.1	133.2	154.6	180.5	193.6	207.6	230.8	261.9	016
	34.3	36.8	40.8	43.5	53.2	72.9	75.9	78.4	83.4	89.3	017
	18.7	22.4	27.1	34.3	42.5	48.6	53.2	58.6	67.4	78.2	018
	32.7	38.8	50.6	60.9	77.0	89.0	93.6	103.5	127.3	152.1	019
	79.0	89.2	102.2	120.5	142.6	170.6	196.5	226.0	261.5	299.8	020
	-12.6	-11.9	-7.2	-13.4	5.3	18.1	34.0	25.8	43.5	65.3	021
	596.3	670.8	792.0	912.0	1082.6	1266.1	1385.6	1500.3	1737.3	1970.5	022
	608.9	682.8	799.2	925.4	1077.2	1248.0	1351.6	1474.5	1693.9	1905.3	023
	444.5	482.3	558.8	649.3	767.1	916.4	1019.2	1122.5	1258.8	1411.9	024
	48.4	57.3	72.2	88.2	108.8	123.9	130.5	149.1	182.8	213.9	025
	97.7	112.7	142.2	192.7	249.0	250.1	282.8	350.5	400.1	425.2	026
	-4.9	6.8	7.0	7.2	11.2	2.2	5.6	3.1	7.2	0.4	027
	160.3	181.9	226.9	260.2	296.4	369.4	393.7	462.4	572.6	696.9	028
	136.2	179.0	215.3	280.1	358.5	406.7	459.9	586.9	679.4	828.7	029
	-0.9	20.8	7.4	8.0	3.3	-7.3	-20.4	-26.2	-48.2	-14.4	030
	591.4	616.9	658.6	699.4	720.7	716.5	718.9	734.2	766.6	803.7	031
	145.7	150.4	155.3	160.0	160.7	162.9	163.6	167.1	171.5	173.0	032
	12.3	11.2	11.7	11.4	11.1	10.8	11.5	11.6	10.8	11.4	033
	146.5	154.6	169.3	179.2	183.9	183.1	179.9	181.3	190.4	203.5	034
	17.9	15.8	17.8	18.8	18.7	19.6	19.7	20.3	23.1	26.1	035
	28.5	31.7	33.2	39.9	41.9	35.3	36.3	38.3	41.8	44.5	036
	86.9	90.0	95.2	102.7	107.4	108.0	109.8	112.5	116.9	123.4	037
	33.1	35.1	37.9	40.2	41.1	41.3	41.9	42.9	44.9	47.5	038
	18.5	21.5	23.8	27.3	30.0	29.1	29.2	29.9	31.5	33.9	039
	28.7	29.7	32.3	33.5	36.4	36.9	37.0	38.1	40.1	41.4	040
	73.3	76.8	82.0	86.6	89.5	89.5	90.1	92.3	95.6	99.2	041
	-12.3	-11.1	-6.0	-10.2	3.7	10.3	18.2	22.1	29.2	27.7	042
	579.1	605.9	652.6	689.2	724.4	726.8	737.1	756.3	795.7	831.4	043
	591.4	616.9	658.6	699.4	720.7	716.5	718.9	734.2	766.6	803.7	044
	434.8	452.4	480.6	504.6	531.8	543.8	561.5	578.6	600.1	623.0	045
	43.7	45.8	49.9	53.4	57.0	55.8	55.3	58.7	62.3	64.6	046
	95.1	101.6	118.3	143.8	165.4	141.9	151.0	164.1	176.4	185.7	047
	-4.8	6.5	5.7	5.5	7.6	1.1	3.3	2.3	4.4	1.5	048
	160.6	171.5	196.5	213.9	217.9	231.5	241.4	256.5	307.2	349.7	049
	138.0	177.5	212.4	244.6	269.1	266.1	289.3	322.5	369.3	427.0	050
	0.1	16.7	20.0	22.8	10.2	8.5	-4.3	-3.5	-14.5	6.3	051

	Item	1978	1979	1980	1981	1982	1983	1984	1985
	Investment Financing, at current prices								
052	Gross domestic capital formation	51.5	62.6	70.9	77.3	88.4	109.2	106.7	82.0
053	Gross national saving	44.8	55.1	64.3	74.3	76.5	95.2	109.3	91.7
054	Gross domestic saving [b]	45.4	54.5	64.8	75.4	80.1	101.0	125.3	107.5
055	Net factor income from abroad	-0.7	0.6	-0.5	-1.1	-3.6	-5.8	-16.0	-15.8
056	Foreign saving	7.8	9.7	12.4	10.5	22.0	30.7	21.5	3.7
057	Net transfer from abroad [c]	1.9	1.8	2.0	2.3	1.8	4.0	2.6	3.4
058	Net borrowing from abroad	5.9	7.8	10.4	8.1	20.2	26.7	18.9	0.3
	Per Capita GNP, Pesos								
059	Current prices	3638	4327	5035	5663	6174	6978	9531	10172
060	Constant *1985* prices	11940	12367	12595	12684	12724	12601	11209	10172
	PRODUCTION							*Thousand metric tons;*	
	Agriculture, crop year								
061	1. Sugarcane [d]	3282	3199	22326	22651	24434	24014	23944	17542
062	2. Coconut [e]	4195	4296	13369	14190	13146	12368	11738	12828
063	3. Rice (rough)	7199	7515	7647	7911	8334	7295	7829	8806
064	4. Corn (shelled)	2796	3090	3050	3296	3404	3134	3250	3863
065	5. Banana	3156	3582	3283	3201	3364	3016	3058	3127
066	6. Rubber	54	59	96	100	98	96	141	146
067	7. Coffee	119	116	110	121	122	122	125	137
068	8. Abaca	130	148	108	99	100	84	86	81
	Mining								
069	1. Chromite ore [f]	540	556	496	439	322	267	261	272
070	2. Copper metal	264	298	304	302	292	271	233	222
071	3. Iron ore [f]	2	6	–	6	6	3	–	–
	Manufacturing								
072	1. Cement	4201	6857	4516	4008	4393	4559	3662	3080
073	2. Cotton yarns	32	36	38	36	36	20	25	23
	Production Indexes								*Period*
074	Agriculture, *1979-81 = 100*	92.7	96.5	99.7	103.8	103.9	102.3	102.0	99.8
075	Mining, *1978 = 100*	100.0	109.4	119.8	114.5	109.2	100.2	89.7	102.2
076	Manufacturing, *1978 = 100*	100.0	125.5	159.5	184.5	209.6	243.6	330.7	384.0
	ENERGY								*Annual*
	Crude petroleum, *'000 m.t.*								
077	Production	–	1169	494	253	487	665	531	394
078	Exports	–	–	–	–	–	–	–	–
079	Imports	10022	9122	8832	8289	9636	8128	7154	6472
080	Consumption	9987	10070	9650	8681	8584	8545	7611	7595
	Coal, *'000 m.t.*								
081	Production	255	263	329	331	538	1020	1216	1262
082	Exports	–	–	–	–	–	–	–	–
083	Imports	52	1	2	13	120	120	71	505
084	Consumption	259	233	281	270	332	1056	1692	2393
	Electricity, *Mn kWh* [g]								
085	Production	15587	17804	17883	18583	19406	21454	21180	22767
086	Consumption	15587	17804	17883	18583	19406	21454	21180	22766
	Retail prices, *P/litre*								
087	Gasoline, premium	...	2.20	4.59	4.88	5.19	5.48	7.71	8.40
088	Diesel	...	1.40	2.65	2.94	3.11	3.44	5.67	6.42
	PRICE INDEXES								*Period*
089	Consumer (Philippines), *1988 = 100*	26.8	31.2	36.6	43.1	46.8	49.3	72.5	89.5
090	Food [h]	27.5	31.6	36.3	42.8	45.7	47.8	72.1	89.0
091	Non-food	...	...	...	...	...	...	...	...

1986	1987	1988	1989	1990	1991	1992	1993	1994	1995	
92.8	119.5	149.2	199.9	260.2	252.3	288.4	353.6	407.4	425.7	052
103.3	131.2	161.1	174.6	206.7	225.8	235.8	228.7	295.8	344.7	053
115.9	143.1	168.2	188.0	201.3	207.7	201.8	202.9	252.3	279.5	054
-12.6	-11.9	-7.2	-13.4	5.3	18.1	34.0	25.8	43.5	65.3	055
-11.5	9.1	-4.4	33.4	56.8	19.3	32.2	98.7	63.3	66.6	056
7.1	9.3	6.4	16.0	4.5	8.3	7.6	16.3	24.1	43.5	057
-18.6	-0.3	-10.8	17.4	52.3	11.0	24.6	82.4	39.3	23.1	058
10647	11696	13488	15176	17447	19878	21206	22398	25316	28043	059
10341	10563	11113	11468	11674	11411	11282	11291	11596	11833	060

Calendar year

14831	13797	17275	21425	18667	21825	21802	22915	24695	18679	061
14335	13731	12482	11810	11940	11291	11405	11328	11207	12183	062
9247	8540	8971	9459	9319	9673	9129	9434	10538	10541	063
4091	4278	4428	4522	4854	4655	4619	4798	4519	4128	064
3193	3157	3067	3190	2913	2951	3059	3069	3112	3082	065
146	147	156	172	185	181	172	174	178	181	066
145	140	142	156	134	133	128	124	122	124	067
84	82	84	88	81	85	84	81	91	86	068
202	189	171	248	263	210	112	8	11	...	069
217	214	216	192	180	148	124	136	112	...	070
15	–	–	6	8	7	5	10	–	...	071
3283	3987	5449	6035	6498	6913	6667	7961	9571	...	072
9	9	37	38	31	...	...	...	...	...	073

averages

107.0	105.6	106.0	112.3	118.6	115.9	117.9	120.0	122.2	124.3	074
85.1	104.6	110.5	130.4	187.9	233.9	314.4	235.6	182.0	...	075
464.2	530.4	647.2	732.7	807.7	920.4	951.9	1025.9	1120.6	...	076

values

344	278	297	256	235	148	445	452	223	142	077
–	–	–	–	–	–	323	1078	176	92	078
6887	8681	10049	10064	11372	10883	12186	10049	11840	15945	079
7350	8971	10358	10331	11489	11001	9353	10525	11737	15717	080
1235	1208	1358	1360	1243	1325	1661	1582	1449	1318	081
–	–	–	–	–	–	–	–	–	–	082
959	615	1330	1076	1344	1435	1104	1274	1113	1095	083
1844	2016	2539	2133	2378	2833	2549	2845	2929	2904	084
21797	22642	24538	25573	25215	25654	28814	26818	30459	33426	085
21797	22642	24539	25573	25215	25654	28814	21899	24593	26862	086
7.15	7.15	6.93	5.91	9.74	14.33	10.00	10.00	9.67	9.67	087
5.16	4.96	4.81	3.81	5.98	7.53	7.50	7.00	7.01	7.01	088

averages

89.1	91.8	100.0	112.2	128.1	152.0	165.6	178.2	194.3	210.0	089
87.6	90.9	100.0	114.0	127.6	147.2	157.3	166.9	180.7	197.9	090
...	...	100.0	109.6	128.7	158.9	177.3	194.1	213.6	227.3	091

	Item	1978	1979	1980	1981	1982	1983	1984	1985
092	Consumer (Metro Manila), *1978\ 1988 = 100*	100.0	119.3	141.5	158.7	176.2	195.3	291.5	351.9
093	Food [h]	100.0	118.8	136.9	153.8	165.9	179.8	279.9	329.0
094	Non-food	100.0	119.8	145.8	163.2	185.8	209.7	302.3	373.2
095	Wholesale (Metro Manila), *1978 = 100*	100.0	119.0	140.8	161.1	179.0	208.0	346.5	409.3
096	Implicit GDP deflator, *1985 = 100*	30.5	35.0	40.0	44.7	48.5	55.4	85.0	100.0
	MONEY AND BANKING [i]								*Million Pesos;*
097	Money supply (M1)	16995	18906	22622	23579	23556	32571	33737	35893
098	Currency in circulation	8127	9168	10160	11604	12660	19587	21764	24029
099	Demand deposits	8868	9738	12462	11975	10896	12984	11973	11864
100	Quasi-money	23475	26741	33279	42509	55956	64534	77419	89638
101	Money supply (M2)	40470	45647	55901	66088	79512	97105	111156	125531
102	Foreign assets (net)	-7508	-15381	-23169	-32479	-57848	-102570	-138183	-155884
103	Domestic credit	66830	84705	106790	130183	161063	201959	209179	198090
104	Claims on govt. sector (net)	9082	10469	14534	18807	32033	46437	52749	53130
105	Claims on private sector	51406	65417	81221	98245	110861	127984	123047	111045
106	Claims on other financial insts.	6342	8819	11035	13131	18169	27538	33383	33915
107	Other items	-18852	-23677	-27720	-31616	-23703	-2284	40160	83325
	Deposit Money Banks								
108	Demand deposits	9602	11397	13535	14312	11939	19597	15747	14935
109	Savings deposits	17314	20884	23047	27017	33445	42268	48452	58437
110	Time deposits	16737	23717	36048	37933	47846	57168	73017	75301
111	Domestic credits outstanding	65427	81996	95527	112898	130310	171482	174678	161351
	Interest Rates								
	On deposits [j]								*Percent;*
112	Savings	7.0	9.0	9.0	9.8	9.8	9.7	9.9	10.8
113	Time: 6 months	9.0	11.0	14.0	14.6	14.5	13.4	20.1	18.8
114	12 months	10.0	12.0	14.0	13.0	13.9	14.2	17.4	19.8
115	On loans and discounts [k]	12.7	12.7	13.5	17.1	18.2	19.3	26.7	28.2
	GOVERNMENT FINANCE								*Million Pesos;*
	Central Government								
116	Current revenue	24073	29470	34731	35933	38205	45632	56861	68961
117	Taxes	20441	25956	30533	31423	33779	39524	50118	61253
118	Non-taxes	3632	3514	4198	4510	4426	6108	6743	7708
119	Current expenditure	19230	20608	24516	26390	31746	34522	42873	55275
120	Current surplus/deficit	4843	8862	10215	9543	6459	11110	13988	13686
121	Capital receipts [l]	–	–	–	–	–	–	–	–
122	Capital expenditure	6772	8351	12927	20760	18646	16148	19630	23149
123	Capital account surplus/deficit	-6772	-8351	-12927	-20760	-18646	-16148	-19630	-23149
124	Net lending	238	853	675	929	2218	2393	4423	1678
125	Overall surplus/deficit	-2167	-342	-3387	-12146	-14405	-7431	-10065	-11141
	Financing								
126	Domestic borrowing	2510	911	2126	9516	8527	4632	16268	13252
127	Foreign borrowing	1852	3185	2404	5992	4597	5437	2004	-340
128	Foreign grants [m]	...	...	...	...	...	...	...	...
129	Use of cash balances [n]	-2195	-3754	-1143	-3362	1281	-2638	-8207	-1771
	Expenditure by Function, Central Govt.								
130	Total [o]	26768	32640	37404	48154	48924	53418	68625	87390
131	General public services	4635	5924	6516	9301	9940	10707	10621	13590
132	Defence	4394	4738	4975	5447	5951	6526	5391	7132
133	Education	3064	3419	4762	5806	6413	6263	7988	11288
134	Health	892	1172	1390	1734	2136	2485	2293	3113
135	Social security & welfare	427	465	721	1907	1238	1418	644	753
136	Housing & community amenities	579	1364	934	1289	1373	1871	1177	672
137	Economic services [p]	10601	12565	14523	18773	16981	15700	20948	19377
138	Agriculture	...	...	2289	3241	3889	3534	3594	4804
139	Industry	...	...	1305	2759	2275	1905	725	972
140	Electricity, gas & water	...	...	3637	4313	2798	1661	1675	2813

1986	1987	1988	1989	1990	1991	1992	1993	1994	1995	
370.5	395.5	435.3 I	109.6	127.3	153.6	172.4	190.3	209.8	226.8	092
342.4	364.6	409.7 I	109.7	124.5	144.6	154.8	165.9	177.6	190.8	093
396.6	424.9	459.1 I	109.5	130.0	162.2	189.1	213.4	240.1	227.3	094
410.6	444.0	498.5	550.7	607.5	689.3	720.6	712.6	770.8	796.8	095
103.0	110.7	121.3	132.3	149.5	174.2	188.0	200.8	221.0	237.1	096

As of end of period

42694	52416	59718	78530	89012	101374	112092	133877	151952	184931	097
29264	35372	40638	52823	61921	69394	74298	84083	95675	110892	098
13430	17044	19080	25707	27091	31980	37794	49794	56277	74039	099
96780	105855	136203	172561	208295	242683	269781	341839	451052	570260	100
139474	158271	195921	251091	297307	344057	381873	475716	603004	755191	101
-144947	-137752	-122833	-114525	-157624	-92805	-18002	-31537	-35169	-88425	102
170999	155444	166462	203818	267510	269049	277100	682064	821551	1084011	103
69100	34122	25802	31927	47356	31709	-18599	274080	299812	335328	104
87262	107434	127623	157935	204196	218585	272255	382781	484377	701001	105
14637	13888	13037	13956	15958	18755	23444	25203	37362	47682	106
113422	140579	152292	161798	187421	167813	122775	-174811	-183378	-240395	107

23217	23013	23555	29525	32607	39101	43457	54516	63598	80984	108
74204	84439	110039	136714	181070	213198	265973	359396	468810	583598	109
48606	49456	65154	86152	97066	198741	117152	141855	160663	209243	110
135871	150793	185096	234018	291024	330555	396428	525204	684526	935244	111

Period averages

8.0	4.5	4.1	6.2	10.9	11.0	10.6	8.3	8.0	8.0	112
11.0	7.4	11.8	14.2	20.3	19.1	14.0	10.1	11.0	8.9	113
11.5	10.0	11.9	14.5	17.3	15.4	12.8	10.1	10.0	10.2	114
17.3	13.3	16.0	19.5	24.3	23.5	19.4	14.6	15.0	14.6	115

Fiscal year ending 31 December

79046	101821	111457	150245	178640	217778	240067	258890	335428	340849 *	116
65491	85923	90352	122462	151700	182275	208705	230170	271305	309978 *	117
13555	15898	21105	27783	26940	35503	31362	28720	64123	30871 *	118
66921	96265	113595	144632	177993	196523	219505	234563	277275	...	119
12125	5556	-2138	5613	647	21255	20562	24327	58153	...	120
–	–	–	808	–	–	903	–	–	18486 *	121
28428	16566	17056	23264	41749	49045	36974	44584	41897	...	122
-28428	-16566	-17056	-22456	-41749	-49045	-36071	-44584	-41897	...	123
15148	7077	5415	4082	-1646	1568	2201	3149	702	3686 *	124
-31451	-18087	-24609	-20925	-39456	-29358	-17710	-23406	15554	9294 *	125

28449	34337	35088	20450	15144	34368	138248	-28566	-10351	19624 *	126
3580	6781	4242	8210	4126	6880	14390	12910	-11578	-12895 *	127
199	1393	1404	1357	2262	3009	1744	1515	732	880 *	128
-777	-24425	-16124	-9092	17924	-14899	-136672	37547	5643	-16903 *	129

114505	155502	167407	173340	255755	293161	328137	313749	373778	384700	130
14631	12559	15731	17453	23566	26465	32845	48259	50722	58900	131
7611	12549	18298	19766	22688	24944	26321	19912	21998	24300	132
14838	17040	22022	27378	33528	33510	40110	38986	51728	55300	133
3570	4088	5564	6488	7962	9178	9791	6969	9236	10100	134
834	1005	1147	1574	2163	3751	4865	3266	4269	5800	135
1550	443	595	624	679	1159	769	1465	4659	5300	136
28113	25038	26091	39522	51891	63807	74006	64228	81953	84100	137
...	7475	8428	12964	15067	20239	21721	15487	18243	17300	138
...	1158	1146	1474	1681	2632	1316	2442	2642	2900	139
...	3173	1624	2978	10659	4810	7199	8933	5124	4600	140

	Item	1978	1979	1980	1981	1982	1983	1984	1985
141	Transport and communications	...	...	4569	5762	5803	5859	6848	7541
142	Other economic services	...	...	2723	2698	2216	2741	8106	3247
143	Others	2176	2993	3583	3897	4892	8448	19563	31465
	Provincial and Other Local Govts.								
144	Revenue	2926	3999	4573	5102	5929	6700	7349	8510
145	Tax	2012	2723	3281	3805	4501	5040	5454	6199
146	Non-tax	914	988	925	873	968	1208	1370	1564
147	Subsidy/grants	–	288	368	424	460	452	525	748
148	Expenditure	3715	3781	4490	5092	5713	6545	7616	8508
	EXTERNAL TRADE							*Million US dollars;*	
149	Exports, fob	3425	4601	5788	5722	5021	5005	5391	4629
150	Imports, cif	5143	6613	8295	8479	8263	7979	6428	5445
151	Trade balance	-1718	-2012	-2507	-2757	-3242	-2974	-1037	-816
	Exports, by SITC section								
152	Food and live animals	673	852	1402	1339	1129	955	941	824
153	Beverage and tobacco	32	37	34	56	58	38	34	31
154	Crude materials excl. fuels	892	1235	1446	1075	868	746	564	480
155	Mineral fuels, etc.	10	11	38	42	33	114	87	42
156	Animal, vegetable oil & fats	623	748	573	538	403	523	606	372
157	Chemicals	59	112	89	105	95	86	105	151
158	Basic manufactures	306	419	532	473	335	369	371	468
159	Machines, transport equipment	75	88	127	161	168	254	417	309
160	Misc. manufactured goods	322	466	610	704	612	612	532	537
161	Unclassified goods	433	633	937	1229	1320	1308	1734	1415
	Exports, by principal commodity								
162	1. Coconut oil	621	742	567	533	401	516	580	347
163	2. Copper concentrates	250	440	545	429	312	249	115	84
164	3. Centrifugal and refined sugar	197	212	624	567	416	299	246	169
165	4. Logs and lumber	230	343	273	202	202	223	195	130
166	5. Copra	136	89	47	34	49	4	–	–
	Imports, by SITC section								
167	Food and live animals	346	412	572	644	744	594	477	483
168	Beverage and tobacco	47	52	52	57	69	76	36	79
169	Crude materials excl. fuels	258	306	322	217	224	210	157	168
170	Mineral fuels, etc.	1090	1468	2358	2556	2190	2196	1705	1512
171	Animal, vegetable oil & fats	15	20	20	20	18	29	36	15
172	Chemicals	575	732	811	839	834	856	682	641
173	Basic manufactures	762	1012	1070	946	1123	1011	624	549
174	Machines, transport equipment	1411	1798	1958	1894	1772	1683	1129	760
175	Misc. manufactured goods	137	150	211	211	207	189	108	112
176	Unclassified goods	502	663	921	1095	1082	1135	1474	1126
	Direction of Trade							*Million US dollars;*	
177	Exports, Total	3425.8	4602.4	5787.0	5720.7	5019.8	4932.0	5342.6	4614.0
178	1. United States	1159.2	1390.0	1593.6	1770.8	1588.5	1792.6	2031.5	1658.3
179	2. Japan	828.2	1214.2	1540.0	1253.9	1149.1	983.7	1034.4	874.5
180	3. Singapore	71.4	65.6	112.6	129.2	111.6	139.3	321.3	249.8
181	4. United Kingdom	90.0	136.5	146.6	193.1	189.9	233.7	223.9	166.3
182	5. Hong Kong	90.4	158.0	192.0	221.7	197.9	158.4	234.2	186.6
183	6. Netherlands	280.1	359.9	365.8	319.6	189.9	221.6	167.5	145.0
184	7. Thailand	10.0	18.9	63.0	25.3	14.4	19.9	9.0	83.1
185	8. Germany	142.9	226.7	255.1	240.3	202.8	208.3	175.5	174.1
186	9. Korea, Rep. of	66.4	141.2	203.0	198.3	151.5	148.7	98.7	75.0
187	10. France	53.7	122.3	94.9	84.4	82.4	91.3	95.8	87.3

1986	1987	1988	1989	1990	1991	1992	1993	1994	1995	
...	9184	12945	16916	17064	27079	28302	22723	31853	28800	141
...	4048	1948	5190	7420	9047	15468	14643	24091	30500	142
43358	82780	77959	60535	113278	130347	139430	130664	149213	140900	143
8661	8923	13359	15281	19062	23900	27434	44210	...	...	144
6537	6777	8053	9654	13005	16484	23086	38166	...	...	145
1390	1513	1702	3170	3365	4019	3804	5399	...	...	146
734	633	3604	2457	2693	3396	544	645	...	...	147
8719	9587	11245	13892	18022	23682	24444	37829	...		148

Calendar year

1986	1987	1988	1989	1990	1991	1992	1993	1994	1995	
4842	5720	7074	7821	8186	8840	9824	11375	13483	17447	149
5394	7187	8731	11171	13042	12856	15465	18773	22638	28341 q	150
-552	-1467	-1657	-3350	-4856	-4016	-5641	-7398	-9155	-10894	151
873	888	1056	1100	1075	1228	1132	1329	1333	1339	152
29	28	32	34	58	86	54	44	45	42	153
519	535	709	729	551	482	492	388	411	531	154
66	97	153	118	181	211	238	229	215	263	155
346	397	425	392	375	311	495	370	491	844	156
243	245	256	279	261	304	269	262	306	343	157
434	469	687	741	742	704	683	800	874	1116	158
392	553	676	940	972	1210	1671	2119	2907	3869	159
587	758	953	1196	1375	1440	1657	1773	1982	2245	160
1353	1750	2127	2292	2596	2864	3133	4061	4920	6855	161
333	380	408	377	361	299	481	358	474	826	162
90	109	216	237	207	174	140	109	112	134	163
87	60	60	89	111	115	88	102	61	66	164
131	155	157	137	20	20	19	26	10	18	165
18	32	28	25	20	19	11	7	9	13	166
459	513	788	999	1213	892	1115	1268	1506	2108	167
75	112	97	93	90	109	133	136	237	169	168
259	325	456	587	595	666	680	775	977	1237	169
920	1307	1161	1495	1946	1921	2159	2162	2161	2623	170
15	15	20	26	27	24	37	26	41	42	171
778	1009	1128	1317	1479	1440	1618	1813	2191	2616	172
700	1030	1331	1927	1931	1835	2331	2814	3143	3959	173
839	1193	1726	2663	3375	3235	4422	6146	7585	9109	174
119	153	201	283	325	369	454	623	776	1002	175
1230	1530	1823	1781	2061	2365	2516	3010	4022	5476	176

Calendar year

1986	1987	1988	1989	1990	1991	1992	1993	1994	1995	
4806.8	5696.1	7034.2	7753.9	8193.8	8839.6	9828.5	11271.2	13433.0	17318.0	177
1709.3	2060.4	2512.0	2934.6	3103.6	3151.4	3843.2	4341.5	5178.3	6216.5	178
851.6	980.4	1415.5	1581.4	1622.0	1771.3	1745.4	1811.3	2019.8	2760.1	179
153.6	196.4	220.8	217.3	239.6	229.5	252.3	378.2	706.9	993.0	180
228.3	245.4	325.7	325.7	350.5	371.6	466.7	534.1	637.3	909.7	181
220.0	277.0	343.8	302.0	330.5	391.6	463.5	546.3	650.5	825.1	182
214.4	310.4	314.4	326.7	357.1	338.4	406.2	357.9	515.2	785.4	183
66.7	124.7	123.3	154.8	156.4	220.8	98.4	166.8	0.0	735.8	184
240.6	290.9	297.3	333.3	413.6	502.4	521.7	579.8	664.2	699.7	185
112.3	98.3	160.5	160.4	229.5	227.9	176.0	220.4	291.3	426.5	186
109.8	125.3	164.1	151.4	144.0	164.9	178.9	208.9	184.4	206.1	187

	Item	1978	1979	1980	1981	1982	1983	1984	1985
188	Imports, Total	5143.2	6612.9	8294.9	8477.3	8262.5	7863.0	6262.1	5351.4
189	1. Japan	1412.9	1510.6	1651.3	1608.9	1661.9	1342.1	851.1	749.5
190	2. United States	1083.7	1511.3	1950.9	1930.6	1860.9	1831.3	1713.5	1343.8
191	3. Saudi Arabia	275.7	385.0	825.4	1070.0	941.7	840.5	430.0	276.5
192	4. Hong Kong	113.0	158.9	203.1	224.0	219.6	264.9	242.4	209.2
193	5. Korea, Rep. of	56.9	97.7	145.4	118.1	160.6	161.3	155.3	214.0
194	6. Singapore	53.3	85.6	132.5	114.1	230.1	289.8	119.4	126.8
195	7. Germany	197.5	294.4	345.4	336.2	355.9	379.5	203.4	148.7
196	8. Australia	194.0	234.4	244.4	243.3	256.1	199.0	148.6	179.5
197	9. Malaysia	58.7	93.1	162.1	182.4	122.0	158.9	354.8	390.2
198	10. United Kingdom	184.4	208.4	190.5	175.9	173.3	177.8	147.3	106.7
	Trade Indexes [r]								**1985 = 100;**
	Quantum index								
199	Exports	78.3	85.6	103.3	137.8	124.4	128.2	138.2	100.0
200	Imports	139.8	152.6	154.5	152.5	162.4	155.8	119.3	100.0
	Unit value index								
201	Exports	94.5	116.2	121.1	87.3	85.2	82.9	83.1	100.0
202	Imports	67.6	79.6	98.6	99.5	92.4	92.7	97.3	100.0
203	Terms of trade [s]	139.9	146.0	122.8	87.7	92.2	89.4	85.4	100.0
	BALANCE OF PAYMENTS								**Million US dollars;**
204	Merchandise exports, fob	3425	4601	5788	5722	5021	5005	5391	4629
205	Merchandise imports, fob	-4732	-6142	-7727	-7946	-7667	-7487	-6070	-5111
206	Trade balance	-1307	-1541	-1939	-2224	-2646	-2482	-679	-482
207	Other goods, services and income	-107	-311	-399	-309	-1040	-740	-823	0
208	Credit	1484	1655	2222	2896	2983	3127	2626	3288
209	Debit	-1591	-1966	-2621	-3205	-4023	-3867	-3449	-3288
210	Unrequited transfer	312	355	434	472	486	472	386	379
211	Private	197	229	300	325	322	237	118	172
212	Official	115	126	134	147	164	235	268	207
213	Current balance	-1102	-1497	-1904	-2061	-3200	-2750	-1116	-103
214	Direct investment	121	92	-2	196	132	221	122	49
215	Portfolio investment	-21	-72	-100	-21	-115	-109	-105	-32
216	Other long-term capital	891	1151	1032	1332	1548	1392	478	2787
217	Other short-term capital	-90	-495	324	-28	108	-618	549	-1731
218	Change in NFA - commercial banks [t]								
219	Net errors and omissions [u]	78	174	140	-392	-421	-437	146	1110
220	Monetization of gold	32	41	128	400	277	183	169	221
221	Allocation of SDRs	–	28	29	27	–	–	–	–
222	Overall balance [v]	-91	-578	-353	-547	-1671	-2118	243	2301
223	Monetary movements	91	578	353	547	1671	2118	-243	-2301
	INTERNATIONAL RESERVES								**Million US dollars;**
224	Total	1881	2416	3140	2574	1711	864	890	1116
225	Gold, national valuation	118	166	294	508	823	117	288	501
226	Foreign exchange	1746	2216	2846	2064	885	746	574	550
227	Reserve position in the Fund	–	–	–	–	–	–	9	26
228	SDRs	17	34	–	2	3	1	19	39
	EXCHANGE RATES								**Pesos per**
229	End of period	7.375	7.415	7.600	8.200	9.171	14.002	19.760	19.032
230	Average of period	7.366	7.378	7.511	7.900	8.540	11.113	16.699	18.607
	EXTERNAL INDEBTEDNESS								**Million US dollars;**
231	Total outstanding and disbursed	10772	13282	17417	20786	24412	24211	24357	26640
232	Long term	6252	7154	8817	10231	12088	13696	14011	16314
233	Public and publicly guaranteed	4161	5082	6363	7471	8859	10571	11300	13714
234	Private non-guaranteed	2091	2071	2454	2761	3229	3125	2711	2600

	1986	1987	1988	1989	1990	1991	1992	1993	1994	1995	
	5211.0	6936.8	8661.8	11170.8	12992.6	12944.5	14562.2	17638.2	22534.3	28284.1	188
	886.6	1148.5	1503.0	2174.0	2396.6	2517.0	3086.8	4021.6	5447.2	6366.9	189
	1293.4	1539.4	1822.6	2132.4	2538.4	2609.6	2625.5	3531.8	4162.1	5129.9	190
	232.6	221.5	118.3	268.7	620.4	690.3	873.6	740.0	994.2	1696.7	191
	258.5	308.6	388.6	500.3	576.5	614.3	720.9	879.1	1145.9	1451.7	192
	168.3	201.0	347.8	444.6	498.8	638.6	696.8	901.9	1169.9	1400.1	193
	126.8	237.4	353.1	519.7	508.1	475.4	550.9	979.1	1488.6	1289.9	194
	216.6	282.1	342.0	436.2	563.2	489.6	669.9	616.0	798.3	990.3	195
	161.6	220.2	309.4	393.1	407.7	420.1	406.7	475.2	632.5	813.8	196
	215.1	233.5	246.9	282.6	287.6	403.5	412.9	357.5	486.8	603.7	197
	110.3	147.8	170.4	181.3	266.5	225.3	299.8	380.1	405.5	565.9	198

Period averages

	1986	1987	1988	1989	1990	1991	1992	1993	1994	1995	
	116.6	124.2	138.2	155.0	166.2	171.8	...	...	...	...	199
	119.7	158.0	191.3	229.3	246.4	250.6	...	...	...	...	200
	88.8	97.7	107.7	105.7	102.7	104.7	...	...	...	...	201
	82.3	82.7	82.1	87.2	94.0	90.0	...	...	...	...	202
	107.9	118.1	131.2	121.3	109.3	116.3	102.6	99.1	101.3	102.7	203

Calendar year

	1986	1987	1988	1989	1990	1991	1992	1993	1994	1995	
	4842	5720	7074	7821	8186	8840	9824	11375	13483	17447	204
	-5044	-6737	-8159	-10419	-12206	-12051	-14519	-17597	-21333	-26391	205
	-202	-1017	-1085	-2598	-4020	-3211	-4695	-6222	-7850	-8944	206
	715	–	-80	312	739	1515	3020	2507	3964	6177	207
	3791	3454	3592	4586	4842	5624	7443	7497	10550	15412	208
	-3076	-3454	-3672	-4274	-4103	-4109	-4423	-4990	-6586	-9235	209
	441	573	775	830	714	827	817	699	936	880	210
	235	376	500	473	357	473	473	398	460	431	211
	206	197	275	357	357	354	344	301	476	449	212
	954	-444	-390	-1456	-2567	-869	-858	-3016	-2950	-1887	213
	146	362	983	559	528	529	675	864	1289	1079	214
	-6	-36	3	284	-48	125	62	-52	269	1201	215
	732	159	-519	381	406	922	666	2105	1313	1219	216
	-824	80	-303	-89	19	349	660	-148	1002	-56	217
					120	-181	459	-547	465	1309	218
	-39	-222	505	484	1231	983	-302	515	260	-2397	219
	279	365	314	288	218	245	130	113	154	177	220
	–	–	–	–	–	–	–	–	–	–	221
	1242	264	593	451	-93	2103	1492	-166	1802	645	222
	-1242	-264	-593	-451	93	-2103	-1492	166	-1802	-645	223

As of end of period

	1986	1987	1988	1989	1990	1991	1992	1993	1994	1995	
	2527	2014	2111	2376	2048	4526	5339	5921	7121	7775	224
	799	1046	1108	959	1124	1280	935	1245	1104	1403	225
	1675	913	951	1365	868	3186	4283	4546	5866	6235	226
	47	55	52	51	55	56	120	120	127	129	227
	6	–	–	1	1	4	1	10	24	8	228

US dollar

	1986	1987	1988	1989	1990	1991	1992	1993	1994	1995	
	20.530	20.800	21.335	22.440	28.000	26.650	25.096	27.699	24.418	26.214	229
	20.386	20.568	21.095	21.737	24.311	27.479	25.512	27.120	26.417	25.714	230

As of end of year

	1986	1987	1988	1989	1990	1991	1992	1993	1994	1995	
	28206	29786	29011	28722	30614	32456	32997	35926	39302	...	231
	21559	24729	24052	23592	25277	26428	26637	29682	32522	...	232
	19265	22895	22442	22403	24076	25065	25607	27472	29577	...	233
	2294	1834	1610	1189	1201	1362	1030	2209	2945	...	234

	Item	1978	1979	1980	1981	1982	1983	1984	1985
235	Short term	3863	5315	7556	9421	11325	9420	9460	9157
236	Use of IMF credit	658	813	1044	1133	999	1095	885	1168
	Debt service								*Transactions*
237	Principal repayments on LT debt	950	962	541	725	974	827	528	588
238	Interest on long-term debt	309	494	579	826	929	945	931	938
239	Interest on short-term debt	0	0	875	1307	1452	1016	926	750
	Average terms of new commitments								
240	Interest (%)	7.6	8.8	9.9	10.3	10.8	8.5	7.5	8.5
241	Maturity (years)	16.6	15.9	16.6	15.7	16.3	16.7	15.0	10.7
242	Grace period (years)	4.8	5.1	5.3	4.8	5.2	5.3	3.9	2.8
243	Grant element (%)	16.2	9.5	4.0	1.3	-2.9	10.6	12.9	7.8

Footnotes:

a   From 1978, data were based on the household population of 15 years old and over as working age using past quarter reference period of the third quarter results of the Integrated Survey of Households (ISH) until 1986. For 1987 onwards, the past week is used as the reference period and figures were based on the results of the October rounds of the ISH.

b   Estimated as GDP less private and government consumption expenditures.

c   Includes government interest payments on public debt and capital transfers from abroad.

d   Includes sugarcane used for centrifugal sugar, muscovado, panocha and molasses.

e   Includes nuts used for making copra, desiccated coconut, home-made oil, food nuts, and for commercial manufacturing.

f   In thousand dry metric tons (DMT).

g   Production refers to the amount of electric power that is generated while consumption refers to the amount of electric power that is demanded.

h   Includes beverages and tobacco.

i   Data from 1980 onwards relate to the new expanded commercial banks' concept which includes the Land Bank of the Philippines.

j   Data for 1978-80 refer to ceiling rates. Data for 1981 refer to quoted rates of ten selected commercial banks. Thereafter, data refer to the weighted average interest rates (WAIR) of sample commercial banks.

k   Data are the WAIR on all loans outstanding of commercial banks. From 1982-89, data refer to WAIR on all maturities.

l   Refers to extraordinary income.

m   Reclassified from non-tax revenues beginning 1986.

n   Includes change in cash and non-budgetary accounts beginning 1986.

o   On obligation basis excluding lending account.

p   Agriculture includes agrarian reform and natural resources; industry includes trade and tourism.

q   Excludes lease of aircraft amounting to US$146.8 million.

r   Unit value indexes of imports are based on CIF value while those of exports are based on FOB value.

s   Estimated from national accounts data from 1992 to 1995.

t   Beginning 1990, commercial bank transactions have been reclassified from monetary capital to capital and financial transactions based on the revised BOP methodology under which commercial bank's transactions, because of foreign exchange liberalization, are now considered autonomous or undertaken independently for their own sake.

u   Include data on revaluation adjustments, unremittable arrears/adjustments and purchase of collateral when available.

v   Data from 1982 onwards are based on the new concept of net international reserve computation under the 1983 standby agreement.

1986	1987	1988	1989	1990	1991	1992	1993	1994	1995	
5382	3797	3865	3953	4426	4943	5259	5035	5716	...	235
1266	1260	1094	1176	912	1086	1100	1210	1064	...	236
during the year										
1036	1223	1203	888	1475	1479	2637	2703	2170	2486 *	237
1144	1340	1583	1675	1572	1457	1335	1759	1628	1880 *	238
400	365	341	402	100	73	94	309	403	...	239
5.3	5.4	5.1	5.5	6.3	5.1	5.7	5.2	5.4	...	240
23.4	21.4	22.4	20.1	21.9	22.9	18.6	15.8	16.0	...	241
6.1	6.4	7.0	5.9	7.3	6.6	4.6	5.2	6.1	...	242
33.4	32.0	35.7	30.4	27.2	35.7	25.8	27.1	26.3	...	243

	Item	1978	1979	1980	1981	1982	1983	1984	1985
001	POPULATION [a]	2.35	2.38	2.28	2.32	2.37	2.41	2.44	*Million;* 2.48
									Thousand;
002	LABOR FORCE [b]	995	1056	1116	1188	1253	1293	1304	1288
003	Employed	959	1021	1077	1154	1221	1251	1270	1235
004	Agriculture	18	15	17	13	12	13	10	9
005	Manufacturing	271	295	324	350	360	348	348	314
006	Mining	1	2	1	1	3	3	2	3
007	Others	669	709	735	790	846	887	910	909
008	Unemployed	36	35	39	34	32	42	35	53
009	Unemployment rate, % [c]	3.6	3.3	3.5	2.9	2.6	3.2	2.7	4.1
	NATIONAL ACCOUNTS *At Current Market Prices*								*Million Singapore dollars;*
010	GDP by Industrial Origin	17830.4	20523.0	25090.7	29339.4	32669.9	36732.8	40047.9	38923.5
011	Agriculture	273.7	295.2	322.0	356.2	349.1	330.9	339.7	292.3
012	Mining	37.5	42.1	82.2	104.7	128.1	140.6	132.2	111.3
013	Manufacturing	4575.9	5702.5	7312.7	8361.5	8153.5	8907.9	9863.4	9184.3
014	Electricity, gas and water	351.1	422.1	555.0	477.5	600.9	702.7	773.0	796.0
015	Construction	1118.8	1236.6	1613.2	2163.7	3146.1	4202.5	4943.7	4167.9
016	Trade	4283.3	4844.8	5435.1	5840.0	6387.5	6667.4	6885.5	6636.3
017	Transport and communications	2554.7	2852.5	3522.2	4063.0	4435.8	4891.9	5222.3	5234.5
018	Finance	3191.4	3738.6	4944.0	6653.2	7756.6	8872.0	9962.7	10652.0
019	Public administration								
020	Others [d]	1444.0	1388.6	1304.3	1319.6	1712.3	2016.9	1925.4	1848.9
021	Net factor income from abroad	-43.0	-78.9	-902.2	-1148.2	-894.2	-171.7	767.2	1406.9
022	GNP	17787.4	20444.1	24188.5	28191.2	31775.7	36561.1	40815.1	40330.4
023	Expenditure on GDP	17830.4	20523.0	25090.7	29339.4	32669.9	36732.8	40047.9	38923.5
024	Private consumption	10149.1	11245.2	12911.3	14329.3	15282.5	16202.1	17569.5	17552.9
025	Government consumption	1964.7	2033.6	2447.4	2788.6	3570.4	3995.3	4333.0	5548.5
026	Gross fixed capital formation	6365.1	7519.6	10203.1	12784.7	15505.7	17464.2	19122.2	16424.8
027	Increase in stocks	592.3	1380.3	1424.5	802.3	153.1	131.6	295.1	126.4
028	Net exports of goods and services	-897.6	-1445.1	-2215.8	-1633.5	-1440.6	-663.8	-1113.0	-945.7
029	Statistical discrepancy	-343.2	-210.6	320.2	268.0	-401.2	-396.6	-158.9	216.6
	At Constant 1985 Prices								
030	GDP by Industrial Origin	24046.0	26284.7	28832.5	31603.1	33772.3	36537.2	39572.5	38923.5
031	Agriculture	314.9	321.2	325.1	319.4	303.4	311.0	326.5	292.3
032	Mining	52.5	60.0	65.0	83.5	104.0	122.0	120.2	111.3
033	Manufacturing	6790.3	7727.3	8500.1	9290.6	8965.4	9216.4	9907.6	9184.3
034	Electricity, gas and water	491.4	536.5	578.0	620.4	650.2	707.8	762.1	796.0
035	Construction	1730.6	1852.8	2055.8	2418.4	3299.0	4266.7	4927.2	4167.9
036	Trade	4767.6	5095.6	5452.8	5755.0	6091.9	6374.2	6738.9	6636.3
037	Transport and communications	2663.1	3046.4	3448.5	3896.8	4351.7	4678.1	5131.8	5234.5
038	Finance	4511.1	5022.2	5919.9	6873.2	7563.6	8400.0	9441.0	10652.0
039	Public administration								
040	Others [d]	2724.5	2622.7	2487.3	2345.8	2443.1	2461.0	2217.2	1848.9
041	Net factor income from abroad	-53.6	-72.0	-608.8	-765.2	-1269.3	-431.9	986.7	1406.9
042	GNP	23992.4	26212.7	28223.7	30837.9	32503.0	36105.3	40559.2	40330.4
043	Expenditure on GDP	24046.0	26284.7	28832.5	31603.1	33772.3	36537.2	39572.5	38923.5
044	Private consumption	13168.1	13971.4	14809.7	15491.3	16086.4	16852.1	17711.6	17552.9
045	Government consumption	2976.3	2961.9	3241.5	3411.6	3863.8	4235.9	4457.2	5548.5
046	Gross fixed capital formation	8199.9	9257.7	11126.6	12810.3	15405.7	17067.7	18677.4	16424.8
047	Increase in stocks	931.0	1596.7	1516.1	730.7	144.0	242.2	273.0	126.4
048	Net exports of goods and services	-1119.3	-1318.5	-1495.2	-1088.6	-2044.9	-1669.6	-1431.4	-945.7
049	Statistical discrepancy	-110.0	-184.5	-366.2	247.8	317.3	-191.1	-115.3	216.6
	Investment Financing at current prices								
050	Gross domestic capital formation	6957.4	8899.9	11627.6	13587.0	15658.8	17595.8	19417.3	16551.2

	1986	1987	1988	1989	1990	1991	1992	1993	1994	1995	
As of 1 July											
	2.52	2.55	2.60	2.65	2.71	2.76	2.82	2.87	2.93	2.99	001
Calendar year											
	1299	1329	1378	1425	1516	1554	1619	1636	1693	1748	002
	1215	1267	1333	1394	1486	1524	1576	1592	1649	1701	003
	10	11	6	6	6	4	5	4	5	4	004
	307	339	379	404	422	430	434	429	423	408	005
	1	1	1	1	1	0	0	0	0	1	006
	897	916	947	983	1057	1090	1137	1159	1221	1288	007
	84	63	46	31	30	30	43	44	44	47	008
	6.5	4.7	3.3	2.2	2.0	1.9	2.7	2.7	2.6	2.7	009
Calendar year											
	39263.9	43569.3	51515.9	59205.6	67705.3	75137.1	80250.4	92825.0	106178.6	118629.0	010
	244.5	221.5	203.5	190.0	176.6	165.4	170.9	166.7	186.5	206.4	011
	75.6	57.3	48.1	58.2	81.7	76.1	38.7	38.3	55.0	59.0	012
	10304.9	12209.0	15461.4	17346.2	19393.1	21191.4	21236.7	24524.3	27674.3	31635.9	013
	1075.4	962.4	1155.5	1131.6	1250.0	1280.0	1353.3	1571.1	1740.3	1869.7	014
	3289.2	3042.4	2996.7	3227.4	3724.0	4799.3	6212.2	6772.4	7975.6	8555.4	015
	6608.6	7471.5	8997.4	10280.9	12590.6	13898.1	14346.8	16500.2	19122.4	21652.1	016
	5332.8	5941.3	6899.3	7987.4	8715.6	9991.3	10168.7	11494.5	12986.3	14130.0	017
	9930.5	11074.6	12464.5	14774.6	17835.1	19857.8	22235.5	26738.6	30575.8	34187.3	018
											019
	2402.4	2589.3	3289.5	4209.3	3938.6	3877.7	4487.6	5018.9	5862.4	6333.2	020
	949.0	-428.7	-136.3	445.3	427.4	7.3	1436.3	-792.7	15.7	858.0	021
	40212.9	43140.6	51379.6	59650.9	68132.7	75144.4	81686.7	92032.3	106194.3	119487.0	022
	39263.9	43569.3	51515.9	59205.6	67705.3	75137.1	80250.4	92825.0	106178.6	118629.0	023
	18311.7	20540.5	23910.7	26916.1	30062.6	32751.9	35273.8	40353.2	43945.8	46878.6	024
	5270.2	5314.6	5336.9	6013.3	6779.7	7435.8	7626.6	8497.1	8947.6	10101.8	025
	14132.0	14405.4	15666.6	18905.8	21577.8	25090.6	28907.9	33003.9	36421.9	39851.2	026
	584.6	1893.3	1663.2	1459.1	2771.0	1008.4	423.8	2564.6	-1032.2	-522.9	027
	143.1	589.1	4526.7	5969.5	5988.4	9293.1	8587.9	8556.2	18342.0	21792.9	028
	822.3	826.4	411.8	-58.2	525.8	-442.7	-569.6	-150.0	-446.5	527.4	029
	39830.2	43710.3	48792.3	53497.5	58289.8	62364.5	66255.0	73161.3	80587.2	87752.5	030
	260.8	234.0	205.4	191.8	177.3	160.6	162.4	158.5	167.3	180.2	031
	94.3	93.4	74.8	75.9	69.0	80.4	55.0	42.5	38.9	42.3	032
	9955.8	11673.2	13773.2	15121.5	16557.6	17458.2	17887.3	19678.6	22224.9	24518.7	033
	839.9	926.6	1012.1	1085.9	1203.3	1281.1	1353.5	1450.7	1582.4	1682.6	034
	3234.2	2916.8	2804.2	2843.5	3042.5	3690.4	4499.9	4863.3	5668.0	6150.8	035
	6653.2	7358.4	8573.3	9308.7	10327.5	11309.5	11737.6	12688.1	13849.1	15093.8	036
	5677.4	6165.6	6807.6	7481.1	8160.9	8785.7	9341.9	10358.5	11496.8	12778.8	037
	10541.6	11665.1	12476.6	13709.2	15343.1	16628.3	17758.8	19973.0	21626.3	23423.9	038
											039
	2573.0	2677.2	3065.1	3679.9	3408.6	2970.3	3458.6	3948.1	3933.5	3881.4	040
	2347.6	-1222.1	-613.7	-310.1	-686.4	-1069.8	-1067.0	-1549.8	-2089.6	-2477.2	041
	42177.8	42488.2	48178.6	53187.4	57603.4	61294.7	65188.0	71611.5	78497.6	85275.3	042
	39830.2	43710.3	48792.3	53497.5	58289.8	62364.5	66255.0	73161.3	80587.2	87752.5	043
	18333.3	20106.0	22811.7	24751.2	26625.3	28254.1	29951.8	33102.4	34798.0	36655.2	044
	5606.8	5653.9	5316.4	5615.8	6234.9	6753.5	6893.1	7621.6	7628.3	8574.5	045
	14381.4	14296.4	14844.9	17182.4	18949.4	21500.8	24156.1	27087.6	29020.4	31343.9	046
	637.4	1889.7	954.3	705.4	2152.4	757.8	359.9	1421.3	-989.8	-468.2	047
	262.0	1183.3	4429.7	4924.8	3988.2	4951.4	4799.7	4275.2	10998.9	13141.5	048
	609.3	581.0	435.3	317.9	339.6	146.9	94.4	-346.8	-868.6	-1494.4	049
	14716.6	16298.7	17329.8	20364.9	24348.8	26099.0	29331.7	35568.5	35389.7	39328.3	050

Item		1978	1979	1980	1981	1982	1983	1984	1985
051	Gross national saving	5673.6	7165.3	8829.8	11073.3	12922.8	16363.7	18912.6	17229.0
052	Gross domestic saving [e]	5716.6	7244.2	9732.0	12221.5	13817.0	16535.4	18145.4	15822.1
053	Net factor income from abroad	-43.0	-78.9	-902.2	-1148.2	-894.2	-171.7	767.2	1406.9
054	Foreign saving	940.6	1524.0	3118.0	2781.7	2334.8	835.5	345.8	-461.2
055	Net transfer from abroad	-88.4	-76.1	-227.6	-322.8	-438.8	-454.2	-475.1	-469.0
056	Net borrowing from abroad	1029.0	1600.1	3345.6	3104.5	2773.6	1289.7	820.9	7.8
	Per Capita GNP, Singapore dollars								
057	Current prices	7569	8590	10609	12151	13407	15171	16728	16262
058	Constant *1985* prices	10210	11014	12379	13292	13714	14981	16623	16262
	PRODUCTION								*Thousand metric tons;*
	Manufacturing								
059	1. Fuel oil [f]	10154	10340	6457	7560	8259	8155	9294	8025
060	2. Diesel oil [f]	6780	6566	4619	6490	7074	6569	6044	5999
061	3. Aviation kerosene [f]	4708	5033	3709	4003	4099	4290	4929	3878
062	4. Cement	1628	1808	1952	2253	2695	3153	2511	1897
063	5. Animal feed	300	306	334	255	238	210	223	167
	Production Indexes								*Period*
064	Agriculture, *1979-81 = 100*	104.3	96.2	96.2	111.1	81.1	95.8	105.7	105.9
065	Mining	...	...	...	...	...	...	...	...
066	Manufacturing, *1992 = 100*	36.7	42.2	47.4	52.0	49.1	50.2	54.7	50.7
	ENERGY								*Annual*
	Crude petroleum, *'000 m.t.*								
067	Production	–	–	–	–	–	–	–	–
068	Exports	320	434	338	50	276	465	352	398
069	Imports	33579	34928	30925	35969	38715	39392	36326	35754
070	Consumption	27785	29192	32587	37125	35200	36200	35395	34395
	Coal, *'000 m.t.*								
071	Production	–	–	–	–	–	–	–	–
072	Exports	0	1	1	0	0	0	0	0
073	Imports	0	0	0	1	0	0	1	0
074	Consumption	0	1	0	1	0	0	1	0
	Electricity, *Mn kWh*								
075	Production	5898	6483	6968	7462	7883	8665	9452	9917
076	Consumption	5214	5744	6198	6660	7000	7698	8399	8871
	Retail prices, *S$/litre*								
077	Gasoline, premium	0.77	0.81	1.00	1.07	1.06	1.10	1.25	1.38
078	Diesel	0.27	0.35	0.63	0.70	0.69	0.61	0.57	0.56
	PRICE INDEXES								*Period*
079	Consumer, *Oct 1992 - Sept 1993 = 100*	65.8	68.5	74.4	80.4	83.6	84.6	86.8	87.2
080	Food	73.9	76.0	81.9	89.8	94.2	94.6	96.0	94.7
081	Non-Food	61.0	64.2	70.2	75.0	77.2	78.5	81.2	82.6
082	Wholesale, *1990 = 100* [g]	84.0	96.0	114.9	119.3	114.2	110.1	109.4	107.0
083	Implicit GDP deflator, *1985 = 100*	74.2	78.1	87.0	92.8	96.7	100.5	101.2	100.0
	MONEY AND BANKING								*Million Singapore dollars;*
084	Money supply (M1)	4926	5706	6135	7242	8157	8608	8866	8785
085	Currency in circulation	2583	2941	3137	3382	3996	4335	4619	4739
086	Demand deposits	2343	2765	2998	3860	4161	4272	4247	4046
087	Quasi-money	5936	7194	9930	12429	14647	16918	18255	19363
088	Money supply (M2)	10862	12900	16065	19671	22804	25526	27121	28148
089	Foreign assets (net)	-701	-404	-772	-1930	-2673	-5222	-6672	-6933
090	Domestic credit	13369	16628	21537	27881	33331	39005	42176	43320
091	Claims on govt. sector (net)	–	–	–	–	–	–	–	–
092	Claims on private sector [h]	10802	13922	18118	23736	27850	32705	35552	36149
093	Claims on other financial insts. [i]	2567	2706	3419	4145	5481	6300	6624	7171

1986	1987	1988	1989	1990	1991	1992	1993	1994	1995	
16631.0	17285.5	22132.3	26721.5	31290.4	34956.7	38786.3	43182.0	53300.9	62506.6	051
15682.0	17714.2	22268.3	26276.2	30863.0	34949.4	37350.0	43974.7	53285.2	61648.6	052
949.0	-428.7	-136.0	445.3	427.4	7.3	1436.3	-792.7	15.7	858.0	053
-1092.1	-160.4	-4390.4	-6414.8	-6415.8	-9300.4	-10024.2	-7763.5	-18357.7	-22650.9	054
-398.4	-492.2	-602.2	-714.6	-802.9	-863.4	-878.1	-968.8	-1121.9	-1259.1	055
-693.7	331.8	-3788.2	-5700.2	-5612.9	-8437.0	-9146.1	-6794.7	-17235.8	-21391.8	056
15958	16918	19761	22510	25141	27226	28967	32067	36244	39962	057
16737	16662	18530	20071	21256	22208	23116	24952	26791	28520	058

Calendar year

8423	7925	8435	10445	7790	...	...	...	...	...	059
5680	7523	8540	9773	10925	...	...	...	...	...	060
4451	5063	5661	5260	5141	...	...	...	...	...	061
1875	1550	1684	1476	1926	...	...	...	...	...	062
112	117	127	138	119	...	...	...	...	...	063

averages

104.8	104.3	76.5	93.4	93.3	72.9	55.8	41.7	52.3	52.5	064
...	...	...	...	...	...	...	...	...	...	065
55.1	64.7	76.5	84.2	92.6	97.6	100.0	110.2	124.5	137.3	066

values

–	–	–	–	–	–	...	...	...	...	067
90	98	1600	185	19	1	...	...	...	...	068
35100	33184	34390	36776	42680	45026	46336	...	...	...	069
34910	35686	34090	36091	40861	44525	...	...	...	...	070
–	–	–	–	–	–	...	...	...	...	071
0	0	0	0	0	0	...	...	...	...	072
0	0	0	0	1	0	...	...	...	...	073
0	0	0	0	0	0	...	...	...	...	074
10577	11814	13018	14039	15618	16597	17543	18962	20676	22057	075
9476	10617	11735	12688	14194	15089	15948	17194	18901	20240	076
0.98	0.95	0.91	1.01	1.10	1.23	1.22	1.20	1.20	1.20	077
0.40	0.44	0.39	0.43	0.51	0.51	0.49	0.49	0.47	0.47	078

averages

86.0	86.4	87.8	89.8	92.9	96.1	98.3	100.5	103.6	105.4	079
93.5	93.3	94.6	96.0	96.7	98.2	99.5	100.3	103.9	106.2	080
81.5	82.3	83.7	86.3	90.7	94.9	97.6	100.6	103.5	105.1	081
90.8	97.6	95.8	98.3	100.0	95.9	91.7	89.2	87.3	87.4	082
98.6	99.7	105.6	110.7	116.2	120.5	121.1	126.9	131.8	135.2	083

As of end of period

9821	11031	11958	13745	15261	16430	18516	22882	23411	25350	084
5033	5440	5997	6610	7109	7497	8279	8942	9420	9907	085
4788	5591	5961	7135	8152	8933	10236	13940	13991	15443	086
21134	26058	30130	37801	46584	53112	57213	59249	70570	76617	087
30955	37089	42088	51546	61845	69542	75729	82131	93981	101967	088
-3449	-1576	512	2793	460	2706	5152	1424	1689	-3931	089
41843	44715	49251	59802	68185	76571	83617	94484	107354	127932	090
–	–	–	–	–	–	–	–	–	–	091
34438	36444	40445	49263	56161	62677	67528	76924	89027	106762	092
7405	8271	8806	10538	12024	13894	16089	17560	18327	21170	093

Item	1978	1979	1980	1981	1982	1983	1984	1985
094 Other items [j]	-1806	-3324	-4700	-6280	-7854	-8257	-8383	-8239
Deposit Money Banks								
095 Demand deposits	2732	3244	3484	4441	4781	4983	4857	4700
096 Savings deposits	1211	1395	1692	2168	2917	4080	4870	5983
097 Time deposits	6045	7473	10788	13315	15620	17100	18192	17941
098 Domestic credits outstanding	9399	12059	16158	21250	25336	30145	32743	33775
Interest Rates [k]								*Per cent;*
On deposits								
099 Savings	3.82	5.40	8.03	9.83	7.20	6.24	6.93	5.66
100 Time: 6 months	5.14	6.45	9.28	10.82	7.56	6.49	7.03	5.23
101 12 months	5.65	6.76	9.03	10.86	7.95	6.77	7.16	5.57
GOVERNMENT FINANCE [l]								*Million Singapore dollars;*
Central Government								
102 Current revenue [m]	3738.8	4603.0	5903.5	7862.2	9128.5	10631.8	10059.2	9511.3 l
103 Taxes	2948.7	3401.3	4415.3	5467.4	6469.4	7464.0	7635.2	6724.4 l
104 Non-taxes	790.1	1201.7	1488.2	2394.8	2659.1	3167.8	2424.0	2786.9 l
105 Current expenditure [n]	2728.3	3161.7	3714.0	4499.0	5047.0	5727.3	6536.9	6641.7 l
106 Current surplus/deficit	1010.5	1441.3	2189.5	3363.2	4081.5	4904.5	3522.3	2869.6 l
107 Capital receipts [o]	1260.3	1171.0	1826.9	1523.4	1871.5	2411.2	5557.8	3996.9 l
108 Capital expenditure [p]	2172.9	2324.2	3682.8	5189.8	5031.0	6424.7	7246.9	8588.1 l
109 Capital account surplus/deficit	-912.6	-1153.2	-1855.9	-3666.4	-3159.5	-4013.5	-1689.1	-4591.2 l
110 Net lending	–	–	–	–	–	–	–	– l
111 Overall surplus/deficit	97.9	288.1	333.6	-303.2	922.0	891.0	1833.2	-1721.6 l
Financing								
112 Domestic borrowing (net)	1975.8	1689.0	2205.4	–	1300.0	6190.5	12.1	10.0 l
113 Foreign borrowing (net)	46.7	9.5	15.7	13.8	30.4			l
114 Foreign grants	–	–	–	–	–	–	–	– l
115 Use of cash balances	-2120.4	-1986.6	-2554.7	289.4	-2252.4	-7081.5	-1845.3	1711.6 l
Expenditure by Function, Central Govt.								
116 Total	5214.8	6328.2	9268.9	10175.6	12130.2	15035.0	14882.3	19015.2 l
117 General public services [q]	299.6	366.6	432.5	715.3	816.3	1065.9	946.1	1064.1 l
118 Defense	944.5	995.6	1266.8	1495.1	1607.6	1527.8	2424.0	2705.4 l
119 Education	472.8	562.7	689.2	906.4	1304.9	1638.7	1798.5	1805.6 l
120 Health	212.7	229.9	279.3	348.1	378.5	424.0	466.2	504.5 l
121 Social security & welfare	10.7	10.8	10.9	11.9	11.9	12.2	561.8	5042.2 l
122 Housing & community amenities	1122.3	1310.4	1557.1	1967.8	2835.0	4111.0	3117.6	489.8 l
123 Economic services	1209.1	1166.4	2210.5	2091.4	2011.9	1929.4	3144.0	2273.3 l
124 Agriculture	12.6	18.1	20.4	22.4	29.2	24.4	36.8	39.6 l
125 Industry	459.6	583.6	1281.2	1253.0	976.1	696.9	750.3	509.0 l
126 Electricity, gas & water	273.4	–	20.0	–	–	–	–	70.0 l
127 Transport and communications	336.0	427.0	595.2	546.9	498.4	703.6	1924.7	1131.6 l
128 Other economic services	127.5	137.7	293.7	269.1	508.2	504.5	432.2	523.1 l
129 Others	943.1	1685.8	2822.6	2639.6	3164.1	4326.0	2424.1	5130.3 l
EXTERNAL TRADE								*Million Singapore dollars;*
130 Exports, fob	22986	30940	41452	44290	44473	46155	51340	50179
131 Imports, cif	29601	38334	51345	58248	60245	59505	61134	57818
132 Trade balance	-6615	-7394	-9893	-13958	-15772	-13350	-9794	-7639
Exports, by SITC section								
133 Food and live animals	1488	1674	2008	2125	2388	2025	2895	2193
134 Beverage and tobacco	100	132	157	174	217	210	210	241
135 Crude materials excl. fuels	3483	4413	4700	3665	2781	3388	3410	2700
136 Mineral fuels, etc.	5329	7414	11966	14176	14617	12970	16179	16452
137 Animal, vegetable oil & fats	514	858	1096	820	780	628	1540	1535
138 Chemicals	870	1124	1418	1556	1722	1956	2464	2717
139 Basic manufactures	2260	2842	3442	3670	3839	3683	3625	3598
140 Machines, transport equipment	5715	8217	11089	11779	11546	14678	16865	16567

1986	1987	1988	1989	1990	1991	1992	1993	1994	1995	
-7439	-6050	-7675	-11050	-6800	-9735	-13040	-13776	-15062	-22034	094
5423	6658	6636	8019	9170	10291	11635	15766	15788	17538	095
7426	8482	9025	9952	10010	11981	14209	16895	16900	23501	096
17610	21009	26508	34972	44407	49529	52137	49878	65083	67390	097
31680	34269	37752	46253	52744	58543	63429	72618	84726	102035	098

Period averages

4.25	3.06	2.73	2.93	3.50	3.69	2.14	1.62	2.31	2.81	099
4.06	3.09	3.05	3.68	5.11	4.97	3.09	2.54	3.00	3.77	100
4.25	3.47	3.56	4.42	5.51	5.06	3.34	2.84	3.54	4.11	101

Fiscal year beginning 1 April

10411	12947	13856	15710	17872	19919	21417	20656	23713	24252 *	102
5208	5957	7519	9618	10254	11924	13675	...	...	...	103
5203	6990	6337	6092	7618	7995	7742	...	...	...	104
6802	9722	8107	8999	10867	12365	12209	12896	14043	18507 *	105
3609	3225	5749	6711	7005	7554	9208	7760	9670	5745 *	106
4560	858	603	1557	3764	3315	5200	...	...	...	107
4635	5549	3635	4116	3356	3601	3649	...	...	...	108
-75	-4691	-3032	-2559	408	-286	1551	...	...	...	109
2973	-301	-768	-1737	221	813	589	2595	5578	9028 *	110
561	-1165	3485	5889	7192	6455	10170	...	...	...	111
-373	1217	-3386	-5846	-7104	-6430	-10155	...	...	...	112
-188	-52	-99	-43	-88	-25	-15	...	...	...	113
–	–	–	–	–	–	–	...	...	...	114
–	–	–	–	–	–	–	...	...	...	115
11437	15271	11742	13115	14223	15966	15858	...	...	...	116
1382	2246	1245	1244	1403	2046	1956	...	...	...	117
2172	2231	2492	2837	3409	3523	3891	...	...	...	118
2076	2204	2231	2369	2828	3655	3532	...	...	...	119
464	548	608	613	652	994	964	...	...	...	120
182	196	236	282	300	344	365	...	...	...	121
1638	1483	1387	1249	870	808	1061	...	...	...	122
2272	2383	1878	2617	2389	1714	1830	...	...	...	123
26	27	28	32	94	55	46	...	...	...	124
7	7	75	31	26	28	24	...	...	...	125
...	...	...	...	...	...	...	...	...	...	126
1214	1534	1092	759	710	709	534	...	...	...	127
1025	815	683	1795	1559	922	1226	...	...	...	128
1251	3980	1665	1904	2372	2882	2259	...	...	...	129

Calendar year

48986	60266	79051	87117	95206	101880	103351	119473	147327	167515	130
55545	68415	88227	96864	109806	114195	117530	137603	156396	176313	131
-6559	-8149	-9176	-9747	-14600	-12315	-14179	-18130	-9069	-8799	132
2626	2717	3285	3037	2734	3033	2987	2910	3542	3554	133
332	387	553	886	1388	1841	1969	2389	2448	2274	134
2459	3003	4047	3721	2915	2522	2278	2132	2193	2405	135
12361	12198	12353	13443	17295	17371	13510	14612	14075	13858	136
880	796	886	1016	761	722	747	610	574	718	137
2840	3762	5199	5737	5970	6680	6732	7663	8418	9999	138
3633	4523	6529	7084	6651	7320	7115	7756	8856	10614	139
18901	26274	37939	43142	47733	51697	56939	69641	94199	110007	140

	Item	1978	1979	1980	1981	1982	1983	1984	1985
141	Misc. manufactured goods	1725	2122	2572	2919	2832	3084	3408	3378
142	Unclassified goods	1502	2144	3004	3406	3751	3533	743	798
	Exports, by principal commodity								
143	1. Petroleum products	5256	7302	11810	13954	14288	12557	12849	13418
144	2. Telecommunication apparatus [r]	1062	1723	2718	2642	2197	2390	3162	3150
145	3. Clothing (except fur)	672	811	913	990	980	1002	1171	1177
146	4. Crude rubber	2460	3069	3292	2454	1743	2106	2135	1492
147	5. Fixed vegetable oils	348	685	841	582	561	452	1116	1128
	Imports, by SITC section								
148	Food and live animals	2183	2553	2916	3270	3602	3504	4158	3535
149	Beverage and tobacco	176	207	276	282	340	416	461	501
150	Crude materials excl. fuels	2470	3108	3417	2776	2306	2625	2510	1988
151	Mineral fuels, etc.	7082	9673	14889	19831	20480	18612	16961	17031
152	Animal, vegetable oil & fats	491	829	1001	722	672	632	1436	1381
153	Chemicals	1598	2178	2687	2756	2791	2982	3096	2890
154	Basic manufactures	4566	5737	7237	8080	8407	8090	8045	7082
155	Machines, transport equipment	8608	11344	15304	16475	17219	18046	19420	18317
156	Misc. manufactured goods	2071	2194	2951	3413	3852	3947	4197	4194
157	Unclassified goods	356	511	667	643	576	651	850	898
	Direction of Trade							*Million US dollars;*	
158	Exports, Total	10132	14239	19377	20970	20787	21832	24070	22812
159	1. United States	1626	1967	2424	2770	2612	3954	4823	4830
160	2. Malaysia	1408	2039	2908	3269	3669	3843	3902	3539
161	3. Hong Kong	719	961	1496	1837	1751	1482	1488	1454
162	4. Japan	981	1366	1560	2124	2262	2008	2255	2148
163	5. Thailand	395	610	844	883	799	944	1154	949
164	6. Germany	335	485	584	534	455	507	576	512
165	7. United Kingdom	320	443	500	497	423	498	644	626
166	8. China, People's Rep. of	58	170	307	179	240	213	243	333
167	9. Korea, Rep. of	177	230	289	293	317	457	382	281
168	10. Netherlands	183	331	367	347	357	254	295	290
169	Imports, Total	13061	17643	24013	27571	28176	28158	28667	26237
170	1. Japan	2509	3004	4311	5188	5044	5075	5261	4486
171	2. Malaysia	1673	2481	3323	3412	3778	4088	4306	3736
172	3. United States	1664	2527	3389	3484	3632	4261	4179	3988
173	4. Thailand	360	501	475	473	530	506	633	544
174	5. Korea, Rep. of	148	195	274	313	347	428	368	423
175	6. Hong Kong	323	385	494	517	589	600	601	493
176	7. Saudi Arabia	1724	1850	2930	5095	4413	3077	2665	920
177	8. Germany	494	650	784	764	895	766	782	716
178	9. China, People's Rep. of	342	411	629	772	881	827	1347	2268
179	10. United Kingdom	492	629	811	824	799	778	748	770
	Trade Indexes								
	Quantum index, *1972 = 100*							*Period*	
180	Exports	189	227	266	...	...	...	...	...
181	Imports	159	185	213	...	...	...	...	...
	Unit value index, *1990 = 100* [s]								
182	Exports	87.8	102.6	126.5	131.2	127.2	121.1	116.4	114.2
183	Imports	87.3	98.5	115.2	116.9	111.8	108.9	108.2	105.3
184	Terms of Trade	100.6	104.2	109.8	112.2	113.8	111.2	107.6	108.5
	BALANCE OF PAYMENTS [t]							*Million US dollars;*	
185	Merchandise exports, fob	9587	13400	18200	19662	19435	20429	22662	21533
186	Merchandise imports, fob	-12090	-16450	-22401	-25785	-26197	-26252	-26733	-24361
187	Trade balance	-2503	-3050	-4201	-6123	-6762	-5823	-4071	-2828

1986	1987	1988	1989	1990	1991	1992	1993	1994	1995	
4042	5556	7111	7815	8500	9229	9593	9768	11185	12552	141
912	1050	1151	1235	1260	1465	1482	1993	1838	1532	142
10022	9625	9639	13333	17156	17191	13360	14424	13850	13631	143
3690	5972	8954	10144	11474	11797	11897	14371	18859	18367	144
1470	2096	2491	2715	2867	3008	2948	2500	2322	2075	145
1335	1535	2274	1885	1405	1089	966	779	785	949	146
336	363	455	450	349	305	278	219	247	280	147
3866	3952	4667	4463	4315	4645	4837	5033	5218	5153	148
542	595	730	1013	1426	1557	1652	2074	2141	2024	149
1905	2267	2999	2663	2371	2092	1867	1968	1939	2086	150
10995	12526	12422	13408	17399	16050	14987	14912	13788	14204	151
720	792	941	924	753	849	878	834	641	753	152
3246	4082	5809	7412	8441	8307	8855	9615	10114	11385	153
7614	9537	12994	13785	14168	14998	15046	16013	16523	19191	154
20781	27534	38299	42838	49065	53433	56331	71916	88306	102055	155
4887	6054	7999	8814	10450	10792	11718	13415	15428	17390	156
991	1078	1367	1545	1420	1473	1359	1823	2298	2072	157

Calendar year

22501	28696	39318	44769	52753	59219	63475	74071	96376	88497	158
5257	7000	9370	10432	11215	11674	13396	15074	18093	17537	159
3327	4101	5332	6110	6873	8800	7932	10497	19029	11066	160
1462	1815	2456	2823	3429	4260	4962	6425	8383	9172	161
1931	2598	3394	3828	4616	5133	4825	5526	6766	6224	162
821	1215	2144	2465	3490	3706	3955	4213	5355	5808	163
708	927	1367	1645	2134	2509	2695	2941	3421	3165	164
590	815	1145	1554	1683	1796	1844	2216	2607	3056	165
571	737	1193	1199	799	858	1113	1905	2098	3089	166
324	473	771	866	1173	1393	1305	2062	2532	2081	167
344	530	675	719	1132	1551	1980	1921	2571	1582	168
25513	32626	43869	49694	60954	66271	72181	85393	102287	121456	169
5078	6675	9632	10612	12263	14115	15202	18663	22511	25306	170
3400	4511	6431	6518	8257	10128	10609	14042	16725	17090	171
3819	4786	6824	8522	9801	10501	11882	13955	15630	16761	172
737	1017	1186	1253	1670	2107	2681	3518	4885	7942	173
592	877	1264	1488	1776	1889	2129	2747	3915	7162	174
601	860	1210	1422	1879	1992	2203	2689	3456	5438	175
630	1355	1924	2388	3265	3398	3366	2962	3667	3960	176
841	1122	1625	1807	2178	2115	2358	2605	3446	4015	177
1430	1412	1691	1698	2095	2227	2253	2404	2885	3850	178
866	1034	1274	1396	1870	1905	2014	2235	2819	3542	179

averages

...	...	...	...	...	...	...	...	...	...	180
...	...	...	...	...	...	...	...	...	...	181
98.1	101.5	100.0	99.5	100.0	94.6	88.4	86.4	82.9	...	182
92.9	100.6	101.1	100.9	100.0	96.8	93.5	91.6	90.7	...	183
105.6	100.9	98.9	98.6	100.0	97.7	94.5	94.3	91.4	...	184

Calendar year

21336	27464	38987	43712	52199	58312	64521	75051	95804	85382 *	185
-23402	-29910	-40338	-45593	-55813	-60946	-67866	-80046	-96038	-85365 *	186
-2066	-2446	-1351	-1881	-3614	-2634	-3345	-4995	-234	17 *	187

Item	1978	1979	1980	1981	1982	1983	1984	1985
188 Other goods, services and income	2090	2349	2745	4807	5671	5428	3909	3038
189 Credit	4191	5248	7039	9705	10952	10600	9184	8197
190 Debit	-2101	-2899	-4294	-4898	-5281	-5172	-5275	-5159
191 Unrequited transfer	-39	-35	-107	-153	-205	-215	-223	-213
192 Private	-36	-31	-104	-145	-194	-207	-214	-205
193 Official	-3	-4	-3	-8	-11	-8	-9	-8
194 Current balance	-452	-736	-1563	-1469	-1296	-610	-385	-3
195 Direct investment	187	669	1138	1675	1298	1085	1209	808
196 Portfolio investment	-127	-78	13	-48	-29	-49	-152	175
197 Other long-term capital	239	226	312	84	565	-252	-285	34
198 Other short-term capital	714	181	119	456	475	1679	808	-319
199 Net errors and omissions	104	255	643	211	163	-794	329	642
200 Overall balance	665	517	662	909	1176	1059	1524	1337
201 Allocation of SDRs	–	7	7	8	–	–	–	–
202 Monetary movements	-665	-524	-669	-917	-1176	-1059	-1524	-1337
INTERNATIONAL RESERVES								*Million US dollars;*
203 Total	5302.7	5818.5	6566.8	7549.2	8479.7	9264.2	10416.0	12846.6
204 Foreign exchange [u]	5285.6	5774.1	6491.0	7443.4	8350.6	9130.0	10291.3	12685.5
205 Reserve position in the Fund	17.1	28.3	56.5	73.8	74.7	71.7	67.8	88.6
206 SDRs	–	16.1	19.3	32.0	54.4	62.5	56.9	72.5
EXCHANGE RATES								*Singapore dollars*
207 End of period	2.1635	2.1590	2.0935	2.0478	2.1085	2.1270	2.1780	2.1050
208 Average of period	2.2740	2.1746	2.1412	2.1127	2.1400	2.1131	2.1331	2.2002
EXTERNAL INDEBTEDNESS								*Million US dollars;*
209 Total outstanding & disbursed	1377	1730	2071	2263	3607	3911	4128	4407
210 Long-term	1284	1573	1870	2018	3098	3271	3455	3806
211 Public and publicly guaranteed	1134	1323	1320	1318	...	...	...	...
212 Private non-guaranteed	150	250	550	700	...	...	...	...
213 Short-term	93	157	201	245	509	640	673	601
214 Use of IMF credit	0	0	0	0	0	0	0	0
								Transactions
Debt service								
215 Principal repayments on LT debt	466	163	354	217	298	344	295	982
216 Interest on long-term debt	97	105	143	184	241	310	293	283
217 Interest on short-term debt	...	...	...	...	179	57	69	52
Average terms of new commitments								
218 Interest (%)	10.3	8.6	9.7	11.4	10.5	9.6	9.6	10.1
219 Maturity (years)	8.6	8.5	10.6	9.0	11.2	11.5	10.2	9.6
220 Grace period (years)	1.8	3.1	1.7	3.1	3.5	5.6	1.8	5.1
221 Grant element (%)	-1.8	4.9	0.6	-6.9	-4.3	3.9	0.9	-1.1

Footnotes:

a   Mid-year estimates except for the 1980 and 1990 figures which are the results of population censuses. Figures for 1978-79 refer to total population present in Singapore. From 1980 they refer to Singapore residents (citizens and permanent residents) residing in Singapore.
b   Data from 1978 to 1980 refer to persons aged ten years and over; thereafter, data refer to persons aged fifteen years and over. Figures are based on the annual labor force surveys conducted in June of each year except for the 1980 and 1990 figures which are based on censuses.
c   Data from 1986 onwards are based on the average for the year.
d   Including import duties less imputed bank service charges.
e   Gross domestic product less domestic consumption expenditure.
f   Prior to 1980 data include products processed for third party overseas.
g   Refers to Domestic Supply Price Index.
h   Bills discounted or purchased in Singapore plus loans and advances.
i   Investment in securities and equities in Singapore plus money at call with discount houses. Discount houses ceased operations in 1987.
j   Residual item.
k   Rates refer to the average quoted by ten leading banks.

	1986	1987	1988	1989	1990	1991	1992	1993	1994	1995	
	2567	2523	3533	5190	7238	7821	10038	10805	12963	11869 *	188
	8439	10348	13162	16417	21884	24301	26621	29153	34301	31115 *	189
	-5872	-7825	-9629	-11227	-14646	-16480	-16583	-18348	-21338	-19246 *	190
	-183	-234	-299	-366	-443	-500	-539	-637	-778	-690 *	191
	-172	-170	-209	-241	-274	-341	-405	-484	-598	-528 *	192
	-11	-64	-90	-125	-169	-159	-134	-153	-180	-162 *	193
	318	-157	1883	2943	3181	4687	6154	5173	11951	11196 *	194
	1529	2630	3537	2004	3541	3855	1034	3232	3411	3574 *	195
	-548	252	-293	-76	-1037	-907	1621	306	784	879 *	196
	187	-316	-204	-154	-1109	-977	-1838	-1777	-2479	-1349 *	197
	-1612	-2096	-2052	-1318	3292	-1226	-2143	3749	71	5414 *	198
	681	793	-1209	-664	-2410	-1228	1285	-3161	-8957	-12643 *	199
	555	1106	1662	2735	5458	4204	6113	7522	4781	7071 *	200
	–	–	–	–	–	–	–	–	–	–	201
	-555	-1106	-1662	-2735	-5458	-4204	-6113	-7522	-4781	-7071 *	202

As of end of period

	1986	1987	1988	1989	1990	1991	1992	1993	1994	1995	
	12939.0	15227.0	17072.0	20345.0	27749.0	34133.0	39885.0	48360.0	58176.6	68695.1	203
	12750.9	14999.6	16861.0	20136.0	27535.0	33931.0	39661.0	48066.0	57889.6	68349.1	204
	97.8	112.2	105.0	105.0	98.0	86.0	156.0	216.0	252.0	297.0	205
	90.3	115.2	106.0	104.0	116.0	116.0	68.0	78.0	35.0	49.0	206

per US dollar

	1986	1987	1988	1989	1990	1991	1992	1993	1994	1995	
	2.1750	1.9985	1.9462	1.8944	1.7445	1.6305	1.6449	1.6080	1.4607	1.4143	207
	2.1774	2.1060	2.0124	1.9503	1.8125	1.7276	1.6290	1.6158	1.5274	1.4174	208

As of end of year

	1986	1987	1988	1989	1990	1991	1992	1993	1994	1995	
	3787	4196	4191	4575	4204	4825	4705	5511	7903	...	209
	3239	3620	3588	3892	3468	3913	3717	4609	6873	...	210
	...	...	...	...	...	...	...	...	...	...	211
	...	...	...	...	...	...	...	...	...	...	212
	548	576	603	683	736	912	988	902	1030	...	213
	0	0	0	0	0	0	–	–	–	...	214

during the year

	1986	1987	1988	1989	1990	1991	1992	1993	1994	1995	
	642	712	276	505	226	260	...	...	...	...	215
	234	198	233	295	301	234	...	...	...	...	216
	39	39	47	58	59	49	...	...	...	...	217
	9.2	5.2	...	...	...	...	...	...	...	...	218
	11.6	6.8	...	...	...	...	...	...	...	...	219
	5.6	4.9	...	...	...	...	...	...	...	...	220
	2.7	21.3	...	...	...	...	...	...	...	...	221

l Data from 1986 might not be comparable with those for earlier years because of changes in the definition of the items reflected in each of the related footnote.

m Data refer to the revenue credited to the Consolidated Revenue Account (CRA).

n Before 1986, data on current expenditure refer to the payments from the CRA and the Sinking Fund Account (SFA) but exclude transfer to the Development Fund Account and the contributions to the SFA. Expenditures on goods and services for fixed capital formation have been excluded from the expenditure of the CRA. From 1986-1991, however, data refer only to expenditures paid out of the CRA.

o Before 1986, data refer to other sources of Development Fund, henceforth, data refer to land sales and other capital sales.

p For 1978-85, data refer to total uses of Development Fund plus expenditure on goods and services for fixed capital formation. For 1986 onward, data refer to development expenditure.

q Includes public order and safety.

r Figures exclude gramophones, dictating machines and other sound recorders and reproducers.

s Refers to price index.

t For 1995, data up to the third quarter only.

u Data include gold holdings.

	Item	1978	1979	1980	1981	1982	1983	1984	1985
001	**POPULATION**	214	218	225	233	241	249	258	*Thousand;* 267
									Thousand;
002	**LABOR FORCE**	...	...	...	...	...	...	...	...
003	Employed [a]	17.4	18.2	19.6	20.7	20.8	21.1	22.7	24.0
004	Agriculture	5.9	6.0	6.1	7.2	7.2	7.0	7.6	8.0
005	Manufacturing	1.1	1.7	2.1	1.8	1.8	1.8	1.8	1.7
006	Mining	0.0	0.0	0.0	0.0	...	...	0.1	0.1
007	Others	10.3	10.5	11.4	11.8	11.8	12.3	13.2	14.1
008	Unemployed	...	...	...	...	...	...	...	...
009	Unemployment rate, %	...	...	...	...	...	...	...	...
	NATIONAL ACCOUNTS [b]							*Million Solomon Island dollars;*	
	At Current Factor Cost								
010	GDP by Industrial Origin	64.0	85.0	91.0	104.0	115.0	132.0	195.9	210.1
011	Agriculture	...	...	...	...	...	...	106.9	108.5
012	Mining	...	...	...	...	...	...	-0.4	-1.5
013	Manufacturing	...	...	...	...	...	...	7.2	8.0
014	Electricity, gas and water	...	...	...	...	...	...	1.7	2.2
015	Construction	...	...	...	...	...	...	7.4	9.0
016	Trade	...	...	...	...	...	...	21.1	22.1
017	Transport and communications	...	...	...	...	...	...	10.4	10.8
018	Finance	...	...	...	...	...	...	11.3	13.0
019	Public administration }	...	...	...	...	...	...		
020	Others	...	...	...	...	...	...	30.4	38.1
021	Indirect taxes less subsidies	6.0	10.0	11.0	15.0	18.0	28.0	25.8	26.9
022	GDP at current market prices	70.0	95.0	102.0	119.0	133.0	160.0	221.7	236.9
	At Current Market Prices								
023	Expenditure on GDP	70.0	95.0	102.0	119.0	133.0	160.0	221.7	236.9
024	Private consumption	...	...	...	...	...	...	122.0	152.0
025	Government consumption	...	...	...	...	...	...	52.1	66.6
026	Gross fixed capital formation	...	...	...	...	...	...	43.0	49.9
027	Increase in stocks	...	...	...	...	...	...	7.9	12.2
028	Exports of goods and services	...	...	...	...	...	...	135.2	121.1
029	Less: Imports of goods and services	...	...	...	...	...	...	138.5	164.9
030	Statistical discrepancy	...	...	...	...	...	...	–	–
	*At Constant 1977 mp	1984 fc*								
031	GDP by Industrial Origin	66.0	83.0	163.4	176.2	174.9	183.0	196.1	201.6
032	Agriculture [c]	...	...	85.8	94.1	94.4	100.0	108.1	106.9
033	Mining	...	...	0.0	-0.0	-0.1	-0.1	-0.4	-1.4
034	Manufacturing	...	...	7.1	6.4	6.6	6.6	6.0	6.8
035	Electricity, gas and water	...	...	1.3	1.4	1.5	1.6	1.7	1.9
036	Construction [d]	...	...	8.0	10.2	7.2	8.3	7.6	9.8
037	Trade	...	...	17.2	18.5	19.1	17.6	21.1	22.1
038	Transport and communications	...	...	8.2	8.7	8.3	8.7	10.3	10.8
039	Finance	...	...	3.1	3.5	4.6	4.7	5.5	5.4
040	Public administration }	...	...						
041	Others	...	...	32.7	33.2	33.4	35.5	36.2	39.3
042	Indirect taxes less subsidies	...	...	...	...	...	...	...	...
043	GDP at constant market prices	...	...	...	...	...	...	...	...
	Per Capita GDP, Solomon Island dollars								
044	Current prices	327	436	453	511	552	641	859	886
045	Constant *1977* mp	*1984* fc	308	381	726	756	725	733	759	754

1986	1987	1988	1989	1990	1991	1992	1993	1994	1995	
As of 1 July										
277	287	297	308	319	330	342	355	368	382	001
Calendar Year										
...	...	...	...	...	...	...	...	...	...	002
24.0	23.8	24.8	25.4	26.1	26.6	26.8	29.6	...	...	003
8.4	6.6	7.0	7.5	7.5	7.7	6.4	8.1	...	...	004
1.8	2.2	2.2	2.2					...	...	005
0.1	0.1	0.1	0.1	2.3	2.1	2.0	2.8	...	...	006
13.7	14.9	15.6	15.6	16.3	16.8	18.4	18.6	...	...	007
...	...	...	...	...	...	...	...	...	...	008
...	...	...	...	...	...	...	...	...	...	009
Calendar year										
221.1	252.4	306.8	328.0	...	...	...	...	...	...	010
110.0	111.8	...	...	...	...	...	...	...	...	011
-2.6	-2.2	...	...	...	...	...	...	...	...	012
10.1	8.0	...	...	...	...	...	...	...	...	013
2.6	3.1	...	...	...	...	...	...	...	...	014
11.4	11.3	...	...	...	...	...	...	...	...	015
18.9	35.5	...	...	...	...	...	...	...	...	016
13.0	13.7	...	...	...	...	...	...	...	...	017
14.6	16.7	...	...	...	...	...	...	...	...	018
		...	...	...	...	...	...	...	...	019
43.3	54.4	...	...	...	...	...	...	...	...	020
31.4	40.4	49.6	56.4	...	...	...	...	...	...	021
252.5	292.8	356.4	384.4	426.0	506.0	612.0	781.0	...	...	022
252.6	292.7	356.4	384.4	426.0	506.0	612.0	781.0	...	...	023
159.3	184.9	253.6	300.0	...	...	...	...	...	...	024
84.1	106.3	123.8	133.4	...	...	...	...	...	...	025
63.6	59.6	122.1	...	...	...	...	...	...	...	026
2.5	7.9	10.0	...	...	...	...	...	...	...	027
132.9	163.6	227.0	249.0	...	...	...	...	...	...	028
189.8	229.6	380.1	405.9	...	...	...	...	...	...	029
–	–	–	...	...	...	...	...	...	...	030
200.1	204.8	215.8	230.6	234.0	243.1	252.2	...	...	...	031
101.9	95.0	102.1	112.2	114.5	117.6	128.8	...	...	...	032
-2.5	-2.8	-0.7	-0.8	-0.7	-0.7	–	...	...	...	033
7.2	8.7	8.7	8.9	8.9	9.0	9.6	...	...	...	034
2.0	2.0	2.2	2.6	2.3	2.2	2.3	...	...	...	035
10.7	9.4	9.5	10.2	10.4	10.5	...	...	...	...	036
21.5	22.4	20.2	23.4	22.2	23.3	25.1	...	...	...	037
11.3	10.2	10.6	12.4	14.0	17.5	17.6	...	...	...	038
6.2	7.1	7.2	7.8	8.9	8.0	8.4	...	...	...	039
							...	...	...	040
41.8	52.7	56.0	54.0	53.5	55.8	60.4	...	...	...	041
...	...	...	...	...	...	...	...	...	...	042
...	...	...	...	...	...	...	...	...	...	043
913	1022	1200	1250	1337	1532	1788	2200	...	...	044
723	714	727	750	734	736	737	...	...	...	045

Item	1978	1979	1980	1981	1982	1983	1984	1985
PRODUCTION								*Thousand metric tons;*
Agriculture								
046 1. Copra	28	34	29	34	32	28	43	42
047 2. Palm oil & kernel	13	15	17	21	23	24	24	24
048 3. Rice, paddy	8	10	14	14	11	9	7	6
049 4. Cocoa	0.23	0.31	0.35	0.59	0.67	1.17	1.71	1.72
050 5. Timber, *'000 cu. m.*	274	299	299	365	388	395	423	378
051 6. Fish	17	24	23	25	21	35	36	31
Production Indexes								*Period*
052 Agriculture, *1979-81 = 100*	87.2	96.7	95.3	108.0	108.6	110.4	116.3	118.2
053 Mining	...	...	...	...	...	...	...	...
054 Manufacturing	...	...	...	...	...	...	...	...
ENERGY								*Annual*
Electricity, *Mn kWh*								
055 Production	20	21	23	24	25	25	28	29
056 Consumption	20	21	23	24	25	25	28	29
PRICE INDEXES						*4th Quarter 1977*	*4th Quarter 1984 = 100;*	
057 Consumer [e]	...	...	129.9	151.2	170.8	182.4	202.6 I	105.7
058 Food	...	...	133.7	159.8	180.3	192.2	220.7 I	106.0
059 Non-food	...	...	126.5	143.5	162.4	173.6	186.4 I	105.4
060 Implicit GDP deflator, *1977 = 100*I *1984 = 100*	106.1	114.5 I	55.7	59.0	65.8	72.1	99.9	104.2
MONEY AND BANKING							*Thousand Solomon Island dollars;*	
061 Money supply (M1)	7820	10990	15140	14230	15780	18430	28320	28330
062 Currency in circulation	3850	4840	5660	6420	7150	9300	12750	13890
063 Demand deposits	3970	6150	9480	7810	8630	9130	15570	14440
064 Quasi-money	19480	28570	23870	17920	23900	29160	35910	37590
065 Money supply (M2)	27290	39560	39010	32150	39680	47590	64230	65920
066 Foreign assets (net)	24240	31500	22490	11670	18070	25290	40910	24360
067 Domestic credit	3850	8830	20400	28060	33110	30210	40220	62240
068 Claims on govt. sector (net)	-1850	-4310	130	3800	7150	4210	9270	14500
069 Claims on private sector	5700	13140	17340	21390	22450	20560	29880	47100
070 Claims on other financial insts.	–	–	2930	2870	3510	5440	1070	640
071 Other items	-800	-770	-3880	-7580	-11500	-7910	-16900	-20680
Deposit Money Banks								
072 Demand deposits	3970	6150	9480	7810	8630	9130	15570	14450
073 Savings deposits }								
074 Time deposits }	19480	28570	23870	17920	23900	29160	35910	37590
075 Domestic credits outstanding	5790	13670	23000	28290	30320	28930	40400	56250
GOVERNMENT FINANCE [f]							*Thousand Solomon Island dollars;*	
Central Government								
076 Current revenue	13530	19754	22824	29723	33648	34255	47236	52449
077 Taxes	10860	16640	18355	24655	29296	28941	43735	47482
078 Non-taxes	2670	3115	4469	5068	4352	5314	3502	4967
079 Current expenditure	16740	20075	24357	30852	34489	39235	46107	58980
080 Current surplus/deficit	-3210	-321	-1533	-1128	-841	-4981	1130	-6531
081 Capital receipts	70	1181	570	189	192	112	464	740
082 Capital expenditure	6720	11835	11816	10980	11896	10706	10137	15735
083 Capital account surplus/deficit	-6650	-10654	-11246	-10791	-11704	-10595	-9672	-14995
084 Net lending	3940	3351	4287	4631	3343	3844	2700	1289
085 Overall surplus/deficit	-13800	-14326	-17067	-16550	-15888	-19419	-11242	-22815
Financing								
086 Foreign grants	14680	11384	13465	7335	5512	6042	4710	2052
087 Foreign borrowing	690	2028	3426	3248	4994	7647	4353	...
088 Domestic borrowing	-10	2119	3123	2958	4706	6459	-2136	...
089 Use of cash balances	-1560	-1205	-2948	3010	676	-727	4315	...

	1986	1987	1988	1989	1990	1991	1992	1993	1994	1995	
Calendar year											
	32	27	29	34	34	25	29	29	22	...	046
	18	14	18	25	28	30	35	38	37	...	047
	2	–	–	–	–	–	–	–	–	...	048
	1.89	2.68	2.65	3.30	2.73	2.46	2.18	3.30	3.34	...	049
	471	322	310	298	436	352	392	547	438	...	050
	44	32	42	37	29	50	43	32	39	...	051
averages											
	108.9	103.0	111.0	122.0	129.0	135.0	139.0	134.0	136.0	137.4	052
	...	...	...	...	...	...	...	...	...	...	053
	...	...	...	...	...	...	...	...	...	...	054
values											
	30	30	30	30	30	30	30	...	...	...	055
	30	30	30	30	30	30	30	...	...	...	056
Period averages											
	120.1	133.3	156.3	178.8	194.5	223.7	247.8	270.5	306.4	...	057
	118.0	127.4	146.7	180.8	196.0	228.9	255.1	278.2	309.6	...	058
	122.0	139.3	158.8	175.0	192.9	218.4	240.2	268.1	306.8	...	059
	110.5	123.3	142.2	142.3	...	...	...	...	...	...	060
As of end of period											
	30380	37230	49030	50900	64460	79540	104910	123930	162880	...	061
	13580	16840	20210	22650	25220	27800	30830	42110	50230	...	062
	16800	20390	28820	28250	39240	51740	74080	81820	112650	...	063
	41650	59760	79040	76680	75650	94020	111120	125880	149700	...	064
	72030	96980	128070	127580	140110	173560	216030	249810	312580	...	065
	40830	63340	79720	50180	34450	20880	73080	60610	52630	...	066
	63240	71300	91990	129900	161640	210040	220120	256260	312450	...	067
	10400	9390	16760	31940	72760	128390	139720	170700	205390	...	068
	51620	55020	69520	92230	82310	75640	72220	84220	107060	...	069
	1220	6890	5710	5730	6570	6010	8180	1340	–	...	070
	-32040	-37660	-43640	-52500	-55980	-57360	-77170	-67060	-52500	...	071
	16800	20390	28820	28250	39230	51740	74080	81820	112650	...	072
											073
	41650	59760	79040	76680	75650	94020	111120	120320	149700	...	074
	63450	80870	103020	125780	128560	151710	179150	217790	260110	...	075
Fiscal year ending 31 December											
	57475	69440	82140	116200	124400	138800	169400	...	...	...	076
	52104	63570	72760	99400	108500	120800	150900	...	...	...	077
	5370	5870	9380	16800	15900	18000	18500	...	...	...	078
	65731	77100	92430	125200	146600	190700	208800	...	...	...	079
	-8257	-7660	-10290	-9000	-22200	-51900	-39400	...	...	...	080
	4	10	300	200	1500	–	–	...	...	...	081
	30326	48630	45830	19800	20900	20700	82300	...	...	...	082
	-30322	-48620	-45530	-19600	-19400	-20700	-82300	...	...	...	083
	1569	7970	14700	2400	4900	2000	-1900	...	...	...	084
	-40148	-64250	-70520	-31000	-46500	-74600	-119800	...	...	...	085
	25394	30200	37560	25700	21600	15500	84100	...	...	...	086
	...	35140	20360	-11700	-10100	-1900	1700	...	...	...	087
	...	-1090	12600	17000	35000	61000	34000	...	...	...	088
	...							...	...	...	089

Item	1978	1979	1980	1981	1982	1983	1984	1985
Expenditure by Function, Central Govt.								
090 Total	23460	31911	36173	41832	46385	49942	56244	74715
091 General public services	8600	5277	6505	6993	7922	8681	10308	12399
092 Defence	–	–	–	–	–	–	–	–
093 Education	3040	3925	4886	6149	7557	10948	11921	13920
094 Health	2620	3061	3857	4246	4800	5304	6298	6686
095 Social security & welfare	270	693	691	1124	937	1322	641	643
096 Housing & community amenities [g]	660	981	1435	3307	1956	2667	2419	894
097 Economic services	8250	11690	11985	10298	11985	11503	12595	19003
098 Agriculture	3420	3664	4527	4974	5739	5416	5600	7156
099 Industry	270	177	189	178	169	125	3	0
100 Electricity, gas & water	370	887	857	1279	1230	890	633	992
101 Transport & communications	3770	6340	5814	3130	3983	4128	5166	9556
102 Economic infrastructure								
103 Other economic services	420	622	598	738	865	945	1193	1300
104 Others	20	6283	6815	9716	11228	9517	12063	21171
EXTERNAL TRADE							*Thousand Solomon Island dollars;*	
105 Exports, fob	32949	59260	60797	57554	56560	71225	118563	103806
106 Imports, fob I cif [h]	30767	50573	61462	65974	57432	70632	83838	102664
107 Trade balance	2182	8687	-665	-8420	-872	593	34725	1142
Exports, by SITC section								
108 Food & live animals	8786	18551	25412	23820	15852	31598	32484	37063
109 Beverage & tobacco	94	67	132	95	80	152	105	88
110 Crude materials excl. fuels	15630	32835	27219	24958	31785	29887	64912	50453
111 Mineral fuels, etc.	–	–	–	–	–	–	–	–
112 Animal vegetable oil & fats	4653	6590	6650	7094	6820	7789	17134	12382
113 Chemicals	–	–	–	–	–	–	–	–
114 Basic manufactures	–	–	–	–	–	–	–	–
115 Machines, transport equipment	–	–	–	–	–	–	–	–
116 Misc. manufactured goods	–	–	–	–	–	–	–	–
117 Unclassified goods	3786	1217	1384	1587	2023	1799	3928	3820
Exports, by principal commodity								
118 1. Fish (fresh, frozen, smoked & canned)	7554	16932	23179	21965	13966	29200	28799	31956
119 2. Timber (rough)	6837	14721	14904	14728	21385	18792	28742	23709
120 3. Copra	10212	16067	10476	8050	8078	8375	32199	23471
121 4. Palm oil	4653	6590	5832	7080	6820	7789	17135	12382
122 5. Cocoa	596	648	637	893	895	2259	3366	5009
Imports, by SITC section [h]								
123 Food & live animals	4934	6362	6630	6998	8510	8210	13146	15660
124 Beverage & tobacco	1466	1906	1804	2343	2131	2723	3746	3948
125 Crude materials excl. fuels	241	222	417	594	544	801	1236	887
126 Mineral fuels, etc.	3547	6483	9873	15192	14405	17857	19061	20829
127 Animal vegetable oil & fats	170	583	402	334	511	741	788	1806
128 Chemicals	2779	3308	3161	3830	3756	4205	5043	6120
129 Basic manufactures	5840	8825	10203	12099	9142	12605	13554	16181
130 Machines, transport equipment	8460	18945	24045	19309	13259	18472	20051	27002
131 Misc. manufactured goods	3048	3724	4719	5023	4939	4798	6735	9792
132 Unclassified goods	282	215	208	252	235	220	479	442
Direction of Trade							*Million US dollars;*	
133 Exports, Total	39.6	69.8	73.3	66.4	57.3	62.2	89.8	69.8
134 1. Japan	7.9	16.5	19.3	24.6	33.5	26.5	28.4	36.4
135 2. United Kingdom	7.7	11.2	9.3	7.9	8.3	7.0	11.7	9.9
136 3. Netherlands	1.1	10.3	9.3	7.9	2.1	1.6	9.3	7.4
137 4. United States	2.5	5.1	15.0	14.9	0.5	7.0	1.1	1.7
138 5. Australia	1.1	1.1	1.7	2.0	1.6	1.2	2.1	1.6

1986	1987	1988	1989	1990	1991	1992	1993	1994	1995	
96057	125730	138260	...	...	...	...	...	...	...	090
13793	16750	21320	...	...	...	...	...	...	...	091
–	–	–	...	...	...	...	...	...	...	092
15019	17130	30940	...	...	...	...	...	...	...	093
6746	8440	8580	...	...	...	...	...	...	...	094
922	1270	1050	...	...	...	...	...	...	...	095
2924	6130	4640	...	...	...	...	...	...	...	096
37368	54040	47980	...	...	...	...	...	...	...	097
16794	29960	23830	...	...	...	...	...	...	...	098
36	2430	1060	...	...	...	...	...	...	...	099
1792	2860	5110	...	...	...	...	...	...	...	100
17388	15380	17850	...	...	...	...	...	...	...	101
			...	...	...	...	...	...	...	102
1358	3410	130	...	...	...	...	...	...	...	103
19285	21970	23750	...	...	...	...	...	...	...	104

Calendar year

114890	128299	170577	171447	178109	228713	301176	411441 *	491664 *	...	105
104325	134943 |	203298	259471	231036	305713 *	326609 *	443625 *	437023 *	...	106
10565	-6644	-32721	-88024	-52927	-77000 *	-25433 *	-32184 *	54641 *	...	107

60141	63060	87315	74146	66119	127520	112005	...	...	...	108
82	20	227	–	29	–	–	...	...	...	109
43288	50636	61552	69668	79595	69799	136601	...	...	...	110
–	–	–	–	–	–	–	...	...	...	111
5611	6901	12343	18229	20399	18205	36043	...	...	...	112
–	–	–	–	–	–	–	...	...	...	113
–	–	–	–	–	–	–	...	...	...	114
–	–	–	–	–	–	–	...	...	...	115
–	–	–	–	–	–	–	...	...	...	116
5768	7682	9140	9404	11967	13189	16527	...	...	...	117

52927	52580	78740	74234	53184	106415	86709	82687	98584	...	
33953	35067	36902	38631	56526	51092	104020	221725	267071	...	119
5951	10256	15656	20974	10936	10370	19806	18533	18368	...	120
5611	6902	12343	18230	17931	14108	24217	35808	36919	...	121
6472	9540	7442	7904	10501	13472	6290	16804	9700	...	122

17474	20225 |	34771	36596	36211	39919	45812	...	...	...	123
4073	4231 |	6575	7919	7580	7478	9477	...	...	...	124
822	791 |	1681	1836	2064	3103	3950	...	...	...	125
19678	19881 |	23055	25062	30440	41002	39421	...	...	...	126
784	799 |	1023	903	1358	3051	2360	...	...	...	127
4924	9035 |	13881	11120	11710	16859	15626	...	...	...	128
16373	27696 |	40161	51691	55257	62259	59564	...	...	...	129
30767	39281 |	61989	94568	58660	99682	111741	...	...	...	130
8505	12451 |	19285	24742	24433	26476	33354	...	...	...	131
925	553 |	877	5034	3323	5884	5304	...	...	...	132

Calendar year

65.3	64.3	81.9	74.8	72.3	81.6	128.6	131.1	125.6	153.0	133
24.2	22.9	28.3	24.8	31.2	36.8	49.3	83.1	79.0	91.4	134
5.7	8.9	11.9	12.7	8.7	11.0	9.3	3.2	3.8	12.8	135
1.8	1.3	1.4	5.0	2.2	4.2	5.9	8.1	9.1	4.8	136
0.0	4.6	3.1	0.1	2.8	0.2	2.1	3.4	0.8	4.6	137
2.6	2.4	3.9	5.4	3.3	1.2	1.8	1.8	1.7	3.8	138

	Item	1978	1979	1980	1981	1982	1983	1984	1985
139	6. Thailand	0.0	0.0	0.0	0.0	0.0	3.9	4.3	5.7
140	7. Singapore	3.6	2.2	1.0	0.5	0.2	0.4	2.1	0.1
141	8. Germany	1.4	2.4	4.2	3.3	1.0	2.6	4.6	1.1
142	9. Hong Kong	0.1	0.0	0.0	0.0	0.0	0.1	0.6	0.1
143	10. Korea, Rep. of	0.0	0.0	0.0	0.6	0.8	3.1	6.0	1.6
144	Imports, Total [i]	37.6	59.2	75.7	82.9	57.7	62.1	65.6	69.2
145	1. Australia	11.8	17.6	23.1	24.2	19.5	20.0	23.8	25.6
146	2. Singapore	3.6	7.3	11.1	18.8	10.1	11.3	9.4	7.2
147	3. Japan	4.6	10.6	14.5	11.7	8.1	11.7	9.9	13.7
148	4. New Zealand	2.3	3.8	5.2	7.7	4.8	4.2	5.3	6.2
149	5. Hong Kong	1.5	1.9	2.2	1.9	1.8	1.3	1.7	2.1
150	6. Papua New Guinea	1.3	2.1	4.0	4.1	1.2	1.2	1.6	1.2
151	7. United States	1.6	2.1	2.4	3.3	3.2	2.5	2.2	1.4
152	8. United Kingdom	3.6	8.0	6.4	5.5	2.6	1.8	2.1	2.8
153	9. China, People's Rep. of	1.2	1.8	1.8	2.0	1.9	1.7	2.6	2.6
154	10. Germany	1.5	0.9	0.9	0.7	1.0	0.7	1.2	0.9
	Trade Indexes								*1982 = 100;*
	Quantum index								
155	Exports	73.1	93.2	96.1	104.9	100.0	120.6	133.3	121.7
156	Imports [j]	79.4	100.5	89.4	83.3	100.0	89.2	135.3	161.0
	Unit value index								
157	Exports	79.1	113.4	112.1	97.9	100.0	105.7	157.4	150.9
158	Imports [j]	76.2	77.6	94.4	98.9	100.0	105.0	110.9	109.2
159	Terms of Trade [j]	103.8	146.1	118.8	99.0	100.0	100.7	141.9	138.2
	BALANCE OF PAYMENTS								*Million US dollars;*
160	Merchandise exports, fob	35	68	73	66	58	62	93	71
161	Merchandise imports, fob	-35	-58	-74	-76	-59	-61	-68	-72
162	Trade balance	-0	10	-1	-10	-1	1	26	-1
163	Other goods, services & income	-16	-20	-31	-29	-17	-15	-29	-29
164	Credit	5	6	12	13	19	20	15	16
165	Debit	-21	-25	-43	-42	-37	-34	-44	-45
166	Unrequited transfer	19	20	20	12	6	11	12	9
167	Private	2	2	1	-6	-6	-4	-3	-3
168	Official	17	18	19	18	11	15	15	12
169	Current balance	3	10	-12	-26	-12	-3	9	-21
170	Direct investment	5	4	2	0	1	0	2	1
171	Portfolio investment	–	–	–	–	–	–	–	–
172	Other long-term capital }								
173	Other short-term capital }	2	3	1	7	15	13	-13	8
174	Net errors & omissions	6	-9	-	13	2	-6	-7	-3
175	Overall balance	15	8	-9	-7	5	5	-9	-15
176	Allocation of SDRs	–	–	–	–	–	–	–	–
177	Monetary movements	-15	-8	9	7	-5	-5	9	15
	INTERNATIONAL RESERVES								*Million US dollars;*
178	Total	29.2	37.0	29.6	21.6	37.2	47.3	44.7	35.6
179	Foreign exchange	29.2	36.3	27.5	20.2	35.8	45.1	42.9	34.2
180	Reserve position in the Fund	–	0.6	0.9	0.0	0.0	0.5	0.5	0.6
181	SDRs	–	0.1	1.2	1.4	1.4	1.7	1.3	0.9
	EXCHANGE RATES [k]								*Solomon Islands dollars*
182	End of period	0.8692	0.8582	0.7975	0.8889	1.0449	1.2214	1.3435	1.6126
183	Average of period	0.8737	0.8660	0.8298	0.8702	0.9711	1.1486	1.2737	1.4808

1986	1987	1988	1989	1990	1991	1992	1993	1994	1995	
14.8	7.8	11.9	9.8	4.8	4.7	5.4	5.0	2.7	3.0	139
0.4	0.6	0.9	2.1	0.9	1.5	4.1	3.1	2.5	2.9	140
2.1	2.7	2.4	1.6	3.1	3.2	2.9	3.1	3.2	2.6	141
0.4	0.4	0.6	0.6	0.7	3.0	3.2	2.4	1.4	1.2	142
2.9	3.9	2.6	2.2	6.0	7.8	17.9	0.0	0.0	0.0	143
60.9	67.7	97.8	114.7	89.8	105.3	165.3	120.3	122.8	143.7	144
24.0	28.0	44.4	41.7	30.6	31.3	35.3	42.0	45.4	60.2	145
4.9	6.3	5.2	9.1	8.6	16.2	16.0	22.1	15.1	17.5	146
10.2	12.9	15.8	27.5	18.9	23.1	20.9	13.0	16.6	14.3	147
4.6	5.4	8.1	8.6	7.0	7.8	7.5	9.8	10.3	11.7	148
1.8	1.6	2.7	2.9	3.2	3.7	4.5	4.5	4.5	5.2	149
0.9	1.3	1.4	2.4	2.5	2.5	2.8	3.3	3.8	4.4	150
2.3	2.0	2.9	3.1	5.5	4.5	53.9	2.6	1.1	2.8	151
2.5	3.0	5.1	3.4	1.3	2.1	1.1	2.5	1.6	1.4	152
2.1	2.4	3.2	4.4	1.4	1.1	1.3	1.4	1.2	1.3	153
3.3	0.8	1.3	0.8	0.8	0.8	3.3	1.0	0.6	1.0	154

Period averages

1986	1987	1988	1989	1990	1991	1992	1993	1994	1995	
149.6	109.6	121.3	119.5	129.2	136.8	132.8	...	...	...	155
165.5	151.0	170.0	186.1	109.6	112.1	101.9	...	...	...	156
135.0	202.9	242.9	246.5	227.8	215.3	221.7	...	...	...	157
126.0	145.9	206.0	188.2	319.4	312.5	343.5	...	...	...	158
107.1	139.1	117.9	131.0	71.3	68.9	64.5	...	...	...	159

Calendar year

1986	1987	1988	1989	1990	1991	1992	1993	1994	1995	
64	63	82	75	70	83	102	...	...	...	160
-67	-69	-105	-94	-77	-92	-87	...	...	...	161
-4	-6	-23	-20	-7	-9	14	...	...	...	162
-38	-38	-53	-57	-59	-66	-52	...	...	...	163
20	26	26	30	28	33	37	...	...	...	164
-58	-64	-78	-87	-86	-99	-89	...	...	...	165
29	19	37	43	38	38	36	...	...	...	166
0	-0	5	6	5	2	2	...	...	...	167
29	19	32	37	33	36	34	...	...	...	168
-12	-25	-38	-33	-28	-36	-2	...	...	...	169
-1	8	2	12	10	15	14	...	...	...	170
–	–	–	–	–	–	–	...	...	...	171
										172
-1	1	42	14	12	1	8	...	...	...	173
-4	9	-11	-5	-9	8	-6	...	...	...	174
-18	-7	-5	-13	-14	-13	14	...	...	...	175
–	–	–	–	–	–	–	...	...	...	176
18	7	5	13	14	13	-14	...	...	...	177

As of end of period

1986	1987	1988	1989	1990	1991	1992	1993	1994	1995	
29.6	36.8	39.6	26.2	17.6	8.5	23.5	20.1	13.7	...	178
27.4	35.8	38.9	25.4	16.5	7.7	22.7	19.3	12.9	...	179
0.6	0.7	0.7	0.7	0.8	0.8	0.7	0.7	0.7	0.8	180
1.6	0.2	–	0.1	0.4	0.1	0.1	0.0	0.0	0.0	181

per US dollar

1986	1987	1988	1989	1990	1991	1992	1993	1994	1995	
1.9865	1.9743	2.1182	2.3969	2.6137	2.7949	3.0998	3.2478	3.3289	...	182
1.7415	2.0033	2.0825	2.2932	2.5288	2.7148	2.9281	3.1877	3.2914	...	183

	Item	1978	1979	1980	1981	1982	1983	1984	1985
	EXTERNAL INDEBTEDNESS							*Million US dollars;*	
184	Total outstanding & disbursed	11.5	13.8	19.4	23.4	28.0	34.4	44.0	65.9
185	Long-term	9.5	12.8	17.4	19.5	22.3	27.9	36.9	53.9
186	Public and publicly-guaranteed	9.5	12.8	17.4	19.5	22.3	27.9	36.9	53.9
187	Private non-guaranteed	0.0	0.0	0.0	0.0	0.0	0.0	0.0	0.0
188	Short-term	2.0	1.0	2.0	3.0	3.0	3.0	4.0	9.0
189	Use of IMF credit	0.0	0.0	0.0	0.9	2.7	3.5	3.1	3.0
	Debt service							*Transactions*	
190	Principal repayments on LT debt	0.0	0.0	0.0	0.0	0.0	0.0	0.7	0.8
191	Interest on long-term debt	0.0	0.0	0.0	0.1	0.1	0.1	1.1	1.7
192	Interest on short-term debt	0.0	0.0	0.3	0.4	0.3	0.3	0.3	0.5
	Average terms of new commitments								
193	Interest (%)	0.8	1.0	1.0	0.9	0.3	3.3	7.8	5.4
194	Maturity (years)	31.7	39.7	39.8	34.4	33.6	34.0	16.9	29.3
195	Grace period (years)	8.5	10.1	10.3	8.3	8.0	8.5	5.7	6.2
196	Grant Element (%)	71.6	78.3	78.3	71.7	78.0	57.5	17.0	40.1

Footnotes:

a   Refers to wage and salary employees. Figures are as of end-June.
b   No breakdown of GDP by industrial origin nor by expenditure at current prices was available from the Statistics Office from 1978-83. Details may not add up to total due to roun
c   Includes nonmonetary food.
d   Includes nonmonetary construction.
e   Refers to the retail price index of Honiara.
f   From 1985-92, figures are still preliminary.
g   Include other community and social services.
h   Before 1988, data on imports are on fob basis.
i   Imports are on fob basis.
j   Import indexes relate to food imports only.
k   On October 24, 1977, the Solomon islands dollar was introduced at par with the Australian dollar and both currencies had legal tender status until June 30, 1978. After that date, t
    Solomon Islands dollar became the sole legal tender in Solomon Islands as issued by the Solomon Islands Monetary Authority.

1986	1987	1988	1989	1990	1991	1992	1993	1994	1995	
As of end of year										
77.6	98.5	104.8	100.8	121.6	130.4	95.2	151.1	165.1	...	184
71.1	94.9	101.5	99.4	104.3	99.4	93.4	145.0	154.1	...	185
71.1	94.9	101.5	99.4	104.3	99.4	93.4	94.9	99.6	...	186
0.0	0.0	0.0	0.0	0.0	0.0	0.0	50.1	54.5	...	187
3.0	1.4	1.6	0.0	16.6	31.0	1.8	6.1	11.0	...	188
3.5	2.2	1.7	1.4	0.7	0.0	0.0	0.0	0.0	...	189
during the year										
1.0	1.2	3.2	5.9	7.1	8.6	5.2	7.2	13.8	11.7 *	190
1.8	2.0	3.5	3.6	3.1	2.7	1.5	2.6	3.1	3.3 *	191
0.4	0.2	0.1	0.1	0.5	1.4	0.9	0.2	0.5	...	192
4.7	1.0	0.0	0.0	2.2	1.0	4.2	0.8	0.0	...	193
24.6	39.5	0.0	0.0	18.0	41.3	18.5	39.5	0.0	...	194
5.5	10.3	0.0	0.0	11.7	9.6	5.0	10.0	0.0	...	195
39.4	78.0	0.0	0.0	57.9	77.9	36.3	80.3	0.0	...	196

Item	1978	1979	1980	1981	1982	1983	1984	1985
								Million;
001 **POPULATION**	14.19	14.47	14.75	15.01	15.19	15.42	15.60	15.84
								Thousand;
002 **LABOR FORCE**	5700	5392	...	5017	...	...	...	5972
003 Employed	4828	4600	...	4119	...	...	...	5132
004 Agriculture	...	...	...	1876	...	...	...	2531
005 Mining	...	...	...	34	...	...	...	67
006 Manufacturing	...	...	...	409	...	...	...	648
007 Others	...	...	...	1801	...	...	...	1886
008 Unemployed	872	792	...	897	...	...	...	840
009 Unemployment rate, %	15.3	14.7	...	17.9	...	...	...	14.1
NATIONAL ACCOUNTS								Million Rupees;
At Current Market Prices								
010 GDP by Industrial Origin	44562	54920	68338	84526	97528	119202	147343	157763
011 Agriculture	12098	15199	17900	22787	25258	30468	37293	38505
012 Mining	587	646	910	1078	1159	1420	1209	1226
013 Manufacturing	10070	10890	12422	14028	14644	17933	24301	26180
014 Electricity, gas and water	169	352	547	1003	1542	1611	2507	2999
015 Construction	2476	3702	6502	8037	8651	9902	11306	11939
016 Trade	8949	9896	11331	16168	19732	23901	26951	29062
017 Transport and communications	3371	4848	6962	7383	9748	11635	15621	17429
018 Finance	845	1243	1785	2463	3617	4897	6121	6456
019 Public administration	2660	2969	3573	4162	5379	7260	8237	9244
020 Others	3337	5175	6406	7417	7798	10175	13797	14723
021 Net factor income from abroad	-232	-240	-432	-1868	-1959	-3214	-3401	-3445
022 GNP	44330	54680	67906	82658	95569	115988	143942	154318
023 Expenditure on GDP	44562	54920	68338	84526	97528	119202	147343	157763
024 Private consumption	31892	40052	53458	64581	77310	93075	108312	118100
025 Government consumption	4851	5447	6667	7456	10407	12727	15442	19170
026 Gross fixed capital formation	9481	14058	22243	23955	27926	31584	34262	37651
027 Increase in stocks [a]	375	1672	992	2200	642	181	-489	2844
028 Exports of goods and services	14835	17660	21434	25892	27148	32016	44285	42394
029 Less: Imports of goods and services	16872	23969	36456	39558	45905	50381	54469	62396
030 Statistical discrepancy	–	–	–	–	–	–	–	–
At Constant 1975 I 1990 Prices								
031 GDP by Industrial Origin	31492	33406	35308	37266	39199	41062	43136	45301
032 Agriculture	8812	9209	9357	10058	10372	10994	10200	11146
033 Mining	436	411	475	500	479	575	693	673
034 Manufacturing	6866	7043	7071	7327	7281	7064	8300	8812
035 Electricity, gas and water	132	166	181	203	222	226	253	274
036 Construction	1505	1650	1947	2208	2157	2172	2200	2248
037 Trade	5925	6794	7564	8059	9408	10162	10907	11422
038 Transport and communications	2782	3000	3460	3564	3658	4043	4531	4607
039 Finance	387	426	493	562	714	757	832	897
040 Public administration	2208	2195	2206	2236	2256	2272	2298	2334
041 Others	2439	2512	2554	2550	2652	2797	2922	2888
042 Net factor income from abroad	-104	-101	-169	-696	-748	-1062	-1101	944
043 GNP	31388	33305	35139	36570	38451	40000	42035	46245
044 Expenditure on GDP	31492	33406	35308	37266	39199	41062	43136	45301
045 Private consumption	25961	28569	31610	35390	37721	39188	39599	41987
046 Government consumption	3654	3688	3626	3593	4208	3919	3953	4876
047 Gross fixed capital formation	5237	5722	6911	7306	7425	7324	6680	6635
048 Increase in stocks [a]	3178	424	-1398	-3337	-3858	-2885	-1849	-3963
049 Exports of goods and services	7091	7746	8131	8375	9212	8936	10312	10828
050 Less: Imports of goods and services	13629	12743	13572	14061	15509	15420	15559	15062
051 Statistical discrepancy	–	–	–	–	–	–	–	–

	1986	1987	1988	1989	1990	1991	1992	1993	1994	1995	
As of 1 July											
	16.13	16.37	16.60	16.81	16.99	17.25	17.41	17.62	17.83 *	18.04 *	001
Calendar year											
	...	...	...	...	5915	5894	5947	6066	6143	...	002
	...	...	...	...	4951	5084	5158	5227	5300	...	003
	...	...	...	...	2360	2114	2380	2011	1833	...	004
	...	...	...	...	80	46	52	114	769	...	005
	...	...	...	...	699	680	635	690	320	...	006
	...	...	...	...	1812	2244	2091	2412	2378	...	007
	...	...	...	...	964	810	789	839	843	...	008
	...	...	...	...	16.3	13.7	13.3	13.8	13.7	...	009
Calendar year											
	172442	188822	218774	248230	317904	369720	421755	499708	579159	...	010
	39529	43174	51074	56774	72788	81926	88840	...	...	...	011
	1670	2194	3024	3605	4570	4048	4418	...	...	...	012
	26913	29701	34852	41415	54943	62798	72293	...	...	...	013
	3062	3457	3986	4250	5635	6500	7417	...	...	...	014
	13197	14207	15349	17505	21592	24858	27564	...	...	...	015
	32716	35373	41643	44564	61784	75248	91086	...	...	...	016
	19661	20236	22305	23877	29614	35269	40493	...	...	...	017
	7743	8370	10152	11585	14267	17103	21877	...	...	...	018
	11124	12708	15915	19675	24123	28852	29826	...	...	...	019
	16827	19402	20474	24980	28588	33118	37942	...	...	...	020
	-3871	-4699	-5266	-5739	-6685	-7367	-7819	-5978	-8028	...	021
	168571	184123	213508	242491	311219	362353	413936	493730	571131	...	022
	172442	188822	218774	248230	317904	369720	421755	499708	579159	...	023
	130728	138754	163092	184379	233961	270927	313525	363580	420298	...	024
	22990	26204	30331	32585	41836	50767	53965	65745	75429	...	025
	38494	43948	47848	50968	64817	86463	96632	120778	145972	...	026
	1365	-153	1389	4219	2654	-779	-2973	-2709	6257	...	027
	42602	50763	57885	68666	97117	107016	135114	168858	195805	...	028
	63737	70694	81771	92587	122481	144674	174508	216544	264602	...	029
	–	–	–	–	–	–	–	–	–	...	030
	47236	48003	49336	50310	317904	333231	347822	371876	392884	...	031
	11224	10562	10837	10528	72788	74072	72722	77670	80204	...	032
	918	1133	1465	1819	4570	3405	3182	3642	4142	...	033
	9345	9670	9911	10227	54943	59227	64549	70675	76829	...	034
	294	304	315	321	5635	6019	6327	7138	7807	...	035
	2419	2557	2596	2616	21592	21928	23310	25364	27192	...	036
	11983	12422	12772	13077	61784	65184	71602	76483	81259	...	037
	4718	4803	4829	4775	29614	31164	32913	34558	36090	...	038
	932	989	1049	1112	14267	15209	16121	17862	19559	...	039
	2380	2475	2502	2750	24123	25643	25884	26753	27633	...	040
	3023	3088	3060	3085	28588	31380	31212	31731	32169	...	041
	-991	-961	-1048	-1049	-6685	-7090	-6915	-5421	-6189	...	042
	46245	47042	48288	49261	311219	326141	340907	366455	386695	...	043
	47236	48003	49336	50310	317904	333231	347822	371876	392884	...	044
	44192	44429	46906	48018	233961	236488	250829	...	...	...	045
	5714	5846	5855	5530	41836	45737	45917	...	...	...	046
	6463	6931	6394	6239	64817	70555	73714	...	...	...	047
	-3844	-3695	-4260	-5459	2654	17780	13161	...	...	...	048
	11550	11735	12098	13091	97117	101196	116375	...	...	...	049
	16839	17243	17657	17109	122481	138526	152174	...	...	...	050
	–	–	–	–	–	–	–	...	...	...	051

307

	Item	1978	1979	1980	1981	1982	1983	1984	1985
	Investment Financing, at current prices								
052	Gross domestic capital formation	9856	15730	23235	26155	28568	31765	33773	40495
053	Gross national saving	7587	9181	7781	10621	7852	10186	20188	17048
054	Gross domestic saving	7819	9421	8213	12489	9811	13400	23589	20493
055	Net factor income from abroad	-232	-240	-432	-1868	-1959	-3214	-3401	-3445
056	Foreign saving	2269	6549	15454	15534	20716	21579	13585	23447
	Per Capita GNP, Rupees								
057	Current prices	3124	3779	4604	5507	6292	7522	9225	9741
058	Constant *1975 I 1990* prices	2212	2302	2382	2436	2531	2594	2694	2919
	PRODUCTION							*Thousand metric tons;*	
	Agriculture								
059	1. Rice (paddy)	1891	1917	2133	2230	2156	2484	2420	2661
060	2. Coconut, *Mn nuts*	2207	2393	2026	2258	2521	2312	1942	2958
061	3. Sugar	17	20	26	350	350	375	578	754
062	4. Cassava	586	535	449	526	572	722	682	580
063	5. Tea	199	206	191	210	188	179	208	214
064	6. Rubber	156	153	133	124	125	140	142	138
065	7. Maize	35	26	22	24	24	29	38	30
066	8. Cotton	4	4	2	6	5	2	71	3
	Mining								
067	1. Llmenite	33	55	29	80	68	80	40	115
068	2. Rutile	12	15	13	13	7	8	6	9
069	3. Graphite	11	10	7	7	9	5	6	7
	Manufacturing								
070	1. Cigarettes, *Mn*	5098	4637	5226	5539	5803	5859	5726	6063
071	2. Cement (Portland)	573	592	551	921	469	447	402	339
072	3. Tyre, *'000*	173	188	195	156	166	171	161	165
073	4. Rubber, natural	156	153	133	124	125	140	142	138
074	5. Steel	61	76	59	73	47	48	44	18
075	6. Paper & paper products	25	22	21	24	22	22	20	24
076	7. Sugar	26	19	27	25	24	22	20	20
077	8. Milk, *Mn. liters*	...	...	...	309	163	168	172	179
	Production Indexes								*Period*
078	Agriculture, *1979-81 = 100*	91	98	100	101	100	107	100	109
079	Mining	...	...	...	...	...	...	...	...
080	Manufacturing	...	...	...	...	...	...	...	...
	ENERGY								*Annual*
	Crude petroleum, *'000 m.t.*								
081	Imports	1444	1444	1861	1711	1941	1492	1733	1657
082	Consumption	1476	1378	1781	1725	1905	1465	1721	1689
	Electricity, *Mn kWh*								
083	Production	1377	1589	1668	1871	2066	2114	2261	2470
084	Consumption	1148	1286	1365	1502	1684	1792	1876	2061
	Retail prices, *Rs/litre*								
085	Gasoline, *premium*	...	6.60	8.80	10.00	10.00	12.25	13.50	13.50
086	Diesel	...	2.31	4.62	5.94	5.94	7.24	8.13	8.13
	PRICE INDEXES								*Period*
087	Consumer, *1952 = 100*	227.8	252.3	318.2	375.4	416.1	474.2	553.1	561.2
088	Food	237.5	263.3	339.7	399.6	450.4	506.3	598.0	598.4
089	Wholesale, *1974 = 100*	156.7	171.6	229.5	268.5	283.3	354.1	444.7	377.1
090	Implicit GDP deflator, *1975 I 1990 = 100*	141.5	164.4	193.5	226.8	248.8	290.3	341.6	348.3

1986	1987	1988	1989	1990	1991	1992	1993	1994	1995	
39859	43795	49237	55187	67471	85684	93659	118069	152229	...	052
14853	19165	20085	25527	35422	40659	46446	64405	75404	...	053
18724	23864	25351	31266	42107	48026	54265	70383	83432	...	054
-3871	-4699	-5266	-5739	-6685	-7367	-7819	-5978	-8028	...	055
25006	24630	29152	29660	32049	45025	47213	53664	76825	...	056
10453	11246	12863	14425	18318	21010	23783	28023	32032	...	057
2868	2873	2909	2930 I	18318	18910	19587	20799	21688	...	058

Calendar year

2588	2127	2477	2063	2538	2389	2340	2570	2684	...	059
3039	2291	1936	2484	2532	2184	1196	2200	2599	...	060
737	660	629	686	760	856	61	70	...	...	061
486	427	492	424	384	378	302	309	299	...	062
211	213	227	207	233	241	179	232	242	...	063
138	122	122	111	113	104	106	104	105	...	064
41	42	39	31	33	34	29	33	32	...	065
15	15	15	...	...	...	...	...	...	...	066
130	132	63	98	66	60	37	77	62	...	067
8	7	5	6	5	3	3	3	2	...	068
7	7	6	4	5	6	2	...	...	...	069
6111	5873	4328	5136	5621	5790	5649	5218	...	...	070
557	642	632	596	578	620	650	551	...	...	071
185	212	203	200	382	392	276	184	...	...	072
138	122	122	111	113	104	106	108	...	...	073
49	32	38	33	35	50	56	41	...	...	074
27	27	25	18	19	23	26	29	31	...	075
22	16	54	54	57	66	60	69	...	...	076
176	275	226	238	292	301	...	...	...	...	077

averages

108	94	95	92	101	96	93	99	105	107	078
...	...	...	...	...	...	...	...	...	...	079
...	...	...	...	...	...	...	...	...	...	080

values

1639	1704	1894	1275	1779	1626	1297	1800	1898	...	081
1696	1609	1817	1552	1757	1726	1897	2008	2180	...	082
2652	2708	2799	2858	3149	3376	3540	3979	4364	3551 *	083
2232	2253	2371	2353	2608	2742	2916	3275	2582	...	084
13.50	13.50	13.50	20.00	30.00	30.00	31.08	35.00	35.00	...	085
8.13	8.13	8.13	9.60	11.00	11.00	11.35	12.20	11.40	...	086

averages

606.0	652.8	744.1	830.2	1008.6	1131.5	1260.4	1408.4	1527.4	1644.6	087
641.1	697.0	802.0	884.6	1090.9	1220.3	1366.0	1519.4	1654.1	1846.9 *	088
366.0	414.9	488.7	532.9	651.1	710.8	773.0	831.8	873.4	945.4	089
365.1	393.4	443.4	493.4 I	100.0	111.0	121.3	134.4	147.4	...	090

	Item	1978	1979	1980	1981	1982	1983	1984	1985
	MONEY AND BANKING								*Million Rupees;*
091	Money supply (M1)	5936	7669	9428	10024	11760	14748	16824	18761
092	Currency in circulation	3015	3774	4181	4823	5988	7200	8561	9816
093	Demand deposits	2921	3895	5247	5202	5772	7548	8263	8946
094	Quasi-money	4957	7387	10432	14423	18750	22509	26604	29648
095	Money supply (M2)	10893	15056	19860	24447	30510	37257	43428	48409
096	Foreign assets (net)	5590	6808	3631	2940	2450	3155	9951	9183
097	Domestic credit	10675	14971	25804	33967	42398	49293	49927	59226
098	Claims on govt. sector (net)	4226	6267	13095	17277	21828	21918	18703	24785
099	Claims on private sector	6449	8704	12709	16690	20570	27375	31224	34441
100	Claims on other financial insts.	–	–	–	–	–	–	–	–
101	Other items	-5372	-6722	-9575	-12460	-14338	-15191	-16450	-20000
	Deposit Money Banks								
102	Demand deposits	3643	4834	6688	6511	7271	9068	10339	11466
103	Savings deposits ⎫								
104	Time deposits ⎬	4897	7509	10604	14624	19798	24208	28779	33041
105	Domestic credits outstanding	8828	11948	17000	21152	25361	31416	35103	38702
	Interest rates								*Per cent;*
	On deposits								
106	Savings	8.4	8.4	12.0	12.0	12.0	12.0	12.0	12.0
107	Time: 6 months	11.5	11.5	16.5	18.3	15.6	19.0	16.0	14.0
108	12 months	14.5	14.5	20.0	21.0	18.5	20.5	18.0	15.0
	GOVERNMENT FINANCE								*Million Rupees;*
	Central Government								
109	Current revenue	11061	11966	13022	14775	16210	23317	34061	36249
110	Taxes	10324	11015	12158	13696	14737	19912	29939	30442
111	Non-taxes	737	951	864	1079	1473	3405	4122	5807
112	Current expenditure	9849	10825	12319	14646	18339	21999	24630	32645
113	Current surplus/deficit	1212	1141	703	129	-2129	1318	9431	3604
114	Capital receipts	–	–	–	–	–	–	–	–
115	Capital expenditure	4655	6917	12123	11255	15431	15866	19915	21530
116	Capital account surplus/deficit	-4655	-6917	-12123	-11255	-15431	-15866	-19915	-21530
117	Net lending	2400	1450	3946	2113	-258	1772	3292	1059
118	Overall surplus/deficit	-5843	-7226	-15366	-13239	-17302	-16320	-13776	-18985
	Financing								
119	Domestic borrowing	1990	3900	8708	5694	9673	7489	3181	8569
120	Foreign borrowing	3292	2347	3516	48880	4744	6313	6492	7109
121	Foreign grants	661	1390	2619	2721	3376	3473	3293	3307
122	Use of cash balances	-100	-411	523	-44056	-491	-955	810	–
	Expenditure by function, Central Govt.								
123	Total	17672	20309	28534	29492	35287	41838	51284	55173
124	General public services [b]	1617	2174	2607	2889	4294	4010	5147	5193
125	Defence	309	393	458	479	486	979	1275	4614
126	Education	1140	1391	1846	2020	2484	2831	3109	4453
127	Health	697	1004	1342	999	1128	2045	1751	2091
128	Social security & welfare	37	53	75	73	92	86	106	4900
129	Housing & community amenities	302	670	204	201	293	231	261	705
130	Economic services	1282	2248	2915	2654	2889	3920	4699	21494
131	Agriculture	495	777	1165	1139	1357	1958	2093	10683
132	Industry	40	56	86	134	160	242	322	1369
133	Electricity, gas and water	...	...	...	...	...	...	...	1499
134	Transport and communications	747	1415	1664	1381	1372	1720	2284	5397
135	Other economic services	...	...	...	...	...	...	110	2546
136	Others	12288	12376	19087	20177	23621	27736	34936	11723
	Provincial and Other Local Govts.								
137	Revenue	369	388	488	632	785	959	1197	...
138	Tax	...	...	...	...	...	...	...	...

1986	1987	1988	1989	1990	1991	1992	1993	1994	1995	
As of end of period										
21179	25082	32379	35338	39878	47055	50057	59355	70461	70306 *	091
11570	13495	18487	19650	22120	24852	27280	32133	...	...	092
9609	11588	13892	15688	17758	22202	22777	27222	...	...	093
29681	33253	35568	41095	51139	65043	79741	100781	121209	140703 *	094
50860	58335	67947	76433	91017	112098	129798	160136	191670	211009 *	095
9180	9291	7059	4732	10207	17305	...	...	...	...	096
64109	75566	96867	102321	119864	134226	...	...	...	...	097
27285	34414	46851	49981	54833	55870	...	...	...	...	098
36824	41152	50016	52340	65031	78356	...	...	...	...	099
–	–	–	–	–	–	...	...	...	...	100
-22429	-26522	-35979	-30620	-39053	-39434	...	...	...	...	101
12236	13861	18313	21439	26885	27270	32091	34592	41708	...	102
										103
33875	38492	41818	48548	61700	81816	98776	124745	148882	...	104
41339	49054	57709	66831	81642	94251	112635	125182	143221	...	105
Period averages										
12.0	12.0	11.0	14.0	14.0	14.0	14.0	14.0	14.0	12.0	106
10.3	10.0	10.8	12.0	14.5	15.5	14.8	14.6	12.7	...	107
11.3	11.3	12.3	15.8	16.0	15.0	16.8	15.5	13.5	13.6	108
Fiscal year ending 31 December										
37238	42145	41749	53979	67964	76179	85781	98339	110038	136701 *	109
31272	35119	35946	47513	61206	68157	76353	85891	99417	118171 *	110
5966	7026	5803	6466	6758	8022	9428	12448	10621	18530 *	111
33966	39560	46132	56884	71771	83756	89639	102288	127084	148351 *	112
3272	2585	-4383	-2905	-3807	-7577	-3858	-3949	-17046	-11650 *	113
–	–	–	–	–	–	–	–	–	–	114
23236	22816	22878	20750	19529	25304	24948	33662	30391	40774 *	115
-23236	-22816	-22878	-20750	-19529	-25304	-24948	-33662	-30391	-40774 *	116
1991	1518	7522	4530	8514	10467	2386	4510	10293	10003 *	117
-21955	-21749	-34783	-28185	-31850	-43348	-31192	-42121	-57730	-62427 *	118
9143	11356	21067	12373	16986	16149	15552	24241	37696	34915 *	119
9061	5716	7128	5926	11644	19329	7361	9855	11778	18582 *	120
3753	4677	6588	6407	6697	7870	8280	8025	8257	8930 *	121
-2	–	–	3479	-3477	–	-1	–	-1	–	122
59873	65190	74103	83805	97796	116414	119261	134543	...	...	123
5546	6788	11464	12520	14824	11916	13547	16236	...	...	124
4351	6001	4732	4073	6736	10317	12876	15413	...	...	125
5027	4853	5891	8141	9571	9128	12541	14056	...	...	126
2246	3380	3918	4639	4964	5229	6541	7064	...	...	127
5269	6151	7620	9760	11998	19281	18569	21232	...	...	128
1029	1148	705	1003	935	919	1186	1078	...	...	129
25507	23393	25175	22903	23393	29947	24277	26463	...	...	130
9553	9570	7811	6210	6197	6983	7288	6576	...	...	131
1236	1302	526	879	302	402	533	1860	...	...	132
2526	3300	5531	5135	6477	6840	5660	4361	...	...	133
9316	6833	7877	7804	6919	12229	5571	10432	...	...	134
2876	2388	3430	2875	3498	3493	5225	3234	...	...	135
10898	13476	14598	20766	25375	29677	29724	33001	...	...	136
...	...	...	...	...	...	...	...	...	...	137
...	...	...	...	...	...	...	...	...	...	138

	Item	1978	1979	1980	1981	1982	1983	1984	1985
139	Non-tax	...	...	...	...	...	...	...	...
140	Subsidy/grants	...	...	...	...	...	...	...	...
141	Expenditure	300	320	561	714	948	1164	1375	...
	EXTERNAL TRADE								*Million Rupees;*
142	Exports, fob	13206	15273	17388	20199	21124	25183	37006	35035
143	Imports, cif	14687	22560	33637	35530	36876	42021	46913	49069
144	Trade balance	-1481	-7287	-16249	-15331	-15751	-16838	-9908	-14034
	Exports, by SITC section								
145	Food and live animals	7850	7510	7882	8724	8801	10969	18850	14904
146	Beverage and tobacco	34	52	26	81	42	47	91	58
147	Crude materials excl. fuels	3186	3765	3439	3688	3390	3794	4366	3822
148	Mineral fuels, etc.	775	1475	2663	2578	2729	2402	3214	3053
149	Animal, vegetable oil & fats	329	518	53	205	369	473	315	953
150	Chemicals	219	516	531	351	455	491	299	932
151	Basic manufactures	132	191	740	710	1197	1485	1331	1665
152	Machines, transport equipment	24	39	70	512	444	335	523	911
153	Misc. manufactured goods	609	1146	1872	3057	3656	5069	7963	8278
154	Unclassified goods [c]	18	16	17	23	16	21	28	63
	Exports, by principal commodity								
155	1. Tea	6401	5722	6170	6444	6342	8295	15764	12003
156	2. Rubber	2021	2491	2590	2889	2323	2852	3301	2566
157	3. Desiccated coconut	639	775	701	768	598	902	1177	1333
158	4. Copra	10	13	5	42	57	74	73	99
159	5. Coconut oil	323	509	49	200	347	433	304	951
	Imports, by SITC section								
160	Food and live animals	47	51	61	6559	4510	6920	6624	9211
161	Beverage and tobacco	468	595	528	56	127	120	173	147
162	Crude materials excl. fuels	2433	3961	8170	706	706	892	941	1211
163	Mineral fuels, etc.	20	72	55	8676	11557	10047	12096	10575
164	Animal, vegetable oil & fats	1149	1874	2814	104	87	167	384	315
165	Chemicals	2335	4606	5843	150	2504	2833	3900	4438
166	Basic manufactures	3501	5599	8371	6557	7059	8346	9290	10547
167	Machines, transport equipment	325	525	938	7893	8735	11035	11422	10010
168	Misc. manufactured goods	137	150	114	1137	1453	1588	1989	1882
169	Unclassified goods [c]	137	206	114	142	98	132	176	182
	Direction of Trade								*Million US dollars;*
170	Exports, Total	873.8	978.1	1039.1	1023.8	996.2	1053.8	1435.6	1264.9
171	1. United States	59.3	101.8	115.7	145.7	142.9	184.2	279.6	282.0
172	2. Germany	36.2	58.0	54.9	57.7	55.7	65.3	70.0	68.8
173	3. United Kingdom	66.5	79.1	77.1	67.7	66.1	51.9	72.0	68.7
174	4. Belgium-Luxembourg	4.6	4.5	5.1	5.8	12.9	14.5	9.0	19.2
175	5. Japan	49.1	66.6	33.1	34.2	49.9	50.9	61.1	64.2
176	6. France	11.0	16.2	14.9	16.5	15.5	14.7	20.1	15.4
177	7. Netherlands	23.5	31.1	28.3	23.4	31.6	31.2	33.9	44.1
178	8. United Arab Emirates	4.0	5.1	6.6	8.6	10.7	6.6	8.2	12.8
179	9. Italy	19.7	27.4	22.0	16.7	21.5	18.3	17.4	14.7
180	10. Singapore	17.8	10.1	11.8	22.8	37.4	35.5	15.4	45.9
181	Imports, Total	963.7	1449.0	2028.7	1905.7	1773.2	1794.8	1845.6	1831.8
182	1. Japan	101.9	193.0	258.9	260.9	269.9	318.1	307.9	283.0
183	2. Singapore	26.0	87.3	91.3	98.9	106.0	148.0	102.1	73.7
184	3. India	86.3	149.9	96.7	76.7	72.9	115.4	111.5	74.7
185	4. Hong Kong	13.7	33.2	41.7	51.9	41.3	53.9	59.0	57.5
186	5. United Kingdom	89.5	129.4	192.2	112.7	116.3	121.4	86.9	96.4

1986	1987	1988	1989	1990	1991	1992	1993	1994	1995	
...	...	...	...	...	...	...	...	...	...	139
...	...	...	...	...	...	...	...	...	...	140
...	...	...	...	...	...	...	...	...	...	141

Calendar Year

1986	1987	1988	1989	1990	1991	1992	1993	1994	1995	
34092	39861	47092	55511	76624	82225	107509	137994	158660	138126 *	142
51282	59750	70320	75353	105559	127831	149780	181381	221527	176360 *	143
-17189	-19889	-23228	-19842	-28936	-45606	-42272	-43387	-62867	-38234 *	144
11938	13801	17969	17728	25051	23405	21749	27922	31131	...	145
72	79	131	148	252	558	1870	1982	1950	...	146
4053	4986	5946	6247	2945	4169	4269	4671	6335	...	147
1920	135	359	523	529	342	2354	3026	3259	...	148
704	257	203	790	301	92	190	239	377	...	149
666	933	1140	1073	1794	2054	1543	1924	1830	...	150
2935	7130	5949	8013	31655	34539	53368	66629	77559	...	151
1110	668	695	790	2216	2670	1950	2976	3645	...	152
10008	11870	14713	20199	8873	12088	19138	26069	28834	...	153
50	...	1	...	3001	2306	1078	2556	3740	...	154
9253	10654	12299	13664	19823	17867	14893	19911	20964	11370 *	155
2622	2929	3706	3112	3080	2641	2960	3086	3582	3244 *	156
848	1101	618	1023	1427	1546	2372	1565	2088	1183 *	157
88	79	102	148	120	187	188	167	199	110 *	158
673	242	175	749	296	37	105	116	189	112 *	159
6463	5969	9463	9517	17677	20486	21636	20305	30759	...	160
253	320	426	410	587	1146	1755	2152	2715	...	161
6512	8121	9082	8740	9037	12978	16291	19965	24966	...	162
6579	9095	7557	8075	13307	14007	13309	13979	13774	...	163
287	346	607	508	558	752	1031	2327	1494	...	164
4684	5312	7092	6506	12870	12407	14096	16989	20115	...	165
8121	9154	12033	12444	19435	24204	23627	31666	46983	...	166
11606	12860	14292	14520	21459	26728	34620	43726	54347	...	167
6770	8107	9663	14549	10456	14829	23391	30331	26467	...	168
6	479	107	83	173	294	41	44	38	...	169

Calendar year

1986	1987	1988	1989	1990	1991	1992	1993	1994	1995	
1162.7	1334.3	1460.8	1540.0	1895.3	1987.5	2488.1	2859.5	3288.2	3858.6	170
302.3	354.4	367.3	400.0	490.4	559.0	850.2	1006.8	1066.3	1235.4	171
82.3	100.1	103.8	95.4	126.5	148.8	214.9	227.5	268.4	329.0	172
67.5	73.3	79.8	88.4	107.9	126.2	172.8	203.5	259.2	296.4	173
36.6	27.2	52.2	83.3	96.9	78.8	136.2	176.8	198.1	223.8	174
64.8	66.3	83.7	89.0	102.3	101.6	129.9	148.0	171.4	211.1	175
16.3	25.3	25.1	39.1	43.6	63.5	91.5	86.1	123.9	119.8	176
46.0	38.1	47.2	44.8	48.7	59.0	99.1	107.6	114.7	106.0	177
15.0	21.6	17.9	20.3	27.7	73.1	28.0	92.1	99.5	109.4	178
14.2	13.8	15.3	21.1	36.6	37.2	48.0	42.5	52.2	67.3	179
27.9	30.8	39.1	36.3	44.7	67.5	33.3	48.7	51.9	60.3	180
1829.4	2056.4	2278.8	2087.5	2636.4	3061.1	3473.7	4005.4	5115.6	6274.7	181
318.9	304.2	305.1	261.1	325.2	358.4	422.3	452.6	500.4	472.4	182
71.8	100.1	92.9	93.9	102.5	135.0	241.5	208.0	371.3	430.7	183
79.2	83.5	91.0	66.2	118.0	220.1	306.7	342.9	366.9	425.7	184
85.4	129.8	116.6	109.2	120.3	212.5	244.8	312.4	349.5	399.9	185
102.7	140.4	126.5	126.1	145.9	166.3	177.0	184.8	258.7	275.2	186

	Item	1978	1979	1980	1981	1982	1983	1984	1985
187	6. United States	77.0	77.8	88.9	129.3	115.1	115.9	164.0	129.4
188	7. Thailand	3.1	10.7	9.9	14.5	15.0	19.0	14.0	21.4
189	8. France	44.3	30.9	79.8	39.9	37.0	48.8	22.2	32.0
190	9. China, People's Rep. of	29.0	66.8	51.2	39.2	42.0	42.0	36.2	70.7
191	10. Germany	53.3	78.5	71.0	90.5	76.3	75.4	88.1	98.4
	Trade Indexes								*1985 = 100*
	Quantum index								
192	Exports	82	83	81	83	88	83	97	100
193	Imports	63	78	89	92	92	101	105	100
	Unit value index								
194	Exports	55	60	69	70	69	88	113	100
195	Imports	29	44	63	81	85	89	93	100
196	Terms of Trade	188	136	110	87	82	99	122	100
	BALANCE OF PAYMENTS								*Million US dollars;*
197	Merchandise exports, fob	846.0	981.4	1064.7	1065.5	1013.7	1064.1	1462.3	1315.3
198	Merchandise imports, fob	-999.3	-1449.4	-2051.2	-1876.9	-1994.1	-1921.3	-1928.1	-2044.3
199	Trade balance	-153.3	-468.0	-986.5	-811.4	-980.4	-857.2	-465.8	-729.0
200	Other goods, services and income	7.6	47.4	51.9	4.2	-15.1	-60.0	-68.2	-134.2
201	Credit	124.4	192.1	278.5	312.7	334.5	341.4	336.8	328.6
202	Debit	-116.8	-144.7	-226.6	-308.5	-349.6	-401.4	-405.0	-462.8
203	Unrequited transfer	79.6	192.2	274.7	365.6	426.4	444.4	479.0	443.2
204	Private	21.9	48.4	136.7	203.6	264.0	273.7	276.4	265.5
205	Official	57.7	143.8	138.0	162.0	162.4	170.7	202.6	177.7
206	Current balance	-66.1	-228.4	-659.9	-441.6	-569.1	-472.8	-55.0	-420.0
207	Direct investment	1.5	47.0	42.9	49.2	63.6	37.7	32.6	25.0
208	Portfolio investment	...	...	...	...	...	...	...	...
209	Other long-term capital	157.7	165.2	197.9	330.4	455.6	375.9	337.1	304.2
210	Other short-term capital	7.3	0.1	157.5	20.0	7.1	37.6	-25.5	4.4
211	Net errors and omissions	-3.2	52.7	29.9	9.8	-0.2	32.6	-10.0	-7.6
212	Valuation adjustments	22.9	-1.8	51.3	-0.6	-8.3	2.7	-10.5	55.3
213	Overall balance	120.1	34.8	-180.4	-32.8	-51.3	13.7	268.7	-38.7
214	Allocation of SDRs	...	15.5	15.6	13.1	...	...	...	...
215	Monetary Movements	-120.1	-50.3	164.8	19.7	51.3	-13.7	-268.7	38.7
	INTERNATIONAL RESERVES								*Million US dollars;*
216	Total	406	535	262	342	365	308	522	462
217	Gold, national valuation	9	18	16	14	13	11	11	10
218	Foreign exchange	363	488	246	304	338	278	505	445
219	Reserve position in the Fund	–	–	–	1	7	18	6	7
220	SDRs	34	29	–	23	7	1	0	0
	EXCHANGE RATES								*Rupees*
221	End of period	15.505	15.445	18.000	20.550	21.320	25.000	26.280	27.408
222	Average of period	15.611	15.572	16.534	19.246	20.812	23.529	25.438	27.163
	EXTERNAL INDEBTEDNESS								*Million US dollars;*
223	Total outstanding and disbursed	1372.7	1553.8	1841.3	2234.8	2625.2	2884.0	2992.0	3540.0
224	Long-term	967.6	1016.3	1230.5	1515.7	1867.0	2155.5	2393.0	2937.1
225	Public and publicly guaranteed	967.2	1015.2	1227.2	1511.7	1864.8	2115.3	2349.3	2838.6
226	Private non-guaranteed	0.4	1.1	3.3	4.0	2.5	40.2	44.3	98.5
227	Short-term	110.0	136.0	219.8	203.9	275.9	283.6	194.7	206.3
228	Use of IMF credit	295.1	401.5	391.0	515.2	482.3	445.1	404.8	396.6

1986	1987	1988	1989	1990	1991	1992	1993	1994	1995	
117.6	118.0	152.7	137.0	207.3	174.5	161.9	131.3	217.3	310.9	187
39.7	40.2	42.0	88.9	85.2	99.1	98.5	109.2	204.4	290.9	188
25.0	34.6	51.6	35.8	41.1	34.8	44.0	50.5	311.9	169.3	189
87.1	63.7	104.9	102.6	112.7	101.5	122.9	149.9	160.3	263.1	190
85.8	90.0	102.7	70.8	86.9	101.9	129.4	138.4	163.3	197.5	191

Period averages

105	104	101	103	120	125	144	164	184	...	192
101	101	96	90	95	108	119	137	154	...	193
94	114	130	155	220	233	304	382	430	...	194
101	112	131	148	199	234	282	351	416	...	195
93	102	99	105	111	100	108	109	103	...	196

Calendar year

1209.7	1395.5	1477.2	1558.4	1983.9	2039.5	2459.0	2863.6	3208.2	...	197
-1973.2	-2075.1	-2240.2	-2225.6	-2686.4	-3036.7	-3477.1	-4013.6	-4769.4	...	198
-763.5	-679.6	-763.0	-667.2	-702.5	-997.2	-1018.1	-1150.0	-1561.2	...	199
-129.1	-156.8	-153.6	-155.7	-97.5	-91.2	-33.8	37.7	10.3	...	200
378.4	398.3	411.7	404.9	533.2	601.8	689.5	747.1	897.6	...	201
-507.5	-555.1	-565.3	-560.6	-630.7	-693.0	-723.3	-709.4	-887.3	...	202
467.4	493.7	527.4	515.8	540.7	605.0	645.8	722.0	790.4	...	203
284.9	313.3	320.3	328.5	362.4	401.8	462.5	561.4	627.2	...	204
182.5	180.4	207.1	187.3	178.3	203.2	183.3	160.6	163.2	...	205
-425.2	-342.7	-389.2	-307.1	-259.3	-483.4	-406.1	-390.3	-760.5	...	206
28.0	58.6	43.5	17.6	32.3	63.7	121.3	188.7	158.2	...	207
...	...	...	...	9.7	32.1	25.4	67.8	27.1	...	208
310.0	207.6	202.8	176.9	363.5	479.6	291.9	447.2	561.4	...	209
-13.4	41.3	14.9	98.7	67.0	81.4	97.3	147.4	261.9	...	210
-11.6	-68.9	22.8	-35.9	-45.2	65.9	57.8	69.0	-1.3	...	211
50.5	64.3	14.7	-37.7	23.1	-22.7	...	...	...	...	212
-61.7	-39.8	-90.5	-87.5	191.1	216.6	187.6	529.8	246.8	...	213
...	...	...	...	...	...	...	...	...	...	214
61.7	39.8	90.5	87.5	-191.1	-216.6	-187.6	-529.8	-246.8	...	215

As of end of period

363	290	232	255	433	695	964	1629	2046	2088	216
10	10	10	10	10	10	37	–	–	–	217
353	279	222	231	422	685	899	1601	2016	2057	218
–	0	0	0	0	0	28	28	30	30	219
0	1	0	13	0	0	0	0	0	1	220

per US dollar

28.520	30.763	33.033	40.000	40.240	42.580	46.000	49.562	49.980	54.048	221
28.017	29.445	31.807	36.047	40.063	41.372	43.830	48.322	49.415	51.252	222

As of end of year

4079.7	4748.3	5199.0	5169.3	5840.1	6544.8	6419.0	6793.1	7811.0	...	223
3548.3	4198.3	4264.0	4409.4	5036.0	5749.8	5724.0	6035.5	6687.1	...	224
3452.3	4081.5	4150.7	4277.5	4934.2	5651.1	5625.0	5945.7	6597.4	...	225
96.0	116.8	113.3	131.9	101.8	98.7	99.0	89.8	89.7	...	226
184.6	273.3	577.0	394.2	394.2	394.2	231.0	241.5	506.7	...	227
346.8	276.7	359.4	365.7	409.9	400.8	464.0	516.1	617.2	...	228

	Item	1978	1979	1980	1981	1982	1983	1984	1985
	Debt service								*Transactions*
229	Principal repayments on LT debt	65.7	49.5	51.0	45.5	75.0	73.9	91.4	111.4
230	Interest on long-term debt	24.7	27.6	32.8	49.5	69.0	92.3	106.2	116.5
231	Interest on short-term debt	15.3	25.9	35.8	35.8	26.9	24.4	18.6	15.6
	Average terms of new commitments								
232	Interest (%)	2.4	3.8	3.9	5.0	8.0	3.0	5.3	3.1
233	Maturity (years)	36.7	32.7	30.5	33.5	26.2	36.1	26.6	36.2
234	Grace Period (years)	9.0	8.0	7.7	8.2	6.1	9.3	7.5	9.2
235	Grant element (%)	63.3	52.7	50.4	49.4	24.4	60.8	37.8	59.0

Footnotes:

a   Includes statistical discrepancy.
b   Classified as civil administration and public order and safety.
c   Includes re-exports.

1986	1987	1988	1989	1990	1991	1992	1993	1994	1995	
during the year										
148.5	206.3	208.2	194.8	167.0	164.9	249.0	239.2	241.5	335.5 *	229
121.6	126.8	124.9	111.5	121.9	128.1	133.5	138.0	134.1	161.4 *	230
14.3	29.4	26.0	22.2	31.7	33.0	18.8	13.0	13.8	...	231
2.9	3.0	2.0	3.7	1.8	2.4	2.5	2.3	2.3	...	232
32.3	31.8	35.0	28.7	34.7	30.7	29.8	30.9	29.1	...	233
8.9	8.9	9.8	7.1	9.5	8.3	9.1	9.0	9.1	...	234
56.8	57.4	67.5	52.2	69.3	60.8	60.4	61.9	60.5	...	235

	Item	1978	1979	1980	1981	1982	1983	1984	1985
001	**POPULATION**	16.97	17.31	17.64	17.97	18.30	18.60	18.87	*Million;* 19.14
002	**LABOR FORCE**	6337	6515	6629	6764	6959	7266	7491	*Thousand;* 7651
003	Employed	6231	6432	6547	6672	6810	7069	7308	7429
004	Agriculture	1553	1380	1277	1257	1284	1317	1286	1297
005	Manufacturing	1916	2083	2152	2162	2168	2282	2497	2501
006	Mining	60	57	56	54	51	46	41	35
007	Others	2702	2912	3062	3199	3307	3424	3484	3596
008	Unemployed	106	83	82	92	149	197	183	222
009	Unemployment rate, %	1.7	1.3	1.2	1.4	2.1	2.7	2.4	2.9
	NATIONAL ACCOUNTS *At Current Market Prices*								*Billion New Taiwan dollars;*
010	GDP by Industrial Origin	991.6	1195.8	1491.1	1773.9	1900.0	2100.0	2343.1	2473.8
011	Agriculture	93.0	102.2	114.6	129.5	147.0	153.3	148.4	143.1
012	Mining	10.0	11.1	14.1	15.4	14.7	14.5	14.1	14.0
013	Manufacturing	353.3	429.3	537.1	631.2	668.9	754.7	879.5	929.1
014	Electricity, gas and water	24.6	27.8	37.5	59.4	63.4	77.4	88.0	99.5
015	Construction	60.1	74.0	93.3	100.7	95.4	97.5	99.9	102.0
016	Trade	119.8	147.4	196.1	235.2	252.9	273.6	308.3	327.9
017	Transport and communications	59.4	70.0	89.1	105.6	113.8	126.9	146.5	158.6
018	Finance	108.2	145.0	189.4	219.9	233.3	244.4	277.6	305.1
019	Public administration	95.4	116.0	144.3	184.3	208.0	221.5	239.2	254.3
020	Others	67.6	73.0	75.6	92.7	102.3	136.2	141.5	140.1
021	Net factor income from abroad	-2.3	0.4	-2.1	-9.7	-0.7	3.3	25.4	41.3
022	GNP	989.3	1196.2	1489.0	1764.3	1899.3	2103.3	2368.5	2515.0
023	Expenditure on GDP	991.6	1195.8	1491.1	1773.9	1900.0	2100.0	2343.1	2473.8
024	Private consumption	497.6	604.5	767.7	922.2	1002.3	1085.4	1189.5	1261.6
025	Government consumption	150.3	184.5	237.2	285.7	320.6	340.3	371.8	399.4
026	Gross fixed capital formation	255.6	335.9	456.4	494.0	490.9	478.4	496.3	466.3
027	Increase in stocks	24.1	57.5	47.5	35.8	-11.7	14.4	23.1	5.0
028	Exports of goods and services	519.4	637.6	783.3	920.9	952.5	1114.3	1317.5	1341.3
029	Less: Imports of goods and services	455.4	624.1	801.0	884.7	854.7	932.9	1055.1	999.8
030	Statistical discrepancy	–	–	–	–	–	–	–	–
	At Constant 1991 Prices								
031	GDP by Industrial Origin	1798.4	1945.4	2087.5	2216.1	2294.8	2488.7	2752.4	2888.8
032	Agriculture	148.9	155.9	152.7	152.1	155.9	158.7	161.5	165.1
033	Mining	19.2	18.2	18.9	19.1	18.0	18.1	17.6	17.4
034	Manufacturing	624.3	673.4	739.8	796.1	813.2	906.7	1038.3	1072.5
035	Electricity, gas and water	43.0	47.1	50.3	50.9	53.6	62.5	70.7	79.8
036	Construction	118.8	127.1	137.1	139.7	134.0	131.3	134.0	137.0
037	Trade	225.6	244.7	264.9	281.3	296.4	321.7	359.8	384.3
038	Transport and communications	97.4	108.6	119.7	132.4	142.8	156.6	175.5	187.5
039	Finance	213.4	258.9	285.3	277.6	286.1	293.0	334.2	363.3
040	Public administration	232.0	248.6	262.5	280.5	296.9	311.6	332.2	350.9
041	Others	75.8	63.0	56.2	86.4	98.0	128.6	128.6	130.9
042	Net factor income from abroad	-4.1	0.7	-2.9	-11.6	-0.8	3.8	29.3	47.6
043	GNP	1794.3	1946.1	2084.6	2204.5	2294.0	2492.4	2781.7	2936.4
044	Expenditure on GDP	1798.4	1945.4	2087.5	2216.1	2294.8	2488.7	2752.4	2888.8
045	Private consumption	920.6	1018.3	1070.2	1118.1	1179.8	1267.7	1393.9	1482.3
046	Government consumption	332.8	359.4	386.8	402.1	428.3	448.2	481.8	512.1
047	Gross fixed capital formation	402.4	454.1	520.8	541.6	543.2	532.5	556.2	530.2
048	Increase in stocks	33.2	68.2	46.4	31.9	-11.2	12.9	20.8	3.9
049	Exports of goods and services	658.3	697.9	753.6	824.6	842.9	987.4	1164.4	1192.9
050	Less: Imports of goods and services	548.9	652.4	690.4	702.1	688.2	760.1	864.7	832.6
051	Statistical discrepancy	–	–	–	–	–	–	–	–

1986	1987	1988	1989	1990	1991	1992	1993	1994	1995	
As of 1 July										
19.36	19.56	19.79	20.01	20.23	20.46	20.66	20.85	21.04	21.22	001
Calendar year										
7945	8183	8246	8390	8423	8569	8764	8874	9081	9210	002
7733	8022	8107	8258	8283	8439	8632	8746	8939	9045	003
1317	1226	1113	1066	1064	1093	1065	1005	976	954	004
2635	2821	2802	2796	2653	2598	2585	2483	2485	2449	005
33	31	28	24	20	19	18	19	18	15	006
3748	3944	4164	4372	4546	4729	4964	5239	5460	5627	007
212	161	139	132	140	130	132	128	142	165	008
2.7	2.0	1.7	1.6	1.7	1.5	1.5	1.4	1.6	1.8	009
Calendar year										
2855.2	3237.1	3523.2	3938.8	4307.0	4810.7	5337.7	5874.5	6376.5	6907.7	010
158.3	171.7	177.4	192.9	180.1	182.4	192.2	214.8	227.6	243.7	011
13.8	15.0	15.9	16.6	16.6	17.8	25.3	31.5	21.0	21.5	012
1123.5	1259.0	1308.7	1361.1	1434.5	1603.8	1692.2	1790.4	1849.2	1948.5	013
99.8	110.9	106.9	113.2	121.1	128.3	144.8	158.9	168.2	176.0	014
107.9	126.0	148.2	175.8	203.3	225.7	266.0	309.9	338.8	361.6	015
370.1	417.5	467.1	532.0	612.0	702.9	799.7	888.7	979.0	1109.9	016
176.2	198.5	220.5	244.9	265.3	297.9	335.8	376.0	417.5	457.5	017
334.2	400.0	490.5	638.5	719.8	781.5	905.1	1030.0	1206.1	1325.1	018
268.9	289.6	333.3	382.7	458.4	532.2	588.1	633.5	677.7	727.0	019
202.4	248.7	254.7	281.3	295.8	338.1	388.5	440.9	491.3	536.9	020
70.6	66.0	88.3	90.4	105.0	117.1	103.3	96.0	78.0	74.7	021
2925.8	3303.0	3611.5	4029.3	4412.0	4927.8	5440.9	5970.5	6454.5	6982.4	022
2855.2	3237.1	3523.2	3938.8	4307.0	4810.7	5337.7	5874.5	6376.5	6907.7	023
1366.5	1542.5	1781.4	2103.7	2358.7	2635.5	2988.8	3345.9	3772.5	4108.9	024
422.9	466.2	529.9	616.4	739.6	836.8	907.9	939.6	960.8	997.8	025
517.5	622.6	733.7	869.6	965.6	1066.6	1240.0	1390.9	1460.7	1591.2	026
-16.8	44.3	100.2	53.9	28.5	53.8	89.2	87.2	61.4	51.0	027
1658.7	1855.4	1914.5	1953.3	2014.0	2280.5	2315.7	2598.8	2812.8	3374.5	028
1093.6	1294.0	1536.5	1657.9	1799.3	2062.5	2203.8	2487.9	2691.8	3215.7	029
–	–	–	–	–	–	–	–	–	–	030
3225.1	3636.0	3921.1	4243.9	4472.8	4810.7	5136.0	5460.5	5817.4	6169.8	031
165.0	174.7	176.5	175.6	179.2	182.4	177.1	186.7	178.6	182.9	032
17.3	17.4	17.4	17.5	16.9	17.8	18.5	20.0	19.6	19.8	033
1235.2	1396.8	1455.8	1509.6	1502.9	1603.8	1655.8	1697.3	1794.7	1903.3	034
83.7	92.3	101.5	108.5	116.9	128.3	135.0	145.1	154.0	163.6	035
144.3	158.1	176.0	194.0	212.7	225.7	250.9	282.8	299.0	311.7	036
415.1	467.9	518.7	575.7	637.9	702.9	775.0	846.8	904.2	975.5	037
204.2	224.6	242.8	260.3	276.8	297.9	322.4	345.4	367.0	394.9	038
397.8	467.6	562.1	682.3	749.1	781.5	863.0	938.0	1049.7	1113.3	039
362.1	382.4	413.8	442.6	487.8	532.2	564.6	590.0	610.5	632.9	040
200.4	254.2	256.4	277.9	292.5	338.1	373.6	408.2	440.3	471.9	041
80.9	75.3	99.6	97.5	109.0	117.1	98.7	89.4	69.7	64.3	042
3306.0	3711.3	4020.7	4341.4	4581.8	4927.8	5234.7	5549.9	5887.1	6234.1	043
3225.1	3636.0	3921.1	4243.9	4472.8	4810.7	5136.0	5460.5	5817.4	6169.8	044
1594.7	1773.0	2011.0	2273.6	2455.8	2635.5	2869.0	3103.6	3369.7	3541.4	045
532.4	577.8	628.4	692.3	779.0	836.8	874.6	879.5	869.1	872.1	046
584.5	690.6	790.6	908.1	978.8	1066.6	1214.7	1319.3	1394.4	1484.8	047
-17.1	46.0	103.0	54.8	30.2	53.8	88.8	88.2	61.2	45.6	048
1529.6	1818.0	1909.0	2005.4	2021.3	2280.5	2402.3	2574.7	2715.0	3065.9	049
999.1	1269.4	1520.8	1690.3	1792.3	2062.5	2313.3	2504.7	2592.0	2840.0	050
–	–	–	–	–	–	–	–	–	–	051

	Item	1978	1979	1980	1981	1982	1983	1984	1985
	Investment Financing, at current prices								
052	Gross domestic capital formation	279.7	393.4	503.9	529.8	479.2	492.9	519.4	471.4
053	Gross national saving [a]	340.2	399.3	480.6	553.0	571.1	675.9	800.5	844.2
054	Gross domestic saving	343.6	406.9	486.2	566.1	577.0	674.3	781.8	812.8
055	Net factor income from abroad	-2.3	0.4	-2.1	-9.7	-0.7	3.3	25.4	41.3
056	Net transfer from abroad	-1.1	-8.0	-3.4	-3.4	-5.3	-1.7	-6.7	-9.9
057	Foreign saving	-60.5	-5.9	23.3	-23.2	-91.8	-183.0	-281.1	-372.8
058	Net borrowing from abroad	-60.5	-5.9	23.3	-23.2	-91.8	-183.0	-281.1	-372.8
	Per Capita GNP, '000 New Taiwan dollars								
059	Current prices	58	69	84	98	104	113	125	131
060	Constant *1991 prices*	106	112	118	123	125	134	147	153
	PRODUCTION								*Thousand metric tons;*
	Agriculture								
061	1. Sugarcane	7941	9363	8851	8422	8275	7070	6545	6823
062	2. Rice (brown)	2444	2450	2354	2375	2483	2485	2244	2174
063	3. Citrus fruits	374	399	374	389	391	379	354	419
064	4. Maize	107	99	115	96	118	143	190	226
065	5. Pineapple	250	245	229	181	145	115	124	150
066	6. Sweet potatoes	463	1225	1055	834	741	560	424	369
067	7. Bananas	182	227	214	185	203	196	203	199
068	8. Sorghum	9	6	9	12	13	14	32	87
	Mining								
069	1. Limestone	12857	13126	12822	13221	11378	13183	12936	12645
070	2. Marble	4464	5376	7721	8686	8356	9054	9333	10072
071	3. Salt	341	366	722	351	262	79	218	174
	Manufacturing								
072	1. Cement	11461	11897	14062	14342	13432	14810	14234	14418
073	2. Steel bars	2969	1933	2109	2557	2531	2607	2671	2334
074	3. Fertilizer	1881	1872	1959	1517	1074	1118	1243	1164
075	4. Paper	394	451	490	471	482	477	463	515
076	5. Wheat flour	452	425	416	460	495	499	513	520
077	6. Sugar (Refined)	782	872	726	797	641	646	622	646
078	7. Cotton fabrics, *Mn m.*	...	...	...	1549	1379	1403	1134	1303
079	8. Cotton yarn	...	...	...	202	206	210	232	245
	Production Indexes								*1991 = 100;*
080	Agriculture	73.1	78.8	79.7	78.6	80.0	83.2	85.8	88.4
081	Mining	234.6	224.1	224.6	204.9	184.2	179.0	173.1	159.0
082	Manufacturing	44.3	46.8	49.7	51.5	51.9	59.1	66.5	68.1
	ENERGY								*Annual*
	Crude petroleum, *'000 k.l.*								
083	Production	247	231	211	183	139	135	136	118
084	Exports	...	...	...	...	...	...	...	...
085	Imports	17130	17436	18107	17184	18924	20093	20420	18837
086	Consumption	...	...	...	...	...	...	...	...
	Coal, *'000 m.t.*								
087	Production	2884	2720	2574	2446	2384	2236	2011	1858
088	Exports	4	6	6	8	...	...	...	...
089	Imports	1002	1900	4637	4777	5612	6405	7513	10091
090	Consumption	...	...	...	...	...	...	...	...
	Natural gas, *Mn cu. m.*								
091	Production	1961	1893	1959	1669	1418	1471	1480	1327
	Electricity, *Mn kWh*								
092	Production	35846	39547	42607	41928	42724	47473	51476	54803
093	Consumption	33345	37044	39821	39308	40776	45195	48967	51434

1986	1987	1988	1989	1990	1991	1992	1993	1994	1995	
500.7	666.9	833.9	923.4	994.1	1120.4	1329.2	1478.1	1522.1	1642.2	052
1125.2	1272.2	1245.2	1253.0	1293.9	1448.8	1539.1	1659.2	1685.2	1799.6	053
1065.8	1228.4	1211.9	1218.7	1208.8	1338.5	1441.0	1589.0	1643.1	1801.0	054
70.6	66.0	88.3	90.4	105.0	117.1	103.3	96.0	78.0	74.7	055
-11.2	-22.2	-55.0	-56.1	-19.8	-6.7	-5.2	-25.9	-35.9	-76.1	056
-624.5	-605.2	-411.3	-329.6	-299.8	-328.4	-209.9	-181.0	-163.2	-157.4	057
-624.5	-605.2	-411.3	-329.6	-299.8	-328.4	-209.9	-181.0	-163.2	-157.4	058
151	169	183	201	218	241	263	286	307	329	059
171	190	203	217	226	241	253	266	280	294	060

Calendar year

1986	1987	1988	1989	1990	1991	1992	1993	1994	1995	
6002	5163	6767	6628	5581	4536	5668	4577	5275	4769 *	061
1974	1900	1845	1865	1807	1819	1628	1820	1679	1687 *	062
386	523	560	569	529	544	527	507	468	427 *	063
272	307	321	329	339	375	390	406	397	376 *	064
158	193	228	231	235	241	226	277	252	252 *	065
324	345	255	206	200	224	204	188	181	196 *	066
151	204	229	198	201	197	196	213	184	173 *	067
97	103	118	77	102	110	108	112	105	98 *	068
12463	12407	13653	14069	13923	15351	16885	13085	13297	13270	069
10386	10791	11361	12231	11349	11945	14706	17836	17855	17064	070
136	100	111	170	83	195	26	176	186	221	071
14806	15663	17281	18043	18458	19399	21464	23971	22722	22470	072
2756	3264	3892	4871	5754	6305	7331	8459	8432	7709	073
1556	1513	1592	1600	1622	1620	1614	1558	1633	1766	074
622	707	806	795	831	895	945	938	1026	1050	075
572	619	620	619	622	629	635	654	682	711	076
535	539	567	491	490	399	487	445	475	402	077
1592	1536	1277	1360	1287	1178	1092	957	970	774	078
286	320	344	350	334	370	351	321	341	324	079

Period averages

1986	1987	1988	1989	1990	1991	1992	1993	1994	1995	
88.1	95.2	96.6	96.4	98.5	100.0	97.6	103.5	100.4	104.0	080
148.6	143.9	140.8	125.3	110.0	100.0	95.9	94.9	95.3	102.7	081
78.6	87.3	90.4	93.7	93.0	100.0	104.0	106.4	112.6	117.6	082

values

1986	1987	1988	1989	1990	1991	1992	1993	1994	1995	
105	148	140	135	182	110	72	65	69	62	083
...	...	...	...	...	...	...	...	...	...	084
18839	20233	21334	24130	24684	24333	26517	28639	27654	33588	085
...	...	...	...	...	...	...	...	...	...	086
1725	1499	1225	784	472	403	335	328	285	235	087
...	...	...	...	...	...	...	...	...	...	088
10685	14022	17454	16780	18467	18382	22092	25294	26688	28680	089
...	...	...	...	...	...	...	...	...	...	090
1209	1223	1395	1405	1304	987	855	827	908	942	091
61590	68382	74782	84055	90201	99176	105528	115205	124635	113117	092
57669	63298	70406	76997	82647	91249	97375	106028	113467	120968	093

	Item	1978	1979	1980	1981	1982	1983	1984	1985
	Retail prices, *NT $/litre*								
094	Gasoline, premium	14.0	21.0	26.0	28.0	28.0	26.0	26.0	26.0
095	Diesel	5.7	10.0	13.0	14.5	14.5	14.0	14.0	14.0
	PRICE INDEXES								*1991 = 100;*
096	Consumer	54.7	60.0	71.5	83.1	85.6	86.7	86.8	86.6
097	Food	58.9	62.9	72.9	85.5	88.9	90.1	87.9	85.9
098	Wholesale	76.2	86.7	105.4	113.5	113.3	111.9	112.4	109.5
099	Implicit GDP deflator, *1991 = 100*	55.1	61.5	71.4	80.0	82.8	84.4	85.1	85.6
	MONEY AND BANKING								*Billion New Taiwan dollars;*
100	Money supply (M1)	300.3	323.4	396.8	451.6	517.5	612.9	669.7	751.5
101	Currency in circulation [b]	78.6	88.3	110.4	128.3	138.3	159.6	168.2	182.8
102	Demand deposits [c]	221.7	235.1	286.4	323.3	379.2	453.3	501.5	568.7
103	Quasi-money	413.9	458.9	556.8	679.8	888.7	1164.7	1464.6	1881.7
104	Money supply (M2)	714.2	782.3	953.6	1131.4	1406.2	1777.6	2134.3	2633.2
105	Foreign assets (net)	203.0	202.5	195.2	245.7	355.9	554.9	771.6	1168.7
106	Domestic credit	597.0	699.3	924.3	1112.7	1336.6	1534.0	1716.0	1851.9
107	Claims on govt. sector (net) [d]	35.8	38.5	112.5	188.4	252.1	230.2	196.7	183.8
108	Claims on private sector	550.4	651.6	802.2	917.8	1072.1	1296.2	1507.2	1625.5
109	Claims on other financial insts.	10.8	9.2	9.6	6.5	12.4	7.6	12.1	42.6
110	Other items	-85.8	-119.5	-165.9	-227.0	-286.3	-311.3	-353.3	-387.4
	Deposit Money Banks [e]								
111	Demand deposits	...	...	...	...	...	...	...	...
112	Savings deposits	...	...	...	...	...	...	...	...
113	Time deposits [f]	313.4	341.8	406.1	463.6	604.6	802.3	1012.6	1264.3
114	Domestic credits outstanding [g]	637.7	750.0	959.5	1080.5	1270.1	1475.3	1649.3	1742.2
	Interest rates								*Per cent;*
	On deposits								
115	6 months (time deposit)	6.75	10.25	11.00	11.50	8.00	7.50	7.00	5.75
116	12 months (time saving deposit)	9.50	12.50	12.50	13.00	9.00	8.50	8.00	6.25
	On loans & discounts								
117	Export credit [h]	6.50	10.50	10.50	11.00	8.25	8.00	7.75	6.25
	GOVERNMENT FINANCE								*Billion New Taiwan dollars;*
	Central Government								
118	Current revenue	209.6	179.5	208.0	241.3	277.8	289.2	312.0	336.7
119	Taxes	168.2	127.4	152.3	175.9	182.4	181.1	203.9	211.4
120	Non-taxes	41.4	52.1	55.7	65.4	95.4	108.1	108.1	125.3
121	Current expenditure	131.9	108.4	152.9	185.8	217.8	234.9	242.6	275.8
122	Current surplus/deficit	77.7	71.1	55.1	55.5	60.0	54.3	69.4	60.9
123	Capital receipts	24.0	4.5	9.0	11.0	10.4	6.9	4.4	5.4
124	Capital expenditure	95.0	63.8	70.1	79.2	82.1	71.0	68.8	71.2
125	Capital account surplus/deficit	-71.0	-59.3	-61.1	-68.2	-71.7	-64.1	-64.4	-65.8
126	Overall surplus/deficit	6.7	11.8	-6.0	-12.7	-11.7	-9.8	5.0	-4.9
	Financing								
127	Domestic borrowing	12.7	5.8	-1.5	0.3	8.5	17.6	-2.5	6.7
128	Foreign borrowing	107.6	2.7	-0.9	-0.6	...	-0.6	-0.3	...
129	Foreign grants	5.7	0.6	3.0	...	...	...	...	...
130	Use of cash balances	-132.7	-20.9	5.4	13.0	3.2	-7.2	-2.2	-1.8
	Expenditure by Function, Central Govt.								
131	Total	130.1	172.2	223.9	265.0	299.9	305.9	311.4	347.0
132	General public services }	69.8	96.4	118.3	168.6	191.3	196.4	189.3	207.9
133	Defence }								
134	Education	7.8	4.9	7.7	11.7	13.2	17.0	16.8	18.7
135	Health	...	1.1	1.3	2.1	3.4	4.0	4.1	4.7
136	Social security & welfare	15.3	12.4	16.4	22.9	34.0	38.7	43.2	48.9

1986	1987	1988	1989	1990	1991	1992	1993	1994	1995	
19.0	17.0	14.5	14.5	18.5	17.5	17.0	16.1	16.5	16.9	094
11.0	10.5	10.0	10.0	13.0	12.5	12.0	11.4	11.7	11.9	095

Period averages

87.2	87.6	88.8	92.7	96.5	100.0	104.5	107.5	111.9	116.0	096
88.0	89.1	90.3	96.0	99.2	100.0	108.7	112.2	119.4	124.5	097
105.9	102.4	100.8	100.5	99.8	100.0	96.3	98.8	100.9	108.3	098
88.5	89.0	89.9	92.8	96.3	100.0	103.9	107.6	109.6	112.0	099

As of end of period

1137.9	1568.2	1950.5	2068.7	1931.9	2165.3	2434.4	2806.4	3148.5	3178.1	100
231.0	285.0	320.6	348.4	354.7	387.7	436.1	470.4	507.0	516.0	101
906.9	1283.2	1629.9	1720.3	1577.2	1777.6	1998.3	2336.0	2641.5	2662.1	102
2161.0	2606.8	2970.3	3603.2	4299.3	5267.2	6430.2	7399.2	8490.0	9455.6	103
3298.9	4175.0	4920.8	5671.9	6231.2	7432.5	8864.6	10205.6	11638.5	12633.7	104
1649.1	1982.0	2062.8	2005.7	2169.6	2254.8	2183.6	2301.3	2491.3	2573.0	105
1913.9	2144.2	2928.7	3806.3	4456.8	5630.6	7235.0	8669.9	10102.3	11168.8	106
150.2	11.0	-79.7	47.1	107.1	361.3	461.1	604.0	721.6	901.0	107
1732.2	2110.2	2982.9	3723.2	4324.5	5243.4	6748.5	8033.4	9357.9	10244.7	108
31.5	23.0	25.5	36.0	25.2	25.9	25.4	32.5	22.8	23.1	109
-264.1	48.8	-70.7	-140.1	-395.2	-452.9	-554.0	-765.6	-955.1	-1108.1	110
...	...	...	...	...	...	...	...	...	...	111
...	...	...	...	...	...	...	...	...	...	112
1370.5	1534.4	1840.5	2463.4	3070.7	3800.1	4541.3	5455.8	6266.9	7016.6	113
1917.3	2296.6	3190.0	4142.8	4640.1	5687.7	7270.7	8431.2	9897.9	10795.6	114

Period averages

6.25	6.25	6.25	9.25	8.75	7.53	7.25	7.10	6.75	6.25	115
6.25	6.25	6.25	9.25	9.50	8.27	7.90	7.60	7.35	6.75	116
5.50	5.50	5.50	6.50	6.50	...	...	...	...	...	117

Fiscal year ending 30 June

362.1	387.6	440.4	569.1	701.0	617.9	743.9	800.3	879.9	932.7	118
234.4	265.7	320.3	431.5	562.6	507.2	539.9	596.1	655.7	747.9	119
127.7	121.9	120.1	137.6	138.4	110.7	204.0	204.2	224.2	184.8	120
308.4	310.2	350.4	408.9	442.9	523.5	693.1	715.3	707.2	916.0	121
53.7	77.4	90.0	160.2	258.1	94.4	50.8	85.0	172.7	16.7	122
7.5	16.0	14.8	16.4	21.3	31.7	31.2	21.1	23.7	34.9	123
86.5	92.7	102.1	123.9	197.8	233.7	372.4	337.9	308.2	292.7	124
-79.0	-76.7	-87.3	-107.5	-176.5	-202.0	-341.2	-316.8	-284.5	-257.8	125
-25.3	0.7	2.7	52.7	81.6	-107.6	-290.4	-231.8	-111.8	-241.1	126
17.8	30.3	43.6	57.6	-35.9	32.4	179.6	200.6	107.4	90.9	127
-1.4	-2.2	-1.0	...	...	...	...	...	...	...	128
...	...	...	...	...	...	...	...	...	...	129
8.9	-28.8	-45.3	-110.3	-45.7	75.2	110.8	31.2	4.4	150.2	130
395.0	402.8	452.5	532.6	640.7	757.2	1065.5	1053.2	1015.5	1043.9	131
219.7	209.5	259.0	309.9	359.2	432.5	623.1	462.6	437.6	446.2	132
										133
21.6	24.3	25.4	30.7	45.5	61.2	74.4	110.3	111.7	109.2	134
8.7	8.4	13.1	15.2	10.6	15.0	18.5	21.7	18.2	29.5	135
64.7	72.2	63.1	74.1	96.0	118.4	171.7	136.6	141.2	144.0	136

	Item	1978	1979	1980	1981	1982	1983	1984	1985
137	Housing & community amenities	...	1.4	1.5	1.0	1.8	1.3	1.3	1.4
138	Economic services	29.7	53.7	72.4	56.1	52.7	43.7	48.9	54.4
139	Others	7.5	2.3	6.3	2.6	3.5	4.8	7.8	11.0
	Provincial and Other Local Govts.								
140	Revenue	95.1	109.5	147.9	165.4	183.5	181.5	230.5	239.8
141	Tax	60.2	79.3	89.8	115.1	117.1	120.4	147.1	154.1
142	Non-tax	34.9	30.2	58.1	50.3	66.4	61.1	83.4	85.7
143	Subsidy/grants	...	...	...	...	32.5	26.3	22.0	27.8
144	Expenditure	96.8	101.1	143.6	160.8	216.2	197.4	237.0	252.9
	EXTERNAL TRADE							*Billion New Taiwan dollars;*	
145	Exports, fob	468.5	579.3	712.2	829.7	864.3	1005.5	1204.7	1223.0
146	Imports, cif	408.4	532.9	711.4	778.6	736.1	813.9	870.9	801.8
147	Trade balance	60.1	46.4	0.8	51.1	128.2	191.6	333.8	421.2
	Exports, by SITC section								
148	Food & live animals	47.5	51.0	60.9	59.3	59.5	62.9	65.4	68.5
149	Beverage & tobacco	0.3	0.4	0.5	0.5	0.5	0.5	0.3	0.5
150	Crude materials excl. fuels	8.9	11.8	11.9	14.9	18.1	19.5	19.8	22.7
151	Mineral fuels, etc.	10.0	10.2	10.6	16.7	16.5	18.7	22.0	21.8
152	Animal, vegetable oil & fats	0.0	0.0	0.1	0.1	0.1	0.1	0.4	0.1
153	Chemicals	8.9	12.2	18.0	20.3	23.1	25.0	30.7	30.8
154	Basic manufactures	109.8	147.9	163.5	189.3	187.8	219.7	251.1	263.8
155	Machines, transport equipment	109.4	136.6	176.0	212.4	218.9	263.8	339.0	340.7
156	Misc. manufactured goods	173.5	209.1	270.6	316.3	339.7	395.2	476.0	474.0
157	Unclassified goods	0.1	0.1	0.1	0.1	0.1	0.1	0.1	0.1
	Exports, by principal commodity								
158	1. Outer garments, knitted or crocheted	34.7	35.7	42.1	45.2	44.8	49.5	60.8	55.4
159	2. Footwear of plastic	16.3	19.1	29.6	29.9	28.9	32.3	43.1	47.9
160	3. Travel goods, handbags and similar articles	12.8	16.9	23.0	25.1	26.9	30.7	32.8	31.2
161	4. Toys	7.8	10.5	13.4	19.4	20.0	23.9	28.9	23.7
162	5. Thermionic, valves, tubes, transistors, etc.	9.2	12.4	17.5	21.6	22.6	26.0	36.4	34.4
	Imports, by SITC section								
163	Food & live animals	28.9	37.1	43.4	52.6	48.4	54.3	55.5	53.0
164	Beverage & tobacco	3.0	4.3	3.7	3.5	4.6	4.1	4.1	5.3
165	Crude materials excl. fuels	61.5	82.9	97.4	96.9	94.2	104.1	117.3	104.1
166	Mineral fuels, etc.	70.1	94.9	181.4	201.3	179.2	195.3	187.3	172.6
167	Animal, vegetable oil & fats	1.8	2.0	1.7	1.8	2.5	2.5	2.5	2.2
168	Chemicals	44.3	60.4	67.2	71.4	73.4	96.3	102.0	95.5
169	Basic manufactures	57.0	72.2	87.1	88.6	78.1	91.6	105.2	93.3
170	Machines, transport equipment	122.8	155.8	198.6	220.6	205.8	217.9	247.4	223.8
171	Misc. manufactured goods	18.2	22.5	29.6	39.6	47.9	45.8	47.3	50.2
172	Unclassified goods	0.8	0.8	1.3	2.4	2.0	2.2	2.3	1.8
	Direction of Trade							*Million US dollars;*	
173	Exports, Total	12687	16103	19811	22611	22204	25123	30456	30726
174	1. United States	5010	5652	6760	8158	8758	11334	14868	14773
175	2. Hong Kong	858	1140	1551	1897	1565	1644	2087	2540
176	3. Japan	1570	2249	2173	2454	2365	2477	3186	3461
177	4. Germany	572	743	1076	906	788	851	868	805
178	5. United Kingdom	323	406	472	566	528	617	691	650
179	6. Canada	327	415	460	568	510	728	916	945
180	7. Australia	334	419	539	677	644	634	834	747
181	8. Saudi Arabia	322	476	545	607	719	760	728	590
182	9. New Zealand	18	29	36	50	54	55	73	76
183	10. Iran	37	24	40	84	8	64	14	12

1986	1987	1988	1989	1990	1991	1992	1993	1994	1995	
4.1	3.3	4.4	3.5	5.3	5.3	9.8	8.3	7.0	13.0	137
69.6	76.9	76.3	87.4	108.6	106.3	136.8	260.9	237.6	224.7	138
6.6	8.2	11.2	11.8	15.5	18.5	31.2	52.8	62.2	77.3	139
257.2	272.2	345.8	442.0	461.0	505.8	688.4	684.7	737.9	775.1	140
160.7	182.9	212.2	264.1	263.4	290.0	398.5	468.5	502.9	542.3	141
96.5	89.3	133.6	177.9	197.6	215.8	289.9	216.2	235.0	232.8	142
32.8	27.7	46.2	56.3	72.7	100.4	134.4	113.3	106.6	109.3	143
279.4	278.6	330.7	756.1	588.8	682.8	749.8	721.5	852.3	899.1	144
Calendar year										
1507.0	1707.6	1731.8	1747.8	1802.8	2040.8	2048.0	2239.0	2456.0	2950.4	145
917.0	1113.9	1423.1	1385.7	1471.8	1690.8	1817.1	2034.7	2261.7	2743.7	146
590.0	593.7	308.7	362.1	331.0	350.0	230.9	204.3	194.4	206.7	147
90.1	94.0	84.9	71.5	71.6	84.4	77.1	81.7	88.8	98.8	148
0.4	0.5	0.9	0.7	0.6	1.2	1.3	1.4	1.8	1.8	149
24.4	24.8	29.1	32.2	31.6	33.3	32.5	33.4	40.5	53.3	150
15.7	13.8	10.7	10.6	10.8	11.8	13.3	15.3	15.1	20.7	151
0.1	0.1	0.2	0.2	0.5	0.4	0.5	0.4	0.7	0.8	152
40.9	45.0	59.7	63.7	74.8	93.8	96.2	113.7	143.6	199.2	153
307.1	343.6	357.6	363.2	384.9	438.9	435.7	488.2	578.6	684.4	154
438.6	551.2	610.2	648.0	705.2	799.4	840.0	989.6	1113.3	1419.9	155
589.7	634.4	578.3	555.1	520.5	574.7	548.4	512.7	471.8	468.2	156
0.1	0.1	0.1	2.6	2.5	2.8	3.0	2.7	1.9	2.4	157
67.5	67.1	53.5	50.9	37.9	45.2	39.7	36.9	43.9	43.4	158
60.4	59.7	50.5	39.1	26.3	21.9	14.5	10.7	8.3	6.1	159
34.9	34.8	28.2	25.4	22.1	21.5	18.3	13.7	13.1	12.5	160
27.4	29.0	19.2	11.7	10.3	10.7	10.3	11.1	10.7	10.6	161
41.8	50.1	62.9	81.2	94.5	120.1	147.0	240.9	322.8	478.2	162
50.5	48.7	59.4	63.5	68.0	72.6	75.3	79.4	91.6	99.8	163
3.9	7.9	7.6	9.2	8.0	9.2	11.9	15.6	18.2	24.6	164
121.0	131.2	141.3	134.7	119.5	142.3	128.6	133.7	151.0	172.3	165
119.3	117.9	113.1	116.4	160.1	156.8	141.6	150.2	156.6	189.2	166
2.1	1.9	2.0	2.1	2.6	3.0	3.2	3.9	4.6	6.3	167
133.1	149.1	180.8	180.4	186.1	229.7	217.1	238.9	286.0	364.4	168
130.3	161.6	205.7	231.2	227.3	296.9	311.8	380.9	398.6	486.6	169
297.1	386.3	468.4	500.0	544.0	604.1	714.4	801.1	882.8	1102.3	170
57.8	68.1	93.7	71.1	85.8	102.8	116.6	143.2	179.6	208.8	171
2.0	41.3	151.0	77.3	70.3	73.3	96.6	87.9	92.6	88.2	172
Calendar year										
39862	53679	60667	66304	67214	76178	81470	85091	93049	111659	173
19014	23685	23467	24036	21746	22321	23572	23587	24337	26407	174
2921	4123	5587	7042	8556	12431	15415	18453	21262	26106	175
4560	6986	8772	9065	8338	9189	8894	8977	10221	13157	176
1275	1988	2340	2564	3183	3869	3599	3504	3251	3839	177
966	1548	1907	2102	1979	2072	2205	2171	2173	2409	178
1272	1561	1584	1759	1559	1624	1643	1538	1458	1430	179
870	1103	1359	1538	1279	1354	1428	1450	1632	1756	180
627	706	630	557	459	616	563	533	456	450	181
120	173	212	224	195	194	201	206	234	253	182
14	14	6	11	35	84	114	82	43	43	183

Item	1978	1979	1980	1981	1982	1983	1984	1985
184	Imports, Total	11027	14774	19733	21200	18888	20287	21959	20102
185	1. Japan	3678	4561	5353	5929	4780	5587	6442	5549
186	2. United States	2376	3381	4673	4766	4563	4646	5042	4746
187	3. Germany	412	636	722	646	788	692	768	846
188	4. Australia	322	454	512	593	644	682	778	801
189	5. Hong Kong	153	205	250	309	307	299	370	320
190	6. Saudi Arabia	649	865	1419	1797	1969	1925	1971	1361
191	7. United Kingdom	244	296	289	302	270	308	294	262
192	8. Canada	106	132	249	268	316	361	400	369
193	9. New Zealand	39	49	59	67	71	90	90	75
194	10. Iran	91	30	173	0	0	32	0	7
	Trade Indexes								*1991 = 100;*
	Quantum index								
195	Exports	27.8	29.6	32.8	35.4	37.4	44.8	52.5	55.9
196	Imports	23.9	26.6	30.4	30.3	29.4	34.5	36.5	36.3
	Unit Value Index								
197	Exports	82.7	95.8	106.3	114.8	113.3	110.0	112.5	107.2
198	Imports	101.1	118.4	138.4	152.2	148.3	139.6	141.2	130.8
199	Terms of trade	81.8	80.9	76.8	75.4	76.4	78.8	79.7	82.0
	BALANCE OF PAYMENTS								*Million US dollars;*
200	Merchandise exports, fob	12602	15829	19575	22408	21776	25028	30185	30470
201	Merchandise imports, fob	-10413	-14509	-19498	-20583	-18130	-18760	-20952	-19297
202	Trade balance	2189	1320	77	1825	3646	6268	9233	11173
203	Other goods, services & income	-522	-917	-895	-1215	-1262	-1813	-2088	-1727
204	Credit	1824	2585	3052	3671	3915	3803	4548	4954
205	Debit	-2346	-3502	-3947	-4886	-5177	-5616	-6636	-6681
206	Unrequited transfer	-28	-222	-95	-91	-136	-42	-169	-247
207	Private	-20	-222	-92	-85	-126	-41	-169	-244
208	Official	-8	–	-3	-6	-10	-1	–	-3
209	Current balance	1639	181	-913	519	2248	4413	6976	9199
210	Direct investment	110	122	124	91	71	130	131	261
211	Portfolio investment	45	-79	60	85	145	41	-50	-46
212	Other long-term capital	198	439	1027	1149	1626	906	-1205	-1234
213	Other short-term capital	84	-420	-254	3473	-2179	-1797	-1470	-2143
214	Net errors & omissions	-125	-205	-363	-326	-498	-351	-408	490
215	Overall balance	1951	38	-319	4991	1413	3342	3974	6527
216	Monetization	–	-17	267	111	100	156	119	156
217	Allocations of SDRs	–	75	-75	–	–	–	–	–
218	Monetary movement	-1951	-96	127	-5102	-1513	-3498	-4093	-6683
	INTERNATIONAL RESERVES								*Million US dollars;*
219	Total	...	1517	2574	7694	9063	12541	16480	23520
220	Gold, national valuation	...	125	369	459	531	682	816	964
221	Foreign exchange	1406	1392	2205	7235	8532	11859	15664	22556
222	Reserve position in the fund	...	...	...	...	...	...	...	...
223	SDRs	...	...	...	...	...	...	...	...
	EXCHANGE RATES								*New Taiwan dollars*
224	End of period	36.000	36.100	36.010	37.840	39.910	40.270	39.470	39.850
225	Average of period	37.054	36.048	36.015	36.849	39.124	40.065	39.597	39.849

	1986	1987	1988	1989	1990	1991	1992	1993	1994	1995	
	24181	34983	49673	52265	54716	62861	72007	77061	85349	103550	184
	8255	11841	14825	16031	15998	18858	21767	23186	24786	30266	185
	5433	7648	13007	12003	12612	14114	15771	16723	18043	20771	186
	1144	1634	2133	2594	2668	3013	3919	4220	4784	5683	187
	883	1000	1336	1631	1660	2018	2056	2097	2225	2575	188
	379	754	1922	2205	1446	1947	1781	1729	1533	1843	189
	910	1075	1237	1375	1539	1679	1465	1502	1333	1763	190
	357	792	1113	927	1154	1124	1358	1192	1529	1643	191
	486	652	954	996	839	1040	1178	1119	1251	1594	192
	91	134	166	210	191	266	289	310	352	446	193
	24	36	33	3	167	291	296	213	312	438	194

Period averages

	1986	1987	1988	1989	1990	1991	1992	1993	1994	1995	
	70.6	82.5	83.4	88.9	90.2	100.0	103.9	108.0	114.6	121.2	195
	45.2	60.7	76.6	84.2	88.2	100.0	113.4	119.5	122.6	133.2	196
	104.7	101.5	101.8	96.3	98.0	100.0	96.6	101.6	105.0	119.3	197
	119.9	108.5	109.9	97.4	98.7	100.0	94.8	100.7	109.1	121.8	198
	87.3	93.5	92.6	98.9	99.2	100.0	101.9	100.9	96.3	98.0	199

Calendar year

	1986	1987	1988	1989	1990	1991	1992	1993	1994	1995	
	39552	53298	60319	65875	66823	75535	80723	84329	92242	110709	200
	-22635	-33013	-46485	-49672	-51895	-59781	-67956	-72742	-80258	-97127	201
	16917	20285	13834	16203	14928	15754	12767	11587	11984	13582	202
	-341	-1590	-1733	-2693	-3424	-3488	-4406	-3891	-4473	-5724	203
	6745	8179	11246	14070	14249	16250	18072	20539	20795	23775	204
	-7086	-9769	-12979	-16763	-17673	-19738	-22478	-24430	-25268	-29499	205
	-297	-696	-1924	-2125	-735	-251	-207	-982	-1357	-2854	206
	-304	-703	-1921	-2117	-730	-230	-168	-955	-1316	-2817	207
	7	7	-3	-8	-5	-21	-39	-27	-41	-37	208
	16279	17999	10177	11385	10769	12015	8154	6714	6154	5004	209
	261	11	-3161	-5347	-3913	-583	-990	-1534	-1085	-2502	210
	69	-371	-1711	-902	-1006	45	445	1067	905	-1106	211
	-1913	-2225	-1402	-1512	-1682	-2289	-2913	-2133	-1780	512	212
	8520	12983	-5182	-4369	-8549	600	-3450	-2062	563	-6772	213
	108	-306	-114	-35	463	-129	121	-511	-135	337	214
	23324	28091	-1393	-780	-3918	9659	1367	1541	4622	-4527	215
	223	992	2629	18	0	0	3	6	6	0	216
	–	–	–	–	–	–	–	–	–	–	217
	-23547	-29083	-1236	762	3918	-9659	-1370	-1547	-4628	4527	218

As of end of period

	1986	1987	1988	1989	1990	1991	1992	1993	1994	1995	
	47623	79445	79292	79052	78064	88325	88308	89298	98273	95911	219
	1313	2697	5395	5828	5623	5920	6002	5725	5819	5601	220
	46310	76748	73897	73224	72441	82405	82306	83573	92454	90310	221
	...	...	...	...	...	...	...	...	...	...	222
	...	...	...	...	...	...	...	...	...	...	223

per US dollar

	1986	1987	1988	1989	1990	1991	1992	1993	1994	1995	
	35.500	28.550	28.170	26.160	27.108	25.748	25.403	26.626	26.240	27.265	224
	37.838	31.740	28.588	26.407	26.893	26.815	25.164	26.387	26.457	26.486	225

Item	1978	1979	1980	1981	1982	1983	1984	1985
EXTERNAL INDEBTEDNESS								*Million US dollars;*
226 Total outstanding & disbursed	...	...	...	...	9631.0	10867.0	9645.0	9146.0
227 Long-term	...	...	...	...	7177.0	7666.0	6383.0	5786.0
228 Public and publicly-guaranteed	2935.1	3082.4	4107.4	4795.5	5661.1	6289.8	5534.5	4764.5
229 Private non-guaranteed	...	...	...	...	...	...	...	...
230 Short-term	...	...	...	...	2454.0	3201.0	3262.0	3360.0
231 Use of IMF credit	...	...	...	...	–	–	–	–
Debt service								*Transactions*
232 Principal repayments on LT debt	420.5	480.2	717.0	661.5	890.0	1019.0	1537.0	1520.0
233 Interest on long-term debt	245.7	277.7	408.2	589.9	793.0	729.0	551.0	521.0
234 Interest on short-term debt	...	...	...	...	351.0	282.0	336.0	271.0

Footnotes:

a   Includes net transfers from abroad.
b   Refers to net currency issued and cash in the vaults.
c   Refer to demand deposits adjusted of net checking accounts, passbook deposits and passbook savings deposits.
d   Include claims on official entities.
e   Data on deposit money banks exclude those of the Central Bank of China.
f   Include time deposits and time saving deposits.
g   Computed as total assets of deposit money banks less foreign assets and cash in vaults.
h   The ceilings and floors on lending rates have been removed since July 19, 1989.

	1986	1987	1988	1989	1990	1991	1992	1993	1994	1995	
As of end of year											
	12757.0	20102.0	18595.0	17890.0	18459.0	19900.0	19858.0	23243.0	26162.0	...	226
	4357.0	3170.0	3063.0	2742.0	2843.0	3244.0	2599.0	3486.0	6043.0	...	227
	3236.2	1889.6	1528.8	1145.5	898.1	713.5	455.4	395.4	360.4	...	228
	...	...	...	...	...	...	...	...	...	...	229
	8400.0	16932.0	15532.0	15148.0	15616.0	16656.0	17259.0	19757.0	20119.0	...	230
	–	–	–	–	–	–	–	–	–	...	231
during the year											
	974.0	1675.0	298.0	260.0	383.0	750.0	...	...	...	...	232
	384.0	285.0	210.0	260.0	203.0	210.0	...	...	...	...	233
	399.0	873.0	1298.0	1380.0	1277.0	968.0	...	...	...	...	234

	Item	1978	1979		1980	1981	1982	1983	1984	1985
001	**POPULATION**	44.46	45.46		46.72	47.74	48.74	49.73	50.71	*Million;* 51.68
002	**LABOR FORCE** [a, b]	21895	21420		22728	24579	25749	25849	26744	*Thousand;* 27115
003	Employed	21738	21230		22524	24366	24831	25184	25999	25853
004	Agriculture	16018	15019		15943	17528	16985	17401	18130	17675
005	Manufacturing	1478	1725		1789	1742	2007	1843	1986	2067
006	Mining	30	39		37	61	65	51	117	69
007	Others	4212	4447		4755	5035	5774	5888	5764	6042
008	Unemployed	157	190		204	213	918	614	611	995
009	Unemployment rate, %	0.7	0.9		0.9	0.8	3.5	2.4	2.3	3.7
	NATIONAL ACCOUNTS *At Current Market Prices*									*Million Baht;*
010	GDP by Industrial Origin	488226	558861	I	662482	760356	841569	920989	988070	1056496
011	Agriculture	119638	134148	I	153960	162390	156098	184752	173642	167026
012	Mining	16608	18498	I	11727	11208	13416	14106	18543	25962
013	Manufacturing	97658	117611	I	142504	172143	179438	203837	226360	231598
014	Electricity, gas and water	5667	6499	I	6373	10814	15601	17093	18609	24955
015	Construction	24393	27004	I	29383	34696	39890	46632	52427	53903
016	Trade	90299	96875	I	116711	138594	161738	152380	175026	193810
017	Transport and communications	27462	32179	I	34894	41648	54350	56613	65078	78075
018	Finance	31560	36149	I	20503	21833	25542	30875	33491	35271
019	Public administration	19829	23484	I	30718	33361	39815	44704	45090	48679
020	Others	55112	66414	I	115709	133669	155681	169997	179804	197217
021	Net factor income from abroad	-3622	-6225	I	-5394	-12035	-12922	-6701	-11451	-17598
022	GNP	484604	552636	I	657088	748321	828647	914288	976619	1038898
023	Expenditure on GDP	488226	558861	I	662482	760356	841569	920989	988070	1056496
024	Private consumption	314983	364028	I	433585	496417	534991	599560	628937	657365
025	Government consumption	54583	66798	I	81433	97007	110167	118577	130100	142923
026	Gross fixed capital formation	123249	142859	I	183987	212821	226728	262138	282599	286999
027	Increase in stocks	14247	9191	I	9073	12817	-3573	13931	8616	11405
028	Exports of goods and services	97082	126150	I	159734	181325	192870	185222	216401	245252
029	Less: Imports of goods and services	117721	163740	I	201180	229029	207282	251184	258557	274073
030	Statistical discrepancy	1803	13575	I	-4150	-11002	-12332	-7255	-20026	-13375
	At Constant 1972 I 1988 Prices									
031	GDP by Industrial Origin	271378	285797	I	913733	967706	1019501	1076432	1138353	1191255
032	Agriculture	61856	60726	I	184576	194023	198825	208312	217518	227324
033	Mining	7435	7691	I	6861	8327	11022	11659	16167	21553
034	Manufacturing	58337	63163	I	211031	224294	230235	255995	271855	268133
035	Electricity, gas and water	4874	5376	I	15614	17525	20732	21171	23230	26959
036	Construction	13037	12855	I	41882	44690	48008	53772	59390	59269
037	Trade	45593	46779	I	163680	177866	183928	181627	189102	197432
038	Transport and communications	15717	17932	I	65669	60230	69607	72308	80548	85922
039	Finance	20412	21796	I	28292	26922	29738	34657	37181	38145
040	Public administration	12272	14125	I	37756	41454	43514	48074	47448	50913
041	Others	31845	35354	I	158372	172375	183892	188857	195914	215605
042	Net factor income from abroad	-1767	-2778	I	-3049	-9285	-9595	-3627	-10806	-18768
043	GNP	269611	283019	I	910684	958421	1009906	1072805	1127547	1172487
044	Expenditure on GDP	271378	285797	I	913733	967706	1019501	1076432	1138353	1191255
045	Private consumption	174705	187526	I	607226	620549	634507	682669	712971	723199
046	Government consumption	33823	39066	I	106938	122904	124424	130959	141572	151252
047	Gross fixed capital formation	65524	68107	I	269627	287170	285784	327409	346643	333644
048	Increase in stocks	8150	2186	I	6452	12424	-6561	13450	11921	12230
049	Exports of goods and services	46963	51858	I	195231	213116	237964	223726	262337	288017
050	Less: Imports of goods and services	51236	61930	I	271199	272723	232838	309125	332719	290571
051	Statistical discrepancy	-6551	-1016	I	-542	-15734	-23779	7344	-4372	-26516

	1986	1987	1988	1989	1990	1991	1992	1993	1994	1995	
As of 1 July											
	52.65	53.43	54.33	55.21	55.84	56.57	57.29	58.01	58.71	59.40	001
Calendar year											
	27754	29419	30318	31206	31750	32143	32906	32845	...	...	002
	26612	27516	29274	30612	30844	31138	32450	32153	...	...	003
	17750	17679	19407	20402	19726	18777	19705	18245	...	...	004
	2063	2433	2458	2770	3133	3465	3600	3961	...	...	005
	42	55	43	44	54	55	62	57	...	...	006
	6757	7349	7366	7396	7931	8841	9083	9890	...	...	007
	966	1712	927	433	710	869	456	494	...	...	008
	3.5	5.8	3.1	1.4	2.2	2.7	1.4	1.5	...	...	009
Calendar year											
	1133397	1299913	1559804	1856992	2186026	2507029	2827158	3163914	3600907 *	4162200 *	010
	177537	204521	252346	279947	274658	316769	347965	322666	369053 *	455700 *	011
	19753	22221	26599	31885	34835	39372	42306	47047	48599 *	51800 *	012
	270605	315291	403034	496714	594014	707911	779093	893344	1014952 *	1216300 *	013
	28888	33279	35298	42466	47746	53461	65507	75825	83923 *	95400 *	014
	55715	62641	74449	102123	136235	168278	190529	222466	267999 *	295000 *	015
	189986	223129	266257	309816	387012	427641	473244	526994	592016 *	667500 *	016
	88202	99344	116611	138084	156586	176953	204878	238092	267933 *	307100 *	017
	37102	49980	66220	84668	120551	134212	182780	231711	286000 *	324600 *	018
	50681	52726	56488	64621	76556	86926	105392	117676	127436 *	147400 *	019
	214928	236781	262502	306668	357833	395506	435464	488093	542996 *	601400 *	020
	-22437	-22394	-24770	-23668	-27438	-40120	-56506	-68664	-77652 *	-91100 *	021
	1110960	1277519	1535034	1833324	2158588	2466909	2770652	3095250	3523255 *	4071100 *	022
	1133397	1299913	1559804	1856992	2186026	2507029	2827158	3163914	3600907 *	4162200 *	023
	695784	781064	885008	1030563	1233353	1392578	1552086	1740597	1977996 *	2276300 *	024
	144564	147224	156710	176798	205354	231127	280203	315979	353824 *	405500 *	025
	292193	359269	478534	642876	881764	1043799	1112645	1272461	1466381 *	1780600 *	026
	1043	3078	29820	8299	21214	27199	17855	5171	8689 *	13800 *	027
	290170	375597	514922	648490	745286	885794	1031800	1176331	1406057 *	1727600 *	028
	267131	368317	536596	696101	909456	1062258	1152866	1313368	1577751 *	2014300 *	029
	-23226	1998	31406	46067	8511	-11210	-14565	-33257	-34289 *	-27300 *	030
	1257177	1376847	1559804	1749952	1946192	2110867	2282107	2470757	2686739 *	2920200 *	031
	228191	228346	252346	276569	263806	281028	298026	292279	308321 *	314700 *	032
	21511	24107	26599	28227	31053	36085	37959	40606	43608 *	44000 *	033
	294521	341750	403034	467632	540940	604357	672651	747467	816619 *	939800 *	034
	29890	31515	35298	42259	46841	51750	57115	62164	68497 *	74800 *	035
	60138	66060	74449	95554	116606	132494	138700	151879	172815 *	179100 *	036
	207211	229859	266257	296919	338730	363299	374805	406821	439463 *	473000 *	037
	92046	100585	116611	128754	146796	157417	174043	190300	208676 *	231100 *	038
	39404	51834	66220	80426	108111	113843	148916	182716	214488 *	230600 *	039
	52329	53717	56488	57277	61363	65258	66180	68122	69668 *	70800 *	040
	231936	249074	262502	276335	291946	305336	313712	328403	344584 *	362300 *	041
	-23761	-23310	-24770	-22154	-23675	-32406	-44005	-51975	-54486 *	-75000 *	042
	1233416	1353537	1535034	1727798	1922517	2078461	2238102	2418782	2632253 *	2845200 *	043
	1257177	1376847	1559804	1749952	1946192	2110867	2282107	2470757	2686739 *	2920200 *	044
	748896	813783	885008	984184	1110000	1183337	1275466	1386999	1501363 *	1632800 *	045
	150208	150637	156710	160822	171944	482589	194276	204200	219681 *	219500 *	046
	331353	392408	478534	586318	759870	856451	914396	1011296	1121573 *	1279700 *	047
	142	1776	29820	8432	20652	25266	14119	4402	8224 *	11700 *	048
	332419	404905	514922	623825	709648	804327	918046	1030978		1368200 *	049
	287873	384479	536596	651608	810738	906655	976965	1105563	-164102 *	1506900 *	050
	-17968	-2183	31406	37979	-15184	-334448	-57231	-61555		-84800 *	051

	Item	1978	1979		1980	1981	1982	1983	1984	1985
	Investment Financing, at current prices									
052	Gross domestic capital formation	137496	152050	I	193060	225638	223155	276069	291215	298404
053	Gross national saving	116329	123880	I	146803	159720	188815	202796	222520	244497
054	Gross domestic saving	119951	130105	I	152197	171755	201737	209497	233971	262095
055	Net factor income from abroad	-3622	-6225	I	-5394	-12035	-12922	-6701	-11451	-17598
	Per Capita GNP, Baht									
056	Current prices	10900	12157	I	14064	15675	17001	18384	19257	20101
057	Constant *1972I 1988* prices	6064	6226	I	19492	20076	20720	21571	22233	22686
	PRODUCTION								*Thousand metric tons;*	
	Agriculture [c]									
058	1. Sugar cane	20244	12460		18652	30260	23916	23325	25053	24000
059	2. Tapioca roots	16358	11101		17744	20000	19000	20000	19263	15255
060	3. Rice	16791	16910		16800	17800	17200	19436	19888	20599
061	4. Maize	3030	3300		3150	4000	3350	3900	4500	5030
062	5. Rubber	467	531		501	502	552	587	629	722
063	6. Coconut	688	628		537	710	861	882	902	981
064	7. Mung beans	259	251		261	284	281	288	352	323
065	8. Jute and kenaf	310	260		210	208	230	233	205	266
066	9. Cotton	74	143		193	176	122	119	79	102
	Mining									
067	1. Gypsum	280.9	352.4		412.0	540.4	753.4	760.4	1110.7	1273.5
068	2. Marl	1459.7	2261.7		1938.6	1786.7	457.5	...	...	...
069	3. Fluorite ore [d]	259.8	259.5		294.4	271.0	280.6	237.7	295.2	354.6
	Manufacturing									
070	1. Cement	5044.5	5203.7		5336.8	6262.5	6609.0	7263.5	8240.0	7915.7
071	2. Sugar	1664.2	1841.7		855.6	1665.1	2768.1	2035.3	2431.1	2293.6
072	3. Synthetic fiber	90.8	99.0		103.2	117.7	101.8	110.5	115.2	126.5
073	4. Tin plate	44.0	64.8		70.2	78.8	62.2	73.1	92.0	68.2
074	5. Galvanized iron sheet	84.8	101.5		124.0	151.6	126.9	123.7	153.8	128.7
075	6. Jute products	164.3	190.9		202.4	198.7	190.8	174.3	192.9	157.1
	Production Indexes								*Period*	
076	Agriculture, *1979-81 = 100*	97.7	95.4		100.0	105.5	106.7	110.0	113.1	121.7
077	Mining, *1988 = 100*	65.7	72.6		75.3	71.4	68.7	65.8	76.9	77.2
078	Manufacturing, *1988 = 100*	50.4	54.6		56.2	59.8	61.2	66.4	70.9	70.6
	ENERGY								*Annual*	
	Crude petroleum, *'000 m.t.*									
079	Production	8	9		8	17	16	351	788	1158
080	Exports	0	27		0	0	0	0	0	0
081	Imports	8254	8800		8382	8182	7271	7930	6902	6745
082	Consumption	8378	8782		8180	7932	7672	7813	7630	7942
	Coal *'000 m.t.*									
083	Production	...	...		0	2	2	0	0	0
084	Exports	0	0		1	1	0	1	1	0
085	Imports	13	4		15	15	99	99	145	214
086	Consumption	13	4		14	16	101	98	144	214
	Electricity, *Mn kWh*									
087	Production	13204	13362		15112	16124	17450	19770	22029	24179
088	Exports	6	7		8	9	13	25	22	20
089	Imports	222	788		766	740	752	701	710	723
090	Consumption	13420	13087		15870	16855	18189	20446	22717	24882
	Retail prices, *Baht/litre*									
091	Gasoline	...	...		...	...	13.45	12.73	11.70	11.70
092	Diesel	2.64	3.95		6.47	7.39	7.39	7.06	6.70	6.70

1986	1987	1988	1989	1990	1991	1992	1993	1994	1995	
293236	362347	508354	651175	902978	1070998	1130500	1277632	1475070 *	1794400 *	052
276895	357480	499522	633008	738329	874065	957200	1059215	1219051 *	1427800 *	053
299332	379874	524292	656676	765767	914185	1013706	1127879	1296703 *	1518900 *	054
-22437	-22394	-24770	-23668	-27438	-40120	-56506	-68664	-77652 *	-91100 *	055
21099	23911	28256	33204	38657	43605	48359	53357	60008 *	68536 *	056
23425	25334	28256	31293	34430	36739	39063	41696	44833 *	47898 *	057

Calendar year

1986	1987	1988	1989	1990	1991	1992	1993	1994	1995	
24441	27200	36670	33560	40563	47430	34712	37569	50459	54616	058
19554	22300	24264	20700	19705	20356	20203	19091	15374	17340	059
19026	17072	20653	21858	17026	19809	20184	19098	20125	20550	060
4300	2310	4500	4100	3800	3600	3400	3300	3900	4060	061
782	921	975	1180	1250	1340	1500	1553	1737	1810	062
1024	1048	1102	1150	1141	1103	1129	1170	1148	1130	063
301	267	333	356	303	304	261	231	256	253	064
240	212	182	165	191	139	140	139	116	82	065
57	74	106	86	97	129	99	67	78	79	066
1665.6	3030.9	4549.0	5477.2	5753.4	7196.4	7111.1	7454.8	8142.8	8533.2	067
...	295.5	136.1	535.1	366.9	717.7	675.3	563.7	561.6	610.6	068
197.1	104.6	76.3	98.4	94.8	62.1	56.5	48.4	23.7	24.1	069
7913.6	9850.4	11514.4	15024.6	18053.9	19163.7	21711.1	26299.9	29929.3	33445.4	070
2607.2	2432.2	2864.7	3836.8	3382.9	4031.0	4857.3	3650.5	3973.7	5201.8	071
134.9	142.4	155.6	202.3	225.0	306.1	359.9	397.7	468.3	540.8	072
104.4	119.3	148.2	149.5	173.1	190.4	226.4	222.4	236.7	250.5	073
140.9	171.7	190.0	200.6	208.5	213.3	217.3	249.8	307.4	370.0	074
198.5	195.6	191.6	191.6	152.3	136.5	132.1	118.9	117.3	76.0	075

averages

1986	1987	1988	1989	1990	1991	1992	1993	1994	1995	
112.8	113.0	124.7	130.3	124.3	133.6	134.3	132.6	137.3	139.7	076
76.4	84.8	100.0	108.6	123.9	143.2	149.0	158.6	168.8	171.0	077
75.2	85.5	100.0	119.0	135.0	145.0	160.0	177.0	193.3	216.3	078

values

1986	1987	1988	1989	1990	1991	1992	1993	1994	1995	
1132	956	1088	1066	1196	1222	1317	1247	1324	...	079
0	0	0	0	0	0	0	0	0	...	080
7171	7860	7502	10143	10860	10996	13792	16096	18124	...	081
8427	8769	8973	11118	11937	12337	15151	17442	19448	...	082
0	0	0	0	0	0	16	12	...	...	083
0	1	0	0	0	0	0	0	...	...	084
183	219	304	300	162	331	342	659	...	...	085
183	218	304	300	162	331	355	672	...	...	086
25932	29992	33964	37406	44175	50186	57098	63405	70488	...	087
17	18	20	23	31	40	41	49	57	...	088
758	416	430	643	652	595	481	645	920	...	089
26673	30390	34374	32834	38342	43398	49304	56279	65752	...	090
9.50	8.90	8.85	8.45	9.15	10.06	9.29	9.09	8.57	...	091
6.45	6.30	6.28	6.10	6.72	8.03	7.83	7.84	7.39	...	092

	Item	1978	1979	1980	1981	1982	1983	1984	1985
	PRICE INDEXES								*Period*
093	Consumer (Bangkok), *1990 = 100*	48.0	52.9	63.4	71.9	75.8	78.3	78.9	81.4
094	Food	51.2	55.9	66.5	73.5	76.0	80.0	79.1	77.5
095	Non-Food	45.5	50.7	61.2	70.8	75.6	77.2	78.8	84.2
096	Consumer (Whole Kingdom), *1990 = 100*	49.4	54.3	65.0	73.3	77.1	80.0	80.7	82.6
097	Food	52.6	57.4	68.7	75.9	78.1	82.0	81.1	79.1
098	Non-Food	47.1	52.0	62.4	71.2	76.4	78.4	80.3	85.0
099	Wholesale, *1985 = 100*	68.5	76.2	91.5	100.3	101.2	103.3	100.1	100.0
100	Implicit GDP deflator, *1972I 1988*	179.9	195.5 I	72.5	78.6	82.5	85.6	86.8	88.7
	MONEY AND BANKING								*Billion Baht;*
101	Money supply (M1)	54.7	63.5	71.6	73.9	78.9	83.0	88.8	85.9
102	Currency in circulation	33.2	40.8	45.9	47.8	54.0	59.6	63.5	64.0
103	Demand deposits	21.5	22.7	25.7	26.1	25.0	23.4	25.2	21.9
104	Quasi-money	125.6	142.0	180.2	219.0	284.9	367.5	449.1	507.6
105	Money supply (M2)	180.3	205.5	251.8	292.9	363.8	450.5	537.9	593.5
106	Foreign assets (net)	27.4	33.1	42.4	34.3	38.6	16.5	28.3	37.9
107	Domestic credit	213.4	257.5	305.9	357.3	437.5	549.7	643.9	697.9
108	Claims on govt. sector (net)	48.4	54.8	74.7	92.9	124.5	135.3	154.4	156.9
109	Claims on private sector e	149.3	182.8	206.1	241.6	286.7	384.3	447.2	495.6
110	Claims on other financial insts.	15.8	19.9	25.0	22.8	26.3	30.1	42.3	45.4
111	Other items	-60.5	-85.0	-96.5	-98.7	-112.2	-115.7	-134.3	-142.2
	Deposit Money Banks								
112	Demand deposits	23.5	25.4	28.3	29.7	28.2	25.7	27.9	25.8
113	Savings deposits	15.0	18.2	28.1	38.6	61.7	95.5	106.0	117.1
114	Time deposits	117.8	129.4	157.7	188.7	231.4	282.9	358.4	409.4
115	Domestic credits outstanding f	115.6	140.4	156.5	180.6	214.1	283.8	338.0	376.7
	Interest Rates								*Per cent;*
	On deposits								
116	Savings	4.50	5.50	8.00	9.00	9.00	9.00	9.00	9.00
117	Time: 6 months	7.00	7.00	10.00	11.00	11.00	11.00	13.00	13.00
118	12 months	8.00	9.00	12.00	13.00	13.00	13.00	13.00	13.00
	On loans and discounts								
119	Commercial bills	15.00	15.00	18.00	19.00	19.00	17.50	17.50	17.50
120	Export credit	15.00	15.00	18.00	19.00	19.00	17.50	17.50	17.50
121	Other commercial g	12.50	15.00	18.00	19.00	19.00	17.50	17.50	17.50
	GOVERNMENT FINANCE h								
	Central Government								*Million Baht;*
122	Current revenue	65208	78675	95557	111843	115980	143436	148242	160652
123	Taxes	60252	73637	88473	100906	105076	129062	136246	144947
124	Non-taxes	4956	5038	7084	10937	10904	14374	11996	15705
125	Current expenditure	58518	70166	94370	105259	125904	137355	154481	166937
126	Current surplus/deficit	6690	8509	1187	6584	-9924	6081	-6239	-6285
127	Capital receipts	–	–	–	–	–	–	–	–
128	Capital expenditure	18991	19290	26603	28185	31113	29733	27747	33091
129	Capital account surplus/deficit	-18991	-19290	-26603	-28185	-31113	-29733	-27747	-33091
130	Net lending	–	–	–	–	417	1967	2911	2630
131	Non-budgetary surplus/deficit	-14	-2146	1767	372	-2331	-1104	1362	-3079
132	Overall surplus/deficit	-12315	-12927	-23649	-21229	-43785	-26723	-35535	-45085
	Financing								
133	Domestic borrowing (net)	13900	12863	25666	22106	43545	25375	35869	31588
134	Foreign borrowing (net) }	-620	-928	-1207	-1023	779	928	-715	14190
135	Foreign grants }								
136	Use of cash balances	-965	992	-810	146	-539	420	381	-693

	1986	1987	1988	1989	1990	1991	1992	1993	1994	1995	
averages											
	82.9	85.0	88.2	93.8	100.0	105.4	109.2	113.3	119.8	126.6	093
	77.5	79.1	82.8	91.2	100.0	106.3	110.2	114.1	123.2	132.9	094
	86.6	89.1	92.0	95.7	100.0	104.6	108.4	112.7	117.2	122.1	095
	84.2	86.3	89.6	94.4	100.0	105.7	110.0	113.7	119.5	126.4	096
	79.6	81.4	85.5	92.6	100.0	107.0	111.8	114.2	122.1	132.0	097
	87.2	89.5	92.3	95.6	100.0	104.8	108.8	113.4	117.7	122.7	098
	99.6	105.5	114.2	119.4	123.5	132.0	132.3	131.7	136.8	148.2	099
	90.2	94.4	100.0	106.1	112.3	118.8	123.9	128.1	134.0 *	142.5 *	100
As of end of period											
	103.4	132.4	148.5	174.7	195.4	222.4	249.7	296.2	346.4	388.3	101
	72.1	86.7	99.0	119.0	137.5	149.3	180.2	208.6	241.9	284.1	102
	31.4	45.7	49.5	55.7	58.0	73.1	69.6	87.6	104.5	104.2	103
	569.3	676.2	807.6	1032.4	1333.7	1610.0	1868.1	2210.9	2482.9	2922.3	104
	672.8	808.6	956.1	1207.1	1529.1	1832.4	2117.8	2507.1	2829.4	3310.6	105
	80.9	107.5	145.7	247.5	307.1	413.7	449.0	453.9	147.9	7.6	106
	740.7	871.2	1007.4	1207.3	1531.7	1768.6	2087.0	2560.4	3300.7	4059.6	107
	173.4	175.5	128.1	68.6	17.5	-86.7	-147.8	-205.5	-289.8	-395.9	108
	516.9	630.4	811.4	1062.1	1427.8	1742.5	2099.3	2614.1	3399.4	4203.2	109
	50.4	65.3	67.9	76.6	86.4	112.8	135.5	151.8	191.0	252.3	110
	-148.8	-170.2	-197.0	-247.7	-309.7	-349.9	-418.2	-507.3	-619.2	-756.6	111
	33.6	48.1	51.8	57.3	58.1	72.9	75.1	92.4	117.1	157.5	112
	164.1	234.1	283.4	365.4	398.3	443.0	528.0	677.2	750.5	734.7	113
	425.9	464.3	552.0	702.8	975.3	1223.6	1421.2	1644.2	1868.4	2331.5	114
	386.6	462.7	602.6	796.8	1086.3	1333.2	1617.3	2028.4	2630.1	3283.7	115
As end of period											
	7.25	5.50	6.25-7.25	7.25	10.00-12.00	8.50	6.00-6.50	5.00	5.00	5.00	116
	9.50	7.00	7.00-9.50	9.50	13.00-15.50	10.50	8.00-9.00	7.00	8.25-10.00	10.25-11.00	117
	9.50	7.25	7.75-9.50	9.50-10.25	12.00-15.50	10.50	8.50	7.00	8.25-10.25	10.25-11.00	118
	15.00	15.00	15.00	15.00	19.00	19.00	16.00-16.50	14.50	14.00-14.75	16.00-16.50	119
	15.00	15.00	15.00	15.00	19.00	19.00	16.00-16.50	14.50	14.00-14.75	16.00-16.50	120
	15.00	15.00	15.00	15.00	19.00	19.00	16.00-16.50	14.50	14.00-14.75	16.00-16.50	121
Calendar year											
	169925	202021	258169	327149	411652	462608	511317	574932	680455	777286	122
	154202	185690	241745	302057	385742	427214	456572	522229	619408	711095	123
	15723	16331	16424	25092	25910	35394	54745	52703	61047	66191	124
	173557	180671	193542	226179	249210	283718	327092	375758	395557	441973	125
	-3632	21350	64627	100970	162442	178890	184225	199174	284898	375313	126
	–	–	–	–	–	–	–	–	–	–	127
	30722	31317	29547	37619	55263	78520	115519	145189	183659	200348	128
	-30722	-31317	-29547	-37619	-55263	-78520	-115519	-145189	-183659	-200348	129
	7024	...	109	2241	1177	–	–	–	–	–	130
	-741	...	1601	-381	-497	7337	4105	5847	-3753	-8718	131
	-42119	-5539	36572	60730	105505	107707	72811	59832	97486	166247	132
	50249	10638	-28824	-11150	-11864	-46872	-28613	-44347	-58872	-30574	133
	-6452	-3271	-4537	-6197	-39217	-3780	-17354	-4353	-17426	-4855	134
											135
	-1678	-1828	-3211	-43383	-54424	-57055	-26844	-11132	-21188	-130818	136

	Item	1978	1979	1980	1981	1982	1983	1984	1985
	Expenditure by Function, Central Govt.								
137	Total	77509	89456	120973	133444	157017	167088	182228	200028
138	General public services	9526	12429	17705	19424	18134	24556	24304	25765
139	Defense	15310	17336	24398	25917	31350	31685	36034	43184
140	Education	...	...	...	...	...	...	...	...
141	Health	...	...	...	...	...	...	...	...
142	Social security & welfare	23831	27703	35474	37586	47940	50524	55419	58949
143	Housing & community amenities	...	...	...	...	...	...	...	...
144	Economic services	17012	17093	22804	26218	27902	27969	28573	30534
145	Others	11830	14895	20592	24299	31691	32354	37898	41596
	EXTERNAL TRADE								**Million Baht;**
146	Exports, fob	83065	108179	133197	153001	159728	146472	175237	193366
147	Imports, cif	108899	146161	188686	216746	196616	236609	245155	251169
148	Trade balance	-25834	-37982	-55489	-63745	-36888	-90137	-69918	-57803
	Exports, by SITC section								
149	Food & live animals	40617	50087	59338	80038	86371	73755	86482	86582
150	Beverage & tobacco	1173	1266	1393	1758	2599	1860	1698	1648
151	Crude materials excl. fuels	12571	17862	19095	16722	15134	16288	18875	19611
152	Mineral fuels, etc.	14	33	86	37	40	30	411	2448
153	Animal, vegetable oil & fats	40	22	222	232	298	270	432	583
154	Chemicals	444	722	936	1191	1253	1673	2187	2440
155	Basic manufactures	17479	23532	29474	26941	26587	26002	29187	35860
156	Machines, transport equipment	2719	3972	7618	7662	8293	8356	11959	16977
157	Misc. manufactured goods	4213	6149	8467	11731	13404	14756	19558	24030
158	Unclassified goods	1982	2691	3777	2650	2060	1332	1286	1433
159	Re-exports	1813	1843	2791	4039	3689	2150	3162	1754
	Exports, by principal commodity								
160	1. Textile products	6866	8795	9643	12570	14005	14351	19155	23578
161	2. Rice	10424	15592	19508	26336	22510	20157	25932	22524
162	3. Precious stones	1707	2250	3240	4486	4671	6214	6129	6350
163	4. Jewelry	352	502	533	526	578	1028	1254	2168
164	5. Shrimp, fresh & frozen	1500	2372	1961	2136	2764	3164	2799	3439
165	6. Rubber	8030	12351	12351	10841	9490	11787	13004	13567
166	7. Tapioca products	10892	9891	14887	16446	19752	15387	16600	14969
	Imports, by SITC section								
167	Food & live animals	2846	3899	5763	5795	5061	6501	7511	9442
168	Beverage & tobacco	1013	1214	1518	1588	2327	1268	1681	2256
169	Crude materials excl. fuels	7316	11415	10755	13297	11516	14376	15418	16491
170	Mineral fuels, etc.	22851	32647	58733	65100	60765	57065	57353	56719
171	Animal, vegetable oil & fats	272	473	1458	903	438	781	1130	493
172	Chemicals	14979	21794	22352	26761	24848	31804	31681	35166
173	Basic manufactures	18479	26345	28152	34512	30597	39034	38913	42135
174	Machines, transport equipment	33635	37742	43102	54371	46503	68361	71988	70550
175	Misc. manufactured goods	4843	7919	10959	10899	11195	14039	15525	14045
176	Unclassified goods [i]	2665	2713	5894	3520	3366	3380	3955	3872
	Direction of Trade								**Million US dollars;**
177	Exports, Total	4086.2	5300.9	6501.3	7026.9	6934.6	6367.7	7414.2	7122.9
178	1. United States	450.5	593.8	823.1	905.5	880.8	953.2	1273.0	1401.6
179	2. Japan	829.5	1125.7	981.8	995.6	951.1	960.3	965.1	951.4
180	3. Singapore	330.9	451.6	502.7	550.8	500.7	517.9	623.3	565.6
181	4. Hong Kong	218.2	258.3	329.8	337.3	341.6	316.6	281.3	287.9
182	5. Germany	169.3	215.3	269.4	226.7	232.5	222.0	244.1	266.3
183	6. Malaysia	211.2	233.6	292.4	319.9	355.7	285.3	350.8	354.8
184	7. United Kingdom	63.1	97.4	121.7	113.1	131.7	130.0	164.6	173.2
185	8. Netherlands	599.1	600.4	859.8	855.0	912.8	690.6	740.5	506.0
186	9. France	80.7	98.5	107.1	130.2	132.0	122.6	127.5	132.7
187	10. Belgium-Luxembourg	73.0	95.9	161.9	74.2	75.2	62.3	70.6	85.5

1986	1987	1988	1989	1990	1991	1992	1993	1994	1995	
204279	211988	223089	263798	304473	362238	442611	521066	579216	642321	137
25761	26995	28059	35360	42947	46350	54929	55652	62640	73651	138
41125	41485	44149	47830	57422	62090	74076	75564	85400	96331	139
...	...	...	...	...	...	...	...	...	...	140
										141
60156	63421	65647	79760	95097	115700	153381	194421	220300	242417	142
										143
29928	31357	30924	40038	53420	85040	107741	145597	158590	169964	144
47309	48730	54310	60810	55587	53058	52484	49832	52286	59958	145
Calendar year										
233383	299853	403570	516315	589813	725630	824643	935862	1137600	1404253	146
241358	334209	513114	662679	844448	958831	1033244	1166595	1369035	1772257	147
-7975	-34356	-109544	-146364	-254635	-233201	-208601	-230733	-231435	-368004	148
101629	109341	137566	173474	166311	192016	210961	201576	235504	266744	149
1565	1428	1613	1777	2291	3401	4493	3858	4155	3549	150
20529	26751	35649	35337	33854	36984	40519	40336	56173	79781	151
1832	2099	3069	3700	4904	7220	8088	9639	8511	8956	152
225	307	180	160	164	166	168	176	543	497	153
3381	4528	4838	6457	8332	13998	15203	20388	24174	43548	154
43392	58751	76865	93563	108151	120871	136153	177578	189599	254861	155
24851	35522	63789	91801	130913	175692	220133	281136	380776	477068	156
33166	57773	75980	102709	126251	164155	178474	189948	227386	253947	157
1525	2590	2771	6216	6987	8790	9026	9473	8692 }	15302	158
1288	763	1250	1121	1655	2337	1425	1754	2087 }		159
31268	48555	58625	74027	84472	109524	111837	116669	133469	140331	160
20315	22703	34676	45462	27770	30516	36214	32947	39188	48759	161
8150	11550	13958	16419	22045	23438 }	36582	41030	44684	50864	162
5014	8257	9725	11974	12813	12465 }					163
4391	5749	9698	16057	20454	26681	31696	37843	49155	50205	164
15116	20539	27189	26423	23557	24954	28925	29180	41820	59851	165
19086	20661	21844	23974	23136	24368	29611	21736	18774	18003	166
13087	13946	24062	29999	33562	41915	44823	42371	45395	51306	167
1996	1515	2625	3529	5481	5625	5379	6134	6043	6549	168
16184	24669	34589	45143	54051	59356	65801	70254	78435	93692	169
32354	44177	38829	59819	78346	87661	83758	86457	91621	117663	170
153	175	480	663	635	685	983	1063	1244	1795	171
38794	50876	63657	74204	85591	88345	104321	113941	135521	179042	172
43655	65384	108516	149806	186902	231966	224363	238761	275283	364897	173
74215	108662	204144	251001	348248	388213	440712	536098	660201	31820	174
15553	16854	23957	29051	24781	28667	30742	37044	38600	46421	175
5367	7951	12255	19464	26851	26398	32362	34472	36692	879072	176
Calendar year										
8864.3	11563.2	15910.3	20174.8	23071.6	28811.0	32472.4	37157.7	46043.9	56919.5	177
1606.1	2163.3	3200.4	4357.7	5240.4	6067.7	7302.7	8005.0	9525.8	10226.6	178
1260.3	1731.7	2544.5	3421.5	3969.5	5134.8	5686.0	6299.8	7727.7	9302.6	179
786.9	1049.3	1224.1	1431.9	1695.7	2335.9	2822.5	4458.7	6167.3	7750.2	180
354.1	488.3	710.8	869.2	1037.8	1347.8	1506.7	1959.7	2387.2	2779.1	181
412.0	573.4	737.0	818.0	1198.2	1469.7	1427.5	1479.2	1597.4	1726.6	182
381.3	387.6	472.9	585.0	575.0	684.1	841.5	1040.8	1671.8	2266.6	183
283.1	416.9	588.2	745.7	936.5	1028.4	1172.2	1188.4	1345.5	1594.3	184
646.7	776.2	870.4	974.9	1114.6	1247.8	1404.9	1156.5	1258.6	1628.4	185
201.7	284.3	379.5	441.5	563.4	699.4	739.7	773.3	810.3	1033.4	186
89.1	133.4	212.5	257.3	348.3	662.4	458.1	724.9	661.2	737.7	187

	Item	1978	1979	1980	1981	1982	1983	1984	1985
188	Imports, Total	5355.2	7164.3	9212.6	9954.1	8531.5	10282.9	10415.3	9259.5
189	1. Japan	1645.4	1843.2	1952.4	2413.6	2003.6	2815.6	2802.5	2450.3
190	2. United States	734.8	1122.6	1332.4	1296.5	1144.1	1299.0	1408.9	1052.0
191	3. Singapore	217.5	335.4	598.6	695.4	541.5	635.8	822.2	688.9
192	4. Germany	310.0	388.7	401.6	426.8	331.5	481.1	436.7	500.4
193	5. Malaysia	67.2	122.0	165.9	268.5	444.1	553.8	504.7	547.0
194	6. Korea, Rep. of	81.4	116.6	197.5	139.0	156.0	243.6	291.1	186.3
195	7. China, People's Rep. of	83.9	241.9	416.6	320.7	233.7	265.2	318.0	222.7
196	8. United Kingdom	204.8	230.6	246.5	266.2	218.4	234.4	242.1	233.2
197	9. Australia	120.9	160.1	173.4	194.0	166.4	186.1	212.3	152.8
198	10. France	70.0	123.7	93.4	176.5	126.9	156.3	166.1	249.1
	Trade Indexes								*1990 = 100*
	Quantum index								
199	Exports	25.2	26.9	28.0	31.2	35.0	31.7	38.2	41.1
200	Imports	29.4	33.8	35.2	34.2	30.3	38.6	39.4	37.1
	Unit value index								
201	Exports	55.3	67.7	80.0	82.4	76.6	77.7	77.0	79.1
202	Imports	43.8	51.1	63.4	74.9	76.9	72.5	73.6	80.1
203	Terms of trade	126.4	132.5	126.2	109.9	99.7	107.1	104.6	98.7
	BALANCE OF PAYMENTS								*Million US dollars;*
204	Merchandise exports, fob	4045	5234	6448	6902	6835	6308	7337	7077
205	Merchandise imports, fob	-4903	-6785	-8349	-8932	-7566	-9169	-9263	-8410
206	Trade balance	-858	-1551	-1901	-2030	-731	-2861	-1926	-1333
207	Other goods, services and income	-334	-595	-384	-708	-458	-303	-386	-358
208	Credit	1088	1429	2125	2352	2576	2919	3078	3165
209	Debit	-1422	-2024	-2509	-3060	-3034	-3222	-3464	-3523
210	Unrequited transfer	40	60	216	169	183	277	175	166
211	Private	6	23	75	50	75	153	60	47
212	Official	34	37	141	119	108	124	115	119
213	Current balance	-1152	-2086	-2069	-2569	-1006	-2887	-2137	-1525
214	Direct investment	50	51	187	287	187	355	411	159
215	Portfolio investment	76	180	96	45	69	15	-6	141
216	Other long-term capital	520	1246	1824	2020	1128	1105	1405	1326
217	Other short-term capital	715	500	-64	120	58	33	666	227
218	Deposit Money Banks	...	...	...	...	...	672	67	-533
219	Net errors and omissions	-233	20	-180	143	-517	593	85	133
220	Overall balance	-24	-89	-206	46	-81	-114	491	-72
221	Allocation of SDRs	–	24	25	24	–	–	–	–
222	Monetary movements	24	65	181	-70	81	114	-491	72
	INTERNATIONAL RESERVES								*Million US dollars;*
223	Total	2557	3129	3026	2727	2652	2556	2688	3003
224	Gold, national valuation	548	1286	1466	995	1114	949	768	813
225	Foreign exchange	1974	1794	1552	1671	1513	1561	1890	2157
226	Reserve position in the Fund	–	–	–	–	–	30	28	32
227	SDRs	35	49	8	61	25	16	2	1
	EXCHANGE RATES								*Baht per*
228	End of period	20.39	20.43	20.63	23.00	23.00	23.00	27.15	26.65
229	Average of period	20.34	20.42	20.48	21.82	23.00	23.00	23.64	27.16
	EXTERNAL INDEBTEDNESS								*Million US dollars;*
230	Total outstanding and disbursed	5029	6645	8297	10852	12238	13902	15013	17552
231	Long-term	2686	3938	5646	7116	8351	9557	10558	13230
232	Public and publicly guaranteed	1747	2695	3943	5017	6034	6902	7186	9860
233	Private non-guaranteed	939	1243	1703	2099	2317	2655	3372	3370

	1986	1987	1988	1989	1990	1991	1992	1993	1994	1995	
	9165.4	12998.3	20298.2	25372.9	33407.9	37924.5	40686.1	46064.7	54334.2	69761.4	188
	2420.8	3376.3	5493.3	7736.1	10143.9	11037.7	11905.2	13963.4	16442.1	21761.1	189
	1312.0	1619.7	2752.5	2841.5	3600.4	3989.3	4776.1	5379.4	6445.7	7620.6	190
	600.9	1012.2	1510.5	1871.0	2479.8	2989.8	2970.2	2969.1	3439.8	4164.9	191
	527.3	771.0	1090.0	1311.0	1701.8	2094.5	2164.6	2482.1	3212.5	3733.7	192
	384.8	521.3	425.8	649.7	1125.4	1190.5	1595.2	1674.4	2640.5	3020.0	193
	218.1	311.1	562.3	741.5	1045.5	1593.5	1785.5	1947.8	1978.4	2604.1	194
	263.1	503.9	679.4	744.4	1107.0	1149.4	1219.5	904.5	1388.2	2027.6	195
	294.7	409.4	600.2	650.9	906.8	849.0	944.2	1059.3	1151.1	1446.4	196
	161.1	227.5	347.1	508.0	560.7	661.8	912.4	951.3	1070.9	1357.3	197
	150.4	197.6	490.9	409.7	817.2	521.4	944.0	916.9	750.9	1756.1	198

Period averages

	48.2	58.2	71.9	89.4	100.0	119.4	133.8	149.5	177.0	203.3	199
	38.4	49.2	68.4	82.5	100.0	108.7	116.7	130.8	150.5	177.0	200
	82.1	87.8	95.2	98.0	100.0	103.3	104.5	105.5	108.9	117.9	201
	74.4	80.5	88.8	95.1	100.0	104.4	104.9	105.2	107.5	120.2	202
	110.3	109.1	107.1	103.0	100.0	98.9	99.6	100.3	101.3	98.1	203

Calendar year

	8829	11609	15855	19939	22881	28330	32244	36553	44649	56036	204
	-8442	-11976	-17812	-22751	-29493	-34053	-36104	-40606	-48041	-63793	205
	387	-367	-1957	-2812	-6612	-5723	-3860	-4053	-3392	-7757	206
	-338	-161	201	171	-737	-1959	-2874	-2823	-5537	-5996	207
	3337	4171	5951	7053	8486	9498	10828	13211	14213	18790	208
	-3675	-4332	-5750	-6882	-9223	-11457	-13702	-16034	-19750	-24786	209
	225	225	236	246	213	299	646	750	1128	626	210
	64	100	46	47	26	186	604	717	1067	587	211
	161	125	190	199	187	113	42	33	61	39	212
	274	-303	-1520	-2395	-7136	-7383	-6088	-6126	-7801	-13127	213
	261	182	1080	1731	2402	1415	1544	1404	922	1153	214
	97	499	447	1429	457	48	531	4128	1373	3102	215
	-268	-61	-167	1159	793	3234	2188	1864	2311	5008	216
	348	224	1518	1630	4489	2042	1707	2685	2066	3556	217
	-835	239	850	-297	1603	4598	3682	434	5511	9060	218
	567	154	246	734	1182	194	-521	-475	-207	-1516	219
	444	934	2454	3991	3790	4148	3043	3914	4175	7236	220
	—	—	—	—	—	—	—	—	—	—	221
	-444	-934	-2454	-3991	-3790	-4148	-3043	-3914	-4175	-7236	222

As of end of period

	3776	5211	7112	10508	14273	18416	21182	25440	30279	36945	223
	972	1204	1015	993	968	899	823	967	947	963	224
	2736	3906	5997	9461	13247	17287	20012	24078	28884	35463	225
	35	41	39	38	45	222	335	373	416	474	226
	33	60	61	16	13	8	12	22	32	45	227

US dollar

	26.13	25.07	25.24	25.69	25.29	25.28	25.52	25.54	25.09	25.16 [j]	228
	26.30	25.72	25.29	25.70	25.59	25.52	25.40	25.32	25.15	24.89 [k]	229

As of end of year

	18505	20305	21674	23452	28204	35894	39612	45836	60990	...	230
	14596	16669	16211	17067	19881	23402	24885	26095	31811	...	231
	11488	13832	13195	12428	12570	13358	13427	14553	16672	...	232
	3108	2837	3016	4640	7311	10044	11459	11542	15140	...	233

	Item	1978	1979	1980	1981	1982	1983	1984	1985
234	Short-term	2094	2340	2303	2878	3041	3305	3551	3200
235	Use of IMF credit	249	367	348	858	846	1040	903	1122
	Debt service								*Transactions*
236	Principal repayments on LT debt	606	640	782	628	801	1015	1384	1661
237	Interest on long-term debt	195	321	473	710	714	750	848	913
238	Interest on short-term debt	276	338	328	442	337	349	300	377
	Average terms of new commitments								
239	Interest (%)	7.0	7.8	9.5	10.0	9.3	8.2	8.8	8.3
240	Maturity (years)	17.4	17.4	16.8	17.3	19.0	20.2	16.7	18.5
241	Grace period (years)	5.1	4.7	5.3	5.1	5.5	7.1	6.1	9.8
242	Grant element (%)	19.8	16.7	6.6	4.6	5.7	13.2	8.8	11.5

Footnotes:

a   Prior to 1986, the labor force refers to the population aged 11 years and over; thereafter, the labor force definition has been changed to refer to the population aged 13 years and over.

b   For 1983-93, item includes seasonally inactive labor force.

c   For the crop year.

d   Prior to 1988, item includes metallurgical and low-grade ores.

e   Refers to claims on non-financial public enterprises and claims on business and household sectors.

f   Refers to loans and overdrafts.

g   Refers to discount rates for bills on raw materials for industrial use and bills on sales on credit of industrial products.

h   The use of foreign funds is excluded from expenditure items, therefore, foreign disbursements are not shown under financing items.

i   Includes gold.

j   Refers to end of November only.

k   Refers to average for January to November only.

1986	1987	1988	1989	1990	1991	1992	1993	1994	1995	
2840	2664	4800	6112	8322	12492	14727	19740	29179	...	234
1069	972	662	273	1	0	0	0	0	...	235

during the year

2021	1887	2585	2404	2984	2261	3197	6311	5947	4357 *	236
1026	1055	1123	1087	1357	1782	1876	1820	1823	2041 *	237
228	205	360	491	650	874	834	989	1468	...	238

5.6	5.2	5.5	7.4	5.1	5.0	6.5	4.3	4.8	...	239
18.5	19.1	17.0	12.9	21.3	19.0	17.9	20.0	16.7	...	240
7.5	6.4	5.8	4.8	6.8	4.7	6.2	5.4	4.9	...	241
29.1	31.9	28.8	13.1	35.5	33.4	23.2	37.7	31.2	...	242

	Item	1978	1979	1980	1981	1982	1983	1984	1985
001	**POPULATION** [a]	90.9	91.4	91.8	92.2	92.7	93.2	93.6	*Thousand;* 94.1
002	**LABOR FORCE** [b]	...	...	25.1	...	...	...	30.9	*Thousand;* ...
003	Employed	...	...	20.6	...	...	...	29.5	...
004	Agriculture	...	...	9.0	...	...	...	14.7	...
005	Manufacturing ⎫								
006	Mining ⎬	...	...	1.2	...	...	...	0.9	...
007	Others ⎭	...	...	10.4	...	...	...	13.9	...
008	Unemployed	...	...	4.5	...	...	...	1.4	...
009	Unemployment rate, %	...	...	17.9	...	...	...	4.5	...
	NATIONAL ACCOUNTS *At Current Factor Cost*								*Thousand Pa'anga;*
010	GDP by Industrial Origin	31027	34710	40583	46897	52519	57880	63118	72518
011	Agriculture	12966	14478	15623	18317	20032	21000	23800	27400
012	Mining	195	225	321	418	430	412	394	408
013	Manufacturing	2303	2690	2843	2261	2458	2665	3770	4114
014	Electricity, gas and water	343	372	339	523	506	581	689	687
015	Construction	1497	1967	2361	2863	3126	5422	5412	5596
016	Trade	4439	4761	6806	6869	7758	8040	8361	10120
017	Transport and communications	1825	1999	3108	4423	4688	4948	4825	5576
018	Finance	2270	2566	2704	4131	4325	4745	4905	5806
019	Public administration ⎫								
020	Others ⎭	5189	5652	6477	7092	9196	10067	10962	12811
021	Indirect taxes less subsidies	5290	5249	6190	7266	8674	9679	10093	13480
022	GDP at current market prices	36318	39959	46773	54163	61193	67559	73211	85998
023	Net factor income from abroad	665	1338	2238	3360	3007	1742	2327	3787
024	GNP at current market prices	36983	41297	49011	57523	64200	69301	75538	89785
	At Current Market Prices								
025	Expenditure on GDP	36318	39959	46773	54163	61193	67559	73211	85998
026	Private consumption [c]	34451	39015	43392	53234	54408	72198	70694	85786
027	Government consumption	5344	5962	6936	7596	10343	9661	11585	13729
028	Gross fixed capital formation	8963	11236	13582	15332	17939	18171	17252	20004
029	Increase in stocks	1754	1218	476	679	1167	1655	290	2686
030	Exports of goods and services	10456	10421	14061	13744	16882	12605	19480	25910
031	Less: Imports of goods and services	24650	27893	31674	36422	39546	46731	46090	62117
032	Statistical discrepancy	–	–	–	–	–	–	–	–
	At Constant 1974/75 ǀ 1984/85 Factor Cost								
033	GDP by Industrial Origin	23153	23846	25198 ǀ	64301	66758	67961	69579	72518
034	Agriculture	10447	10373	10636 ǀ	24985	25945	23300	25500	27400
035	Mining	163	187	194 ǀ	579	566	500	434	408
036	Manufacturing	1412	1446	1468 ǀ	3131	3238	3234	4141	4114
037	Electricity, gas and water	255	312	349 ǀ	570	552	582	622	687
038	Construction	1063	1305	1438 ǀ	3965	4193	6570	5922	5596
039	Trade	2974	3050	3270 ǀ	9369	9837	9743	9196	10120
040	Transport and communications	1471	1543	2040 ǀ	5657	5945	5996	5307	5576
041	Finance	1807	1887	1903 ǀ	5123	5340	5647	5485	5806
042	Public administration ⎫								
043	Others ⎭	3562	3743	3901 ǀ	10922	11142	12389	12972	12811
044	Indirect taxes less subsidies	3478	3043	3211 ǀ	9962	11026	11365	11126	13480
045	GDP at *1974/75 ǀ 1984/85* market prices	26631	26889	28409 ǀ	74263	77784	79326	80705	85998
046	Net factor income from abroad	489	911	1334 ǀ	...	...	...	...	...
047	GNP at *1974/75 ǀ 1984/85* market prices	27120	27800	29743 ǀ	...	...	...	...	...

	1986	1987	1988	1989	1990	1991	1992	1993	1994	1995	
As of 1 July	94.5	95.0	95.5	96.0	96.4	96.9	97.4	97.7	97.1	97.7	001
Calendar year											
	23.7	...	...	...	32.0	...	...	...	35.0	...	002
	21.6	...	...	...	30.7	...	...	...	34.6	...	003
	10.6	...	...	...	11.7	...	...	...	13.6	...	004
											005
	0.6	...	...	...	4.7	...	...	...	7.7	...	006
	10.4	...	...	...	14.3	...	...	...	13.3	...	007
	2.1	...	...	...	1.3	...	...	...	0.4	...	008
	9.0	...	...	...	4.1	...	...	...	1.3	...	009
Fiscal year ending 30 June											
	86246	98288	104069	114186	123429	143249	158840	169252	178314	182025 *	010
	33600	38200	39500	41952	43351	52879	60536	65379	63843	63990 *	011
	391	435	532	625	578	477	527	548	617	482 *	012
	4489	4779	5588	6847	7543	7634	8140	8710	9715	9514 *	013
	1091	1299	1184	1799	1951	2295	2525	2752	2940	3126 *	014
	6606	6118	6190	7127	7759	7402	8227	9151	10615	10615 *	015
	11624	13036	15264	16593	17754	21534	23475	24883	27309	26995 *	016
	6772	8469	10816	10705	11573	11507	12650	13054	13677	14015 *	017
	6706	8399	7372	7750	7791	9732	11934	12672	14074	17111 *	018
											019
	14967	17553	17623	20788	25129	29789	30826	32103	35524	36177 *	020
	15775	18349	20752	20768	23482	28819	26028	29357	29777	31212 *	021
	102021	116637	124821	134954	146911	172068	184868	198609	208091	213237 *	022
	5603	4814	8569	5423	5490	5317	4228	...	...	...	023
	107624	121451	133390	140377	152401	177385	189096		...	...	024
	102021	116637	124821	134954	146911	172068	184868	198609	208091	213237 *	025
	106352	110628	130506	134747	134333	164840	173456	...	...	...	026
	16106	19428	20334	23303	28152	35026	35000	...	...	...	027
	22965	26212	26005	27043	26504	27429	28614	...	...	...	028
	1654	-349	2913	320	710	2369	3500	...	...	...	029
	26232	36072	28380	33597	46670	34132	38304	...	...	...	030
	71288	75354	83317	84056	89458	91728	94006	...	...	...	031
	–	–	–	–	–	–	–	...	...		032
	74241	76214	73987	75377	73316	77310	79990	82209	86899	88479 *	033
	27600	28100	25400	26542	25205	27683	29710	30502	32655	34412 *	034
	353	326	366	377	319	244	247	257	289	238 *	035
	3896	3563	3839	4242	4154	3905	3863	4085	4097	3913 *	036
	660	948	975	1016	1147	1202	1223	1247	1296	1378 *	037
	5725	4898	4707	5018	5143	4327	4375	4681	5275	5170 *	038
	10073	9757	10498	10002	9776	11015	11141	11671	12498	12292 *	039
	5868	6339	7438	6453	6373	5886	6004	6123	6411	6550 *	040
	5804	6497	5484	5345	5056	4623	5068	5234	5828	5954 *	041
											042
	14262	15786	15280	16382	16143	18425	18359	18409	18550	18572 *	043
	13579	14228	14753	13709	13949	15553	13107	14368	14221	14833 *	044
	87820	90442	88740	89086	87265	92863	93097	96577	101120	103312 *	045
	...	...	...	...	...	...	...	...	...	...	046
	...	...	...	...	...	...	...	...	...	...	047

	Item	1978	1979	1980	1981	1982	1983	1984	1985
	Investment Financing, at current prices								
048	Gross domestic capital formation	10717	12454	14058	16011	19106	19826	17542	22690
049	Gross national saving	-2812	-3680	-1317	-3307	-551	-12558	-6741	-9730
050	Gross domestic saving	-3477	-5018	-3555	-6667	-3558	-14300	-9068	-13517
051	Net factor income from abroad	665	1338	2238	3360	3007	1742	2327	3787
052	Foreign saving	13529	16134	15375	19318	19657	32384	24283	32420
053	Net transfer from abroad	7549	9331	10728	12879	23019	32491	24641	30487
054	Net borrowing from abroad	5980	6804	4646	6439	-3362	-107	-358	1933
	Per Capita GDP, Tongan dollars								
055	Current prices	400	437	510	587	660	725	782	914
056	Constant *1974/75| 1984/85* prices	293	294	309 |	805	839	851	862	914
	PRODUCTION							*Thousand metric tons;*	
	Agriculture								
057	1. Coconuts	75	75	100	98	50	50	55	52
058	2. Copra	9	8	13	12	4	4	6	5
059	3. Bananas	2	3	2	3	1	2	3	3
	Production Indexes							*Period*	
060	Agriculture, *1979-81 = 100*	93.9	96.3	101.5	102.1	92.6	91.0	94.3	92.2
061	Mining	...	...	...	...	...	...	...	...
062	Manufacturing	...	...	...	...	...	...	...	...
	ENERGY							*Annual*	
	Electricity, *Mn kWh*								
063	Production	7	9	10	12	12	12	12	12
064	Consumption	7	9	10	12	12	12	12	12
	PRICE INDEXES							*Period*	
065	Consumer, *November 1995 = 100*	23.9	25.2	30.8	35.4	39.2	43.0	43.1	50.3
066	Implicit GDP deflator, *1974/75 = 100| 1984/85 = 100*	136.4	148.6	164.6 |	72.9	78.7	85.2	90.7	100.0
	MONEY AND BANKING							*Thousand Pa'anga;*	
067	Money supply (M1)	4277	4387	5224	5185	6975	6573	9017	9985
068	Currency in circulation	2152	1936	2123	2404	2602	2452	2819	2732
069	Demand deposits	2125	2451	3101	2780	4374	4120	6198	7253
070	Quasi-money	5871	6415	7481	8222	8709	9488	10407	13928
071	Money supply (M2)	10148	10802	12705	13407	15684	16061	19424	23913
072	Foreign assets (net)	...	...	10327	10091	10564	9886	15265	17905
073	Domestic credit	...	...	1631	2562	4263	4841	2717	4129
074	Claims on gov't sector (net)	...	...	-1942	-2706	-3490	-4569	-6745	-8846
075	Claims on private sector	...	...	3573	5268	7752	9411	9462	12975
076	Claims on other financial insts.	...	...	—	—	—	—	—	—
077	Other items	...	...	747	753	857	1333	1443	1880
	Interest Rates							*Percent;*	
	On deposits								
078	Savings	...	...	4.00	5.00	5.00	5.00	5.00	5.00
079	Time: 6 months	...	...	5.25	5.50	5.50	5.50	5.50	5.50
080	over 12 months	...	...	5.50	6.00	6.00	6.00	6.00	6.00
	On loans and discounts								
081	Commercial bills	...	...	...	...	...	...	...	...
082	Export credit	...	...	8.50	8.50	8.50	8.50	8.50	8.50
083	Other commercial	...	...	8.50	8.50	8.50	8.50	8.50	8.50

1986	1987	1988	1989	1990	1991	1992	1993	1994	1995	
24619	25863	28918	27363	27214	29798	32114	...	...	...	048
-14834	-8605	-17450	-17673	-10084	-22481	-19360	...	...	...	049
-20437	-13419	-26019	-23096	-15574	-27798	-23588	...	...	...	050
5603	4814	8569	5423	5490	5317	4228	...	...	...	051
39453	34468	46368	45036	37298	52279	51474	...	...	...	052
37542	43396	37050	42819	53141	46596	49579	...	...	...	053
1911	-8928	9318	2217	-15843	5683	1895	...	...	...	054
1080	1228	1307	1406	1524	1776	1898	2034	2144	2183	055
929	952	929	928	905	958	956	989	1042	1057	056

Calendar year

70	45	32	30	25	25	25	25	25	25	057
8	4	2	2	2	2	2	2	2	...	058
5	4	2	1	1	1	1	1	1	...	059

averages

96.1	91.1	87.6	88.6	87.3	85.2	86.4	84.9	82.5	82.4	060
...	...	...	...	...	...	...	...	...	...	061
...	...	...	...	...	...	...	...	...	...	062

values

12	16	20	22	22	22	23	23	...	...	063
12	16	20	22	22	22	23	23	...	...	064

averages

61.2	64.1	70.4	73.3	81.3	88.9	96.0	96.9	97.8	98.2	065
116.2	129.0	140.7	151.5	168.4	185.3	198.6	205.6	205.8	206.4 *	066

As of 30 June

11288	14266	16998	14822	16445	17895	19797	19110	19310	22840	067
4214	4390	5647	5436	5626	6238	5642	6070	6810	7420	068
7074	9876	11351	9386	10819	11657	14155	13040	12500	15420	069
15687	21775	19729	22775	23827	26049	34089	31920	36230	42170	070
26974	36040	36727	37597	40272	43944	53886	51030	55540	65010	071
16315	26470	34753	33269	33107	32897	38056	...	...	31570	072
8762	7667	16356	20654	28979	34011	40204	...	...	52090	073
-6755	-10539	-6426	-11807	-6524	490	5569	...	...	...	074
15517	18207	22782	32461	35503	33521	34635	...	...	...	075
–	–	–	–	–	–	–	...	...	...	076
1897	1903	-14382	-16326	-21814	-22964	-24374	...	...	-18650	077

Period averages

5.00	5.00	5.00	6.25	6.25	6.25	5.75	3.75	4.25	4.25	078
5.00	5.00	5.00	7.00	7.00	7.00	6.75	4.25	4.67	4.67	079
5.75	5.75	5.75	7.25	8.00	8.00	6.00	5.00	5.25	6.23	080
										081
...	...	...	...	...	...	...	...	...	...	
8.50	8.50	8.50	13.00	13.00	13.00	...	...	...	...	082
8.50	8.50	8.50	13.00	13.00	13.00	...	...	...	...	083

	Item	1978	1979	1980	1981	1982	1983	1984	1985
	GOVERNMENT FINANCE								*Thousand Pa'anga;*
	Central Government								
084	Current revenue	8627	8722	10597	12571	15723	18260	17999	22628
085	Taxes	6147	6265	7453	8926	10374	11995	12366	15729
086	Non-taxes	2480	2457	3144	3645	5349	6265	5633	6899
087	Current expenditure	8515	8932	10538	11758	16266	16985	17839	21266
088	Current surplus/deficit	112	-210	59	813	-543	1275	160	1362
089	Capital receipts	1844	3350	2745	5035	3073	3544	6178	5093
090	Capital expenditure	1890	2653	2879	4762	3809	3352	4200	5752
091	Capital account surplus/deficit	-46	697	-134	273	-736	192	1978	-659
092	Overall surplus/deficit	66	487	-75	1086	-1279	1467	2138	703
	Financing								
093	Domestic borrowing	224	621	42	250	235	–	991	28
094	Foreign borrowing	7183	729	374	2678	790	1126	565	1124
095	Foreign grants	...	1731	2130	1907	2103	1938	4132	3337
096	Use of cash balances	-7473	-3568	-2471	-5921	-1849	-4531	-7826	-5192
	Expenditure by Function, Central Govt. [d]								
097	Total	8515	8932	10538	11758	16266	16984	17839	21266
098	General public services	2386	2443	2925	3252	4785	4336	4998	5951
099	Defence	305	314	378	440	605	624	704	898
100	Education	1404	1481	1605	1764	2153	2293	2434	2856
101	Health	1126	1201	1475	1636	2143	2188	2311	2598
102	Social security & welfare	153	200	258	205	286	296	373	448
103	Housing & community amenities	–	–	–	–	–	–	–	–
104	Economic services	2963	3004	3264	3805	5484	6132	5886	6704
105	Agriculture	937	976	1054	1181	1359	1248	1222	1369
106	Industry	179	211	231	239	325	341	363	408
107	Electricity, gas & water	–	–	–	–	–	–	–	–
108	Transport and communications	1700	1682	1786	2168	3483	4167	3685	4364
109	Other economic services	147	135	193	217	317	376	616	563
110	Others	178	289	633	656	810	1115	1133	1812
	EXTERNAL TRADE								*Thousand Pa'anga;*
111	Exports, fob	5078	7012	7168	7487	4288	6455	10439	7783
112	Imports, cif	22318	26210	30135	35088	41205	41664	46614	58930
113	Trade balance	-17240	-19198	-22967	-27602	-36917	-35209	-36175	-51147
	Exports, by SITC section								
114	Food and live animals	1639	2415	2243	2318	1598	2478	3947	3360
115	Beverage and tobacco	–	–	–	1	–	–	–	–
116	Crude materials excl. fuels	3037	1872	1377	2396	273	300	91	106
117	Mineral fuels, etc.	–	–	–	–	–	–	6	6
118	Animal, vegetable oil & fats	–	1871	3045	1172	1291	2118	5013	2742
119	Chemicals	2	0	4	6	4	2	14	5
120	Basic manufactures	95	75	48	128	154	110	107	197
121	Machines, transport equipment	35	337	45	341	100	171	376	331
122	Misc. manufactured goods	173	347	291	1028	734	957	594	665
123	Unclassified goods	97	96	116	98	134	320	292	371
	Exports, by principal commodity								
124	1. Squash	...	...	–	–	–	–	–	–
125	2. Fish	...	...	...	...	...	...	...	...
126	3. Vanilla Beans	181	47	261	277	629	619	1048	401
127	4. Bananas	182	302	395	507	88	303	856	823
128	5. Coconut oil	–	1870	3045	1172	1291	2118	5013	2742
129	6. Desiccated coconut	716	1044	660	751	230	424	761	526

1986	1987	1988	1989	1990	1991	1992	1993	1994	1995	

Fiscal year ending 30 June

26832	29819	34357	33690	40900	47440	46230	52280	54740	58218 *	084
18471	20965	24268	24724	27440	33730	31120	36870	39320	41602 *	085
8362	8854	10089	8966	13460	13710	15120	15410	11320	16616 *	086
26940	32018	33857	34829	44457	47440	51080	49920	50370	55504 *	087
-108	-2198	500	-1139	-3557	0	-4850	2360	4370	2714 *	088
6509	8723	6437	9798	10377	...	...	...	...	...	089
7756	7048	6429	6335	11251	...	...	...	...	...	090
-1247	1675	7	3464	-874	...	...	...	...	...	091
-1355	-523	508	2325	-4431	...	...	...	...	...	092
										093
–	–	680	1591	37	...	...	...	...	...	094
821	537	21	164	575	...	...	...	...	...	095
5028	6699	3672	5968	5521	...	...	...	...	...	096
-4494	-6713	-4880	-10048	-1702	...	...	...	...	...	
26940	32018	33857	34829	44457	47440	51080	49920	50370	55504 *	097
8035	10812	10510	12455	17807	16780	15640	15350	15550	15742 *	098
1011	1149	1081	1194	1935	1820	2760	1650	1810	3169 *	099
3694	4239	4570	5010	5873	8950	8620	9130	9080	9882 *	100
3158	3321	3666	3900	4152	5310	5930	5890	6270	6667 *	101
503	636	557	623	628	890	1010	1310	1630	1362 *	102
–	–	–	–	–	–	–	–	–	– *	103
7910	8303	8384	8250	8556	11210	11640	11080	10970	11526 *	104
1620	1597	1678	1761	1947	2620	2820	2680	2640	2309 *	105
470	524	632	722	846	...	...	...	...	...	106
–	–	–	–	–	–	–	–	–	– *	107
5238	5531	5317	5079	5093	6470	6630	6390	6100	6102 *	108
581	652	757	688	671	...	...	...	...	3115 *	109
2628	3558	5090	3396	5507	2470	5500	5530	5070	7156 *	110

Calendar year

9484	9553	10555	12183	15299	21465	17409	21970	17747	18022	111
59616	68460	70689	68334	78989	76817	84271	85220	91210	98077	112
-50132	-58907	-60134	-56151	-63691	-55352	-66862	-63250	-73463	-80055	113
5117	5407	5658	7263	10891	17675	13897	20237	16281	16678	114
–	1	18	0	21	0	0	–	0	0	115
251	175	94	68	24	40	113	122	744	486	116
		–		–				–	–	117
2010	1616	1173	850	399	418	437	126	–	–	118
22	0	–	–	0	129	40	33	64	68	119
357	379	897	967	1354	1651	1230	716	389	277	120
339	526	235	349	451	200	610	6	101	71	121
1080	1103	1667	2125	1810	967	925	693	142	322	122
309	347	814	560	349	386	157	39	26	122	123
–	–	–	1983	4838	12445	8675	12870	8750	8405	124
...	1193	2295	1100	1278	1397	1411	2160	3160	4342	125
1686	1217	1385	2074	2765	2857	2084	2750	2650	2802	126
1482	1234	658	206	103	0	0	460	70	0	127
2010	1616	1102	850	399	418	437	120	–	–	128
721	552	392	13	0	0	0	–	–	–	129

347

	Item	1978	1979	1980	1981	1982	1983	1984	1985
	Imports, by SITC section								
130	Food and live animals	6220	6989	7095	8638	8936	9922	10967	13266
131	Beverage and tobacco	1585	1677	1954	1929	2317	2414	2615	3101
132	Crude materials excl. fuels	1120	739	1627	1797	3129	2139	2947	3096
133	Mineral fuels, etc.	2311	2635	4291	5836	5715	6622	6528	7598
134	Animal, vegetable oil & fats	24	20	27	38	39	123	73	145
135	Chemicals	1139	1632	1699	1888	2646	2621	2794	3854
136	Basic manufactures	4353	4756	5975	6590	9418	7150	9306	10849
137	Machines, transport equipment	3786	5769	5101	5503	6029	6508	6356	11247
138	Misc. manufactured goods	1732	1893	2227	2802	2821	4007	4813	5477
139	Unclassified goods	49	100	139	68	156	157	215	297
	Direction of Trade								*Million US dollars;*
140	Exports, Total	6.3	7.8	8.2	8.6	4.4	5.3	8.8	5.0
141	1. Japan	0.1	0.4	0.0	0.0	0.0	0.0	0.0	0.1
142	2. United States	0.0	0.1	1.1	0.0	0.4	0.4	0.8	0.2
143	3. New Zealand	1.8	2.7	2.4	2.5	1.7	2.4	5.2	2.4
144	4. Hong Kong	0.0	0.0	0.0	0.1	0.0	0.0	0.0	0.0
145	5. Fiji	0.1	1.0	0.2	0.6	0.2	0.1	0.0	0.3
146	6. Australia	0.0	2.8	2.8	2.8	1.8	2.0	1.8	1.7
147	7. American Samoa	0.0	0.0	0.2	0.3	0.1	0.1	0.1	0.3
148	8. France	0.1	0.0	0.0	0.0	0.0	0.0	0.0	0.0
149	9. Germany	0.9	0.0	0.0	0.0	0.0	0.0	0.0	0.0
150	10. United Kingdom	1.3	0.0	0.2	0.4	0.0	0.0	0.6	0.0
151	Imports, Total	27.5	29.3	34.3	40.3	41.8	37.5	40.9	41.2
152	1. New Zealand	9.8	10.0	13.0	14.4	15.6	13.1	15.4	16.0
153	2. Australia	5.9	8.0	10.8	16.5	9.8	10.1	9.8	10.1
154	3. Fiji	5.9	1.5	1.7	1.9	3.0	2.2	2.0	2.2
155	4. United States	0.0	1.0	2.2	1.9	4.0	2.3	2.2	2.4
156	5. United Kingdom	1.5	2.6	1.2	0.8	0.6	0.8	0.6	0.8
157	6. Japan	3.3	2.4	2.1	2.2	2.6	3.5	4.7	3.2
158	7. Hong Kong	1.0	0.7	0.6	0.6	0.5	0.5	0.5	0.6
159	8. Germany	0.0	0.2	0.1	0.1	0.1	0.2	0.3	0.8
160	9. China, People's Rep. of	0.0	0.4	0.6	0.5	0.7	0.5	0.7	0.5
161	10. Singapore	0.0	1.3	1.3	0.4	2.7	3.2	2.3	0.8
	Trade Indexes								*1990 = 100;*
162	Terms of trade	104	141	96	109	104	102	102	98
	BALANCE OF PAYMENTS								*Million US dollars;*
163	Merchandise exports, fob	8	5	8	7	7	3	6	7
164	Merchandise imports, fob	-18	-22	-29	-36	-35	-36	-30	-32
165	Trade balance	-10	-17	-21	-29	-28	-33	-24	-25
166	Other goods, services and income	2	4	5	7	8	3	4	3
167	Credit	7	8	11	12	14	12	14	16
168	Debit	-5	-4	-6	-5	-6	-9	-10	-13
169	Unrequited transfer	8	11	13	15	23	30	20	21
170	Private	8	11	13	16	...	15	14	18
171	Official	0	0	0	-1	...	15	6	3
172	Current balance	0	-2	-3	-7	3	0	0	-1
173	Direct investment	...	...	...	...	...	...	...	0
174	Portfolio investment	...	...	...	...	...	...	...	0
175	Other long-term capital	4	3	3	3	1	0	1	1
176	Other short-term capital	...	...	...	...	...	1	3	1
177	Net errors and omissions	...	...	-5	-5	3	-1	1	2
178	Overall balance	4	1	-5	-9	7	0	5	3
179	Allocation of SDRs	...	...	...	...	...	...	...	...
180	Monetary movements	-4	-1	5	9	-7	0	-5	-3

1986	1987	1988	1989	1990	1991	1992	1993	1994	1995	
13566	14755	17741	16514	18150	16520	18172	19632	22520	22323	130
3476	3640	3203	3244	3563	3123	3248	3818	4040	4521	131
2085	3213	2635	2872	4158	3618	4033	3800	4990	4760	132
7340	6952	6853	7411	10451	12147	10756	11587	10972	12135	133
127	123	179	166	175	186	196	263	358	359	134
5186	4476	4604	4306	4994	6224	5204	5990	7580	6833	135
13904	12511	13454	13311	14221	11905	19163	16650	18130	19028	136
9136	16175	15472	13669	14491	14641	16230	16030	15420	20311	137
4679	6355	6029	6520	8075	8057	6951	7170	6830	7442	138
117	260	520	323	711	396	319	280	370	367	139

Calendar year

5.8	6.7	9.7	10.2	12.7	17.4	18.5	22.6	22.3	19.9	140
0.0	0.1	0.7	1.6	3.8	9.6	8.7	12.5	11.3	8.4	141
1.0	1.0	2.0	2.8	3.3	2.8	3.1	4.2	5.7	6.0	142
2.3	2.7	2.8	3.2	2.5	1.4	1.2	0.8	0.8	1.1	143
0.0	0.0	0.0	0.0	0.0	0.0	0.0	0.1	0.3	0.9	144
0.0	0.0	0.4	0.1	0.2	0.4	0.3	0.3	0.4	0.4	145
1.7	1.8	1.5	2.0	1.9	1.5	1.4	1.3	0.5	0.4	146
0.5	0.6	0.3	0.5	0.5	0.3	0.2	0.2	0.3	0.3	147
0.0	0.0	0.0	0.0	0.2	0.2	0.0	0.0	0.0	0.2	148
0.0	0.0	0.0	0.0	0.0	0.0	0.0	0.2	0.0	0.2	149
0.1	0.0	0.0	0.0	0.0	0.0	0.0	0.1	0.5	0.2	150
39.9	47.9	63.0	59.7	66.9	64.2	64.4	68.3	85.6	93.3	151
15.4	17.2	16.8	16.5	20.1	17.5	17.9	22.7	26.3	27.7	152
11.3	12.3	15.8	12.1	13.4	15.1	14.2	9.6	13.3	14.4	153
2.6	4.2	5.7	5.5	8.1	9.2	9.1	10.8	12.3	14.2	154
1.5	4.4	4.5	6.3	6.9	5.8	5.5	5.9	6.5	8.1	155
1.1	0.0	0.7	0.8	0.7	0.6	0.2	2.4	1.2	5.3	156
4.6	4.2	4.3	3.9	4.0	5.3	7.6	3.0	9.7	2.9	157
0.5	0.5	1.1	1.0	1.0	0.9	0.4	0.7	0.5	0.6	158
0.4	0.4	0.4	0.4	0.3	0.3	0.0	0.3	0.2	0.5	159
0.6	0.8	2.2	0.7	0.9	1.1	0.2	0.3	0.6	0.5	160
0.8	1.9	2.7	4.2	4.2	0.9	0.3	0.0	0.0	0.0	161

Period averages

95	94	98	101	100	98	104	110	...	...	162

Fiscal year ending 30 June

6	7	7	10	9	11	16	12	17	14 *	163
-33	-38	-47	-47	-54	-58	-47	-48	-57	-62 *	164
-27	-31	-40	-37	-45	-47	-31	-37	-40	-48 *	165
1	7	4	1	13	-1	-2	0	-4	2 *	166
17	25	26	25	35	24	21	21	23	25 *	167
-16	-18	-22	-23	-23	-25	-23	-21	-27	-23 *	168
25	30	29	34	45	45	35	41	36	37 *	169
22	24	23	24	31	30	28	35	32	33 *	170
3	7	6	10	14	15	7	7	4	4 *	171
-1	6	-7	-2	13	-3	1	4	-8	-9 *	172
0	0	0	0	0	0	1	0	2	2 *	173
0	–	-0	-0	-0	-1	1	-0	–	0 *	174
-1	0	4	1	-15	-2	-1	3	1	2 *	175
1	-1	1	0	2	5	3	-0	0	-1 *	176
2	2	0	-1	1	0	-1	0	0	-2 *	177
1	8	-2	-1	0	-1	4	7	-5	-8 *	178
...	...	...	...	...	...	...	...	...	...	179
-1	-8	2	1	0	1	-4	-7	5	8 *	180

	Item	1978	1979	1980	1981	1982	1983	1984	1985
	INTERNATIONAL RESERVES								*Million US dollars;*
181	Total [e]	10.1	12.6	13.8	14.0	15.6	21.0	26.0	27.5
182	Gold, national valuation	...	...	...	...	...	...	...	...
183	Foreign exchange	10.1	12.6	13.8	14.0	15.6	21.0	26.0	26.7
184	Reserve position in the Fund	–	–	–	–	–	–	–	0.8
185	SDRs	–	–	–	–	–	–	–	–
	EXCHANGE RATES								*Pa'anga*
186	End of period	0.8692	0.9046	0.8470	0.8866	1.0198	1.1086	1.2080	1.4686
187	Average of period	0.8737	0.8946	0.8782	0.8702	0.9859	1.1100	1.1395	1.4319
	EXTERNAL INDEBTEDNESS								*Million US dollars;*
188	Total outstanding and disbursed	...	...	...	...	...	...	...	...
189	Long-term	...	...	...	...	...	...	...	...
190	Public and publicly guaranteed	...	...	...	...	...	...	...	...
191	Private non-guaranteed	0.0	0.0	0.0	0.0	0.0	0.0	0.0	0.0
192	Short-term	...	...	...	...	...	...	...	...
193	Use of IMF credit	0.0	0.0	0.0	0.0	0.0	0.0	0.0	0.0
	Debt service								*Transactions*
194	Principal repayments on LT debt	...	...	...	...	...	...	...	...
195	Interest on long-term debt	...	...	...	...	...	...	...	...
196	Interest on short-term debt	...	...	...	...	...	...	...	...
	Average terms of new commitments								
197	Interest (%)	...	...	...	...	...	...	...	...
198	Maturity (years)	...	...	...	...	...	...	...	...
199	Grace period (years)	...	...	...	...	...	...	...	...
200	Grant element (%)	...	...	...	...	...	...	...	...

Footnotes:

a   Revised estimates.
b   Figures for 1980, 1984 and 1990 relate to estimates based on sample surveys undertaken for each respective year.
c   Private consumption expenditure is a residual item with figures for statistical discrepancy included therein.
d   Refers to recurrent expenditures only.
e   Total reserves exclude gold.

	1986	1987	1988	1989	1990	1991	1992	1993	1994	1995	
As of end of period											
	22.5	28.9	30.5	24.9	31.3	32.3	31.8	37.1	35.5	28.7	181
	...	...	...	...	...	...	...	...	...	...	182
	21.5	27.8	29.4	23.7	30.0	30.2	29.6	34.8	33.1	26.9	183
	0.9	1.1	1.0	1.0	1.1	1.1	1.6	1.6	1.8	1.8	184
	0.0	0.1	0.1	0.2	0.2	1.1	0.5	0.6	0.7	0.1	185
per US dollar											
	1.5042	1.3841	1.1703	1.2585	1.2958	1.3317	1.3902	1.3793	1.2584	1.2703	186
	1.4960	1.4282	1.2750	1.2612	1.2800	1.2961	1.3471	1.3841	1.3202	1.2709	187
As of end of year											
	28.9	36.1	37.6	39.2	53.6	45.0	43.4	44.3	64.4	...	188
	28.4	35.6	37.0	38.1	44.4	44.2	42.6	43.7	63.4	...	189
	28.4	35.6	37.0	38.1	44.4	44.2	42.6	43.7	63.4	...	190
	0.0	0.0	0.0	0.0	0.0	0.0	0.0	0.0	0.0	...	191
	0.5	0.5	0.6	1.1	9.2	0.8	0.8	0.6	1.0	...	192
	0.0	0.0	0.0	0.0	0.0	0.0	0.0	0.0	0.0	...	193
during the year											
	0.7	0.8	0.8	0.8	1.0	1.1	1.0	1.2	2.1	2.3 *	194
	0.3	0.3	0.4	0.4	0.5	0.4	0.5	0.5	0.6	0.7 *	195
	0.0	0.0	0.1	0.1	0.4	0.1	0.0	0.1	0.1	...	196
	3.2	1.3	1.0	2.2	0.8	1.0	0.0	1.6	0.0	...	197
	31.3	34.2	43.1	31.2	39.2	39.2	0.0	39.5	0.0	...	198
	7.7	8.3	9.9	8.7	10.1	9.8	0.0	8.6	0.0	...	199
	57.3	67.7	78.4	63.0	78.7	77.6	0.0	69.3	0.0	...	200

	Item	1978	1979	1980	1981	1982	1983	1984	1985
									Thousand;
001	**POPULATION**	...	7.36	...	...	...	8.23	8.20	8.23
	NATIONAL ACCOUNTS [a]							*Thousand Australian dollars;*	
	At Current Factor Cost								
002	GDP by Industrial Origin	...	...	...	...	...	...	...	...
003	Agriculture	...	...	...	328	252	410	489	546
004	Mining }	...	...	...					
005	Manufacturing }	...	...	...	48	52	63	86	108
006	Electricity, gas and water	...	...	...	...	...	65	64	92
007	Construction	...	...	...	354	407	307	344	481
008	Trade	...	...	...	1458	810	1044	1082	561
009	Transport and communications	...	...	...	-547	-311	-232	-68	41
010	Finance	...	...	...	167	206	244	259	340
011	Public administration }	...	...	...	1775	1804	1953	2021	2227
012	Others }	...	...	...	525	512	581	671	638
013	Indirect taxes less subsidies	...	...	...	...	...	...	...	...
014	GDP at current market prices	...	...	...	4109	3732	4435	4947	5034
015	Net factor income from abroad	...	...	...	...	...	...	...	...
016	GNP at current market prices	...	...	...	...	...	...	...	...
017	Expenditure on GDP	...	...	...	4109	3732	4435	4947	5034
018	Private consumption	...	...	...	...	...	...	...	...
019	Government consumption	...	...	...	...	...	...	...	...
020	Gross fixed capital formation	...	...	...	...	...	...	...	...
021	Increase in stocks	...	...	...	...	...	...	...	...
022	Exports of goods and services	...	...	...	...	...	...	...	...
023	Less: Imports of goods and services	...	...	...	...	...	...	...	...
024	Statistical discrepancy	...	...	...	...	...	...	...	...
	At Constant 1988 Factor Cost								
025	GDP by Industrial Origin	...	...	...	...	...	...	...	...
026	Agriculture	...	...	...	...	...	...	...	...
027	Mining	...	...	...	...	...	...	...	...
028	Manufacturing	...	...	...	...	...	...	...	...
029	Electricity, gas and water	...	...	...	...	...	...	...	...
030	Construction	...	...	...	...	...	...	...	...
031	Trade	...	...	...	...	...	...	...	...
032	Transport and communications	...	...	...	...	...	...	...	...
033	Finance	...	...	...	...	...	...	...	...
034	Public administration }	...	...	...	...	...	...	...	...
035	Others }	...	...	...	...	...	...	...	...
036	Indirect taxes less subsidies	...	...	...	...	...	...	...	...
037	GDP at *1988* market prices	...	...	...	...	...	...	...	...
038	Net factor income from abroad	...	...	...	...	...	...	...	...
039	GNP at *1988* market prices	...	...	...	...	...	...	...	...
	Investment Financing, at current prices								
040	Gross domestic capital formation	...	...	...	...	...	...	...	...
041	Gross national saving	...	...	...	...	...	...	...	...
042	Gross domestic saving	...	...	...	...	...	...	...	...
043	Net factor income from abroad	...	...	...	...	...	...	...	...
044	Foreign saving	...	...	...	...	...	...	...	...
045	Net transfer from abroad	...	...	...	...	...	...	...	...
046	Net borrowing from abroad	...	...	...	...	...	...	...	...
	Per Capita GDP, Australian dollars								
047	Current factor cost	...	...	...	...	...	...	...	...
048	Constant *1988* factor cost	...	...	...	...	...	...	...	...

1986	1987	1988	1989	1990	1991	1992	1993	1994	1995	
As of 1 July										
8.37	8.46	8.67	8.85	9.04	9.04	9.20	9.35	9.51	9.67 *	001
Calendar year										
6257	7033	9087	10079	11432 *	13326 *	14151 *	14690 *	16025 *	...	002
1151	1037	1802	2481	3329 *	3675 *	3722 *	4040 *	4198 *	...	003
				186 *	193 *	346 *	209 *	241 *	...	004
111	157	580	621	276 *	336 *	350 *	316 *	298 *	...	005
106	124	134	196	98 *	100 *	163 *	173 *	266 *	...	006
842	1012	1587	1799	696 *	870 *	1387 *	1596 *	532 *	...	007
568	1138	1275	809	2924 *	3388 *	3388 *	3397 *	4543 *	...	008
279	285	446	696	173 *	915 *	566 *	-15 *	748 *	...	009
688	712	865	913	1004 *	1095 *	1133 *	1385 *	1517 *	...	010
2455	2498	2244	2387	2745 *	2754 *	3096 *	3590 *	3682 *	...	011
57	71	154	177						...	012
281	551	544	301	609 *	780 *	929 *	485 *	1360 *	...	013
6538	7584	9632	10379	12041 *	14105 *	15079 *	15176 *	17385 *	...	014
...	...	...	...	...	...	...	...	...	...	015
...	...	...	...	...	...	...	...	...	...	016
6538	7584	9632	10379	12041 *	14105 *	15079 *	15176 *	17385 *	...	017
...	...	...	...	8680 *	11043 *	7975 *	11587 *	23635 *	...	018
...	...	...	...	3750 *	3610 *	4196 *	5201 *	5411 *	...	019
2568	2127	4828	5499	3163 *	2998 *	5343 *	5254 *	3780 *	...	020
-	-	211	295	3020 *	3076 *	2834 *	2662 *	3309 *	...	021
...	...	...	...	329 *	461 *	230 *	200 *	250 *	...	022
...	...	...	...	6901 *	7083 *	5499 *	9728 *	19000 *	...	023
...	...	...	...	–	–	–	–	–	...	024
...	...	9087	8910	10672 *	12064 *	12260 *	11347 *	13251 *	14183 *	025
...	...	1802	2145	...	...	...	...	...	3152 *	026
...	...	291	226	...	...	...	...	...	317 *	027
...	...	289	283	...	...	...	...	...	452 *	028
...	...	134	196	...	...	...	...	...	345 *	029
...	...	1587	1280	...	...	...	...	...	1963 *	030
...	...	1275	818	...	...	...	...	...	2043 *	031
...	...	446	646	...	...	...	...	...	599 *	032
...	...	865	877	...	...	...	...	...	1390 *	033
...	...	2398	2439	...	...	...	...	...	3922 *	034
...	...	...	...	...	...	...	...	...	...	035
...	...	...	...	...	...	...	...	...	...	036
...	...	...	...	...	...	...	...	...	...	037
...	...	...	...	...	...	...	...	...	...	038
...	...	...	...	...	...	...	...	...	...	039
2568	2127	5039	5794	6183 *	6074 *	8176 *	7916 *	7089 *	...	040
										041
...	...	...	...	...	...	...	...	...	...	042
...	...	...	...	...	...	...	...	...	...	043
...	...	...	...	...	...	...	...	...	...	044
...	...	...	...	...	...	...	...	...	...	045
...	...	...	...	...	...	...	...	...	...	046
747	832	1048	1139	1265 *	1474 *	1539 *	1571 *	1685 *	...	047
...	...	1048	1007	1181 *	1334 *	1333 *	1213 *	1393 *	1466 *	048

Item	1978	1979	1980	1981	1982	1983	1984	1985
PRODUCTION								*Metric tons;*
Agriculture, *crop year*								
049 1. Copra	...	...	...	294	243	234	680	333
ENERGY								*Annual*
Electricity, *'000 kWh*								
050 Production	...	...	...	...	...	...	...	...
051 Exports	...	...	...	...	...	...	...	...
052 Imports	...	...	...	...	...	...	...	...
053 Consumption	...	...	...	...	...	...	...	...
PRICE INDEXES								*Period*
054 Consumer (Funafuti), *4th Quarter 1983*								
Nov. 1983 = 100	...	...	75.8	84.8	91.7	100.0	103.8	107.6 l
055 Food	...	...	80.0	88.8	92.8	100.0	104.0	109.6 l
056 Non-food	...	...	72.3	81.5	90.8	100.0	103.6	105.9 l
GOVERNMENT FINANCE								*Thousand Australian dollars;*
Central Government								
057 Current revenue	...	...	1999	2168	2361	2280	2497	2700
058 Taxes	...	...	697	661	705	703	891	837
059 Non-taxes	...	...	1302	1507	1656	1577	1606	1863
060 Current expenditure	...	...	2786	3163	3102	3285	3512	3919
061 Current surplus/deficit	...	...	-787	-995	-741	-1005	-1015	-1219
062 Capital receipts	...	...	...	–	–	–	–	–
063 Capital expenditure	...	...	...	2180	1872	645	1024	881
064 Capital account surplus/deficit	...	...	...	-2180	-1872	-645	-1024	-881
065 Net lending	...	...	...	–	–	–	–	–
066 Overall surplus/deficit	...	...	...	-3175	-2613	-1650	-2039	-2100
Financing								
067 Domestic borrowing	...	...	...	...	...	...	...	...
068 Foreign borrowing	...	...	...	...	...	...	...	...
069 Foreign grants	...	...	804	1388	951	1002	1060	969
070 Use of cash balances	...	...	...	...	...	...	...	...
Expenditure by Function, Central Gov't.								
071 Total	...	...	...	4062	4123	2554	5301	3531
072 General public services [b]	...	...	...	394	717	492	2507	692
073 Defence	...	...	...	...	...	...	...	...
074 Education	...	...	...	691	472	532	645	1129
075 Health	...	...	...	187	30	43	13	141
076 Social security & welfare [c]	...	...	...	11	141	13	25	10
077 Housing & community amenities	...	...	...	304	88	115	92	33
078 Economic services	...	...	...	2319	2569	1046	1881	1428
079 Agriculture [d]	...	...	...	1016	1081	301	694	612
080 Industry	...	...	...	...	...	...	...	...
081 Electricity, gas & water [e]	...	...	...	53	602	149	151	318
082 Transport and communications	...	...	...	1142	758	552	945	428
083 Other economic services [f]	...	...	...	108	128	44	91	70
084 Others [g]	...	...	...	156	106	313	138	98
EXTERNAL TRADE								*Thousand Australian dollars;*
085 Exports, fob	...	...	672	2123	853	770	1396	526
086 Imports, cif	...	...	3147	2592	2789	2964	3949	4127
087 Trade balance	...	...	-2475	-469	-1936	-2194	-2553	-3601

	1986	1987	1988	1989	1990	1991	1992	1993	1994	1995	
Calendar year											
	239	64	88	415	257	...	...	...	...	...	049
values											
	...	...	...	...	...	...	...	...	...	...	050
	...	...	...	...	...	...	...	...	...	...	051
	...	...	...	...	...	...	...	...	...	...	052
	843	962	1025	1025	1120	...	...	...	...	...	053
averages											
	114.0	117.8	125.4	128.6	131.2	141.6	144.7	148.0	150.1	157.6	054
	113.4	117.3	126.6	124.5	122.7	129.5	136.0	139.4	144.9	153.0	055
	114.7	118.3	124.2	132.6	139.4	153.2	153.0	156.2	155.1	161.9	056
Fiscal year ending 31 December											
	2931	...	...	...	...	...	...	...	...	...	057
	1055	...	...	...	...	...	...	...	...	...	058
	1876	...	...	...	...	...	...	...	...	...	059
	3971	...	...	...	...	...	...	...	...	...	060
	-1040	...	...	...	...	...	...	...	...	...	061
	–	...	...	...	...	...	...	...	...	...	062
	...	...	...	...	...	...	...	...	...	...	063
	...	...	...	...	...	...	...	...	...	...	064
	...	...	...	...	...	...	...	...	...	...	065
	...	...	...	...	...	...	...	...	...	...	066
	...	...	...	...	...	...	...	...	...	...	067
	...	...	...	...	...	...	...	...	...	...	068
	900	...	...	...	...	...	...	...	...	...	069
	...	...	...	...	...	...	...	...	...	...	070
	4666	7438	...	...	...	...	...	...	...	...	071
	753	1316	...	...	...	...	...	...	...	...	072
	...	...	...	...	...	...	...	...	...	...	073
	831	1255	...	...	...	...	...	...	...	...	074
	182	249	...	...	...	...	...	...	...	...	075
	54	15	...	...	...	...	...	...	...	...	076
	65	111	...	...	...	...	...	...	...	...	077
	2296	4234	...	...	...	...	...	...	...	...	078
	752	532	...	...	...	...	...	...	...	...	079
	...	...	...	...	...	...	...	...	...	...	080
	702	191	...	...	...	...	...	...	...	...	081
	759	3356	...	...	...	...	...	...	...	...	082
	83	155	...	...	...	...	...	...	...	...	083
	485	258	...	...	...	...	...	...	...	...	084
Calendar year											
	184	112	261	312	178 *	...	...	...	...	...	085
	4056	4947	6788	5170	...	...	...	...	...	...	086
	-3872	-4835	-6527	-4858	...	...	...	...	...	...	087

Item	1978	1979	1980	1981	1982	1983	1984	1985
Exports, by principal commodity								
088 1. Stamps	...	...	605	2098	651	454	665	372
089 2. Copra	...	...	67	25	11	61	308	152
090 3. Handicrafts	...	...	–	–	–	–	2	2
091 4. Garments	...	...	...	–	–	–	–	–
Imports, by SITC section								
092 Food and live animals	...	...	920	785	648	816	965	1098
093 Beverage and tobacco	...	...	245	118	131	157	164	124
094 Crude materials excl. fuels	...	...	59	68	97	117	55	112
095 Mineral fuels, etc.	...	...	407	421	484	415	462	514
096 Animal, vegetable oil & fats	...	...	7	6	7	8	15	10
097 Chemicals	...	...	173	114	88	205	199	206
098 Basic manufactures	...	...	520	405	553	502	871	737
099 Machines, transport equipment	...	...	418	353	464	365	588	839
100 Misc. manufactured goods	...	...	331	276	263	303	554	404
101 Unclassified goods	...	...	68	46	54	76	76	83
Direction of Trade							*Million US dollars;*	
102 Exports, Total	...	...	...	0.1	0.1	0.2	1.4	0.2
103 1. United States	...	...	...	–	–	–	–	–
104 2. South Africa	...	...	...	...	...	...	...	...
105 3. Columbia	...	...	...	...	...	...	...	...
106 4. Belgium-Luxembourg	...	...	...	–	–	–	–	–
107 5. Germany	...	...	...	–	–	–	–	–
108 6. Russia	...	...	...	...	...	...	...	...
109 7. Poland	...	...	...	...	...	...	...	–
110 8. France	...	...	...	–	–	–	–	–
111 9. Italy	...	...	...	–	–	–	–	–
112 10. Switzerland	...	...	...	–	–	–	–	–
113 Imports, Total	...	...	...	3.9	5.4	2.9	3.6	3.3
114 1. Fiji	...	...	...	1.4	1.5	1.2	1.2	1.4
115 2. Australia	...	...	...	1.3	1.8	1.2	1.3	0.9
116 3. Switzerland	...	...	...	–	–	–	–	–
117 4. United States	...	...	...	–	–	–	–	–
118 5. New Zealand	...	...	...	1.0	0.3	0.4	0.8	0.6
119 6. Germany	...	...	...	–	–	–	–	–
120 7. Netherlands	...	...	...	–	–	–	–	–
121 8. France	...	...	...	–	–	–	–	0.4
122 9. Italy	...	...	...	–	0.1	–	0.2	–
123 10. United Kingdom	...	...	...	0.2	–	–	–	–
BALANCE OF PAYMENTS							*Thousand Australian dollars;*	
124 Merchandise exports, fob	...	...	772	2123	853	770	1375	600
125 Merchandise imports, fob	...	...	-3062	-2529	-4147	-2855	-3844	-4178
126 Trade balance	...	...	-2290	-406	-3294	-2085	-2469	-3578
127 Other goods, services and income	...	...	-1162	-1319	-997	-1318	-1429	384
128 Credit	...	...	...	...	...	...	...	5263
129 Debit	...	...	...	...	...	...	...	-4879
130 Unrequited transfer	...	...	...	4266	5542	3889	6500	4011
131 Private	...	...	...	...	...	...	...	...
132 Official	...	...	...	...	...	...	...	...
133 Current balance	...	...	...	2541	1251	486	2602	817
134 Direct investment	...	...	...	...	...	...	...	...
135 Portfolio investment	...	...	...	...	...	...	...	...
136 Other long-term capital	...	...	...	...	...	...	...	...
137 Other short-term capital	...	...	...	...	...	...	...	...

1986	1987	1988	1989	1990	1991	1992	1993	1994	1995	
161	92	253	133	147 *	...	...	...	...	...	088
19	16	–	73	29 *	...	...	...	...	...	089
4	4	8	6	2 *	...	...	...	...	...	090
–	–	–	100 *	...	...	...	...	...	...	091
1195	1295	1653	1514	...	...	...	...	...	...	092
282	218	248	202	...	...	...	...	...	...	093
35	134	156	240	...	...	...	...	...	...	094
564	645	803	660	...	...	...	...	...	...	095
7	15	28	21	...	...	...	...	...	...	096
267	254	321	369	...	...	...	...	...	...	097
502	947	1623	1001	...	...	...	...	...	...	098
615	951	1134	632	...	...	...	...	...	...	099
521	389	742	455	...	...	...	...	...	...	100
68	99	80	76	...	...	...	...	...	...	101

Calendar year

1986	1987	1988	1989	1990	1991	1992	1993	1994	1995	
0.2	0.1	0.3	0.4	0.8	1.7	5.3	2.1	1.4	2.2	102
–	–	–	–	–	–	2.9	1.3	–	–	103
...	...	...	...	–	–	–	0.4	0.9	1.4	104
...	...	...	...	–	–	0.0	0.1	0.1	0.2	105
–	–	0.2	0.1	0.1	0.2	0.1	0.1	0.1	0.2	106
–	–	–	–	–	–	0.2	0.1	0.1	0.0	107
...	...	...	...	...	...	–	0.1	–	–	108
–	–	–	–	–	–	0.0	0.0	–	–	109
–	–	–	–	–	0.0	0.1	–	0.1	–	110
–	–	–	0.0	–	0.0	–	0.0	–	–	111
–	–	–	0.1	–	0.0	0.0	0.0	–	–	112
3.1	4.1	4.8	5.8	3.9	2.3	9.2	12.6	16.9	15.2	113
1.3	1.9	3.0	2.3	–	–	2.5	5.0	7.5	10.0	114
1.2	1.7	1.1	1.0	1.3	1.1	1.8	2.8	6.7	2.6	115
–	–	–	–	–	0.0	–	0.9			116
–	–	–	–	–	–	2.4	1.7	0.1	0.3	117
0.4	0.5	0.1	0.0	0.1	0.0	0.8	0.4	0.8	0.6	118
–	–	–	0.0	0.0	0.0	0.0	0.5	0.3	0.2	119
–	–	0.2	0.1	0.1	0.1	0.1	0.1	0.6	0.2	120
–	–	–	–	0.0	–	0.0	0.3	–	–	121
–	–	–	0.1	0.1	0.1	0.2	0.3	0.1	–	122
–	–	0.1	0.2	1.1	0.2	0.3	0.1	0.2	0.5	123

Calendar year

1986	1987	1988	1989	1990	1991	1992	1993	1994	1995	
475	266	589	456	322	473	297	328	337	347	124
-4339	-7465	-6332	-6349	-6231	-6673	-6892	-9457	-9835	-10327	125
-3864	-7199	-5743	-5894	-5909	-6200	-6595	-9129	-9498	-9980	126
753	493	50	633	1963	1263	1227	1627	1659	1693	127
5750	5764	5042	5720	7471	7883	8847	9800	9996	10196	128
-4997	-5271	-4991	-5087	-5508	-6619	-7620	-8173	-8337	-8503	129
5112	5962	4809	4476	6030	5312	12889	9381	9397	9031	130
...	...	...	...	...	...	...	...	...	...	131
...	...	...	...	...	...	...	...	...	...	132
2001	-744	-884	-785	2084	376	7521	1879	1558	744	133
...	...	...	...	...	...	...	...	...	...	134
...	...	...	...	...	...	...	...	...	...	135
...	...	...	...	...	...	...	...	...	...	136
...	...	...	...	...	...	...	...	...	...	137

	Item	1978	1979	1980	1981	1982	1983	1984	1985
									Thousand;
001	**POPULATION** [a]	101.61 I	112.45	115.06	116.30	120.00	123.50	126.90	129.10
									Thousand;
002	**LABOR FORCE**	...	...	...	...	...	...	...	...
003	Employed	...	51.13	...	...	...	...	...	...
004	Agriculture	...	39.28	...	...	...	...	...	...
005	Manufacturing	...	0.99	...	...	...	...	...	...
006	Mining	...	0.08	...	...	...	...	...	...
007	Others	...	10.78	...	...	...	...	...	...
008	Unemployed [b]	...	...	...	...	...	...	...	...
009	Unemployment rate, %	...	...	...	...	...	...	...	...
	NATIONAL ACCOUNTS								*Million Vatu;*
	At Current Market Prices								
010	GDP by Industrial Origin	...	...	...	...	...	10150	12339	12534
011	Agriculture	...	...	...	...	...	2649	3543	3693
012	Manufacturing	...	...	...	...	...	312	431	481
013	Electricity, gas and water	...	...	...	...	...	157	196	202
014	Construction	...	...	...	...	...	302	325	335
015	Trade	...	...	...	...	...	3627	4301	4046
016	Transport and communications	...	...	...	...	...	757	867	873
017	Finance	...	...	...	...	...	819	800	1027
018	Public administration	...	...	...	...	...	1393	1597	1710
019	Others [c]	...	...	...	...	...	134	279	167
020	Net factor income from abroad	...	...	...	...	...	-497	-399	402
021	GNP	...	...	...	...	...	9653	11940	12936
022	Expenditure on GDP	...	...	...	...	...	10150	12339	12534
023	Private consumption	...	...	...	...	...	5450	6306	7091
024	Government consumption	...	...	...	...	...	3660	4068	4501
025	Gross fixed capital formation	...	...	...	...	...	2142	2491	2849
026	Increase in stocks	...	...	...	...	...	463	458	695
027	Exports of goods and services	...	...	...	...	...	5934	7757	6391
028	Less: Imports of goods and services	...	...	...	...	...	7326	8424	9067
029	Statistical discrepancy	...	...	...	...	...	-173	-317	74
	At Constant 1983 Prices								
030	GDP by industrial origin	...	...	...	...	...	10150	10846	10966
031	Agriculture	...	...	...	...	...	2649	2831	2771
032	Manufacturing	...	...	...	...	...	312	419	466
033	Electricity, gas and water	...	...	...	...	...	157	192	192
034	Construction	...	...	...	...	...	302	293	282
035	Trade	...	...	...	...	...	3627	3741	3753
036	Transport and communications	...	...	...	...	...	757	808	770
037	Finance	...	...	...	...	...	819	772	967
038	Public administration	...	...	...	...	...	1393	1542	1629
039	Others [c]	...	...	...	...	...	134	249	136
040	Net factor income from abroad	...	...	...	...	...	-497	-385	378
041	GNP	...	...	...	...	...	9653	10461	11344
042	Expenditure on GDP	...	...	...	...	...	10150	10846	10966
043	Private consumption	...	...	...	...	...	5450	6035	6079
044	Government consumption	...	...	...	...	...	3660	3928	4237
045	Gross fixed capital formation	...	...	...	...	...	2142	2370	2619
046	Increase in stocks	...	...	...	...	...	463	435	634
047	Exports of goods and services	...	...	...	...	...	5934	6309	5652
048	Less: Imports of goods and services	...	...	...	...	...	7326	8245	8737
049	Statistical discrepancy	...	...	...	...	...	-173	14	482

1986	1987	1988	1989	1990	1991	1992	1993	1994	1995	
As of 1 July										
132.50	136.00	139.50	142.94	147.30	151.50	155.60	159.80	164.20	168.40	001
Calendar year										
...	...	...	...	...	...	...	...	...	...	002
...	...	...	66.60	...	...	...	...	...	...	003
...	...	...	49.81	...	...	...	...	...	...	004
...	...	...	0.89	...	...	...	...	...	...	005
...	...	...	...	...	...	...	...	...	...	006
...	...	...	15.89	...	...	...	...	...	...	007
...	...	...	12.97	...	...	...	...	...	...	008
...	...	...	...	...	...	...	...	...	...	009
Calendar year										
12179	13404	15006	16351	17900	19212	20523	21959	...	...	010
2958	2881	2933	3122	3582	3400	3759	4153	...	...	011
471	613	702	880	1050	1280	1260	1276	...	...	012
200	189	206	254	339	358	378	393	...	...	013
445	696	859	945	1033	1125	1080	1247	...	...	014
3802	4393	4967	5254	5771	6499	6884	7114	...	...	015
909	1085	1216	1375	1517	1609	1726	1845	...	...	016
1434	949	1458	1576	1744	1877	2022	2179	...	...	017
1893	1909	2144	2037	1985	2241	2458	2737	...	...	018
67	689	521	908	879	823	956	1015	...	...	019
511	-865	-425	553	1283	-1028	-1707	-1970	...	...	020
12690	12539	14581	16904	19183	18184	18817	19989	...	...	021
12179	13404	15006	16351	17900	19212	20523	21959	...	...	022
7406	8198	9562	10545	11267	11301	11662	11701	...	...	023
4604	4544	4969	4881	5054	5868	5988	6029	...	...	024
3580	4417	4170	5470	7241	5258	5645	6075	...	...	025
620	320	441	606	488	500	520	540	...	...	026
4417	5144	5508	6008	8301	9677	9677	9743	...	...	027
8253	9084	9213	10588	13714	12045	12270	13262	...	...	028
-195	-135	-431	-571	-737	-1347	-699	1133	...	...	029
10743	10789	10850	11222	11758	12271	12391	12888	...	...	030
2539	2383	2148	2229	2566	2515	2563	2773	...	...	031
467	588	684	774	871	1002	930	889	...	...	032
190	180	191	214	235	229	199	204	...	...	033
368	514	598	638	651	671	613	696	...	...	034
3378	3452	3460	3482	3636	3987	4125	4147	...	...	035
741	735	776	847	857	890	907	902	...	...	036
1285	757	1064	1062	1118	1140	1168	1238	...	...	037
1721	1614	1564	1390	1290	1380	1440	1576	...	...	038
54	566	365	586	534	457	446	463	...	...	039
460	-690	-287	347	759	-657	-1056	-1206	...	...	040
11203	10099	10563	11569	12517	11614	11335	11682	...	...	041
10743	10789	10850	11222	11758	12271	12391	12888	...	...	042
6118	6051	6330	6591	6884	7221	7217	7165	...	...	043
4123	3814	3817	3462	3382	3749	3705	3692	...	...	044
3183	3321	2847	3378	3998	3359	3943	3720	...	...	045
559	267	350	433	325	319	322	331	...	...	046
5001	4421	4232	4507	6115	5919	5988	5966	...	...	047
7754	7696	7362	7407	9121	7697	7593	8121	...	...	048
-487	611	636	258	175	-599	-741	135	...	...	049

Item	1978	1979	1980	1981	1982	1983	1984	1985
Per Capita GNP, Vatu								
050 Current prices	...	...	...	...	...	78162	94100	100201
051 Constant *1983* prices	...	...	...	...	...	78162	82435	87870
PRODUCTION							*Thousand metric tons;*	
Agriculture								
052 1. Coconut	346	340	240	356	294	314	372	322
053 2. Copra	50	49	34	46	36	37	48	39
054 3. Maize	1	1	1	1	1	1	1	1
055 4. Cocoa	1	1	1	1	1	1	1	1
056 5. Bananas	1	1	1	1	1	1	1	1
Production Indexes							*Period*	
057 Agriculture, *1979-81 = 100*	103.6	103.3	89.7	108.0	95.1	105.0	115.2	107.3
058 Mining	...	...	...	...	...	...	...	...
059 Manufacturing	...	...	...	...	...	...	...	...
ENERGY							*Annual*	
Electricity, *Mn kWh*								
060 Production	19	20	20	20	21	23	24	25
061 Consumption	19	20	20	20	21	23	24	25
Retail Prices, *Vatu/litre* [d]								
062 Gasoline, premium	23.2	32.0	45.0	61.0	66.0	64.5	69.0	71.5
063 Diesel	17.7	24.8	32.0	47.0	51.0	50.3	47.0	54.0
PRICE INDEXES							*Period*	
064 Consumer (Vila) *Q1 76* ꞁ *Q1 90 = 100* [e]	115.7	120.6	134.1	170.9	181.4	184.4	194.6	196.7
065 Food (Vila) [e]	116.6	119.7	135.3	183.6	185.3	180.5	182.7	178.2
066 Implicit GDP deflator, *1983 = 100*	...	...	...	...	...	100.0	113.8	114.3
MONEY AND BANKING							*Million Vatu;*	
067 Money supply (M1)	1282	1380	1306	1261	1448	1822	2093	2182
068 Currency in circulation	92	132	144	597	613	735	887	940
069 Demand deposits [f]	1190	1248	1162	664	835	1087	1206	1242
070 Quasi-money	...	...	...	2380	4429	5945	8390	8937
071 Money supply (M2)	...	...	...	3641	5877	7767	10483	11119
072 Foreign assets (net)	...	...	...	2293	3957	5831	9356	9904
073 Domestic credit	...	...	...	3124	3080	2892	2744	1955
074 Claims on govt. sector (net) [g]	...	...	...	-1332	-887	-617	-1235	-1348
075 Claims on private sector	...	...	...	3135	3252	3492	3497	3287
076 Claims on other financial insts.	...	...	...	1321	715	17	482	16
077 Other items	...	...	...	-1776	-1160	-956	-1617	-740
Deposit Money Banks								
078 Demand deposits	...	...	...	851	1110	1525	2104	1679
079 Savings deposits ⎫	...	...	...	2312	4149	5528	7533	8490
080 Time deposits ⎭								
081 Domestic credits outstanding	...	...	...	3135	3252	3492	3497	3287
GOVERNMENT FINANCE							*Million Vatu;*	
Central Government								
082 Current revenue	1153	1419	1263	1366	1607	1892	2503	2809
083 Taxes	684	941	942	1020	1265	1468	2037	2290
084 Non-taxes	469	478	321	346	342	424	466	519
085 Current expenditure	3363	3728	2026	2043	2327	2419	2658	3130
086 Current surplus/deficit	-2210	-2309	-763	-677	-720	-527	-155	-321
087 Capital receipts	–	–	–	–	–	–	–	–
088 Capital expenditure	193	389	...	2690	2580	2138	2226	2625
089 Capital account surplus/deficit	-193	-389	...	-2690	-2580	-2138	-2226	-2625
090 Overall surplus/deficit	-2403	-2698	...	-3367	-3300	-2665	-2381	-2946

1986	1987	1988	1989	1990	1991	1992	1993	1994	1995	
95774	92199	104523	118259	130231	120026	120929	125088	...	...	050
84551	74257	75720	80936	84976	76660	72847	73104	...	...	051

Calendar year

343	338	304	242	357	262	260	259	259	259	052
42	36	30	24	45	28	27	28	30	...	053
1	1	1	1	1	1	1	1	1	...	054
1	2	1	2	2	2	1	3	1	...	055
1	1	1	11	11	12	12	13	13	...	056

averages

113.6	112.0	102.7	94.5	122.6	106.6	101.8	106.8	106.7	106.7	057
...	...	...	...	...	...	...	...	...	...	058
...	...	...	...	...	...	...	...	...	...	059

values

25	24	26	26	26	27	29	30	31	31	060
25	24	26	26	26	27	29	30	31	...	061
69.0	81.0	84.0	84.0	87.0	92.0	86.0	87.5	89.0	...	062
50.0	...	...	...	...	...	...	...	...	...	063

averages

206.1	82.3	89.6	96.6	101.1	107.2	112.3	117.1	120.2	122.3	064
188.2	218.2	242.5	266.9	280.5	103.7	104.2	110.0	110.5	114.8	065
113.4	124.3	138.3	145.7	152.2	156.6	165.6	170.4	...	...	066

As of end of period

2139	2742	2510	3062	2668	3399	3794	3954	3953	4055	067
873	977	937	1011	915	1129	1105	1212	1351	1401	068
1266	1765	1573	2051	1753	2270	2689	2742	2602	2654	069
10963	10360	9790	13440	15694	19209	18206	20210	21307	22957	070
13102	13102	12300	16502	18362	22608	22000	24164	25260	27012	071
11196	11669	11393	14921	16699	20430	19056	20890	19731	21832	072
2710	1987	2415	3396	4638	4131	6164	6340	7238	7779	073
-775	-2092	-2033	-1494	-1412	-2096	-1844	-1702	-1411	-1126	074
3485	4079	4446	4887	6048	6223	7911	7942	8630	8905	075
–	–	2	3	3	4	97	100	19	–	076
-804	-554	-1508	-1815	-2975	-1953	-3220	-3066	-1709	-2599	077
1904	3102	2441	3270	2918	3361	4233	4448	4339	4175	078
9919	8687	8558	11907	14143	18172	16981	18712	18139	21435	079
										080
3482	4078	4365	4799	5966	6223	7911	7944	8500	8905	081

Fiscal year ending 31 December

2798	3291	3718	4135	4935	4710	5054	5136	5812	5940	082
2357	2836	3322	3379	3991	3574	3820	3846	4868	4721	083
441	455	396	756	944	1136	1234	1290	944	1219	084
3499	3323	3372	4051	4522	4693	5112	5373	5431	5939	085
-701	-32	346	84	413	17	-58	-237	381	1	086
–	–	–	–	–	–	–	–	–		087
2621	2552	3849	3361	2881	2211	1280	1326	1384	...	088
-2621	-2552	-3849	-3361	-2881	-2211	-1280	-1326	-1384	...	089
-3322	-2584	-3503	-3277	-2468	-2194	-1338	-1563	-1003	...	090

	Item	1978	1979	1980	1981	1982	1983	1984	1985
	Financing								
091	Domestic borrowing [h]	–	–	...	–	–	–	–	–
092	Foreign borrowing	–	–	...	-23	26	-21	-19	43
093	Foreign grants	2285	2214	...	3934	3350	2601	3120	2740
094	Use of cash balances [i]	118	484	...	-544	-76	85	-720	163
	Expenditure by Function, Central Govt.								
095	Total	3555	4117	2025	2042	2326	2374	2657	3129
096	General public services	1037	1550	634	788	992	1049	1136	1356
097	Defence	–	–	–	–	–	–	–	–
098	Education	1652	1625	662	599	608	605	692	785
099	Health	322	362	268	275	353	365	406	434
100	Social security & welfare	6	6	11	21	28	25	35	42
101	Housing & community amenities	–	–	–	–	–	–	–	–
102	Economic services	538	574	450	331	321	311	365	479
103	Agriculture	88	92	62	70	95	98	112	134
104	Industry	–	–	–	–	–	–	–	–
105	Electricity, gas & water	–	–	–	–	–	–	–	–
106	Transport and communications	49	54	147	145	164	156	179	241
107	Other economic services	401	428	241	116	62	57	74	104
108	Others [j]	–	–	–	28	24	19	23	33
	EXTERNAL TRADE								*Million Vatu;*
109	Exports, fob	3082	3240	2449	2833	2201	2941	4395	3252
110	Imports, cif	4614	5020	4993	5116	5663	6292	6811	7378
111	Trade balance	-1532	-1780	-2544	-2283	-3462	-3351	-2416	-4126
	Exports, by principal commodity								
112	1. Copra	1163	1505	592	1071	710	1308	2734	1392
113	2. Beef	150	139	75	160	184	193	142	186
114	3. Cocoa	188	95	94	117	57	183	135	133
115	4. Timber	35	47	1	21	23	31	147	136
116	5. Reexports [k]	972	831	1056	826	689	1033	911	1017
	Imports, by SITC section [l]								
117	Food & live animals	...	...	...	...	...	1023	1166	1210
118	Beverage & tobacco	...	...	...	...	...	269	310	295
119	Crude materials excl.fuels	...	...	...	...	...	49	49	68
120	Mineral fuels, etc.	...	...	...	...	...	572	560	651
121	Animal, vegetable oil & fats	...	...	...	...	...	24	36	38
122	Chemicals	...	...	...	...	...	320	408	395
123	Basic manufactures	...	...	...	...	...	844	903	1083
124	Machines, transport equipment	...	...	...	...	...	1070	1350	1387
125	Misc. manufactured goods	...	...	...	...	...	806	868	972
126	Unclassified goods	...	...	...	...	...	252	175	286
	Direction of Trade								*Million US dollars;*
127	Exports, Total	42.3	47.1	35.9	32.2	22.9	21.5	44.3	43.1
128	1. Japan	1.9	2.2	1.3	2.1	0.6	1.1	4.0	2.9
129	2. Germany	0.1	0.0	0.0	0.0	0.0	0.0	0.0	0.1
130	3. United States	12.7	11.2	12.1	7.5	5.8	0.0	0.0	0.0
131	4. Spain	0.1	0.0	0.0	0.0	0.0	0.0	0.0	0.0
132	5. United Kingdom	0.4	0.0	0.0	0.1	0.0	0.0	0.1	0.0
133	6. New Caledonia	1.0	0.8	0.9	1.0	1.5	0.9	0.4	0.2
134	7. Australia	0.0	0.1	0.1	0.2	0.2	0.1	0.2	0.4
135	8. Sweden	–	–	–	–	–	–	–	–
136	9. Turkey	–	–	–	–	–	–	–	–
137	10. Chile	–	–	–	–	–	–	–	–

1986	1987	1988		1989	1990	1991	1992	1993	1994	1995	
–	–	–	I	78	150	516	196	128	143	...	091
56	30	88	I	3285	766	873	716	1018	642	...	092
2341	3357	2956	I	1259	485	589	448	369	274	...	093
925	-803	459	I	-1345	1067	216	-22	48	-56	...	094
3499	3323	3942	I	4051	4522	4693	5112	5194	...	...	095
1545	1128	1201	I	921	1071	960	1156	1407	...	...	096
–	292	336	I	328	380	396	446	477	...	...	097
939	924	1045	I	860	888	927	1083	1037	...	...	098
440	408	445	I	424	456	484	517	506	...	...	099
52	38	62	I						...	...	100
–	15	18	I						...	...	101
486	455	835	I	706	818	1059	1085	1046	...	...	102
126	128	149	I	146	169	199	228	209	...	...	103
–	–	292	I	346	409	415	408	402	...	...	104
–	–	–	I	–	–	–	–	–	...	...	105
235	236	272	I	164	143	280	313	302	...	...	106
125	91	122	I	50	97	165	136	133	...	...	107
37	63	–	I	812	909	867	825	721	...	...	108

Calendar year

1841	1943	2033	2579	2204	2042	2677	2758	2911	3173	109
6105	7638	7361	8350	11211	9216	9276	9167	10344	10480 *	110
-4264	-5695	-5328	-5771	-9007	-7174	-6599	-6409	-7433	-7307	111
461	719	953	750	528	528	829	706	894	110	112
149	252	243	262	368	340	336	457	452	427	113
196	207	116	176	247	258	165	154	226	126	114
63	208	106	204	91	86	146	267	308	252	115
768	254	346	723	271	150	313	...	...	...	116
1089	1022	1263	1237	1312	1296	1606	1407	1560	1460 *	117
252	204	368	360	335	374	374	349	423	347 *	118
67	226	88	69	135	136	74	84	69	107 *	119
573	634	584	663	863	938	835	819	672	797 *	120
37	25	31	32	33	34	44	32	36	35 *	121
364	450	421	550	642	593	566	558	674	712 *	122
1062	1624	1430	1492	1911	1621	1378	1498	1976	2057 *	123
1503	1918	1797	2470	3815	2285	2521	2463	3061	3231 *	124
820	983	851	890	1355	1100	978	1098	1186	1075 *	125
138	364	233	251	290	228	233	216	252	239 *	126

Calendar Year

25.6	22.1	33.0	13.9	24.9	22.7	38.4	22.5	25.8	26.8	127
1.7	3.7	2.5	2.6	5.1	4.8	6.5	5.9	6.3	7.3	128
0.0	0.2	8.9	0.3	7.2	7.4	8.4	4.0	3.8	5.3	129
0.0	0.0	7.3	0.0	0.9	1.6	4.9	3.6	3.5	...	130
0.0	0.0	0.3	0.0	0.8	1.7	1.6	2.0	2.4	3.3	131
0.3	0.8	0.0	0.1	0.1	0.3	0.8	2.0	2.3	1.7	132
0.2	0.5	0.6	1.1	1.2	0.8	1.1	1.3	1.5	1.7	133
0.4	0.3	0.7	1.4	1.9	0.9	1.1	1.2	1.2	3.6	134
–	–	–	–	0.0	0.0	0.9	0.7	0.5	0.5	135
–	–	0.0	–	–	–	0.0	0.0	1.0	1.1	136
–	–	0.0	–	0.0	0.0	5.2	0.0	0.7	...	137

Item	1978	1979	1980	1981	1982	1983	1984	1985
138 Imports, Total	56.1	52.6	75.2	58.2	58.9	64.0	58.7	60.2
139 1. Japan	6.8	10.9	6.6	5.8	6.4	6.2	7.6	7.4
140 2. Australia	24.2	17.4	19.0	15.5	16.3	17.8	20.4	21.6
141 3. Italy	0.6	2.4	0.2	0.1	0.2	0.2	0.2	0.3
142 4. Spain	–	–	0.1	0.1	0.1	0.1	0.1	0.1
143 5. New Zealand	3.1	4.3	5.5	3.8	5.1	6.0	5.7	6.6
144 6. Fiji	–	–	6.8	5.9	5.6	3.9	4.3	4.0
145 7. France	7.2	7.7	6.6	4.9	4.6	4.8	5.5	5.0
146 8. Malaysia	–	–	0.0	0.0	0.0	0.0	0.1	0.1
147 9. China, People's Rep. of	–	–	0.4	0.5	0.7	0.7	1.1	1.2
148 10. Hong Kong	–	–	1.6	1.9	2.1	2.3	2.7	2.7
BALANCE OF PAYMENTS								*Million US dollars;*
149 Merchandise exports, fob	41.5	47.3	35.4	32.2	10.7	17.9	32.5	18.7
150 Merchandise imports, fob	-51.2	-58.9	-64.0	-53.5	-43.3	-45.8	-51.5	-52.3
151 Trade balance	-9.7	-11.6	-28.6	-21.3	-32.6	-27.9	-18.9	-33.6
152 Other goods, services and income	-10.8	-7.0	8.4	13.2	1.5	4.1	3.2	4.3
153 Credit	...	...	...	...	42.6	44.6	51.2	64.9
154 Debit	...	...	...	...	-41.1	-40.5	-48.0	-60.6
155 Unrequited transfers	33.5	39.2	49.9	44.8	43.2	32.2	38.6	30.6
156 Official	33.3	38.9	49.9	...	34.7	26.2	28.1	23.9
157 Private	0.2	0.3	–	...	8.2	6.0	6.9	6.8
158 Current balance	13.0	20.6	29.7	36.7	11.8	8.4	19.3	1.3
159 Direct investment	...	...	...	...	6.9	5.9	7.4	4.6
160 Portfolio investment	...	...	...	...	–	–	–	–
161 Other long-term capital	...	...	0.2	...	-44.6	6.3	102.7	-47.2
162 Other short-term capital	...	...	...	...	22.4	-23.4	-137.7	47.7
163 Net errors and omissions [m]	-18.5	-28.1	...	...	6.4	3.8	2.1	-6.6
164 Overall balance	-5.5	-7.5	29.9	36.7	2.9	1.0	-6.2	-0.3
165 Allocation of SDRs	–	–	–	–	–	–	–	–
166 Monetary movements	5.5	7.5	-29.9	-36.7	-2.9	-1.0	6.2	0.3
INTERNATIONAL RESERVES								*Million US dollars;*
167 Total	...	...	...	8.46	5.67	6.59	8.09	10.61
168 Gold, national valuation	...	...	...	–	–	–	–	–
169 Foreign exchange	...	...	...	8.46	4.52	4.93	6.45	8.71
170 Reserve position in the Fund	...	...	...	0.00	1.15	1.64	1.55	1.74
171 SDRs	...	...	...	–	–	0.02	0.09	0.16
EXCHANGE RATES								*Vatu per*
172 End of period	67.56	64.97	72.99	91.23	96.15	101.77	102.58	100.25
173 Average of period	72.94	68.76	68.29	87.83	96.21	99.37	99.23	106.03
EXTERNAL INDEBTEDNESS								*Million US dollars;*
174 Total outstanding and disbursed	5.1	4.8	4.1	3.0	4.0	10.5	12.9	15.9
175 Long-term	5.1	4.8	4.1	3.0	4.0	3.5	4.9	6.9
176 Public and publicly guaranteed	5.1	4.8	4.1	3.0	4.0	3.5	4.9	6.9
177 Private non-guaranteed	–	–	–	–	–	–	–	–
178 Short-term	–	–	–	–	–	7.0	8.0	9.0
179 Use of IMF credit	–	–	–	–	–	–	–	–
Debt Service								*Transactions*
180 Principal repayments on LT debt	0.3	0.4	0.3	0.3	0.3	0.3	0.4	0.4
181 Interest on long-term debt	0.2	0.3	0.2	0.2	0.2	0.2	0.1	0.1
182 Interest on short-term debt	–	–	–	–	–	0.8	0.8	0.8

1986	1987	1988	1989	1990	1991	1992	1993	1994	1995	
55.7	67.8	67.7	258.8	285.7	108.6	107.3	195.8	153.1	135.4	138
7.2	8.7	6.3	148.3	173.9	29.7	16.4	68.2	64.9	61.9	139
20.3	23.5	29.4	18.5	25.0	28.2	27.3	42.5	33.8	32.0	140
0.1	0.1	0.4	23.5	50.8	21.1	24.7	23.1	13.2	1.3	141
0.0	0.0	0.0	23.5	0.0	2.4	0.0	24.7	0.1	0.1	142
5.4	9.5	7.1	8.1	7.8	7.5	7.0	8.1	8.2	9.7	143
2.7	4.2	4.7	7.1	0.0	0.0	4.4	5.3	6.0	7.0	144
4.2	3.2	3.3	2.9	6.6	6.1	6.0	4.8	5.2	4.6	145
0.1	0.1	0.3	0.0	0.1	0.0	0.1	6.2	3.2	1.2	146
0.9	1.1	1.3	1.3	2.1	1.1	7.7	1.3	7.5	1.9	147
2.1	2.1	2.7	2.0	2.6	4.3	2.7	2.9	2.6	3.2	148
Calendar year										
8.8	13.7	15.4	13.7	13.7	14.9	17.8	17.4	20.7	...	149
-46.8	-57.1	-57.9	-57.9	-79.3	-74.0	-66.8	-64.7	-83.5	...	150
-38.0	-43.4	-42.5	-44.2	-65.6	-59.1	-49.0	-47.3	-62.8	...	151
6.6	-0.2	4.6	15.4	34.9	14.8	13.2	12.0	7.0	...	152
71.4	67.3	63.4	63.7	92.1	91.0	87.5	87.2	92.4	...	153
-64.8	-67.5	-58.8	-48.3	-57.2	-76.1	-74.3	-75.2	-85.4	...	154
28.6	52.2	22.7	16.5	24.5	30.6	22.7	22.8	27.5	...	155
21.3	32.3	...	...	...	...	...	...	...	...	156
7.2	5.8	...	...	...	...	...	...	...	...	157
-2.8	-5.3	-15.2	-12.3	-6.2	-13.7	-13.1	-12.4	-28.3	...	158
2.0	12.9	10.8	9.2	13.1	25.5	26.5	26.7	29.8	...	159
–	–	–	–	–	–	–	–	–		160
11.9	16.0 }	17.0	23.8	17.1	-34.1	14.5	9.6	-13.9	...	161
-0.9	-9.5 }								...	162
-5.3	-15.1	-17.3	-13.0	-19.4	19.3	-27.1	-20.4	6.3	...	163
4.8	-1.1	-4.7	7.7	4.7	-3.1	0.7	3.4	-6.1	...	164
–	–	–	–	–	–	–	–	–	...	165
-4.8	1.1	4.7	-7.7	-4.7	3.1	-0.7	-3.4	6.1	...	166
As of end of period										
21.42	40.17	40.67	35.08	37.69	39.84	42.46	45.59	43.58	...	167
–	–	–	–	–	–	–	–	–		168
19.23	37.55	38.10	32.44	34.69	36.69	39.31	41.96	39.63	...	169
1.94	2.26	2.15	2.12	2.29	2.30	2.21	3.42	3.63	3.70	170
0.24	0.37	0.42	0.53	0.71	0.84	0.93	0.21	0.31	0.43	171
US dollar										
116.24	100.56	105.05	110.70	109.25	110.79	119.00	120.80	112.08	113.74	172
106.08	109.85	104.43	116.04	117.06	111.68	113.39	121.58	116.41	112.11	173
As of end of year										
18.1	23.7	26.8	30.3	40.3	39.3	40.4	42.4	46.5	...	174
8.1	13.7	15.3	20.8	30.7	38.1	39.6	39.4	41.5	...	175
8.1	13.7	15.3	20.8	30.7	38.1	39.6	39.4	41.5	...	176
–	–	–	–	–	–	–	–	–	...	177
10.0	10.0	11.5	9.5	9.6	1.2	0.8	3.0	5.0	...	178
–	–	–	–	–	–	–	–	–		179
during the year										
0.6	2.2	0.8	0.5	1.1	0.9	0.9	0.9	1.0	...	180
0.4	0.5	0.5	0.7	0.6	0.4	0.6	0.5	0.7	...	181
0.6	0.8	1.1	0.7	0.7	0.4	0.1	0.1	0.2	...	182

	Item	1978	1979	1980	1981	1982	1983	1984	1985
	Average terms of new commitments								
183	Interest (%)	–	–	–	–	3.8	2.9	13.6	4.5
184	Maturity (years)	–	–	–	–	16.3	29.6	15.4	27.0
185	Grace period (years)	–	–	–	–	3.6	8.1	0.5	4.7
186	Grant element (%)	–	–	–	–	33.2	56.1	-17.6	37.7

Footnotes:

a. Mid-year estimates based on the 1979 Census except for 1989 which is the result of the 1989 Census. There was no country data for 1978 and the value supplied was ADB's own estimate.
b. Data for 1989 includes not economically active population, i.e., those which by their definition neither did economic work nor looked for work during the reference period.
c. Include real estate and business services, other community, social and personal services less imputed banking charges.
d. End of period data until 1982, average of quarterly figures thereafter.
e. Data referring to base period Q1 1976 are for the low-income group only.
f. Exclude deposits of the Government of Vanuatu but include deposits of non-reporting (i.e., exempt) banks and other institutions held with reporting banks.
g. Include claims on public enterprises.
h. Refers to transfers from the recurrent budget and STABEX fund and receipts from non-government organization for 1989-93.
i. Refers to the balancing item for financing of the overall surplus/deficit for 1989-93.
j. Include social security & welfare and housing and community amenities for 1989-93.
k. Include frozen fish only for 1978-82. From 1983 onward, data include other re-export commodities excluding petroleum.
l. Refers to goods for home consumption only.
m. Includes capital flows for 1978.

1986	1987	1988	1989	1990	1991	1992	1993	1994	1995	
1.5	8.6	1.0	1.2	–	2.1	1.0	–	–	...	183
38.2	14.5	39.5	35.8	–	37.9	39.8	–	–	...	184
9.3	2.0	10.1	10.4	–	8.6	10.1	–	–	...	185
72.3	7.0	77.9	75.2	–	67.6	78.7	–	–	...	186

	Item	1978	1979	1980	1981	1982	1983	1984	1985
001	**POPULATION**	51.42	52.46	53.72	54.93	56.17	57.37	58.65	*Million;* 59.87
	LABOR FORCE								*Million;*
002	Employed [a]	20.4	21.0	21.6	22.5	23.5	24.4	25.1	26.0
003	Agriculture	14.0	14.6	15.1	15.8	16.6	17.3	18.2	18.8
004	Manufacturing [b]	2.1	2.2	2.3	2.4	2.5	2.7	2.7	2.8
005	Mining								
006	Others	4.3	4.2	4.2	4.3	4.4	4.4	4.2	4.4
007	Unemployed	...	...	...	...	...	...	...	...
008	Unemployment rate, %	...	...	...	...	...	...	...	...
	NATIONAL ACCOUNTS [c]								
	At Current Market Prices								*Billion dong;*
009	NMP I GDP by Industrial Origin [d]	1.9	2.2	2.6	6.0	13.4	18.1	28.4 I	75.6
010	Agriculture [e]	0.9	1.0	1.3	3.3	7.1	8.9	13.6 I	35.7
011	Mining								
012	Manufacturing	0.5	0.5	0.5	1.4	3.4	4.6	7.5 I	22.7
013	Electricity, gas and water								
014	Construction	0.1	0.1	0.1	0.1	0.4	0.6	0.9 I	3.4
015	Trade	0.3	0.4	0.5	0.9	2.0	2.9	4.9 I	10.9
016	Transport and communications	0.0	0.0	0.1	0.1	0.2	0.3	0.4 I	1.2
017	Finance	...	...	...	...	...	...	... I	...
018	Others [f]	0.1	0.2	0.1	0.2	0.3	0.8	1.1 I	1.7
019	Net factor income from abroad	...	...	...	...	...	...	...	...
020	GNP	...	...	...	...	...	...	...	...
	At Current Market Prices								
021	Expenditure on NMP I GDP	1.9	2.2	2.6	6.0	13.4	18.1	28.4 I	75.6
022	Private consumption	...	...	...	...	...	...	...	...
023	Government consumption	...	...	...	...	...	...	...	...
024	Gross fixed capital formation	...	...	...	...	...	...	...	...
025	Increase in stocks								
026	Exports of goods and services	...	...	...	...	...	...	...	...
027	Less: Import of goods and services	...	...	...	...	...	...	...	...
028	Statistical discrepancy	...	...	...	...	...	...	...	...
	At Constant 1982 I 1989 Prices								
029	NMP I GDP by Industrial Origin [d]	12.4	12.2	12.0	12.3	13.4	14.3	15.5 I	164.1
030	Agriculture [e]	5.7	5.8	6.1	6.4	7.1	7.6	7.9 I	83.4
031	Mining								
032	Manufacturing	3.8	3.6	3.1	3.1	3.5	3.7	4.2 I	46.3
033	Electricity, gas and water								
034	Construction	0.5	0.5	0.4	0.4	0.4	0.4	0.5 I	5.0
035	Trade	2.0	1.9	1.8	1.8	2.0	2.0	2.3 I	22.1
036	Transport and communications	0.3	0.3	0.2	0.2	0.3	0.3	0.3 I	2.9
037	Finance	...	...	...	...	...	...	... I	...
038	Others [f]	0.3	0.2	0.3	0.3	0.3	0.4	0.4 I	4.4
039	Net factor income from abroad	...	...	...	...	...	...	...	...
040	GNP							...	...
	Investment Financing, at current prices								
041	Gross domestic capital formation	...	...	...	...	...	...	...	...
042	Gross national saving	...	...	...	...	...	...	...	...
043	Gross domestic saving	...	...	...	...	...	...	...	...
044	Net factor income from abroad	...	...	...	...	...	...	...	...
	Per Capita NMP I GDP, Dong								
045	Current prices	37	42	48	109	239	315	484 I	1263
046	Constant *1982* I *1989* prices	241	233	223	224	239	249	264 I	2741

	1986	1987	1988	1989	1990	1991	1992	1993	1994	1995	
As of 1 July	61.11	62.45	63.73	64.77	66.23	67.77	69.41	71.03	72.51 *	73.96 *	001
Calendar year	27.4	28.5	28.5	28.9	30.3	31.0	31.8	32.7	33.7	34.7 *	002
	19.8	20.2	20.4	20.7	21.7	22.3	23.0	23.7	23.6	23.9 *	003
	2.9	3.0	3.1	3.2	3.4	3.4	3.5	3.5	3.9	4.2 *	004
	4.7	5.3	5.0	5.0	5.2	5.3	5.4	5.5	6.2	6.6 *	006
											007
	...	...	...	...	...	...	...	...	...	...	008
Calendar year											
	394.9	1899.2	9751.3	17413.9	41955.0	76707.0	110535.0	136571.0	170258.0	222840.0 *	009
	159.4	832.8	5082.9	8411.5	15720.0	30314.0	36468.0	39320.0	47082.0	61387.0 *	010
											011
	111.0	525.3	2012.1	3631.3	7900.0	15193.0	23956.0	29371.0	37535.0	48912.0 *	012
											013
	13.3	58.2	343.8	847.1	1613.0	3059.0	6179.0	10101.0	12946.0	15892.0 *	014
	75.8	317.0	1421.7	3078.4	5460.0	9742.0	15281.0	17549.0	23072.0	30284.0 *	015
	3.8	17.3	138.4	259.2	1449.0	2860.0	4662.0	6036.0	6924.0	8747.0 *	016
			...	...	516.0	1108.0	1567.0	2318.0	3457.0	5580.0 *	017
	31.6	148.6	752.4	1186.4	9297.0	14431.0	22422.0	31876.0	39242.0	52038.0 *	018
											019
	...	...	...	...	...	...	...	...	...	...	020
	394.9	1899.2	9751.3	17413.9	41955.0	76707.0	110535.0	136571.0	170258.0	222840.0 *	021
	...	...	...	...	35559.0	62755.0	88943.0	106440.0	127043.0	180522.0 *	022
	...	...	...	...	5177.0	6204.0	6371.0	10279.0	14132.0		023
	...	...	...	...	5272.0	11560.0	19498.0	34020.0	43375.0	60488.0 *	024
											025
	...	...	...	...	15120.0	20294.0	33037.0	40286.0	42314.0	67548.0 *	026
	...	...	...	...	18996.0	24219.0	37553.0	52582.0	59098.0	88367.0 *	027
	...	...	...	...	-177.0	113.0	239.0	-1872.0	2492.0	2649.0 *	028
	174.8	180.6	188.9	194.0	29526.0	31286.0	33991.0	36735.0	39982.0	43780.0 *	029
	84.6	81.7	86.5	92.0	11642.0	11894.0	12751.0	13235.0	13751.0	14369.0 *	030
											031
	48.4	53.9	56.0	54.7	5500.0	6042.0	6925.0	7766.0	8771.0	9768.0 *	032
											033
	5.0	5.3	5.1	5.2	1129.0	1186.0	1317.0	1558.0	1860.0	2138.0 *	034
	23.4	24.3	25.8	26.5	3486.0	3654.0	3877.0	4109.0	4478.0	4891.0 *	035
	3.1	3.3	3.3	3.1	744.0	792.0	842.0	897.0	960.0	1066.0 *	036
	...	...	...	...	368.0	448.0	495.0	578.0	710.0	998.0 *	037
	10.3	12.1	12.2	12.5	6657.0	7270.0	7784.0	8592.0	9452.0	10550.0 *	038
	...	...	...	...	...	...	...	...	...	...	039
	...	...	...	...	...	...	...	...	...	...	040
	...	...	...	...	5272.0	11560.0	19498.0	34020.0	43375.0	60488.0 *	041
	...	...	...	...	...	...	...	...	...	...	042
	...	...	...	...	1219.0	7748.0	15221.0	19852.0	29083.0	42318.0 *	043
	...	...	...	...	...	...	...	...	...	...	044
	6462	30411	153017	268841	633446	1131806	1592604	1922723	2348062	3012980 *	045
	2860	2892	2964	2995	445790	461622	489747	517176	551400	591942 *	046

	Item	1978	1979	1980	1981	1982	1983	1984	1985
	PRODUCTION								*Thousand metric tons;*
	Agriculture								
047	1. Paddy rice	10040	10758	11647	12415	14390	14743	15506	15875
048	2. Coconut	199	326	311	349	406	518	523	612
049	3. Maize	485	475	418	416	437	467	525	587
050	4. Rubber	46	43	41	44	46	47	47	48
051	5. Coffee	6	5	8	5	5	5	4	12
052	6. Tea	19	21	21	21	25	25	27	28
	Mining								
053	1. Coal	6000	5500	5300	6000	6100	6235	4900	5700
054	2. Salt	530	526	437	430	516	794	713	677
	Manufacturing								
055	1. Cigarettes, *Mn*	7952	7040	7032	10440	13886	18476	21236	21012
056	2. Cement	843	705	641	538	710	907	1296	1503
057	3. Chemical fertilizers	607	260	360	268	230	289	460	532
058	4. Sugarcane	2847	3446	4388	3934	4467	5693	6567	5560
	Production index								*Period*
059	Agriculture, *1979-81 = 100*	89.2	93.8	101.6	104.2	113.6	115.3	121.7	121.5
	ENERGY								*Annual*
	Crude petroleum, *'000 m.t.*								
060	Production	...	...	...	...	...	...	...	...
061	Exports	...	...	...	...	...	...	...	...
062	Imports	...	...	...	...	...	...	...	...
063	Consumption	...	...	...	...	...	...	...	...
	Coal, *'000 m.t.*								
064	Production	6000	5500	5300	6000	6100	6235	4900	5700
065	Exports	1430	759	656	921	778	491	549	766
066	Imports	...	...	...	...	...	...	...	...
067	Consumption	...	...	...	...	...	...	...	...
	Electricity, *Mn kWh*								
068	Production	...	...	3600	3800	4100	4300	5000	5230
069	Exports	...	...	...	...	...	...	...	...
070	Imports	...	...	...	...	...	...	...	...
071	Consumption	...	...	2700	2800	3000	3100	3600	3800
	PRICE INDEXES								*Period*
072	Retail, 1985 = 100 [g]	...	...	...	...	...	...	...	100.0
073	Food	...	...	...	...	...	...	...	100.0
074	Implicit NMP I GDP deflator, *1982*I *1989*	15.3	18.0	21.7	48.8	100.0	126.6	183.2 I	46.1
	MONEY AND BANKING [h]								*Billion dong;*
075	Money Supply (M1)	...	...	...	...	...	...	...	...
076	Currency in circulation	...	...	...	...	...	...	...	...
077	Demand deposits [i]	...	...	...	...	...	...	...	...
078	Quasi-money [j]	...	...	...	...	...	...	...	...
079	Money supply (M2)	...	...	...	...	...	...	...	...
080	Foreign assets (net)	...	...	...	...	...	...	...	...
081	Domestic credit	...	...	...	...	...	...	...	...
082	Claims on gov't sector (net)	...	...	...	...	...	...	...	...
083	Claims on private sector [k]	...	...	...	...	...	...	...	...
084	Claims on other financial inst. [l]	...	...	...	...	...	...	...	...
085	Other items	...	...	...	...	...	...	...	...
	Deposit Money Banks								
086	Demand deposits	...	...	...	...	...	1.6	3.1	17.1
087	Savings deposits }								
088	Time deposits }	...	...	...	...	...	0.6	0.8	2.6

1986	1987	1988	1989	1990	1991	1992	1993	1994	1995	
Calendar year										
16003	15103	17000	18996	19225	19622	21590	22837	23528	24856	047
711	791	857	922	894	1053	1140	1207	1277	1200	048
570	561	815	838	671	672	707	882	1144	1144	049
50	52	50	51	58	65	67	96	129	130	050
19	21	31	41	59	67	72	131	166	166	051
30	29	30	30	32	33	36	38	38	38	052
6392	6839	6860	3849	4600	4729	5019	5899	5690	7452	053
763	847	850	643	593	583	594	650	469	560	054
22364	19630	17754	23288	24990	25500	30460	33052	36600	39850	055
1540	1665	1954	2088	2534	3127	3926	4849	5371	5731	056
516	485	503	373	354	450	530	713	845	918	057
4965	5470	5700	5345	5398	6131	6437	6083	7550	7912	058
averages										
130.0	136.6	139.4	147.9	151.4	153.5	161.4	170.3	176.0	183.4	059
values										
...	...	...	...	2700	3850	5520	6261	7000	7700	060
...	...	...	...	2617	3917	5446	6153	6942	7600	061
...	...	...	...	2851	2572	3143	4091	4513	4969	062
...	...	...	...	2860	2560	3134	4060	4985	4950	063
6392	6839	6860	3849	4600	4729	5019	5899	5690	7452	064
752	233	349	579	789	1173	1623	3432	2137	2800	065
										066
...	...	...	3270	3838	3156	3469	2547	3983	4652	067
5700	6200	7000	8000	8790	9307	9818	10851	12693	14867	068
...	...	...	...	...	...	...	...	...	...	069
...	...	...	...	...	...	...	...	...	...	070
4200	4600	5000	5700	6200	6600	6859	7809	9177	11795	071
averages										
587.2	2446.9	10054.2	19686.0	26851.8	49165.6	67750.2	73373.4	80270.5 *	...	072
653.2	2864.9	13024.0	...	...	...	...	...	...	...	073
225.9	1051.6	5162.1	8976.2 ⎮	142.1	245.2	325.2	371.8	425.8	509.0 *	074
As of end of period										
109	442	2327	5324	7678	11947	18931	24882 ⎮	28894	36159	075
55	205	1024	2352	3735	6419	10579	14218 ⎮	18624	19170	076
54	237	1303	2972	3943	5528	8352	10664 ⎮	10271	16989	077
3	29	242	2095	3680	8354	8213	7406 ⎮	9530	11061	078
112	471	2569	7419	11358	20301	27144	32288 ⎮	38424	47220	079
-23	210	284	1004	2626	8503	10593	6231 ⎮	6940	10851	080
153	532	2633	6717	9960	14111	17121	27112 ⎮	37951	46843	081
19	80	669	2600	4032	3956	1912	3903 ⎮	4551	4472	082
4	76	255	511	620	1026	2770	7698 ⎮	12936	18292	083
130	376	1709	3606	5308	9129	12439	15511 ⎮	20464	24079	084
-18	-271	-348	-302	-1228	-2313	-570	-1055 ⎮	-6467	-10473	085
38.7	149.6	428.0	...	...	...	...	...	...	...	086
										087
7.1	53.2	120.0	...	...	...	...	...	...	...	088

Item	1978	1979	1980	1981	1982	1983	1984	1985
Interest rates								*Percent;*
On deposits								
089 Savings	...	...	...	...	...	...	...	...
090 Time: 6 months	...	...	...	...	...	...	...	...
091 Time: 12 months [m]	...	...	...	...	...	...	2.5	2.5
GOVERNMENT FINANCE								*Billion dong;*
Central Government								
092 Current revenue	...	...	...	...	...	...	9	19
093 Taxes [n]	...	...	...	...	...	...	2	3
094 Non-taxes	...	...	...	...	...	...	7	16
095 Current expenditure	...	...	...	...	...	...	9	24
096 Current surplus/deficit	...	...	...	...	...	...	1	-5
097 Capital receipts	...	...	...	...	...	...	–	–
098 Capital expenditure	...	...	...	...	...	...	3	11
099 Capital account surplus/deficit	...	...	...	...	...	...	-3	-11
100 Overall surplus/deficit	...	...	...	...	...	...	-2	-16
Financing								
101 Domestic borrowing	...	...	...	...	...	...	1	9
102 Foreign borrowing	...	...	...	...	...	...		
103 Foreign grants	...	...	...	...	...	...	2	6
104 Use of cash balances	...	...	...	...	...	...	-1	1
EXTERNAL TRADE [o]								*Million US dollars;*
105 Exports. fob	648	587	339	401	527	617	650	699
106 Imports, cif [p]	1485	1599	1314	1382	1472	1527	1745	1857
107 Trade balance	-837	-1012	-976	-981	-946	-910	-1095	-1159
Exports, by SITC section								
108 Food & live animals	...	...	...	...	...	...	...	...
109 Beverage & tobacco	...	...	...	...	...	...	...	...
110 Crude materials excl. fuels	...	...	...	...	...	...	...	...
111 Mineral fuels, etc.	...	...	...	...	...	...	...	...
112 Animal, vegetable oil & fats	...	...	...	...	...	...	...	...
113 Chemicals	...	...	...	...	...	...	...	...
114 Basic manufactures	...	...	...	...	...	...	...	...
115 Machines, transport equipment	...	...	...	...	...	...	...	...
116 Misc. manufactured goods	...	...	...	...	...	...	...	...
117 Unclassified goods	...	...	...	...	...	...	...	...
Exports, by principal commodity								
118 1. Rice	...	...	...	...	...	...	...	...
119 2. Coffee	...	...	...	...	...	...	...	...
120 3. Frozen shrimp	...	...	...	...	...	...	...	...
121 4. Rubber	...	...	...	...	...	30	31	30
122 5. Coal	...	...	...	...	...	28	26	40
Imports, by SITC section								
123 Food & live animals	...	...	...	...	...	...	...	...
124 Beverage & tobacco	...	...	...	...	...	...	...	...
125 Crude materials excl. fuels	...	...	...	...	...	...	...	...
126 Mineral fuels, etc.	...	...	...	...	...	...	...	...
127 Animal, vegetable oil & fats	...	...	...	...	...	...	...	...
128 Chemicals	...	...	...	...	...	...	...	...
129 Basic manufactures	...	...	...	...	...	...	...	...
130 Machines, transport equipment	...	...	...	...	...	...	...	...
131 Misc. manufactured goods	...	...	...	...	...	...	...	...
132 Unclassified goods	...	...	...	...	...	...	...	...

	1986	1987	1988	1989	1990	1991	1992	1993	1994	1995	

As of end of period

					2.4	2.1	1.0	0.8	0.7	...	089
	...	...	...	...	...	...		1.7	1.7	...	090
	8.9	10.8	19.2	42.6	...	...	...	...	...	...	091

Fiscal year ending 31 December

83	380	1617	3899	6153	9731	18746	27906	38299	51646 *	092
18	68	455	2716	4810	8381	15116	24507	33577	45271 *	093
65	312	1162	1183	1343	1350	3630	3399	4722	6375 *	094
87	399	2161	5045	7062	9946	17260	27410	33355	41662 *	095
-4	-19	-544	-1146	-909	-215	1486	496	4944	9984 *	096
–	–	–	–	–	622	2277	2594	3826	1649 *	097
33	116	549	1626	2124	2135	6450	9600	11300	12800 *	098
-33	-116	-549	-1626	-2124	-1513	-4173	-7006	-7474	-11151 *	099
-37	-135	-1093	-2772	-3033	-1728	-2687	-6510	-2530	-1167 *	100
23	92	737	1700	1173	393	1373	2500	2330	2697 *	101
										102
14	43	356	1072	1860	1335	1314	4010	200	-1530 *	103
-1	1	–	–	–	–	–	–	–	–	104

Calendar year

789	854	1038	1946	2404	2087	2581	2985	4054	5220	105
2155	2455	2757	2566	2752	2338	2541	3924	5826	7510	106
-1366	-1601	-1719	-620	-348	-251	40	-939	-1772	-2290	107
337	369	414	690	826	767	963	1121	1536	...	108
21	23	28	16	18	2	4	4	3	...	109
150	164	232	230	327	317	329	230	310	...	110
34	36	44	424	500	631	868	981	1002	...	111
8	8	10	9	10	2	5	6	11	...	112
10	10	13	14	18	8	11	14	12	...	113
54	57	70	91	107	81	92	143	217	...	114
1	1	2	1	1	6	7	20	98	...	115
165	175	215	452	575	271	303	463	700	...	116
9	9	11	19	22	2	–	3	165	...	117
22	17	27	290	305	234	418	363	245	538	118
61	50	58	81	92	76	91	111	328	495	119
75	93	133	109	152	178	185	225	296	...	120
30	31	32	47	66	50	67	74	134	145	121
34	11	14	24	33	48	62	52	75	79	122
121	134	180	159	114	136	147	119	185	...	123
2	2	15	13	12	41	56	34	57	...	124
92	104	102	89	90	77	20	54	121	...	125
453	514	716	623	641	542	644	710	743	...	126
0	1	1	1	1	4	1	12	11	...	127
335	358	399	429	450	430	540	656	995	...	128
364	444	612	546	612	527	513	759	778	...	129
704	801	632	621	742	450	472	1037	1494	...	130
59	70	73	61	67	109	119	254	580	...	131
24	26	27	23	23	22	29	289	863	...	132

	Item	1978	1979	1980	1981	1982	1983	1984	1985
	Direction of Trade							Million US dollars;	
133	Exports, Total	...	...	...	141.4	179.1	204.6	250.0	690.8
134	1. Japan	46.6	43.5	44.4	33.9	32.6	34.5	46.5	32.3
135	2. Singapore	13.0	14.8	16.3	11.9	19.3	30.4	44.4	36.2
136	3. Germany	4.0	4.3	5.9	5.0	3.6	4.7	5.3	2.0
137	4. Australia	0.8	0.1	0.2	0.2	0.6	4.0	3.8	2.4
138	5. France	4.1	5.2	4.5	6.6	5.5	6.9	7.5	12.3
139	6. China, People's Rep. of	37.0	0.0	0.0	0.0	0.0	0.0	0.0	0.0
140	7. Hong Kong	18.8	15.4	20.2	30.3	74.1	63.9	80.0	47.6
141	8. Malaysia	0.5	0.2	0.2	0.2	2.0	7.6	7.8	0.0
142	9. Korea, Rep. of	3.0	13.2	4.4	4.6	0.0	2.8	0.0	15.5
143	10. Netherlands	0.0	0.0	0.0	0.1	0.2	1.4	0.4	0.0
144	Imports, Total	...	...	...	565.7	434.7	408.0	524.8	1840.4
145	1. Singapore	44.9	52.9	54.4	79.0	38.2	49.5	78.6	23.8
146	2. Korea, Rep. of	3.0	2.2	9.6	0.1	0.0	0.0	0.0	2.8
147	3. Japan	239.8	128.3	124.9	120.0	101.4	131.3	130.6	142.1
148	4. Hong Kong	32.8	20.0	33.3	29.9	65.3	60.9	81.0	28.6
149	5. China, People's Rep. of	17.9	0.0	0.0	0.0	0.0	0.0	0.0	0.0
150	6. France	109.9	109.6	66.0	88.1	25.7	35.8	30.0	6.9
151	7. Thailand	12.9	23.5	13.7	0.4	0.6	1.0	9.4	0.0
152	8. Indonesia	1.3	0.0	0.0	0.0	0.0	0.4	2.2	0.0
153	9. Malaysia	0.3	1.3	0.1	0.0	0.6	1.0	0.3	0.0
154	10. Germany	54.7	59.6	21.8	20.5	8.1	4.5	8.9	4.3
	BALANCE OF PAYMENTS							Million US dollars;	
155	Merchandise exports, fob	...	...	...	...	...	588	665	746
156	Merchandise imports, fob	...	...	...	...	...	-1310	-1560	-1590
157	Trade balance [q]	...	...	...	...	...	-722	-895	-844
158	Other goods, services & income	...	...	...	...	...	...	...	...
159	Credit	...	...	...	...	...	...	...	...
160	Debit	...	...	...	...	...	...	...	...
161	Unrequited transfer [r]	...	...	...	...	...	-8	-31	-47
162	Private	...	...	...	...	...	...	...	...
163	Official	...	...	...	...	...	...	...	...
164	Current balance	...	...	...	...	...	-730	-926	-891
165	Direct investment	...	...	...	...	...	...	...	...
166	Portfolio investment	...	...	...	...	...	...	...	...
167	Other long-term capital [s]	...	...	...	...	...	...	...	...
168	Other short-term capital	...	...	...	...	...	...	...	...
169	Net errors & omissions	...	...	...	...	...	...	...	...
170	Overall balance	...	...	...	...	...	...	...	...
171	Allocations of SDRs	...	...	...	...	...	...	...	...
172	Monetary movement [t]	...	...	...	...	...	...	...	...
	INTERNATIONAL RESERVES							Million US dollars;	
173	Total	...	...	...	...	...	...	16	16
174	Gold, national valuation	...	...	...	...	...	...	4	4
175	Foreign exchange	...	...	...	...	...	...	12	12
176	Reserve position in the fund	...	...	...	...	...	...	...	...
177	SDRs	...	...	...	...	...	...	...	...
	EXCHANGE RATES							Dong per	
178	End of period [u]	...	...	...	...	...	...	12	15
179	Average of period	...	...	...	...	...	...	...	...
	EXTERNAL INDEBTEDNESS							Million US dollars;	
180	Total outstanding & disbursed	...	...	...	...	9639	11287	9352	10345
181	Long-term	1620	2266	2603	2596	9451	11146	9199	10112
182	Public and publicly guaranteed	...	...	...	...	...	...	...	...
183	Private non-guaranteed	...	...	...	...	...	...	...	...

	1986	1987	1988	1989	1990	1991	1992	1993	1994	1995	
Calendar year											
	341.0	419.1	528.2	1936.2	2364.0	2081.2	2566.8	3581.6	4502.9	5674.7	133
	75.9	131.9	177.7	261.0	340.3	719.3	833.9	975.6	1227.3	1559.9	134
	0.0	0.0	0.0	70.7	194.5	425.0	401.7	320.4	408.9	474.3	135
	7.7	7.0	11.9	8.7	41.3	6.7	34.4	264.3	377.7	518.4	136
	8.4	13.2	16.9	0.8	7.7	5.2	21.4	171.7	211.2	212.7	137
	13.5	16.7	10.7	79.7	115.7	83.1	132.3	159.5	205.3	279.0	138
	0.0	0.0	0.0	0.3	7.8	19.3	95.6	111.4	173.8	284.8	139
	96.5	102.9	123.3	78.9	243.2	223.3	201.7	126.2	134.5	157.8	140
	15.0	12.6	24.6	2.5	5.0	14.5	68.4	84.5	101.4	124.6	141
	0.0	0.0	0.0	25.0	26.7	51.3	93.5	82.4	103.4	10.6	142
	0.6	0.4	0.4	0.2	6.4	16.2	20.1	54.4	91.8	92.6	143
	590.3	613.9	792.3	2561.7	2726.1	2296.1	2504.3	6150.9	8398.4	...	144
	0.0	0.0	0.0	41.3	497.0	722.2	821.6	1078.4	1461.0	1694.7	145
	0.0	0.0	0.0	15.6	53.1	152.1	211.2	801.1	1130.1	1479.0	146
	209.2	198.8	212.9	105.6	169.0	157.7	239.4	705.5	708.0	...	147
	65.5	74.1	104.6	102.6	196.9	194.8	142.9	561.1	575.9	700.6	148
	0.0	0.0	0.0	0.0	4.6	18.4	31.8	304.3	375.9	718.0	149
	38.3	41.1	56.4	52.5	123.0	147.9	161.7	308.7	312.5	354.1	150
	1.2	4.8	5.1	2.3	17.0	14.2	41.2	127.3	279.5	483.8	151
	32.3	27.0	21.2	0.5	9.8	49.4	39.8	188.8	196.0	211.7	152
	1.5	3.8	6.8	0.9	0.8	6.2	35.9	150.7	175.4	271.1	153
	10.3	14.7	17.9	5.2	118.6	101.2	40.6	135.4	165.3	229.4	154
Calendar year											
	785	861	733	1320	1731	2042	2475	2985	4054	5198	155
	-2155	-2191	-1412	-1670	-1772	-2105	-2535	-3532	-5244	-7543	156
	-1370	-1330	-679	-350	-41	-63	-60	-547	-1190	-2345	157
	...	...	-68	-237	-356	-160	-71	-484	-278	-77	158
	...	...	...	...	...	...	...	...	...	...	159
	...	...	...	...	...	...	...	...	...	...	160
	-53	-30	...	...	138	90	123	264	302	290	161
	...	...	...	...	-	35	59	70	170	140	162
	...	...	...	...	138	55	64	194	132	150	163
	-1423	-1360	-747	-587	-259	-133	-8	-767	-1166	-2132	164
	...	...	...	100	120	220	260	300	1048	1780	165
	...	...	...	...	...	...	...	...	...	...	166
	...	...	360	412	-47	-191	52	-597	-275	93	167
	...	...	41	-213	48	-88	-41	117	124	311	168
	...	...	26	66	-4	142	-197	-109	-140	125	169
	...	...	-320	-222	-142	-50	66	-1056	-409	177	170
	...	...	...	...	...	...	...	...	...	...	171
	...	...	320	222	142	50	-66	1056	409	-177	172
As of end of period											
	15	15	15	...	...	...	...	...	...	...	173
	5	5	5	...	...	...	...	...	...	...	174
	10	10	10	...	...	...	...	...	...	...	175
	...	...	...	...	...	...	...	...	...	...	176
	...	...	...	...	...	...	...	...	...	...	177
US dollar											
	18	225	900	4300	5016	9080	11209	10850	...	...	178
	...	...	...	...	...	...	...	...	...	...	179
As of end of period											
	11413	14451	15248	19516	22268	22450	23840	24360	25115	...	180
	11043	13999	14703	18443	20753	20763	21418	21825	22226	...	181
	...	...	...	18443	20753	20763	21418	21825	22226	...	182
	...	...	...	0	0	0	0	0	0	...	183

	Item	1978	1979	1980	1981	1982	1983	1984	1985
184	Short-term	...	...	...	...	188	141	153	233
185	Use of IMF credit	...	...	...	...	–	–	–	–
	Debt service								*Transactions*
186	Principal repayments on LT debt	15	72	56	13	27	112	13	15
187	Interest on long-term debt	29	112	160	144	60	27	24	141
188	Interest on short-term debt	...	...	...	...	13	14	11	9
	Average terms of new commitments								
189	Interest (%)	...	...	...	...	...	...	...	...
190	Maturity (years)	...	...	...	...	...	...	...	...
191	Grace period (years)	...	...	...	...	...	...	...	...
192	Grant element (%)	...	...	...	...	...	...	...	...

Footnotes:

a   Refers to total number of persons engaged in the activity regardless of age and sex.

b   Includes mining and electricity, gas and water.

c   In 1985, there was a revaluation of the currency whereby 10 old dong = 1 new dong. Data for current prices prior 1985 were adjusted based on the value of the new dong.

d   Estimates of Net Material Product (NMP) are computed under the Material Product System (MPS), while estimates of GDP are computed under the UN System of National Accounts (SNA). The basic difference between the two systems is the exclusion of non-material services and depreciation in the MPS. From 1990 onwards, GDP estimates are presented following a directive from the government on the application of SNA from MPS in the country.

e   For 1978-1989, agriculture refers to pure agriculture sector only. Commercial fishing is included in the industry sector while forestry is included in the others section. For 1990 onwards, agriculture includes forestry.

f   Includes state management, science, education, health, sports, housing, tourism, hotel, repairs of personal consumer goods and other goods.

g   From 1989 onwards, indexes were derived using computed growth rates.

h   Beginning 1994, there has been an expansion in the monetary survey to include additional banks.

i   Includes time deposits.

j   Refers to foreign currency deposits.

k   Includes cooperatives.

l   Refers to claims on state enterprises.

m   Refers to maximum interest per annum for state enterprise deposits. Data for 1989 refers to end of August 1989 and are staff estimates based on monthly interest rates.

n   Prior to 1989, data exclude those from state enterprises. From 1989 onwards, data include government, cooperatives, private sector and state enterprises.

o   Trade with non-convertible areas were valuated using the conversion rate 1 ruble = 1 dollar for 1986-91.

p   Includes foreign aid in goods.

q   For 1988-1990, non-convertible trade is valued at transferable ruble 2.4 = $1.0. From 1991 onwards, trade with the former Council of Mutual Economic Assistance has been denominated in convertible currencies.

r   Includes services.

s   Includes medium-term loans.

t   Refers to changes in net foreign assets and arrears.

u   Prior to 1989, data refer to the official exchange rate for non-commercial transactions.

1986	1987	1988		1989	1990	1991	1992	1993	1994	1995	
370	452	545	I	965	1403	1584	2324	2435	2607	...	184
–	–	–	I	108	112	102	98	100	282	...	185
during the year											
72	56	13	I	181	131	174	399	264	183	2131 *	186
176	303	199	I	63	50	32	80	75	79	354 *	187
10	13	19	I	26	23	15	19	26	32	...	188
...	...	...		5.0	2.2	1.3	2.3	2.1	1.6	...	189
...	...	...		10.0	14.1	5.0	25.0	31.3	29.8	...	190
...	...	...		4.0	6.2	2.7	8.4	8.1	9.0	...	191
...	...	...		23.3	43.0	20.8	57.2	61.7	68.3	...	192

Item	1978	1979	1980	1981	1982	1983	1984	1985
Production Indexes								*Period*
048 Agriculture, *1979-81 = 100*	87.7	99.1	101.9	99.0	106.0	99.3	97.4	101.7
049 Mining	...	...	...	...	...	...	...	...
050 Manufacturing, *1982 = 100*[a]	...	...	...	...	100.0	108.0	109.3	125.4
ENERGY								*Annual*
Electricity, *Mn kWh*								
051 Production	28	31	31	30	39	32	33	35
052 Consumption	28	30	31	30	39	26	28	30
PRICE INDEXES						*Aug. 1971-July 1972*		*1980 = 100;*
053 Consumer	198.2	75.2	100.0	120.5	142.6	166.4	185.7	202.6
054 Food	207.9	73.9	100.0	120.2	145.6	167.6	182.3	200.2
055 Non-food	182.2	77.7	100.0	121.0	138.2	164.7	190.5	206.0
056 Implicit GDP deflator, *1984 = 100*	...	...	...	...	73.8	86.4	100.0	99.6
MONEY AND BANKING[b]								*Million Tala;*
057 Money supply (M1)	6.8	8.5	11.8	14.0	16.5	16.5	18.6	19.5
058 Currency in circulation	2.6	3.6	3.9	5.5	6.2	5.5	7.1	8.4
059 Demand deposits[c]	4.2	4.9	7.9	8.5	10.3	11.0	11.5	11.1
060 Quasi-money[d]	5.9	9.7	10.6	9.1	14.7	25.0	24.2	32.4
061 Money supply (M2)	12.7	18.3	22.4	23.1	31.2	41.5	42.8	52.0
Interest Rates								*Per cent;*
On deposits[e]								
062 Savings	4.0	4.0	4.0	6.0	6.0	8.0	8.0	7.2
063 Time: 6 months	5.5	5.5	7.0	10.0	10.0	15.0	15.0	13.3
064 12 months	6.0	6.0	8.0	11.5	11.5	17.0	17.0	15.3
GOVERNMENT FINANCE								*Thousand Tala;*
Central Government[f]								
065 Current revenue	18215	21070	24903	24269	28309	41000	59100	71170
066 Taxes	14641	16626	20445	20251	23878	34100	49900	59520
067 Non-taxes	3574	4444	4458	4018	4431	6900	9200	11650
068 Current expenditure	14294	16848	21100	25100	31700	29000	34900	41890
069 Current surplus/deficit	3921	4222	3803	-831	-3391	12000	24200	29280
070 Capital receipts	–	–	–	–	–	–	–	–
071 Capital expenditure[g]	22947	27779	31400	31600	31300	39000	68300	60560
072 Capital account surplus/deficit	-22947	-27779	-31400	-31600	-31300	-39000	-68300	-60560
073 Net lending[h]	–	–	–	–	–	2500	–	–
074 Overall surplus/deficit	-19026	-23557	-27597	-32431	-34691	-29500	-44100	-31280
Financing								
075 Domestic borrowing	2380	2400	6300	6500	5200	-2800	8400	2270
076 Foreign borrowing	14690	18460	–	–	–	5000	10400	2470
077 Foreign grants[i]	31	1068	12600	12100	13100	27300	25300	26540
078 Use of cash balances	1925	1629	8697	13831	16391	–	–	–
Expenditure by Function, Central Govt.								
079 Total	37241	44626	54014	58287	61802	65732	31703	34110
080 General public services	4231	4986	6231	6470	7177	6907	9590	10174
081 Defence	–	–	–	–	–	–	...	...
082 Education	3562	4229	5918	5751	6053	7394	6853	7765
083 Health	3811	4262	4867	5237	6624	6354	5091	5798
084 Social security & welfare	–	–	–	–	–	–	...	...
085 Housing & community amenities	169	185	239	273	284	286	...	...
086 Economic services	24031	29511	34250	38237	39188	40803	5916	6326
087 Agriculture	8374	11551	17790	17987	17355	17428	1375	1442
088 Industry	–	–	–	–	–	–	...	...
089 Electricity, gas & water	–	–	–	–	–	–	...	...
090 Transport and communication	1724	2125	2303	2471	2613	2432	1156	2516
091 Other economic services	13933	15835	14157	17779	19220	20943	3385	2368
092 Others	1437	1453	2509	2319	2476	3988	4253	4047

	1986	1987	1988	1989	1990	1991	1992	1993	1994	1995	
averages											
	101.2	108.0	106.0	110.0	100.0	89.0	87.0	94.0	93.8	93.8	048
	...	...	...	...	...	...	...	...	...	...	049
	130.2	132.3	135.9	129.9	118.1	105.1	105.1	98.7	103.4	129.6	050
values											
	45	46	46	50	50	47	48	55	59	62	051
	45	46	46	50	50	47	48	55	52	54	052
Period averages											
	214.3	224.1	243.6	258.8	298.3	294.1	319.2	324.7	384.3	388.0	053
	213.1	219.1	239.4	246.5	296.4	272.1	302.7	299.9	377.2	377.4	054
	215.9	231.2	248.1	276.5	300.5	325.5	342.9	360.0	...	...	055
	104.1	108.3	126.5	125.9	141.7	203.9	218.7	211.8	252.9	272.3 *	056
As of end of period											
	21.6	28.7	30.3	33.2	47.3	42.9	38.1	44.7	47.2	60.9	057
	9.2	10.5	10.7	12.5	12.9	14.0	12.3	14.9	16.8	21.6	058
	12.5	18.2	19.5	20.7	34.4	29.0	25.8	29.8	30.4	39.3	059
	41.5	52.0	56.7	68.3	73.7	75.8	81.5	77.6	90.9	107.3	060
	63.2	80.7	87.0	101.5	121.0	118.7	119.6	122.3	138.1	168.2	061
Period averages											
	7.4	7.5	7.5	7.5	5.9	6.9	5.0	3.8	3.0	3.0	062
	13.1	12.0	12.0	12.0	8.5	9.4	7.5	6.5	6.5	6.5	063
	15.0	...	...	...	9.2	10.4	8.5	7.5	7.5	7.5	064
Fiscal year ending 31 December I 30 June											
	77540	91450	106020	111730	125570 I	...	147050	157190	169310	141700	065
	60760	69020	72690	81510	91690 I	...	121350	127910	138290	108200	066
	16780	22430	33330	30220	33880 I	...	25700	29280	31020	33500	067
	44940	47500	51130	57650	68860 I	...	92990	95790	103210	89000	068
	32600	43950	54890	54080	56710 I	...	54060	61400	66100	52700	069
	–	–	–	–	– I	...	–	–	–	–	070
	60030	78260	75590	87950	112350 I	...	135840	175580	127690	100800	071
	-60030	-78260	-75590	-87950	-112350 I	...	-135840	-175580	-127690	-100800	072
	–	–	–	–	– I	...	–	–	–	61700	073
	-27430	-34310	-20700	-33870	-55640 I	...	-81780	-114180	-61590	-109800	074
	-10670	-11130	-24130	-9390	-10840 I	...	13170	22270	-200	22100	075
	2130	8040	2290	3560	20480 I	...	30430	40050	27470	87800	076
	35980	37400	42540	39700	46000 I	...	38180	51860	34320	...	077
	–	–	–	–	– I	...	–	–	–	...	078
	40261	40532	...	...	...	...	...	...	...	...	079
	10825	11374	...	...	...	...	...	...	...	...	080
			...	...	...	...	...	...	...	...	081
	9624	9691	...	...	...	...	...	...	...	...	082
	6758	7141	...	...	...	...	...	...	...	...	083
	...	...	...	...	...	...	...	...	...	...	084
	...	...	...	...	...	...	...	...	...	...	085
	8351	9165	...	...	...	...	...	...	...	...	086
	1550	1583	...	...	...	...	...	...	...	...	087
	...	...	...	...	...	...	...	...	...	...	088
	...	...	...	...	...	...	...	...	...	...	089
	476	565	...	...	...	...	...	...	...	...	090
	6325	7017	...	...	...	...	...	...	...	...	091
	4703	3161	...	...	...	...	...	...	...	...	092

	Item	1978	1979	1980	1981	1982	1983	1984	1985
	EXTERNAL TRADE [j]							*Thousand Tala;*	
093	Exports, fob [k]	8169	14981	15828	11149	16249	27410	34155	36195
094	Imports, cif	38566	60947	57439	69660	60118	75100	93282	115074
095	Trade balance	-30397	-45966	-41611	-58511	-43869	-47690	-59127	-78879
	Exports, by SITC section								
096	Food and live animals	7689	5692	5718	5139	5841	5350	23917	5372
097	Beverage and tobacco	–	6	358	824	1176	1932	2303	2137
098	Crude materials excl. fuels	167	8322	8745	4214	4031	7069	...	...
099	Mineral fuels, etc.	–	3	3	–	11	2	...	...
100	Animal, vegetable oil & fats	–	6	–	54	3664	11109	...	...
101	Chemicals	100	45	46	62	36	17	...	...
102	Basic manufactures	35	18	24	14	37	6	...	...
103	Machines, transport equipment	–	–	–	–	–	–	...	...
104	Misc. manufactured goods	28	69	58	82	35	21	...	...
105	Unclassified goods	153	820	876	760	1418	1904	...	...
	Exports, by principal commodity								
106	1. Taro	1127	1187	1048	2136	2126	2371	2753	5113
107	2. Copra	3614	8782	8405	3924	2760	1398	–	954
108	3. Cocoa	2645	3642	3013	1436	985	4617	2258	2356
109	4. Timber	281	266	324	289	1271	541	1258	817
110	5. Banana	56	152	440	241	597	407	27	28
	Imports, by SITC section								
111	Food and live animals	8545	12414	12353	13236	13270	15198	19879	26800
112	Beverage and tobacco	2188	1728	1481	1272	1133	1914	2507	2400
113	Crude materials excl. fuels	829	925	1575	629	1502	812	1063	800
114	Mineral fuels, etc.	2865	5758	9561	12576	9214	13133	17200	19400
115	Animal, vegetable oil & fats	308	412	423	396	2230	392	513	800
116	Chemicals	2370	2715	3450	3078	3503	4221	5528	5700
117	Basic manufactures	8043	11239	13067	12467	13917	15243	19964	21300
118	Machine, transport equipment	9872	21918	11708	22837	10955	14968	19604	27100
119	Misc. manufactured goods	3545	3613	3809	3113	4294	5279	6914	8200
120	Unclassified goods	1	225	12	56	100	82	107	2600
	Direction of Trade							*Million US dollars;*	
121	Exports, Total	10.0	18.6	17.2	11.3	13.3	16.8	19.8	27.3
122	1. Australia	0.3	0.2	0.3	0.2	1.3	2.2	2.8	2.9
123	2. New Zealand	3.9	3.7	4.4	3.7	3.6	4.0	4.9	5.2
124	3. American Samoa	0.6	1.8	1.2	1.6	1.3	0.8	1.4	1.1
125	4. Japan	0.7	0.0	0.8	0.3	1.1	0.3	0.0	0.2
126	5. United States	0.4	1.6	1.0	1.3	3.7	5.5	7.1	16.2
127	6. Germany	1.7	5.6	1.8	1.4	0.8	2.0	0.9	1.3
128	7. Hong Kong	0.0	0.0	0.0	0.0	0.0	0.0	0.0	0.0
129	8. Fiji	0.1	0.1	0.0	0.0	0.1	0.0	0.1	0.1
130	9. Pakistan	0.0	0.0	0.0	0.0	0.0	0.0	0.0	0.0
131	10. Spain	0.0	0.0	0.0	0.0	0.0	0.0	0.0	0.0
132	Imports, Total	53.8	71.3	62.6	67.1	49.8	51.2	50.3	50.7
133	1. New Zealand	17.5	19.4	20.2	16.4	15.5	15.8	15.7	16.2
134	2. Australia	8.3	11.9	12.7	11.0	10.8	11.7	10.9	0.0
135	3. Japan	10.6	7.4	5.9	6.0	5.9	6.2	6.0	8.3
136	4. Fiji	2.0	2.2	2.0	2.1	2.7	2.9	2.8	1.9
137	5. United States	5.0	5.7	5.4	15.6	4.8	4.9	4.9	3.0
138	6. Singapore	3.3	3.9	6.9	6.9	2.8	2.8	2.8	0.6
139	7. Germany	1.4	13.2	1.2	1.4	1.0	1.1	1.1	0.9
140	8. American Samoa	0.1	0.0	0.1	0.1	0.0	0.0	0.0	0.0
141	9. Hong Kong	0.7	0.9	0.9	0.5	0.4	0.4	0.4	0.6
142	10. United Kingdom	1.5	1.8	3.5	2.8	0.8	0.8	0.8	0.9

	1986	1987	1988	1989	1990	1991	1992	1993	1994	1995	
Calendar year											
	23487	24968	31397	29206	20494	15515	14349	16511	8849	21674	093
	105375	131009	155120	171220	186120	225337	271325	263691	202944	228041	094
	-81888	-106041	-123723	-142014	-165626	-209822	-256976	-247180	-194095	-206367	095
	5120	...	...	...	...	...	...	...	...	...	096
	1321	...	...	...	...	...	...	...	...	...	097
	...	...	...	...	...	...	...	...	...	...	098
	...	...	...	...	...	...	...	...	...	...	099
	...	...	...	...	...	...	...	...	...	...	100
	...	...	...	...	...	...	...	...	...	...	101
	...	...	...	...	...	...	...	...	...	...	102
	...	...	...	...	...	...	...	...	...	...	103
	...	...	...	...	...	...	...	...	...	...	104
	...	...	...	...	...	...	...	...	...	...	105
	4335	5077	5201	5849	3502	6878	4696	9509	86	105 *	106
	1049	65	1970	3237	1101	–	–	–	58	2193	107
	3185	2622	1260	2143	803	502	6	–	–	–	108
	592	396	1084	135	21	10	22	31	163	140 *	109
	39	40	24	34	3	20	2	103	217	258 *	110
	...	...	...	...	...	...	...	...	...	...	111
	...	...	...	...	...	...	...	...	...	...	112
	...	...	...	...	...	...	...	...	...	...	113
	...	...	...	...	...	...	...	...	...	...	114
	...	...	...	...	...	...	...	...	...	...	115
	...	...	...	...	...	...	...	...	...	...	116
	...	...	...	...	...	...	...	...	...	...	117
	...	...	...	...	...	...	...	...	...	...	118
	...	...	...	...	...	...	...	...	...	...	119
	...	...	...	...	...	...	...	...	...	...	120
Calendar year											
	10.5	11.1	14.7	12.7	11.6	7.6	5.8	6.4	3.5	58.3	121
	2.3	2.3	2.4	1.1	1.7	2.1	0.7	0.8	0.5	50.8	122
	3.1	4.2	4.0	4.5	3.9	3.4	3.0	3.3	1.6	3.7	123
	1.7	1.1	1.1	1.2	1.1	0.9	1.0	1.1	0.7	0.8	124
	0.0	0.0	0.1	0.1	0.1	0.0	0.0	0.0	0.1	1.1	125
	1.0	1.9	1.1	1.0	0.8	0.6	0.7	0.8	0.1	0.5	126
	2.0	1.3	3.3	3.4	1.6	0.0	0.0	0.0	0.0	0.5	127
	0.0	0.0	0.0	0.0	0.5	0.0	0.0	0.0	0.1	0.2	128
	0.0	0.0	0.3	0.4	0.2	0.0	0.0	0.0	0.0	0.0	129
	0.0	0.0	0.3	0.0	0.0	0.0	0.0	0.0	0.0	0.0	130
	0.0	0.0	0.0	0.0	0.0	0.0	0.0	0.0	0.0	0.0	131
	47.9	62.0	69.2	76.9	83.2	99.0	110.0	102.6	80.3	136.5	132
	14.2	18.3	20.4	22.7	26.1	37.8	42.5	39.9	29.9	50.4	133
	0.0	0.0	0.0	0.0	9.0	19.8	24.0	16.8	16.0	27.5	134
	5.7	7.3	8.2	9.1	7.3	9.4	5.5	11.0	7.6	29.8	135
	1.8	2.3	2.6	2.9	1.5	6.4	11.6	9.9	9.8	11.4	136
	7.1	9.2	10.3	11.4	8.0	10.3	8.9	10.8	9.2	8.3	137
	0.1	0.1	0.1	0.1	0.1	1.5	0.6	1.3	1.4	1.6	138
	2.8	3.6	4.1	4.5	4.2	1.9	1.5	2.1	1.2	1.2	139
	0.0	0.0	0.0	0.0	0.0	1.9	1.8	1.2	1.0	1.1	140
	0.4	0.5	0.6	0.6	1.2	1.8	2.1	1.3	0.9	0.8	141
	1.3	1.6	1.8	2.0	1.3	0.6	1.1	0.8	0.3	1.0	142

	Item	1978	1979	1980	1981	1982	1983	1984	1985
	Trade Indexes [1]								1974 I 1982-1988 = 100;
	Quantum index								
143	Exports	83	112	134	... I	93	116	88	103
144	Imports	...	...	...	... I	85	87	93	100
	Unit value index								
145	Exports	122	165	136	... I	63	85	143	122
146	Imports	...	...	...	... I	67	82	95	109
147	Terms of trade	...	...	...	... I	94	104	151	112
	BALANCE OF PAYMENTS								*Thousand US dollars;*
148	Merchandise exports, fob	9740	18130	17220	10780	13460	17690	18340	16120
149	Merchandise imports, fob	-47660	-67150	-56860	-51380	-45310	-44120	-45550	-46600
150	Trade balance	-37920	-49020	-39640	-40600	-31850	-26430	-27210	-30480
151	Other goods, services and income	-4340	-7880	-8970	-6760	-6530	-6010	-5640	-2660
152	Credit	3910	3630	8450	7610	8320	9270	8870	11010
153	Debit	-8250	-11510	-17420	-14370	-14850	-15280	-14510	-13670
154	Unrequited transfer	24160	34860	35690	32240	31760	35940	33500	34900
155	Private	12140	13460	18740	18560	18630	20330	20270	23630
156	Official	12020	21400	16950	13680	13130	15610	13230	11270
157	Current balance	-18100	-22040	-12920	-15120	-6620	3500	650	1760
158	Direct investment	–	–	–	–	–	–	–	–
159	Portfolio investment	–	–	–	–	–	–	–	–
160	Other long-term capital }								
161	Other short-term capital }	7800	19470	8190	2630	-80	2580	4560	-470
162	Net errors and omissions	3560	1670	2270	6800	3520	1100	2000	3920
163	Overall balance	-6740	-900	-2460	-5690	-3180	7180	7210	5210
164	Allocation of SDRs	–	–	–	–	–	–	–	–
165	Reserves and related items	6740	900	2460	5690	3180	-7180	-7210	-5210
	INTERNATIONAL RESERVES								*Million US dollars;*
166	Total	4.8	4.8	2.8	3.3	3.5	7.2	10.6	14.0
167	Gold, national valuation	...	...	...	...	...	...	...	...
168	Foreign exchange	4.7	4.8	2.8	3.3	3.5	6.8	10.4	14.0
169	Reserve position in the Fund	-	–	–	–	–	–	–	–
170	SDRs	0.1	–	–	0.0	0.0	0.4	0.2	0.0
	EXCHANGE RATES								*Tala per*
171	End of period	0.7145	0.9111	0.9292	1.0992	1.2371	1.6203	2.1829	2.3063
172	Average of period	0.7363	0.8262	0.9193	1.0341	1.2073	1.5491	1.8623	2.2453
	EXTERNAL INDEBTEDNESS								*Million US dollars;*
173	Total outstanding and disbursed	41.2	52.6	60.2	63.7	69.8	74.6	75.5	76.0
174	Long term	36.6	46.3	53.4	54.8	58.5	58.6	63.0	63.7
175	Public and publicly guaranteed	36.6	46.3	53.4	54.8	58.5	58.6	63.0	63.7
176	Private non-guaranteed	0.0	0.0	0.0	0.0	0.0	0.0	0.0	0.0
177	Short term	0.0	0.0	1.0	1.4	5.0	8.1	2.7	1.4
178	Use of IMF credit	4.6	6.3	5.8	7.5	6.3	7.9	9.8	10.9
	Debt service								*Transactions*
179	Principal repayments on LT debt	1.6	2.1	2.2	1.7	1.8	2.8	2.9	3.6
180	Interest on long-term debt	1.2	1.6	2.2	1.7	1.3	1.1	1.4	1.6
181	Interest on short-term debt	0.0	0.0	0.2	0.1	0.2	0.6	0.4	0.1

1986	1987	1988	1989	1990	1991	1992	1993	1994	1995	
Calendar year										
106	97	97	91	67	43	37	37	24	61	143
93	109	120	112	121	142	166	153	115	118	144
82	92	119	119	112	139	150	173	144	138	145
107	114	126	147	151	151	155	164	167	179	146
77	81	94	81	74	92	97	105	86	77	147
Calendar year										
10510	11770	15090	12870	8850	6480	5820	6430	3530	8770	148
-42840	-55790	-66570	-66990	-70000	-77620	-89900	-87370	-69010	-80330	149
-32330	-44020	-51480	-54120	-61150	-71140	-84080	-80940	-65480	-71560	150
-110	2020	9410	14190	16010	920	-3170	-2530	14460	21390	151
14600	19180	29780	35380	42260	37950	42810	40110	47170	60390	152
-14710	-17160	-20370	-21190	-26250	-37030	-45980	-42640	-32710	-39000	153
39680	49290	50010	52750	52400	41570	34750	44800	56810	60300	154
28400	36390	35470	38150	39720	31000	34750	28380	23820	25000	155
11280	12900	14540	14600	12680	10570	–	16420	32990	35300	156
7240	7290	7940	12820	7260	-28650	-52500	-38670	5790	10130	157
–	–	–	–	–	–	–	–	–	–	158
–	–	–	–	–	–	–	–	–	–	159
										160
-740	3150	490	480	9400	18600	19950	15550	-7600	-4690	161
900	-1850	1670	-2610	-5660	7970	19820	13820	-4190	-2160	162
7400	8590	10100	10690	11000	-2080	-12730	-9300	-6000	3280	163
–	–	–	–	–	–	–	–	–	–	164
-7400	-8590	-10100	-10690	-11000	2080	12730	9300	6000	-3280	165
As of end of period										
23.8	37.2	49.2	55.1	69.0	67.8	61.2	50.7	50.8	55.3	166
...	...	...	...	...	...	...	...	...	...	167
22.8	35.3	45.9	54.1	64.8	64.1	57.7	47.1	46.9	51.3	168
–	–	0.0	0.0	0.0	0.0	0.9	0.9	1.0	1.0	169
1.0	1.9	3.3	0.9	4.2	3.7	2.6	2.7	2.9	3.0	170
US dollar										
2.1978	2.0109	2.1482	2.2899	2.3332	2.4486	2.5575	2.6076	2.4516	2.5272	171
2.2358	2.1218	2.0804	2.2702	2.3152	2.3083	2.4663	2.5699	2.5276	2.4757	172
As of end of year										
75.7	80.6	75.9	73.7	91.9	140.6	117.9	194.3	154.9	...	173
64.6	71.4	71.1	71.9	91.0	113.3	117.8	140.9	154.7	...	174
64.6	71.4	71.1	71.9	91.0	113.3	117.8	140.9	154.7	...	175
0.0	0.0	0.0	0.0	0.0	0.0	0.0	0.0	0.0	...	176
1.0	1.0	1.0	0.2	0.1	27.1	0.1	53.4	0.2	...	177
10.1	8.2	3.8	1.6	0.8	0.2	0.0	0.0	0.0	...	178
during the year										
4.0	2.7	2.8	3.3	3.2	2.9	3.2	2.7	3.6	2.9 *	179
1.3	1.3	1.3	1.0	1.2	1.1	1.4	1.4	1.4	1.5 *	180
0.1	0.1	0.1	0.0	0.0	0.7	0.0	1.3	0.0	...	181

Item	1978	1979	1980	1981	1982	1983	1984	1985
Average terms of new commitments								
182 Interest (%)	5.7	2.9	0.4	1.2	0.8	1.0	6.0	1.0
183 Maturity (years)	22.9	37.5	40.1	34.5	12.2	40.6	12.7	41.7
184 Grace period (years)	6.4	8.7	20.6	8.4	4.5	10.3	3.8	10.1
185 Grant element (%)	35.5	63.5	86.0	69.5	47.2	80.2	27.0	79.3

Footnotes:

a   For 1982-93, figures refer to volume indices of industrial production.

b   Data for July 1977 relate to the Bank of Western Samoa only. Subsequent figures cover both the Bank of Western Samoa and the Pacific Commercial Bank Ltd. Up to December 1989, data were reported as of the last Wednesday of the month. This reporting date was changed to the last day of the month beginning January 1990.

c   Excludes deposits of the government and the banking system.

d   Time deposits exclude deposits of the government.

e   Effective 15 September 1986, the rates for term deposits in excess of WS$ 20,000 and all rates for terms over six months have been opened to negotiation between a customer and his bank.

f   For 1984-90, figures represent estimates of the Treasury department and the Central Bank. Data are provisional.

g   Includes development expenditure, net treasury advances and capital account. The 1983 figure includes revaluation of IMF subscription.

h   Mainly net loans and advances to non-financial public enterprises, capital subscriptions and land purchases. Includes errors and omissions. After 1983, net loans and advances to public enterprises and others are included in net treasury advances, while Government's purchases of shares in public and private enterprises are incorporated in the capital account. Net treasury advances and capital account are subsumed in capital expenditure.

i   Includes project, and cash and commodity grants, all of which were assumed to be externally derived.

j   Excludes trade data for Yasaki and imports by foreign diplomatic missions to Western Samoa.

k   Beginning June 1991, exports were derived from Central Bank information.

l   Indices for exports exclude re-exports from 1982 onwards.

1986	1987	1988	1989	1990	1991	1992	1993	1994	1995	
1.3	0.8	1.9	0.9	0.8	1.6	0.5	0.8	...	...	182
34.9	50.1	21.2	37.9	39.9	32.4	29.1	39.0	...	...	183
8.5	10.1	7.8	10.3	10.3	7.4	10.3	8.2	...	...	184
70.6	84.1	57.3	78.0	80.7	67.6	76.7	78.0	...	...	185

SOURCES

SOURCES

AFGHANISTAN

Population	–	ESCAP, *SYAP 1994* and past issues. For 1994-95, ADB staff estimates.
Labor Force	–	Central Statistics Office (CSO), 3 July 1991 and past communication.
National Accounts	–	For 1978-81, CSO, 9 January 1991 and past communication. For 1982-89, ESCAP, *SYAP 1994* and past issues. For 1990-93, UNDP, 11 March 1996.
Production Agriculture	–	FAO, *PY 1994* and past issues. For rice, maize and wheat, 1987-95, FAO, Statistics Division, 22 May 1996 and past communication.
Mining	–	ESCAP, *SYAP 1994* and past issues.
Manufacturing	–	For 1978, CSO, *Statistical Information of Afghanistan, 1975-78*. For 1979 - 85, CSO, 3 July 1991 and past communication. For 1986-91, ESCAP, *SYAP 1994*.
Production Index Agriculture	–	For 1978-80, 1994-95, FAO, Statistics Division, 22 May 1996 and past communication. For 1981-93, FAO, *PY 1994* and past issues.
Energy	–	UN, *ESY 1992* and past issues.
Price Indexes	–	For 1978-88, CSO, 3 July 1991 and past communication. For 1989-92, UNDP, 11 March 1996.
Money and Banking	–	IMF, *IFS Yearbook 1995* and *IFS*, April 1996.
Government Finance	–	ESCAP, *SYAP 1994* and past issues.
External Trade	–	ESCAP, *SYAP 1994* and past issues.
Direction of Trade	–	IMF, *DOTS* tape, May 1996.
Balance of Payments	–	IMF, *IFS Yearbook 1995* and *IFS,* April 1996.
International Reserves Exchange Rates	–	IMF, *IFS* tape, May 1996.
External Indebtedness	–	For 1978-91, OECD, *FEDDC 1992 Survey* and past issues. For 1992-94, OECD, *External Debt Statistics Annual Report 1995* and past issues.

BANGLADESH

Population	–	ADB staff estimates. (Census data from UN, *Demographic Yearbook 1994).*
Labor Force	–	Bangladesh Bureau of Statistics (BBS), 7 May 1996 and past communication.

National Accounts	–	For 1978-92, BBS, *Monthly Statistical Bulletin*, June 1995 and past issues. For 1993-95, BBS, 7 May 1996.
Production	–	BBS, 7 May 1996 and past communication.
Production Indexes Agriculture	–	FAO, Statistics Division, 22 May 1996 and past communication.
Mining Manufacturing }	–	For 1978-93, BBS, *Monthly Statistical Bulletin*, June 1995 and past issues. For 1994-95, BBS, 7 May 1996.
Energy	–	For 1978-83, UN, *ESY 1984* and past issues. For 1984-94, BBS, *Monthly Statistical Bulletin*, June 1995 and past issues. For 1992-95 data on natural gas, BBS, 22 May 1996.
Price Indexes	–	BBS, 7 May 1996 and past communication.
Money and Banking	–	For 1978-85, Bangladesh Bank, *Bangladesh Bank Bulletin*, July-September 1994 and past issues. For 1986-95, Bangladesh Bank, 8 April 1996.
Interest Rates	–	BBS, 28 March 1991 and Bangladesh Bank through ADB, Bangladesh Resident Mission (BRM), 8 May 1995.
Government Finance	–	BBS, 7 May 1996 and past communication.
External Trade	–	For 1978-86, BBS, 18 April 1995 and past communication. For 1987-95, Bangladesh Bank, 8 April 1996.
	–	Trade by SITC: For 1978-86, BBS, 18 April 1995 and past communication. For 1989-93, UN, ESCAP, *Foreign Trade Statistics of Asia and the Pacific, 1989-93*.
Direction of Trade	–	IMF, *DOTS* tape, May 1996.
Trade Indexes	–	BBS, 18 April 1995.
Balance of Payments	–	BBS, 7 May 1996 and past communication.
International Reserves Exchange Rates }	–	IMF, *IFS* tape, May 1996.
External Indebtedness	–	WB, *WDT 1996* (STARS version).

BHUTAN

Population	–	For 1978-80, Central Statistics Organization (CSO), *Revised Series on GDP of Bhutan*, May 1989. For 1981-95, UN, Population Division, *Interpolated National Populations by Sex and Age: 1950-2025, 1992 Revision*.
Labor Force	–	ESCAP, *SYAP 1991* and past issues.
National Accounts	–	For 1980-94, CSO, *National Accounts Statistics*, September 1995 and past issues. For 1995, CSO, 5 January 1996.

Production
Agriculture
- For 1978-86, FAO, *Agrostat* PC 2.0, 1993 (Diskette).
  For 1987-93, FAO, *PY 1994* and past issues.
  For 1994-95, FAO, Statistics Division, 22 May 1996 and past communication.

Production Indexes
Agriculture
- For 1978-93, FAO, *PY 1994* and past issues.
  For 1994-95, FAO, Statistics Division, 22 May 1996.

Energy
- For 1978-92, UN, *ESY 1992* and past issues.
  For 1993-94, IMF estimates, September 1994 and October 1995.

Price Indexes
- For 1979-85, CSO, *Statistical Yearbook of Bhutan (SYB) 1988* and past issues.
  For 1986-94, Royal Monetary Authority of Bhutan (RMAB), *Selected Economic Indicators (SEI)*, June 1995 and past issues.

Money and Banking
Money supply:
- For 1980-82, CSO, *SYB 1987*.
  For 1983-94, RMAB, *SEI*, June 1995 and past issues.

Interest rates :
- For 1982-86 interest rates on savings deposits, CSO, *Round Table Meeting 1992*.
  For 1982-86 interest rates on time deposits, CSO, *SYB 1990*.
  For 1987-95, IMF estimates, September 1994 and October 1995.

Government Finance
Central Government expenditure :
- For 1978-80, Ministry of Foreign Affairs, 19 November 1981 and ADB, *Economic Report (ER)*, July 1983.
  For 1981-82, CSO, *SYB 1990*.
  For 1983-89, RMAB, *SEI*, June 1992.
  For 1990-95, IMF estimates, September 1994 and October 1995.

Expenditure by function :
- For 1982-89, ESCAP, *SYAP 1994* and past issues.
  For 1990-95, IMF estimates, September 1994 and October 1995.

External Trade
- For 1980-85, CSO, *SYB 1990* and past issues.
  For 1986-94, RMAB, *SEI*, June 1995 and past issues.

Exports, by principal commodity:
- For 1981-88, CSO, *SYB 1990*.
  For 1989-94, IMF estimates, September 1994 and October 1995.

Balance of Payments
- For 1978-80, ADB, *ER*, July 1983 and Ministry of Foreign Affairs, 19 November 1981.
  For 1981-86, IMF, *IFS Yearbook 1994*.
  For 1987-95, RMAB, *SEI*, June 1995 and past issues.

International Reserves }
Exchange Rates   }
- IMF, *IFS* tape, May 1996.

External Indebtedness
- WB, *WDT 1996* (STARS version).

CAMBODIA

Population	–	For 1978-92, WB, *World Tables 1994*. For 1993-95, National Institute of Statistics (NIS), 2 June 1996.
National Accounts	–	NIS, 23 January 1996 and past communication.
Production Agriculture	–	For rice and maize, FAO, Statistics Division, 22 May 1996 and past communication. For rubber, logs and fish, for 1980-87, WB, *Cambodia: Agenda for Rehabilitation and Reconstruction*, June 1992. For 1988-92, IMF, *Cambodia: Recent Economic Developments*, 23 April 1993. For 1993-95, NIS, 2 June 1996.
Production Index Agriculture	–	For 1978-93, FAO, *PY 1994* and past issues. For 1994-95, FAO, Statistics Division, 22 May 1996.
Energy	–	For 1987, WB, *Cambodia: Agenda for Rehabilitation and Reconstruction*, June 1992. For 1988-92, Cambodian authorities and IMF staff estimates.
Price Indexes	–	National Bank of Cambodia (NBC), 15 January 1996 and past communication.
Money and Banking	–	For 1987-94, NBC, 15 January 1996 and past communication. For 1995, Ministry of Economy and Finance (MEF), *Monthly Bulletin of Statistics*, February 1996.
Government Finance	–	For 1986-90, data provided by the Cambodian authorities and IMF estimates and projections. For 1991-93, MEF, 11 May 1995. For 1994-95, NIS, 2 June 1996.
	–	Expenditure by function: For 1986-87, data provided by the Cambodian authorities and IMF estimates and projections. For 1988-93, WB, *Cambodia: From Rehabilitation to Reconstruction, An Economic Report*, January 1994. For 1994, NIS, 4 May 1995.
External Trade	–	For 1987-92, ADB Economic Mission, May 1995. For 1993-95, NIS, 2 June 1996.
		Exports by principal commodity: For 1986-88, IMF, *Cambodia: Recent Economic Developments*, 23 April 1993. For 1989-94, ADB, *ERBOP: Kingdom of Cambodia*, August 1995.
Direction of Trade	–	IMF, *DOTS* tape, April 1995.
Balance of Payments	–	For 1986, WB, *Cambodia: From Rehabilitation to Reconstruction, An Economic Report*, January 1994. For 1987-92, NBC, May 1995 and past communication. For 1993-95, NBC, *Economic and Monetary Statistics Review*, February 1996.
International Reserves	–	IMF, *IFS* tape, May 1996.

Exchange Rates	—	For 1981-91, NBC, January 1993.
		For 1992-95, IMF, *IFS* tape, May 1996.
External Indebtedness	—	WB, *WDT 1996* (STARS version).

CHINA, People's Republic of

Population	—	For 1978-81, ESCAP, *SYAP 1990*.
		For 1982-94, State Statistical Bureau (SSB), *Statistical Yearbook of China (SYC) 1995* and past issues.
		For 1995, SSB, 25 March 1996.
Labor Force	—	SSB, *SYC 1995* and past issues and SSB, 25 March 1996.
National Accounts	—	For current prices by industrial origin, SSB, 25 March 1996.
		For current prices by expenditure, SSB, *SYC 1995* and SSB, 25 March 1996.

Production
    Agriculture — For rice, wheat and maize, for 1978-94, FAO, Basic Data Unit, 14 February 1995 and past communication.
For rice, wheat and maize, for 1995, SSB, 25 March 1996.
For the other agricultural products, for 1979-94, SSB, *SYC 1995* and past issues.
For the other agricultural products, for 1995, SSB, 25 March 1996.

    Mining }
    Manufacturing } — SSB, *SYC 1995* and past issues.

Production Indexes
    Agriculture — FAO, *PY 1994* and FAO, Basic Data Unit, 14 February 1995 and past communication.

    Mining — People's Bank of China (PBC), 27 March 1988.

    Manufacturing — For 1978-87, PBC, 27 March 1988 and for 1988-89, PBC, 9 January 1990.

Energy
    Crude Petroluem }
    Coal }
    Natural Gas } — SSB, *SYC 1995* and past issues; SSB, 25 March 1996 and past communication.
    Electricity }

Price Indexes	—	SSB, *SYC 1995* and past issues.
Money and Banking	—	IMF, *IFS* tape, May 1996 and SSB, 14 March 1994 and past communication.
Government Finance	—	For 1978-91, SSB, *SYC 1994* and past issues.
		For 1992-94, SSB, 25 January 1996 and past communication.
External Trade	—	For total trade and by SITC, SSB, *SYC 1995* and past issues, and SSB, 25 March 1996.
		For exports by principal commodity, SSB, 25 March 1996.
		For 1978-86, terms of trade, unit value indexes of exports and imports, ADB Mission to SSB, April 1988.

For 1987-88, terms of trade, ADB, *ERBOP - PRC*, May 1989.
For 1989-91, terms of trade, 25 February 1994 and past communication.

Direction of Trade — IMF, *DOTS* tape, May 1996.

Balance of Payments — For 1978-81, WB, *Report No. 4072-CHA*.
For 1982-88, IMF, *IFS Yearbook 1995*.
For 1989-94, IMF, *IFS*, May 1996.

International Reserves } — For 1978-88, IMF, *IFS Yearbook 1995*.
Exchange Rates } For 1989-94, IMF, *IFS*, May 1996.

External Indebtedness — WB, *WDT 1996* (STARS version).

COOK ISLANDS

Population — For 1978, ESCAP, *SIAP*, December 1978.
For 1979-80, Statistics Office (SO), 23 January 1985 and past communication.
For 1981-90, ESCAP, *SYAP 1993* and past issues.
For 1991-95, SO, 04 March 1996.

Labor Force — For 1979, SO, 07 February 1980.
For 1980, SO, *Cook Islands Key Facts 1983*.
For 1981, SO, *Cook Islands Statistical Bulletin, Economic Indicator, I and II Quarters 1986*, September 1986.
For 1982-86, ADB, *National Accounts of the Cook Islands 1982 to 1986*.
For 1989-90, SO, *Cook Islands Survey of Employment, Wages and Salaries*, September 1989 and September 1990.
For 1991 and 1993, SO, 07 April 1995 .

National Accounts — For 1982-89, SO, *Cook Islands National Accounts 1982 to 1990*, December 1991.
For 1990-1995, SO, 04 March 1996 and past communication.

Energy — For 1978-81, SO, 07 February 1980.
For 1982-85, SO, *Cook Islands Quarterly Statistical Bulletin*, August 1987.
For 1986-90, UN, *ESY 1990* and past issues.
For 1991-95, SO, 04 March 1996 and past communication.

Price Indexes
Consumer — For 1978, SO, 08 May 1988 .
For 1979-80, ESCAP, *SIAP*, December 1981 and past issues.
For 1981, SO, *Cook Islands Statistical bulletin, Economic Indicator, IV Quarter 1985*, 25 August 1986.
For 1982-86, SO, *Cook Islands Quarterly Bulletin*, August 1987.
For 1987, SO, 11 May 1988.
For 1988 , ESCAP, *SIAP*, March 1990.
For 1989-91, SO, *Cook Islands Statistical Bulletin, Rarotonga Consumer Price Index*, December 1991 and past issues.
For 1992-95, SO, 04 March 1996 and past communication.

Food — For 1978-88, ESCAP, *SIAP*, March 1992 and past issues.
For 1989-91, SO, *Cook Islands Statistical Bulletin, Rarotonga Consumer Price Index*, December 1991 and past issues.
For 1992-95, SO, 04 March 1996 and past communication.

Government Finance	–	For 1978-81, SO, 08 February 1984 and past communication.
		For 1982-85, SO, *Cook Islands Statistical Bulletin, Economic Indicator,*
		I and II Quarters 1986, September 1986.
		For 1986-95, SO, 14 February 1996 and past communication.

External Trade – For total exports, 1978-80, SO, *Cook Islands External Trade*, July 1986.
For total exports, 1981-85, SO, *Cook Islands Statistical Bulletin, Economic Indicator*,
September 1986 and past issues.
For total exports, 1986-89, SO, *Cook Islands Statistical Bulletin*, June 1990
and past issues.
For total exports, 1990-95, SO, 04 March 1996 and past communication.
For exports by SITC section, 1978-85, SO, *Cook Islands External Trade*, July 1986.
For exports by SITC section, 1986-89, SO, *Cook Islands Statistical Bulletin,*
Economic Indicator, II Quarter 1988 and II Quarter 1990.
For exports by SITC section, 1990-95, SO, 14 February 1996 and past communication.
For exports by principal commodity section, 1978-85, SO, *Cook Islands External*
Trade, July 1986.
For exports principal commodity section, 1986-89, SO, *Cook Islands Statistical*
Bulletin, Economic Indicator, II Quarter 1988 and II Quarter 1990.
For exports principal commodity section, 1990-95, SO, 04 March 1996
and past communication.
For total imports and by SITC section, 1978-80, SO, *Cook Islands External trade*,
July 1986.
For total imports and by SITC section, 1981-89, SO, *Cook Islands Quarterly Statistical*
Bulletin, June 1990 and past issues.
For total imports and by SITC section, 1990, SO, *Cook Islands Imports Statistics 1990*,
January 1992 and past issues.
For total imports and by SITC section, 1991-92, SO, *Cook Islands Quarterly Statistical*
Bulletin, Economic Indicator, 4th quarter 1992.
For total imports and by SITC section, 1993-95, SO, 04 March 1996
and past communication.

Exchange Rates – IMF, *IFS*, May 1996 and past issues.

FIJI

Population – For 1978-94, Bureau of Statistics (BS), *Current Economic Statistics (CES)*,
October 1995.
For 1995, ADB staff estimate.

Labor Force – For 1978-94, BS, *CES*, October 1995.
For 1995, BS, 27 March 1996.
For 1983-94 data on unemployment and unemployment rate, BS, 26 April 1995
and past communication.

National Accounts – For 1978-93, BS, *CES*, October 1995 and past issues.
For 1994, BS, 8 February 1996 and past communication.

Net factor income from abroad:
For 1978-87, NCDS, *South Pacific Economic and Social Database*, March 1996.
For 1988-94, BS, 26 April 1995.

Production
Agriculture – For 1978-94, BS, *CES*, October 1995 and past issues.
For 1995, FAO, Statistics Division, 22 May 1996.

Manufacturing	–	For 1978-94, BS, *CES*, October 1995 and past issues.

Production Indexes
Agriculture	–	For 1978-93, FAO, *PY 1994* and past issues.
		For 1994-95, FAO, Statistics Division, 22 May 1996.

Mining	–	For 1978-85, BS, *CES*, April 1988 and past issues.
		For 1986-89, Reserve Bank of Fiji, *Quarterly Review*, September 1990 and past issues.
		For 1990-92, BS, 31 March 1993 and past communication.
		For 1993, BS, *Statistical News, No. 50, 1994*, 06 October 1994.

Manufacturing	–	For 1978-85, BS, *CES*, April 1988 and past issues.
		For 1986-94, BS, 8 February 1996 and past communication.

Energy		Coal:
	–	For 1978-92, UN, *ESY 1992* and past issues.
		Electricity:
	–	For 1978-79, UN, *WES 1981*.
		For 1980-94, BS, 8 February 1996 and past communication.

Price Indexes	–	BS, *Statistical News*, 31 January 1996 and past issues.

Money and Banking	–	For 1978-94, BS, *CES*, October 1995 and past issues.
		For 1995, BS, 27 March 1996.

Government Finance	–	BS, 27 March 1996 and past communication.
		Expenditure by Function:
	–	For 1978-89, BS, *CES*, April 1991 and past issues.
		For 1990-95, BS, 27 March 1996 and past communication.

External Trade	–	For 1978-94, BS, *CES*, October 1995 and past issues.
		For 1995, BS, 27 March 1996.
		For exports by SITC, 27 March 1996 and past communication.

Trade Indexes	–	NCDS, *South Pacific Economic and Social Database*, March 1996.

Direction of Trade	–	IMF, *DOTS* tape, May 1996.

Balance of Payments	–	BS, 8 February 1996 and past communication.

International Reserves	–	IMF, *IFS* tape, May 1996.
Exchange Rates		

External Indebtedness	–	WB, *WDT 1996* (STARS version).

HONG KONG

Population	–	For 1978-88, Census and Statistics Department (CSD), *Monthly Digest of Statistics (MDS)*, October 1994 and past issues.
		For 1989-94, CSD, *Hongkong Social and Economic Trends (1995 Edition)*, October 1995 and past issues.
		For 1995, CSD, 15 April 1996.

Labor Force	—	For 1978-93, CSD, *MDS*, October 1994 and past issues. For 1994-95, CSD, 15 April 1996 and past communication.
National Accounts	—	CSD, *Estimates of Gross Domestic Product, 1961-1995*.
Production Agriculture	—	For 1978-92, CSD, *Hong Kong Annual Report 1994* and past issues. For 1993-95, CSD, 15 April 1996 and past communication.
Mining Manufacturing }	—	For 1978-95, CSD, 15 April 1996 and past communication.
Production Indexes Agriculture	—	FAO, Statistics Division, 22 May 1996 and past communication.
Manufacturing	—	For 1978-94, CSD, 15 April 1996 and past communication.
Energy Coal	—	CSD, 15 April 1996 and past communication.
Electricity	—	For 1978-92, *Hong Kong Energy Statistics, 3rd Quarter 1993* and past issues; UN, *ESY 1992* and past issues. For 1993-95, CSD, 15 April 1996.
Retail Prices	—	CSD, 15 April 1996 and past communication.
Price Indexes	—	For 1978-93, CSD, *MDS*, October 1994 and past issues. For 1994-95, CSD, 15 April 1996 and past communication.
Money and Banking	—	For 1978-93, CSD, *MDS*, October 1994 and past issues. For 1994-95, CSD, 15 April 1996. For deposit money banks and interest rates, CSD, 15 April 1996 and past communication.
Government Finance	—	CSD, 15 April 1996 and past communication.
External Trade	—	For 1978-93, CSD, *MDS*, October 1994 and past issues. For 1994-95, CSD, 15 April 1996 and past communication.
Direction of Trade	—	IMF, *DOTS* tape, May 1996.
Exchange Rates	—	For 1978-93, CSD, *MDS*, October 1994 and past issues. For 1994-95, CSD, 15 April 1996 and past communication.
External Indebtedness	—	For public long term debt, short-term debt and use of IMF credit, 1978-81, WB, *WDT 1986-87*. For long-term debt and short-term debt, 1982-91, OECD, *FEDDC, 1992 Survey*. For long-term, short-term and total debt, 1992-94, OECD, *External Debt Statistics Annual Report 1995* and past issues. For debt service, 1978-81, WB, *WDT 1986-87*. For debt service, 1982-91, OECD, *FEDDC, 1992 Survey*. For average terms of new commitments, WB, *WDT 1986-87*.

INDIA

Population	– For 1978-94, Central Statistical Organisation (CSO), 26 June 1995 and past communication. For 1995, ADB staff estimate.
Labor Force	– CSO, 26 June 1995 and past communication.
National Accounts	– For 1978/79-1979/80 and 1981/82-1986/87, CSO, 15 June 1994 and past communication. For 1980/81 & 1987/88-1990/91, CSO, *National Accounts Statistics 1995*. For 1991/1992, Ministry of Finance (MOF), *Economic Survey 1995-96*. For 1992/93-1994/95, CSO, 21 March 1996. For 1995/96, Institute of Economic Growth, 26 December 1995.

Production
   Agriculture   – For 1978/79-1984/85, CSO, 30 March 1987 and past communication and CSO, *Monthly Abstract of Statistics*, September 1988 and past issues.
For 1985/86-1993/94, CSO, 26 June 1995 and past communication.
For 1994/95, MOF, *Economic Survey 1995-96*.

   Mining   – For 1978/79-1979/80, 1981/82-1982/83, 1988/89-1993/94, CSO, 26 June 1995 and past communication.
For 1980/81, 1983/84-1987/88 and 1994/95, CSO, *Monthly Abstract of Statistics*, June 1995 and past issues.

   Manufacturing   – For 1978/79-1979/80, 1982/83-1984/85, 1990/91-1993/94, CSO, 26 June 1995 and past communication.
For 1980/81-1981/82, 1985/86-1989/90 and 1994/95, CSO, *Monthly Abstract of Statistics*, June 1995 and past issues.

Production Indexes
   Agriculture   – For 1978-86, FAO, *PY 1994* and past issues.
For 1987-95, FAO, Statistics Division, 22 May 1996 and past communication.

   Mining   – For 1982/83, CSO, *Statistical Abstract India*, 1989.
For 1981/82, 1983/84-1989/90, CSO, *Monthly Abstract of Statistics*, November 1993 and past issues.
For 1978/79-1980/81, 1990/91-1993/94, CSO, 26 June 1995 and past communication.

   Manufacturing   – For 1978/79-1980/81, CSO, *Statistical Abstract India*, 1982 and CSO, 30 March 1987 and past communication.
For 1982/83, CSO, *Statistical Abstract India*, 1989.
For 1981/82, 1983/84-1989/90 and 1994/95, CSO, *Monthly Abstract of Statistics*, June 1995 and past issues.
For 1990/91-1994/95, CSO, 21 March 1996 and past communication.

Energy
   Crude Petroleum

   Coal   – CSO, 26 June 1995 and past communication.

   Natural Gas

   Electricity   – CSO, 21 March 1996 and past communication.

Retail Prices	–	CSO, 26 June 1995 and past communication.
Price Indexes		Consumer:
	–	For 1978-88, 1993-95, CSO, 21 March 1996 and past communication.
		For 1989-92, CSO, *Monthly Abstract of Statistics*, June 1995 and past issues.
		Wholesale:
	–	For 1978-89, 1993-95, CSO, 21 March 1996 and past communication.
		For 1990-92, CSO, *Monthly Abstract of Statistics*, June 1995 and past issues.
Money and Banking		Money Supply and Deposit Money Banks:
	–	CSO, 26 June 1995 and past communication.
		Interest Rates:
	–	CSO, 21 March 1996 and past communication.
Government Finance	–	Reserve Bank of India (RBI), *Report on Currency and Finance*, 1993-94 and past issues.
External Trade		Total Exports and Imports:
	–	For 1978/79-1986/87, CSO, *Monthly Abstract of Statistics*, June 1995 and past issues.
		For 1987/88, RBI, *Report on Currency and Finance*, 1989-90.
		For 1988/89-1994/95, CSO, 21 March 1996 and past communication.
		Trade by SITC Section:
	–	For 1978/79-1986/87, CSO, *Monthly Abstract of Statistics*, October 1991 and past issues.
		For 1987/88, RBI, *Report on Currency and Finance*, 1989-90.
		For 1988/89-1993/94, CSO, 26 June 1995 and past communication.
		Trade by Principal Commodity:
	–	For 1978/79-1979/80, 1981/82, 1987/88-1993/94, CSO, 26 June 1995 and past communication.
		For 1980/81, 1982/83-1986/87, CSO, *Monthly Abstract of Statistics*, October 1991 and past issues.
Trade Indexes	–	For 1978/79-1979/80, 1981/82 and 1989/90-1994/95, CSO, 21 March 1996 and past communication.
		For 1980/81, 1983/84-1988/89, CSO, *Monthly Abstract of Statistics*, June 1995 and past issues.
Direction of Trade	–	IMF, *DOTS* tape, May 1996.
Balance of Payments	–	For 1978-88, IMF, *IFS Yearbook 1995* and past issues.
		For 1989-92, IMF, *IFS*, April 1996.
International Reserves } Exchange Rates }	–	For 1978-88, IMF, *IFS Yearbook 1995*. For 1989-95, IMF, *IFS* tape, May 1996.
External Indebtedness	–	WB, *WDT 1996* (STARS version).

INDONESIA

Population	–	For 1978-89, Central Bureau of Statistics (CBS), *Population Projection of Indonesia, 1985-2005* and past issues.
		For 1990-95, CBS, *Statistical Yearbook of Indonesia (SY) 1994*.

Labor Force
– For 1978-88, CBS, 4 April 1991 and past communication.
For 1989-93, Bank Indonesia (BI), 11 May 1995.
For 1994, ADB, *ERBOP for Indonesia*, April 1995.

National Accounts
– For 1978-83, BI, 29 March 1993 and past communication.
For 1984-87, CBS, *National Income of Indonesia 1986-1991* and past issues.
For 1988-95, CBS, 3 May 1996 and past communication.

Production
Agriculture
For all products except copra:
– For 1978-80, FAO, *Agrostat* PC 2.0, 1993 (Diskette).
For 1981-95, CBS, *Economic Indicators (EI)*, April 1996.

For copra:
– For 1978-1985, CBS, *SY 1990* and past issues.
For 1986-1993, ADB, *ERBOP for Indonesia*, April 1995.

Mining
– CBS, *EI*, April 1996 and past issues.

Manufacturing
– For 1978-87, CBS, *EI*, January 1989 and past issues.
For 1988-94, BI, 11 May 1995.

Production Indexes
Agriculture
– For 1978-86, FAO, *PY 1993* and past issues.
For 1987-95, FAO, Statistics Division, 22 May 1996 and past communication.

Manufacturing
– CBS, *EI*, November 1991 and past issues.
For 1989-93, CBS, *SY 1994*.
For 1994, CBS, *EI*, April 1996.

Energy
Crude Petroleum :
– For 1978-83, UN, *ESY 1990* and past issues.
For 1984-93, BI, 05 April 1994 and past communication.

Coal :
– For 1978-87, CBS, 29 May 1993 and past communication.
For 1988-94, BI, 11 May 1995.

Natural Gas :
– For 1978-92, UN, *ESY 1992* and past issues.

Electricity :
– For 1978-87, UN, *ESY 1990* and past issues.
For 1988-93, BI, 11 May 1995.

Retail Prices:
– For 1978-89, BI, 28 December 1990 and past communication.
For 1990-94, CBS, 31 March 1995.

Price Indexes	CPI :
	— For 1978-84, CBS, 4 April 1991 and past communication. For 1985-90, BI, *Indonesian Financial Statistics (IFS)*, December 1993 and past issues. For 1990-93, BI, 11 May 1995. For 1994-95, BI, *IFS*, March 1996.
	WPI:
	— BI, 11 May 1995 and past communication. For 1994, CBS, 07 February 1996. For 1995, BI, *IFS*, March 1996.
Money and Banking	Money Supply and Deposit Money Banks:
	— For 1978, CBS, *EI*, September 1984. For 1979-94, BI, *Weekly Report*, December 1995 and past issues. For 1990-95, BI, *IFS*, March 1996. For 1995 data on savings and time deposits of deposit money banks, BI, 10 April 1996.
	Domestic credits outstanding:
	— For 1978, CBS, *EI*, September 1984 and past issues. For 1979-94, BI, *Weekly Report*, December 1995 and past issues. For 1990-95, BI, *IFS*, March 1996.
	Interest Rates:
	— For 1977-87, BI, 20 March 1990 and past communication. For 1988-92, BI, *IFS*, January 1995 and past issues For 1993-95, BI, 10 April 1996 and past communication.
Government Finance	— For 1977-88, BI, *IFS*, January 1995 and past issues. For 1989-94, BI, 11 May 1995. For 1995, ADB data file.
	Expenditure by Function:
	— BI, *Report for the Financial Year 1994/95* and past issues.
External Trade	Total Trade and Trade by SITC Section:
	— For 1978-80, CBS, *SY 1985* and past issues. For 1981-95, CBS, *EI*, April 1996.
	Trade by Principal Commodity :
	— For 1978-95, CBS, *EI*, April 1996 and past issues.
Trade Indexes	Quantum Indexes:
	— For 1978-80, CBS, 28 October 1982 and past communication. For 1987-94, BI, 11 May 1995 and past communication.
	Unit Value Indexes and Terms of Trade:
	— For 1978-80, CBS, 28 October 1982 and past communication. For 1983-88, CBS, *EI*, December 1995. For 1989-94, BI, 11 May 1995 and past communication.
Direction of Trade	— For 1978-94, IMF, *DOTS* tape, May 1996.
Balance of Payments	— IMF, *IFS Yearbook 1995* and *IFS*, April 1996.

International Reserves }   –   IMF, *IFS* tape, May 1996.
Exchange Rates

External Indebtedness   –   WB, *WDT 1996* (STARS version).

KAZAKSTAN

Population	– For 1981-94, State Committee on Statistics and Analysis (Goskomstat), *Statistical Bulletin, No.3/95.* For 1995, Goskomstat, 09 April 1996.
Labor Force	– For 1980, 1985-90, Goskomstat, *Statistical Bulletin, No.3/95.* For 1991-95, Goskomstat, 09 April 1996.
National Accounts	NMP by Industrial Origin and by Expenditure: – WB, *Statistical Handbook of the States of the Former USSR (SHSFUSSR) 1994* and past issues. Goskomstat, 09 April 1996. GDP at current market prices: – For 1980-92, WB, *World Tables 1994.* For 1993-94, ADB, *ERBOP*, October 1995. GDP at constant market prices: – For 1990-94, ADB, *ERBOP*, October 1995.

Production
    Agriculture }
    Mining   }   –   Goskomstat, 09 April 1996.
    Manufacturing }

  Production Indexes   –   Goskomstat, 09 April 1996.

Energy
    Production   –   For crude petroleum and coal, Goskomstat, 09 April 1996.
                        For natural gas and electricity, Goskomstat, *Statistical Bulletin, No. 3/95.*

    Exports }   –   For 1991-93, ADB, *ERBOP*, October 1994.
    Imports }   For 1994-95, Goskomstat, 09 April 1996.

    Consumption   –   ADB, *ERBOP*, October 1994.

Price Indexes   –   ADB, *ERBOP*, October 1995.

Money and Banking   –   ADB, *ERBOP*, October 1995.

Government Finance   –   Goskomstat, 09 April 1996.

External Trade   –   For 1990-93, ADB, *ERBOP*, October 1994 and 1995.
                           For 1994-95, IMF, *DOTS tape*, May 1996.

Direction of Trade   –   IMF, *DOTS* tape, May 1996.

Balance of Payments   –   Goskomstat, 09 April 1996.

| International Reserves | – | ADB, *ERBOP*, October 1995. |

| Exchange Rates | – | For 1987-91, WB, *SHSFUSSR 1994*.
For 1992, ADB, *ERBOP*, October 1995.
For 1993-95, Goskomstat, 09 April 1996. |

| External Indebtedness | – | WB, *WDT 1996* (STARS version). |

KIRIBATI

| Population | – | For 1978-90, NCDS, *South Pacific Economic and Social Database*, March 1996.
For 1991-95, ADB staff estimates. |

| Labor Force | – | For 1978, MOF, SO, *Kiribati 1979-1987: A Compendium of Statistics*, 1987.
For 1985, MOF, SO, *Kiribati Statistical Yearbook 1988*.
For 1990, ADB, *Kiribati Country Survey*, December 1992. |

| National Accounts | – | For 1978, Republic of Kiribati, National Development Plan.
For 1979-81, MOF, SO, *Kiribati Statistical Yearbook 1988*.
For 1982-92, ADB, *Kiribati Country Survey*, December 1992. |

Production
Agriculture   –   For 1978-88, MOF, SO, *Kiribati Statistical Yearbook 1988*.
     For 1989-91, ADB, *Kiribati Country Survey*, December 1992.

| Energy | – | For 1978-92, UN, *ESY 1992* and past issues. |

| Price Indexes | – | For 1978, ADB, *Economic Survey*, August 1983.
For 1979-83, MOF, SO, *Kiribati 1979-1987: A Compendium of Statistics*, 1987.
For 1984-88, MOF, SO, *Kiribati Statistical Yearbook 1988*.
For 1989-95, MOF, SO, *Retail Price Index*, March 1996. |

| Money and Banking | – | For 1978-79, ADB, Economic Mission, October 1979.
For 1982-86, ADB Economic Mission, February 1988; ADB, *Economic Survey of Kiribati*, June 1988. |

| Government Finance | – | For 1978, ADB, Economic Mission, October 1979.
For 1979-81, MOF, SO, *Statistical Bulletin for the Kiribati Aid Donors Meeting*, 29 May 1985.
For 1982-83, ADB, *Economic Survey of Kiribati*, June 1988.
For 1984, ADB, *Bank Operational Strategy for the Republic of Kiribati*, June 1991.
For 1985-94, MOF, SO, *Government Finance Statistics 1985-94*, September 1995.
For 1995, ADB data file. |

External Trade	–	For total trade and by SITC Section: For 1978-94, MOF, SO, *1994 International Trade - Exports and Imports*, November 1995 and past issues.
		By Principal Commodity:
	–	For 1978, MOF, SO, *1985 International Trade - Imports and Exports*, October 1986. For 1979-81, MOF, SO, *Kiribati Statistical Yearbook 1988*. For 1982-94, MOF, SO, *1994 International Trade - Exports and Imports*, November 1995 and past issues.

| Direction of Trade | – | IMF, *DOTS* tape, May 1996. |

Balance of Payments	—	For 1978, MOF, 12 January 1977 and ADB Economic Mission, October 1979. For 1979-81, MOF, SO, *Kiribati Statistical Yearbook 1988.* For 1982-84, ADB, *Kiribati Country Survey*, December 1992. For 1985-94, MOF, SO, *Balance of Payments Statistics 1985-1994*, December 1995. For 1995, ADB data file.
International Reserves	—	For 1978-79, ADB, Economic Mission, October 1979. For 1980-82, ADB, *Economic Survey*, August 1983. For 1983-85, MOF, SO, 7 March 1986 and past communication.
Exchange Rates	—	IMF, *IFS* tape, April 1996.
External Indebtedness	—	WB, *WDT 1994-95* and past issues.

KOREA, Republic of

Population	—	National Statistical Office (NSO), *Korea Statistical Yearbook 1995* and past issues.
Labor Force	—	For 1978-94, NSO, *Monthly Statistics of Korea*, January 1996 and past issues. For 1995, NSO, 9 April 1996.
National Accounts	—	For 1978-92, Bank of Korea (BOK), 28 April 1994. For 1993-95, NSO, *Monthly Statistics of Korea*, March 1996.
Production	—	For 1978-94, NSO, *Korea Statistical Yearbook 1995* and past issues. For 1995, NSO, 9 April 1996.
Production Indexes Agriculture	—	FAO, Statistics Division, 22 May 1996 and past communication.
Mining	—	For 1978-94, NSO, *Korea Statistical Yearbook 1995* and past issues.
Manufacturing	—	For 1995, NSO, 9 April 1996.
Energy	—	NSO, 25 January 1996 and past communication.
Price Indexes	—	For 1978-95, NSO, *Monthly Statistics of Korea*, March 1996 and past issues.
Money and Banking	—	BOK, *Monthly Statistical Bulletin*, February 1996 and past issues.
Government Finance	—	BOK, 26 January 1996 and past communication.
External Trade	—	For 1978-94, NSO, *Korea Statistical Yearbook 1995* and past issues. For 1995, NSO, *Monthly Statistics of Korea*, February - March 1996. For Exports by Principal Commodity: BOK, *Monthly Statistical Bulletin*, February 1996 and past issues.
Direction of Trade	—	IMF, *DOTS* tape, May 1996.
Balance of Payments	—	For 1978-95, BOK, *Monthly Statistical Bulletin*, February 1996 and past issues.

International Reserves }   –   IMF, *IFS* tape, April 1996.
Exchange Rates

External Indebtedness   –   WB, *WDT 1996* (STARS version).

KYRGYZ Republic

Population	– For 1980, WB, *Statistical Handbook 1994, States of the Former USSR*. For 1985-90, National Statistical Committee (Natstatcom), 25 July 1995. For 1991-95, ADB data file.
Labor Force	– For 1980, 1985-94, WB, *Statistical Handbook 1994, States of the Former USSR* and Natstatcom, 25 July 1995.
National Accounts	– For 1990-95, Natstatcom, 12 April 1996.
Production Agriculture	– For 1978-79, Natstatcom, 12 April 1996. For 1980-94, Natstatcom, 25 July 1995. For 1995, Natstatcom, 12 April 1996.

Production Indexes
  Agriculture
  Industry
	– For 1978-95, Natstatcom, 12 April 1996.
	– For 1980-94, Natstatcom, 25 July 1995.

Energy	– For coal, 1992, ADB, *Economic Report (ER) on the Kyrgyz Republic*, November 1994. For electricity, 1980-94, Natstatcom, 25 July 1995.
Price Indexes	– For 1990-94, ADB, *ERBOP*, October 1995. For 1995, ADB data file.
Money and Banking	– For 1991-92, ADB, *ER*, November 1994. For 1993-94, ADB, *ERBOP*, October 1995. For 1995, Natstatcom, 12 April 1996. For deposit money banks, 1995, Natstatcom, 12 April 1996.
Government Finance	– For 1987-92, ADB, *ER*, November 1994. For 1993-95, Natstatcom, 12 April 1996. For expenditure by function, 1987-95, Natstatcom, 12 April 1996.
External Trade	– For 1992-93, Natstatcom, 25 July 1995. For 1994-95, Natstatcom, 12 April 1996.
Direction of Trade	– For 1988-93, ADB, *ER*, November 1994. For 1994, Natstatcom, 25 July 1995. For 1995, Natstatcom, 12 April 1996.
Balance of Payments	– For 1992-93, Natstatcom, 25 July 1995. For 1994-95, Natstatcom, 12 April 1996.
International Reserves	– For 1993-95, ADB, *ERBOP*, October 1995.

Exchange Rates	–	For 1992-94, ADB, *ERBOP*, October 1995.
		For 1995, Natstatcom, 12 April 1996.
External Indebtedness	–	WB, *WDT 1996* (STARS version).

LAO People's Democratic Republic

Population	–	For 1978-79, UN, *MBS*, February 1987 and past issues.
		For 1980-84 , State Statistical Centre (SSC), *10 Years of Socio -Economic Development in Lao PDR*, 1985.
		For 1985-89, SSC, *Basic Statistics About the Social and Economic Development of Lao PDR (1975-1990).*
		For 1990-91, SSC, 19 March 1992.
		For 1992, SSC, *Basic Statistics About the Social and Economic Development of Lao PDR (1992).*
		For 1993-94, National Statistical Centre (NSC), 30 May 1996.
		For 1995, ADB staff estimate.
National Accounts	–	For 1981-93, Bank of Lao PDR, 24 June 1994.
		For 1994, NSC, 30 May 1996.
		For 1995, ADB, *ERBOP: Lao PDR*, 10 May 1996.
Production		
Agriculture	–	For 1978-84, 1994, FAO, *PY 1994* and past issues.
		For 1985-93, FAO, Statistics Division, 14 February 1995 and past communication.
		For 1995, ADB, *ERBOP: Lao PDR*, 10 May 1996.
Mining	–	For 1978-80, UN, *SYAP 1990* and past issues.
		For 1981-86, ADB, *Economic Report on Lao PDR* , November 1988.
		For 1987-89, SSC, *Basic Data About the Social and Economic Development of Lao PDR (1989).*
		For 1990-92, SSC, 19 July 1993 and past communication.
		For 1993-95, NSC, 30 May 1996.
Production Indexes		
Agriculture	–	FAO, Statistics Division, 22 May 1996 and past communication.
Energy	–	For 1978-84, UN, *1988 ESY* and past issues.
		For 1985-92, SSC, *Basic Data About the Social and Economic Development of Lao PDR (1992).*
		For 1993-95, NSC, 30 May 1996.
Price Indexes	–	For 1978-85, ADB, Programs Department, 24 September 1987.
		For 1988-95, *Basic Statistics About the Socio-Economic Development in the Lao PDR (1975-1995).*
Money and Banking	–	For 1981-84, ADB, *Economic Report of Lao PDR*, November 1988.
		For 1985-86, ADB, *ERBOP: Lao PDR*, August 1992.
		For 1987-93, Bank of Lao PDR , 24 June 1994.
		For 1994-95, NSC, 30 May 1996.
Government Finance	–	For 1978-80, ADB, Programs Department, 24 September 1987.
		For 1981-83, ADB, *Economic Report on Lao PDR*, November 1988.
		For 1984-88, ADB, *ERBOP: Lao PDR*, August 1992.
		For 1989-93, Bank of Lao PDR, 24 June 1994.
		For 1994-95, NSC 30 May 1996.

External Trade	–	For 1978 , ESCAP, *SYAP 1985.*
		For 1979-80, ADB, Programs Department, 24 September 1987.
		For 1981-83, ADB, *Economic Report on Lao PDR*, November 1988.
		For 1984-86, ADB, *ERBOP: Lao PDR*, November 1990.
		For 1987-92, Bank of Lao PDR, 28 February 1994.
		For 1993-95, NSC, 30 May 1996.

| Direction of Trade | – | IMF, *DOTS* tape, May 1996. |

Balance of Payments	–	For 1978-80, ADB, Economic Mission, March 1984.
		For 1981-83, ADB, *Economic Report on Lao PDR*, November 1988.
		For 1984-90, Bank of Lao PDR, 28 February 1994.
		For 1991-95, NSC, 30 May 1996.

International Reserves	–	For 1978-80, ADB, *Economic Memorandum on Lao PDR*, July 1981.
		For 1981-84, ADB, *Economic Report on Lao PDR*, November 1988.
		For 1985-88, ADB, *ERBOP: Lao PDR*, August 1992 and past issues.
		For 1989-95, IMF, *IFS*, April 1996.

| Exchange Rates | – | IMF, *IFS* tape, May 1996. |

| External Indebtedness | – | WB, *WDT 1996* (STARS version). |

MALAYSIA

Population	–	For 1978, Department of Statistics (DOS), 31 March 1993.
		For 1979-91, Ministry of Finance (MOF), *Economic Report 1994/95* and past issues.
		For 1992-94, DOS, 17 April 1995 and past communication.
		For 1995, MOF, *Economic Report 1995/96.*

| Labor Force | – | For 1978-95, MOF, *Economic Report 1995/96* and past issues. |

| National Accounts | – | For 1978-95, MOF, *Economic Report 1995/96* and past issues. |

Production
Agriculture ⎫
⎬ – For 1978-93, Bank Negara of Malaysia (BNM), *Quarterly Bulletin*, September 1994 and past issues.
Mining ⎭ For 1994, DOS, 17 April 1995.
For 1995, MOF, *Economic Report 1995/96.*

| Manufacturing | – | For 1978-93, BNM, *Quarterly Bulletin*, September 1994 and past issues. |
| | | For 1994-95, DOS , 08 April 1996 and past communication. |

Production Indexes
| Agriculture | – | For 1978-86, FAO, *PY 1993* and past issues |
| | | For 1987-95, FAO, Statistics Division, 22 May 1996 and past communication. |

| Mining | – | For 1978-93, BNM, *Quarterly Bulletin*, March 1995 and past issues. |
| | | For 1994-95, DOS, 08 April 1996 and past communication. |

| Manufacturing | – | For 1978-92, BNM, *Quarterly Bulletin*, March 1995 and past issues. |
| | | For 1993-95, DOS, 08 April 1996 and past communication. |

Energy

Crude Petroleum	–	For 1978-91, DOS, 05 April 1993 (excluding crude petroleum consumption). For 1978-91, UN, *ESY 1994* and past issues (for crude petroleum consumption). For 1992, UN, *ESY 1994.* For 1993-94, DOS, 17 April 1995 (for crude petroleum production).
Coal	–	For 1978-92, UN, *ESY 1994* and past issues. For 1993-94, DOS,17 April 1995 (for coal production).
Natural Gas	–	UN, *ESY 1994* and past issues.
Electricity	–	For 1978-91, UN, *ESY 1994* and past issues. For 1992-94, DOS, 09 February 1996 and past communication.
Retail Prices	–	DOS, 08 April 1996 and past communication.
Price Indexes	–	DOS, 08 April 1996 and past communication.
Money and Banking	–	For 1978-1994, BNM, *Quarterly Bulletin*, March 1995 and past issues. For interest rates, BNM, 24 April 1996 and past communication.
Government Finance	–	Central Government: For 1978-94, BNM, *Quarterly Bulletin*, March 1995 and past issues. For 1995, MOF, *Economic Report 1995/96.*
	–	Expenditure by Function: For 1978-94, BNM, *Quarterly Bulletin*, March 1995 and past issues. For 1995, BNM, 24 April 1996.
External Trade	–	For 1978-93, BNM, *Quarterly Bulletin*, September 1994 and past issues. For 1994, DOS, 17 April 1995. For 1995, MOF, *Economic Report 1995/96.*
Trade Indexes	–	For 1978-84, MOF, *Economic Report 1986/87* and past issues. For 1985-87, DOS, 23 December 1988 (except Quantum Index-Imports). For 1984-87, DOS, 29 April 1991 (Quantum Index-Imports only).
Direction of Trade	–	IMF, *DOTS* tape, May 1996.
Balance of Payments	–	For 1978-80, IMF, *IFS Yearbook 1991* and past issues. For 1981-95, DOS, 08 April 1996 and past communication.
International Reserves Exchange Rates	–	For 1978-87, IMF, *IFS Yearbook 1994.* For 1988-95, IMF, *IFS*, April 1996.
External Indebtedness	–	WB, *WDT 1996* (STARS version).

MALDIVES

Population	–	For 1978-79, Maldives Monetary Authority (MMA), 11 April 1993 and past communication. For 1980-95, Department of External Resources (DER), 06 May 1996.
Labor Force	–	MMA, 11 April 1993 and past communication.

National Accounts	GDP by Expenditure, at Current Market Prices:
	— For 1980-84, MMA, 11 April 1993 and past communication.
	For 1985-95, DER, 06 May 1996.

National Accounts
     GDP by Expenditure, at Current Market Prices:
  – For 1980-84, MMA, 11 April 1993 and past communication.
     For 1985-95, DER, 06 May 1996.

     GDP by Industrial Origin, at Constant Prices:
  – For 1981-84, MMA, 11 April 1993 and past communication.
     For 1985-95, DER, 06 May 1996.

     GDP by Expenditure, at Constant Prices:
  – For 1981-90, MMA, 11 April 1993 and past communication.
     For 1991-95, DER, 06 May 1996 and past communication.

     GNP and NFIA at Constant Prices:
  – For 1982-90, MMA, 11 April 1993 and past communication.
     For 1991, DER, 29 March 1994.

Production
    Fisheries
  – For 1978-84, Ministry of Planning and Environment (MPE), *Statistical Yearbook 1992* and past issues.
     For 1985-94, DER, 06 May 1996.

Production Indexes
    Agriculture
  – FAO, Statistics Division, 22 May 1996 and past communication.

Energy
    Electricity
        Production
  – For 1977-82, ESCAP, *SYAP 1991* and past issues.
     For 1983-89, MPE, *National Development Plan 1991-1993*, Vol 1.
     For 1990-91, MPE, *Statistical Yearbook 1992*.
     For 1992-95, DER, 03 February 1996 and past communication.

        Consumption
  – For 1978-82, ESCAP, *SYAP 1991* and past issues.
     For 1983-89, MPE, *National Development Plan 1991-1993*, Vol 1.
     For 1990-92, ESCAP, *SYAP 1994*.

    Retail Prices
  – For 1978-83, MPE, *Statistical Yearbook 1984*.
     For 1984-92, MMA, 30 January 1993 and past communication.
     For 1993, DER, 29 March 1994.

Price Indexes
  – DER, 06 May 1996.

Money and Banking
  – MMA, 22 April 1996.

Government Finance
    Central Government
  – For 1978-87, MMA, 11 April 1993 and past communication.
     For 1988-95, DER, 06 May 1996 and past communication.

    Expenditure
    by Function
  – For 1982-87, MPE, 11 April 1993.
     For 1988-95, DER, 06 May 1996 and past communication.

External Trade
  – For 1978-85, DER, 06 May 1996.
     For 1986-95, MMA, 22 April 1996.

    Exports by principal
    commodity
  – For 1978-84, MPE, *Statistical Yearbook 1986*.
     For 1985-94, DER, 06 May 1996.

Direction of Trade	—	IMF, *DOTS* tape, May 1996.
Trade Indexes	—	DER, 12 February 1995.
Balance of Payments	—	For 1978-85, IMF, *IFS* tape, April 1995. For 1986-95, MMA, 22 April 1996.
International Reserves Exchange Rates	—	IMF, *IFS* tape, May 1996.
External Indebtedness	—	WB, *WDT 1996* (STARS version).

MARSHALL ISLANDS

Population	—	Office of Planning and Statistics (OPS), *Marshall Islands Statistical Abstract 1995* and OPS, 14 March 1996.
Labor Force	—	For 1980 and 1988, OPS, *Marshall Islands Statistical Abstract 1995*.
National Accounts		GDP at Current Prices:
	—	OPS, *Marshall Islands Statistical Abstract 1995*.
		GDP at Constant 1991 Prices:
	—	OPS, 16 May 1996.
Production Agriculture	—	OPS, *Marshall Islands Statistical Abstract 1995* and past issues.
Energy Electricity	—	OPS, *Marshall Islands Statistical Abstract 1995*.
Price Indexes	—	OPS, *Marshall Islands Statistical Abstract 1995* and past issues.
Government Finance	—	For 1985/86-1989/90, IMF estimates, 7 February 1992. For 1990/91- 1993/94, OPS, 11 April 1995 and past communication.
External Trade	—	OPS, *Marshall Islands Statistical Abstract 1995* and past issues.
Direction of Trade	—	OPS, *Marshall Islands Statistical Abstract 1995*.
Balance of Payments	—	IMF estimates, 7 February 1992.

MICRONESIA, Fed. States of

Population	—	For 1980, Office of Planning and Statistics (OPS), *Second National Development Plan 1992-1996*. For 1985-95, Federated States of Micronesia (FSM), *Responding to the Challenges: A Report Presented to the Asian Development Bank's Consultative Group of Donors Meeting (Responding to the Challenges)*, Manila, 6 December 1995.
Labor Force	—	OPS, *Second National Development Plan 1992-1996*.

| National Accounts | — | For 1983, ADB, *Economic Report on The Federated States of Micronesia*, February 1991.
For 1986-95, FSM, *Responding to the Challenges*, Manila, 6 December 1995. |

Production
Agriculture — IMF estimates, 22 February 1992.

| Government Finance | — | For 1988-90, OPS, *Second National Development Plan 1992-1996*.
For 1991-95, FSM, *Responding to the Challenges*, Manila, 6 December 1995. |

| External Trade | — | For 1978-83, NCDS, *South Pacific Economic and Social Database,* March 1996.
For 1984-86, ADB, *Economic Report on The Federated States of Micronesia*, February 1991.
For 1987-91, OPS, *Trade Bulletin No. 5*, November 1992. |

Direction of Trade

Exports:
— For 1988, ADB, *Economic Report on the Federated States of Micronesia*, February 1991.
For 1991, OPS, *Trade Bulletin No. 5*, November 1992.

Imports:
— OPS, *Trade Bulletin No. 5*, November 1992.

| Balance of Payments | — | For 1983, ADB, *Economic Report on The Federated States of Micronesia*, February 1991.
For 1986-90, IMF estimates, 22 May 1992. |

MONGOLIA

Population — State Statistical Office (SSO), *Mongolian Economy and Society in 1994, Statistical Yearbook*.
For 1995, SSO, 17 May 1996.

Labor Force — SSO, 17 May 1996 and past communication.
Unemployed:
For 1987-89, ADB, Economic Mission, July 1993.
For 1990-95, SSO, 17 May 1996.

National Accounts

GDP by Industrial Origin at Current Market Prices:
— For 1980-94, SSO, Statistical tables provided to consultant, December 1995.
For 1995, SSO, 17 May 1996.

GDP by Expenditure at Current Market Prices:
— For 1980-94, SSO, *Statistical Yearbook 1995* and past issues.
For 1995, SSO, 17 May 1996.

At Constant Prices:
— SSO, 17 May 1996.

Production
Agriculture
Mining   } — SSO, 17 May 1996.
Manufacturing

Production Indexes
  Agriculture   –   For 1978-92, FAO, *PY 1994* and past issues.
                                   For 1993-95, FAO, Statistics Division, 22 May 1996 and past communication..

Energy
  Coal   –   For 1980-84, ADB, *Economic Report on the Mongolian People's Republic, Part II*, September 1991.
                                   For 1985-94, SSO, *Statistical Yearbook 1994*.
                                   For 1995, SSO, 17 May 1996.

  Electricity   –   For 1981-84, ADB, *Economic Report on the Mongolian People's Republic, Part II*, September 1991 and SSO, 6 March 1992.
                                   For 1980, 1985-94, SSO, *Statistical Yearbook 1994*.
                                   For 1995, SSO, 17 May 1996.

  Retail prices   –   For 1980, 1988-90, ADB, *Economic Report on the Mongolian People's Republic, Part II*, September 1991 and ADB, *Mongolia: A Centrally Planned Economy in Transition*, 1992.
                                   For 1986-87 and 1991, SSO, 6 March 1992.
                                   For 1992, ADB, Economic Mission, July 1993.

Price Index   –   For 1978-89, IMF, *The Mongolian People's Republic: Toward a Market Economy*, April 1991.
                                   For 1990, SSO, 6 March 1992.
                                   For 1991-93, SSO, *Mongolian Economy and Society in 1993, Annual Statistical Yearbook*.
                                   For 1994-95, SSO, 05 April 1995 and 07 February 1996.

Money and Banking   –   For 1980, 1986-88, ADB, *Mongolia: A Centrally Planned Economy in Transition*, 1992.
                                   For 1985, ADB, *Economic Report on the Mongolian People's Republic, Part I*, September 1991.
                                   For 1989, ADB, *ERBOP, Mongolia*, June 1995.
                                   For 1990-95, Mongol Bank, *Monthly Statistical Bulletin*, March 1996.

                                   Interest rates:
                         –   For 1985-86 and 1989, ADB, *Mongolia: A Centrally Planned Economy in Transition*, 1992.
                                   For 1987-88, ADB, *Economic Report on the Mongolian People's Republic, Part I*, September 1991.
                                   For 1990-91, ADB, *ERBOP, Mongolia*, June 1995.
                                   For 1992-95, Mongol Bank, *Monthly Statistical Bulletin*, March 1996.

Government Finance   Central Government:
                         –   For 1978-88, ADB, *Mongolia: A Centrally Planned Economy in Transition*, 1992.
                                   For 1989-90, ADB, *ERBOP, Mongolia*, June 1995.
                                   For 1991-95, SSO, *Statistical Yearbook 1995* and past issues.

                                   Expenditure by Function:
                         –   For 1978-90, ADB, *Mongolia: A Centrally Planned Economy in Transition*, 1992.
                                   For 1991-95, SSO, *Statistical Yearbook 1995* and past issues.

External Trade   –   SSO, 17 May 1996.

Direction of Trade   –   SSO, *Statistical Yearbook 1995*.

Trade Indexes   –   For 1980-90, ADB, *Mongolia: A Centrally Planned Economy in Transition*, 1992.

Balance of Payments	–	For 1980-86, ADB, *Mongolia: A Centrally Planned Economy in Transition*, 1992.
		For 1987-88, IMF, April 1992.
		For 1989-94, ADB, *ERBOP, Mongolia*, June 1995.
International Reserves	–	For 1980-91, ADB, *Mongolia: A Centrally Planned Economy in Transition*, 1992.
		For 1992-95, IMF, *IFS* tape, May 1996.
Exchange Rates	–	For 1980-91, ADB, *Mongolia: A Centrally Planned Economy in Transition*, 1992.
		For 1992-93, SSO, 20 January 1994.
		For 1994-95, IMF, *IFS* tape, May 1996.
External Indebtedness	–	WB, *WDT 1996* (STARS version) and past issues.

MYANMAR

Population	–	For 1978/79-1995/96, Ministry of National Planning and Economic Development (MNPED), *The Union of Myanmar, Review of the Financial, Economic and Social Conditions (RFESC) for 1994/95* and past issues.
Labor Force	–	For 1978/79-1989/90, Central Statistical Organization (CSO), 4 April 1990 and past communication.
		For 1990/91-1994/95, MNPED, *RFESC 1994/95* and past issues.
		For 1995/96, MNPED, 8 April 1996.
		For labor force and unemployment, 1990/91-1995/96, CSO, 9 April 1996.
		For unemployment, 1978/79-1982/83, UN, *Monthly Bulletin of Statistics*, April 1984 and past issues.
National Accounts	–	For 1978/79-1995/96, MNPED, *RFESC 1994/95* and past issues.
Production		
Agriculture	–	For 1978/79, CSO, 9 April 1986.
		For 1979/80-1995/96, CSO, 9 April 1996.
Mining	–	For 1978/79-1995/96, CSO, 9 April 1996.
Manufacturing	–	For 1978/79-1995/96, CSO, 9 April 1996 and past communication.
Production Indexes		
Agriculture	–	FAO, Statistics Division, 22 May 1996 and past communication.
Mining ⎫	–	For 1978/79-1984/85, CSO, 18 April 1994 and past communication.
Manufacturing ⎭		For 1985/86-1995/96, MNPED, *RFESC 1994/95* and past issues.
Energy	–	For crude petroleum, 1978-82, UN, *ESY 1988* and past issues.
		For crude petroleum, 1983-92, UN, *SYAP 1994*.
		For coal, 1978-95, CSO, 9 April 1996 and past communication, and UN, *SYAP 1994*.
		For natural gas, 1978-82, UN, *ESY 1988* and past issues.
		For natural gas, 1983-88, CSO, 22 May 1995 and past communication.
		For electricity, 1978-95, CSO, 9 April 1996 and past communication, and UN, *SYAP 1994*.
		For retail prices, CSO, 22 May 1995 and past communication.
Price Indexes		
CPI	–	For 1978/79-1995/96, CSO, 9 April 1996 and past communication.
WPI	–	For 1978/79-1984/85, CSO, 28 March 1989.

Money and Banking	–	For 1978/79-1995/96, CSO, 9 April 1996 and past communication.
Government Finance	–	For 1978/79-1995/96, CSO, 9 April 1996 and past communication.
External Trade	–	For 1978-1989/90, CSO, 22 May 1995 and past communication. For 1990/91-1993/94, CSO, *Statistical Abstract 1994*. For 1994/95, CSO, 9 April 1996.
Direction of Trade	–	IMF, *DOTS* tape, May 1996.
Trade Indexes	–	MNPED, *RFESC 1994/95* and past issues.
Balance of Payments	–	For 1978-88, IMF, *IFS Yearbook 1995*. For 1989-91, IMF, *IFS*, May 1996.
International Reserves } Exchange Rates }	–	For 1978-88, IMF, *IFS Yearbook 1995*. For 1989-95, IMF, *IFS*, May 1996.
External Indebtedness	–	WB, *WDT 1996* (STARS version).

NEPAL

Population	–	For 1978-90, Central Bureau of Statistics (CBS), *Statistical Yearbook of Nepal 1995*. For 1991-95, CBS, 22 April 1996.
National Accounts	–	Ministry of Finance (MOF), *Economic Survey (ES) (Revised) 1994/95*, October 1995.
Production Agriculture	–	For 1978-94, MOF, *ES 1994/95*, October 1995. For 1995, CBS, 22 April 1996.
Manufacturing	–	MOF, *ES 1994/95*, October 1995. For fertilizer, Nepal Rastra Bank (NRB), 15 April 1993.
Production Indexes Agriculture	–	For 1978-1993, FAO, *PY 1994*. For 1994-95, FAO, Statistics Division, 22 May 1996.
Manufacturing	–	MOF, *ES 1994/95*, October 1995.
Energy	–	For coal, NRB, 15 April 1993. For electricity, MOF, *ES 1994/95*, October 1995.
	–	Retail prices: For 1978-91, CBS, 29 April 1992 and past communication. For 1992-95, NRB, 2 June 1996.
Price Indexes	–	For 1978-84, NRB, *Quarterly Economic Bulletin (QEB)*, mid-January 1993. For 1985-94, MOF, *ES 1994/95*, October 1995. For 1995, CBS, 8 February 1996 and NRB, 2 June 1996.
Money and Banking	–	For 1978-93, MOF, *ES 1994/95*, October 1995. For 1994-95, NRB, 2 June 1996. For 1992-95 data on interest rates on time deposit, CBS, 8 February 1996.

Government Finance	—	For 1978-94, MOF, *ES 1994/95*, October 1995. For 1995, NRB, 2 June 1996. For data on financing, NRB, 2 June 1996.
External Trade	—	For 1978-93, MOF, *ES 1994/95*, October 1995. For 1994-95, NRB, 2 June 1996.
Direction of Trade	—	IMF, *DOTS* tape, May 1996.
Balance of Payments	—	For 1978-94, IMF, *IFS Yearbook 1995* and *IFS*, April 1996. For 1995, NRB, 2 June 1996.
International Reserves } Exchange Rates	—	IMF, *IFS* tape, May 1996.
External Indebtedness	—	WB, *WDT 1996* (STARS version).

PAKISTAN

Population	—	For 1978-93, Federal Bureau of Statistics (FBS), *Monthly Statistical Bulletin*, February 1994. For 1994-95, FBS, 15 April 1996.
Labor Force	—	FBS, 15 April 1996 and past communication.
National Accounts	—	For 1978-82, FBS, *National Accounts of Pakistan, 1988-89* and past issues. For 1983-90, FBS, *Monthly Statistical Bulletin*, February 1994. For 1991-95, FBS, 15 April 1996 and past communication.
Production	—	For 1978-87, FBS, *Pakistan Statistical Yearbook 1991* and past issues. For 1988-91, FBS, *Monthly Statistical Bulletin*, February 1994 and past issues. For 1992-95, FBS, 15 April 1996.
Production Indexes Agriculture	—	For 1978-93, FAO, *PY 1994* and past issues. For 1994-95, FAO, Statistics Division, 22 May 1996 and past communication.
Mining	—	For 1978-88, FBS, *Pakistan Statistical Yearbook 1991* and past issues. For 1989-94, FBS, 12 April 1995 and past communication. For 1995, Gov't . of Pakistan, Finance Division, *Economic Survey 1994-95*.
Manufacturing	—	For 1978-87, FBS, *Pakistan Statistical Yearbook 1991* and past issues. For 1988-92, FBS, *Monthly Statistical Bulletin*, February 1994. For 1993-95, FBS, 15 April 1996.
Energy	—	FBS, 12 April 1995 and past communication.
Price Indexes	—	For 1978-91, FBS, *Monthly Statistical Bulletin*, February 1994 and past issues. For 1992-95, FBS, 15 April 1996.
Money and Banking	—	FBS, 22 May 1996 and past communication.
Government Finance	—	For 1978-81, State Bank of Pakistan (SBP), *Annual Report 1982/83* and past issues. For 1982-95, Gov't. of Pakistan, Finance Division, *Economic Survey 1994-95* and past issues.

External Trade	–	For 1978-87, FBS, *Pakistan Statistical Yearbook 1991* and past issues. For 1988-91, FBS, *Monthly Statistical Bulletin*, February 1994 and past issues. For 1992-95, FBS, 15 April 1996.
Direction of Trade	–	IMF, *DOTS* tape, May 1996.
Balance of Payments	–	FBS, 7 January 1996 and past communication.
International Reserves Exchange Rates	–	IMF, *IFS* tape, May 1996.
External Indebtedness	–	WB, *WDT 1996* (STARS version) .

PAPUA NEW GUINEA

Population	–	For 1978-80, National Statistics Office (NSO), 9 October 1985. For 1981-95, ADB staff estimates based on intercensal growth rates from 1980 and 1990 national population censuses.
National Accounts	–	For 1978-84, NSO, 13 March 1990 and past communication. For 1985-91, NSO, *National Economic Accounts 1987-1991* and past issues. For 1992-93, NSO, 22 April 1994. For 1994, Ministry of Finance and Planning, *Economic and Development Policies: Budget Papers 1993.*
Production Agriculture	–	FAO, *PY 1994* and past issues. For 1994 data on rice, FAO, Statistics Division , 22 May 1996.
Mining	–	Bank of Papua New Guinea (BPNG), *Quarterly Economic Bulletin*, December 1994 and past issues.
Manufacturing	–	ESCAP, *SYAP 1994* and past issues.
Production Indexes Agriculture	–	FAO, Statistics Division, 22 May 1996 and past communication.
Energy	–	UN, *ESY 1991* and past issues.
Price Indexes	–	For 1978, BPNG, *Quarterly Economic Bulletin*, December 1985. For 1979-83, NSO, 9 April 1987. For 1984-92, NSO, *Consumer Price Indexes,* September Quarter 1994 and past issues. For 1993, NSO, 22 April 1994.
Money and Banking	–	BPNG, *Quarterly Economic Bulletin*, December 1994 and past issues. For 1995, NSO, 03 May 1996.
Government Finance	–	For 1978-81, NSO, 30 January 1989 and past communication. For 1982-88, NSO, *Government Finance Statistics, 1984-1988* and past issues. For 1990-93, NSO, 28 April 1994. For 1989 and 1994, NCDS, *South Pacific Economic and Social Database*, March 1995. For 1995, NSO, 03 May 1996.
External Trade	–	NSO, 03 May 1996 and past communication.

Direction of Trade	–	IMF, *DOTS* tape, May 1996.
Trade Indexes	–	NSO, *Statistical Bulletins on Export Price Indexes and Import Price Indexes*, December 1992 and past issues.
Balance of Payments	–	IMF, *IFS* tape, May 1996.
International Reserves Exchange Rates }	–	IMF, *IFS* tape, May 1996.
External Indebtedness	–	WB, *WDT 1996* (STARS version).

PHILIPPINES

Population	–	National Statistical Coordination Board (NSCB), *1995 Philippine Statistical Yearbook (PSY)* and past issues.
Labor Force	–	For 1978-94, NSCB, *1995 PSY* and past issues. For 1995, Bureau of Labor and Employment Statistics, *Current Labor Statistics*, October 1995.
National Accounts	–	For 1978-91, NSCB, *The National Accounts of the Philippines (Base Year: 1985), 1946-90*, May 1994. For 1992, NSCB, *1995 PSY*. For 1993-95, NSCB, *The National Accounts of the Philippines (Base Year: 1985), CY 1993 to CY 1995*, February 1996.
Production Agriculture	–	For 1978-93, NSCB, *1995 PSY* and past issues. For 1994-95, NSCB, 19 April 1996.
Mining	–	NSCB, *1995 PSY* and past issues.
Manufacturing	–	For 1978-86, National Economic and Development Authority, 7 April 1988 and past communication. For 1987-94, NSCB, *1995 PSY*.
Production Indexes Agriculture	–	For 1978-86, FAO, *Agrostat* 1993 (diskette). For 1987-95, FAO, Statistics Division, 22 May 1996 and past communication.
Mining	–	NSCB, 19 April 1996.
Manufacturing	–	NSCB, 19 April 1996.
Energy	–	For 1978-93, NSCB, 04 May 1995. For 1994-95, Department of Energy, 31 May 1996. For retail prices, NSCB, 19 April 1996 and past communication.
Price Indexes	–	For 1978-94, NSCB, *1995 PSY* and past issues. For 1995, NSCB, 19 April 1996 and past communication.
Money and Banking	–	Bangko Sentral ng Pilipinas (BSP), 23 May 1996.

Government Finance	–	For 1978-85, NSCB, 19 April 1996. For 1986-95, Bureau of Treasury, 27 February 1996.
Provincial and other local governments	–	For 1978-92, NSCB, 11 April 1994 and past communication. For 1993, NSCB, *1995 PSY*.
External Trade	–	BSP, 31 May 1996. For exports by principal commodity, 1978-94, NSCB, *1995 PSY* and past issues. For exports by principal commodity, 1995, NSCB, 19 April 1996.
Direction of Trade	–	IMF, *DOTS* tape, May 1996.
Trade Indexes	–	For 1978-91, NSCB, 11 April 1994. For 1992-95, ADB staff estimates.
Balance of Payments	–	For 1978-85, NSCB, 19 April 1996. For 1986-95, BSP, 27 May 1996.
International Reserves Exchange Rates	–	IMF, *IFS* tape, May 1996.
External Indebtedness	–	WB, *WDT 1996* (STARS version).

SINGAPORE

Population	–	Department of Statistics (DOS), 8 April 1996 and past communication.
Labor Force	–	DOS, 8 April 1996.
National Accounts	–	DOS, 8 April 1996 and past communication.
Production Manufacturing	–	Economic Development Board (EDB), 22 March 1993 and past communication.
Production Indexes Agriculture	–	FAO, Statistics Division, 22 May 1996 and past communication.
Manufacturing	–	EDB, 20 March 1996.
Energy Crude Petroleum	–	UN, *ESY 1991* and past issues. For 1992 data on imports, Trade Development Board (TDB), 17 March 1993.
Coal	–	UN, *ESY 1991* and past issues.
Electricity	–	DOS, 8 April 1996.
Retail Prices	–	DOS, 8 April 1996.
Price Indexes	–	DOS, 8 April 1996.
Money and Banking	–	DOS, 8 April 1996.

Government Finance	–	For 1978-85, DOS, 26 March 1987 and past communication. For 1986-92, IMF, *Government Finance Statistics Yearbook 1994*. For 1993-95, Ministry of Finance, (MOF), 24 February 1996.
External Trade	–	For 1978-83, DOS, *Yearbook of Statistics 1994* and past issues. For 1984-95, TDB, 20 March 1996 and past communication.
Direction of Trade	–	IMF, *DOTS* tape, May 1996.
Balance of Payments	–	DOS, 25 January 1996 and past communication.
International Reserves } Exchange Rates	–	IMF, *IFS* tape, April 1996.
External Indebtedness	–	For 1978-81, WB, *WDT 1988-89* and past issues. For 1982-91, OECD, *FEDDC 1992 Survey* and past issues. For 1992, OECD, *External Debt Statistics Annual Report 1994*. For 1993-94, OECD, *External Debt Statistics 1995 Edition*. For average terms of new commitments, WB, *WDT 1988-89* and past issues.

SOLOMON ISLANDS

Population	–	For 1978-80, ESCAP, *SYAP 1990* and past issues. For 1981-95, Statistics Office (SO), *Solomon Islands 1993 Statistical Yearbook (SISY)*, August 1995.
Labor Force	–	SO, *1993 SISY*, August 1995.
National Accounts	–	For GDP at current prices, 1978-83, SO, 1 July 1986. For GDP at current prices, 1984-87, SO, *Statistical Bulletin No. 22/89, National Accounts of Solomon Islands 1984-87*. For GDP at current prices, 1988-89, NCDS, *South Pacific Economic and Social Database*, March 1995. For GDP at current prices, 1990-93, IMF, *Recent Economic Developments*, 25 February 1994. For GDP at constant prices, 1978-79, SO, 1 July 1986. For GDP at constant prices, 1980-89, Central Bank of Solomon Islands (CBSI), *Quarterly Review*, December 1991 and past issues. For GDP at constant prices, 1990-91, CBSI, *Annual Report 1991*. For GDP at constant prices, 1992, SO, 20 April 1995.
Production Agriculture	–	For 1978-92, SO, *1993 SISY*, August 1995 and past issue. For 1993-94, CBSI, *Annual Report 1994*.
Production Index Agriculture	–	For 1978-86, FAO, *Agrostat* 1993 (diskette). For 1987-95, FAO, Statistics Division, 22 May 1996 and past communication.
Energy	–	For 1978-80, UN, *WES Yearbook* 1981 and past issues. For 1981, UN, Energy Statistics Unit, 13 February 1985. For 1982-92, UN, *1992 ESY* and past issues.
Price Indexes	–	SO, *1993 SISY*, August 1995 and past issue.

Money and Banking	–	For 1978-88, IMF, *IFS Yearbook 1995*.
		For 1989-94, IMF, *IFS*, May 1996.
Government Finance	–	For 1978-86, SO, *1985/86 SISY*.
		For 1987-88, IMF, *Government Finance Statistics Yearbook 1995*.
		For 1989-92, NCDS, *South Pacific Economic and Social Database*, March 1996.
External Trade	–	For 1978-92, SO, *1993 SISY* and past issue.
		For 1993-94, CBSI, *Annual Report 1994*.
Direction of Trade	–	IMF, *DOTS* tape, May 1996.
Trade Indexes	–	SO, *1993 SISY*, August 1995.
Balance of Payments	–	For 1978-87, IMF, *IFS Yearbook 1995*.
		For 1988-92, IMF, *IFS*, May 1996.
International Reserves ⎫	–	IMF, *IFS* tape, May 1996.
Exchange Rates ⎭		
External Indebtedness	–	WB, *WDT 1996* (STARS version).

SRI LANKA

Population	–	For 1978-90, Department of Census and Statistics (DCS), 19 April 1991 and past communication.
		For 1991-93 Central Bank of Sri Lanka (CBSL), *Annual Report 1993* and past issues.
		For 1994-95, ADB staff estimates.
Labor Force	–	For 1978-94, DCS, 7 April 1995 and past communication.
National Accounts	–	For 1978-94, DCS, 23 January 1996 and past communication.
Production		
Agriculture	–	For 1978-90, DCS, 14 April 1992 and past communication.
		For 1991-94, CBSL, *CBSL Bulletin*, August 1995.
Mining	–	For 1978-91, DCS, 14 April 1992 and past communication.
		For 1991-94, CBSL, *CBSL Bulletin*, August 1995,.
Manufacturing	–	For 1978-79 and 1985-91, DCS, 14 February 1983 and past communication.
		For 1980-84, CBSL, 30 August 1984.
		For 1985-91, DCS, 14 April 1992.
		For 1992-94, CBSL, *CBSL Bulletin*, August 1995.
Production Index		
Agriculture	–	For 1978-84, FAO, *PY 1990* and past issues.
		For 1985-95, FAO, Statistics Division, 22 May 1996 and past communication.
Energy	–	For 1978-84, UN, Energy Statistics Unit, 13 February 1985 and past issues.
		For 1985-87, DCS, 30 December 1988 and past communication.
		For 1988, CBSL, *CBSL Bulletin*, June 1989.
		For 1989-95, CBSL, 19 January 1996 and past communication.

		Crude Petroleum:
	–	For 1978-91, DCS, 14 April 1992 and past communication.
		For 1992-94 and revisions, CBSL, 12 April 1995.
Price Indexes	–	For 1978-1991, CBSL, *CBSL Bulletin*, August 1995 and past issues.
		For 1992-95 and revisions, CBSL, 19 January 1996.
Money and Banking	–	For 1978-92, CBSL, *CBSL Bulletin*, July 1993 and past issues.
		For 1983-95 and revisions, CBSL, 19 January 1996 and past communication.
Government Finance	–	For 1978-91, CBSL, 23 January 1995 and past communication.
		For 1992-95 and revisions, CBSL, 19 January 1996.
External Trade		For Total Trade and by Principal Commodity:
	–	For 1978-94, CBSL, *CBSL Bulletin*, August 1995 and past issues.
		For 1995, CBSL, 19 January 1996 and past communication.
		By SITC Section:
	–	For 1978-80, DCS, 24 March 1987 and past communication.
		For 1981-85, ESCAP, *Foreign Trade Statistics of Asia and the Pacific, 1983-87.*
		For 1986-94, CBSL, 12 April 1995 and past communication.
Trade Indexes	–	For 1978-94, CBSL, *CBSL Bulletin*, August 1995 and past issues.
Direction of Trade	–	IMF, *DOTS* tape, May 1996.
Balance of Payments	–	For 1978-79, DCS, 14 February 1983.
		For 1980-94 and some revisions, CBSL, 19 January 1996 and past communication.
International Reserves } Exchange Rates }	–	IMF, *IFS* tape, May 1996.
External Indebtedness	–	WB, *WDT 1996* (STARS version).

TAIPEI,China

Population	–	Directorate-General of Budget, Accounting and Statistics (DGBAS), 27 March 1996 and past communication.
Labor Force	–	For 1978-94, DGBAS, *Monthly Bulletin of Statistics of the Republic of China (MBROC)*, February 1996 and past issues.
		For 1995, DGBAS, 27 March 1996.
National Accounts	–	For 1978-93, DGBAS, *National Income in Taiwan Area of the Republic of China 1995.*
		For 1994-95, DGBAS, 27 March 1996.
Production Agriculture	–	For 1978-94, DGBAS, *Statistical Yearbook of China (SYROC) 1995* and past issues.
		For 1995, DGBAS, 27 March 1996.
Mining } Manufacturing }	–	For 1978-91, DGBAS, *Monthly Statistics of the Republic of China (MSROC)*, February 1994 and past issues.
		For 1992-95, DGBAS, 27 March 1996 and past communication.

Production Indexes
   Agriculture ⎫
   Mining ⎬   – For 1978-94, DGBAS, *SYROC 1995*.
   Manufacturing ⎭   For 1995, DGBAS, 27 March 1996.

Energy   – DGBAS, 27 March 1996 and past communication.

   Retail Prices   – DGBAS, 27 March 1996 and past communication.

Price Indexes   – DGBAS, *MBROC*, February 1996 and past issues.

Money and Banking   – Central Bank of China (CBC), *Financial Statistics Monthly*, January 1996 and past issues, and DGBAS, 27 March 1996 and past communication.

   Deposit Money Banks ⎫ – DGBAS, 27 March 1996 and past communication.
   Interest Rates ⎭

Government Finance   – DGBAS, 27 March 1996 and past communication.

External Trade   – For 1978-85, Department of Statistics (DOS), *Monthly Statistics of Exports and Imports*, September 1994 and past issues.
For 1986-95, DGBAS, 27 March 1996 and past communication.
For principal export commodities, DGBAS, *MSROC*, February 1994 and past issues, and DGBAS, 27 March 1996 and past communication.
For terms of trade, DGBAS, 27 March 1996 and past communication.

Direction of Trade   – DGBAS, 27 March 1996 and past communication.

Balance of Payments   – For 1978-91, CBC, *Balance of Payments*, December 1994 and past issues.
For 1992-94, CBC, *Financial Statistics*, January 1996 and past issues.
For 1995, DGBAS, 27 March 1996.

International Reserves ⎫ – For 1978-1994, CBC, *Financial Statistics*, January 1996 and past issues.
Exchange Rates ⎭   For 1995, DGBAS, 27 March 1996.

External Indebtedness   – For total debt outstanding & disbursed, long-term and short-term debt, for 1982-91, OECD, *FEDDC, 1992 Survey* and past issues.
For total debt, long-term and short-term debt, for 1992, OECD, *External Debt Statistics Annual Report 1994*.
For total debt, long-term and short-term debt, for 1993-94, OECD, *External Debt Statistics 1995*.
For public and publicly-guaranteed long-term debt, for 1978-94, CBC, *Balance of Payments*, December 1995 and past issues.
For principal repayments on LT debt and interest on long-term debt, for 1978-81, DGBAS, 21 March 1989 and past communication.
For principal repayments on LT debt and interest on long-term and short-term debt, for 1982-91, OECD, *FEDDC*, 1992 Survey.

THAILAND

Population	—	For 1978-82, National Statistics Office (NSO), 3 March 1987 and past communication.
		For 1983-86, NSO, *Statistical Handbook of Thailand 1990*.
		For 1987-95, Office of the National Economic and Social Development Board (NESDB), *Population Projections for Thailand, Whole Kingdom 1990-2020* and past issues.

Labor Force
— For 1978-79, NSO, *Report of the Labor Force Survey (Round 2)*, July-September 1972-79 and past issues.
For 1980-84, NSO, 3 March 1987 and past communication.
For 1985, Bank of Thailand (BOT), 25 March 1991.
For 1986-91, NSO, *Report of the Labor Force Survey, Whole Kingdom (Round 3)* as quoted in NSO, 31 March 1992 and 13 April 1993.
For 1992, BOT, 4 April 1994.
For 1993, NSO, *Report of the Labor Force Survey, Whole Kingdom* as quoted in NSO, 20 April 1995 .

National Accounts
For GDP by Industry at Current Prices and Constant Prices, and GDP by Expenditure at Current Prices:
— For 1978-79, BOT, 24 March 1989.
For 1980-88, NESDB as quoted in BOT, 04 April 1994.
For 1989-94, NESDB, *National Income of Thailand 1994*.
For 1995, BOT, 9 May 1996.

For GDP by Expenditure at Constant Prices:
— For 1978-79, BOT, 24 March 1989.
For 1980-88, NESDB as quoted in BOT, 04 April 1994.
For 1989-94, NESDB, *National Income of Thailand 1994*.
For 1989-93, BOT, 9 May 1996 (for exports of goods and services, imports of goods and services and statistical discrepancy).
For 1995, BOT, 9 May 1996.

Investment Financing items:
— For 1978-79, BOT, 24 March 1989.
For 1980-90, NESDB as quoted in BOT, 04 April 1994.
For 1991, NESDB, *National Income of Thailand 1993* as quoted in NSO, 20 April 1995.
For 1992-94, BOT, 26 January 1996.
For 1995, BOT, 9 May 1996.

Production
Agriculture
— For 1978-93, BOT, *Quarterly Bulletin*, September 1995 and past issues.
For 1994-95, BOT, 9 May 1996.

Mining
— For 1990-94, BOT, *Quarterly Bulletin*, September 1995 and past issues.
For 1995, BOT, 9 May 1996.

Manufacturing
— For 1978-93, BOT, *Quarterly Bulletin*, September 1995 and past issues.
For 1994-95, BOT, 9 May 1996.

Production Indexes
Agriculture
— For 1978-86, FAO, *PY 1994* and past issues.
For 1987-95, FAO, Statistics Division, 22 May 1996 and past communication.

Mining
— BOT, 9 May 1996 and past communication.

Manufacturing	–	For 1978-87, BOT, 4 January 1991 and past communication. For 1988-93, BOT, *Quarterly Bulletin*, September 1995 and past issues. For 1994-95, BOT, 9 May 1996.
Energy Crude Petroleum	–	For 1978-88, UN, *ESY 1991* and past issues. For 1989-90, National Energy Administration, *Thailand Energy Situation* as quoted in NSO, 31 March 1992. For 1991-93, Department of Energy Affairs, Ministry of Science, Technology and Environment as quoted in NSO, 20 April 1995 and past communication. For 1994, BOT, 10 April 1995.
Coal	–	For 1978-88, UN, *ESY 1991* and past issues. For 1989-90, National Energy Administration, *Thailand Energy Situation* as quoted in NSO, 31 March 1992. For 1991-93, Department of Energy Affairs, Ministry of Science, Technology and Environment as quoted in NSO, 20 April 1995 and past communication.
Electricity	–	For 1978-88, UN, *ESY 1991* and past communication. For 1989-93, Department of Energy Affairs, Ministry of Science, Technology and Environment as quoted in NSO, 20 April 1995 and past communication. For 1994, BOT, 10 April 1995.
Retail Prices	–	For 1990-94, BOT, *Quarterly Bulletin*, September 1995 and past issues.
Price Indexes	–	For 1978-94, BOT, *Quarterly Bulletin*, September 1995 and past issues. For 1995, BOT, 9 May 1996.
Money and Banking	–	Money Supply: For 1978-81, BOT, 12 April 1988. For 1982, BOT, *Quarterly Bulletin*, June 1989 (except currency in circulation and demand deposits). For 1982, BOT, 12 April 1988 (for currency in circulation and demand deposits only). For 1983-94, BOT, *Quarterly Bulletin*, September 1995 and past issues. For 1995, BOT, 9 May 1996. Deposit Money Banks: For 1978-94, BOT, *Quarterly Bulletin*, September 1995 and past issues. For 1995, BOT, 9 May 1996. Interest Rates: For 1978-94, BOT, *Quarterly Bulletin*, September 1995 and past issues. For 1995, BOT, 9 May 1996. BOT, 9 May 1996 and past communication (for rates on loans and discounts).
Government Finance	–	For 1978-92, BOT, *Quarterly Bulletin*, September 1995 and past issues (except net lending and non-budgetary surplus/deficit). For 1993-95, BOT, 9 May 1996 and past communication. BOT, 9 May 1996 and past communication (for net lending and non-budgetary surplus/deficit). By Expenditure: For 1978-94, BOT, *Quarterly Bulletin*, September 1995 and past issues. For 1995, BOT, 9 May 1996.

External Trade	–	For 1978-94, BOT, *Quarterly Bulletin*, September 1995 and past issues. For 1995, BOT, 9 May 1996.
Direction of Trade	–	IMF, *DOTS* tape, May 1996.
Trade Indexes	–	For 1978-94, BOT, *Quarterly Bulletin*, September 1995 and past issues. For 1995, BOT, 9 May 1996.
Balance of Payments	–	BOT, 9 May 1996 and past communication.
International Reserves Exchange Rates	–	IMF, *IFS* tape, May 1996.
External Indebtedness	–	WB, *WDT 1996* (STARS version).

TONGA

Population	–	Statistics Department (SD), 23 April 1996.
Labor Force	–	For 1980, ADB Mission, January 1983. For 1984, SD, 12 February 1985. For 1986 and 1990, SD, *Statistical Abstract 1993*, August 1993. For 1994, SD, 23 April 1996.
National Accounts	–	For 1978-80, SD, *Statistical Abstract 1983*, December 1983. For 1981-95, SD, 23 April 1996.
Production Agriculture	–	For 1978-92, ESCAP, *SYAP 1993* and past issues. For 1993-95, FAO, Statistics Division, 22 May 1996 and past communication.
Production Index Agriculture	–	For 1978-86, FAO, *Agrostat* 1993 (diskette). For 1987-95, FAO, Statistics Division, 22 May 1996 and past communication.
Energy	–	For 1978-91, ESCAP, *SYAP 1993* and past issues. For 1992-93, SD, 06 February 1995.
Price Indexes	–	SD, 23 April 1996.
Money and Banking	–	For 1978-92, SD, *Statistical Abstract 1993*, August 1993 and past issues. For 1993-95, SD, 15 May 1996 and past communication. For foreign assets, domestic credit, and other items, 1978-79, SD, 19 April 1991 and past communication. For interest rates, SD, 23 April 1996 and past communication.
Government Finance	–	For 1978-90, SD, *Statistical Abstract 1993*, August 1993 and past issues. For 1991-95, SD, 23 April 1996.
External Trade	–	For 1978-92, SD, *Statistical Abstract 1993*, August 1993 and past issues. For 1993-95, SD, 23 April 1996.
Direction of Trade	–	IMF, *DOTS* tape, May 1996.

Balance of Payments	–	For 1978-89, SD, *Statistical Abstract 1993*, August 1993 and past issues. For 1990-95, SD, 23 April 1996.
International Reserves } Exchange Rates	–	IMF, *IFS* tape, May 1996.
External Indebtedness	–	WB, *WDT 1996* (STARS version).

TUVALU

Population	–	For 1979-91, National Center for Development Studies (NCDS), *South Pacific Economic and Social Database*, March 1996. For 1992-95, ADB, *Tuvalu Economic Situation, Policies and Prospects*, September 1994.
National Accounts	–	For 1981-89, NCDS, *South Pacific Economic and Social Database*, March 1996. For 1990-94, Ministry of Finance, Economic Planning, Commerce and Industry (MFECI), Central Statistics Division, 25 January 1996. For 1995, ADB, *Tuvalu Economic Situation, Policies and Prospects*, September 1994.
Production	–	For 1981-83, Australian International Development Assistance Bureau (AIDAB), *Tuvalu Economic Situation and Development Prospects*, February 1993. For 1984-90, NCDS, *South Pacific Economic and Social Database*, March 1996.
Energy	–	NCDS, *South Pacific Economic and Social Database*, March 1996.
Price Indexes	–	For 1980-85, AIDAB, *Tuvalu Economic Situation and Development Prospects*, February 1993. For 1986-95, MFECI, Central Statistics Division, 25 January 1996.
Government Finance	–	NCDS, *South Pacific Economic and Social Database*, March 1996.
External Trade	–	For 1980-89, AIDAB, *Tuvalu Economic Situation and Development Prospects*, February 1993. For 1990, ADB, *Tuvalu Economic Situation, Policies and Prospects*, September 1994.
Direction of Trade	–	IMF, *DOTS* tape, May 1996.
Balance of Payments	–	For 1980-84, NCDS, *South Pacific Economic and Social Database*, March 1996. For 1985-95, ADB, *Tuvalu Economic Situation, Policies and Prospects*, September 1994.
Exchange Rates	–	IMF, *IFS* tape, May 1996.

VANUATU

Population	–	For 1978, ADB, *Economic Report on Vanuatu*, March 1982. For 1979-95, National Planning and Statistics Office (NPSO), *Statistical Bulletin (SB)*, *Statistical Indicators*, 1st Quarter 1995 and past issues.
Labor Force	–	For 1979, NPSO, *Report on the Census of Population*, 1979. For 1989, NPSO, *Vanuatu National Population Census*, May 1989.

National Accounts	–	For 1983-84, NPSO-ADB, *National Accounts of Vanuatu 1983-1987.* For 1985-93, NPSO, *SB, Statistical Indicators*, 1st Quarter 1995.
Production 　Agriculture	–	FAO, *PY 1994* and past issues. For 1995 data on coconut, FAO, Statistics Division, 22 May 1996.
Production Indexes 　Agriculture	–	FAO, Statistics Division, 22 May 1996 and past communication.
Energy 　Electricity	–	For 1978-82, UN, Energy Statistics Unit, 8 December 1983 and 13 February 1985. For 1983-90, UN, *ESY 1991* and past issues. For 1991-95, Statistics Office, 7 February 1996.
Retail Prices	–	For 1978-87, NPSO, 18 April 1988 and 12 March 1986. For 1988-94, NPSO, *SB, Statistical Indicators*, 1st Quarter 1995 and past issues.
Price Indexes	–	For 1978-90, NPSO, *SB, Consumer Price Indexes 1988-1990* and past issues. For 1991-94, NPSO, *SB, Statistical Indicators*, 1st Quarter 1995. For 1995, NCDS, *South Pacific Economic and Social Database*, March 1996.
Money and Banking	–	For 1978-80, ADB Economic Mission, August 1981. For 1981-83, Central Bank of Vanuatu (CBV), *Quarterly Economic Review*, June 1986. For 1984-85, NPSO, *SB, Monetary and Banking Statistics*, 3rd Quarter 1988 and past issues. For 1986-88, NPSO, 12 January 1990. For 1989-91, NPSO, *SB, Statistical Indicators*, 2nd Quarter 1992. For 1992-95, NCDS, *South Pacific Economic and Social Database*, March 1996. For Deposit Money Banks: NCDS, *South Pacific Economic and Social Database*, March 1996.
Government Finance	–	For 1978-79, ADB Economic Mission, August 1981. For 1980-88, NPSO, 21 March 1989 and 12 January 1990. For 1989-95, NCDS, *South Pacific Economic and Social Database*, March 1996.
External Trade	–	For 1978-87, NPSO, *SB, Statistical Indicators*, 2nd Quarter 1992 and past issues. For 1988-94, Statistics Office, 7 February 1996 and past communication. For 1995, NCDS, *South Pacific Economic and Social Database*, March 1996.
Direction of Trade	–	IMF, *DOTS* tape, May 1996.
Trade Indexes	–	NPSO, 12 January 1988.
Balance of Payments	–	For 1978, Ministry of Finance and Bureau of Statistics as cited in ADB, *Economic Report on Vanuatu*, March 1982. For 1979-80, NPSO, 26 September 1983. For 1981, CBV, *Annual Report* 1984. For 1982-93, IMF, *IFS*, April 1996 and past issues.
International Reserves Exchange Rate	–	IMF, *IFS* tape, May 1996.
External Indebtedness	–	WB, *WDT 1996* (STARS version).

VIET NAM

Population	–	For 1978-79, General Statistical Office (GSO), 27 March 1992.
		For 1980-84, GSO, *Statistical Data of the Socialist Republic of Viet Nam 1976-1989*.
		For 1985-94, GSO, *Statistical Yearbook 1994*.
		For 1995, ADB, *Asian Development Outlook 1996 and 1997*.
Labor Force	–	For 1978-84, 1986-89, GSO, 27 March 1992.
		For 1985, 1990-93, GSO, *Statistical Yearbook 1994*.
		For 1994-95, GSO, 06 May 1996.
National Accounts	–	GSO, 06 May 1996 and past communication.

Production
   Agriculture

Paddy:
– For 1978-79, FAO, Statistics Division, 14 February 1995 and past communication.
For 1980-91, GSO, *Statistical Yearbook 1994*.
For 1992-95, GSO, 06 May 1996 and past communication and
ADB, Economic Mission, 16 April 1996 .

Coconut and Maize:
– For 1978-91, FAO, Statistics Division, 14 February 1995 and past communication.
For 1992-95, GSO, 06 May 1996 and past communication and
ADB, Economic Mission, 16 April 1996 .

Rubber, Coffee and Tea:
– For 1978-79, ESCAP, *SYAP 1990* and past issues.
For 1980-91, GSO, *Statistical Yearbook 1994*.
For 1992-95, GSO, 06 May 1996 and past communication.

   Mining
– For 1978-84, ESCAP, *SYAP 1994* and past issues.
For 1985-89, GSO, 26 March 1994 and past communication.
For 1990-91, GSO, *Statistical Yearbook 1993*.
For 1992-95, GSO, 06 May 1996 and ADB, Economic Mission, 16 April 1996.

   Manufacturing
– For 1978-84, ESCAP, *SYAP 1994* and past issues.
For 1985-89, GSO, 26 March 1994 and past communication.
For 1990, GSO, *Statistical Yearbook 1993*.
For 1991-95, GSO, 06 May 1996 and past communication and
ADB, Economic Mission, 16 April 1996.

Production Indexes
   Agriculture
– For 1978-86, FAO, *PY 1994* and past issues.
For 1987-95, FAO, Statistics Division, 22 May 1996 and past communication.

Energy
   Crude Petroleum
– GSO, 06 May 1996 and past communication.

   Coal
Production:
– For 1978-84, ESCAP, *SYAP 1994* and past issues.
For 1985-89, GSO, 26 March 1994 and past communication.
For 1990-91, GSO, *Statistical Yearbook 1993*.
For 1992-95, GSO, 06 May 1996 and ADB, Economic Mission, 16 April 1996.

Exports and Imports:
– GSO, 06 May 1996 and past communication.

Electricity	Production:
	— For 1978-89, GSO, 26 March 1994 and past communication.
	For 1990-91, GSO, *Statistical Yearbook 1993*.
	For 1992-95, GSO, 06 May 1996 and past communication.
	Consumption:
	— GSO, 06 May 1996 and past communication.
Price Indexes	— For 1985-88, GSO, *Statistical Data of the Socialist Republic of Viet Nam 1976-1989*.
	For 1989-93 (growth rates), IMF, *Economic Review: Viet Nam 1994*, November 1994.
	For 1994 (growth rate), GSO, 10 March 1995.
Money and Banking	Money Supply:
	— For 1986-88, ADB, *ERBOP - Socialist Republic of Viet Nam*, September 1993 and past issues.
	For 1989-92, ADB, *Economic Update - Socialist Republic of Viet Nam*, December 1994.
	For 1993-95, ADB, Economic Mission, 16 April 1996
	Deposit Money Banks and Interest Rates:
	— ADB, *Economic Report of the Socialist Republic of Viet Nam*, October 1989.
	Interest Rates:
	— For 1984-88, ADB, *ERBOP - Socialist Republic of Viet Nam*, September 1993 and past issues (for time deposits: 12 months).
	For 1989, ADB, *Economic Update - Socialist Republic of Viet Nam*, December 1994 (for time deposits: 12 months).
	For 1990-94, GSO, 06 May 1996 (for savings and time deposits: 6 months).
Government Finance	— For 1984-88, ADB, *Economic Report of the Socialist Republic of Viet Nam*, October 1989.
	For 1989-90, GSO, 26 March 1994 and past communication.
	For 1991-95, ADB, Economic Mission, 16 April 1996.
External Trade	Total Trade:
	— For 1978-79, IMF, *IFS Yearbook 1994*.
	For 1980-93, GSO, *Statistical Yearbook 1994*.
	For 1992-94, GSO, 06 May 1996 and past communication.
	For 1995, ADB, Economic Mission, 16 April 1996.
	Trade by SITC Section:
	— GSO, 06 May 1996 and past communication.
	Exports by Principal Commodity:
	— For 1983-93, GSO, 06 July 1995 and past communication.
	For 1994, GSO, 06 May 1996 (for frozen shrimp only).
	For 1994-95, ADB, Economic Mission, 16 April 1996 (for other export items, excluding frozen shrimp).
Direction of Trade	— IMF, *DOTS* tape, May 1996.
Balance of Payments	— For 1983-87, ADB, *Economic Report of the Socialist Republic of Viet Nam*, October 1989.
	For 1988, ADB, *ERBOP - Socialist Republic of Viet Nam*, September 1993.
	For 1989, ADB, *Economic Update - Socialist Republic of Viet Nam*, December 1994.
	For 1990-95, ADB, Economic Mission, 16 April 1996.

International Reserves	–	ADB, *Economic Report of the Socialist Republic of Viet Nam*, October 1989.
Exchange Rates	–	For 1984-85, ADB, *Economic Report of the Socialist Republic of Viet Nam*, October 1989. For 1986-93, GSO, 26 March 1994 and past communication.
External Indebtedness	–	For 1978-88, OECD, *FEDDC 1992 Survey* and past issues. For 1989-95, WB, *WDT 1996* (STARS version).

WESTERN SAMOA

Population	–	For 1978-80, Ministry of Finance (MOF), *The 1985 Budget Statement*, 16 October 1984; Department of Statistics (DOS), 21 November 1984 and past communication. For 1981-86, DOS, *Quarterly Statistical Bulletin*, July-December 1986. For 1987-92, ESCAP, *SYAP 1993*. For 1993-95, ADB staff estimates.
National Accounts	–	For 1982-87, ADB, *Economic Survey on Western Samoa*, October 1988. For 1988, IMF, *Report on Western Samoa*, 2 February 1989. For 1989-94, Central Bank of Samoa (CBS), 23 March 1995 and past communication. For 1995, ADB staff estimates.
Production	–	For copra, 1978-92, FAO, *PY 1992* and past issues. For coconut, 1978-80, FAO, *PY 1982* and past issues. For coconut, 1981-94, FAO, Basic Data Unit, 14 February 1995 and past communication.
Production Indexes Agriculture	–	For 1978-86, FAO, *Agrostat* 1993 (diskette). For 1987-95, FAO, Statistics Division, 22 May 1996 and past communication.
Manufacturing	–	For 1982-93, CBS, *Central Bank of Samoa Bulletin*, December 1994 and past issues. For 1994-95, CBS, 11 April 1996.
Energy	–	For 1978-82, UN, *WES Yearbook 1980* and computer printouts, 1982. For 1983-84, DOS, 20 December 1984. For 1985, DOS, *Quarterly Statistical Bulletin*, July-December 1986 and past issues. For 1986-91, UN, *ESY 1991* and past issues. For 1992-95, CBS, 12 February 1996.
Price Indexes	–	For 1978-79, MOF, *The 1982 Budget Statement*, 13 November 1981. For 1980-82, DOS, 8 February 1984. For 1983-93, CBS, *Central Bank of Samoa Bulletin*, December 1994 and past issues. For 1994-95, CBS, 12 February 1996.
Money and Banking	–	For 1978, MOF, *The 1983 Budget Statement*, 8 February 1983 and past issues. For 1979-80, DOS, *Quarterly Statistical Bulletin*, January-June 1981. For 1981-83, DOS, 8 February 1984; DOS, *Annual Statistical Abstract 1985*. For 1984-93, CBS, *Central Bank of Samoa Bulletin*, December 1994 and past issues. For 1994, CBS, 23 March 1995 and past communication. For 1995, ADB data file.
Government Finance	–	For 1978-79, MOF, *The 1983 Budget Statement*, 8 February 1983 and past issues. For 1980-82, DOS, 6 February 1985.

For 1983-93/94, CBS, *Central Bank of Samoa Bulletin*, September 1995
and past issues.
For 1994/95, ADB data file.

External Trade	–	For 1978, DOS, *Quarterly Statistical Bulletin*, January-June 1981 and past issues.
		For 1979-82, DOS, *Annual Statistical Abstract 1985*.
		For 1983-94, CBS, *Central Bank of Samoa Bulletin*, September 1995 and past issues.
		For 1995, CBS, 11 April 1996.
Trade Indexes	–	For 1978, DOS, *Quarterly Statistical Bulletin*, January-June 1981 and past issues.
		For 1979-80, DOS, *Annual Statistical Abstract 1985*.
		For 1982-94, CBS, *Central Bank of Samoa Bulletin*, September 1995 and past issues.
		For 1995, CBS, 11 April 1996.
Direction of Trade	–	IMF, *DOTS* tape, May 1996.
Balance of Payments	–	For 1978-87, IMF, *IFS Yearbook 1995*.
		For 1988-93, IMF, *IFS*, February 1996.
		For 1994-95, CBS, 11 April 1996.
International Reserves Exchange Rates }	–	IMF, *IFS* tape, April 1996.
External Indebtedness	–	WB, *WDT 1996* (STARS version).